Approaches to Aboriginal Education in Canada

D1606752

Approaches to Aboriginal Education in Canada

SEARCHING FOR SOLUTIONS

Frances Widdowson and
Albert Howard, editors

Brush
Education Inc.

Brush Education Inc.
www.brusheducation.ca
contact@brusheducation.ca

Cover design: Carol Dragich, Dragich Design; Illustration of wampum pattern: Julia Jungwirth; Photo of braid pattern: © Zheng Dong | Dreamstime.com
Copy edit: Kirsten Craven

This book collects previously published articles in their original forms. Wherever possible, we have updated and edited citations for usefulness and consistency. Where updating was not possible, we have included the authors' original citation information for your reference.

Printed and manufactured in Canada
Ebook edition available at Amazon, Kobo, and other e-retailers.

Library and Archives Canada Cataloguing in Publication
Approaches to Aboriginal education in Canada : searching for solutions / Frances Widdowson and Albert Howard, editors.
Includes bibliographical references.
Issued in print and electronic formats.
ISBN 978-1-55059-456-0 (pbk.).–ISBN 978-1-55059-457-7 (epub).–ISBN 978-1-55059-476-8 (pdf).–ISBN 978-1-55059-477-5 (mobi)

1. Native peoples–Education–Canada.   I. Widdowson, Frances, 1966-, editor of compilation   II. Howard, Albert, editor of compilation
E96.2.A66 2013   371.829'97071   C2013-902688-6   C2013-902689-4

Produced with the assistance of the Government of Alberta, Alberta Multimedia Development Fund. We also acknowledge the financial support of the Government of Canada through the Canada Book Fund for our publishing activities.

Government of Alberta

Canadian Heritage

Patrimoine canadien

Dedication

In Memoriam
Larry Gaynor
1939–2010

Contents

Acknowledgements

There are many people who should be thanked for assisting us with this project.

First of all, we would like to thank a number of people at Mount Royal University for providing a scholarly environment where open and honest debate is encouraged, not suppressed. These people include Duane Bratt and Bruce Foster, the present and previous chairs of the Department of Policy Studies, Manuel Mertin and Sabrina Reed, the previous dean and previous associate dean of the Faculty of Arts, and Robin Fisher (the previous provost and vice-president, academic). All of these individuals were instrumental in supporting the Aboriginal policy forums where Aboriginal education policy was debated. Miriam Carey also provided guidance that was helpful in developing the Bertrand Russell quadrant in the Exchanges section of the book. Elaine Mullen contributed to the development of our ideas about critical thinking and their application to the introduction. Walter Bruno has been a great source of support in encouraging the free exchange of ideas about Aboriginal policy and identity politics in general. Jeffrey Keshen, the new dean of Arts, also should be commended for encouraging a climate of civil debate at Mount Royal University.

There are also a number of political scientists to be thanked for encouraging open debate on Aboriginal policy. These include Janet Ajzenstat, Kathy Brock, Alan Cairns, Katherine Fierlbeck, Tom Flanagan, Rhoda Howard-Hassmann, and Leo Panitch.

Furthermore, David Newhouse and Elizabeth Rata are thanked for contributing original work to this volume. Both scholars have been very helpful and open in sharing their thoughts concerning Aboriginal education.

We would like to thank the students in Widdowson's segment of Policy Studies 5010 (Selected Topics in Public Policy), upon which this book was modelled. They have been an inquisitive group, whose questions contributed to our investigation of this topic. Tom Widdowson's comments on the manuscript were especially helpful.

Finally, special gratitude is owed to Fraser Seely for encouraging us to take on this project and to Lauri Seidlitz for her organizational skills as managing editor. They have made our experience working with Brush Education stimulating and enjoyable.

Introduction

Hunting Assumptions[1] in the Search for Solutions

● ● ● ● ● ● ● ● ● ● ● ● ● ● ● ● ● ● ● ●

> For a teacher to mandate in advance—either explicitly
> or implicitly—that only one ideological interpretation or
> outcome is permitted in a discussion or assignment is to
> contradict a fundamental tenet of critical thinking. That tenet
> holds that all involved—including teachers—must always
> be open to reexamining the assumptions informing their
> ideological commitments. (Brookfield, 2012, p. 134)

On February 25, 2010, we travelled to Edmonton, Alberta, to give a presentation at the Greater Edmonton Teachers' Convention Association (GETCA). The event would impress upon us the constraints on honest discussions about Aboriginal education, eventually leading to our decision to edit this volume.

The speaking engagement, to occur the following day, was the result of an invitation from Hope Knudsen, the president of the association. Ms. Knudsen had heard one of us (Frances Widdowson) being interviewed by Michael Enright about our book *Disrobing the Aboriginal Industry: The Deception behind Indigenous Cultural Preservation*. After listening to Widdowson's arguments, Knudsen thought our research and observations would be of great interest to teachers (Knudsen, personal communication, August 5, 2009). Consequently, she asked Widdowson to make a submission to the convention, and the proposed talk, "Speaking Frankly about Aboriginal Education," was added to the program.

Upon checking into our hotel, we received a message inviting us to have a drink with conference organizers that evening. We were informed during the meeting that GETCA was under pressure to have Widdowson excluded from the program. Fortunately, the association was standing firm but was concerned about the reception Widdowson might receive; Widdowson assured the convention organizers that she was not worried and hoped that her presence would encourage much needed debate on Aboriginal education. It was then decided that another session, presented by an Aboriginal member of the association, Patrick Loyer, would be cancelled so that he could comment on Widdowson's speech (presumably so that GETCA could meet the opponents' demands).

Although the presentation did not result in the acrimony feared by GETCA organizers, the matter did not end there. After arriving back in Calgary, Widdowson received a telephone call from Andrew Hanon, a journalist at the *Edmonton Sun*. Hanon informed Widdowson that a professor from the University of Alberta, Cora Weber-Pillwax, and two of her graduate students, had issued a press release entitled "ATA Invites Racism into Alberta Classrooms" (2010). The press release asserted that "the Alberta Teachers Association is complicit in furthering … racist and assimilationist views" by inviting Widdowson to speak. The evidence used to support this assertion was Widdowson's observation, in an interview given in 2009, that "there is no history of literacy, science and mathematics in aboriginal societies, and therefore little expertise exists to improve native educational levels." Widdowson's criticisms about the relevance of Aboriginal traditions to modern educational processes were claimed to be "a threat to the sense of security of every Aboriginal child in Alberta" and "a direct attack on Aboriginal students in this province" (Weber-Pillwax, Rost, & Auger, 2010). Weber-Pillwax and her graduate students had concluded that "we cannot trust that the ATA would support and promote the safeguarding of our children now that we have witnessed their support of professional development that denies the existence of Aboriginal knowledge and, essentially, of Aboriginal humanity" (Andrew Hanon, personal communication, March 4, 2010; Hanon, 2010).

The events that transpired at the GETCA convention exemplify a disturbing trend in the discussion of Aboriginal policy today. As Alan Cairns (2001), a long-time observer of Aboriginal affairs, has pointed out, "Aboriginal policy is extremely politicized, and subject to taboos which constrain both Aboriginal and non-Aboriginal participants" (p. 155). These taboos prevent dissenting opinions from being expressed, narrowing the range of views considered. This makes effective policy development difficult, because the validity and accuracy of the assumptions behind current initiatives are rarely analyzed, and alternatives are not explored.

The attempt to shut down Widdowson's speech in Edmonton was certainly not the first use of this tactic. At the Canadian Political Science Association conference in 2008, for example, a number of political scientists debated whether to have Widdowson charged under hate speech provisions of the Criminal Code for suggesting that Indigenous theories and methodologies did not meet the standards of rigour demanded in the discipline of political science (Shimo, 2009; Widdowson, 2009; Ajzenstat, 2008). Further opposition was encountered at the Aboriginal Research Policy Conference in 2009, when some participants threatened a boycott if we were allowed to speak. Conference organizers again stood up to the pressure, but our presentation was removed from its original placement on a panel and held separately at the request of another presenter.

These problems are particularly acute with respect to discussions specifically about Aboriginal education. Although a variety of perspectives exist, there is a reluctance to incorporate alternative viewpoints in edited anthologies. This circumstance is illustrated by the volumes on Aboriginal education published over the last 25 years. All of these edited anthologies embrace what we refer to as parallelist assumptions. They make no attempt to include other perspectives that would challenge the existing orthodoxy with respect to Aboriginal education.

The objective of this book is to break down these barriers to discussion and debate, allowing a diversity of views to be represented in one volume. Readers can examine the assumptions of each, and evaluate the accuracy and validity of the evidence used to support the various perspectives. This will encourage critical thinking in assessing the merits of opposing viewpoints, and begin the process of considering what course of action should be pursued.[2]

It should be mentioned that even the publication of this book has been subject to the censorial attitudes that have come to hinder discussions about Aboriginal education. Just as the book was going through the final stages of its preparation, Weber-Pillwax—this time in her capacity as one of the editors of the *Canadian Journal of Native Education*—again acted to restrict the open discussion of ideas. Although permission for publication had already been granted by the journal to reprint four articles, Weber-Pillwax's interference led two authors—Marie Battiste and Paul Berger—to request that their articles be withdrawn from the volume. As a result, this book's coverage of parallelist perspectives is not as complete as was originally intended.

Hunting Assumptions in Parallelist and Integrationist Approaches

In attempting to understand Aboriginal education in Canada, two quite distinct outlooks are evident. They entail very different goals and assumptions, and thus provide a basis for categorizing the many proposals intent on improving Aboriginal education in Canada. The images on the cover of this book represent these two theoretical positions.

The first, and most prevalent, perspective argues for Aboriginal self-determination and autonomy from the rest of Canadian society. This "parallelist" position advocates Aboriginal education functioning in a separate realm from non-Aboriginal education, with different content, teaching practices, and forms of organization. Parallelism is represented on this book's cover by the wampum belt showing two rows running side by side but never coming together.

Integrationist assumptions are quite different from those held by parallelists. From an integrationist perspective, Aboriginal educational success is perceived in terms of the successful participation of Aboriginal people in a common scientific and humanistic educational system. Educational achievement is determined according to whether all students, including those of Aboriginal ancestry, meet universal standards such as thinking critically, writing clearly, and understanding mathematical relationships. Represented on the cover of this book by the different strands of yarn retaining their unique character, but interwoven to create a stronger whole, integrationist perspectives assume that all people can contribute to improving humanity's common understanding of the universe.

Although parallelist and integrationist approaches often put forward contradictory assumptions, it is important to point out that discussions about Aboriginal education do not always fall neatly into the two camps. Parallelism and integrationism each exist within a spectrum. The articles in this book illustrate that parallelist approaches rarely reject all European influences on Aboriginal education, and integrationists often argue that a certain amount of Aboriginal autonomy in the Canadian education system is necessary. Parallelism and integrationism, therefore, constitute ideal types; various degrees of difference can exist within these categories.

Parallelism: Self-Determination and Traditional Cultural Revitalization

The term *parallelism* was coined by Alan Cairns (2000), who described it as "Aboriginal and non-Aboriginal communities travelling side by side, coexisting but not getting in each other's way" (p. 6). Parallelism can be found in a number of Aboriginal education anthologies,[3] as well as the five-volume report of the Royal Commission on Aboriginal Peoples (RCAP).[4] Furthermore, it is the viewpoint overwhelmingly expressed in the most significant journal devoted to the subject of Aboriginal education in Canada—the *Canadian Journal of Native Education.*

In the parallelist view, Aboriginal–non-Aboriginal relations are visualized as "two parallel rows of purple wampum that represent two vessels travelling upon the river" (Edward J. Cross, as cited in RCAP, 1996, Vol. 4, p. 120). Each row of purple shells represents the "laws, traditions, customs, language and spiritual beliefs" of Aboriginal and non-Aboriginal peoples (Cross, as cited in RCAP, 1996, Vol. 4, p. 120).[5] So accepted is the two-row wampum metaphor, in fact, that it is a dominant image in many discussions of Aboriginal policy. It is the motif used throughout Cannon and Sunseri's edited book *Racism, Colonialism, and Indigeneity in Canada.*[6] In their introduction, Cannon and Sunseri (2011a) discuss the two-row wampum belt as a treaty document that shows that Aboriginal peoples are "sovereign nations whose inherent rights were granted by the Creator," and racism is even defined "as something that violates the ancient principles set out in Two Row Wampum" (pp. xiv–xv, xix).

This vision of parallelism is supported by social movements espousing an ideology referred to as "the politics of identity and entitlement" (Ball, Dagger, Christian, & Campbell, 2013, pp. 221–246). In these movements, groups come to identify with one another because of a history of shared oppression and exclusion. Their attempts to achieve emancipation include efforts to change the social beliefs that justify their marginalization and inhibit their capacity for liberation. The lack of recognition of marginalized group identities is viewed as discriminatory and oppressive, resulting in demands that these movements be portrayed in a positive light and compensated for past ill-treatment (Ball et al., 2013, p. 223).[7]

The politics of identity and entitlement has led parallelist approaches to focus on the lack of public recognition of Indigenous nationhood and sovereignty—aspirations that Indigenous movements point out have been repeatedly suppressed by colonization. This loss of political independence, according to parallelists, has prevented Aboriginal people from asserting control over their lives, resulting in impoverishment, low educational levels, and social pathologies (Monture-Angus, 1995, pp. 26, 51–52; Schissel & Wotherspoon, 2003, pp. 22, 29). It also, parallelists point out, has resulted in the destruction of Aboriginal cultural features. The retention of Aboriginal traditions is regarded as essential because Aboriginal culture is understood as being innate (RCAP, 1996, Vol. 1, pp. xxiii–xxiv), a view that has similarities to the primordialist nationalist paradigm.[8] Aboriginal culture is assumed to be tied to ancestry, as Aboriginal traditions are understood as instructions from the Creator that have been passed down from one generation to another.[9] This results in the parallelist argument that the diminished usage of Aboriginal languages, and erosion of spiritual beliefs, is a form of genocide.[10] These cultural characteristics are perceived as being inextricably connected to Aboriginal identity (Alfred, 2009, p. 7; Alfred, 2004, pp. 89, 95), and so Aboriginal well-being is linked to their revitalization in a separate educational system.[11]

In contrast to universalist notions of progress found in integrationist perspectives, parallelist assumptions are culturally and epistemologically relativist[12]—an ideological position characteristic of postmodernism.[13] This is seen in the labelling of the Canadian education system as "Eurocentric"—the implication being that modern educational methods are applicable only to those with European heritage. This label is used by parallelists, in fact, to challenge the idea of universal educational standards (Schissel & Wotherspoon, 2003, pp. 21–23).

Nowhere is the relativist character of parallelism more apparent than in discussions about Aboriginal epistemology. Sometimes it is argued that there are two knowledge systems—one Aboriginal and one that exists among white settler Canadians (Ermine, 1995, pp. 101–112); at other times it is maintained that each Aboriginal group has its own epistemology drawn from its unique tribal experiences and interaction with the spirit world (Redwing Saunders & Hill, 2007, p. 1019; Battiste, 1986, p. 25).

While parallelists stress the difference between Aboriginal and non-Aboriginal education, there is also a tendency advocating a merging of the two paths, proposing that participation in the former will facilitate Aboriginal participation in the latter (Schissel & Wotherspoon, 2003, p. 28; Brant Castellano, Davis, & Lahache, 2000c, p. xiv). In fact, many argue that preserving Aboriginal culture will enable Aboriginal peoples to *more* fully participate in Canadian society (Brant Castellano, Davis, & Lahache, 2000c, p. xiv; RCAP, 1996, Vol. 4, pp. 522, 530–531; Schissel & Wotherspoon, 2003, p. 28). Another argument is for Aboriginal cultural features to be incorporated into the Canadian educational system, which would simultaneously enhance Aboriginal success in the mainstream and improve the Canadian system (Friesen & Friesen, 2002; RCAP, 1996, Vol. 1, pp. 684–685).

These arguments result in the proposition that more funding is required for building a separate Aboriginal educational system, and to some extent, to radically transform mainstream education (Barman, Hébert, & McCaskill, 1986a, pp. 16–17; Brant Castellano, Davis, & Lahache, 2000b, p. 251).

Although parallelist approaches are the most prevalent in discussions of Aboriginal education policy, this viewpoint has been challenged by a number of academics and educational professionals. These critics espouse what can be loosely characterized as integrationism. These approaches oppose parallelism's focus on promoting Aboriginal difference over the common values and knowledge that are required to contribute to humanity as a whole. They also reject parallelism's reliance on cultural and epistemological relativism.

Integrationism: Inclusion, Universality, and Progress

In contrast to parallelism, integrationism rejects the idea that the future for Aboriginal–non-Aboriginal relations can be improved by encouraging an autonomous and culturally different Native educational system. It sees parallelist arguments as being equivalent to the "separate but equal" logic that opposed black integration in the United States. Integrationist proponents are universalist, not relativist, in their underlying assumptions about the development and acquisition of knowledge, maintaining that educational progress has been a continuum throughout history. All should be able to enjoy the fruits of human educational development, integrationists assert; they argue that improving the educational achievement of all, including the performance of Aboriginal peoples in the conventional system, should be the focus.

There is a binary distinction in integrationist approaches, however. One is informed by liberalism and the other by the political economy tradition. Liberal integrationist approaches regard individual freedom, not group identity, as the important agent for change in determining the good life (Ball et al., 2013, p. 40). Freedom of the individual can be nourished by removing obstacles—discriminatory laws, racist attitudes, traditions, etc.—that thwart a person's ability to choose how they want to live their life (Ball et al., 2013, p. 41). It is assumed that all individuals have the capacity to use reason to determine what is in their best interest, and any attempt to link a person's status to heredity, or limit individual freedom by excessive government regulation or appealing to group solidarity, is questioned.

With respect to Aboriginal peoples in Canada, liberal assumptions can be seen most clearly in Tom Flanagan's book *First Nations? Second*

Thoughts—views that first appeared in the Liberal government's 1969 White Paper on Indian Policy. In his book, Flanagan (2000) argues against most government intervention on the grounds that it prevents individuals from being free and prosperous (p. 8). He opposes government policies that provide people with different legal rights based on unchangeable qualities such as race and sex, as this impedes the free association of individuals (Flanagan, 2000, p. 8–9). As a result, Flanagan (2000) promotes transferring funding directly to Aboriginal peoples so that government interference can be limited (pp. 197–198). He laments band council control over Aboriginal communities, arguing that this threatens individual freedom and impedes economic efficiency (Flanagan, 2001, p. 154).

Revisions to liberalism, however, challenge Flanagan's classical liberal assumptions about minimal government intervention and equality under the law. Put forward most comprehensively by Alan Cairns (2000) in his book *Citizens Plus: Aboriginal Peoples and the Canadian State*, this reform liberal position asserts that ensuring equal legal and political rights is not sufficient to obtain Aboriginal consent in the Canadian political system. Aboriginal peoples need to have their culture recognized by the Canadian state, according to Cairns, if the political system is to become legitimate in the eyes of the Native population. Unlike the case of parallelism, Aboriginal culture is not promoted for its own sake. It is intended to facilitate Aboriginal acceptance of Canadian citizenship—an integrationist goal;[14] Cairns (2001) is opposed to Flanagan's insistence on "a common, uniform citizenship" because this does not recognize Aboriginal peoples' desire for autonomy, recognition, and dignity (pp. 155, 158). Cairns (2001) advocates a positive role for the state to address Aboriginal poverty and the state of crisis that exists in Aboriginal communities (pp. 156–157).

While Flanagan and Cairns do not devote much time to discussing Aboriginal education specifically, other commentators with similar assumptions have. These liberal perspectives focus on the removal of obstacles that prevent Aboriginal people from achieving the same participation rates and educational levels as the rest of the Canadian population, and often refer to individual qualities to explain educational deficits (Schissel & Wotherspoon, 2003, pp. 17–18). They argue that Aboriginal participation in Canadian society can only be brought about through the unencumbered operation of market forces, and this should be facilitated, as much as possible, by the educational system. Special bureaucratic structures devoted to Aboriginal education and legal preferences should be eliminated as these obstruct individual choice, stifle innovation, and reduce incentives for the Native population to compete with others and take responsibility for their own lives (Schissel and Wotherspoon, 2003, p. 18; Wotherspoon & Satzewich, 2000, p. xxii). As Tom Flanagan (2000) argues, "most aboriginal advocates define 'doing better' as succeeding not by their own efforts, but by getting something from the oppressors," including "the attainment of land and natural resources, bigger budgetary appropriations, and financial compensation for residential schools ..." (p. 195). This, according to Flanagan (2000), "does not produce independence and prosperity (p. 195).

When cultural factors are examined in liberal approaches, they are perceived in terms of the extent to which they aid or impede individual integration into the wider society. "Cultural deficit approaches," for example, maintain that certain cultural features in Aboriginal traditions have been detrimental to educational success (Schissel & Wotherspoon, 2003, p. 21; Nagler, 1975, p. 32). These views were prominent in educational anthropology in the 1960s (St. Denis, 2011, p. 178), where it was maintained that certain cultural beliefs and practices made it more likely for marginalized minorities to fail.

Recent developments in liberal approaches to Aboriginal education have shied away from focusing on traditional cultural features as obstacles to Aboriginal educational success. Instead, Aboriginal culture is seen as being helpful in certain contexts. The "cultural discontinuity thesis," for example, maintains that the failure to recognize Aboriginal culture in the educational system has slowed the pace of integration and maintained the gap between Aboriginal and non-Aboriginal students. According to this view, Aboriginal cultures need to be included in the educational system to help students make the transition to an alien cultural framework (Schissel & Wotherspoon, 2003, pp. 21–22).[15] Other liberal perspectives argue that an individual's freedom can be enhanced by cultural supports or "social capital," which is cultivated by the revitalization of Aboriginal political communities (Schissel & Wotherspoon, 2003, p. 19). It is pointed out that a high level of education among Aboriginal people reduces income and employment gaps (Schissel & Wotherspoon, 2003, p. 19), and promoting Aboriginal culture could be used to obtain higher attendance and graduation rates (Abele, Dittburner, & Graham, 2000, p. 8). New legal frameworks also are proposed to facilitate Aboriginal integration into the Canadian educational system. What is needed is more Aboriginal involvement in the development of educational policy to ensure that the Canadian educational system provides appropriate choices and is responsive to Aboriginal concerns.

As can be seen from these recent theoretical developments, some liberal approaches to Aboriginal education argue for a certain amount of cultural revitalization and political autonomy in the Canadian system.[16] As such, these approaches share some of the characteristics of parallelism. Liberal arguments proposing increasing control for Aboriginal peoples, however, still stress the need for common goals and participation in Canadian society. While parallelism stresses the importance of Aboriginal identity with respect to Indigenous self-determination, liberals are concerned with identity only to the extent that it enables the freedom of the individual to flourish. Preserving Aboriginal culture is not seen as an end in itself, only as a means to enhance Aboriginal participation in the Canadian educational system and in the wider society.

As well as differences existing between liberalism and parallelism, there is diversity within integrationism; perspectives influenced by the political economy tradition, in particular, take issue with liberalism's individualistic assumptions. They are critical of the economic inequalities that are not addressed by the liberal promotion of increasing choice, enhancing social capital, and obtaining consent. These ideals of liberalism, according to political economists, disregard the fact that individual well-being and self-actualization are elusive in the context of economic inequality. Political economists assume that "true freedom—freedom from exploitation and alienation, the freedom to develop one's human powers to their fullest—can flourish only in a classless society" (Ball et al., 2013, p. 133).

Political economy approaches, however, share similarities with liberal ones in that they are products of the Enlightenment and therefore accept the notion of historical progress.[17] Progress is envisioned not in terms of individual freedom, as in liberalism, but in the tendency of productive forces to develop.[18] The development of productive forces generates greater surpluses that make improvements in socially beneficial goods and services, including modern education, possible (Trotsky, 1965, pp. 56, 78). Although the human tendency to increase control over nature is linked to the human species' capacity to reason, as well as increases in scientific knowledge and self-awareness, these are the necessary result, not the cause, of historical progress (Trotsky, 1965, p. 64; 1967, p. 21).

Recognizing the tendency of productive forces to develop does not mean that political economists believe that capitalism is "the end of history," as is the case with liberalism (Fukuyama, 1992). This is because increases in productive capacity are thwarted by the conflicts that are created between classes—defined in terms of those who own the means of production (land, factories, etc.) and those who are forced to work for those who do. Economic disparities are also complicated by the processes of colonization when the expansion of the capitalist system brought peoples with vastly different levels of development together, as occurred with respect to Aboriginal–non-Aboriginal relations in Canada. Since political economists argue that relatively unproductive economies limit institutional complexity and the capacity for human understanding (Trotsky, 1967, p. 21), they would agree with liberals that some aspects of Aboriginal culture contribute to the relative deprivation of the Native population in a capitalist society. Political economists, however, would also assert that the capitalist system acts to maintain the isolation and marginalization of many Aboriginal people, entrenching their low educational levels. The problem, for political economists, is that universal education and other public services have not been provided to the level that will address the developmental differences between societies based on hunting and gathering and horticulture and those that have developed industrial processes. Political economists claim that the socialist provision of intensive educational services—based on need, not market forces—would enable academic achievement to be substantially improved in the marginalized Canadian Aboriginal population.

On the surface, it may appear that political economy approaches are similar to those of parallelism because both recognize colonialism's contribution to the educational difficulties being experienced by the Aboriginal population. Parallelism, however, differs in that it focuses on the lack of recognition of Aboriginal nationhood and cultural identity, not class exploitation. Political economists, on the contrary, argue that it is one's productive contribution to socially necessary goods and services (Ball et al., 2013, pp. 121, 169), not entitlements based on original occupancy or tribal position, that should determine a person's socially granted rights. They would oppose the idea of exclusively owned Aboriginal lands and hereditary control over the allocation of educational programs; they would argue that goods and services should benefit all equally, not just those with tribal connections. Political economy approaches embrace "the power and importance of universal humanitarian idealism" but maintain this idealism should be "grounded in the reality of material conditions rather than in the illusory distortions of ideology" (Rata, 2000, p. xvi).

Political economists maintain that the material conditions determining Aboriginal-non-Aboriginal relations in general, and Aboriginal education in particular, are rooted in the combination of

Aboriginal societies with capitalism (Rata, 2003, p. 45). This results in Aboriginal kinship relations being used to distribute the surpluses created by a capitalist economy. Unlike precontact Aboriginal relations, which occurred in the context of subsistence economies, Aboriginal tribal relations in a capitalist environment result in profound inequalities. These inequalities are disguised by a neotraditionalist ideology that assumes that tribal politics are transcendentally communal or socialistic (Rata, 2005, pp. 275–276). Political economists also point out that Aboriginal tribal incorporation into the capitalist system is actually *supported* by modern states, as this helps to break down the welfare state and the system of organized labour that emerged during the post-war period (Rata, 1999, p. 239).

The neotraditionalist ideology that has justified tribal control over the distribution of resource rents, compensation packages, and government transfers is at the heart of the problems facing Aboriginal education, according to political economists. Instead of Aboriginal peoples joining forces with the working class to wage a struggle to recapture control over education in the interests of all, political economists note that monetary transfers for educational programs become a revenue stream for privileged tribal leaders. It is pointed out that the substandard education that is provided by tribal governments is legitimated by relativist assumptions that deny the possibility of academic standards. The promotion of Native spirituality that is justified by relativism is not only inconsistent with the evidence-based approaches that are needed to develop the knowledge required for survival in an industrial and information-based economy (Widdowson, 2006, p. 625); it also is perceived to obscure the low educational levels in Aboriginal communities, thereby entrenching the position of tribal elites. Political economists argue that Aboriginal demands for tribally controlled education constitute a rolling back of the progress that has been made toward universal, publicly funded education.

Political economy, therefore, differs from parallelism in that it does not see public education for Aboriginal peoples as a form of colonialist domination. The problem is not that the state is providing education to Aboriginal students but the fact that, in a capitalist society, administrative functions are usurped by dominant class interests (Communist Students, 2011). Political economists note that education, like many other services, is socially necessary, but it needs to be refashioned so that it will serve humanity, not the interests of a particular class. Therefore, they would exhort all Canadians, including Aboriginal peoples, to fight for universal free education, based on scientific and humanistic principles, as this is a progressive gain for the working class and therefore humanity as a whole.

Because common ownership, the public provision of universal educational programs, and educational planning are all promoted in political economy approaches, they have been criticized by both parallelism and liberalism. Liberalism criticizes political economy for its top-down approach to education. Because liberals maintain that the individual is best able to determine their own interests, any promotion of increasing the government role in society is regarded with suspicion.[19] Parallelism, on the other hand, sees political economists as failing to understand the flourishing and renewal of Aboriginal cultures, and the political agency that has enabled the Native population to resist colonialism. Parallelists view any attempt to identify developmental differences as an attempt to justify the oppression of Aboriginal peoples. They object to characterizing Aboriginal cultural features as undeveloped,[20] viewing Native economic, political, and intellectual traditions as viable in the modern context and a benefit to Aboriginal peoples and society more generally (Widdowson, 2006, pp. 224–225; Widdowson & Howard, 2009).

Regardless of how one chooses to classify different approaches to Aboriginal education, the points of contention remain clear. The crucial debate that needs to occur concerns the role that Aboriginal traditions will play in the educational system, and the degree of Aboriginal autonomy that would be beneficial. Are the knowledge and educational practices found in mainstream education more developed than those that exist in Aboriginal traditions? Can all Aboriginal traditions be used to improve Aboriginal circumstances, or just some? Are these traditions to be used merely as a tool for integration, or is their preservation a goal in its own right? Can Aboriginal traditions enhance mainstream education, or would their characteristics constitute a violation of modern scientific and humanistic principles? It is hoped that the chapters that follow in this volume will shed some light on these questions.

The Structure of the Book

In order to help readers to "hunt assumptions" so that the search for solutions can really begin, the book is divided into three parts. Part I contains a selection of articles that are representative of parallelist approaches. Parallelist approaches are discussed first because they constitute the vast majority of articles on Aboriginal education in the literature.

The section on parallelist approaches contains two articles that provide general commentary on Aboriginal education. It was originally intended to include an article by Marie Battiste here, as she is one of the most significant theorists articulating the case for parallelism in Aboriginal education, but due to the intervention by Cora Weber-Pillwax, mentioned earlier, this chapter had to be deleted. These general articles on Aboriginal education are followed by specific chapters on different areas of education: early childhood, primary, and secondary schooling; post-secondary education; and teacher training. A very interesting article on primary and secondary schooling in Nunavut also has been removed from this section because permission to publish was rescinded by one of its authors, as noted previously.

Part II of the book contains a number of articles that can be categorized as "integrationist" in their intent. These include approaches from liberal and political economy perspectives. This part begins with general articles containing liberal assumptions, followed by more specific articles pertaining to liberal perspectives on post-secondary education. Chapters articulating liberal perspectives are followed by general and specific articles from political economists.

Part III, the final part of the book, is called "Exchanges." In this section, we have given the different perspectives the opportunity to speak directly with one another. In the first exchange, a parallelist responds to a contributor with liberal assumptions. The second exchange is between a parallelist and a political economist. Fortunately, the intervention of Weber-Pillwax did not prevent the inclusion of this parallelist article (by David Newhouse). And since parallelism is the dominant perspective in the literature on Aboriginal education, this approach, exemplified by the arguments of Newhouse, has been given the opportunity to make the final response.

REFERENCES

Abbott Mihesuah, D., & Cavender Wilson, A. (Eds.). (2004). *Indigenizing the academy: Transforming scholarship and empowering communities*. Lincoln: University of Nebraska Press.

Abele, F., Dittburner, C., & Graham, K.A. (2000). Towards a shared understanding in the policy discussion about Aboriginal education. In M. Brant Castellano, L. Davis, & L. Lahache (Eds.), *Aboriginal education: Fulfilling the promise* (pp. 3–24). Vancouver: University of British Columbia Press.

Abele, F., & Stasiulis, D. (1989). Canada as a "white settler colony": What about Natives and immigrants? In W. Clement & G. Williams (Eds.), *The new Canadian political economy* (pp. 240–277). Kingston, ON: McGill-Queen's University Press.

Ajzenstat, J. (2008, August 28). Harvey Mansfield on Canada. *The Idea File*. Retrieved March 2013, from http://janetajzenstat.wordpress.com/2008/08/28/harvey-mansfield-on-canada/

Alfred, T. (2000). Of white heroes and old men talking. *Windspeaker, 18*(2), p. 4.

Alfred, T. (2004). Warrior scholarship: Seeing the university as a ground of contention. In D. Abbott Mihesuah & A. Cavender Wilson (Eds.), *Indigenizing the academy: Transforming scholarship and empowering communities* (pp. 88–99). Lincoln: University of Nebraska Press.

Alfred, T. (2009). *Peace, power, righteousness: An Indigenous manifesto* (2nd ed.). Toronto: Oxford University Press.

Alfred, T. (2011). Colonial stains on our existence. In M.J. Cannon & L. Sunseri (Eds.), *Racism, colonialism, and indigeneity* (pp. 3–10). Toronto: Oxford University Press.

Ball, T., Dagger, R., Christian, W., & Campbell, C. (2013). *Political ideologies and the democratic ideal* (third Canadian edition). Toronto: Pearson.

Barman, J., Hébert, Y., & McCaskill, D. (1986a). The legacy of the past: An overview. In J. Barman, Y. Hébert, & D. McCaskill (Eds.), *Indian education in Canada: The legacy* (Vol. 1) (pp. 1–22). Vancouver: University of British Columbia Press.

Barman, J., Hébert, Y., & McCaskill, D. (Eds.). (1986b). *Indian education in Canada: The legacy.* (Vol. 1). Vancouver: University of British Columbia Press.

Barman, J., Hébert, Y., & McCaskill, D. (Eds.). (1987). *Indian education in Canada: The challenge.* (Vol. 2). Vancouver: University of British Columbia Press.

Battiste, M. (1986). Micmac literacy and cognitive assimilation. In J. Barman, Y. Hébert, & D. McCaskill (Eds.), *Indian education in Canada volume 1: The legacy* (pp. 23–44). Vancouver: University of British Columbia Press.

Battiste, M. (Ed.). (2000). *Reclaiming Indigenous voice and vision.* Vancouver: University of British Columbia Press.

Battiste, M., & Barman, J. (Eds.). (1995). *First Nations education in Canada: The circle unfolds.* Vancouver: University of British Columbia Press.

Battiste, M., & Henderson, J. (2011). Eurocentrism and the European ethnographic tradition. In M.J. Cannon & L. Sunseri (Eds.), *Racism, colonialism, and indigeneity in Canada* (pp. 11–19). Toronto: Oxford University Press.

Binda, K.P., & Calliou, S. (Eds.). (2001). *Aboriginal education in Canada: A study in decolonization.* Mississauga, ON: Canadian Educators' Press.

Brant Castellano, M., Davis, L., & Lahache, L. (Eds.). (2000a). *Aboriginal education: Fulfilling the promise.* Vancouver: University of British Columbia Press.

Brant Castellano, M., Davis, L., & Lahache, L. (2000b). Conclusion: Fulfilling the promise. In M. Brant Castellano, L. Davis, & L. Lahache (Eds.), *Aboriginal education: Fulfilling the promise* (pp. 251–255). Vancouver: University of British Columbia Press.

Brant Castellano, M., Davis, L., & Lahache, L. (2000c). Introduction. In M. Brant Castellano, L. Davis, & L. Lahache (Eds.), *Aboriginal education: Fulfilling the promise* (pp. xi–xviii). Vancouver: University of British Columbia Press.

Brookfield, S.D. (2012). *Teaching for critical thinking: Tools and techniques to help students question their assumptions.* San Francisco: John Wiley & Sons.

Cairns, A. (2000). *Citizens plus: Aboriginal peoples and the Canadian State.* Vancouver: University of British Columbia Press.

Cairns, A. (2001, Summer). An exchange on Aboriginal policy. *Inroads, 21*, 108–116, 120–122.

Callinicos, A. (1995). *Theories and narratives: Reflections on the philosophy of history.* Cambridge, UK: Polity Press.

Cannon, M.J., & Sunseri, L. (2011a). Not disappearing: An introduction to the text. In M.J. Cannon & L. Sunseri (Eds.), *Racism, colonialism, and indigeneity in Canada* (pp. xiii–xxvi). Toronto: Oxford University Press.

Cannon, M.J., & Sunseri, L. (Eds.). (2011b). *Racism, colonialism, and indigeneity in Canada.* Toronto: Oxford University Press.

Cohen, G.A. (2000). *Karl Marx's theory of history: A defence.* Princeton: Princeton University Press.

Communist Students. (2011, October 8). *Marx and Education*. Retrieved March 2013, from http://communiststudents.org.uk/?p=7089

Corntassel, J., & Spak, S. (2010, Fall). Lighting the eighth fire: The liberation, resurgence, and protection of Indigenous nations [review]. *Wicazo Sa Review, 25*(2), 135–138. http://dx.doi.org/10.1353/wic.2010.0014

Ermine, W. (1995). Aboriginal epistemology. In M. Battiste & J. Barman (Eds.), *First Nations education in Canada: The circle unfolds* (pp. 101–112). Vancouver: University of British Columbia Press.

Flanagan, T. (2000). *First nations? Second thoughts*. Montreal: McGill-Queen's University Press.

Flanagan, T. (2001, Summer). An exchange on Aboriginal policy. *Inroads, 21*, 103–107, 117–118.

Friesen, J.W., & Friesen, V.L. (2002). *Aboriginal education in Canada: A plea for integration*. Calgary, AB: Detselig Enterprises Ltd.

Fukuyama, F. (1992). *The end of history and the last man*. New York: Free Press.

Green, J. (2003). Decolonization and recolonization in Canada. In W. Clement & L.F. Vosko (Eds.), *Changing Canada: The political economy of transformation* (pp. 51–78). Montreal: McGill-Queen's University Press.

Hanon, A. (2010, March 4). A lesson in racism. *Edmonton Sun*.

Hobsbawm, E. (2002). *On History*. London: Abacus.

Johnston, D. (1986). The quest of the Six Nations Confederacy for self-determination. *University of Toronto Faculty of Law Review, 44*(1), 1–32.

Koptie, S.W. (2010). Kanehsatà:ke: Canadian colonial aporias. *Social Studies, 6*(1), 137–155.

Mercredi, O., & Turpel, M.E. (1993). *In the rapids: Navigating the future of First Nations*. Toronto: Viking.

Monture-Angus, P. (1995). *Thunder in my soul: A Mohawk woman speaks*. Halifax, NS: Fernwood.

Monture-Angus, P. (1999). *Journeying forward: Dreaming First Nations' independence*. Halifax, NS: Fernwood Publishing.

Morris, S., McLeod, K., & Danesi, M. (Eds.). (1993). *Aboriginal languages and education: The Canadian experience*. Oakville, ON: Mosaic Press.

Nagler, M. (1975). *Natives without a home*. Don Mills, ON: Longman Canada Limited.

Paquette, J., & Fallon, G. (2010). *First Nations education policy in Canada: Progress or gridlock?* Toronto: University of Toronto Press.

Rata, E. (1999). The theory of neotribal capitalism. *RE:view, 22*(3), 231–288.

Rata, E. (2000). *The political economy of neotribal capitalism*. Maryland: Lexington Books.

Rata, E. (2003). Late capitalism and ethnic revivalism. *Anthropological Theory, 3*(1), 43–63. http://dx.doi.org/10.1177/1463499603003001751

Rata, E. (2005). Rethinking biculturalism. *Anthropological Theory, 5*(3), 267–284. http://dx.doi.org/10.1177/1463499605055960

Redwing Saunders, S., & Hill, S.M. (2007). Native education and in-classroom coalition-building: Factors and models in delivering an equitous authentic education. *Canadian Journal of Education, 30*(4), 1015–1045. http://dx.doi.org/10.2307/20466677

Royal Commission on Aboriginal Peoples (RCAP). (1996). *Final report of the Royal Commission on Aboriginal Peoples*. (Vols. 1, 4). Ottawa: Supply and Services Canada.

Schissel, B., & Wotherspoon, T. (2003). *The legacy of school for Aboriginal people: Education, oppression and emancipation*. Toronto: Oxford University Press.

Shimo, A. (2009, February 25). Tough critique or hate speech. Retrieved from http://www2.macleans.ca/2009/02/25/tough-critique-or-hate-speech

Simpson, L. (2008). Our elder brothers: The lifeblood of resurgences. In L. Simpson (Ed.), *Lighting the eighth fire: The liberation, resurgence, and protection of Indigenous nations* (pp. 73–89). Winnipeg, MB: Arbeiter Ring Publishing.

Smith, A.D. (2001). *Nationalism.* Cambridge, UK: Polity Press.

Sokal, A., & Bricmont, J. (1998). *Fashionable nonsense: Postmodern intellectuals' abuse of science.* New York: Picador USA.

St. Denis, V. (2011). Rethinking culture theory in Aboriginal education. In M.J. Cannon & L. Sunseri (Eds.), *Racism, colonialism, and indigeneity in Canada* (pp. 177–187). Toronto: Oxford University Press.

Stiffarm, L.A. (Ed.). (1998). *As we see ... Aboriginal pedagogy.* Saskatoon, SK: University Extension Press.

Styres, S., Singa, D., Bennett, S., & Bomberry, M. (2010). Walking in two worlds: Engaging the space between Indigenous community and academia. *Canadian Journal of Education, 33*(3), 617–648.

Trotsky, L. (1965). *The revolution betrayed: What is the Soviet Union and where is it going?* (M. Eastman, Trans.). New York: Merit Publishers. (Original work published 1937)

Trotsky, L. (1967). *The history of the Russian revolution.* (Vol. 1) (M. Eastman, Trans.) London, UK: Sphere Books. (Original work published 1932/1933)

Weber-Pillwax, C., Rost, M., & Auger, S. (2010, February 26). ATA invites racism into Alberta classrooms. Retrieved March 2013, from http://blogs.mtroyal.ca/fwiddowson/files/2010/03/Press-Release-Weber-Pillwax-et-al.pdf

Widdowson, F. (2006). *The political economy of Aboriginal dependency: A critique of the Royal Commission on Aboriginal Peoples.* (Unpublished doctoral dissertation). York University.

Widdowson, F. (2009, July 15). Letter to board of directors of the Canadian Political Science Association. Retrieved March 2013, from http://blogs.mtroyal.ca/fwiddowson/files/2009/11/Professional-Misconduct-and-the-CPSA-Womens-Caucus.pdf

Widdowson, F., & Howard, A. (2009, May). *Development, postmodernism and Aboriginal policy: What are we afraid of?* Paper presented at the Annual Meeting of the Canadian Political Science Association, Carleton University.

Wotherspoon, T., & Satzewich, V. (2000). *First Nations: Race, class, and gender relations.* Regina: Canadian Plains Research Center.

NOTES

1 The words "hunting assumptions" are taken from Brookfield (2012), who maintains that one of the essential processes in critical thinking is "trying to discover what our assumptions are, and then trying to judge when, and how far, these are accurate" (p. 7). According to Brookfield (2012), "you cannot think critically without hunting assumptions; that is, without trying to uncover assumptions and then trying to assess their accuracy and validity, their fit with life" (p. 7).

2 Brookfield (2012) notes that the process of critical thinking involves "(1) identifying the assumptions that frame our thinking and determine our actions, (2) checking out the degree to which these assumptions are accurate and valid, (3) looking at our ideas and decisions (intellectual, organizational, and personal) from several different perspectives, and (4) on the basis of all this, taking informed actions" (p. 1).

3 See, for example, Barman, Hébert, and McCaskill (1986b, 1987); Morris, McLeod, and Danesi (1993); Battiste and Barman (1995); Stiffarm (1998); Brant Castellano, Davis, and Lahache (2000a); Battiste (2000); Binda and Calliou (2001); Abbott Mihesuah and Cavender Wilson (2004); and Cannon and Sunseri (2011b).

4 The parallelist assumptions of RCAP with respect to Aboriginal education are extensively analyzed in Widdowson (2006, especially pp. 586–655).

5 For additional discussions of the application of the two-row wampum metaphor to Aboriginal–non-Aboriginal relations, see Monture-Angus (1999, p. 38); Johnston (1986); Koptie (2010); Mercredi and Turpel (1993, p. 35); and Redwing Saunders and Hill (2007, p. 1021).

6 The two-row wampum image appears on the cover of the Penner Commission of Self-Government's report, and Phil Fontaine refers to it in his response to the "Statement of Reconciliation."

7 For a very good example of the politics of entitlement and identity in the Aboriginal context, see Taiaiake Alfred (2011, pp. 4, 8–9).

8 According to Anthony D. Smith (2001), the *primordialist* paradigm asserts that nations "exist in the first order of time, and lie at the root of subsequent processes and developments" (p. 51). For a discussion of primordialism, see Smith (2001, pp. 51–57).

9 See Styres, Singa, Bennett, and Bomberry (2010, p. 622), and Cannon and Sunseri (2011a, p. xix)

10 See Ball et al. (2013, p. 226). Leanne Simpson (2008), for example, refers to the loss of Indigenous languages as "linguistic genocide" (p. 76).

11 The new field of "Indigenous resurgence," for example, links community health to a reconnection with ancestral circumstances. See, for example, Corntassel and Spak (2010, p. 135).

12 Claims to universality are asserted to be arrogant and narcissistic. See, for example, Battiste and Henderson (2011, pp. 12, 14, 18); Alfred (2011, p. 3); and Styres et al. (2010).

13 *Postmodernism* is defined by Sokal and Bricmont (1998) as "an intellectual current characterized by the more-or-less explicit rejection of the rationalist tradition of the Enlightenment, by theoretical discourses disconnected from any empirical test, and by a cognitive and cultural relativism that regards science as nothing more than a 'narration', a 'myth' or a social construction among many others" (p. 1). For a discussion of the connection between postmodernism and approaches to Aboriginal education in Canada, see Wotherspoon and Satzewich (2000, p. xxiv).

14 This is why parallelists are so opposed to Cairns's views. See, for example, Alfred (2000, p. 4).

15 For a criticism of this view, see St. Denis (2011, p. 178).

16 See, for example, Paquette and Fallon (2010) for an example of an attempt to deal with the problem of "offer[ing] quality education that is authentically and deeply Aboriginal yet meets the curriculum content requirements and standards of the provincial and territorial systems" (p. i).

17 As has been noted by Callinicos (1995), political economy assumes there is "directionality" in history, where "each successive social form represents an increase in some property common to all kinds of society" (p. 102). The property that is common is productive forces.

18 Hobsbawm (2002) has characterized this thusly: "the persistent and increasing capacity of the human species to control the forces of nature by means of manual and mental labour, technology and the organization of production," which is "demonstrated by the growth—particularly in the past few centuries—of production and productive capacity" (p. 41). See also, Callinicos (1995, p. 107), and Cohen (2000, pp. 28–62).

19 Flanagan, in fact, has referred to Canadian Aboriginal policy as a "failure of socialism," since Aboriginal communities are "socialist ghettos, where everyone

works for the government." These comments were made on the program *Studio One*, TV Ontario, May 22, 2001.

20 These arguments are even made in approaches that claim to be associated with the political economy tradition. Green (2003), for example, refers to ideas envisioning "human development [as] an ineluctable trajectory of beneficial improvement correlated with 'our' mastery and exploitation of nature" as the "shared myth of liberalism and socialism" (p. 55), while Abele and Stasiulis (1989) conclude that "there is no particular virtue in seeking a replication of European stages in the evolution of social formations everywhere" (p. 250).

Part I: Parallelist Approaches

Parallelism is the most common perspective in the literature on Aboriginal education. As noted earlier, it is often symbolized by the two-row wampum where Aboriginal and non-Aboriginal communities travel on separate paths controlling their distinctive cultural features. The goal is to enable Indigenous self-determination, including the revitalization of traditional knowledge and educational practices, so that Aboriginal peoples can overcome the oppression brought by colonization. Part I provides a wide range of approaches motivated by these objectives.

The first two articles in Part I provide a general discussion of Aboriginal education from a parallelist standpoint and examine a number of concerns that express this view. The first article is by Verna J. Kirkness, a scholar who has studied Aboriginal education for over 40 years. In this chapter, Kirkness provides a historical overview of Aboriginal education policy and the challenges that continue to face the development of an autonomous Aboriginal educational system. Kirkness maintains that much work still needs to be done to ensure that Aboriginal education is holistic and incorporates traditional values while at the same time embracing modern scientific and technical advancements.

Kirkness's article was to be followed by an article by Marie Battiste, one of the most prolific and well-known scholars writing about Aboriginal education. As was mentioned in the introduction to this book, this article is not included because of the interference of Cora Weber-Pillwax and the subsequent decision of Battiste to rescind permission for reprinting it. In our view, this circumstance exemplifies the continuing censorial climate surrounding the development of Aboriginal education policy and the resulting obstruction of open and honest debate.

Battiste's (1998) article, entitled "Enabling the Autumn Seed: Toward a Decolonized Approach to Aboriginal Knowledge, Language and Education," is available on the Internet and can be accessed from the website of the Mi'kmaq Resource Centre at Cape Breton University. The article is an important representation of parallelism because it attempts to illustrate that the Canadian educational system is colonialist and results in what Battiste calls the cognitive imperialism of Aboriginal students. Battiste charges that colonization has eroded the knowledge required for Aboriginal peoples to heal and develop as self-confident nations. The revitalization and use of Aboriginal languages is essential, according to Battiste, as this will maintain continuity with ancestral traditions. Battiste describes a number of obstacles that prevent Aboriginal knowledge and languages from being recognized and protected, including the stipulation that Aboriginal education must meet provincial curricular standards.

The second article is by Verna St. Denis, who draws attention to the problematic discourse of multiculturalism in discussions about Aboriginal education. St. Denis's focus is somewhat different from that of Kirkness and Battiste in that she is less concerned with cognitive imperialism and cultural revitalization than the other authors. St. Denis, however, is disturbed about the impact of colonialism on Aboriginal education. She maintains that the discourse of multiculturalism accepts colonialist assumptions and perpetuates Aboriginal marginalization. Multiculturalism, according to St. Denis, masquerades as a tolerant and neutral ideology, but, in so doing, undermines assertions about Indigenous sovereignty and the recognition of Aboriginal rights. St. Denis maintains this is one of the reasons why it is difficult for Aboriginal teachers to incorporate meaningful Aboriginal content into the curriculum.

The two general chapters that examine the colonialist nature of Aboriginal education are followed by more specific pieces that focus on different facets of the educational system. These include chapters investigating early childhood education, primary and secondary education, post-secondary education, and Aboriginal teacher education.

Discussion of early childhood education is provided in the chapter by Mai Nguyen, who uses welfare-state and Indigenous-based theories to understand the educational gap between Aboriginal and non-Aboriginal youth. Nguyen suggests that governments must increase the human capital of their citizens by giving them the tools to become productive, but colonialism has diminished Aboriginal peoples' sense of self-worth, eroded their culture, and prevented them from becoming self-determining. Early childhood education must be culturally sensitive and controlled by Aboriginal communities so that Aboriginal children will know who they are, according to Nguyen. This will also enable Aboriginal children to enjoy their early educational experience more, providing a firmer foundation for future academic achievement.

The first chapter that was selected to comment on primary education from a parallelist perspective has been excluded from Part I because of the decision of another author, Paul Berger, in consultation with his co-authors, to rescind permission for publication. Although this article is not available on the Internet, it can be accessed from three library databases provided by ProQuest.[1] Also, the article can be purchased online from British Library Direct.[2]

We are disappointed we could not include this article in Part I, as it provides an examination of some of the problems being experienced by Inuit students in Nunavut—an area that has the lowest educational levels in Canada. In this article, Berger, along with his co-authors Juanita Ross Epp and Helle Møller (2006), observe a clash between Inuit culture and the requirements of the Nunavut school system. This, in conjunction with the region's colonial past, results in absenteeism and low educational performance. To overcome these problems, the authors advocate true Inuit control of education, which involves meaningful consultation, valuing Inuit culture in the school system, and cross-cultural English as a Second Language (ESL) training for teachers. Further, the authors maintain that education in Nunavut should be decolonized by making it more culturally compatible. This would mean that non-Inuit standards for punctuality, attendance and educational achievement would not be imposed. As Berger et al. (2006) put it: "when punctuality, attendance, and achievement concerns are no longer so predictable, it may be because Qallunaat[3] schools have made real strides toward becoming Inuit schools" (p. 201).

The chapter by Wayne Gorman was intended to complement the piece by Berger, Epp, and Møller by examining some of the inequitable learning opportunities that Canadian Native students face. On the basis of interviews with Aboriginal students, Gorman maintains that teachers often create feelings of shame in the classroom through a "hidden curriculum" that conflicts with Aboriginal culture. This hidden curriculum, Gorman asserts, consists of rules and expectations imposed by the dominant culture that disadvantage Native students. According to Gorman, teachers need to be cultural brokers who support, rather than change, the cultural characteristics of Native students.

Gorman's chapter is followed by that of John B. Friesen and Anthony N. Ezeife, who examine some of the problems they perceive to exist with respect to science education in schools. Friesen and Ezeife maintain that visible and meaningful connections need to be made between Western and Aboriginal science, so that Aboriginal students will feel more comfortable in science classrooms. Friesen and Ezeife agree that Aboriginal peoples may need to understand Western society but this should not be at the expense of traditional Native knowledge. To incorporate diverse knowledge systems, Friesen and Ezeife propose the creation of culturally responsive assessment practices. Assessments would consider the cultural backgrounds of students so as to prevent bias and the perpetuation of failure among Aboriginal students. Aboriginal students are disadvantaged, according to Friesen and Ezeife, because Western cultural values are given prominence over Aboriginal traditions. The authors argue this problem should be addressed by connecting the science curriculum to Aboriginal cultural experiences.

In the next chapter, Blair Stonechild examines Aboriginal post-secondary education. His piece gives an overview of the progress that has been made across Canada in achieving Aboriginal control over post-secondary education. This control is necessary, according to Stonechild, because of the colonial nature of post-secondary institutions. His overview, however, points to a number of problems—organizational, financial, and jurisdictional—confronting Aboriginal control over post-secondary education. To address these challenges, Stonechild looks to the tribal college system in the United States for guidance. He also examines the case of the First Nations University of Canada and argues that it illuminates some potential problems that can occur when Aboriginal peoples begin to assert control over an educational institution. This case, according to Stonechild, shows the challenges that face any attempt to create Aboriginal educational institutions in a colonial context.

Linda Goulet and Yvonne McLeod round out Part I with their discussion of Aboriginal teacher education. This chapter describes the use of a cultural camp in Aboriginal adult education. They maintain that outdoor cultural camps are an important element of Aboriginal teacher education because they enable Aboriginal teachers to experience authentic education provided by elders, as well as to affirm their cultural identity and reconnect with the past. Colonialism, Goulet and McLeod argue, severed the connections between Aboriginal peoples and their ancestors. As they claim that creating a positive identity is one of the main objectives of Aboriginal education, Goulet and McLeod stress the importance of Aboriginal teachers acquiring spiritual strength and cultural connections to help their Aboriginal students.

Although they address different facets of Aboriginal education, all of the chapters in Part I share the common assumption that the solution to Aboriginal educational deficits is through more Aboriginal control over the educational system and a revitalization of Aboriginal traditions. They take the relativist position that the standards in the Canadian educational system are reflective of European cultural domination, and that decolonization entails recognizing that there are distinctive Aboriginal ways of knowing, pedagogy, and administrative structures that are more suited to the Aboriginal population's needs.

REFERENCES

Battiste, M. (1998). Enabling the autumn seed: Toward a decolonized approach to Aboriginal knowledge, language, and education. *Canadian Journal of Native Education, 22*(1), 16–27. Retrieved from http://www.cbu.ca/mrc/autumn-seed

Berger, P., Epp, J.R., & Møller, H. (2006). The predictable influences of culture clash, current practice, and colonialism on punctuality, attendance, and achievement in Nunavut schools. *Canadian Journal of Native Education, 29*(2), 182–205.

NOTES

1 The three databases are Canadian Business and Current Affairs Complete, Canadian Business and Current Affairs Education, and Research Library.

2 British Library Document Supply Service, http://direct.bl.uk/bld/PlaceOrder.do?UIN=195619310&ETOC=RN&from=searchengine

3 Berger et al. (2006) note that "by Qallunaat schools we mean schools structured like schools in southern Canada as opposed to schools with large numbers of non-Inuit students or teachers. Some elementary schools in Nunavut are in fact staffed mostly by Inuit, but still function on a southern model" (note 1, p. 201).

1

Aboriginal Education in Canada: A Retrospective and a Prospective

Verna J. Kirkness

This chapter was originally published in the *Journal of American Indian Education* (Fall 1999), *31*(1), pp. 14–30. Reproduced with permission.

Introduction

The year 2000 is a good time to reflect on where we have been and where we want to go in Aboriginal education. During the course of my career in education, which spans over 40 years, I have had the opportunity to work at many levels of education. Similar issues and challenges have existed and continue to exist in post-secondary and in-school education offered to Aboriginal students, both young and old. Though there has been progress in improving access and quality of education for our people, it is clear that much remains to be done. In 1992, I was the principal author of a study commissioned by the Canadian Education Association to determine the state of Aboriginal education in federal, provincial (public and separate), and band schools in Canada. The study, entitled "First Nations and Schools: Triumphs and Struggles," indicated that positive changes began to occur after the policy of "Indian Control of Indian Education" was introduced in 1973. Over the years, I have given many talks on Aboriginal education and written a number of papers on the history of Aboriginal education in Canada that include directions for the future. When asked to submit a paper as a retrospective and prospective of Aboriginal education in Canada for this journal, I went to my file and decided to include two of my papers, one written in 1985 entitled "Indian Education: Past, Present and Future" and the other written in 1998, "Our Peoples' Education: Cut the Shackles, Cut the Crap and Cut the Mustard."

A review of these two papers takes us from our earliest experience in education both informal and formal, albeit briefly, to where we are today. It leaves us to speculate whether we are, in fact, making progress, or whether we are destined to repeat history even at our own hands.

Indian Education: Past, Present, and Future (1985)

The Past: Pre-Contact—Traditional Indian Education

Long before Europeans arrived in North America, Indians had evolved their own form of education. It was an education in which the community was the classroom, its members were the teachers, and each adult was responsible to ensure that each child learned how to live a good life (National Indian Brotherhood, 1973). Central to the teaching was the belief in the Great Spirit. In *The Gospel of the Redman*, it states, "The Redman has the most spiritual civilization the world has ever known … His measure of success is 'How much service have I rendered to my people?' … His mode of life, his thought, his every act are given spiritual significance" (Seton & Seton, 1977). This was expressed in their daily living, in relationship of one to another, in humility, in sharing, in co-operating, in relationship to nature—the land, the animals, in recognition of the Great Spirit, in the way our people thought, felt, and perceived their world. Traditionally, our people's teachings addressed the total being, the whole community, in the context of a viable living culture. Then came the change …

Our Second Past: Contact—Colonial Domination

In the early seventeenth century, European missionaries came to establish schools for Indians. It was believed that this would be the best method of civilizing the "natives." Day or mission schools were the first to be established. The day school concept was largely abandoned in favour of residential (boarding) schools in the 1800s. The highest recorded number of residential schools, which were located all across

Canada, was 80 in 1933. The enrolments ranged anywhere from 50 to over four hundred students of all ages. Most of the residential schools were phased out in the 1960s.

Residential schools were devised as a means of isolating the Indian child from his parents and the influences of the reserve. As one government inspector stated in the mid-1800s:

> Little can be done with him (the Indian child). He can be taught to do a little farming, and at [sic]stock raising, and to dress in a more civilized manner, but that is all. The child who goes to a day school learns little while his tastes are fashioned at home, and his inherited aversion to toil is in no way combatted. (Flood Davin, 1879)

The residential schools were oppressive. Separated from their parents for long periods of time, the students, who ranged in age from three to 18, were subjected to a severe regimen. The boys were expected to clean the stables, attend to the livestock, mend broken machinery, and work in the fields. The girls had to attend to the upkeep of the school, washing and mending clothes, doing kitchen chores, scrubbing floors, and doing other domestic duties. While former students of these schools do not take particular issue with such work, for many years it meant that the students only spent a half-day in the classroom. What was provided was a very basic education designed to prepare the children for a domestic, Christian life.

The residential school was notable for its high mortality rate among the students. At the turn of the century, an estimated 50% of the children who attended these schools did not benefit from the education they received. They died while at the boarding school of diseases such as smallpox and tuberculosis. It is believed that many died of loneliness. Only recently, has the general public become aware of the true devastation suffered by many former residential school students as they reveal the physical, mental, and sexual abuse encountered under this colonial regime.

Having generations of Indian children removed from their parents, denying them a normal childhood and the teachings of their people, resulted in the loss of their cultural traditions including their native languages. It is a dark period in the history of Indian education, the repercussions of which continue to be felt today. The weakening of Indian society as a whole can be attributed to boarding schools. Cultural conflict, alienation, poor self-concept, and lack of preparation for jobs and for life in general derive from this deplorable experience. It is evident that not only are those who actually attended these schools affected but so are their children and their communities.

The government decides on another approach …

Federal Indian Day Schools—Integration

"To civilize and Christianize" gave way in the 1950s to a rise in the number of federally run Indian day schools on reserves to accommodate the closure of residential schools. At the same time, a policy of integration was put into effect. Integration, as it occurred, can be described simply as the process of having Indian students attend public schools. In some cases, residential schools were transformed into student residences and the students attended the nearest public school. In other cases, children were transported from their homes on reserves to adjacent public schools. By the 1970s, the government of Canada had succeeded in making provisions for approximately 60% of Indian students in public schools.

The integration concept was a continuation of government control over the lives of Indian people. It was introduced with little or no consultation with Indian parents, Indian bands, or Indian organizations. No particular preparation of teachers or of curriculum was made to accommodate the children of another culture.

Chief Dan George, in his soliloquy "A Talk to Teachers," made this comment on integration:

> You talk big words of integration in the schools. Does it really exist? Can we talk of integration until there is social integration … unless there is integration of hearts and minds you have only a physical presence … and the walls are as high as the mountain range. (George, c. 1972)

Integration has been, in most schools, "only a physical presence." This approach to education has not been one of true integration where the Indian cultures are respected and recognized. Rather, it has been a process of assimilation where Indians are being absorbed into the non-Indian society.

There has been no notable improvement in the overall achievement of Indian children in integrated schools. Studies on the effects of integration have shown that Indian children reveal patterns that can be identified as alienation and identity conflict. The Indian child is caught between two cultures and is therefore literally outside of, and between, both. The panacea of integration failed to provide the answer to education for Indian students.

It is safe to conclude that federal day schools on reserves had, to this point, provided the scenario most conducive to the Indian child. While schools did little to address the cultural challenges in the curriculum, children were at least able to participate in the life of the community and remain with parents and siblings.

Finally, a monumental breakthrough …

The Present: Late 1960s to 1985 — Indian Control of Indian Education

In the 1960s, Indian leaders began to react to the deplorable conditions of their people. In response to the educational concerns being raised by Indian people, the House of Commons Standing Committee on Indian Affairs prepared a report on Indian education. This report, presented to Parliament on June 22, 1971, unfolded before the Canadian public the educational problems facing Indian people. Some of the findings were:

- A drop-out rate four times the national average (96% of Indian children never finished high school);
- A related unemployment rate averaging 50% for adult males, going as high as 90% in some communities;
- "Inaccuracies and omissions" relating to the Indian contribution to Canadian history in textbooks used in federal and provincial schools;
- An age-grade retardation rooted in language conflict and early disadvantage, which accelerated as the child progressed through the primary and elementary grades;
- Less than 15% of the teachers had specialized training in cross-cultural education and less than 10% had any knowledge of an Indian language;
- The majority of Indian parents were uninformed about the implication of decisions made to transfer children from reserve schools to provincial schools.

From this report, it was obvious that the missionaries and governments had failed in 300 years to administer an effective educational program for Indians. The failure has been attributed to several factors, namely the absence of a clear philosophy of education with goals and objectives, failure to provide a meaningful program based on Indian reality, a lack of qualified teaching staff and inadequate facilities, and, most important, the absence of parental involvement in the education of their children (Indian Tribes of Manitoba, 1971).

In 1969, the Government of Canada issued a white paper on Indian policy, based on the elimination of the special status of Indians. The embittered provincial/territorial Indian organizations responded by issuing their respective positions papers related to their ongoing relationships with the federal government that included treaties and Aboriginal rights, as well as strongly stating their positions on education, housing, health, and on social and economic development.

In the wake of a 1971 school strike in northeast Alberta protesting school facilities on reserves and the release of the standing committee report, education was thrust to the forefront. The National Indian Brotherhood (now known as the Assembly of First Nations) established a working committee to prepare a national position on education. Basing its findings on the various position papers of the provincial territorial Indian organizations, the policy of "Indian Control of Indian Education" was tabled with the government on December 21, 1972. In February 1973, the Minister of Indian Affairs, the Honourable Jean Chrétien, gave official departmental recognition to the policy stating, "I have given the National Indian Brotherhood my assurance that I and my Department are fully committed to realizing the educational goals for the Indian people set forth in the Brotherhood's proposal" (Cardinal, 1977).

"Indian Control of Indian Education" is based on two education principles recognized in Canadian society: parental responsibility and local control. It recognizes that Indian parents must enjoy the same fundamental decision-making rights about their children's education as other parents across Canada. It promotes the fundamental concept of local control that distinguishes the free political system of democratic governments from those of a totalitarian nature. The policy recognizes the need to improve educational opportunities for Indians. It states:

Our aim is to make education relevant to the philosophy and needs of Indian people. We want education to give our children a strong sense of identity with confidence in their personal worth and ability.

We believe in education—

- *as a preparation for total living.*
- *as a means of free choice of where to live and work.*
- *as a means of enabling us to participate fully in our own social, economic, political, and educational advancement. (National Indian Brotherhood, 1973)*

An Indian philosophy of education is in many ways more valid and universal than the one that prevails in educational circles today. Instead of a one-sided view of history, we want our children to learn a Canadian history that attaches honour to the customs, values, accomplishments, and contributions of this country's original inhabitants and first citizens, the Indians of Canada.

We want our children to learn science and technology so that they can promote the harmony of man with nature—not destroy it. We want our children to learn about their fellow men in literature and social studies and, in the process, learn to respect the values and cultures of others.

An Indian philosophy of education looks at learning and teaching as an integral part of living both for the teacher and the child. It is not a five-hour, five-day-a-week exercise for a dozen years or so. It is a life-long commitment (Manuel, c. 1976).

"Indian Control of Indian Education" is a four-point policy dealing with parental responsibility, school programs, teachers, and school facilities:

- Responsibility. Under the terms of the 11 major treaties between and among the Indians and the federal government and the Indian Act, the federal government is obligated to provide funds for the education of Indians. This is an incontestable fact. In no way does the principle of Indian Control of Indian Education contradict or nullify this fundamental federal obligation. The government's financial responsibility does not justify its dominance over the lives of Indian people. This policy statement demands that Indian parents participate as partners with the government in the education of their children.

- Programs. The curriculum must be structured to use the child's awareness of his own cultural environment as a springboard for learning about the outside world. The community must participate in program change. No innovations in curriculum, teaching methods, or pupil-teacher relationships can take root unless parents are convinced of their value.

- Teachers and Counsellors. The federal government must help train Indian teachers and counsellors. Experimentation and flexible structures will allow Indians with talent and ambition to take advantage of training programs. Non-Indian teachers and counsellors should receive additional training to prepare them for cross-cultural situations and teach them how to make curriculum for Indian children more meaningful.

- Facilities. Educational facilities must meet the needs of the local population. Substandard buildings and equipment must be replaced.

Today, over a decade later, we find ourselves confronted with serious problems with the implementation of the policy. In May 1981, a resolution was passed by the Assembly of First Nations indicating national concern regarding the implementation of "Indian Control of Indian Education." The resolution reads:

WHEREAS Indian Control of Indian Education has been endorsed and accepted by both the Indian people and the Department of Indian Affairs, and

WHEREAS the Department of Indian Affairs has promised to actively support the full implementation of Indian Control of Indian Education policy paper of 1973; and

WHEREAS the Department of Indian Affairs has failed to actively support the full implementation of Indian Control of Indian Education as seen by recent moves to cut back on several programs in education; and …

THEREFORE BE IT RESOLVED THAT this Assembly of Chiefs reaffirm the policy and directions as stated in the 1973 Indian Control of Indian Education paper: and …

FURTHER THAT WE DEMAND THAT the Department of Indian Affairs and Northern Development reinstate, maintain and expand the programs which are required to fulfill Band Educational Training and support need; and …

WE FURTHER DEMAND THAT the Department of Indian Affairs and Northern Development make available appropriate financial resources to ensure the highest quality of Indian Control of Indian Education (policy).

A review of the implementation of the policy suggests three specific problem areas, namely, dual administration, funding, and legislation. Dual administration refers to the fact that Indian bands have ended up operating education programs under the strict guidelines of the Department of Indian Affairs. The intent of the policy was that Indian responsibility for education would mean replacing the complex existing bureaucracy, not merely becoming an extension of that bureaucracy.

In terms of funding, the policy states, "The Federal Government must take the required steps to transfer to local Bands the authority and the funds that are allotted for Indian education" (National Indian Brotherhood, 1973). The department provides funding to bands under strict guidelines on an annual basis. This precludes the possibility of priority-setting or innovative planning by local Indian bands.

A further restraining factor is that Indian-controlled schools require an administration that is local. The Department of Indian Affairs, on the other hand, operates within a centralized administration. The cost factor is different. Under the present scheme, this poses additional problems for bands. Not only is funding restricted to given guidelines, it is also inadequate. Treasury Board regulations state that the transfer to local control and administration of education programs by bands should not entail any additional costs.

The most serious problem arises from the lack of legislation (Cardinal, 1977). The Indian Act provides no legal basis for the transfer of education from the control of the Minister of Indian Affairs to Indian bands. It authorizes the minister to enter into agreements with public or separate school boards, provincial/territorial governments, and religious or charitable organizations, but not with Indian bands. The present authority allowing Indian bands to administer education funds derives from various Treasury Board authorities, covering a range of educational and student support services that extend from kindergarten to post-secondary school programs.

These problems are all directly related. If we examine the authority used to accommodate the policy of "Indian Control of Indian Education," it reveals that the lack of legislation enabling the minister to transfer control of education to Indian bands prevents the implementation to occur as it should. This fact relates directly to funding as well as the problem of dual administration. It explains why the concept of Indian-controlled schools by the Indian people became known to the Department of Indian Affairs as band-operated schools. Controlling and operating are two entirely different concepts. To control is to have power over, to exercise directing influence, whereas to operate means to manage or to keep in operation. It is predictable that the difference in perception would lead to misunderstanding and impede the direction of the policy.

However, despite the many problems experienced, progress is noted through various reports and evaluations conducted within the last few years. The involvement of Indian people in the education of their children has resulted in:

- greater retention of students;
- improved attendance;
- inclusion of relevant curriculum;
- better graduation rates;
- development of early childhood programs;
- introduction of adult education programs;
- teaching of native languages (Kirkness & Bowman, 1992).

The Future: 1985 and Beyond—The Answers Are Within Us

Indian people stand at the crossroads in 1985. Our sovereign rights are being contested on the streets and in the courts. The question of our future is a serious one. We are probably facing the greatest challenge of our time. As we consider our options at this time, we must do so with pride, confidence, and commitment in our ability to move forward. As we reflect upon our survival against all odds under colonization, we must remind ourselves of the tremendous strength our people have exhibited in the past and be prepared to carry on with the same determination.

Despite repeated efforts on the part of churches, successive governments, institutions, various interest groups, and individuals, we have not allowed ourselves to become completely assimilated. Through education, we must continue toward the realization of our place in this country. We have shown that despite all odds, we have maintained our identity as Indian people. However, to ensure the future of our people as a unique people, we are going to have to become much more radical in our approach to education. We must put into practice our goals and objectives based on our philosophy of education. To meet this challenge, it will be necessary, in fact, critical, for our people to disestablish many of the current educational practices related to foreign ethos and institutions that have failed to meet our needs.

Our efforts especially over the last decade indicate that this will be a major undertaking. Centuries of outside influences are not easily displaced. The recent initiatives of Aboriginal people have resulted in conservative change because we have continued to rely on theories and practices of the dominant society.

We must heed the counsel of Paulo Freire, the radical Brazilian educator, and mobilize our people through knowledge. Freire states that the act of knowing is in part a political issue because it leads to action (as cited in Giroux, 1979). If we were to follow Paulo Freire's approach, we would engage in a massive campaign to raise the social-political consciousness of every Indian man, woman, and child in Canada to understand his/her oppression and domination. In education, we would raise the awareness of every Indian man, woman, and child about the issues and challenges that impact our education and that only if we act collectively on these issues can we transform the situation. From this reflection would emerge a new knowledge that will help us shape the future as a people united in a common cause.

Our children are our future. We have a tremendous responsibility to ensure that future. The need for radical change, a complete overhaul of the educational system for our people, is the basis of the required change. To do this, we must look within ourselves, our communities, our nations, for "the answers are within us."

As I reflect on this paper, written 15 years ago, I can see our continuing struggle to identify a meaningful education for our people based on the policy of "Indian Control of Indian Education." While the Department of Indian Affairs has removed some of the stringent guidelines, the damage has been done and our bands have become conditioned to follow the path designed for assimilation. One major difference is that we can now articulate what we believe to be Aboriginal education. The major drawback currently facing us is that we have reversed our traditional holistic psychology to one wherein we are going from the parts to the whole. In other words, the most common approach under Indian Control of Indian Education today is to interject parts of our culture into the curriculum rather than having culture as the basis of our curriculum. The following paper may serve to clarify this dilemma.

Our Peoples' Education: Cut the Shackles, Cut the Crap, and Cut the Mustard (1998)

From the scant knowledge that survived the many years of colonialism, we do know that our ancestors had evolved their own form of education. It was an education in which the community and the natural environment were the classroom, and the land was regarded as the mother of the people. Members of the community were the teachers, and each adult was responsible for ensuring that each child learned how to live a good life. Central to the teaching was the belief in the sacred, the Great Spirit.

The development of the whole person was emphasized through teachings often shared in storytelling. Legendary heroes such as the Raven, Wesakachak, Nanabush, and others were used to transmit learning. They were regarded as transformers or "tricksters of learning" through which children learned traditional values such as humility, honesty, courage, kindness, and respect.

Traditional education was strongly linked to the survival of the family and the community. Learning was geared to knowledge necessary for daily living. Boys and girls were taught at an early age to observe and utilize, to cope with and respect their environment. Independence and self-reliance were valued concepts handed down to the young. Through observation and practice, children learned the art of hunting, trapping, fishing, farming, food-gathering, child-rearing, and building shelters. They learned whatever their particular environment offered through experiential learning.

The rites of passage from childhood to adulthood were practiced. In most cultures, puberty rites were recognized through formal and often complex ceremonies. This was a critical time for girls and boys who were making the transition to the responsibilities of being an adult.

Traditional education was largely an informal process that provided the young people with specific skills, attitudes, and knowledge they needed to function in everyday life within the context of a spiritual worldview. Our ancestors' mode of life, thought, and every act was given spiritual significance (Seton & Seton, 1966). Teaching and learning were a "natural process occurring during everyday activities ... ensuring cultural continuity" and a sense of well-being (Armstrong, 1987).

Formal education imposed on our people by the colonizers drastically changed all that! We are all aware of the consequences that continue to plague us today. While the education of our people has not been entirely one of gloom and doom, at least over the last 25 years, we are still faced with the monumental challenge of creating a meaningful education that will not only give hope but a promise of better life for our future generations. I believe this means we must "cut the shackles, cut the crap, and cut the mustard."

Cut the Shackles

In schools and other educational institutions under our authority, we have the right and the opportunity to put in place what we believe to be quality education for our people. We are in charge. We owe it to our people, after decades of oppressive church and government control, to release them from this bondage by creating the kind of education that will truly liberate us so we can have the independence once enjoyed by our ancestors. Our new "independence" education must begin with us; our people, our communities. It must celebrate our cultures, our history, the true account of the way it was, and the way it is. From there, we can build on how it should be and how it will be.

We must seize the opportunity to frame our education within our context. If we fail to do this, we run the risk of doing the greatest disservice to our people by simply mirroring the kind of education provided to us by federal and public schools, a kind of education that has had dismal results for us over many years. We must take a strong stance in shaping our education. To do this, what we need is radical change.

We must begin by disestablishing many of our existing practices based on theories of the society that has dominated us for so many years. Then we must look within ourselves, within our communities, and within our nations to determine which values are important to us, the content of what should be learned and how it should be learned. This new direction must relate to theories firmly based on the traditions of our people.

This means that we must "cut the shackles" and make a new start. It is time for us to forget band-aiding; it is time for us to forget adapting; it is time for us to forget supplementing; it is time for us to forget the so-called standards, all of which have restricted our creativity in determining our own master plan. The authorities would have us believe that we are doing a great injustice to our people by abandoning these practices even though they have been nothing more than compromising approaches that have not worked for us. We must no longer listen to these senseless arguments.

Back in 1972, we believed we could do a better job of educating our people. Through our policy statement "Indian Control of Indian Education" we outlined a national position on education that stated clearly our principles and our goals in education. The two main principles of the policy were "parental responsibility and local control." After years of the church and government making decisions for our people, it was a time for us to reclaim our right to speak for our children, to actively participate in determining what they should learn, how they should learn, and who should teach them.

Sadly, the policy of "Indian Control of Indian Education" has not unfolded as was expected. Two factors have been at play that have negatively affected the process. One was the manipulation of Indian Affairs to have us simply administer the schools as they had in the past. The second was our own peoples' insecurity in taking control and failing to design an education that would be based on our culture, our way of life, and most important, our worldview. For many of our communities that have taken over their own schools and other educational institutions, much time has been lost either emulating the federal or public school systems or merely band-aiding, adapting, or supplementing when they should have been creating a unique and meaningful education. At the base of this attitude is the difficulty to overcome colonial domination.

The greatest challenge is to be radical, to ask the right questions within the community, and to ask the families what they want for their children. Only then will we be practicing what we set out to do in 1972, which was to have the parents set the agenda for education in our communities and then getting on with the plan. We cannot afford to lose any more time, because we have let the opportunity for radical and effective change elude us for far too long. Cut the shackles! Freedom is our only recourse.

Cut the Crap

To move on, we must cut the crap and stop fooling ourselves. From the beginning of our experience with formal education, we have had it drummed into us that education was about mastering the three *R*s. We are told that if we cannot read, 'rite, or do 'rithmetic, we are doomed to failure. We do not argue with this posture but we do take exception to the use of their prescribed methods and their usual authorized textbooks. How, then, should we teach the three *R*s to our children?

The Children of the Earth School in Winnipeg, Manitoba, has the right idea. They have changed the three *R*s to rediscovering (research), respect, and recovering the culture and traditions of our people. We must follow this lead and research our Aboriginal/tribal pedagogy so that the curriculum will accurately reflect our traditions and cultures in what and how we teach. In other words, we must overhaul the existing system and seek more appropriate materials and strategies for teaching.

Our progress has also been hampered by the interpretation of "Indian Control of Indian Education." For people in some of our communities who are making changes in the curriculum, they have taken "local control" literally to mean doing everything themselves for their respective schools. They develop programs, methods, and materials but do not willingly share these with other schools, nor are they prepared to use materials designed by other First Nations schools. This results in duplication and the value of sharing is lost.

I believe this is a mistake. In fact, a mechanism must be made available that will facilitate the sharing of information related to education. For those who are computer-literate, this may already be a possibility through the Internet. Almost 10 years ago, I suggested that a "moccasin disk-line" be created for the sharing of educational materials. This would facilitate communication and enable schools/communities to maintain ownership of their materials, yet share them through sale or barter.

Though it is over 25 years since the policy of "Indian Control of Indian Education" was adopted, there is little evidence of real curriculum change. We must use all our resources to realize quality education, not only for the children but for all our people regardless of their level of study. "Education into culture, not culture into education" must be our practice, and we must believe that "the answers are within us."

This leads me to why I say we must "cut the crap." To illustrate a point, I would like to suggest that we consider a fourth *R*, namely, rhetoric. It is common to hear our political leaders and educators speak very eloquently about the importance of education and what we must do to improve it, not only for today but for future generations.

We know all the right words, we sound like experts, but we fall short when it comes to putting our rhetoric into action.

We have heard, read, and even said many times over the last 25 years that quality education for our people must be based on our culture and on our history, yet we continue to base education on white, urban culture and history.

We say that culture is language and language is culture and that to be Micmac, Ojibwe, Stó:lō, Cree, Haida, we must speak our respective languages, yet we continue to teach our languages for only a few minutes a day in our schools, knowing that this approach is ineffective.

We say that our education must respect our values and customs, yet we encourage competition rather than co-operation, the individual over the group, saving instead of sharing. We are uncomfortable when too much time is spent outdoors learning from the land because we have been conditioned to believe that education occurs in the classroom. We continue to adhere to the established school year, even when it does not suit the life of the community.

The rhetoric goes on and on. We expound on the importance of our elders. We say they are our teachers, our libraries, our archives, yet we rarely include them in a meaningful way. We rarely ask them anything. We are great at having our elders come to say a prayer or tell a story but surely this is not what we mean when we say we must learn from the elders. Elders possess the wisdom and knowledge that must be the focus of all our learning. It is through them that we can understand our unique relationship to the Creator, our connection with nature, the order of things, and the values that enhance the identity of our people.

Not properly acknowledging the elders is probably the most serious mistake we make as we attempt to create a quality education for our people. Let's face it; we can't do it without them. How can we learn about our traditions on which to base our education if we don't ask the elders? There is little written by our people that we can turn to for this information.

If we sincerely believe that our traditions are important to us, we have no other recourse but to go to the elders. I firmly believe that we must know the past in order to understand the present so that we can plan, wisely, for the future. It is up to this generation of educational leaders to tap that valuable resource, because each day, fewer and fewer elders whose knowledge goes back at least two generations are left to teach us what we need to know. When they are gone, their valuable knowledge goes with them. It's like losing a whole library and its archives.

There is more rhetoric. We say that parents must play a major role in the education of their children, yet in many communities parents have no idea what is going on in the school. They are rarely invited to meetings to decide on directions to be taken. They are rarely asked for their original thoughts on how or what should be done in certain situations. School board meetings are often closed meetings. Of course, they are expected to attend on report card day and, if they don't, they are often simply ignored.

"Parental responsibility," as stated in "Indian Control of Indian Education," recognizes that parents must enjoy the same fundamental decision-making rights about their children's education as other parents across Canada. Today, band councils and their designated authorities run our schools. While membership on the band councils and school authorities undoubtedly includes parents, the intention of the policy was to include the parents of all school children in the shaping and running of the schools.

We talk also about the need for balance in our learning. We say that we must not only address the mind, but we must also address spiritual, emotional, and physical growth as well. Is there evidence of this balance in your school? Are children still deprived of recess or physical education classes as a punishment for a misdemeanour? How is spiritual and emotional growth addressed?

Finally, let's remind ourselves of our ancestors' relationship to the land. The land is our mother, Mother Earth. Are we teaching our children to respect the earth, to be environmentally aware? Are we, in our communities, practicing the kind of behaviour that is appropriate of a child toward a mother?

There is no doubt that we have mastered the art of expressing what education for our people should be. The rhetoric is there, but where is the substance? I believe that what we are saying is inarguable. The problem comes with turning that rhetoric into action and doing those things we say are conducive to learning for our children rather than continuing to do the same old thing in the same old way. That is why I am advocating that we must first "cut the shackles," free ourselves from mirroring a system that has not worked, then we must "cut the crap," by less talk and more action. And finally we must "cut the mustard," which is to "practice what we preach."

Cut the Mustard

How do we cut the mustard? How do we get the job done? We must take a good, hard look at the education we are providing in our communities. I don't mean that we should have a formal evaluation with some high-powered, high-priced consultants, who know nothing about our communities, who come in and do the job. Many communities have experienced this pitfall and found that what was recommended did not resemble anything that was said by them in the data collection. It was evident that the evaluators had a blueprint solution for Aboriginal education that was not necessarily valid for all communities.

What has to happen is that people of the community must come together (mothers, fathers, grandparents, high school and post-secondary students, members of band councils/school boards, etc.) to address five simple questions about the education in their community. These questions, framed several years ago by my colleague Clive Linklater, have been effective for those who have used them to evaluate and to design an innovative education plan for their school/community.

The first two questions are "Where are we now? How did we get to where we are?" By addressing these questions, you will have done your own evaluation. You will have considered the history of education in your community. This might include having no formal school, having children taught informally through traditional teachings, having your children leave the family and community for a number of years, or having your children attend public schools in a nearby town or city. Why were these good or bad? If you have always had a school in your community, under which jurisdiction has education been most effective? Why?

Questions three, four, and five deal with the formulation of your own model of education. "Where do we want to go? How will we get to where we want to go? How will we know when we are there?" Deciding on the kind of education you want for your children does not preclude the inclusion of certain programs and courses currently offered to them. It means that the focus of teaching and learning is based on your community's philosophy, goals, and objectives that become central to everything that follows. Therefore, what you initiate and what you want to keep must correspond to that framework.

Considering the kind of education required provides the members of your community with an opportunity to share ideas on what would constitute an ideal education for your people as we approach the twenty-first century. It would typically include traditional values, a holistic approach, and technological and scientific advances of the modern age. How do we get to where you want to go? This question refers to implementing your concept of an ideal education. It will be necessary to discuss the factors that will assist in the process and which factors might hinder the process. In the case of the latter, thought will have to be given to how these obstacles can be addressed.

Finally, how will you know when you are there? You will know you have achieved your goal of quality education when your children are enjoying the challenge of school/learning, when their self-esteem and self-confidence is evident, when your children are proud of who they are, and when their links with the older generations are made. You will know you have achieved your goal when the majority of children who enter your system graduate and go on to further education or get a job, when they are living happy and fulfilled lives of their own making. This list could go on and on. What is clear is that it could take several years before you see the results of today's efforts, much as it has taken many years to realize the devastation caused by residential schools and other forms of colonial schooling.

There is, therefore, an urgency to cut the shackles, cut the crap, and cut the mustard. Our "independence" education will be based on a marriage of the past and the present. It will honour our cultures that include our values, our languages, and our peoples' contributions to the development and progress of this vast country. Most importantly, in your quest for a meaningful education for your school/community, you will have found that the answers you have been seeking can be found within yourselves/within your own communities.

As a retrospective, Aboriginal education in Canada can be described as historically ineffective. While formal education has been available in some form or another for over 300 years, only recently have Aboriginal people themselves been involved in its design and delivery. Since the policy of "Indian Control of Indian Education" was introduced 27 years ago, there have been definite signs of improvement. However, while these modest changes have resulted in many more students graduating from university, we still have a very serious attrition rate at every level of education.

The two papers have tended to relate to the in-school program but a wider application can be made, as the challenges facing young people in school are the same challenges faced in post-secondary and adult education. I discuss this in "First Nations and Higher Education: The Four R's—Respect, Relevance, Reciprocity, Responsibility" (Kirkness & Barnhardt, 1991).

The prospective of Aboriginal education in Canada, as I see it, begins with process rather than content. We must engage not only parents, which is paramount, but we must engage the whole community to take ownership of what is to be in Aboriginal education the twenty-first century. Together with teachers, the school authority, they must decide what they want for their children both now and in the future. They must adhere to the philosophy and principles they set in place. Only then can we/they realize the significance of the rhetoric cited in the last paper and begin to see Aboriginal education as a holistic and cultural phenomenon.

REFERENCES

Armstrong, J.C. (1987). Traditional Indigenous education: A natural process. *Canadian Journal of Native Education, 14*(3), 14–19.

Assembly of First Nations (1981). Conference proceedings. Assembly of Chiefs. Ottawa: Author.

Canadian Education Association. (1984). *Recent developments in Native education.* Toronto: Author.

Cardinal, H. (1977). *The rebirth of Canada's Indians.* Edmonton, AB: Hurtig Publishers.

Charters-Voght, O. (1991). Indian control of Indian education: The path of the Upper Nicola Band. *Canadian Journal of Native Education, 18*(2), 111–143.

Department of Indian Affairs. (1980). *Indian education policy review: Phase I.* Ottawa: Author.

Flood Davin, N. (1879). *Report on industrial schools for Indians and Halfbreeds.* Ottawa: Indian Affairs Branch.

George, D. (c. 1972). A talk with teachers. Unpublished Soliloquy.

Giroux, H. (1979). Paulo Freire's approach to radical educational theory and practice. *Curriculum Inquiry, 9*(3), 257–272. http://dx.doi.org/10.2307/3202124

Government of Canada. (1971). *Report of the Standing Committee on Indian Affairs.* Ottawa: Author.

Indian Tribes of Manitoba. (1971). *Wahbung: Our tomorrows.* Winnipeg, MB: Manitoba Indian Brotherhood.

Kirkness, V.J. (1986). *Indian control of Indian education: Over a decade later. Mokakit Indian Education Research Association, Selected Papers.* Vancouver: University of British Columbia Press.

Kirkness, V.J. (1987). Indian education: Past, present and future. *Aurora—The Professional Journal of the N.W.T. Teachers, 5*(1), 19–26.

Kirkness, V.J., & Barnhardt, R. (1991). First Nations and higher education: The four *R*'s—respect, relevance, reciprocity, responsibility. *Journal of American Indian Education, 30*(3), 1–15.

Kirkness, V.J., & Bowman, S. (1992). *First Nations and schools: Triumphs and struggles.* Toronto: Canadian Education Association.

Manuel, G. (c. 1976). Indian control of Indian education. Unpublished article.

National Indian Brotherhood. (1973). *Indian Control of Indian Education.* Ottawa: Author.

Seton, E., & Seton, J.M. (1966). *The Gospel of the Redman.* Winnipeg, MB: Mary Scorer Books.

Seton, E., & Seton, J.M. (1977). *The Gospel of the Redman.* Winnipeg, MB: Mary Scorer Books.

2

Silencing Aboriginal Curricular Content and Perspectives through Multiculturalism: "There Are Other Children Here"

Verna St. Denis

Recently I was invited to join a provincial discussion about the high school social science curriculum. One area of contention was whether all students should be required to take a course that would combine and integrate social studies, history, and Native studies. Aware that integration of Native studies content into existing courses could easily result in the erasure of Native studies, I suggested, at that provincial meeting, that all students should take such a course if its starting point and continued foundation was Native studies. One participant, in response to this suggestion, stated, "Aboriginal people are not the only people here."

This comment, "Aboriginal people are not the only people here," suggests that it would be wrong to privilege Aboriginal history, knowledge, and experience in the teaching of one high school course in Canadian history and social studies. This comment conveys a recurring sentiment that defends public education as a neutral multicultural space but also effectively tempers Aboriginal educational initiatives. This chapter explores how multicultural discourses impact the reception of Aboriginal teachers, and the Aboriginal knowledge, history, and experience they bring into Canadian public schools. I argue that what happens to Aboriginal teachers in Canadian public schools as they attempt to include Aboriginal content and perspectives is a microcosm of what happens at the political and national levels in regard to Aboriginal peoples' claims to land and sovereignty in Canada. Some of the experiences of Aboriginal teachers in public schools help us to develop a deeper understanding of why Aboriginal political leaders reject having their rights negotiated within a multicultural framework.

I will begin this chapter with a brief discussion of multicultural policy and legislation in Canada. Then I will review some of the general criticisms of multiculturalism and, most importantly, some of the basic reasons Aboriginal people reject having their claims and rights framed within multiculturalism (see, for example, Paine, 1999; Day & Sadik, 2002; Mackey, 2002, 2005; Lawrence & Dua, 2005; Short, 2005; Rutherford, 2010). The chapter then draws on data from two recent studies that have explored the experiences of Aboriginal teachers as they seek to include Aboriginal content and perspectives in public schools (St. Denis, Bouvier, & Battiste, 1998; St. Denis, 2010). By inciting multiculturalism, public schools effectively limit meaningful incorporation of Aboriginal content and perspectives in public schools.

Multiculturalism in Canada

In Canada, official multiculturalism was a political strategy that was introduced as a way to address contesting language, cultural, and land claims within the nation, and it has since been widely explained, defended, and critiqued (see, for example, Fleras & Elliot, 1992; Légaré, 1995; Kymlicka, 1996; Mackey, 2002; Wood & Gilbert, 2005). In 1971, then Prime Minister Pierre Trudeau institutionalized a policy of multiculturalism and this policy was made into national law by the Brian Mulroney government in 1988 as the Multicultural Act.[1] The initial 1971 multicultural policy was an attempt to respond to the demands of French-language speakers, an increasing culturally diverse citizenry, and Aboriginal people. As has been observed, multiculturalism was "introduced so that bilingualism would not create extra problems" (Wood & Gilbert, 2005, p. 682). The Multicultural Act of 1988 was intended to address the concerns of multiple ethnic groups, such as Ukrainians, who wanted recognition of their presence and contributions to Canada (Wood & Gilbert, 2005). Multiculturalism was also intended to acknowledge the need for increased understanding between ethnic groups, and the need to address racial discrimination (Fleras & Elliot, 1992, p. 75). Within the context of historical and ongoing colonization in Canada, both policies, in fact, prevent possibilities for antiracism and anticolonialism (Day, 2000; Mackey, 2002; Lawrence & Dua, 2005).

Scholars have examined the shortcomings of multiculturalism (see, for example, Povinelli, 1998; Paine, 1999; Curthoys, 2000; Chakrabarty, 2001; Day & Sadik, 2002; Mackey, 2002, 2005; Lawrence & Dua, 2005; Short, 2005; Wood & Gilbert, 2005; Rutherford, 2010; James, 2011). First, multiculturalism encourages social division in that it "separates, intensifies misunderstanding and hostility, and pits one group against another in the competition for power and resources" (Fleras & Elliot, 1992, p. 132). Next, multiculturalism is regressive because it is "derelict in combating social inequality" (Fleras & Elliot, 1992, p. 134). Third, multiculturalism permits a form of participation on the part of those designated as "cultural others" that is limited to the decorative and includes "leisure, entertainment, food, and song and dance" (Fleras & Elliot, 1992, p. 136). Finally, multiculturalism is "impractical" and "inadequate" for "sorting out the conflicting claims of individuals, minority groups, vested interests and a centralized state" (Fleras & Elliot, 1992, p. 140). These four assertions begin to identify the ways in which multicultural policies and practices prevent an anticolonial analysis.

In Canada, both Aboriginal people and racialized immigrants are concerned with the use of multicultural discourses to manage and silence competing interests within the nation. Although Aboriginal and racialized immigrants have similar concerns with multiculturalism, they also have very distinct ones. For example, racialized immigrants of colour are concerned that multiculturalism does not address racism and anti-immigration sentiments but may even provoke them (Mackey, 2002; James, 2011). Aboriginal peoples are concerned with Indigenous sovereignty and asserting rights based on their original and continuing occupation of the land (Paine, 1999; Day & Sadik, 2002; Mackey, 2002, 2005; Lawrence & Dua, 2005; Short, 2005; Rutherford, 2010). In other words, Aboriginal groups suggest that multiculturalism is a form of colonialism and works to distract from the recognition and redress of Indigenous rights. Racism also impacts upon Aboriginal groups, and multiculturalism can justify public expressions of anti-Aboriginal sentiments. Discourses of multiculturalism enable racism and colonialism, and thereby impact and limit the work of Aboriginal teachers.

Aboriginal Critiques of Multiculturalism

A brief explanation of how Aboriginal people position themselves within Canada is helpful to understand why they reject multiculturalism as a framework to negotiate Aboriginal sovereignty. Aboriginal peoples continue to argue that they are Indigenous sovereign nations because of their original continuing occupation and rights to the land (Paine, 1999; Day & Sadik, 2002; Mackey, 2002, 2005; Lawrence & Dua, 2005; Short, 2005; Rutherford, 2010). Aboriginal groups explain "their rights are pre-contact, in place before the law of the Settler state" (Paine, 1999, p. 329). They "never willingly ceded their land or political autonomy … [and] hold distinct moral claims as *dispossessed first nations*" (Short, 2005, p. 272, emphasis in original). Turner (2006) explains that Aboriginal sovereignty is a "normative political concept for several overlapping reason[s]: Aboriginal people assert it, constitutions recognize it, comprehensive and specific land claims are negotiated because of it, and public policies have been designed and implemented to undermine it" (p. 69). Multiculturalism is one example of a public policy that has served to undermine Aboriginal sovereignty.

Undermining Aboriginal sovereignty occurs through a number of processes and practices. Multiculturalism helps to erase, diminish, trivialize, and deflect from acknowledging Aboriginal sovereignty and the need to redress Aboriginal rights (Légaré, 1995; Mackey, 2005; Short, 2005). Multiculturalism is dependent "upon the deep structures of colonial discourse" (Day & Sadik, 2002, p. 6). These deep structures of colonial discourse are overlapping and intersecting but include historical, political, and educational thought and practice. Although Aboriginal people insist that an understanding of historical relationships is key to understanding Aboriginal sovereignty, normative Canadian history refuses to recognize Aboriginal interpretations of history (Turner, 2006); this refusal, in turn, places limits on understanding Aboriginal sovereignty.

History limits understanding of Aboriginal sovereignty by "rarely discuss[ing] the history of colonial relations, specifically the continual dispossession and marginalization of Aboriginal peoples" (Mackey, 2005, p. 19). Even in recent gestures toward "truth and reconciliation," the innocence of the colonizing governments is defended. At the 2009 G20 meetings, Prime Minister Stephen Harper stated that Canada has "no history of colonialism" (Ljunggren, 2009). This public denial of the colonization of Aboriginal people can surely be reassuring to a very select group of people, particularly those invested in dominant Canadian historical narratives that continue to "efface the history of ill-treatment that Aboriginal peoples have endured at the hands of the Canadian state" (Day & Sadik, 2002, pp. 14–15). Histories of racism and the brutal colonization of Aboriginal peoples are routinely ignored, minimized, and erased (Day & Sadik, 2002; Mackey, 2002; Lawrence & Dua, 2005; Montgomery, 2005). This minimizing and erasure of brutal colonization has profound detrimental effects for Aboriginal people.

Multiculturalism works against Aboriginal sovereignty and anticolonialism in its production of national histories that imagine Canada as a socially just and successful multicultural state. Normative Canadian history produces Canada as a nation that is "tolerant" and "innocent." As Francis (1997) argued, "the myth of the master race" is a production of Canadian history as benign, serving to promote the belief that "colonists were the innocent victims of Indian aggression" and reassurance that despite brutal colonization, "no colonist ever killed an Indian who wasn't asking for it" (p. 75). Many Canadians take enormous pride in the constructed identity of their nation as one that is innocent of any wrongdoing (Backhouse, 1999). Representing Canadians as innocent of wrongdoing constructs them as "tolerant" "victims of multiculturalism" (Mackey, 2002, pp. 88, 22). Produced as advocates of fairness and equality, Canadians can feel legitimate in rejecting Aboriginal claims to justice. As Légaré (1995) asserted, through this insistence on innocence and tolerance, Aboriginal people are "constructed as the oppressors of ordinary Canadians" (p. 359). This may explain why a suggestion that Native studies become the foundation of a combined course in history and social studies in Canada would be met with a response like "Aboriginal people are not the only people here," because that would for some seem to go far beyond what is required and may even be regarded by some as amounting to injustice.

Aboriginal sovereignty remains an important issue, even though the Canadian state may have come into existence through conquering, having power ceded through treaties, or by simply overrunning Aboriginal communities (Turner, 2006). Aboriginal critics challenge the legitimacy of the current colonial Canadian government to "recognize" and "negotiate" Aboriginal rights within a multicultural framework. Related to this failure is the Canadian government's insistence on "recognition theories" that centre the idea of "recognizing" Aboriginal rights always within the context of a colonial framework, and that thoroughly reject Aboriginal sovereignty (Tully, 2000). Critics of recognition theorists assert that minor "adjustments" to democracy and common law are insufficient to addressing demands for Aboriginal sovereignty (Povinelli, 1998). From the perspective of Aboriginal politics and education, multiculturalism limits a more comprehensive "understanding of Canada as a colonialist state" and diminishes Aboriginal political and educational concerns with "ongoing colonization of Indigenous peoples in the Americas" (Lawrence & Dua, 2005, p. 123).[2]

Multiculturalism can also equate Aboriginal people with racialized minorities and particularly racialized ethnic immigrants. By inaccurately assuming shared commonalities among diverse groups (Dei & Calliste, 2000), multiculturalism erases the specific and unique location of Aboriginal peoples as indigenous to this land by equating them with multicultural and immigrant groups. Aboriginal people adamantly reject this equating of their Aboriginal position with ethnic minorities as a form of colonialism (Curthoys, 2000; Short, 2005). Whether through antiracism or multiculturalism, when colonialism in Canada is left unaddressed, racialized ethnic immigrants are too easily positioned as innocent (Lawrence & Dua, 2005, p. 132). This position ignores the ways in which "people of color in settler formations are settlers on stolen lands ... and historically may have been complicit with on-going land theft and colonial domination of Aboriginal peoples" (Lawrence & Dua, 2005, p. 132). Aboriginal connection to "on-going land claims" remains a key issue (Paine, 1999; Lawrence & Dua, 2005), setting them apart from all others, and in this way they occupy a unique place in Canada, whether in regards to white or more recent settler/immigrants. Aboriginal peoples assert the need for nation-to-nation negotiations and refuse multiculturalism's attempts to reduce them to one of many competing "minority" or "ethnic" groups within the nation.

So far I have argued that Aboriginal peoples reject multiculturalism as an instrument of colonialism. Multiculturalism is dependent on colonial structures because it assumes the legitimacy of the current colonial Canadian government. As multiculturalism ignores ongoing colonialization, the result is a trivializing and erasing of Aboriginal sovereignty. Attempting to equate Aboriginal people with racialized minorities, multiculturalism erases the unique Indigenous/Aboriginal location of Aboriginal peoples. The practices of multiculturalism, which I have discussed in this section, rely on discourses of recognition, tolerance, and fairness, and have tremendous power in educational settings. Inasmuch as non-Aboriginal teachers, administrators, and students accept these discourses, these individuals demonstrate resistance, suspicion, and even resentment toward Aboriginal teachers and the knowledge they bring to public schools. The next section addresses the experiences of Aboriginal teachers in public schools and their attempts to integrate Aboriginal content and perspectives.

Aboriginal Education Encounters with Multiculturalism

At the onset of this chapter, I stated that what happens to Aboriginal teachers in Canadian public schools as they attempt to include Aboriginal content and perspectives is a microcosm of what happens at the political and national levels in regard to Aboriginal peoples' claims to land and sovereignty in Canada. Drawing on qualitative data generated from two studies I have conducted, Aboriginal teachers report on their experiences of incorporating Aboriginal content and perspectives in public schools (St. Denis et al., 1998; St. Denis, 2010). The national politics of denial, resentment, and dismissal of Indigenous rights and sovereignty is also repeated in public schools and detrimentally impacts the work of Aboriginal teachers.

Multiculturalism has been and is used to defend public schools against the need to respond to Aboriginal education. Historically, the need for respectful and meaningful inclusion of Aboriginal education in public schools has long been identified. For example, the Hawthorne (1967, pp. 143–147) report, a comprehensive study of "Indians" in Canada, acknowledged that white racism against Indians was a very real problem and that the attitudes and outlook of white dominant communities needed to change. Yet in its conclusions, this report states, "society and school accept little responsibility for those who cannot conform and the teacher is not in the position to fight an educational system and a society on behalf of a few children out of the many" (Hawthorne, 1967, p. 121). This idea that schools cannot change on behalf of a few Aboriginal children is echoed in the sentiment with which I began this article, that "Aboriginal people are not the only people here" in public schools. Public schools are defended as neutral multicultural spaces where all participants are equally positioned, irrespective of racism and colonialism. In the early 1970s, Trudeau defended Canada as a neutral multicultural nation in which there is "no official culture, nor does any ethnic group take precedence over any other" (James, 2011, p. 194). This idea that Canada does not have an official culture is contested (Mackey, 2002; James, 2011) and the experiences of Aboriginal teachers belie this claim of multicultural neutrality.

Multiculturalism is used as a pretext to justify refusal of an authentic engagement with Aboriginal people, culture, and history. Citing public schools as multicultural spaces permits and enables the expression of "veiled" resentment and resistance to the inclusion of Aboriginal people, culture, and history in public school curricula. The statement, "Aboriginal people are not the only people here," aptly communicates this resentment. Aboriginal teachers in public schools often encounter the discounting of Aboriginal content and perspectives in favour of "existing multicultural curriculum" (St. Denis, 2010, p. 35). Non-Aboriginal colleagues assume the upper "moral" ground, insisting, "with multiculturalism, we can't only focus on one culture" (St. Denis, 2010, p. 35). Multiculturalism in schools suggests that Aboriginal content and perspectives are to be regarded as merely one perspective among many.

Multiculturalism diminishes the importance and need for Aboriginal content and perspectives, just as it facilitates the diminishing of the sovereignty claims of Aboriginal people. As an Aboriginal teacher explained, resistance to Aboriginal content is justified on the basis that "there are other children here" (St. Denis et al., 1998, p. 65). Permitting expressions of resentment and resistance, non-Aboriginal colleagues are confident that they can "question the focus on Aboriginal content" (St. Denis et al., 1998, p. 41) and imply that the presence of Aboriginal teachers is an "intrusion" (St. Denis, 2010, p. 41; St. Denis et al., 1998, p. 64). Public schools are defended as multicultural spaces, notwithstanding criticism of multiculturalism as inadequate to address racism (Vanhouwe, 2007; James, 2011) and ongoing colonialism. Multiculturalism in schools makes it possible for non-Aboriginal teachers and schools to trivialize Aboriginal content and perspectives and at the same time believe that they are becoming more inclusive and respectful.

Aboriginal teachers explain that their non-Aboriginal colleagues need a more meaningful understanding of what it means to incorporate Aboriginal content and perspectives. As one teacher stated, "When non-Aboriginal teachers ask us to deal with Aboriginal issues, they expected us to make bannock … they don't really understand how to make it meaningful" (St. Denis, 2010, p. 36). The folklorization of multiculturalism and culture results in public schools not only trivializing Aboriginal content and perspectives but also conflating multiculturalism with Aboriginal education (Légaré, 1995). This means that there is a very narrow space left for including Aboriginal education, and particularly for understanding what Aboriginal content might be included and how.

For example, one Aboriginal teacher explained, "A little content is allowed, nothing substantial, instead of counting sticks, they count buffalo and call that Aboriginal education" (St. Denis et al., 1998, p. 65). Aboriginal teachers emphasize that teaching about Aboriginal culture and history must go beyond cultural artifacts: "We need the perspective, not just beads and feathers" (St. Denis, 2010, p. 36). As they communicated over and over again, "we don't sit back in our teepees and bead forever, there is only so much beading we can do" (St. Denis et al., 1998, p. 65). Multiculturalism allows schools to assume Aboriginal people, history, and culture are available as mere sources of "enrichment" (Mackey, 2002, p. 98, citing Hage, 1994).

Aboriginal teachers recognize the need for meaningful Aboriginal content and perspectives that address the ways in which racism and colonialism shape the lives of Aboriginal people in Canada. As Aboriginal teachers explain, their non-Aboriginal colleagues are often not open to addressing these issues and "don't want us to make that real" (St. Denis, 2010, p. 36). Aboriginal teachers explain, "people don't want you broaching topics closer to the heart. They only want to talk about fluff" (St. Denis, 2010, p. 35). Part of "making it real" and getting away from "fluff" would involve providing curricular content and teaching practice that exposes the ways in which Aboriginal people have been dehumanized in Canada (Dion, 2007). This may involve non-Aboriginal teachers honestly acknowledging the ways in which Canada has oppressed Aboriginal people in the past, and how Canadian legal institutions continue to dismiss their demands for justice and claims to Aboriginal sovereignty. A defence of schools as multicultural, and the suggestion that attention to historical and ongoing forms of colonialism will result in injustice for non-Aboriginals in the public classroom, act as significant barriers to anticolonialism and antiracism.

Throughout this chapter, I have made the argument that what happens to Aboriginal teachers and Aboriginal content in Canadian public schools is a microcosm of what happens at the political level in regards to Aboriginal people. The prevailing and prevalent policy and practice of multiculturalism enables a refusal to address ongoing colonialism, and even to acknowledge colonialism at all. This leads to the trivializing of issues, to attempts to collapse Aboriginal rights into ethnic and minority issues, and to forcing Aboriginal content into multicultural frameworks. All of these practices deny the reality of Canadian colonialism and reduce efforts for Aboriginal sovereignty and education. The experiences of Aboriginal teachers teach us that just as the Canadian national space is not neutral, so are school spaces not neutral. Dominant cultures regard efforts to address inequality and diversity as a rejection of, and even an intrusion into, broad understandings of self and nation, and so they therefore resist and resent Aboriginal knowledges and history.

Ahmed (2007/2008) has argued that multiculturalism encourages a politics of happiness, whereby those who encounter multiculturalism as racism in disguise or another form of colonialism are socially pressured into silence in order to "maintain signs of getting along"; otherwise, they risk being positioned as the "killjoy" (p. 127). Silencing and further oppression is achieved by suggesting that the "exposure of violence becomes the origins of violence" (Ahmed, 2007/2008, p. 127). Resistance to making Aboriginal content and perspectives in schools "real" is similarly positioned when there is pressure being applied to avoid teaching "difficult knowledge" so that the image of Canada as a fair and just country can be preserved.

Aboriginal teachers are adamant that they are not going away and neither are Aboriginal people. As one Aboriginal teacher stated, "We are not going anywhere. We are still here. And 500 hundred years from now, we will still be here" (St. Denis, 2010, p. 40). If we want success for Aboriginal students in public schools, perhaps our schools and educational institutions must be committed to challenging the Canadian fantasy expressed by Harper, when he made the statement that Canada does not have a history of colonialism. We must start with acknowledging both the past and continuing injustice toward Aboriginal people rather than evading and erasing, so we can become a country committed to justice and fairness.

REFERENCES

Ahmed, S. (2007/2008). Multiculturalism and the promise of happiness. *New Formations, 63*, 121–137.

Backhouse, C. (1999). *Colour-Coded: A legal history of racism in Canada, 1900–1950.* Toronto: University of Toronto Press.

Chakrabarty, D. (2001). Reconciliation and its historiography: Some preliminary thoughts. *UTS Review, 7*(4), 6–16.

Curthoys, A. (2000). An uneasy conversation: The Indigenous and the multicultural. In J. Docker & G. Fischer (Eds.), *Colour and identity in Australia and New Zealand* (pp. 21–36). Sydney, Australia: UNSW Press.

Day, R.J.F. (2000). *Multiculturalism and the history of Canadian diversity.* Toronto: University of Toronto Press.

Day, R.J.F., & Sadik, T. (2002). The BC land question, liberal multiculturalism, and the spectre of Aboriginal nationhood. *BC Studies, 134*, 5–34.

Dei, G.J.S., & Calliste, A. (2000). Mapping the terrain: Power, knowledge and anti-racism education. In G.J.S. Dei & A. Calliste (Eds.), *Power, knowledge and anti-racist education* (pp. 11–22). Halifax, NS: Fernwood Publishing.

Dion, S. (2007). Disrupting molded images: Identities, responsibilities and relationships—teachers and Indigenous subject material. *Teaching Education, 18*(4), 329–342. http://dx.doi.org/10.1080/10476210701687625

Fleras, A., & Elliot, J.E. (1992). *Multiculturalism in Canada: The challenge of diversity.* Scarborough, ON: Nelson Canada.

Francis, D. (1997). *National dreams: Myth, memory and Canadian history.* Vancouver: Arsenal Pulp Press.

Hage, G. (1994). Locating multiculturalism's other: A critique of practical tolerance. *New Formations, 24,* 21–32.

Hawthorne, H.B. (1967). A *survey of the contemporary Indians of Canada: Economic, political, educational needs and policies* (Vol. 1 and 2). Ottawa: Indian Affairs Branch.

James, C.E. (2011). Multicultural education in a color-blind society. In C.A. Grant & A. Portera (Eds.), *Intercultural and multicultural education: Enhancing global interconnectedness* (pp. 191–210). New York: Routledge.

Kymlicka, W. (1996). *Multicultural citizenship: A liberal theory of minority rights.* Oxford: Clarendon Press. http://dx.doi.org/10.1093/0198290918.001.0001

Lawrence, B., & Dua, E. (2005). Decolonizing antiracism. *Social Justice (San Francisco, Calif.), 32*(4), 120–143.

Légaré, E.I. (1995). Canadian multiculturalism and Aboriginal people: Negotiating a place in the nation. *Identities (Yverdon), 1*(4), 347–366. http://dx.doi.org/10.10 80/1070289X.1995.9962515

Ljunggren, D. (2009, September 25). Every G20 nation wants to be Canada, insists PM. Reuters. Retrieved from http://www.reuters.com/article/2009/09/26/columns-us-g20-canada-advantages-idUSTRE58P05Z20090926

Mackey, E. (2002). *The house of difference: Cultural politics and national identity in Canada.* Toronto: University of Toronto Press.

Mackey, E. (2005). Universal rights in conflict: "Backlash" and "benevolent resistance" to Indigenous land rights. *Anthropology Today, 21*(2), 14–20. http://dx.doi.org/10.1111/j.0268-540X.2005.00340.x

Montgomery, K. (2005). Imagining the anti-racist state: Representations of racism in Canadian history textbooks. *Discourse Studies in the Cultural Politics of Education, 26*(4), 427–442. http://dx.doi.org/10.1080/01596300500319712

Paine, R. (1999). Aboriginality, multiculturalism, and liberal rights philosophy. *Ethnos, 64*(3-4), 325–349. http://dx.doi.org/10.1080/00141844.1999.9981607

Povinelli, E. (1998). The state of shame: Australian multiculturalism and the crisis of Indigenous citizenship. *Critical Inquiry, 24*(2), 575–610. http://dx.doi.org/10.1086/448886

Rutherford, S. (2010). Colonialism and the Indigenous present: An interview with Bonita Lawrence. *Race & Class, 52*(1), 9–18. http://dx.doi.org/10.1177/03063968 10371757

Short, D. (2005). Reconciliation and the problem of internal colonialism. *Journal of Intercultural Studies (Melbourne, Vic.), 26*(3), 267–282. http://dx.doi.org/10.1080/07256860500153534

St. Denis, V. (2010, March 10). A *study of Aboriginal teachers' professional knowledge and experience in Canadian public schools.* Ottawa: Canadian Teachers' Federation and Canadian Council on Learning.

St. Denis, V., Bouvier, R., & Battiste, M. (1998, October 31). *Okiskinahamakewak— Aboriginal teachers in Saskatchewan's publicly funded schools: Responding to the flux. Final Report.* Regina, SK: Saskatchewan Education Research Networking Project.

Tully, J. (2000). The struggles of Indigenous peoples for and of freedom. In D. Ivison, P. Patton, & W. Sanders (Eds.), *Political theory and the rights of Indigenous Peoples* (pp. 36–59). Cambridge, UK: Cambridge University Press.

Turner, D. (2006). *This is not a peace pipe: Towards a critical Indigenous philosophy.* Toronto: University of Toronto Press.

Vanhouwe, M.I. (2007). *White teachers, critical race theory and Aboriginal education.* (Unpublished master's thesis). University of Saskatchewan, Saskatoon.

Wood, P., & Gilbert, L. (2005). Multiculturalism in Canada: Accidental discourse, alternative vision, urban practice. *International Journal of Urban and Regional Research, 29*(3), 679–691. http://dx.doi.org/10.1111/j.1468-2427.2005.00612.x

NOTES

1 I draw on Augie Fleras and Jean Leonard Elliott's (1992) book, *Multiculturalism in Canada: The Challenge of Diversity*, as a source for basic information on multiculturalism in Canada.

2 Lawrence and Dua are primarily critiquing antiracism education as failing to recognize colonialism and Indigeneity, but they also do a critique of multiculturalism.

3

Closing the Education Gap: A Case for Aboriginal Early Childhood Education in Canada, a Look at the Aboriginal Head Start Program

Mai Nguyen

This chapter was originally published in the *Canadian Journal of Education* (2011), 34(3), pp. 229–248. Reproduced with permission.

Introduction

Welfare state theory postulates that in order for countries to be economically competitive and successful, governments must increase human capital by providing their citizens with the tools necessary to become productive workers and citizens. One of the crucial tools is education, a right that should be afforded to all citizens. According to some welfare-state theorists (Marshall & Bottomore, 1992; Esping-Andersen, 2002a and 2002b), education is the one social service that can alleviate inherent disadvantages bestowed upon the marginalized of society. More importantly, state investment in early childhood education will diminish welfare problems among future adults—problems such as unemployment, low pay, housing, etc. (Esping-Andersen, 2002a, p. 51). In the Canadian case, Aboriginals largely occupy this socio-economic position. As a colonized minority group they suffer daily tragedies such as chronic unemployment, low wages, and social exclusion. These tragedies are attributed to the historical consequence of colonialism; specifically, the tragedies of military, missionary, and bureaucratic interventions that gradually stripped Indigenous nations of their chosen destinies (Daes, 2000, p. 6). It is on this point that this chapter argues that state-funded early childhood education that focuses on the cultural needs of Aboriginal children and their families will help alleviate their disadvantaged position in society while simultaneously restoring Aboriginal identity and self-worth. This is embedded in the theoretical framework of Indigenous scholars (Archibald, Battiste, Goulet, etc.) who argue that *Eurocentric education* (education focused on the belief systems of the colonizers while simultaneously rejecting and ignoring the worldviews, values, and languages of Aboriginals) cannot rectify the consequences of colonialism on its own. Instead, Aboriginal education needs to be re-framed in an Aboriginal context that will provide Aboriginal children with a sense of self-worth. That is, a sense of who they are and where they come from, which will impact community self-government and self-determination.

In addition, this chapter analyzes data from Statistics Canada, which will provide a recent snapshot of the nonreserve Aboriginal population in Canada. This portrait of the Aboriginal population sheds light upon the disparities between Aboriginals and the general Canadian population, disparities that can be rectified through preventive strategies, such as Aboriginal-specific early child care. Recognizing the eminent need for this, in the 1990s the Canadian federal government began implementing preventative programs like the Aboriginal Head Start (AHS) initiative that focused on the culturally specific needs of Aboriginal children and their families. This chapter will examine the success of AHS and the obstacles facing Aboriginal youth on their journey to higher education. In the end, this chapter concludes that early Aboriginal childhood education is crucial in the development of self-actualization and self-worth for Aboriginal youth. Improvement in these facets of life will bring greater results to the Aboriginal community at large.

The Unfortunate History of Colonization: A Look at the Aboriginal Population Yesterday and Today

It is widely known that Canadian Aboriginals (the terms "Aboriginal" and "Indigenous" will be used interchangeably) are the most disadvantaged and marginalized group in Canadian society. From shorter life expectancy rates to higher crime rates, Aboriginal communities carry a disproportionate burden of society's troubles. The marginalization that is experienced by Aboriginal groups diminishes the groups' capacity to become meaningful participants in Canadian society. This phenomena is not new but one that has deep roots in Canadian history. The genocide of Aboriginal culture via British colonization has ultimately weakened Aboriginal groups' ability for self-determination and has led to their marginalization. The question then is how did this come to be?

The Crown in Canada has been instrumental in the destruction of Aboriginal communities, economies, and culture. In the tradition of empire-building, the British stripped Aboriginals of their land, and attempted to assimilate the Indigenous population and change the power relations within Aboriginal societies. By doing this, the Crown changed what was once an egalitarian society into a class-based society, consequently altering the livelihood of Aboriginal communities. More specifically, the engine behind empire-building—the expansion of the market economy—changed Aboriginal communities toward the capitalist variety. That is, Aboriginal communities began to lose their self-sufficiency and became dependent on the colonizers for their livelihood. More importantly, Aboriginal culture began to change and erode.

To contextualize, the Crown committed cultural genocide through its assimilation processes, stripping Aboriginals of their cultures and, more importantly, their language, which is at the crux of Aboriginal culture. Language, through oral tradition, was the most important mode of communication for Aboriginals. The Department of Indian and Northern Affairs (INAC, formerly DIAND) states, "Language is inextricably linked to culture. It expresses cultural concepts and our understanding of the environment we live in. Put simply, language expresses what matters to society" (INAC, 2005, p. 25). Without an official written language, Aboriginals depended on storytelling and oral tradition to transmit culture and customs, and to convey information (INAC, 2005, p. 26). According to INAC, "Among Canada's native peoples, wise and deliberate speech was an art form and honoured tradition ... both language and gestures were used to communicate information and images" (INAC, 2005, p. 7). The Assembly of First Nations (AFN) (1992) further illustrates this point when stating that

> *Our Native language embodies a value system about how we ought to live and relate to each other ... It gives a name to relations among kin, to roles and responsibilities among family members, to ties with the broader clan group ... There are no*

English words for these relationships … Now, if you destroy our languages you not only break down these relationships, but you also destroy other aspects of our Indian way of life and culture, especially those that describe man's connection with nature, the Great Spirit, and the order of things. Without our languages, we will cease to exist as separate people. (p. 14)

It is these traditions that ensured the livelihood of Aboriginal culture and community daily and intergenerational.

Unfortunately, assimilation processes jeopardized the Aboriginal way of life by forcing a Eurocentric agenda upon Aboriginal communities. As Battiste (Battiste & Barman, 1995) states:

For a century or more, DIAND attempted to destroy the diversity of Aboriginal world-views, cultures, and languages. It defined education as transforming the mind of Aboriginal youth rather than educating it. Through ill-conceived government policies and plans, Aboriginal youth were subjected to a combination of powerful but profoundly distracting forces of cognitive imperialism and colonization. Various boarding schools, industrial schools, day schools, and Eurocentric educational practices ignored or rejected the world-views, languages, and values of Aboriginal parents in the education of their children. The outcome was the gradual loss of these world-views, languages, and cultures and the creation of widespread social and psychological upheaval in Aboriginal communities. (p. viii)

The result of this historical relationship between Aboriginals and the Crown—that involved the dispossession of land, removal of Aboriginal rights and culture, and the destruction of their economies—has been that Aboriginals suffer higher levels of poverty, chronic illnesses, and unemployment (to name a few) compared to that of the general Canadian population (Brady, 1995, p. 364).

Aboriginal Education Yesterday and Today: A Historical and Statistical Analysis

Many scholars (David Walters, Jerry White, Paul Maxim, and Helmar Drost) suggest that Aboriginal inability to resolve these problems is caused by lack of education, a consequence of colonization. As Drost (1994) states, "Unemployment among Aboriginals is higher than for any other ethnic group in Canadian Society. One of the factors considered being a major obstacle for Canadian Aboriginals in finding and securing employment is their relatively low level of general education and occupational skills" (pp. 52–53). Therefore, to gauge the severity of the state of Aboriginal education in Canada and for analytical purposes, it is useful to sketch a portrait of the Aboriginal population in Canada. For the most part, this section will use 2006 and 2007 data from Statistics Canada to illustrate the education gaps between the Aboriginal and Canadian population. These data will demonstrate that the higher the level of educational attainment, the greater the chances of employment. However, even with this in mind, Aboriginal youth continue to fall behind their Canadian counterparts.

According to Statistics Canada in the 2006 Aboriginal Peoples Survey (APS), there are approximately 837,475 off-reserve Aboriginals, with 623,470 Aboriginals living in urban areas, from a group that has surpassed the one million mark. It is estimated that 244,475 of the off-reserve Aboriginals are children aged 14 and under, with 175,410 living in urban areas (Statistics Canada, 2006). More importantly, the Public Health Agency of Canada (2008) notes that, "Currently 38 percent of Aboriginal people are children under the age of 15. This is proportionally twice as high as the rest of the Canadian population." Given this, the future and viability of the Aboriginal community largely depends on the future of Aboriginal children. As the 1996 federal government's Royal Commission on Aboriginal Peoples (RCAP) states,

> We believe that the Creator has entrusted us with the sacred responsibility to raise our families ... for we realize healthy families are the foundation of strong and healthy communities. The future of our communities lies with our children, who need to be nurtured within their families and communities.

Unfortunately, upon examination of the data, the future of Aboriginal children comes into question because, comparatively, they continue to lag behind the general youth population.

According to the 2007 Statistics Canada research paper, *The Aboriginal Labour Force Analysis Series,* prepared by Dominique Perusse, Aboriginal youth do not fare as well compared to the general population in terms of education (see Table 3.1). For instance, 43% of Aboriginal youth (ages 15–24) were enrolled in school compared to 50% of non-Aboriginal youth (p. 19). In addition, it is estimated that two-thirds of the Aboriginal population over the age of 15 have no post-secondary qualifications compared to one-half of the Canadian population over the age of 15 (Statistics Canada, 2001a, 2001b). In

Table 3.1 Aboriginal Education in Canada

Ages 15–24	Enrolled in School	No Secondary Education	No Post-Secondary Education
Aboriginals	43%	48%	66.6%
Non-Aboriginals	50%	26%	50%

Source: Statistics Canada, 2001.

general, among off-reserve Aboriginals ages 20–24, 48% have not completed secondary school while that number is only 26% for the non-Aboriginal counterpart in the same age group (Statistics Canada, 2001a, 2001b).

In terms of employment, Perusse (2007) reveals that 24.1% of off-reserve Aboriginals, ages 15–24, without a high school diploma, were reported to be unemployed (p. 7). However, it is increasingly concerning that even with equivalent education, the gaps persist. Perusse (2007) states, "Aboriginal people with a post-secondary certificate or diploma or a university degree had an employment rate 6.3 percentage points lower than their non-Aboriginal counterpart" (p. 16). While unemployment for Aboriginals ages 15–24 who possessed at least a high school diploma and some post-secondary education was only 12.2%, that number was only 10% for the same non-Aboriginal group (Perusse, 2007, p. 7). Even when examining statistics between Aboriginal groups the gaps continue. As Perusse (2007) notes,

> Education also tends to reduce the unemployment rate for Aboriginal people. The difference in unemployment rates is especially pronounced between those who do not have a high school diploma and those who have one; in 2007, the unemployment rate between these two Aboriginal groups was 14.2% compared to 8.0%. (p. 16)

These data strongly suggest that Aboriginal youth can improve their life chances by prolonging their education. Unfortunately, what is also revealed from these statistics is that Aboriginals continue to lag behind their non-Aboriginal counterparts in terms of employability even when education levels remain the same. The question then is what has prevented Aboriginals from achieving higher education and higher employability? Part of the answer lies with the fact that, historically, Aboriginal education has been controlled by the federal government.

The evolution of Aboriginal education policy in Canada stems from the British North America Act of 1867 and the Indian Act of 1876 (Carr-Stewart, 2001, p. 132). These acts gave the federal government jurisdiction over Aboriginal education policies even though education is an area normally controlled by provincial governments. According to Patrick Brady, the federal government's role in Aboriginal education can be characterized by three distinct phases (Brady, 1995). The first phase, and possibly the most infamous, was the creation of residential schools in which the federal government entered into agreements with numerous Christian denominations to create industrial schools that would partake in the education of Aboriginal children by teaching them the Euro-Canadian way of life (Brady, 1995, p. 350). Aboriginal children were sent away from their homes and forced to reside at the residential schools for extended periods of time and later it was reported that many endured mental, physical, and emotional abuse, ultimately hindering their development. More specifically, Aboriginal families were only allowed to participate in their children's education through consent to send their children away. As Jo-ann Archibald (1995) states,

> This consent was all the involvement that First Nations people were allowed in the education of their children. Religious educational aims focused on conversion and gradual civilization. The "knowledge of most worth" was considered to be Catholicism, English, and later, the general subjects of grammar, spelling, and arithmetic, in this order ... Elders and parents were beginning to see inimical attitudes being instilled in their children. Their First Nations language was forbidden in school and their strong cultural beliefs were dismissed as mere superstition. (p. 293).

Because of this, First Nations parents began to fight back through absenteeism as a form of resistance (Archibald, 1995, p. 293). Though these schools taught industrial skills, many Aboriginal students could not obtain employment in their fields upon leaving school and, therefore, returned to reserves (Archibald, 1995, p. 294). This arrangement existed until after the Second World War (Brady, 1995, p. 350).

The period after the Second World War signified the beginning of phase two and was marked by the new Indian Act of 1951 (Brady, 1995, p. 351). This act allowed the federal government to enter into agreements with provincial governments and permitted Aboriginal children to attend provincially operated schools, but these schools were culturally insensitive to the needs of Aboriginal children. As Archibald (1995) states,

> little attention was paid to the cultural differences of First Nations children ... Cultural differences were later seen as the cause of education problems among First Nations children. Culturally deprived students were helped through remedial or readiness programs which actually separated First Nations children from regular classroom experiences. This created additional social and self-concept barriers for them. (p. 295)

Discerningly, Brady notes that the outcomes of these agreements were significant. He states that "the percentage of Native children attending provincial schools rose from 27 percent in 1963 [Frideres, 1983, as cited in Brady, 1995, p. 315] to 56.3 percent in 1979" (INAC, 1988, as cited in Brady, 1995, p. 351). During this time, many Aboriginal children were placed in non-Aboriginal foster homes or adopted out. This resulted in a great sense of lost identity for these Aboriginal children (Public Health Agency of Canada, 2008).

The third phase was characterized by the *Indian Education Paper phase One of* 1973 that emphasized the need to improve Aboriginal education and transfer control of education back to Aboriginal society (Brady, 1995, p. 351). Brady notes that since the passage of this policy, the enrolment in First Nations-operated schools has almost doubled from 26% to 44% during the period from 1985 to 1991 (Brady, 1995, p. 351). However, it should be noted that these numbers reflect only enrolment among status Indians who live on reserve. Since 1992, it is estimated that approximately 75% to 80% of off-reserve Aboriginal children attend non-Native schools controlled by the provincial governments (Brady, 1995, p. 351). This is concerning because the attendance of Aboriginal students in non-Native schools or under non-Aboriginal-controlled curriculum can be detrimental to the students' success. As Battiste (Battiste & Barman, 1995) states,

> *The federal government has entered into agreements with First Nations bands that require them to adopt provincial curricula as a minimum requirement to assume control of their education. In almost all of these provinces, these curricula are developed away from Aboriginal communities, without Aboriginal input, and written in English. In effect, the curricula serve as another colonial instrument to deprive Aboriginal communities of their knowledge, languages, and cultures. Without Aboriginal languages and knowledge, Aboriginal communities can do little to recover their losses or transform their nations using their legitimate knowledge and languages. (p. 1)*

Historically, the government of Canada has been instrumental in deciding the faith of Aboriginal children through its education policies, which, as this chapter argues, has resulted in the failure of Aboriginals to achieve higher education and employment compared to their non-Aboriginal counterparts.

Understanding State-Funded and Culturally Appropriate Education—Theoretical Framework

Marie Battiste argues that a space for Indigenous Knowledge (IK) needs to be carved out in educational institutions. The lack of such a space has meant that Aboriginal education continues to be Eurocentric. As Battiste (2008) states, "This struggle demands an urgent agenda to effect educational reform ... and to protect and enhance Indigenous heritage and livelihood damaged by colonial assimilation projects, neglect, diminishment, and racism" (p. 85). In the last 40 years, this has come to the forefront in regards to education policies. For example, in 1969, the federal government released its *White Paper Policy* that sought to transfer federal responsibility for First Nations education on reserves to the provinces (Battiste & Barman, 1995, p. viii). Ultimately, the federal government continued to want all Aboriginal students to become absorbed into provincial systems and mainstream society (Battiste & Barman, 1995, p. viii). In objection to this, Aboriginal communities began to mobilize and, according to Battiste (Battiste & Barman, 1995), "argued that Aboriginal communities themselves had the right, based on their Aboriginal status and treaties, to administer educational programs for their children" (p. viii). The acceptance of IK into mainstream education began taking place. As Battiste (2008) states:

> Indigenous Knowledge is being revealed both nationally and internationally as an extensive and valuable knowledge system. It is not only a remedy to the continuing failures of the education system, but also the opening to understanding distinct knowledges that the twenty-first century education must learn to operate in … IK provides a positive approach to dealing with self-doubt and low self-esteem among Indigenous populations. (p. 87)

This is the minimum standard needed for the survival, dignity, and well-being of the Indigenous peoples (Battiste, 2008, p. 89).

These shortfalls in the education system prevent Aboriginal children from developing a strong sense of self and developing greater cognitive skills (Public Health Agency of Canada, 2008). Aboriginal-controlled and culturally appropriate education curricula are both important features of Aboriginal society and must be taken into account during the policy-design process. More importantly, focus on these twin issues must begin at the early stages of development when a sense of identity begins to emerge. More recently there has been an emphasis on the need for Aboriginal control of Aboriginal children's education. Brady (1995) notes, "Native parents in both Canada and the United States are often limited in their ability to influence their children's education, particularly when their children attend schools in non-Native education systems. The key to Native control of Native education would therefore appear to lie in having Native children attend educational institutions controlled by Native peoples" (p. 357).

This has been acknowledged and recognized by the Canadian state. RCAP (1996, as cited in Child Care Canada, 1998) recommends that "the federal, provincial, and territorial governments co-operate to support an integrated early childhood funding strategy that … c) maximizes Aboriginal control over service design and administration … and e) promotes parental involvement and choice in early childhood education options." These recommendations will assist

Aboriginal children in developing a greater sense of self and identity. As the Public Health Agency of Canada (2008) states,

> We are constantly developing our identity, from birth to the end of our lives. We build it based on our relationships to relatives, friends, community, geography, language and other social factors. Identity plays a key role in healthy child development. When a child feels a sense of belonging to family, community and peers he or she is better able to deal with adversity. The importance of identity is particularly true for Aboriginal children's healthy development since community and belonging are such important parts of their cultures' belief systems.

More importantly, Goulet, Dressyman-Lavallee, and McCleod (2001) state that

> Different Aboriginal organizations have identified the need for early childhood programs and child care controlled by Aboriginal people. Studies by the Assembly of First Nations, the Congress of Aboriginal Peoples and the National Association of Friendship Centres all advocate for childcare for a variety of reasons. First is the preparation of children for academic success … But beyond that, they also see early childhood programs as a necessary support to Aboriginal parents striving to overcome a life of poverty through employment or training … Most of all, they see quality early childhood education "as a means of reinforcing Aboriginal identity, instilling the values, attitudes and behaviours that give expression to Aboriginal cultures" (RCAP, Vol. 3, 1996, 449). (pp. 137–138)

The desire to preserve Aboriginal culture means that education policies must be returned to Aboriginal peoples as a form of self-government and must reflect a holistic approach that includes not only governments but also Aboriginal families, elders, and the Aboriginal community as a whole (Turcotte & Zhao, 2004, p. 11). Holistic control over Aboriginal education will lead to a culturally appropriate and acceptable education curriculum and, therefore, lead to better results.

Statistical data has long supported this finding. For example, uncovered in the 2001 APS is the connection between family and language retention. That is, the more children could rely on numerous sources for learning—such as parents, grandparents, school teachers, and extended family—the more likely they were to speak and understand an Aboriginal language (as cited in Turcotte & Zhao, 2004, p. 19). As the survey reveals,

> 38 percent of children who can rely on three sources of assistance are able to speak and understand an Aboriginal language well. This proportion rises to 54 percent for those benefiting from five different sources of assistance, and to 80 percent for those benefiting from seven sources or more for assistance. (as cited in Turcotte & Zhao, 2004, p. 19)

Furthermore, the Aboriginal Education Office of Ontario notes that the lack of cultural understanding among provincial schools can be partially blamed for the low levels of educational attainment experienced by many Aboriginal youths. As the Ministry states, "Factors that contribute to low Aboriginal student outcomes include ... a lack of awareness among teachers of the learning styles of Aboriginal students and a lack of understanding within schools and school boards of Aboriginal cultures, histories and perspectives" (Aboriginal Education Office, 2006). Bernard Schissel and Terry Wotherspoon's 2003 survey of Aboriginal communities came to similar conclusions.

Schissel and Wotherspoon note that there is a positive correlation between cultural education and educational outcomes. According to the authors, 11% of students who received cultural education and 14% who received a little cultural education indicated that they "liked everything about school" (Schissel and Wotherspoon, 2003, p. 92). This is compared to only 6% of students who received no cultural education (Schissel and Wotherspoon, 2003, p. 92). In addition, approximately one-third of students who received no cultural education "liked nothing about school" compared to 22% of students who received cultural education and only 9.5% who received little cultural education (Schissel and Wotherspoon, 2003, p. 92). More importantly, however, the survey reveals that cultural education has an effect on high school dropout rates. Schissel and Wotherspoon (2003) state, "The results illustrate that cultural education is indeed associated with the likelihood that students will stay in school. Just under 40 percent of students with cultural education have dropped out of school at least once, compared to 50 percent of those with no cultural education" (p. 95). Conclusively, there is little doubt that a culturally appropriate curriculum is vital for educational success among Aboriginal youth. This can be achieved when control of Aboriginal education is returned to Aboriginal communities, which historically has not been the case.

Harvey McCue (2006) places blame on the provinces and states, "It should be obvious to anyone that the provincial education system has failed Aboriginal students ... What is needed is a curriculum and pedagogy for Aboriginal schools ... that is culturally appropriate, more applied in content than the status quo, and taught by instructors who are trained in the cultural dimensions of Aboriginal classrooms" (p. 5). There are factors unique to the Aboriginal population, namely the importance attached to Aboriginal-controlled and culturally appropriate curriculum, which must be addressed and implemented in order for Aboriginal youths to succeed as students and as individuals in their Aboriginal community and the Canadian community at large. The next section of this chapter examines how both the federal and provincial governments have approached, and attempted to provide, preventative strategies concerning the issue of Aboriginal education, through government initiatives, more specifically, the Aboriginal Head Start program.

Case Study: Aboriginal Head Start Program

In the mid-1990s, Royal Commissions on Aboriginal peoples and on education highlighted the need to improve Aboriginal education. The federal and provincial governments began to recognize that Aboriginals were largely occupying the lower end of the income strata and bore a disproportionate burden of unemployment, much of which could be related to lower levels of education. Both levels of governments acknowledged the need for action. Informed by welfare-state theory and the Royal Commissions, both levels of government introduced Aboriginal education initiatives concentrating on all stages of education, from preschool to post-secondary education. This section of the chapter will examine the federal government's 1995 early child care initiative, Aboriginal Head Start, regulated by Health Canada (Child Care Canada, 1998).

According to RCAP, there is a strong belief that early childhood experiences are vital for the development of the self. As RCAP (1996) states, "Early childhood is one of the most important points in the learning process. In recent decades, research has confirmed the critical importance of infancy and early childhood as a foundation upon which identity, self-worth and intellectual strength are built" (p. 17). These early years, from ages zero to six, are decisive in determining the success of children later on in the education process. It is important to stress both the federal and provincial government's understanding of this theory. RCAP (1996) states that

> If stresses interfere with the development of a child's capacity for health, self-esteem and intellectual growth before beginning school, the schooling experience soon accentuates the child's "weaknesses." Once they have entered the formal education system, children may never recover the ground lost in these early years. The link between early childhood experiences and success in the formal schooling system has been studied intensively by researchers since the 1960s ... After three decades of examining early childhood interventions, there is strong evidence that such programs do make a difference, particularly if they continue into the elementary school system. There is substantial research showing that children who participate in high quality early childhood development programs are more likely to finish high school and to be employed. (Weikart, 1989, as cited in RCAP, 1996, p. 19)

In addition, the Ontario government in the *Report of the Royal Commission on Learning* emphasizes the same rationale. As the commission states,

> *Children who come through a carefully planned process of early education gain significantly in competence, coping skills, and (not the least important) in positive attitudes towards learning … We're convinced that early childhood education significantly helps in providing a level playing field of opportunity and experience for every child, whatever her background. (Government of Ontario, 1994, as cited in RCAP, 1996, p. 19)*

Both Royal Commissions drive home the point that early childhood education is at the crux of self-development.

In recognition of this, the federal government, with the help of provincial governments and nonprofit Aboriginal organizations, began the AHS initiative that was originally provided for off-reserve Aboriginal families in urban communities and the northern region and later expanded in 1998 (in light of RCAP) to include on-reserve communities (Health Canada, 1998). According to the Public Health Agency of Canada (2004), the key goal of this initiative is to "demonstrate that locally controlled and designed early intervention strategies can provide Aboriginal children with a positive sense of themselves, a desire for learning, and opportunities to develop fully as successful people." It is a half-day, four-days-a-week, preschool experience for children ages zero to six, with an emphasis on children ages three to six (Public Health Agency of Canada, 2004).

AHS sites, as specified in the program's national principles and guidelines, are managed by Aboriginal nonprofit organizations and directly support the parent/caregiver in his/her role as the natural advocate and teacher of the child. According to AHS, "Parents are directly involved in the design, implementation and management of local projects" (Public Health Agency of Canada, 2004). In addition, projects are administered in a holistic framework that allows not only parents and guardians a role, but extended family and community members also play a significant part in the program design, implementation, management, evaluation, and ongoing planning of the project (INAC, 2005). According to Health Canada (1998), "The AHS National Office in Ottawa provides national coordination, leadership, resources, and training, as well as coordinating a national evaluation of the program. A National Aboriginal Head Start Council provides Health Canada with expertise, and ensures project and regional-level input into the operation and management of the program." In essence, the AHS principles and guidelines recognize and affirm the need to provide holistic and community-based approaches to the programs in addition to the recognition and respect of cultural diversity (Public Health Agency of Canada, 1998).

The AHS principles and guidelines are contained in the program's six component areas: Culture and Language, Education and School Readiness, Health Promotion, Nutrition, Social Support, and Parental and Family Involvement. The first two components are of utmost importance here, while the last component merely reinforces the AHS's principles and guidelines. The Culture and Language component is to provide projects that will increase the process of cultural and linguistic revival and retention with the hopes that children will, according to the Public Health Agency of Canada (2004), "aspire to learn their respective languages and participate in their communities' cultures after AHS." The AHS education component is designed to

> support and encourage each Aboriginal child to enjoy life-long learning. More specifically, the projects will encourage each child to take initiatives in learning and provide each child with enjoyable opportunities to learn. This will be done in a manner which is appropriate to both the age and stage of development of the child. The ultimate goal is to engage children in the possibility of learning so that they carry forth the enthusiasm, self-esteem and initiative to learn in the future. (Public Health Agency of Canada, 2004)

The ability to learn is, therefore, pivotal in the development of individuals and is a life-long process. Based on the program's success, AHS has continued to grow strong.

By 1998, three years after the program's inception and with the inclusion of on-reserve communities, there were approximately 99 AHS sites coast to coast (Health Canada, 1998). In the year it was launched, federal funding was announced at $83.7 million over a four-year period, roughly $21 million per year until 1999 (Child Care Canada, 1998). Over the years, federal funding has increased by approximately 20%. For instance, in 2002 funding was estimated at $26 million (Social Union, 2007). By 2006, this amount was increased to $31 million (Social Union, 2007). The incremental increases in funding over the years have also meant a greater increase in accessibility for Aboriginal families. In 2004, there were 126 AHS sites and by 2005 this number had increased to 140 AHS sites (Public Health Agency of Canada, 2004; INAC, 2005). In addition, enrolment has followed the same trajectory. In 1998, available spaces and enrolment was estimated at three thousand (Public Health Agency of Canada, 2004). Since then, enrolment in 2004 increased to four thousand and by 2005 it is reported to have stood at 4,500 (Public Health Agency of Canada, 2004; INAC, 2005). Conclusively, these data suggest that the initiative continues to expand and reach more Aboriginal children and families.

Some examples of AHS sites include the Tiknagin (Chiannou) AHS program in Val d'Or and Senneterre, Quebec (Health Canada, 1998). This site integrates the cultures of the Algonquin, Cree, and Attikamek First Nations (Health Canada, 1998). A six-year-old graduate of this program made national headlines when he saved his family from an evening house fire by employing the fire safety skills he learned at this AHS site (Health Canada, 1998). There is also the Awasisak Cultural Development Program in Prince George, British Columbia, which uses Métis curriculum and is in the process of working with local school districts to establish a Métis kindergarten and a tracking system for AHS graduates as they progress through school (Health Canada, 1998). Last, there is the Mannawasis AHS program located in St. Paul, Alberta. This program educates children in both Cree and English and spirituality is strongly emphasized (Health Canada, 1998).

The continuation of the program and the increase in federal funding and spaces suggest that the program has been popular and effective among the Aboriginal community. According to the 2001 Census, only 4% of Aboriginal children aged 14 had attended Aboriginal preschool programs when they were preschoolers (this would have occurred between 1987 and 1993) (Statistics Canada, 2001b, as cited in Turcotte & Zhao, 2004, p. 13). Within the same Census, 16% of off-reserve Aboriginal children aged six reported attending preschool programs designed for them, such as AHS (Statistics Canada, 2001b, as cited in Turcotte & Zhao, 2004, p. 13). Though the numbers appear minimal, there has been a fourfold increase in enrolment since 1987 and this is considered a significant stride for Aboriginals. In addition, in 1998 Health Canada (1998) stated, "Reports indicate that parents are very pleased with the progress that their children are making and with the opportunity to be involved with Aboriginal Head Start." As one AHS parent notes,

I am the mother of a child who is currently attending the Aboriginal Head Start program. I feel that AHS has made a positive impact on our family life. We are able to understand our child more clearly now. Before our son started school he was unable to put two words together. At one point we had him seeing an Early Childhood Interventionist but unfortunately he showed no signs of speaking more. After being in Head Start for a couple of months I have seen many improvements with his speech. He is able to tell me how his day went and what things he did. (Public Health Agency of Canada, p. 20)

More importantly, the department of Indian and Northern Affairs Canada notes that local evaluations, parents, kindergarten teachers, and community members report significant gains in all areas of children's development, improved family relationships, and the development of parenting skills (INAC, 2005). More specific impact statements and evaluations are currently in the process of being reported. Though it is premature to know the long-term effects of the program on Aboriginal children and on their journey to higher education, the progress that attendees of the schools have made thus far suggests that AHS programs are breaking new ground in education for Aboriginals and their communities.

Conclusion

This chapter has argued that quality early childhood education is one of the strongest defenses against poor socio-economic effects. This is especially the case for Canadian Aboriginal youth. More than any other ethnic group in Canada, Aboriginals have suffered from lower levels of education and employment. Much of this is embedded in Aboriginal-Crown relations, both past and present. Historically, colonization stripped Aboriginal peoples of their lands, society, and culture, therefore leading to a loss of self-identity and self-worth. More recently, the inability to reconcile Aboriginal education curriculum with that of the Canadian education curriculum has meant that education policies still do not work for Aboriginal children. In other words, even with similar education levels, Aboriginal youth are still lagging behind their Canadian counterparts in terms of employability.

As demonstrated in this chapter, such levels can be attributed to the exclusion of Aboriginals from the education policy process, beginning with its creation all the way to the implementation of education policy. Data presented here suggest that Eurocentric curriculum is not sensitive to the needs of Aboriginal children, making it difficult for them to enjoy and stay in school. Informed by Indigenous-based theory, this chapter argues for a holistic approach to Aboriginal education. Such an approach will assist in restoring Aboriginal identity and self-worth back into individuals and their communities at large. Part of this approach is being implemented in the federal government's AHS program designed to address the issues pertaining to Aboriginal education. Though empirical data relating to the program's success are limited, to say the least, there is some evidence to suggest that the program is making significant progress throughout the Aboriginal community and has paved the way for a stronger and increasingly educated Aboriginal population who have, more importantly, a better understanding of who they are and where they come from. These are steps needed to restore self-determination and, ultimately, self-government in Aboriginal communities. As AFN (1998) states,

> Education is one of the most important issues in the struggle for self-government and must contribute towards the objective of self-government. First Nations' governments have the right to exercise their authority in all areas of First Nations education. Until First Nations' education institutions are recognized and controlled by First Nations' governments, no real First Nation education exists. The essential principles are that each First Nation government should make its own decisions and arguments and apply its own values and standards rather than having them imposed from outside. (p. 47)

The federal government's Aboriginal Head Start program is achieving success in helping Aboriginal Canadians work toward these goals, and this author strongly encourages this program's continuation and expansion.

REFERENCES

Aboriginal Education Office. (2006, May). Aboriginal education policy framework: The foundation for improving the delivery of quality education to Aboriginal students in Ontario. *Draft—Aboriginal education policy framework.* Toronto: Ontario Ministry of Education. Retrieved from http://www.curriculum.org/secretariat/files/May24PolicyDraft.pdf

Archibald, J. (1995). Locally developed Native studies curriculum. In M. Battiste & J. Barman (Eds.), *First Nations education in Canada: The circle unfolds* (pp. 288–312). Vancouver: University of British Columbia Press.

Assembly of First Nations (AFN). (1992). *Towards rebirth of First Nations languages.* Ottawa: Assembly of First Nations Education Secretariat.

Assembly of First Nations (AFN). (1998). Tradition and education: Towards a vision of our future. Ottawa: Author.

Assembly of First Nations (AFN). (2003, December). A report of the Assembly of First Nations early childhood development national discussion. In *Assembly of First Nations, First Nations Early Learning and Child Care Action Plan.* (2005, April). Retrieved from http://ruralteammanitoba.cimnet.ca/cim/dbf/AFN_Early_Learning.pdf?im_id=227&si_id=170

Battiste, M. (1998). Enabling the autumn seed: Toward a decolonized approach to Aboriginal Knowledge, language, and education. *Canadian Journal of Native Education, 22*(1), 16–27.

Battiste, M. (2008). The struggle and renaissance of Indigenous Knowledge in Eurocentric education. In M. Villegas, S.R. Neugebauer, & K.R. Venegas (Eds.), *Indigenous Knowledge and education: Site of struggle, strength, and survivance* (pp. 85–92). Cambridge, MA: Harvard Education Review.

Battiste, M., & Barman, J. (1995). *First Nations education in Canada: The circle unfolds.* Vancouver: University of British Columbia Press.

Brady, P. (1995). Two approaches to Native Education: Can reform be legislated? *Canadian Journal of Education, 20*(3), 349–366. Retrieved from http://links.jstor.

org/sici?sici=0380-2361percent28199522percent2920percent3A3percent3C349 percent3ATPATNEpercent3E2.0.COpercent3B2-W. http://dx.doi.org/10.2307/ 1494858

Carr-Stewart, S. (2001). A treaty right to education. *Canadian Journal of Education, 26*(2), 125–123. Retrieved from http://links.jstoLorg/sici?sici=0380-2361percent 282001percent2926percent3A2percent3C125percent3AATRTEpercent3E2.0.CO percent3B2-A. http://dx.doi.org/10.2307/1602197

Child Care Canada. (1998). Aboriginal child care. *Child Care Canada, Childcare Resource and Research Unit* (4th ed.). Toronto: University of Toronto Centre for Urban and Community Studies. Retrieved from http://www.childcarecanada.org/ pt98/abor/aboLhtml

Daes, E.I. (2000). Prologue: The experience of colonization around the world. In M. Battiste (Ed.), *Reclaiming Indigenous Voices and Visions* (pp. 5–8). Vancouver: University of British Columbia Press.

Drost, H. (1994, March). Schooling, vocational training and unemployment: The case of Canadian Aboriginals. *Canadian Public Policy, 20*(1), 52–65. Retrieved from http://links.jstoLorg/sici?sici=0317-0861percent28199403percent2920percent3A1 percent3C52percent3ASVTAUTpercent3E2.0.COpercent. http://dx.doi.org/ 10.2307/3551835

Esping-Andersen, G. (2002a). A child-centred social investment strategy. In G. Esping-Andersen, D. Gallie, A. Hemerijek, & J. Myles (Eds.), *Why we need a new welfare state* (pp. 26–67). Cary, NC: Oxford University Press. http://dx.doi.org/ 10.1093/0199256438.003.0002

Esping-Andersen, G. (2002b). Towards a good society, once again? In G. Esping-Andersen, D. Gallie, A. Hemerijek, & J. Myles (Eds.), *Why we need a new welfare state* (pp. 1–25). Cary, NC: Oxford University Press. http://dx.doi.org/10.1093/ 0199256438.003.0001

Frideres, J. (1983). *Native people in Canada: Contemporary conflicts.* Toronto: Prentice Hall.

Goulet, L., Dressyman-Lavallee, M., & McCleod, Y. (2001). Early childhood education for Aboriginal children: Opening petals. In K.P. Binda (Ed.), *Aboriginal education in Canada: A study in decolonization* (pp. 137–154). Mississauga, ON: Canadian Educators' Press.

Government of Ontario. (1994). *For the love of learning: Report of the Royal Commission on Learning, a short version.* Toronto: Queen's Printer for Ontario.

Health Canada. (1998, October). *Aboriginal Head Start initiative for urban and northern communities.* Ottawa: Author. Retrieved from http://www.hc-sc.gc.calahc-asc/ medialnr-cp/1998/199871bk2e.html.

Indian and Northern Affairs Canada (INAC). (1998). *INAC basic departmental data.* Ottawa: Supply and Services Canada.

Indian and Northern Affairs Canada (INAC). (2005). *Fact Sheet—Aboriginal Head Start in urban and northern communities.* Ottawa: Author. Retrieved from http://www. aincinac.gc.calps/ecde/unce.html.

Marshall, T.H., & Bottomore, T. (1992). *Citizenship and social class.* London, UK: Pluto Press.

McCue, H. (2006, August). *Aboriginal post-secondary education: A think piece.* Ottawa: Centre for Native Policy and Research. Retrieved from http://www.campus2020. calmediaiAboriginalpercent20Post-Secondarypercent20Educationpercent20-percent20Harveypercent20McCue.pdf.

Perusse, D. (2007). *The Aboriginal labour force analysis series.* Ottawa: Statistics Canada. Retrieved from http://www.statcan.gc.calpub/71-588-xl71-588-x200800I-eng.pdf

Public Health Agency of Canada. (1998). *Aboriginal Head Start—urban and northern communities: Principles and guidelines.* Ottawa: Department of Indian and Northern Affairs. Retrieved from http://www.phac-aspc.gc.caldca-dealpublications/pdf/ ahsprincguidee.pdf

Public Health Agency of Canada. (2000). *Aboriginal Head Start urban and northern initiatives: Biennial report 1998/1999 1999/2000*. Ottawa: Health Canada. Retrieved from http://www.phac-aspc.gc.caldcadealpublications/pdflbienniale.pdf

Public Health Agency of Canada. (2004). *AHS program overview*. Ottawa: Government of Canada. Retrieved from http://www.phac-aspc.gc.caldca-dealprogramsmes/ahsoverviewe.html.

Public Health Agency of Canada. (2008). *Aboriginal children: The healing power of cultural identity*. Ottawa: Government of Canada. Retrieved from http://www.phac-aspc.gc.caldca-dealprograms-mes/aboriginal-autochtoneseng.php

Royal Commission on Aboriginal Peoples (RCAP). (1996). *Looking forward looking back* (Vol. 5). Ottawa: Government of Canada.

Schissel, B., & Wotherspoon, T. (2003). *The legacy of school for Aboriginal people: Education, oppression, and emancipation*. Ontario: Oxford University Press.

Siggner, A.J., & Costa, R. (2005). *Aboriginal conditions in Census metropolitan areas, 1981–2001* (Catalogue no. 89–613-MIE-Number 008). Ottawa: Statistics Canada. Retrieved from http://www.statcan.calenglishifreepub/81-004-XIE/2005003/aborig.htm

Social Union. (2007). *Early childhood development activities and expenditures and early learning and child care activities and expenditures: Government of Canada reports 2004–2005 and 2005–2006*. Ottawa: Author. Retrieved from http://www.socialunion.calecdelccae/2007/en/aereport.pdf

Statistics Canada. (1996). *Census of Population*. Ottawa: Author.

Statistics Canada. (2001a). *Aboriginal peoples survey 2001—initial findings: Well-being of the non-reserve Aboriginal population* (Catalogue no. 89–589-XIE). Ottawa: Author.

Statistics Canada. (2001b). *2001 Census of Canada* (Catalogue no. 97F0011XCB2001058). Ottawa: Author. Retrieved from http://www12.statcan.calenglish/census01/products/standardlthemes/RetrieveProductTable.cfm?Temporal=2001&PID=73646&APATH=3&GID=355313&METH=1&PTYPE=55496&THEME=45&FOCUS=0&AID=0&PLACENAME=0&PROVINCE=O&SEARCH=O&GC=O&GK=O&VID=O&VNAMEE=&VNAMEF=&FL=O&RL=O&FREE=O

Statistics Canada. (2006). *Aboriginal peoples in Canada in 2006: Inuit, Métis and First Nations, 2006 Census* (Catalogue no. 97–558-XIE). Ottawa: Author.

Statistics Canada. (2006). *2006 Census* (Catalogue no. 97–558 XCB2006006). Ottawa: Author. Retrieved from http://www12.statcan.gc.calenglish/census06/dataitopics/RetrieveProductTable.cfm?Temporal=2006&PID=89121&GID=614135&METH=1&APATH=3&PTYPE=88971&THEME=73&AID=&FREE=0&FOCUS=&VID=&GC=99&GK=NA&RL=O&TPL=NA&SUB=&d1=0&d2=3.

Tait, H. (1999, Spring). Educational achievements of young Aboriginal adults. Canadian Social Trends, 52 (Catalogue no. 11–008). Ottawa: Statistics Canada. Retrieved from http://dsp-psd.pwgsc.gc.calCollectionRlStatcanl11-008-XIE/0049811-008-XIE.pdf

Turcotte, M., & Zhao, J. (2004, July). A portrait of Aboriginal children living in non-reserve areas: Results from the 2001 Aboriginal peoples survey. *Statistics Canada housing, family and social statistics division* (Catalogue no. 89–597-XIE). Ottawa: Statistics Canada. Retrieved from http://www.statcan.calenglish/freepub/89-597-XIE/2001001/pdf/89-597-XIE2001001.pdf

Weikart, D.P. (1989). *Quality preschool programs: A long-term social investment*. Occasional Paper No. 5. New York: Ford Foundation.

4

Canadian Native Students and Inequitable Learning

Wayne Gorman

This chapter was originally published in *Canadian Social Studies* (Summer 1999) 33(4), p. 114–116. Reproduced with permission.

Introduction

This article is based on a study that consisted, in part, of interviewing Canadian Native students who told their stories about schooling (Gorman, 1999). Inequitable learning opportunities explored in this article are founded upon two divergent cultural practices or social constructs: one of these I characterize as Native, the other as mainstream. Mainstream practice includes rules and expectations of argumentative participation, competitiveness, status projection, and judgement. This affords those with that ethic of discourse a more fulfilling learning opportunity than the one experienced by those without it (Wilson, 1997). These are culturally based ethical behaviours (Bull, 1991; Phillips, 1982) that are not always obvious and that form part of the hidden curriculum. An understanding of social and cultural wholes is crucial for an understanding of what happens in the classroom and how people learn (Wilcox, 1988).

Thinking about their stories, I wondered how Native students differ from other children with backgrounds of poverty, illiteracy, loneliness, and abuse. Attempted cultural genocide and cultural penetration are the distinguishing features affecting these students. As the stories indicated, the legacy of Native educational shaming that has been characterized as "traumatic stress disorder," "residential school syndrome," and "intergenerational dysfunctional relationships" triggers particular responses to social situations that impede learning in mainstream institutions (Gorman, 1999). To comprehend these responses to the teaching environment, we need to examine the development of the Native cultural consciousness and educational experiences.

Cultural Consciousness

Native cultural survival in contemporary society requires an ability to live our values astride two cultures. The critical point is *cultural consciousness*, or the understanding that acculturation colours our perceptions of our experiences and that other people interpret the same experiences through their own cultural lenses. Native cultural consciousness is to nurture peace and harmony and preserve those life-giving energies that maintain life. It is "the suppression of conflict practiced through the ethics of noninterference, noncompetitiveness and emotional restraint" that maintains harmony (Gorman, 1999, p. 535). Equality is expressed in honouring and respecting all things as related and having a purpose for the survival of the whole. The ethic of noninterference encompasses the principles of respect for, and honour of, the individual and one's capacity to become whatever one is to become. "A high degree of respect for every human being's independence leads the Native to view instructing, coercing or attempting to persuade another person as undesirable behaviour" (Wax & Thomas, 1961, p. 535). The practice of instructing is not undesirable in itself; rather, it is how it is done that may be objectionable (Gorman, 1999). "We are very loath to confront people. We are very loath to give advice to anyone if the person is not specifically asking for advice. To interfere or even comment on their behaviour is considered rude" (Ross, 1992, p. 13). It is *shaming*, an act that attacks the very essence of being, that this ethic is meant to curtail. It is an ethic that each person must consider before acting, much like the desire to do no harm and think before you speak (L. Kinnunwa, personal communication, May 29, 1998).

Some Native people perceive direct questions as being rude, since such questions do not allow sufficient time to contemplate the answer, and to comment directly might be considered interference. When direct questions are asked, they are often answered by shrugs or "I dunno!" (L. Kinnunwa, personal communication, May 29, 1998). Or the response might take the form of a rambling story that does not seem related to the question. Looking someone straight in the eye is rude, an indication that you consider the other inferior—a form of shaming. A proper demonstration of respect involves looking down or to the side, with occasional glances up to indicate attentiveness. Within some non-Native cultures, this practice is considered evasive. "Those who have that perception discount what people say when they won't hold eye contact, concluding that they are insincere and untrustworthy" (p. 4). During the interviews, the respondents exhibited Native paraverbal and speech pattern behaviours (Gorman, 1999).

This is obviously a dilemma for Natives: living in two worlds where ethical behaviours may not mesh. The impact of mainstream contact and socialization through the education system disrupts their cognitive maps, "creating marginalizing situations that seldom provide complete cultural guidance and support" for the individual (Stonequist, 1937, p. 217). Some Native children suffer, not only from poverty and abuse, but also from the perception of being continually shamed (Gorman, 1999). This becomes apparent by viewing the mainstream culture through a Native cultural consciousness. Native ethics and transmission of holistic knowledge are continually attacked through schools by fractionalized knowledge that minimizes and trivializes the fundamental beliefs of Native culture.

Educational Experiences

One person in my study, Deanna, characterized the process of shaming as the detribalization of Native children (Gorman, 1999, p. 44). The Native transmission of the knowledge and style of learning was disrupted with the merging of church and state within Indian residential schools, orphanages, and institutionalized education. Detribalization in education means that every activity is controlled by European rules, rules intended to teach obedience to authority and reinforced by shame, strapping, and harsh denial (Fournier & Crey, 1997).

What distinguishes European schooling of Native peoples is the "monitorial method" of teaching (Sterling, 1992). However, Native people traditionally learn by listening, watching, and carrying out gender-appropriate tasks. Natives place their children at the centre of a belief system closely aligned with the natural world. The survival of their societies depends on the communication of a vast amount of spiritual and practical knowledge from the elders to the young, through an exclusively oral tradition and cyclical learning process. Sharing, storytelling, demonstration, observation, and modelling promote long-term learning and critical thinking in a caring way among Native children (Hollihan, 1997). In the modelling method, one is shown how, rather than told how. The teacher does not purport to know more than the student but through demonstration conveys information that the student has the choice of accepting or rejecting. The student is never expected to demonstrate acquired knowledge without being adequately prepared. This reduces performance anxiety, increases loyalty to teachers, strengthens attachments, and promotes group cohesiveness and continuity and enthusiasm for learning.

According to the European model, the child is shaped according to adult expectations, while in the Native world, the child is guided in becoming whatever he is to become. Learning is not a process of shaming, guilt, and absolute obedience to the authority of the teacher and prescribed knowledge. Rather, it is an acceptance or rejection of information provided in a caring and sharing way. The talents, skills, and interests of the Native child are nurtured to fulfillment and are part of a lifelong learning process.

When another person in my study, Ruth, returned to school as an adult, these conditions had not changed (Gorman, 1999). In a class of Native and non-Native students, the teacher triggered her childhood memory of students being berated by teachers. The teacher would ask a question and scold students for wrong answers. She picked on and yelled at students. One embarrassed girl was in tears, and only the encouragement of another Native classmate prevented her from quitting. Such shaming demonstrates the continued assault on students, Native and non-Native, when teachers are not sensitive to cultural reactions to being put on the spot. It also triggered Ruth's own experience with verbal abuse and the feelings of shame she endured as a child. Ruth's story illustrates an insensitive attack on the Native worldview.

A Native instructor was fired from the school because, as Ruth recalls, she was bringing Native culture into the curriculum and the school board objected and tried to change it. Ruth found that the sweats ceremony (*inipi*) helped her with her learning and kept her in school because it brought balance to her life during stressful times. Another example demonstrates the imposition of a prescribed format, ignorant of cultural context: when Ruth's English teacher tried to edit a personal poem Ruth had written, she was disregarding

Ruth's insistence that changes were inappropriate. The teacher was completely insensitive to the Native concept of speaking from the heart, insisting instead on the form and language of the mainstream culture.

The Hidden Curriculum

While the overt abuses of detribalization may not be prominent today, they exist in the hidden curriculum and continue to penetrate Native culture. When mainstream education is considered from a Native perspective, it appears that the youth are being conditioned to accept a particular worldview and are shamed for their own cultural worldview. From the Native perspective, the hidden curriculum is not hidden. For Native students, the exclusion of a whole set of beliefs and values from curricula minimizes, trivializes, and marginalizes their Indigenous values—certainly not as covert as it may seem. The hidden curriculum marginalizes Native people and anyone who does not conform to the norms of the dominant culture as defined by testing—a critical element of a systemic, inequitable, learning opportunity.

The school system determines students' future roles in society through selection, sorting, and distribution. The selection aspect of this system involves a shaming policy through the allocation of marks and assignment to particular class levels of achievement. Suzanne provides a graphic example of shaming—"I scraped bottom that year, so I was at the far end of row three most of the year. I learned about the pecking order, it was humiliating" (Gorman, 1999, p. 66).

The Role of Teachers

Teachers are key agents of socialization of culturally different children (Wilson, 1991). A teacher's prevailing attitude toward the child's potential and capability is transmitted by means of gestures, and oral and written expressions, creating for the child the upper limits of functioning (Rampaul, Singh, & Didyk, 1984). Pedersen, Faucher, and Eaton (1978) demonstrate that when teachers treat students differently according to the expectations they have of them, this affects not only student achievement in school but success in adult life. The critical finding is that "a good teacher shapes both the academic self-concept and achievement of the pupil so that an initial foundation yields cumulative benefits in later stages of life" (Pedersen et al., 1978, p. 29). Rist (1970) illustrates this self-fulfilling prophecy: "If the teacher expects high performance, she receives it, and visa versa" (p. 415). Brophy and Good (1970) see the social culture as constituting the hidden curriculum of discrimination, founded on the authority of middle-class and academic values, against those with different backgrounds and worldviews incompatible with the authorities' expectations of good students.

This self-fulfilling prophecy is evidenced in situations where students faced both negative and positive attitudes from their teachers. Where the interaction was positive, students performed within the norm of the school. Where interaction was negative, students either dropped out of school, sought help from a supportive group, withdrew into another form of learning (e.g., art or reading), or resolved nevertheless to get through it. Though physical violence and overt expressions of racial prejudice (witnessed in residential schools) appear to have largely disappeared, Wilson (1991) found that a significant difference remains in the way students are treated, with geographical location being a factor: students reported that reserve teachers had high expectations and positive interaction with students, whereas teachers in the mainstream school had little or no positive interaction with Native students.

Teacher and student behaviours, particularly paraverbal behaviours, are perhaps more insidious than in the past because they are not explicit and may be perceived as a personal, rather than racial, dislike. Not only are such behaviours perceived as discriminatory and demeaning but they demonstrate the hidden curriculum of conditioning Native students to the kind of rule-obedience that would be required of a labourer. Wilson (1991) also relates how students were channelled into low-level courses because it was assumed they were unable to handle university preparatory work.

Some schools have taken this issue into consideration and have geared their curricula toward the educational and cultural needs of Native learners. But content is not enough. Teachers need to become cultural brokers (Wilson, 1997). Studies have found that student self-concept and self-esteem are affected by ethnicity, culture, expectation, preparedness, deprecation of culture, and racism (Wilson, 1991; Clifton and Roberts, 1988). Students who are treated differently and with low expectations and who feel they are in an unsupportive environment suffer from low self-esteem. For these reasons, educators need to develop strategies that build on, rather than change, the cultural dispositions of students and that emphasize being rather than doing; address the past and present rather than only the future; and promote harmony with nature, rather than subjugation of nature (Clifton and Roberts, 1988).

REFERENCES

Brophy, J., & Good, T. (1970). Teachers communication of differential expectations for children's classroom performance. *Journal of Educational Psychology, 61*(5), 365–374. http://dx.doi.org/10.1037/h0029908

Bull, L. (1991). Indian residential schooling: The Native perspective. *Canadian Journal of Native Education, 18*(Suppl.), 3–63.

Clifton, R., & Roberts, L. (1988). Social psychological dispositions and academic achievement of Inuit and non-Inuit students. *Journal of Educational Research, 34*, 332–343.

Fournier, S., & Crey, E. (1997). *Stolen from our embrace.* Toronto: Douglas & McIntyre.

Gorman, W. (1999). *Words are not enough: Stories of Indigenous learning.* (Unpublished master's thesis). University of Alberta, Edmonton.

Hollihan, K. (1997). Community and the individual: Some thoughts on discipline in traditional Native education. In A. Richardson (Ed.), *Canadian childhood in 1997* (pp. 283–289). Alberta: Kanata Learning Co.

Pedersen, E., Faucher, T., & Eaton, W. (1978). A new perspective on the effects of first-grade teachers on children's subsequent adult status. *Harvard Educational Review, 48*, 1–31.

Phillips, S. (1982). *The invisible culture: Communication in classroom and community of the Warm Spring Indian reservation.* New York: Longmans.

Rampaul, W., Singh, M., & Didyk, J. (1984). The relationship between academic achievement, self-concept, creativity, and teacher expectation among Native children in a northern Manitoba school. *Alberta Journal of Educational Research, 30*, 213–225.

Rist, R. (1970). Student social class and teacher expectations: The self-fulfilling prophecy in ghetto education. *Harvard Educational Review, 40*, 411–451.

Rosenthal, R., & Jacobson, L. (1968). *The study of teaching.* New York: Holt, Rinehart-Winston.

Ross, R. (1992). *Dancing with a ghost: Exploring Indian reality.* Ontario: Octopus Publishing Group.

Sterling, S. (1992). Quaslametko and Yetko: Two grandmother models for contemporary Native education pedagogy. *Canadian Journal of Native Education, 19*, 165–174.

Stonequist, E. (1937). *The marginal man: A study in personality and culture conflict.* New York: Russell & Russell.

Wax, R., & Thomas, R. (1961). American Indians and white people. *Phylon, 22*(4), 305–317. http://dx.doi.org/10.2307/273534

Wilcox, K. (1988). Differential socialization in the classroom: Implications for equal opportunity. In G. Spindler (Ed.), *Doing the ethnography of schooling.* Prospect Heights, IL: Waveland Press.

Wilson, P. (1991). Trauma of Sioux Indian high school students. *Anthropology & Education Quarterly, 22*(4), 367–383. http://dx.doi.org/10.1525/aeq.1991.22.4.05x1194x

Wilson, S. (1997). Teaching Indigenous Canadian children: Adding cultural content is not enough. In A. Richardson (Ed.), *Canadian childhood in 1997.* Alberta: Kanata Learning Company.

5

Making Science Assessment Culturally Valid for Aboriginal Students

John B. Friesen and Anthony N. Ezeife

This chapter was originally published in the *Canadian Journal of Native Education* (2009), 32(2), pp. 24–37. Reproduced with permission.

Developing visible and meaningful connections between Western school science and Aboriginal science will bring school science closer to home experiences for Aboriginal students, giving them greater confidence, increased self-esteem, more initiative, and creativity (Cajete, 1994; Shizha, 2007). Developing these connections is achieved in part through creating culturally responsive assessment practices in science classrooms from a sociocultural perspective. Such a perspective sees knowledge and learning in terms of the relationship between an individual and his or her environment (Gee, 2008; Mislevy, 2006). It is imperative that science assessments reflect the idea that culture and society playa critical role in cognitive development (Solano-Flores & Nelson-Barber, 2001). Science assessments related to Aboriginal experiences and developed in collaboration with Aboriginal community members will have greater cultural validity and develop the connections between Western and Aboriginal science. Attaining greater cultural validity in science assessments occurs when the focus of school science changes from a positivistic, assimilative perspective to a more sociocultural perspective.

Integrating Aboriginal with Western science will encourage teachers to incorporate a sociocultural perspective in their assessment processes, from the planning stages of each assessment to the final interpretation of the results. This infusion of Aboriginal cultural perspectives could help erase cultural bias and establish a need for integrating the reasoning consistent with a sociocultural perspective in assessment practices (Solano-Flores & Nelson-Barber, 2001).

The proportion of the school-aged population with Aboriginal identity is significant and growing, especially in Canada's cities and in some provinces and territories (Statistics Canada, 2005). Between 1996 and 2006, the Aboriginal population grew by 45% compared with 8% for the non-Aboriginal population (Statistics Canada, 2006). Most research on measuring Aboriginal student success focuses on the educational deficits of Aboriginal people; high school and post-secondary education; formal educational settings; and years of schooling and performance on standardized tests as indicators of success in school (Canadian Council on Learning, 2007). As more Aboriginal communities gain control over their own educational programs and create culturally relevant curricula, their leaders have a need "to identify appropriate measurement tools that will help them assess what is working and what is not" in their schools (p. 2). Despite gaining greater control in education, Aboriginal students still face challenges in their goal to achieve parity with non-Aboriginal students (UNESCO, 1997). One of the measurement tools that might help Aboriginal leaders determine what is working and what is not is the measure of the degree of cultural validity of assessments used in science classrooms. In this chapter, we argue that Western science and traditional ecological knowledge (TEK) can be combined in schools to develop meaningful and visible connections between the two. Also, we argue that current science assessments can be modified to give the assessments greater cultural validity, a subset of science assessment validity in general. We believe that integrating Aboriginal science into Western science is particularly important for schools with relatively few Aboriginal students. It is imperative that schools with mainly Aboriginal students do the reverse by integrating Western into Aboriginal science. Integrating Aboriginal science into Western science is especially important for non-Aboriginal students in order to bring Aboriginal scientific knowledge into the epistemological framework of non-Aboriginal students. Non-Aboriginal students can benefit from learning Aboriginal ways of understanding nature.

The idea of reciprocity is important, and integrating Aboriginal science and including Aboriginal people in the learning process may increase Aboriginal student achievement in school science. Snively and Corsiglia (2001) echo this sentiment when they note that reforming the science curriculum to include diverse cultural perspectives and traditions of science are important changes that would be equally important to mainstream students. Barnhardt and Kawagley (2005), in discussing the broader issue of integrating knowledge systems, state,

> *Native people may need to understand Western society, but not at the expense of what they already know and the way they have come to know it. Non-Native people, too, need to recognize the coexistence of multiple worldviews and knowledge systems, and find ways to understand and relate to the world in its multiple dimensions and varied perspectives. (p. 9)*

As well, the Alberta Ministry of Education (2002) program, Aboriginal Studies 10-20-30, was developed to provide a conceptual framework for all students to learn about the diverse Aboriginal cultures in their local areas, Canada, and the world. We believe that the main purpose of student assessment is for learning and that small changes in science assessment practices may lead to big changes in improved Aboriginal student learning.

Definitions

Aboriginal people refer to people of Canadian First Nations, Inuit, and Métis origin. *Aboriginal science* is defined as a metaphor for a large range of Aboriginal processes of thinking, acting, and perceiving that has evolved through human experience with the natural world. Aboriginal science "is a map of natural reality drawn from the experiences of thousands of human generations" (Cajete, 2000, p. 3). A subset of Aboriginal science is *traditional ecological knowledge,* or *TEK.* Snively and Corsiglia (2001) note that TEK is a recent term but that the practices implied by TEK have been in use for thousands of years. Snively and Corsiglia discuss TEK as being guided by traditional wisdom and using observation, questioning, predicting, classifying, interpreting, and adapting in its methodology. TEK, therefore, is defined as representing "experience acquired over thousands of years of direct human contact with the environment" (p. 11). *Indigenous Knowledge* is defined as the educational method of learning through demonstration, observation, and thoughtful storytelling of the natural processes, adapting modes of survival, and obtaining the necessities of life from plants and animals (Barnhardt & Kawagley, 2005). Aikenhead (2001) provides our definition of *Western science* as an ideology that is objective, empirical, nonhumanistic, universal, socially sterile, and unencumbered with human bias. The term *science assessment* refers to assessing in both sciences, Western and Aboriginal, as they are integrated into one entity. *Culture* in this context is defined as those values, beliefs, norms, and expectations that a social community shares in common (Aikenhead & Jegede, 1999). *Validity* is a summary of the existing evidence and the potential consequences of test (assessment) score interpretation and use (Messick, 1989). Lastly, *cultural validity in science assessments* is defined as the ability of science assessments to address the sociocultural influences that guide how students make sense of scientific concepts and how they respond to them (Solano-Flores & Nelson-Barber, 2001).

Traditional Ecological Knowledge (TEK) and Western Science

Aboriginal science is built on respect for, and connectedness with, the land. A Lakota saying, *mitakuye oyasin* (we are all related), focuses on relationships and metaphorically personifies what Aboriginal people perceive as community (Cajete, 2000). One of the connections between Aboriginal science and Western science is in the study of ecology through TEK, which can be received directly from the natural surroundings. TEK accepts intuitive knowledge and looks for a holistic worldview that helps explain it, even if the explanation is spiritual (Dyck, 2001). Archibald (2001) discusses the importance of finding elders who have acquired TEK and have experience passing on this knowledge to younger generations. She delineates the pedagogy she refers to as *storywork*: the combination of the story, the storyteller, and the listener. Archibald emphasizes the importance of prayer, ceremony, song, and the repetition of these rituals to develop a learning atmosphere where students start to appreciate the importance of their rituals. "The understanding of the web of relationships in the 'household' of Nature, is not modern science's sole property. Understanding the relationships scientifically is not enough—living and nurturing these relationships is the key" (Cajete, 2000, p. 95). In the following three sections, we discuss how we can integrate TEK and Western school science, why we should, and some of the challenges of doing so.

How Can We Integrate TEK and Western School Science?

Barnhardt and Kawagley (2005) illustrate the common ground where traditional Native knowledge systems and Western science overlap by using a Venn diagram. Under the heading of Knowledge in the overlap region of the diagram, the authors name plant and animal behaviour, cycles, habitat needs, and interdependence, among other topics. Snively and Corsiglia (2001) create a more specific list related to a number of examples where TEK and Western science could be integrated for school science, including biology, ecology, botany, horticulture, agriculture, and medicine. The authors describe an example in northwest Manitoba where biologists and chemists performing field analysis confirmed that traditional practitioners were often able to detect minute changes in water quality more effectively than contemporary testing equipment. TEK can play a vital role in helping solve global environmental issues through its focus on sustainability and restoration (Kimmerer, 2002; Shizha, 2007). At the State University of New York, case studies about salmon restoration, forest management, and fire ecology are being used to compare perspectives of Indigenous groups with Western scientists (Kimmerer, 2002). Another example comes from Snively and Williams (2006) in the description of their *Aboriginal Knowledge and Science Education Research Project*. Students learned a wealth of Aboriginal culture through studying culturally modified trees (CMTs) on Hansen Island on the coast of British Columbia. The students also gained insight into a model of traditional sustainable forest use as they studied and learned about the cedar forests that have been tended by Aboriginal people for "over 1,200 years" (p. 241).

Discussions of crop production of corn and wild rice and natural fertilization are some specific examples of agricultural science that can be topics of integration. Cajete (2000) notes that the production of corn is one of the most important achievements in agriculture as Aboriginal people learned how to grow, sow, harvest, and prepare corn for eating or storage. Drying corn properly was an important skill that allowed it to be replanted or used to make bread and sugar. Aikenhead (2001) describes the wild rice unit, which involves local rice harvesters from northern Saskatchewan coming to the classrooms to speak to the students about growing wild rice and connect the students to the local culture. The students visit areas that the local harvesters have identified as fertile ground for growing and gain respect for traditional knowledge. The Western science content, such as concepts of habitat, niche, pH, and percent germination, enhance and enrich the local knowledge through broadening students' perspectives. Specific methods for nitrogen fixation, fertilization, and insect control are crop production techniques that came from TEK. The planting of the "three sisters" of corn, beans, and squash with marigold in the same small area called a *milpa* provides nitrates for the soil from the beans and shade for the beans from the corn stalks, which also allows bean and squash vines to grow. The marigolds produce a chemical known now to reduce insects harmful to the crops (Cajete, 2000).

Aboriginal people who have worked with the land for many millennia have generated a vast amount of botanical medical knowledge. Almost 80% of the world's population uses herbal medicine in their primary health care, approximately a quarter of today's pharmaceuticals are directly derived from plants, and half of today's pharmaceuticals are modelled on plants (Ausubel, 1999). Cajete (2000) notes that health was about living in harmony, and corn, tobacco, peyote (a trance-inducing plant), and sage were a few of the plants that played an essential role in connecting the sick with the Spirit World and helping restore their balance. Herbal medicine combined with spiritual and psychological counselling, massages, heat treatment, sweat baths, and other forms of physiotherapy treatments were often used to restore good health.

Why Should We Integrate TEK and Western School Science?

Aboriginal people are underrepresented in science, mathematics, technology, and health-related programs and careers (Aikenhead & Jegede, 1999; MacIvor, 1995; Snively & Williams, 2006). Aboriginal students experience high dropout rates from high school; they are heavily represented in special education classes; and few are in gifted programs (Binda, 2001). Aboriginal students tend to avoid science courses or perform poorly in them (Ezeife, 2003; Hollins, 1996; MacIvor, 1995). Snively and Williams (2006) note that of the Aboriginal students in British Columbia who take grade 11 science courses, a low percentage take the approved science courses for admittance to post-secondary institutions, and this creates barriers for science-related careers. According to the same authors, "This situation arises from a type of science in which Aboriginal knowledge and wisdom are rarely acknowledged and Aboriginal content is seldom if ever legitimized or is considered a token addition" (p. 229). There exists a real need for Aboriginal students to gain expertise in the sciences. MacIvor (1995) notes that science education can contribute to Aboriginal students' intellectual growth, facilitate better decision making, and generally prepare them for jobs in today's economy. She argues that conventional (Western) science needs to be one way to understand our world, but not the only way. In addition, MacIvor argues that land claim settlements that have given control over the management of traditional lands back to the Aboriginal people have represented a huge economic and political victory for some Aboriginal people. Furthermore, TEK provides significant information and perspectives that are missing from [Western] scientific approaches (Kimmerer, 2002).

What Are Some of the Challenges?

White (2006) notes that one of the challenges in merging TEK with Western science stems from the tendency for people to emphasize the differences in orientation and methodology between the two and not their shared perspectives. White notes that even using the term "traditional" is debated because it carries misleading connotations of static, antiquated knowledge from days gone by. Ignas (2004) discusses the feeling of inferiority that Aboriginal students often have when TEK is contrasted with Western science with the "implication being that only [Western] science is fully epistemologically adequate" (p. 55). The problem is countered in part by the designers of the Forests for the Future program: a program of study that dwells on exploring and focusing on the common themes that are uncovered in how TEK and Western scientific knowledge are acquired and communicated (Ignas, 2004). Gaining knowledge through intuition and personal experience runs counter to the Western science perspective, which values objectivity, linear ways of thinking, and the compartmentalization of knowledge and disciplines (Cajete, 2000; Dyck, 2001).

In the context of Western school science, Aikenhead and Jegede (1999) discuss the culture clash that can occur when students from non-Western cultures like Aboriginal cultures are confronted with the language and conventions of many Euro-American teachers in science classrooms. The transition from one social community to another has been identified by Aikenhead and Jegede as *cultural border crossing*, and many Aboriginal students encounter challenging cultural border crossings when engaged in school science. According to Aikenhead and Jegede, student success in school science can be measured by how effectively students negotiate the crossing of cultural borders and the degree of cultural difference that students perceive between their life-world and their science classroom. Ezeife (2003) remarks that students from Western and non-Western cultures share a feeling of foreignness toward school science, but non-Western students feel the alienation to a greater degree. The connection between TEK and Western science should help reduce the feeling of alienation, as well as give Aboriginal students a satisfactory reason for holding onto the concepts discussed in science class without discouraging their own cultural views of nature. Holding onto the concepts means that students should understand the science concept, not necessarily accept the scientifically accepted notion of the concept. Students should be able to explore the differences and similarities between their own beliefs and Western science concepts (Snively & Corsiglia, 2001). This type of learning that involves two or more conflicting schemata held at the same time by a person is called *collateral learning*. There are four types of collateral learning: secured (optimal), dependent, simultaneous, and parallel (Jegede & Aikenhead, 1999). The challenge to educators is to help Aboriginal students attain secured collateral learning in an integrated school science program.

Culturally Valid Assessments in Science

Solano-Flores and Nelson-Barber (2001) stated, "cultural validity refers to the effectiveness with which science assessment addresses the sociocultural influences that shape student thinking" (p. 555). The example below demonstrates how analyzing school science assessments can help us measure the cultural validity of the interpretations of assessment scores used to determine achievement in science.

Solano-Flores and Nelson-Barber (2001) analyzed questions from the 1996 National Assessment of Educational Progress (NAEP). One of the questions they studied was on the idea of erosion. The question gives a diagram of two mountain ranges with a river flowing through a valley between the peaks. One of the mountain ranges is drawn with lower, smooth peaks whereas the other has higher, jagged peaks. The question asks to indicate the picture that shows how the river and mountains look now as opposed to millions of years ago. Solano-Flores and Nelson-Barber interviewed a Latin American girl who incorrectly chose the jagged mountains. The girl did not remember learning about mountains in school and she had no experience of seeing them except for once when she saw mountains on the west coast of California. She did not use the concept of erosion in her explanation, only her personal experience with mountains. The authors argue that the test question privileges students with first-hand experience with flatter mountains and that everyday life experiences are an important influence in student performance. Hinkle (1994) argues that cultural influences on testing can be minimized only through increased awareness, training, and assessment item development. Gorin (2007) observed that most first-year graduate students in educational psychology had a simplistic view of the concept of validity, and Popham (1997) also agrees with this lack of understanding of validity as he states that "most of our teachers and school administrators have, at best, only a murky notion of what validity really is" (p. 10).

From a historical viewpoint, evidence of validity is one of the basic requirements of any measurement process. Early discussions of validity were entrenched in the need to measure a variable of interest for each person as accurately as possible. Validity was defined in terms of the accuracy of this estimate (Kane, 2001). Wilks (1961) defined validity as the extent the process yields a "*true*" measurement of the object. More current validity theory addresses both the consequential, or value, implications of test interpretations and the test use, or social consequences (Messick, 1989). Low scores should not result from missing information that is important to a group of people that, if present, would allow them to demonstrate their competence, nor should low scores result from the presence of irrelevant information that might interfere with the affected student's ability to show his or her competence (Messick, 1998).

From an analytical and constructivism viewpoint, evidence of validity can refer to measurements, or it can refer to a process of legitimizing one's findings. There are various kinds of validity including criterion, concurrent, content, cultural, consequential, and construct validity. It is not the assessment itself that must be validated but the inferences made from the assessment scores and the implications for action based on these scores. Teachers should create assessments with knowledge of students' social situations, as well as their cultural backgrounds. Creating assessments based solely on cultural stereotypes or a single cultural model will not achieve a high degree of cultural validity. This would assume that all students from a particular culture have the same knowledge base associated with the culture, which would be incorrect. Assessments, therefore, must be developed from a sociocultural perspective, combining both the social and cultural contexts, as both play an important role in shaping a student's thinking.

Evidence of validity is always specific to some particular use, and no assessment is valid for all purposes. Validity involves an overall evaluative judgement, and evaluation of valid results must be justified by supporting evidence in terms of the consequences and uses of the interpretations (American Educational Research Association, 1999; Kane, 2006; Linn & Gronlund, 1995). The interpretation refers to the construct or concepts that the assessment is intended to measure. More often than not, however, educators use assessment scores for many purposes, and the same assessment data are used to implement many actions in a school, and invalid inferences made from assessment data have disadvantaged Aboriginal students.

Whether teachers are using assessment data to make instructional decisions or to judge if a student is gaining mastery of certain skills, the consequences and actions taken are possibly unsound if the results-based decisions about the student's achievement are invalid. Hence, much depends on the validity of a teacher's assessment practice and knowledge. Stiggins (2001) discusses a series of studies that he completed to understand more completely the complexity of classroom assessment processes. He uncovered a multitude of uses for school assessment data. Often the same data are used to detect individual students' needs, clarify achievement expectations, assign grades, control behaviour, and evaluate the effectiveness of their instruction. Parents use the same data to decide whether to reward or punish, to seek additional tutoring, and how to allocate family resources. The same study revealed that teachers used a variety of assessment methods, but "few teachers, however, understood how to align these different assessment methods with different kinds of achievement to be assessed, how to sample properly, or how to avoid bias when using the various methods" (Stiggins, 2001, p. 9). Teachers need to be aware of the potential biases in their assessments and strive to eliminate them from their practice, or risk continuation of the cyclic perpetuation of failure for many Aboriginal students.

Modifying Science Assessments

In order to develop science assessments that have greater cultural validity, educators need access to the necessary information, as well as meaningful parental and community participation in assessment development. Science teachers need to begin with what the students know, believe, and practice in their daily lives and focus their instruction and assessment toward new learning (Ezeife, 2003). Educators must collaborate with their cultural communities to develop appropriate assessments that will stem from culturally sensitive instructional practices in order to achieve appropriate learning outcomes and demonstrate that knowledge can be uncovered by both empirical and nonempirical means (Dyck, 2001; Qualls, 1998).

An example of the importance of understanding the communication and socialization style of a culture comes from Solano-Flores and Nelson-Barber (2001), who sought input from Western Alaska's Yup'ik elders to help design a hands-on assessment about making kayaks according to body measurements. Little discussion took place when the elders were asked to solve the kayak problem individually and provide feedback. The teacher involved was uncomfortable in the role of appearing to question the elders' knowledge. Meaningful discussions took place when the elders were asked to solve the problem as a team and offer guidance to the teacher as she solved it out loud. Collaboration with the Yup'ik elders was critical, but changes to the kayak assessment would not have been possible if the communication and socialization styles of the Yup'ik leaders were not understood and honoured.

Teachers need knowledge and an understanding of Aboriginal science in order to integrate TEK into the science curriculum so as to assess students in ways that are culturally valid for Aboriginal students. Developing links between Aboriginal cultures and the science curriculum must start, however, with educators becoming aware of the factors that distinguish their own culture (assuming it is different) from that of the students, while maintaining a positive regard for both cultures. This will contribute to improved cross-cultural communication and facilitate more culturally relevant assessments while also eliminating cultural bias in assessments. Nelson-Barber, Huang, Trumbull, Johnson, and Sexton (2008) analyze science test items for linguistic and cultural loadings as possible sources of item bias. Using this idea from Nelson-Barber et al. to reflect on the following statement from the OECD Programme for International Student Assessment, or PISA (2006), we can see how the statement is biased against Aboriginal students; hence any questions based on it would lack cultural validity.

> Tobacco is smoked in cigarettes, cigars, and pipes. Research shows that tobacco-related diseases kill nearly 13 500 people worldwide every day. It is predicted that, by 2020, tobacco-related diseases will cause 12% of all deaths globally. Tobacco smoke contains many harmful substances. The most damaging substances are tar, nicotine and carbon monoxide. (p. 59)

Two of the questions about the above statement relate to the negative health consequences of tobacco smoke, but for Aboriginal students, tobacco is one of the most sacred plants and historically was used in medicinal and healing rituals, as well as ceremonial and religious practices (Struthers & Hodge, 2004). If a test for item bias were performed on the questions about the adverse effects of tobacco smoke, we might find that Aboriginal students had lower scores as a group. Estrin and Nelson-Barber (1995) suggest that science educators can achieve greater cultural validity from their science assessments if they follow a few guidelines. They suggest that science assessments should use cultural resources with which the children are familiar, use open-ended questions and avoid multiple choice and true/false questions, and also give students plenty of time to complete the task. In addition, they suggest giving students choice about how and when they will be assessed, giving them opportunities to practice, and using co-operative assessment strategies as well as individual strategies to determine an accurate measure of their scientific knowledge of Aboriginal students.

Solano-Flores and Nelson-Barber (2001) note that the cultural validity of science assessments may be increased if cultural differences are considered early in the planning stages of assessments. Hollins (1996) remarks that student learning must involve situated learning experiences that are inquiry-based and initially embedded in Aboriginal cultural practices. A good example of this is discussed in Sutherland (2005), which describes a study with Cree students in Manitoba. The author discusses giving students more opportunity to select their approach to a science topic, including their experiences and their family's while in the bush. Sutherland identified some students as secured collateral learners as they were able to distinguish between science and Indigenous Knowledge and views. Students felt that assignments containing the knowledge of their elders, on moose for example, would get a better grade because of the authority of knowledge that came from those who have plenty of first-hand experience on the topic. This illustrates the positive effects of sociocultural influence on learning for these Aboriginal students as they hold the apprenticeship model of learning and the experiential knowledge of their elders in high regard.

We believe that assessments should guide learning and help teachers make informed decisions about their pedagogy. "Viewing assessment as intrinsic to the instructional process represents a position that, though discrepant with conventional practice, is highly consistent with the first principle of assessment—to make inferences about students that support useful decisions in educational contexts" (Duschl & Gitomer, 1997, p. 39). Duschl and Gitomer also discuss how effective teachers must manage not only materials and behaviour but also reasoning, ideas, and communication. This shift, however, assumes that teachers have access to relevant information that would make it possible to manage reasoning, ideas, and communication. The *Pan-Canadian Protocol for Collaboration on School Curriculum* (Council of Ministers of Education, Canada, 1997), in its vision statement, emphasizes that all Canadian students should develop an evolving combination of the science-related attitudes, skills, and knowledge that they need to acquire inquiry, problem-solving, and decision-making abilities. Duschl and Gitomer posit that assessment activities in classrooms can help to achieve this goal and provide insight into the progress toward it. Less emphasis must be placed on on-demand performance assessments and more emphasis must be placed on establishing a classroom environment that facilitates the acquisition of information that teachers can examine and use to help students learn how to do science.

Little has been done in the past few decades to remedy the dearth of tests that draw on Aboriginal cultural content and learning processes (Estrin & Nelson-Barber, 1995). If current classroom science assessments are developed from Western science perspectives, with little or no integration of Aboriginal science perspectives, the interpretation of Aboriginal students' scores will not be a valid reflection of their scientific knowledge. Standardized tests are similar to classroom science tests with respect to their development from Western perspectives only. Standardized tests have presented difficulties with inappropriate content, tightly timed format, reliance on verbal information, and on-demand testing. The content of most standardized tests does not reflect common experiences for Aboriginal students and this jeopardizes the content validity of inferences for the assessment (Estrin & Nelson-Barber, 1995). Common and Frost (1992) noted that time-limited tests penalize students from cultures that value reflection of thought over quick response for measuring intelligence. In another study, Common and Frost (1994) argued that "standardized measures of intelligence developed for use with one cultural group could not be fairly used with another cultural group unless it was demonstrated that the two cultures were very similar" (p. 70). Because Aboriginal and mainstream Canadian cultures have not been shown to be similar, Common and Frost concluded that it is not appropriate to use standardized IQ tests with Aboriginal people.

We contend that it is critical that assessments be developed in a culturally responsive perspective that allows assessment developers and/or teachers to identify the important cultural influences that shape students' perceptions of science. We agree with Solano-Flores and Nelson-Barber (2001) that assessments need to be developed with an understanding of the subtle nuances of a culture that shapes the worldview of a student. This method of developing assessments will allow students to understand what they are expected to do and how they might approach the problem or question in order to solve it.

Summary

Students from Aboriginal cultural backgrounds are immediately disadvantaged in science classrooms when Western cultural values are given prominence. Many Aboriginal students feel alienated when they realize that the science curriculum has no connection to their cultural experiences. This feeling can lead to frustration, disempowerment, underperformance, and possibly withdrawal from school science (Ezeife, 2003). Science educators need to create a more inclusive curriculum for cultures other than Western culture as our world continues to see large population shifts, multicultural classrooms, and a greater percentage of students from minority and Aboriginal communities. Science teachers need to work toward creating culturally valid assessments that enable Aboriginal students to bridge their cultural worldview smoothly with their school science curriculum and make cultural border crossings easier for Aboriginal students. Canadian science educators must aim to develop assessment tasks that are relevant to Aboriginal students and give them a satisfactory reason for holding onto the concepts discussed in science classes without discouraging their own cultural views of nature. Canada's science education curricula need to integrate traditional ecological knowledge into classroom lessons and ensure that cultural perspectives are taken into account when assessing learners. Cultural perspectives must be integrated from the beginning stages of planning an assessment through to the scoring of the assessment. Canadian science educators require access to relevant traditional ecological knowledge and meaningful community collaboration with Aboriginal elders and other leaders in order to develop appropriate assessments founded on culturally responsive instructional and assessment practices.

REFERENCES

Aikenhead, G.S. (2001). Integrating Western and Aboriginal sciences: Cross-cultural science teachings. *Research in Science Education, 31*(3), 337–355. http://dx.doi.org/10.1023/A:1013151709605

Aikenhead, G.S., & Jegede, O.J. (1999). Cross-cultural science education: A cognitive explanation of a cultural phenomenon. *Journal of Research in Science Teaching, 36*(3), 269–287. http://dx.doi.org/10.1002/(SICI)1098-2736(199903)36:3<269::AID-TEA3>3.0.CO;2-T

Alberta Ministry of Education. (2002). Aboriginal Studies 10-20-30. Edmonton, AB: Alberta Learning. Retrieved May 5, 2009, from http://www.education.alberta.ca/media/654004/abor102030.pdf

American Educational Research Association, American Psychological Association, and the National Council on Measurement in Education. (1999). *Standards for educational and psychological testing.* Washington, DC: Author.

Archibald, J. (2001). Editorial: Sharing Aboriginal knowledge and Aboriginal ways of knowing. *Canadian Journal of Native Education, 25*(1), 1–5.

Ausubel, K. (1999). "It is time to plant": The real green revolution. In G. Cajete (Ed.), *A people's ecology: Explorations in sustainable living* (pp. 53–78). Santa Fe, NM: Clear Light.

Barnhardt, R., & Kawagley, A.O. (2005). Indigenous Knowledge systems and Alaska Native ways of knowing. *Anthropology & Education Quarterly, 36*(1), 8–23. http://dx.doi.org/10.1525/aeq.2005.36.1.008

Binda, K.P. (2001). Native diaspora and urban education: Class, culture, and intractable problems. In K.P. Binda & S. Calliou (Eds.), *Aboriginal education in Canada: A study in decolonization* (pp. 179–194). Mississauga, ON: Canadian Educators' Press.

Cajete, G.A. (1994). *Look to the mountain: An ecology of Indigenous education.* Skyland, NC: Kivaki Press.

Cajete, G.A. (2000). *Native science: Natural laws of interdependence.* Santa Fe, NM: Clear Light.

Canadian Council on Learning. (2007). *Redefining how success is measured in First Nations, Inuit, and Métis learning.* Retrieved July 6, 2008, from http://www.ccl-cca.ca/NR/rdonlyres/212C03D9-7B43-4F94-BAFB-784A3199F06E/0/ Redefining_How _Success_Is_Measured_EN.pdf.

Common, R.W., & Frost, L.G. (1992). The implications of the mismeasurement of Native students' intelligence through the use of standardized intelligence tests. In S. Towson (Ed.), *Educational psychology: Readings for the Canadian context* (pp. 504–516). Peterborough, ON: Broadview Press.

Common, R.W., & Frost, L.G. (1994). Characteristics of gifted native students. In K.P. Binda (Ed.), *Critical issues in First Nations education* (pp. 69–77). Brandon, MB: Brandon University Northern Teacher Education (BUNTEP), Faculty of Education.

Council of Ministers of Education, Canada (CMEC). (1997). *Common framework of science learning outcomes: Pan-Canadian protocol for collaboration on school curriculum.* Ottawa: Author.

Duschl, R.A., & Gitomer, D.H. (1997). Strategies and challenges to changing the focus of assessment and instruction in science classrooms. *Educational Assessment, 4*(1), 37–73. http://dx.doi.org/10.1207/s15326977ea0401_2

Dyck, L. (2001). A personal journey into science, feminist science, and Aboriginal science. In K. James (Ed.), *Science and Native American communities* (pp. 22–28). Lincoln, NE: University of Nebraska Press.

Estrin, E.T., & Nelson-Barber, S. (1995). *Issues in cross-cultural assessments: American Indian and Alaska native students.* Knowledge Brief #12. Washington, DC: Office of Educational Research and Improvement (ED).

Ezeife, A.N. (2003). The pervading influence of cultural border crossing and collateral learning on the learner of science and mathematics. *Canadian Journal of Native Education, 27*(2), 179–194.

Gee, J.P. (2008). A sociocultural perspective on opportunity to learn. In P.A. Moss, D.C. Pullin, J.P. Gee, E.H. Haertel, & L.J. Young (Eds.), *Assessment, equity, and opportunity to learn* (pp. 76–108). New York: Cambridge University Press. http://dx.doi.org/10.1017/CBO9780511802157.006

Gorin, G.S. (2007). Reconsidering issues in validity theory. *Educational Researcher, 36*(8), 456–462. http://dx.doi.org/10.3102/0013189X07311607

Hinkle, J.S. (1994). Practitioners and cross-cultural assessment: A practical guide to information and training. *Measurement and Evaluation in Counselling and Development, 27*(2), 103–115.

Hollins, E.R. (1996). *Culture in school learning: Revealing the deep meaning.* Mahwah, NJ: Erlbaum.

Ignas, V. (2004). Opening the doors to the future: Applying local knowledge in curriculum development. *Canadian Journal of Native Education, 28*(1/2), 49–60.

Jegede, O.J., & Aikenhead, G.S. (1999). Transcending cultural borders: Implications for science teaching. *Journal of Science and Technology Education, 17*(1), 45–66. http://dx.doi.org/10.1080/0263514990170104

Kane, M.T. (2001). Current concerns in validity theory. *Journal of Educational Measurement, 38*(4), 319–342. http://dx.doi.org/10.1111/j.1745-3984.2001.tb01130.x

Kane, M.T. (2006). Validation. In R.L. Brennan (Ed.), *Educational measurement* (4th ed., pp. 17–64). Westport, CT: American Council on Education and Praeger.

Kimmerer, R.W. (2002). Weaving traditional ecological knowledge into biological education: A call to action. *Bioscience, 52*(5), 432–438. http://dx.doi.org/10.1641/0006-3568(2002)052[0432:WTEKIB]2.0.CO;2

Linn, R.L., & Gronlund, N.E. (1995). *Measurement and assessment in teaching* (7th ed.). Englewood Cliffs, NJ: Prentice-Hall.

MacIvor, M. (1995). Redefining science education for Aboriginal students. In M. Battiste & J. Barman (Eds.), *First Nations education in Canada: The circle unfolds* (pp. 73–98). Vancouver: University of British Columbia Press.

Messick, S. (1989). Validity. In R.L. Linn (Ed.), *Educational measurement* (3rd ed., pp. 13–104). New York: Macmillan.

Messick, S. (1998). Test validity: A matter of consequence. *Social Indicators Research, 45*(1/3), 35–44. http://dx.doi.org/10.1023/A:1006964925094

Mislevy, R.J. (2006). Cognitive psychology and educational assessment. In R.L. Brennan (Ed.), *Educational measurement* (4th ed., pp. 257–305). Westport, CT: American Council on Education and Praeger.

Nelson-Barber, S., Huang, C.W., Trumbull, E., Johnson, Z., & Sexton, U. (2008, March). *Elicitory test design: A novel approach to understanding the relationship between test item features and student performance on large-scale assessments.* Paper presented at AERA, New York.

Popham, W.J. (1997). Consequential validity: Right concern—Wrong concept. *Educational Measurement: Issues and Practice, 16*(2), 9–13. http://dx.doi.org/10.1111/j.1745-3992.1997.tb00586.x

OECD Programme for International Student Assessment. (2006). Released PISA items: Science question S439: Tobacco smoking. Retrieved March 18, 2009, from http://www.pisa.oecd.org/dataoecd/13/33/38709385.pdf.

Qualls, A.L. (1998). Culturally responsive assessment: Development strategies and validity issues. *Journal of Negro Education, 67*(3), 296–301. http://dx.doi.org/10.2307/2668197

Shizha, E. (2007). Critical analysis of problems encountered in incorporating Indigenous Knowledge in science teaching by primary school teachers in Zimbabwe. *Alberta Journal of Educational Research, 53*, 302–319.

Snively, G., & Corsiglia, J. (2001). Discovering Indigenous science: Implications for science education. *Science Education, 85*(1), 6–34. http://dx.doi.org/10.1002/1098-237X(200101)85:1<6::AID-SCE3>3.0.CO;2-R

Snively, G., & Williams, L. (2006). The Aboriginal knowledge and science education research project. *Canadian Journal of Native Education, 29*(2), 229–244.

Solano-Flores, G., & Nelson-Barber, S. (2001). On the cultural validity of science assessments. *Journal of Research in Science Teaching, 38*(5), 553–573. http://dx.doi.org/10.1002/tea.1018

Statistics Canada. (2005). *Education indicators in Canada: Report of the pan-Canadian education indicators program.* Retrieved July 6, 2008, from http://www.statcan.ca/english/freepub/81-582-XIE/81-582-XIE2oo6001.htm

Statistics Canada. (2006). *Census.* Retrieved July 8, 2008, from http://www12.statcan.ca/english/census06/analysis/aboriginal/surpass.cfm

Stiggins, R.J. (2001). The unfulfilled promise of classroom assessment. *Educational Measurement: Issues and Practice, 20*(3), 5–15. http://dx.doi. org/10.1111/j.1745-3992.2001.tb00065.x

Struthers, R., & Hodge, F.S. (2004, Sep). Sacred tobacco use in Ojibwe communities. *Journal of Holistic Nursing, 22*(3), 209–225. http://dx.doi.org/10.1177/08980101 04266735 Medline:15296576

Sutherland, D. (2005). Resiliency and collateral learning in science in some students of Cree ancestry. *Science Education, 89*(4), 595–613. http://dx.doi.org/10.1002/sce.20066

UNESCO. (1997). *The UNESCO recommendation against discrimination in education.* Retrieved July 8, 2008, from http://www.cmec.ca/international/discrimination-en.stm.

White, G. (2006). Cultures in collision: Traditional knowledge and Euro-Canadian governance processes in northern land-claim boards. *Arctic, 59*(4), 401–414.

6

A New Deal

Blair Stonechild

Reprinted from *The New Buffalo: The Struggle for Aboriginal Post-Secondary Education in Canada* by Blair Stonechild, published by the University of Manitoba Press, 2006, pp. 117–135. Reproduced with permission.

First Nations dissatisfaction with universities' ability to meet their higher education needs continues. A recent example is outlined by professors Dennis McPherson and Douglas Rabb (2003) in the article "Restoring the Interpretive Circle: Community-Based Research and Education," where the authors refer to the situation that arose at Lakehead University in connection with a grant for US$250,000 from the Rockefeller Foundation to develop Native philosophy. With the help of this funding, a First Nations-based Ayaangwaamizin Academy of Indigenous Learning was established to stimulate philosophical inquiry. In 1999, 16 Aboriginal students involved in this process applied to the qualifying year of Lakehead's Native and Canadian Philosophy M.A. program. All 16 applicants were rejected, and the following year, Lakehead closed what was expected to be Canada's first graduate program in Aboriginal philosophy (McPherson & Rabb, 2003, pp. 157–158). To McPherson and Rabb (2003), the message from the university was clear: "It has told Indians they do not belong there" (p. 159).

They were not the first academics to express disappointment. In reflecting on his 25-year career, Howard Adams viewed much of university teaching as an exercise in neocolonialism: "there are Native Studies programs at almost every large university in Canada and many teacher institutes offering special programs to train Natives to be teachers. But their perspectives and ideologies are quite consistent with mainstream courses .... All of these courses indoctrinate Native students to conservative middle class ideologies. They are intended towards creating an Aboriginal bourgeoisie" (as cited in McPherson & Rabb, 2001, p. 75). McPherson and Rabb (2001) observe: "Adams represents a growing number of Aboriginal academics who have spent their careers encouraging Native students to pursue post-secondary education, only to find that the system has let them down" (p. 75). Marie Battiste and James (Sa'ke'j) Henderson (Battiste & Henderson, 2000) from the University of Saskatchewan also express reservations: "At best Canadian universities and educational systems teach this double consciousness to Indigenous students. Canadian educational systems view Indigenous heritage, identity and thought as inferior to Eurocentric heritage, identity and thought .... Educators still know very little about how Indigenous students are raised and socialized in their homes and communities, and even less about how Indigenous heritage is traditionally transmitted" (pp. 88–89).

While over a dozen mainstream universities offer programs in Native studies, the report of the Royal Commission on Aboriginal Peoples (RCAP) in 1996 acknowledged that Aboriginal peoples still did not enjoy the autonomy to design programs that could best serve their needs. As well, the success rate for Indigenous students was far lower than at Aboriginal-controlled institutions. It urged universities to "continue their efforts to create a more hospitable environment for Aboriginal students" (RCAP, 1996, pp. 520–521). RCAP (1996) recognized that while universities are attempting to integrate Aboriginal needs by creating programs such as Native studies, student completion rates are unacceptably low, often because Aboriginal students feel "isolated in a hostile environment where professors and students express racist attitudes and opinions" (pp. 514–516).

The 2002 report, *Best Practices in Increasing Aboriginal Post-Secondary Enrolment Rates*, prepared for the Council of Ministers of Education, acknowledged that "Almost all Aboriginal education dollars are spent in universities and programs that are not under Aboriginal control. Many of the interviews conducted and much of the literature reviewed for this study demonstrate that whenever Aboriginals are given control over their own programs or institutions, there have been higher rates of success in Aboriginal enrolment and graduation" (Malatest & Associates, 2002, p. 45). It concludes, "Best practices for Aboriginal post-secondary enrolment and retention strategies depend upon Aboriginals exerting control over their own education. A fundamental shift in the post-secondary system would depend on the initiation of increased Aboriginal control at the institutional level" (Malatest & Associates, 2002, p. 46). *Best Practices* noted concern about "often poor or hostile public perception of programs and initiatives geared toward Aboriginal people" (Malatest & Associates, 2002, p. 58). This indicates the need for a campaign of public education and raising awareness.

●   ●   ●   ●   ●   ●   ●   ●   ●   ●   ●   ●   ●   ●   ●

Approximately 80 First Nations higher education programs of various types are funded on a project-driven basis through the Indian Studies Support Program (ISSP), receiving between $10,000 and $700,000 per project. About 90% of these programs are located within First Nations communities. The primary success of these programs is that they have greatly increased access for First Nations students to on-reserve programs generally brokered from mainstream universities.

In eastern Canada, where a tradition of post-Confederation treaty-making did not exist, First Nations control over post-secondary education is the least developed. In the Maritimes, there are no independent, Aboriginal-controlled, higher education institutes. The Micmac-Malecite Institute, opened in 1981, is the only centre for Aboriginal higher education in the Maritimes. Affiliated with the University of New Brunswick, the institute offers a B.Ed. degree to train Aboriginal teachers, a First Nations business administration certificate, and a preparatory bridging year. As well, in Quebec, no major Indigenous-controlled post-secondary institutions have developed since the closing of Manitou Community College in 1979. While the James Bay Cree control their own elementary and secondary education system, they partner with Heritage College for delivery of adult distance-education courses.

In Ontario, the Aboriginal Institutes Consortium, representing nine institutions, was formed to collaborate on common issues such as achieving recognition and accreditation, and obtaining core funding. The institutes delivered 150 programs to 17,906 students over the past seven years. One member of the consortium, the First Nations Technical Institute, was established in 1985 and has offered programs including public administration, social services worker training, community work, health work, small business, computer software, and aviation.

In Manitoba, much of the emphasis has been on establishing "access programs" to increase Aboriginal participation in the province's mainstream public universities. The University of Manitoba has made a major investment in providing improved access. Its Aboriginal Access Program has two recruiters and coordinates a variety of student support initiatives including tutoring, counselling, and mentoring. Access to professional programs at the University of Manitoba includes the Aboriginal Business Education Program, Engineering Access Program, Social Work Distance Education, Health Careers Access Program, and Faculty of Education Access Program (Peter Nunoda, access co-ordinator, University of Manitoba, personal communication, April 25, 2006). The university, which has as many as 2,400 Aboriginal students, officially intends to position itself as the pre-eminent institution for attracting Aboriginal students for higher education in Canada. The success of the access strategy has shown itself not only in enrolments but also in improved Aboriginal student retention, a rate now in excess of 60%.

Yellowquill College, operated by the Dakota Ojibway Council and located in Winnipeg, is the only First Nations–controlled post-secondary institution in Manitoba. The college, which offers a range of preparatory and technical courses, is founded upon the principle that First Nations have the right to determine and offer what they deem to be appropriate programs. In 1993, the Assembly of Manitoba Chiefs passed a resolution calling for a First Nations–controlled post-secondary institute to be established in Manitoba. The City of Winnipeg has expressed openness to creating an urban Indian reserve that could be used for such a purpose. However, the idea remains controversial (Assembly of Manitoba Chiefs, 2003). The chiefs are also now considering how Manitoba's recently created University College of the North can serve their needs.

In Saskatchewan, First Nations University of Canada (FNUC) (originally Saskatchewan Indian Federated College [SIFC]) was born at the initiative of Saskatchewan First Nations elders and leaders who wished to see the formation of an institution of higher learning that would mirror their philosophies, languages, history, and concepts of government. That institution would assist First Nations to find their place in the modern world while keeping First Nations heritage intact. The SIFC was considered a bold experiment in Aboriginal-controlled post-secondary education. While it has enjoyed successes, core funding arrangements have proven inadequate to meet the growing demands of First Nations in the province, let alone the entire country.[1]

In Alberta, tribal colleges, including Red Crow Community College; Old Sun Community College; Blue Quills First Nations College; Maskwachees Cultural College; Bullhead Adult Education Centre; Nechi Training, Research and Health Promotion Institute; Nakoda Education; Pikani Post-Secondary Education; and Yellowhead Tribal Council Education, were formed to provide culturally appropriate education on the reserves. For example, Red Crow College, established in 1986, emphasizes Blackfoot culture, traditions, and knowledge. It also offers programs in leadership training and traditional land use, as well as teacher training in co-operation with the University of Lethbridge and social work in partnership with the University of Calgary.

In British Columbia, the Union of British Columbia Indian Chiefs (UBCIC) voted in 1991 to set up the Institute of Indigenous Government (IIG), an Indigenous-controlled post-secondary institute dedicated to developing self-government skills. In 1993, the province agreed to accredit IIG as a provincial institute under the College and Institute Act, and the IIG's board of governors was appointed by the province, acting upon nominations from the UBCIC. The Nicola Valley Institute of Technology (NVIT), established in 1983 by the First Nations of the Nicola Valley area, in 1995 also became a provincial institute similar to the IIG. Today, NVIT also operates as a private institution under the British Columbia College and Institute Act, with 230 students, 80% of whom are Aboriginal, housed in a new $9-million facility made possible by provincial funding.

●　●　●　●　●　●　●　●　●　●　●　●　●　●　●

Issues of jurisdiction have arisen across the country. In Quebec and the Maritimes, where few First Nations–controlled institutions exist, mainstream universities, some of which receive ISSP funding, play the dominant role in post-secondary education delivery. Standing in stark contrast, section six of the Mi'kmaq Education Act (1998), concerning jurisdiction, states: "The participating First Nations shall have jurisdiction with respect to post-secondary student support funding for members residing on and off First Nations land." In Quebec, the First Nations Education Council (n.d.), based at Wendake, notes that the Assembly of First Nations' (AFN's) document, "First Nations Educational Jurisdiction 2004," called for each region to "establish structures/bodies for the implementation of educational jurisdiction at the local and regional levels." Post-secondary education was identified as one of those areas.

In 1998, the Anishinabek Nation in Ontario signed a Framework for an Education Agreement in Principle that does not limit or abrogate any Aboriginal or treaty rights, the first of its kind in the province. From the perspective of these First Nations, who represent about 2,100 post-secondary students, the agreement is intended to restore their jurisdiction over education matters and enable them to enter into further self-government agreements in the future ("Education self-government," 2000). The agreement also sets out the relationships between the federal and Ontario government, although the latter has not actively participated in the negotiations ("Education agreement in principle," n.d.).

In Manitoba, the Assembly of Manitoba Chiefs signed the Framework Agreement on Indian Education in Manitoba with the federal government in 1990. In one of the introductory clauses of the agreement, federal refusal to accept responsibility for post-secondary education is acknowledged: "And whereas attempts by the parties to negotiate certain issues relating to treaty rights and to post-secondary education have not given rise to acceptable rights … these issues may therefore be addressed outside the scope of this Framework Agreement." This leaves the province of Manitoba, which is not a party to the agreement, to play a principal role.

SIFC, which covers the province through regional campuses and community-based offerings, was given legislative legitimacy in 1994 by the Federation of Saskatchewan Indian Nations' (FSIN's) Saskatchewan Indian Federated College Act, establishing "under First Nations government an autonomous degree-granting University College to serve first Nations people for the purpose of providing university-level education" (Indian Governments of Saskatchewan, 1994). The SIFC was accepted as a full member of the Association of Universities and Colleges of Canada (AUCC) in 1991 on the basis of meeting certain criteria, such as being able to operate free of political interference. Its renaming to FNUC in 2003 is reflective of SIFC's original vision and its funding as a national institution.

In Alberta, the principal approach has been to establish regional tribal colleges, established and controlled by First Nations to meet local community needs. Nine tribal colleges and post-secondary institutes, along with Yellowquill College in Manitoba, have formed the First Nations Adult and Higher Education Consortium to "provide quality adult and higher education controlled entirely by people of the First Nations," as well as to set accreditation standards. Red Crow College is also a member of the American Indian Higher Education Consortium.

In the Government of British Columbia's *Aboriginal Post-Secondary Education and Training Policy Framework* (1995), the province's legal interpretation of its obligations toward Aboriginal post-secondary education is outlined:

> *In the area of education, because the Indian Act, section 4(3) limits the application of the Act to Indians between the ages of 7 and 17 ordinarily resident on a reserve, the responsibility for post-secondary education and for Aboriginal people has resided with the province through legislation regarding public post-secondary education and training.*

The provincial legislation referred to is British Columbia's Private Post-Secondary Education Act. The policy framework was approved in 1995 after a series of forums with Aboriginal political organizations, including the Association of Aboriginal Post-Secondary Institutions (AAPSI), which represents 15 institutions enrolling 1,500 students. Noting that the federal government does not assume responsibility, British Columbia has moved aggressively into the perceived void of First Nations higher education jurisdiction. At the same time, an agreement has been negotiated with the federal government to provide 25% of the funding required to bring First Nations post-secondary education to parity. This approach has been successful because the province has been able to offer major operational funding as well as accreditation, something not possible under the ISSP. The First Nations have tacitly permitted such funding arrangements, perceiving they better meet the immediate needs of their culturally diverse and geographically dispersed communities. In the North, institutions such as Arctic College have been created that can serve a far-flung population and keep students closer to their home communities.

Generally, First Nations in all regions of Canada are issuing declarations and enacting legislation that protects their jurisdiction over all areas of education. However, the federal government's refusal to accept a fiduciary responsibility for First Nations post-secondary education implies that Aboriginal institutions will continue to be forced to partner with mainstream universities and colleges for recognition and additional resources. The forced reorganization of the Institute of Indigenous Government, "BC's first autonomous degree-granting Indigenous-controlled post-secondary institution," by the Province of British Columbia following a 1998 review, suggests that First Nations control in that case was ephemeral (Human Resources and Skills Development Canada, 2006). Should the First Nations eventually feel that such partnership arrangements no longer meet their needs, it is presumed that under First Nations' inherent sovereignty, their own institutions could be set up, although this would entail challenging organizational, financial, and jurisdictional issues.

• • • • • • • • • • • • • • •

The AFN's (2000) *National Report of First Nations Post-Secondary Education Review* found that of post-secondary students nationally, only approximately half were enrolled in university institutions. For example, in 1993, of a total of 17,699 post-secondary students, 9,023 or 50.9% were enrolled in universities, and in 1997, of a total of 23,205 post-secondary students, the proportion of university students stood virtually unchanged at 11,793 or 50.8% (p. 40). That year, these students were predominately enrolled in three main fields: general arts and sciences (25.8%), education (20%), and social sciences and services (16.7%). The areas of least representation were mathematics and physical sciences (1.1%) and agriculture and biosciences (1.4%) (AFN, 2000, p. 42).

One can question whether post-secondary participation of First Nations students is comparable to that of non-Aboriginal students. A closer look suggests that the federal government has fallen far short of achieving its policy goal of parity of First Nations participation in post-secondary education. According to recent Department of Indian Affairs data, 26,800 First Nations students were funded through their Post-Secondary Student Support Program (PSSSP) in 2000–2001 (Hanson/Macleod Institute, 2003, p. 89; Indian and Northern Affairs Canada [INAC], 2001).

According to this breakdown, approximately 13,400 First Nations students were enrolled in universities in 2000, including both full- and part-time students, of which the latter constitute approximately 10% (INAC). In terms of the overall First Nations population, total numbers in 2000 would be approximately 683,200. The participation rate in higher education in 2000 was therefore 13,400 out of 683,200 (Department of Indian Affairs and Northern Development, 2000),[2] or approximately 2% of the First Nations population.

The overall population of Canada in July 2003 was approximately 31,625,000 (Statistics Canada, 2004).[3] According to the AUCC, which represents over 80 higher education institutions, the number of Canadians enrolled in universities in 2003–2004 was 1,028,000.[4] The mainstream participation rate, after excluding 16,000 First Nations students, is 1,012,000 out of 31,625,000 or 3.2%. Comparing this to the First Nations participation rate of 2%, one concludes that the First Nations participation rate in higher education is only 60% that of mainstream society.

To arrive at complete statistics on post-secondary education, the other component of community colleges must be added. According to the Association of Canadian Community Colleges (n.d.), which represents 147 institutions, they have an enrollment of 2,400,000 students.[5] Added to approximately one million non-Aboriginal students in Canadian universities, the total number of Canadian students enrolled in post-secondary education is approximately 3,400,000. Of a total population of 31,625.000, this represents a post-secondary education participation rate of 10.8%. The total number of First Nations post-secondary students, including those at universities and community colleges in 2000, was 26,800. Out of a total First Nations population of 683,200, this would represent a participation rate of 3.9%. This means that the First Nations overall post-secondary participation rate of 3.9% is only 36%, or just over a third of the mainstream society's rate of 10.8%.

Given the lack of growth in the post-secondary budget, which has increased only at approximately 2% per year, consistent with overall Indian Affairs budget increases, this funding has not kept pace with increases in university tuitions, with the result that fewer First Nations students are able to be sponsored. AFN noted that the number of funded students had fallen from a high of 27,157 in 1999 to 25,075 in 2003.[6] The implications of these figures are, first, that the federal government has fallen far short of its stated policy objective of achieving parity in post-secondary participation by First Nations, and, second, that the disparity is beginning to widen. In order to achieve such parity, the federal government would have to triple its current level of funding, bringing it from the $293 million in 2000–2001 to nearly $900 million.

Another controversial issue has arisen recently over the decision by the Canada Revenue Agency in 2004 to tax First Nations post-secondary education payments. Interestingly, the impetus for this move came from the Department of Indian Affairs, whose spokesperson reiterated the federal government's long-standing opinion that such programs are "a matter of social policy not of treaty rights" ("Government to tax Aboriginal post-secondary grants," n.d.). Such a position overlooks the fact that the most recent legal decisions have supported the concept that such rights flow from Indian treaties and hence should not be taxed. Such a move reveals the fundamental contradiction of the department—can it be both trustee of First Nations rights and arm of the federal government? As of the time of writing, the Canada Revenue Agency has indefinitely postponed plans to implement the tax. However, the tax has not been declared invalid.

The other area of concern in a comprehensive post-secondary program, apart from the funding of students to pursue education, is the funding of Aboriginal-controlled post-secondary institutions themselves. According to AUCC, the total amount of funding of various sorts to Canadian universities, be it in tuitions, research funds, capital funds, or government transfers for 2003–2004, amounts to $23,518,660,000 (Statistics Canada). The leading sources of this funding were transfers from other levels of government, provincial governments, and own-source revenue. Applying this amount to the approximately one million non-Aboriginal students in universities suggests that these global resources translate roughly to $23,500 per student.

The average per-student resources of the four sampled universities are $24,476. When compared to this average, the total revenue of the First Nations University, Canada's national university for First Nations, is only 64% of the level of resources received by those provincially funded public universities (see Table 6.1). The First Nations University's revenue comes primarily from the ISSP, comprising 33.4% of its overall revenues, with student tuitions (21.8%) and "nonoperational" funding (15.2%) constituting the other major sources. Despite the recent construction of its facility, made possible only through long-term leasing of half the facility to Indian Affairs, the institution still does not receive funding for capital development or maintenance. This analysis of funding raises other questions, such as whether Aboriginal people, who constitute 3.3% of Canada's population, benefit fairly from the $23.5 billion in total revenues accorded to Canadian universities.[8] If Aboriginal peoples were receiving their 3.3% proportion, they would be benefitting from approximately $775 million in funding resources for higher education alone. Adding an additional proportion for the full range of post-secondary education that includes community colleges would at least double that amount.[9] Métis

Table **6.1** Total Global Revenues per Student at Sample Universities[7]

Institution	Total (Year)	Enrolments (Year)	Revenues (per Student)
University of Toronto	$1,143,395,000 (01–02)	47,265 (01–02)	$24,190
University of Manitoba	463,459,000 (01–02)	23,618 (01–02)	19,623
University of Saskatchewan	524,000,000 (00–01)	20,493 (00–01)	25,569
University of Alberta	919,785,000 (01–02)	32,246 (01–02)	28,524
First Nations University	16,337,381 (01–02)	1,200 (01–02)	13,614

and Inuit populations, who do not have access to the same programs as First Nations, or capital funds for existing or new facilities, experience even greater disparity. These statistics bare the shabby treatment accorded to Aboriginal-controlled post-secondary education in terms of government policy. The underfunding of Aboriginal-controlled institutions, along with the expectation that mainstream universities can fill the need, is an unacceptable evasion of the real issue of failing to fully empower Aboriginal post-secondary education.

In examining post-secondary education funding needs, AFN (2004) stated, "Using conservative estimates, a total of $880,305,332 is required" (p. 16) as shown in Table 6.2.

Such figures expose the underfunding of Aboriginal-controlled institutions when compared to mainstream universities. Under such conditions, Aboriginal students will continue to underperform, and it will be extremely unlikely that they will exceed their current minuscule proportion among the ranks of Ph.D.s or medical doctors and other professionals for many generations.

On March 21, 2000, AFN National Chief Phil Fontaine met with Finance Minister Paul Martin to discuss the federal budget and raised the issue of First Nations post-secondary student underfunding. AFN (2000) reported that Martin "was unaware of this situation and agreed to support increased PSE funding if shown evidence. The National Chief agreed to provide a list of names" (p. 12). A national telephone survey conducted as part of the First Nations Post-Secondary Education Review identified a list of 9,465 individuals who fell within this category (AFN/INAC, 2001). The review also stated: "It is estimated that 39,160 First Nations students will require post-secondary assistance in 2005–2006. For this reason, post-secondary education has become a high political priority for this organization [AFN]" (Bellegarde, 2000).

The PSSSP has managed to achieve only one-third of its goal of attaining post-secondary participation rates comparable with mainstream society. AFN points out that funding by PSSSP had not

Table 6.2 First Nations Post-Secondary Funding Required

$614,199,530	for the PSSSP
$73,703,944	for the ISSP
$110,555,915	for First Nations post-secondary institutes
$79,845,939	for administration
$2,000,000	for the development of a database

substantially increased since 1995–1996, and living allowances have not kept pace with increases in the cost of living. If First Nations are to truly enjoy the full benefits of higher education, including access to effective Aboriginal-controlled institutions, existing post-secondary funding should be immediately tripled to at least $1 billion annually.

A former chief of AFN, Matthew Coon-Come, had also noted that the Liberal government had not kept its promise to remove the cap on post-secondary funding made in the 1993 Liberal "red book":

> *A Liberal Government will remove the cap on postsecondary education specifically to provide adequate funding for Aboriginal students accepted at colleges, universities and vocational institutes, and in adult education programs and professional degree programs. (cited in Bellegarde, 2000, p. 101)*

AFN has indicated that lining the cap on First Nations post-secondary education will be a tangible way in which the new government can demonstrate its purported commitment to embracing Aboriginal issues.

The latest federal initiative of the Liberal government for discussing Aboriginal education policy change, the Roundtable on Lifelong Learning, aims "to seek transformative change." Participants at the roundtable were drawn from a wide spectrum of both Aboriginal and non-Aboriginal experts. The recommendations would become the rationale for increased funding in the Kelowna Accord, signed by Prime Minister Paul Martin and provincial and territorial leaders in November 2005. The accord planned to provide $500 million over five years to enable First Nations post-secondary institutions to be funded at equitable levels and to address inflationary costs and enrolment increases.

The AFN (2004) *Background Paper on Lifelong Learning*, prepared for discussion with First Ministers in 2005, noted:

> *It is time for governments to fund and support the development of First Nations institutions of higher learning that are controlled by First Nations peoples. A variety of First Nations controlled colleges, institutes and community learning centres have already been developed. However, these institutions experience a chronic lack of funding and also the reluctance of mainstream post-secondary institutions to recognize their courses and certificates/degrees. Courses and programs offered by these First Nations institutes of higher learning are highly relevant and valued by First Nations communities; it has been demonstrated that these institutions provide a supportive learning environment and students are encouraged to persist and complete their courses/programs. (p. 16)*

The 2004 Auditor General's report called upon INAC to take action to eliminate the education gap between First Nations and mainstream society. It identified significant weaknesses in the PSSSP's management and accountability framework, including the lack of basic statistical data on programs offered and student enrolment and completion. The scrutiny levelled on First Nations education over the past years and the demand for more accountability for results have placed a great deal of pressure on INAC to demonstrate that gains are being made for the funds expended. First Nations and INAC must work together to find a mechanism through which data can be produced and accountability guaranteed.

* * * * * * * * * * * * * * * *

The example of the tribal college system in the United States has lessons to offer. Six American Indian tribal colleges initially formed the American Indian Higher Education Consortium (AIHEC) in 1973. Tribal colleges were inspired by the self-determination movement of the 1960s and the realization that mainstream universities were not meeting the needs of American Indians living on reservations. The first, the Navajo (now Dine) College, was established in 1968. Today, AIHEC includes 31 tribally mandated and four intertribal universities and colleges that enrol over 33,000 students whose average age is 27 and are 70% female.

In the United States, American Indian and Alaska Natives are eligible for special funding through the Bureau of Indian Affairs, which offered over $30 million in 1994 to 15,000 Native American students in the form of grants averaging $2,412 per student (Malatest & Associates, 2002, p. 25). Tribal colleges are provided government per-student funding under the Tribally Controlled Community College Assistance Act (1978) and later the Tribally Controlled College and University Act, a funding initiative sponsored by President Bill Clinton in 1996 and renewed by President George Bush in 2002. The act recognizes federal responsibilities to assist post-secondary institutions on Indian lands, as they are not eligible for state grants. In 1983, the act allotted $5,280 per American Indian full-time student (approximately $8,000 in 2002 funds). By 1998, the amount allocated was US$6,000, still substantially less than the average at mainstream community colleges ("Tribal colleges spread, marking slow progress," 2003). AIHEC also has its own Tribal College Fund that seeks funding from corporate and philanthropic sources such as the Carnegie and Kellogg foundations to target specific priorities identified by the colleges. In addition, private sources such as Buffy Sainte-Marie's Nihewan Foundation have provided scholarships that have enabled some American Indian students to complete doctoral degrees (Malatest & Associates, 2002, p. 29).

Tribal colleges are successful not only because they provide a culturally affirming environment but also because they are responsive to local community dynamics. One of the successful impacts of tribal colleges has been to assist with the economic development of the reservations. This is accomplished in various ways, including employment, local expenditure, workforce skills development, and fostering entrepreneurship and small business development through tribal business information centres. Local land use and economic opportunities can be researched and technology such as Internet usage can be introduced. The colleges, the majority of which offer two-year programs, employ an average of 81 faculty and staff and generate $2.1 million in salaries per college. Reservations in which tribal colleges exist show higher rates of employment and economic growth, and greater numbers of students remain in the community, making contributions that might otherwise have been directed toward urban centres. For example, the 63% employment rate of graduates of Stonechild College in Rocky Boy Reservation, Montana, stands in contrast to the reservation's overall 28% employment rate. Other positive impacts of post-secondary programs on reservation communities include reduction of dependence on welfare, less drug and alcohol use, and reduced rates of suicide (American Indian Higher Education Consortium, 2000, pp. 5–18).

In spite of insufficient funding, over half the tribal colleges are venturing into using distance-education technology such as Internet-based instruction. Haskell University in Kansas has a distance-education program; Bay Mills Community College, Michigan, offers 50 online courses; and North Dakota tribal colleges have formed a "virtual learning community." This approach recognizes the reality that many students have family or job-related obligations, and that Internet-based instruction offers necessary flexibility. Through the Internet, a virtual library can be created and shared to provide a critical mass of materials for participating institutions. All the institutions have found that distance-education technology has enhanced the achievement of their tribal college mission (Holdsworth & Dahlquist, 2004).

American Indian students who attend a tribal college before transferring to a four-year institution were four times as likely to complete their degree as those who entered as first-year students at mainstream universities (Boyer, 1997). In this sense, tribal colleges have similar successes as historically black colleges, which have demonstrated significantly higher levels of program completion rates for African

Americans. Tribal colleges are "creating bright circles of hope on their reservations" (Ambler, 2005). They have not only revolutionized Indian education but have also become major engines of change in American Indian communities. Regional accreditation agencies in the United States have recognized the validity of judging tribal colleges based upon their abilities to meet their unique mission. This model of Indigenous higher education is spreading around the globe with a network, the World Indigenous Higher Education Consortium, founded at Kananaskis, Alberta, in 2002, representing initiatives in Australia, Canada, Mexico, New Zealand, Sweden, and the United States.

Finally, a cautionary lesson about the pitfalls of Aboriginal control and governance should be learned from the experience at FNUC, where 23 of the board's 31 members were political appointees of FSIN. On February 17, 2005, board Chairman Morley Watson suspended three FNUC senior administrative officers, stating this was necessary in order to investigate allegations of corruption. The repercussions of this controversial political intervention included firing and resignations of faculty and staff who spoke against the actions, turmoil among students, and questions about the institution's credibility within the university community.

The original vision of SIFC had been a broad one: a high-quality university institution that sought the best knowledge of both Aboriginal and non-Aboriginal worlds and was to serve a national and international clientele. A highly capable, talented, and committed team of Aboriginal academics had been gradually drawn to the institution and were on the verge of bringing FNUC to the lofty heights it had aspired to, creating programs equal to, if not better than, Aboriginal programs in mainstream universities. Credibility was such that funding agencies were contemplating major investments in expanded programming. However, the intrusion of February 2005 into FNUC's operations revealed its weaknesses.

The board, using unrestrained power, was able to set in motion a series of events that, due to a lack of checks and balances, caused the institution to collapse like a house of cards. It is clear that the board did not properly assess the situation or anticipate the consequences. A year and a half after the initial intrusion, there has been no reporting of major corruption, despite an audit estimated to have cost $500,000. In retrospect, the actions amounted to a political takeover and radical narrowing of the institution's mission. The international program was disbanded and plans to establish a doctoral program in Indigenous studies were abandoned. These were replaced by an emphasis on delivering teaching programs to First Nations communities in the province. Partners in the academic enterprise, such as the University of Regina, stood by impotently. In a normal situation, one would have expected that checks and balances would come into play to prevent such a disastrous fallout.

At the risk of making the board judgement appear to be the major culprit, it must be pointed out that the foundation for the calamitous fall of FNUC was laid by the federal and provincial governments that underfunded the institution, making it impossible to achieve its ambitious mission. For example, the contribution of the Saskatchewan government to FNUC is to compensate for the enrolment of non-Aboriginal students and in that sense is not directed toward First Nations education.

At a symposium on November 10, 2005, at which Aboriginal scholars from across Canada met to discuss the crisis at FNUC, participants were reminded about the colonialist nature of Canada's history, the usurpation of land and resources, and relegation of Aboriginal peoples to an underprivileged class. One of the unique characteristics that distinguishes FNUC from all other institutions is that it is a university of a colonized people. The events at FNUC, and the trauma produced as factions futilely lashed out against one another, is typical of lateral violence that occurs within colonized populations. Others observed a trend toward fundamentalism in all levels of Aboriginal education—a growing rejection of, and intolerance toward, non-Aboriginal views.

One of the high points of the symposium was a healing testimonial by Ojibway elder Bev Shawanda, who recounted her experiences of being abused and her personal struggle to overcome its impacts. She pointed out that in order to overcome the trauma involved, it is first necessary to recognize that the abuse is occurring before being in a position to rise above it. She pointed out that institutions such as FNUC should be safe places where students can learn about, become empowered by, and resolve to rise above not only the personal but also the collective trauma of colonialism.

Concerns that the governance of FNUC had been tied too closely to FSIN had been long-standing. Doug Cuthand, the first board chairman of SIFC, noted that the intent of the original board was to have Aboriginal chiefs replace administrators once the institution's direction had been set. But the board chair, without the benefit of any studies, defended the political board, stating: "we have our own traditions and ways of doing things and sometimes that is not always kosher with organizations," but that the changes would result in "a top notch university" ("Review needed: board chair," 2005). However, in the eyes of AUCC and the Canadian Association of University Teachers, these actions have raised troubling concerns.

The All Chiefs' Task Force was mandated by the chiefs of Saskatchewan in June 2005 to sort through the issues and recommend how FNUC could best move forward into the future. Major findings included that the board of governors should be reduced in number and depoliticized, that academic freedom must be respected, and that the operations of the institution should be transparent. On May 30, 2006, board Chair Watson responded by announcing the formation of a board that, while smaller at 19 members, is in fact more political. Fifteen of the 19 members are political representatives, and Mr. Watson continues as board chair, something the task force report had specifically recommended against. Former board members representing universities and governments have been removed from the board and assigned to a separate advisory committee. The same week, a report commissioned by FNUC portrayed AUCC as having "non-interest and a lack of advocacy,"[10] something AUCC quickly denied. The report concluded that FNUC should consider other routes of obtaining accreditation.

AUCC announced in June 2006 that, for the first time in its 90-year existence, it would set up a committee to review an institution's continued membership ("University given until mid-June to clean up its act," 2006). Whatever the outcome of this process will be, perhaps the lesson to be learned is that creating, operating, and maintaining an Aboriginal post-secondary institution within a colonialist environment that produces more failures than successes is a daunting challenge.

REFERENCES

Ambler, M. (2005, Spring). Tribal colleges redefining success. *Tribal College Journal, 16*(3), 8–10.

American Indian Higher Education Consortium & Institute for Higher Education Policy. (2000). *Tribal college contributions to local economic development.* Washington, DC: Author.

Assembly of First Nations. (2004, October 20). Background paper on lifelong learning. Ottawa: Author.

Assembly of First Nations (AFN). (2000). *National report of First Nations post-secondary education review.* Ottawa: Author.

Assembly of First Nations/Indian and Northern Affairs Canada. (2001, November). *Draft discussion paper on post-secondary education.* Ottawa: Author.

Assembly of Manitoba Chiefs (2003). *2003 Annual Education Report.* Retrieved from http://www.manitobachiefs.com/education

Association of Canadian Community Colleges. (n.d.). Serving communities. Retrieved from http://www.accc.ca/english/colleges/serving_communities.cfm

Association of Universities and Colleges of Canada (AUCC). *Quick Facts.* Retrieved from http://www.aucc.ca/publications/research/_quick_facts_e.html

Battiste, M., & Henderson, J. (2000). *Protecting Indigenous Knowledge and heritage: A global challenge.* Saskatoon, SK: Purich Publishing.

Bellegarde, P. (2000, August 25). AFN education portfolio, to all First Nations peoples. Covering letter to the National report of First Nations post-secondary education review. Ottawa: Assembly of First Nations.

Boyer, P. (1997). *Native American colleges: Progress and prospects.* Princeton, NJ: Carnegie Foundation for the Advancement of Teaching.

Department of Indian Affairs and Northern Development. (2000, December 17). *Facts from stats.*

Education agreement in principle. (n.d.). Retrieved from http://www.anishinabek.ca/ROJ/edu/gov-AIP.asp

Education self-government agreement-in-principle reached with First Nations within the Anishinabek nation. (2000). *Kahtou News.* Retrieved from http://www.kahtou.com/images/selfeducation

First Nations Education Council. (n.d.). *Responsibilities and education jurisdiction.* Retrieved from http://www.cepn-fnec.com/juridic/resp

Fontaine, P. (n.d.) National Chief Phil Fontaine's response to the Auditor General's recommendations on First Nations education. Assembly of First Nations. Retrieved November 23, 2004, from http://www.afn.ca

Government of British Columbia. (1995). *Aboriginal post-secondary education and training policy framework.* Victoria, BC: Ministry of Advanced Education. Retrieved from http://www.aved.gov.bc.ca/Aboriginal/framework

Government to tax Aboriginal post-secondary grants. Retrieved September 13, 2004, from http://www.meadowlakeprogress.com/story.php?id=111107

Hanson/Macleod Institute. (2003). *Post-secondary evaluation: Draft consolidated report.* Ottawa: Indian and Northern Affairs Canada.

Holdsworth, J., & Dahlquist, J. (2004, April). *Tribal community colleges and on-line distance education.* Paper presented at the 46th Conference for the Study of Community Colleges.

Human Resources and Skills Development Canada. Retrieved July 2006 from http://www11.hrsdc.gc.ca/en/cs/sp/hrsdc/edd/brief/1998-000593/feiig.shtml

Indian and Northern Affairs Canada (INAC). (2001). *Basic departmental data 2001.* Ottawa: Author.

Indian and Northern Affairs Canada (INAC). Retrieved September 10, 2004, from http://www.ainc-inac.gc.ca/nr/nwltr/ sts/1996fs-9_e.html.

Indian Governments of Saskatchewan. (1994, May 26). *An act respecting the Saskatchewan Indian Federated College.*

Liberal Party of Canada. (1993). *Creating opportunity: The Liberal plan for Canada.* Ottawa: Author.

McPherson, D., & Rabb, D. (2001, Spring). Indigeneity in Canada: Spirituality, the sacred and survival. *International Journal of Canadian Studies, 23,* 57–79.

McPherson, D., & Rabb, D. (2003, Fall). Restoring the interpretive circle: Community-Based research and education. *International Journal of Canadian Studies, 28,* 157–158.

Mi'kmaq Education Act. (S.C. 1998, c. 24). Retrieved from http://laws-lois.justice.gc.ca/eng/acts/M-7.6/

Malatest, R.A., & Associates. (2002). *Best practices in increasing Aboriginal post-secondary enrolment rates.* Ottawa: Canadian Council of Ministers of Education.

Review needed: Board chair. (2005, April 15). *Regina Leader-Post.* Retrieved from http://www.canada.com/reginaleaderpost

Royal Commission on Aboriginal Peoples (RCAP). (1996). *Report of the Royal Commission on Aboriginal Peoples.* (Vol. 3). Ottawa: Canada Communications Group.

Statistics Canada. (2004, July 1). Retrieved September 10, 2004, from http://www. statcan.ca/english/edu/clock/population.htm

Statistics Canada. *Universities and colleges revenue and expenditure, provinces and territories.* Retrieved September 13, 2002, from http://www.statcan.ca/english/ Pgdb/govt41a.htm

Tribal colleges spread, marking slow progress. (2003, November 10). *Newsday.* Retrieved from http://www.newsday.com

University given until mid-June to clean up its act. (2006, April 15). *Regina Leader-Post.* Retrieved from http://www.canada.com/reginaleaderpost

---

NOTES

1 The new name of the SIFC, First Nations University of Canada, was announced on June 21, 2003.

2 Based on a population of 658,000 in 1998 and a 1.9% population growth rate.

3 Based upon a July 1, 2004, population estimate of 31,900,034 and an annual growth rate of 0.855%.

4 Of the students, 748,000 attended full time and 280,000 part time.

5 Of these students, 900,000 are described as full-time and 1,500,000 as part-time learners.

6 Assembly of First Nations National Chief Phil Fontaine's (n.d.) response to the Auditor General's recommendations on First Nations education.

7 Statistics have been gleaned from university annual reports and from AUCC's website (http://www.aucc.ca). The enrolment of the First Nations University of Canada is an estimated full-time equivalent that includes class enrolments by University of Regina students. Total revenues include funds from all sources including tuitions, government transfers, capital, and restricted research funding. University enrolments may vary by year slightly, but the statistics are intended to portray a general analysis of funding per student.

8 According to Census Canada 2001 statistics, there were 976,305 Aboriginal people in Canada out of a total population of 29,639,035.

9 When community college post-secondary education is included, the amount of funding resources to which Aboriginal peoples should be entitled would more than double.

10 Pete Shauneen, Briefing document to the Board of Governors, First Nations University of Canada, May 8, 2006. Unpublished document.

7

Connections and Reconnections: Affirming Cultural Identity in Aboriginal Teacher Education

Linda Goulet and Yvonne McLeod

This chapter was originally published in the *McGill Journal of Education* (Fall 2002), 37(3), pp. 355–369. Reproduced with permission.

In this chapter, our cultural camp is described and analyzed to demonstrate how the teaching in our courses affirms the cultural identity of Aboriginal[1] teacher education students through culturally appropriate connections with the land and the elders. Teaching through the venue of the land and elders is essential because it affirms the student's identity and provides an opportunity to reconnect with their past. The elders' teaching in the outdoor education setting not only makes the education holistic, but it also provides opportunities for culturally authentic learning to take place.

Historical Context

Initially, our outdoor courses were just that: courses off campus where instruction took place out of doors. Some cultural components were added, such as tipi-raising and prayers by an elder, but we found that it was not enough.

Aboriginal teacher education needs to consider the historical and societal context in which it takes place. One cannot ignore the impact of past colonial practices on the students in our programs. Many Aboriginal authors have documented the effects of historical and continuing societal, institutional, and personal racism imposed by the colonial process upon Aboriginal peoples (cf. Acoose, 1995; Adams, 1989; Campbell, 1973; Means with Wolf, 1995). Racism has taken its toll on the physical, emotional, social, and spiritual life of Indigenous peoples. It is a testament to the enduring spirit of survival of Indigenous peoples that they always have been, and continue to be, active participants in the resistance against the imposition of oppression by colonization and its inherent racist ideology of superiority (cf. Adams, 1989; Battiste, 2000; Graveline, 1998; Said, 1993). At the same time, colonization has a history of imposing relationships of submission to authority that causes learned irresponsibility. Past schooling practices were very authoritarian, with the curriculum controlled by outsiders and day-to-day interactions controlled by teachers. In any culture, intergenerational connections are the conduit for passing knowledge from one generation to the next, the process needed for cultural retention and renewal. Residential schools, with their isolation and imposition of a foreign language, culture, and ideology, were extremely damaging in severing these connections. Kirkness (1992) states that the legacy of the residential schools was one of cultural conflict, alienation, poor self-concept, and a lack of preparation for independence for jobs and for life in general. In separating children from their families and communities, schooling had a serious impact on Aboriginal peoples in the disruption of intergenerational connections (cf. Binda with Calliou, 2001; Haig-Brown, 1988; Kirkness, 1992; Miller, 1996).

The negative effects of residential schools and other forms of oppression are still felt today, causing the disruption of cultural continuity, leaving individuals without a sense of who they are in the world. The denigration of culture contributes to a sense of unimportance, causing personal dislocation and fragmentation (Brendtro, Brokenleg, & Van Bockern, 1990). Acoose (1995) gives expression to those feelings of fragmentation: "I was overwhelmed with negative feelings and confused because my own way of seeing, being, knowing and understanding the world ... had continuously been assaulted by the canadian [sic] nation's ideological forces" (p. 19). Healing needs to take place as students reconnect with self, others, and the true history of their peoples. As Acoose (1995) says, there is the need for reconnection to those who have gone before in the cultural past: "I began to clearly understand the importance of reconnecting to the collective consciousness of my … ancestors" (p. 20).

In their interviews with graduates of one Aboriginal teacher education program, Friesen and Orr (1998) report that the program affirmed and expanded the student's Aboriginal identity by providing a supportive educational environment. For these students, unlike previous experiences in school, their culture was positively represented in Native studies and Aboriginal language classes. In our program, the students take classes in Indian education, Indian languages, Indian studies, and Indian art. As is the case with other Aboriginal teacher education programs, one of the challenges facing our program is to "look beyond the inclusion of Aboriginal studies and Aboriginal languages as add ons to seek a vision for a uniquely Aboriginal way of schooling" (Hill, 1998, p. 6). Our search for an Aboriginal way of doing our outdoor education courses meant that we needed to make changes.

Change: Alternative Structure and Delivery

When the educational practices are not meeting the needs of the Aboriginal students in a holistic manner, then change is essential. Senge (1990) describes the successful process of change in education. "At the heart of a learning organization is the shift of mind— from seeing ourselves as separate from the world to connected to the world …. a learning organization is a place where people are continually discovering how they create their reality. And how they can change it" (pp. 12–13). Connections are important in any process of educational change but even more so in Aboriginal education. We found that the ones most able to lead students to connect and reconnect with themselves, their past, and the world around them were the elders.[2] We began to ask the elders to take a more prominent role in teaching the courses and found their knowledge and way of teaching provided us with an Aboriginal way of "educating." The elders' teachings reflected an educational philosophy that stressed relationships, strove for balance and harmony, and was holistic in its approach.

Holistic Connection: The Elders' Ways

The elders assisted in promoting change by expanding our capabilities as faculty and students to understand our world and ourselves in a holistic manner; to clarify our shared visions and to improve our shared worldviews. We came to see that it was our responsibility to learn from the elders and the land. The elders' teachings modelled a relationship to the land that was based on interconnectedness and respect. This value is, and has been, at the core of many Aboriginal peoples' beliefs. Long ago, Chief Seattle articulated this viewpoint:

> *Teach your children what we have taught ours. Whatever happens to the earth happens to the children of the earth. The earth does not belong to us; we belong to the earth. All things are connected, like the blood which unites one family .... My people love this earth as the newborn loves its mother's heartbeat .... Care for it as we have cared for it. And with all your strength, with all your mind, with all your heart, preserve it for your children. (Quoted in Gilliland, 1999, p. 36)*

Elders speak for the need for connection: the connection in time and place, of past, present, and future. "From our children will come those braves, who will carry the torches to the places where our ancestors rest ... this is how the void will be filled between the old and the new ways" (Chief Dan George, 1974, p. 55). Elsewhere, other elders have indicated, "a people's sense of place and identity is tied to the land/sea" (Saskatchewan Department of Education, Training and Employment, 2000, p. 19). As the elders took over the teaching in our outdoor education classes, we could see how their teaching provided students with a connectedness to the land and to the past, and how they encouraged these future teachers to make those connections for the children they would teach in the future.

Cultural Camp as Holistic Education

In the change to make our outdoor education program into a cultural camp, we feel we have found one way of doing "uniquely Aboriginal education." Cultural camp aims to enliven Aboriginal education through organized cultural teachings under the leadership of elders, Aboriginal community representatives, Indian education faculty, and Indian education students. It is dedicated to investigating the connections between the land and the elders, and to the practical dimensions of the four aspects of human life (Medicine Wheel Teachings) in the natural and social world. The Medicine Wheel is a symbol used in many different ways by many Indigenous nations. Lillian Dyck (1998) indicates that one can use the Medicine Wheel to understand ideas or to show how all things are living and interconnected. It can be used as a heuristic device or as a framework for thinking about things holistically. "The medicine wheel teaches us that we have four aspects to our nature: the physical, the mental, the emotional, and the spiritual. Each of these aspects must be equally developed in a healthy, well-balanced individual through the development and use of volition (i.e., will)" (Bopp, Bopp, Brown, &

Lane, 1985, p. 12). Students are encouraged to use a Medicine Wheel format (Figure 7.1) when developing lesson plans. For example, by equally developing the four aspects of the Medicine Wheel, students might be better able to plan for balance or harmony in their lesson.

Indian education students are taught to develop lesson plans that have a physical, emotional, mental, and spiritual objective. This holistic approach to attaining knowledge encompasses the four domains. By doing so, the students are able to provide a learning process in a manner that reflects the Aboriginal worldview. According to Lightning (1992), the learning process is described as "a process of internalization and actualization within oneself in a total way" (p. 243). Using the Medicine Wheel strives to support this view in order to encompass "a philosophy of educating for balance, harmony and well-being for the human condition" (p. 253).

The students are introduced to different methods of using the Medicine Wheel so they can work toward a personal development plan based on their personal needs, cultural experiences, and their cultural knowledge (Saskatchewan Department of Education, Training and Employment, 2000). It occurs through affirmation with what is being taught by the elders. Students develop their own holistic perspective regarding their relationships with their spiritual beliefs and practices, with other people, with the land, and with themselves. For example, the use of the Medicine Wheel in daily reflections and journal writing helps students to come to a personal understanding of the four domains in the learning experience. The Medicine Wheel presents students with a framework to help them develop a more informed

Figure 7.1 Lesson Plan Model.

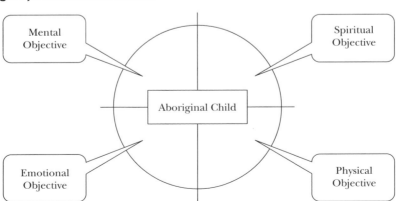

cultural identity and self-worth. The following visual model of the Medicine Wheel may be used to inspire creative writing (Figure 7.2).

This model is based on one way of viewing the Medicine Wheel as described by Gilliland with Reyhner (1988): "The East is symbolic of the sun and the fire and our own creative spirit. The south represents water and our emotions. The West is the place of Mother Earth and our intuition; the place of magic and dreams. North represents air and our minds filled with wisdom as we learn about the mystery of life" (p. 130). Ultimately, the goal for the students is to attain a balanced lifestyle by exploring in a natural way their cultural identity and heritage.

Preparation for Camp

Prior to attending the camp itself, time is spent with the students as a group, planning the activities of the camp together. Readings of traditional learning styles and elders' views of learning are presented and discussed so that students are aware of how to be with elders in the way that is appropriate to the elders' styles of teaching. Observation and listening are emphasized as elders often teach through oratory and activity. Because most of our students' formal learning experiences have been in a Western education system of learning, many of them are not familiar with how teaching and learning takes place with traditional teachers such as elders. For others, the interactions with elders awakens their awareness of learning processes they have experienced culturally, with grandparents or other relatives, but have buried inside under the pressure of Western ways of teaching.

Figure 7.2 Medicine Wheel.

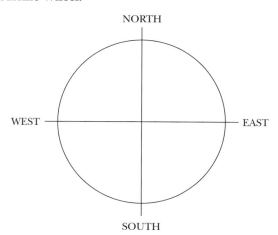

In preparation for living together, camp norms are established, reflecting traditional values that strive to embody individual autonomy and decision making while respecting and considering the well-being of the group as a whole and the maintenance of harmony within the group. The difference in structuring of time is also discussed with the students to prepare them to be flexible since the cultural camp breaks from the usual structuring and sequencing of content and time to a more "organic" flow of activities. We do have a tentative outline of times for activities, but this may change for various reasons. For example, sometimes the weather is not right or an activity with an elder takes much longer than planned. Activities begin when others end or when the elder and/or participants are ready to start.

Students are organized into smaller groups when working with the elders, so these are organized prior to leaving. The small group structure more closely approximates traditional experiential learning situations, providing more opportunity for individual one-on-one interaction with the elder. The group, including elders, students, and faculty, meets as a whole in a circle to start the day and bring it to a close. Although the camp location and activities vary depending on the students, faculty, and elders involved, for the sake of brevity, what follows is an example of what might typically happen in a day at one of our past fall cultural camps.

A Day at Camp

Picture a clear, warm, fall day on the prairies. With your classmates, you travel out of the city chatting excitedly about the days to come. You feel yourself relax as the sky and the vast expanse of the prairie landscape opens up around you. You arrive at a site nestled in the hills of the beautiful Qu'Appelle Valley beside Ketepwa Lake in the traditional lands of the Cree, Saulteaux, and Métis. Accompanying you are your instructors and elders Willie Peigan and Clara and Stanley Pasqua, all from the nearby Pasqua Cree Saulteaux First Nation.

A typical day combines individual reflection with opportunities for experiencing the outdoors from a cultural and elders' perspective. You start your day with a cold wash and a slow walk up the hill to the tipi where you choose to spend time with the elders in a sunrise pipe ceremony and prayer. After a hot breakfast, you participate in traditional fall activities in small groups with the different elders and instructors. Activities might include such things as bannock-making, crushing chokecherries, cutting meat or fish to dry, constructing a drying rack for the meat, or cooking berry soup over the open fire. The camp is a hum of activity as people share work, talk, and laugh.

After lunch, you and your peers gather around the fire or in the tipi to hear the elders talk: they may tell stories, relate personal experiences, or talk about cultural symbols and worldview, such as the importance of the circle. Elder Clara can be heard explaining how the circle relates to the cycles of nature and nature's tendency toward wholeness. Then it's off into the hills, with Elder Clara Pasqua in the lead, to identify different plants used by the Saulteaux people in that area and to pick certain plants or berries. Before supper, you have time to be on your own or do activities with others such as canoeing. After supper, it's back to the tipi or fire for a talking circle to share and reflect upon the day's learning. The evening is usually a time for fun when you may choose to do crafts with Elder Clara, listen to the stories of Elder Stanley Pasqua, dance to the fiddle music provided by Elder Willie Peigan, or sing with an instructor while she plays her guitar.

Camp Setting as Teacher and Healer

The learning experience is different out on the land than it is in the confines of a walled university classroom. The natural beauty of the life and landscape that surround them affect students at camp. When asked how learning differs in the camp setting from the university, Elder Clara Pasqua says that a person doesn't feel so closed when they get out onto the land. A transformation happens when you get out of the enclosure of square buildings, the pavement, and concrete sidewalks of the city. Clara says the students are more open, and she points to her heart—open to their surroundings, to themselves, to others, and to learning—when they are out on the land.

Interaction with the elders at the camp provides different opportunities to connect with the land in a way that acknowledges how the natural world provides the gifts of life. At the camp, students are taught through example that they must live with the laws of nature in order to be sustained by nature. For the first time in their lives, some of the students are able to see how the natural world provides people with the necessities of life.

The elders demonstrate a particular relationship with the land. They talk of the need to value the land, emphasizing the respect that is needed in relationship with it, because it is the land that gives us sustenance and healing through food and medicine. Students gain through lived experiences where they find "parallels between the spiritual attributes of plants and their medicinal properties" (Savinelli, 1997, p. 7). Repeatedly during the day, in gesture or ceremony, the elders show appreciation for the different aspects of life and always remember to give thanks, especially for their food before eating. They model the importance of "giving back" to the land. For example, before taking any plants, Elder Clara performs a quiet ceremony, modelling prayer, offerings, and thankfulness. She will then explain to students that they may now gather sage that can be used both as a medicine and as a *smudge*—a cleansing wash of smoke from a medicine plant. You will hear her explain why and how to show the respect for the land and the life of the plant by "giving back" to the earth when something is taken from it.

Elder Clara also explains how our natural earth can serve as a living guide if we learn to pay attention, just as McGaa (1990) refers to Mother Earth as a "living bible from which one can see, hear, touch, feel and learn a great deal. Nature or Mother Earth was made by the Great Spirit; therefore, there are obviously many revelations that the two-leggeds may learn if they simply have the sense to look" (p. 32).

The students do observe and openly express the impact that the land has upon them. In their daily journals they write about their sense of peace and wholeness. They may include pictures to capture the beauty of life and landscape, or samples of meaningful artifacts they collect. In another activity, after spending some quiet time alone on the land, students are asked to write poetry about their learning from that experience. They often write about the feeling of strong bonds and connections that the land arouses in them, not just with the land but their families that they have left behind. Their poetry has the power to move themselves and others to tears. Often they are astounded by their own creative abilities.

Being in a camp setting builds personal connections with others who are there. First, everyone is in very close proximity with others at the camp for 24 hours a day. All people at the camp develop an intense personal bond through the common participation in different activities. There is time and openness for more personal sharing. For example, a student and instructor who went on a long walk together ended up talking about their common experiences as parents trying to guide daughters through the challenges of their teen years. Years later, the student recalled how much she had appreciated this walk and how important the resulting closeness in their relationship was to her. For the students themselves, many groups have had a propensity for late night storytelling, seeing who can outdo the other with scary stories so that every noise outside the tipi means they need to stay close together for protection and comfort, then laughing at themselves the next day. These close, personal bonds formed at the camp stay with students, instructors, and elders throughout their teacher education program and beyond.

Connecting and Reconnecting through the Elders

One of the most influential ways that our cultural camp reconnects students to the knowledge of their ancestors and forms a positive identity is by having the elders as teachers. Cultural teachings are the foundation of the identity of Aboriginal people, and a positive identity is one of the primary purposes of Aboriginal education. "We want education to give our children a strong sense of identity, with confidence in their personal worth and ability" (National Indian Brotherhood, 1972). It is not just children but also our adult students who, as future teachers of children, need a strong sense of cultural identity and confidence in their personal abilities and worth.

Teaching by the elders is not only important for the information they provide but also by the way in which they do the teaching. "Traditional wisdom is both content and process. It speaks of how things should be done as well as what should be done .... The North American intellectual tradition is, for the most part, an oral one. This means that the transmission of knowledge is an interpersonal and, often, intergenerational process .... Oral societies depend on cultural memory. Elders link the coming generations with the teachings of past generations. The cultural teachings are the foundation of the Aboriginal peoples' identity" (Report of the Royal Commission on Aboriginal Peoples, 1996, pp. 116–117). The importance of this intergenerational link is embedded in the language. In Cree, the root words of great-grandchild (or descendent), *aniskotapan*, are *anis*, which means connectedness, and *otape*, which is to pull or carry, so the literal translation of great-grandchild is one who is connected and pulled or carried along (Keith Goulet, personal communication, 1998).

The teaching relationship used by the elders is a holistic one that models not just the mental and physical but also the incorporation of the spiritual and emotional domain in the learning experience. In addition to ceremonies, Elder Willie Peigan talks about change, how the culture of the Cree has changed in his lifetime and the importance of faith, the belief in yourself, and the ability to find the strength to meet the challenges presented by a changing world. Elder Clara Pasqua may talk specifically to the young women about traditional behaviours of respect and responsibility. Many of our students have not been born into their traditional Aboriginal knowledge, therefore Clara will take the time to explain the significance of the number four, the ceremonies, the dances, the Sweat Lodge, the four-direction offerings in the Pipe Ceremony, and the Sun Dance.

Another aspect of how the elders teach is their use of a mixture of teasing, comical gestures, and laughter. These teaching strategies allow the elders the opportunity to present serious traditional foundations and principles in a way that the students receive the new knowledge with a greater sense of curiosity and interest. The teasing drops the formality of the Western view of teacher and student. The laughter creates a warm feeling that lets the student and teacher get close. Students are able to overcome feelings of shyness and the self-consciousness of trying to do something new when their teachers can laugh at themselves and their own actions. It does not in any way mean this learning is a frivolous endeavour. Elders are able to convey warmth and closeness with a twinkle in their eye without losing sight of the importance, attention, and respect the learning activity deserves.

One might observe that the interaction may not necessarily be face-to-face and that the elders offer a significant wait time for student responses. This allows for active student participation in the discussion. Another notable aspect of their presentation is the use of a natural object during discussion time, such as a stick, stone, or leaf. Elder Clara Pasqua describes the use of this object as either a discipline technique or attention-getter to help the child focus. It may be presented as an artistic or scientific object from the natural world at the appropriate time or during a teachable moment. Elder Clara emphasizes that this teachable moment must come from the heart of the teacher. Cardinal (Kenny, 1997) supports this opinion by stating, "we can use science in different ways but also the elders said make it from the heart, make it beautiful. We always did things beautifully, even our clothes, everything. Art was not a separate world in our language. It was the way we lived" (p. 77). The elders' teaching of this worldview emphasizes interconnectedness to the land, air, water, wildlife, human beings, and spirituality.

Elders are esteemed for both their knowledge and life experiences. They are the source of the Indigenous concepts, values, and knowledge structures that are embedded in the language and ways of being in the culture. Elders are the "keepers of the wisdom, the libraries of Native communities, repositories of knowledge from time immemorial ... [and] are especially attuned to [the three areas] of Stories, Ceremonies, and Values" (Hanohano, 1999, p. 216). The values, worldviews, and ways of being of Aboriginal peoples were embedded in all the elders did; the stories they shared, the ceremonies they performed, the cultural activities they engaged in with the students and faculty.

During the activities, ceremonies, and talking circles, elders share stories of Indigenous wisdom and of their life experiences. Stories told by the elders are the building blocks of awareness and reconnection: a tool of decolonization as the story of the elder usurps the story of the colonizer. "Stories are at the heart of what explorers and novelists say about strange regions of the world; they also become the method colonized people use to assert their own identity and the existence of their own history" (Said, 1993, p. xii). In stories, you see yourself and your people. The stories of the Elders, rather than being from the perspective of "other," are stories of "self," of their life struggles as Aboriginal people. For example, Elder Clara Pasqua tells about the time she and other women from her reserve hand-cuffed themselves together to blockade a highway to get money for education. Elder Stanley Pasqua tells of his struggle as chief to get compensation for flooding of reserve land. Elder Willie Peigan describes how ceremonies were kept alive in a time when they were declared illegal. These and others accounts by the elders have an impact on the students. In stories of their own history, they see their peoples as strong and capable, engaged in the struggle against oppression.

Students are able to reconnect as they are exposed to the true history of their people through the stories of the elders. In the elders' teachings, this reconnecting with the past goes beyond mere awareness to a sense of obligation to both the past and the future. Lee Maracle (Quoted in Henley, 1989) expresses this point in her poem "The Growing Family (I Am Woman)":

> *I know nothing*
> *Of great mysteries*
> *Know less of creation*
> *I do know*
> *That the farther backward*
> *In time that I travel*
> *The more grandmothers*
> *And the farther forward*
> *The more grandchildren*
> *I am obligated to both (p. 281)*

The elders talk about this obligation with reference to learning not only from the present but remembering where we came from and looking to where we are going. Elder Willie reminds students not to forget the past hardships and good times but also to be strong in the present and to be sure of their future. Elder Clara Pasqua emphasizes that we are one with the land—one body, one heart, and one spirit; therefore, we must not forget our grandmothers and we must remember our grandchildren. Each student has an obligation not just to connect with the past but also to bring together the past and the present in order to fulfill obligations with self and, as future teachers, with children, the ones of the future.

Connecting to Self: Strengthening Identity

The cultural camp experience provides students with an experience of unique bonding and a respectful connection to the land, the elders, the faculty, and each other. Students return to their everyday lives with a better understanding of what it means to be Aboriginal. Many express a renewed spiritual strength that helps them accept and work at the challenges of being Aboriginal in our Canadian society. Students who have lost their cultural connections due to residential school effects and/or other historical or societal reasons, begin to recognize that their Aboriginal history is rich with tradition, values, and a life-giving philosophy. This cultural connection creates a renewed interest and respect for both the land and themselves as Aboriginal peoples.

Fulfillment of the Vision

To us, the cultural camp is one way to do "uniquely Aboriginal education." The camp embodies holistic education. All participants are there to share and learn together from one another. The pace of learning is different in that students are given time to reflect and to think about meaning, not just in terms of other people (as in the author of an article or book), but also in terms of the meaning of learnings to themselves and to their own lives. The context is important because the immersion in the natural life and land of the camp helps the participants to be open and true to themselves and each other. The content of the information shared by the elders is crucial in that it provides the bridge to connect students with the past, with the true history of Aboriginal peoples. Students not only learn about the importance of the Aboriginal worldview but also see it in practice, embedded in the actions, activities, ceremonies, and the stories of the elders. They experience a holistic learning relationship that emphasizes the spiritual development of individual gifts and attentions, and that models the emotional in the laughter and tears that are an integral part of the experience.

The threads of cultural discontinuity are pulled together to become an affirmation of cultural continuity. Students reconnect to their past, to the "collective consciousness" of their people. For all participants in the cultural camp, stories reflecting the Aboriginal perspective of history and the experience of working within the philosophy of Aboriginal peoples develop the foundation needed to go forward, secure in the knowledge that all have developed a network of support as we continue to seek new visions for our life today and in the future. For this, we honour and give our respect and thanks to the elders of the cultural camps who have led the way.

> *They told me to tell you the time is now*
> *They want you to know how they feel*
> *So listen carefully, look toward the sun.*
> *The Elders are watching. (Bouchard & Vickers, 1995, p. 105)*

REFERENCES

Acoose, J. (1995). *Iskwewak–kah'ki yaw ni wahkomakanak: Neither Indian princesses nor easy squaws*. Toronto: Women's Press.

Adams, H. (1989). *Prison of grass: Canada from a Native point of view* (2nd ed.). Saskatoon, SK: Fifth House.

Battiste, M. (Ed.). (2000). *Reclaiming Indigenous voice and vision*. Vancouver: University of British Columbia Press.

Binda, K.P., with Calliou, S. (Eds.). (2001). *Aboriginal education in Canada: A study in decolonization*. Mississauga, ON: Canadian Educators' Press.

Bopp, J., Bopp, M., Brown, L., & Lane, P., Jr. (1985). *The sacred tree*. Lethbridge, AB: Four Worlds Development Project.

Bouchard, D., & Vickers, R.H. (1979). Communication. In J. Archibald, E. Hampton, & E. Newton (1995). Organization of educational services in sparsely populated regions of Canada: Research & analysis report. Ottawa: Indian and Northern Affairs Canada.

Brendtro, L., Brokenleg, M., & Van Bockern, S. (1990). *Reclaiming youth at risk: Our hope for the future*. Bloomington, IN: National Educational Service.

Campbell, M. (1973). *Half-breed*. Toronto: McClelland and Stewart.

Dyck, L. (1998). An analysis of Western, Feminist and Aboriginal science using the Medicine Wheel of the Plains Indians. In L. Stiffarm (Ed.), *As we see … Aboriginal pedagogy* (pp. 87–102). Saskatoon, SK: University of Saskatchewan Press.

Friesen, D., & Orr, J. (1998). New paths, old ways: Exploring the places of influence on the role of identity. *Canadian Journal of Native Education, 22*(2), 188–200.

George, Chief Dan. (1974). *My heart soars*. Surrey, BC: Hancock House.

Gilliland, H., with Reyhner, J. (1988). *Teaching the Native American*. Dubuque, IA: Kendall/Hunt Publishing.

Gilliland, H. (1999). *Teaching the Native American*. Dubuque, IA: Kendall/Hunt Publishing.

Graveline, F.J. (1998). *Circle works: Transforming Eurocentric consciousness*. Halifax, NS: Fernwood Publishing.

Haig-Brown, C. (1988). *Resistance and renewal: Surviving the Indian residential school.* Vancouver: Tillacum Library.

Hanohano, P. (1999). The spiritual imperative of Native epistemology: Restoring harmony and balance to education. *Canadian Journal of Native Education, 23*(2), 206–219.

Henley, T. (1989). *Rediscovery, ancient pathways, new directions: Outdoor activities based on Native traditions.* Edmonton, AB: Lone Pine Publishing.

Hill, J. (1998, April). *Queen's university Aboriginal teacher education program: An exercise in partnership.* Paper presented at the American Educational Research Association Annual Meeting, San Diego, CA.

Kenny, C.B. (1997). The sense of art: A First Nations view. *Canadian Journal of Native Education, 22*(1), 77–84.

Kirkness, V.J. (1992). *First Nations and schools: Triumphs and struggles.* Toronto: Canadian Education Association.

Lightning, W. (1992). Compassionate mind: Implications of a text written by elder Louis Sunchild. *Canadian Journal of Native Education, 19*(2), 215–253.

McGaa, E.M. (1990). *Mother earth spirituality: Native American paths to healing ourselves and our world.* New York, NY: HarperCollins.

Means, R., with Wolf, M.J. (1995). *Where White men fear to tread: The autobiography of Russell Means.* New York, NY: St. Martin's Press.

Miller, J.R. (1996). *Shingwauk's vision: A history of Native residential schools.* Toronto: University of Toronto Press.

National Indian Brotherhood. (1972). *Indian Control of Indian Education.* Ottawa: Author.

Report of the Royal Commission on Aboriginal Peoples (RCAP). (1996). *Perspectives and realities* (Vol. 4). Ottawa: Canada Communication Group.

Said, E. (1993). *Culture and imperialism.* New York: Alfred A. Knopf.

Saskatchewan Department of Education, Training and Employment. (2000). *The common curriculum framework for Aboriginal language and culture programs kindergarten to grade 12: Western Canada protocol for collaboration in basic education.* Regina, SK: Author.

Savinelli, A. (1997). *Plants for power.* Taos, NM: Native Scents Inc.

Senge, P. (1990). *The fifth discipline: The art and practice of the learning organization.* New York: Doubleday/Currency.

NOTES

1 In different parts of Canada and the United States different terms are preferred to denote the original peoples of North America. As designated in the Canadian Constitution, we use the term "Aboriginal" in order to be inclusive of First Nations, Métis, and Inuit peoples who are each recognized as distinct groups. Where different terms are used in the context to which we are referring in our writing, we use those terms as well, such as "Indian" to refer to our college and our course names. In the international context, the term "Indigenous" is used.

2 The authors thank Elders Clara and Stanley Pasqua and Elder Willie Peigan from Pasqua First Nation in Saskatchewan. The wisdom provided by them in countless talks and personal interviews provided the foundation for this chapter. The sharing they did with us was done in a traditional manner without formal documentation. We respectfully and gratefully acknowledge their contribution to the development of our understanding of Aboriginal education.

• • • • • • • • • • • • • • • • • •

Part II: Integrationist Approaches

While parallelism is the dominant perspective in theories of Aboriginal educa-tion, a number of other approaches are also engaged. These can be generally labelled "integrationist" in character, and a number of representative contribu-tors are included. These chapters differ from parallelist perspectives in that they propose that the solution to Aboriginal marginalization lies in Aboriginal peoples' capacity to participate in Canadian society and the global environ-ment. The benefits of a scientific and humanistic education are generally taken for granted, as well as is the need for upholding universal educational stan-dards. The focus is on how to ensure that Aboriginal peoples are able to benefit equally from a high-quality education. And while some integrationists accept the need to protect Aboriginal culture and ensure Native autonomy in the Cana-dian educational system, these proposals are meant to facilitate Aboriginal in-tegration, as opposed to perpetuating Aboriginal separation, within the state.

The goal of integration, however, is represented by two distinct visions—one that is influenced by liberalism and the other taking its inspiration from the tradition of political economy. Part II begins with six chapters that represent liberal integrationist perspectives. The first three examine primary and second-ary education generally, and are followed by three that analyze various aspects of post-secondary education. Three chapters from political economists follow the liberal integrationist perspectives.

The first liberal integrationist chapter is by John Richards, one of the most well-known critics of Canadian Aboriginal education policy. In this chapter, Richards discusses the linkage between education, employment, and income, and examines the possible reasons for the educational achievement gap be-tween non-Aboriginal and Aboriginal students (especially for Aboriginal people on reserves). Using data from schools in British Columbia, Richards examines the state of Aboriginal education and provides options for improving it today. These improvements, Richards concludes, should be oriented toward such activities as helping Aboriginal students to meet provincial standards and in-creasing parental choice.

Richards's chapter is followed by a piece that was part of the compilation published from the proceedings of the 2002 Aboriginal Policy Research Confer-ence. In this chapter, Jerry White, Nicholas Spence, and Paul Maxim discuss how the concept of social capital contributes to educational attainment among

Aboriginal students. Using particular policy and program examples from New Zealand, Australia, and Canada, White, Spence, and Maxim try to understand poor Aboriginal educational performance by linking it to the pool of resources and supports that groups rely upon when negotiating the school system. In examining Aboriginal education from the perspective of social capital, the authors point out that group support can be counterproductive if the expectation of educational attainment is low. Instead, linking and bridging with other cultural groups with higher academic achievement has been shown to be significant in raising educational levels.

The next contribution is by Michael Mendelson, a critic of the obsolete legislative structures pertaining to Aboriginal education. In this chapter, Mendelson argues that a legislative vacuum exists with respect to Aboriginal education, resulting in the absence of Aboriginal educational institutions. He identifies the major missing legal elements and proposes new legislative measures that would give Aboriginal peoples the authority required to establish their own school boards and regional education agencies. According to Mendelson, entire system reform is needed. He asserts that the existing system is colonialist and a First Nations Education Act would recognize Aboriginal jurisdiction over education and eliminate paternalistic structures like the Indian Act. These legislative changes, in Mendelson's view, are necessary before Aboriginal education system reform can proceed.

These three general chapters on Aboriginal primary and secondary education are followed by three liberal integrationist perspectives on post-secondary education. The first chapter on post-secondary education, by Calvin Helin and Dave Snow, looks at the specific problem of funding for Aboriginal post-secondary students. Helin and Snow argue that education, generally, is highly correlated with income and employment and maintain that financial problems are a common reason given for why Aboriginal students do not complete post-secondary education. They maintain, however, that one of the existing programs providing funds to Aboriginal students—the Post-Secondary Student Support Program—contains serious flaws. Helin and Snow undertake a comprehensive critique of this program and then explore alternative funding mechanisms that would provide better incentives and empower Native students.

Helin and Snow's chapter is followed by another on post-secondary education. This piece, by Judy Hardes, is a summary of her Capping Project for a master of education degree in educational psychology that concerned strategies for recruiting and retaining Aboriginal students at Lakeland College in Alberta. In this chapter, Hardes discusses the socio-economic, educational, and cultural circumstances that have an impact on Aboriginal students' capacity to complete post-secondary education. Hardes points out that there are a number of cultural features in the Native population that make post-secondary education alienating. She also discusses the debates that surround the provision of special programs for Aboriginal students and outlines a number of strategies that have been proposed to increase the numbers of Native people completing post-secondary education.

The final chapter from a liberal perspective is Robert McGhee's examination of the specific case of Aboriginal participation in the discipline of archaeology. McGhee discusses what he perceives to be a disturbing trend in the discipline—one that he refers to as the acceptance of the flawed concept of Aboriginalism. Aboriginalism, explains McGhee, is the notion that there is such a thing as an essential "authentic" Aboriginality. This concept assumes that Aboriginal peoples are fundamentally different from non-Aboriginals and that their culture is frozen in some distant past. McGhee explores why this concept has taken root in the discipline. He also argues that the acceptance of Aboriginalism has had negative consequences for many scientific disciplines, as well as for Aboriginal people themselves.

The six liberal integrationist chapters are followed by three from the political economy position. The first chapter espousing political economy assumptions is by Albert Howard with Frances Widdowson. This chapter, prepared originally as a paper for the 2009 Aboriginal Policy Research Conference, discusses the taboo he sees facing any researcher studying Aboriginal education policy. He maintains that well-intentioned advocates for Aboriginal aspirations usurp scientific epistemology to deny the reality of a cultural development gap. This taboo prevents discussion of the disparate features that account for much of the difficulty that Native students encounter in education. Howard explores the nature of this gap in detail and argues that it must be acknowledged in order to effectively address the educational problems facing the Aboriginal population. Specifically, he maintains that this gap be addressed through high-quality, publicly funded educational services.

Howard's chapter is followed by a piece by Elizabeth Rata—a New Zealand political economist who studies Maori-settler relations. In this chapter, Rata explores the opposing explanations for the persistent low achievement of Maori students—socio-economic class and culturalism. Rata points out that the culturalist explanation has become dominant, but this view lacks evidential support. Some of the negative implications of culturalism's attempt to institutionalize ethnicity are also examined.

The final chapter from a political economy viewpoint is provided by Frances Widdowson. This piece has been included not only for its content; in its original form, it was the paper mentioned earlier implicated in hate speech allegations by certain members of the Canadian Political Science Association. In this chapter, Widdowson examines the incorporation of Indigenous theories and methodologies into the discipline of political science. She argues that since these theories and methodologies lack the rigour that is demanded in an academic discipline, they present problems for political science and the

Aboriginal people who embrace them. As science is an important contributor to intellectual progress, Widdowson points out that encouraging ethnic exceptionalism and spiritually based worldviews acts to justify Aboriginal isolation and marginalization.

The inclusion of these various integrationist perspectives is intended to stimulate debate on Aboriginal education policy. As will be seen in this part of the book, differences exist not only between parallelists and integrationists but also within integrationism itself. In spite of the differences between integrationists, it is important to point out that they share the assumption that increasing Aboriginal participation in Canadian society is the goal. These approaches vary in the extent to which they argue that Aboriginal culture should be incorporated into the educational system, but they all see this incorporation in terms of its capacity to help Aboriginal peoples enjoy the benefits of a scientific and humanistic education.

8

Schools Matter

John Richards

This chapter was originally published in *Creating Choices: Rethinking Aboriginal Policy*. Toronto: C.D. Howe Institute, 2006. Policy Study No. 43, pp. 56–100. Reproduced with permission.

The Industrial Revolution has permitted dramatic increases in per capita incomes, from nineteenth-century Manchester to twenty-first-century Shanghai. Often, however, it has also painfully disrupted old ways of living and doing things. One of the most painful of those disruptions is that endured by the trapping-hunting-fishing societies of North American Aboriginals.

The essence of the Industrial Revolution is the systematic application of new technologies to work. As industrial technologies have become more complex, the role of formal education has become more important. The benefits of formal education extend, of course, well beyond the narrowly economic. Universal education has been crucial to the emancipation of women, enabling them to pursue careers other than—or in addition to—parenting. And successful democracies need a free press and citizens able to read it, and thereby to understand the broad political issues at stake.

Elites have understood the value of formal education for millennia and their incomes have usually enabled them to acquire it for their children. In the absence of publicly provided education, only a minority among non-elites are able to, or choose to, make the necessary sacrifices for their children's education. No nation, in fact, has succeeded in preparing its citizens sufficiently for a modern industrial economy without providing universal public education—and the provision of such education is now considered a core responsibility of government.

The importance of a country's having an educated, literate population is acknowledged by the United Nations (UN) in its Human Development Index. Each country's index value is based on its per capita income, its life expectancy, and two measures of its education performance: literacy and school enrolment rates. In constructing the index this way, the UN is doing more than simply acknowledging the centrality of a good primary education system to any developing economy. The literacy component also indicates the fraction of a country's population that, lacking education, is likely to be left behind, condemned to low-paying occupations, even if the national economy prospers.

In wealthy industrial societies like Canada, enjoying the benefits of development requires more than simple literacy. Today, one needs, at the minimum, to have completed secondary education, while earning a "good" income increasingly requires some post-secondary training. Most Aboriginals have education levels that are too low to permit them to earn a "good" income. The result is high Aboriginal poverty rates.

Many historical factors enter into explanations of low Aboriginal education levels. History has, for example, made it harder for Aboriginal communities than for many other groups to champion the importance of educational achievement; in this regard, the legacy of family disruptions occasioned by residential schools looms large. But if Aboriginals are to escape poverty, they must become better educated. As I hope to demonstrate in this chapter, the links among education, employment, and income hold as much for Aboriginals as they do for other Canadians. I also take advantage of the data available on Aboriginal student performance in British Columbia to focus on the situation among Aboriginal students attending that province's schools. I finish the chapter with an assessment of options for improving Aboriginal education outcomes.[1]

Education, Work, and Income

To begin to understand the links among education, employment, and income, it is worth looking at a snapshot of income distribution among Aboriginals and comparing it with the distribution among non-Aboriginals. Using data from the *Aboriginal Peoples Survey* (Canada, 2003c), Figure 8.1 illustrates income distributions

Figure 8.1 Income Distributions, Aboriginals On and Off Reserve and Non-Aboriginals, 2000.

A. Ages 25 to 44

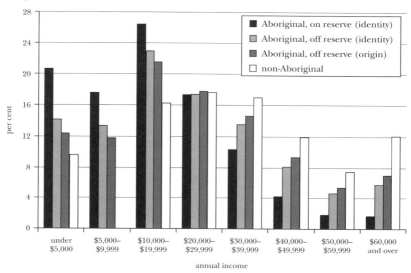

B. Ages 45 to 64

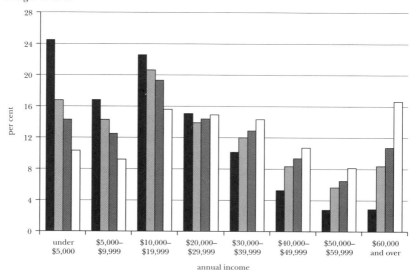

Source: Canada, 2003c.

in 2000 among the 25-to-44 and 45-to-64 age cohorts, but in the case of off-reserve Aboriginals makes a distinction between those who are Aboriginal by identity and those who are Aboriginal by ethnic origin.[2] The reader must bear in mind that these distributions refer to individuals, not to families. They do not take into account the number of dependents an individual supports, nor do they include income in-kind—such as access to band-supplied housing—a category of income much more important for those on reserve than off reserve.

For both age cohorts, Aboriginal median incomes are well below those of non-Aboriginals. This is emphatically so among the on-reserve population, whose median income is less than half that of non-Aboriginals. If one informally defines those with annual income below $20,000 as poor, nearly two-thirds of the on-reserve population, but only one-third of the non-Aboriginal population, are poor. By this admittedly imprecise measure, the poverty rate among off-reserve Aboriginals lies roughly halfway between those for on-reserve Aboriginals and non-Aboriginals. Indeed, the poverty rate among off-reserve Aboriginals by ethnic origin is closer to that for non-Aboriginals than to the rate for the on-reserve population.

If one defines prosperity to mean an annual income above $50,000—a low threshold—a quarter of the older cohort and a fifth of the younger cohort of non-Aboriginals qualify. The corresponding proportions among the on-reserve populations are very low: 6% for the older cohort and 3% for the younger. Similar to the poverty rate, the prosperity rate among off-reserve Aboriginals lies between those for on-reserve populations and non-Aboriginals.

Another way of interpreting the distributions in Figure 8.1 is to use the median income of non-Aboriginals to define economic success. As Table 8.1 shows, according to the 2001 census, just over a third of individuals who identify themselves as Aboriginals and live off reserve had incomes above the non-Aboriginal median, as did a slightly higher fraction of Aboriginal-origin individuals living off reserve. By contrast, only a fifth of Aboriginals living on reserve enjoyed incomes above the non-Aboriginal median.

What emerges from these income distributions is that off-reserve Aboriginal populations are considerably more prosperous than those on reserve. Why such large differences among Aboriginals? The most important explanation, as the following section explores in some detail, is in their relative levels of employment and education.

Table 8.1 Measuring Economic Success, Aboriginals On and Off Reserve and Non-Aboriginals, 2000.

	Aboriginals			
	On-Reserve Identity	**Off-Reserve Identity**	**Off-Reserve Origin**	**Non-Aboriginals**
Ages 24–44				
Median Income, 2000 ($)	13,800	19,700	22,000	29,000
Share with Incomes				
Below $20,000 (%)	65	51	46	34
Above $50,000 (%)	3	10	12	20
Above non-Aboriginal Median (%)	20	34	38	50
Ages 45–64				
Median Income, 2000 ($)	12,800	18,800	22,300	29,900
Share with Incomes				
Below $20,000 (%)	64	52	46	35
Above $50,000 (%)	6	14	17	25
Above non-Aboriginal Median (%)	21	35	40	50

Source: Author's calculations from Canada, 2003c.

The Link between Work and Income

Figure 8.2 draws from the 2001 census to illustrate the relationship between employment and income among selected groups of Canadians in their prime earning years between the ages of 25 and 44.[3] Those in this age group are old enough to have completed their education and training, and young enough to have benefitted from the emphasis on formal education over the past four decades: the oldest entered school in the early 1960s, the youngest in the early 1980s. The figure plots the relationship between income and the employment rate for this age cohort but separates it into six provincial groupings (the six provinces with substantial Aboriginal populations), either Aboriginal or non-Aboriginal, and, for the Aboriginal populations, by residence either on or off reserve. This division thus allocates each of the six provinces' population ages 25 to 44 into one of three categories—18 groups in all.

As the figure reveals, the link between employment and income exists among the various Aboriginal groups as much as it does between Aboriginals and non-Aboriginals. Unambiguously, the

Figure 8.2 Median Incomes of Aboriginals On and Off Reserve and Non-Aboriginals, Ages 25–44, Selected Provinces, by Employment Rate, 2000.

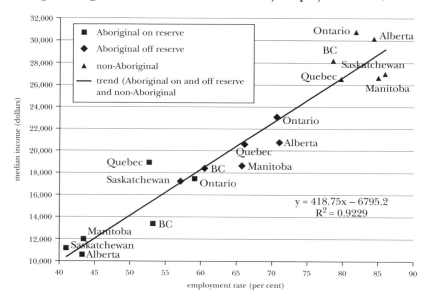

Source: Canada, 2003c.

poorest of the 18 groups are on-reserve Aboriginals living in the Prairie provinces, where median incomes in 2000 were less than $12,000 and employment rates were below 45%. The average of the median incomes of the six off-reserve groups was about 45% higher than that of the six on-reserve groups. The wealthiest Aboriginals, those living off reserve in Ontario, enjoyed twice the median income of on-reserve Prairie Aboriginals. In turn, the six non-Aboriginal groups had, on average, median incomes that were about 45% higher than those of off-reserve Aboriginals. A trend line across all 18 groups reveals that a 10-percentage-point increase in the employment rate is accompanied by an increase of nearly $4,200 in the median income.

In allowing individuals to escape poverty, employment clearly matters a great deal. But, to get a good job, education matters more now than in generations past. A century ago, the large fraction of the labour force employed in Canada's forests, factories, and mines earned good wages regardless of formal education. In the twenty-first century, far fewer such jobs exist. Aggravating the implication of this trend, low-end wages have risen more slowly over the past half-century than high-end wages, resulting in greater wage dispersion (see Organisation for Economic Co-operation and Development [OECD], 1996). For anyone now entering the labour force, limited formal education means fewer job opportunities and wages even lower than average in the jobs available than in decades past.

That the link between education level and income applies as much to Aboriginals as to others in the labour force is evident from Figure 8.3, which again divides the Aboriginal population into those living on and off reserve.[4] As the education level of Aboriginals rises, so does their median income. The figure also reveals that there are, among off-reserve Aboriginals and non-Aboriginals but less evident among on-reserve Aboriginals, three educational steps. The first step up, in terms of increased income, takes place upon completion of high school, which is now the minimum qualification for many entry-level jobs.[5] Those who aspire to reasonably well-paying jobs need to reach at least the second step, completion of a trade certificate. The third step is completion of a university degree.

Figure 8.3 Median Incomes of Aboriginals On and Off Reserve and Non-Aboriginals, by Level of Education, 1995.

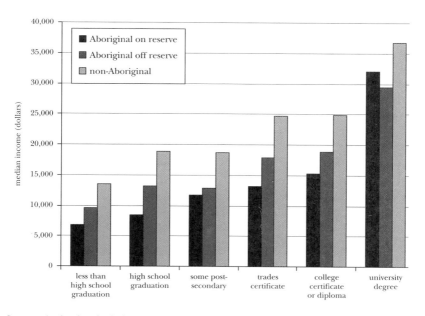

Source: Author's calculations, as reported in Drost and Richards (2003).

Again, looking at the 18 groups of 25-to-44-year-olds from the 2001 census, the employment rate obviously rises with education level, as Figure 8.4 illustrates in terms of high school graduation.[6] A higher education level leads to the possibility of a better-paying job, the rewards from which are likely to outweigh those from nonwork options, such as social assistance.

TWO SNAPSHOTS OF OFF-RESERVE ABORIGINALS

Two recent Statistics Canada studies of social conditions among off-reserve Aboriginals offer further evidence of the links among education, employment, and income. From one study looking at Aboriginal employment in the four western provinces (Canada, 2005a) comes the good news that employment rates among off-reserve Aboriginals with completed post-secondary education and those among non-Aboriginals with comparable education differ by a single percentage point: 82.5 versus 83.5%. There is more good news. At just 1.5 percentage points, the employment gap between non-Aboriginals and Métis has almost closed. Albertans have a reputation as hard workers; their employment rate is traditionally the highest of the 10 provinces.

Figure 8.4 Employment Rate, Aboriginals On and Off Reserve and Non-Aboriginals, Ages 25–44, Selected Provinces, by Percentage with High School Graduation Certificate or Higher Education, 2001.

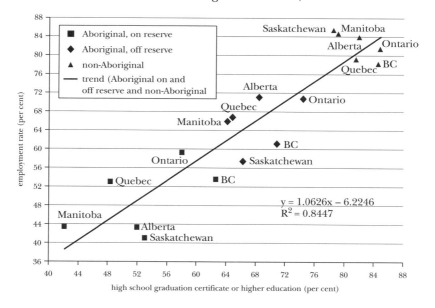

Source: Canada, 2003c.

In another sign of success, the employment rate among off-reserve Alberta Aboriginals—including here both those identifying as Indian and as Métis—now exceeds the rate among non-Aboriginals in British Columbia (see Figure 8.5).

Although off-reserve Aboriginal employment rates have improved since the 2001 census, this study also reveals serious remaining gaps:

- Young off-reserve Aboriginals ages 15 to 24 have an employment rate far below that of young non-Aboriginals: 44 versus 62%.

- Overall, the employment rate remains much higher for non-Aboriginals than for off-reserve Indians: 65 versus 50%. Racism may play a role in explaining low Indian employment rates, but the major factor undoubtedly is low education levels—which reflect the inadequacies of provincially run and band-run schools for Indian children.

- Employment rates are particularly low among off-reserve Aboriginals in Saskatchewan: 8 percentage points lower than in the neighbouring province of Manitoba.

Figure 8.5 Off-Reserve Employment Rate by Racial Identity, Western Provinces, April 2004–March 2005.

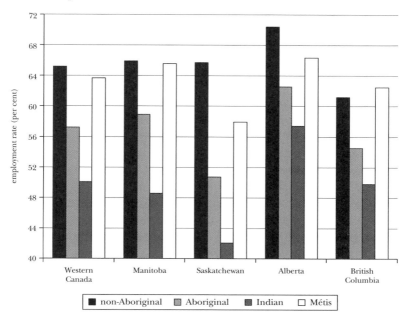

Source: Canada, 2005a, p. 6.

Figure 8.6 Increases in Education Attainment, Aboriginals and Non-Aboriginals, by Sex, Selected Cities, 1981–2001.

A. Males ages 20–24, not in school

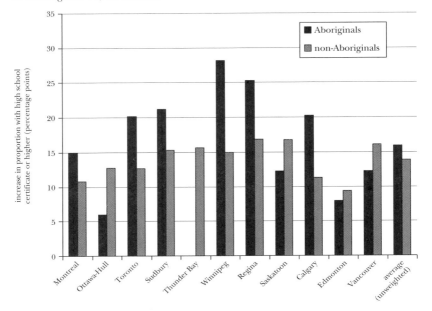

B. Females ages 20–24, not in school

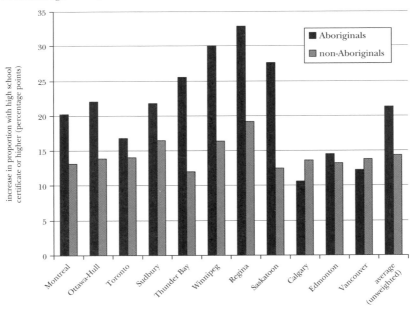

Source: Siggner and Costa, 2005.

The second Statistics Canada report (Siggner and Costa, 2005) examines changes in social outcomes among off-reserve Aboriginals in 11 Canadian cities between 1981 and 2001.[7] One such outcome is the level of education among young Aboriginal adults. Measured by the proportion with a high school certificate or higher, Aboriginal youth are catching up, although a gap remains. As Figure 8.6 shows, increases in Aboriginal education levels generally exceeded those of non-Aboriginals over the two decades—in nine of 11 cities in the case of women, in six of 11 in the case of men. Clearly, improvements have been more significant for girls than for boys.

As Table 8.2 indicates, in 1981 the proportion of young Aboriginal women and men in these cities with high school graduation certification was the same. By 2001, a five-percentage-point gap had emerged in favour of women. (A gender gap of similar size also exists among non-Aboriginals.) Accompanying the increases in Aboriginal education levels, Siggner and Costa (2005) also find that median earnings among Aboriginals increased relative to those among non-Aboriginals in eight of the 11 cities in their study (see Figure 8.7).

Table 8.2 Aboriginal and Non-Aboriginal Population Ages 20–24 Not Attending School and with High School Graduation or Higher Education, by Sex, Selected Cities, 1981 and 2001.

	Aboriginal				Non-Aboriginal			
	Males		Females		Males		Females	
	1981	2001	1981	2001	1981	2001	1981	2001
	(per cent)							
Montreal	64.3	79.3	67.2	87.4	75.1	85.9	78.0	91.1
Ottawa-Hull	70.0	76.0	65.4	87.4	76.2	89.0	79.9	93.8
Toronto	54.2	74.4	64.2	81.0	75.2	87.9	78.6	92.6
Sudbury	52.9	74.1	59.3	81.1	74.1	89.4	75.4	91.9
Thunder Bay	69.7	76.2	44.4	69.9	71.0	86.7	78.1	90.1
Winnipeg	34.5	62.7	37.6	67.6	69.0	84.0	73.3	89.7
Regina	47.5	72.8	32.8	65.7	68.6	85.5	72.9	92.1
Saskatoon	44.8	57.1	42.4	70.0	67.8	84.6	77.2	89.7
Calgary	47.3	67.6	58.8	69.4	72.6	83.9	76.0	89.6
Edmonton	50.0	57.9	52.2	66.7	71.9	81.3	75.3	88.5
Vancouver	54.6	66.9	65.6	77.8	73.1	89.2	79.0	92.8
Averages (unweighted)	53.6	69.5	53.6	74.9	72.2	86.1	76.7	91.1

Source: Siggner and Costa, 2005.

Figure 8.7 Ratios of Aboriginal to Non-Aboriginal Median Employment Incomes, Selected Cities, 1980 and 2000.

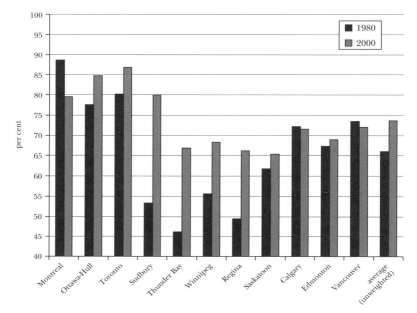

Source: Siggner and Costa, 2005.

A SUMMARY OF THE EDUCATION-INCOME LINK

Figure 8.8 provides a summary of the evidence on the link between education and income. The explanation for a positive link is twofold: higher education increases the employment rate, and it increases earnings among those who are employed. The slope of the trend line among the 12 Aboriginal groups implies that a 10-percentage-point increase in the Aboriginal high school completion rate increases annual median income by $2,900. Admittedly, a satisfactory explanation of comparative incomes requires a far more complex story than reference to high school completion. As Figure 8.8 shows, particularly among the on-reserve populations, there are outliers: Alberta, Saskatchewan, and British Columbia are well below the trend line; Quebec is well above.

Education and Location of Residence

Registered Indians, who make up the majority of Aboriginals who identify in the census as Indians—as opposed to Métis or Inuit—can choose to live either on or off reserve. On reserve, they can participate

Figure 8.8 Median Incomes, Aboriginals On and Off Reserve and Non-Aboriginals, Ages 25–44, Selected Provinces, by Percentage with High School Graduation Certificate or Higher Education, 2000.

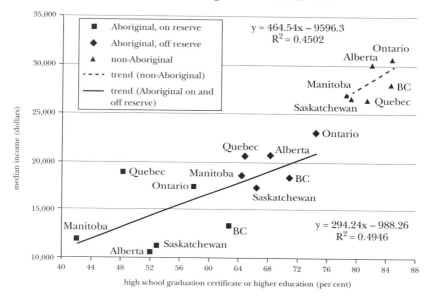

Source: Canada, 2003c.

more readily in the cultural life of the tribe, but the scarcity of well-paying jobs on or near most reserves means that Indians who live there have fewer incentives to invest in formal education than off-reserve Indians. This self-selection dynamic is probably important in explaining low on-reserve education levels; it is also probably part of the explanation for the underperformance of on-reserve schools.

Even if many on-reserve adults willingly forgo off-reserve employ-ment opportunities, on-reserve education attainment remains an important issue if their children are to be able to make a realistic choice, when the time comes, between an on- or off-reserve lifestyle. Figures 8.9–8.11 draw from the 2001 census, which allows for a finer examination of education achievements by area of residence, ethnic identity, and age cohorts than was formerly available. The youngest cohort for which census education data are available is those ages 15 to 24, which permits a tentative forecast of education levels among the next generation, although the evidence is obviously incomplete—many in this cohort are still in school or undertaking some form of post-secondary instruction. Figure 8.9 shows, by place of residence, the percentage of 15-to-24-year-olds among the Aboriginal population with a high school education or better. For comparison, the non-Aboriginal cohort is included. For all identity categories, education levels are highest in large cities (census metropolitan areas, labelled "urban CMA" in Figure 8.9). The results for small cities are somewhat lower, rural non-reserve results are lower yet, and the lowest results are for Indians on reserve.

So far, we have looked mostly at high school attainment levels among Aboriginals, but a more comprehensive survey of their education profiles, both on and off reserve, is revealing. Figure 8.10 summarizes education attainment levels of all Aboriginals and non-Aboriginals ages 15 years and older, as well as for those ages 15 to 24, 25 to 44, and 45 to 64. Figure 8.11 shows the differences between the education levels of the 25-to-44 and 45-to-64 age cohorts of on- and off-reserve Aboriginals and non-Aboriginals.

The good news is that as far as high school graduation rates are concerned, 25-to-44-year-old Aboriginals are better educated than those ages 45 to 64.[8] The bad news is that younger cohorts have not made comparable improvements at the higher education levels. Among off-reserve Aboriginals, the proportion with trades certificates (or

Figure 8.9 High School Certificate or Higher Education, by Identity Group and Area of Residence, 2001.

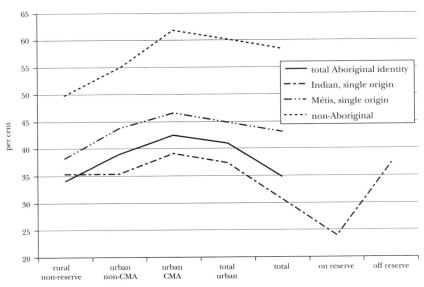

Source: Canada, 2003c.

better) is somewhat higher for 25-to-44-year-olds than for the older cohort. Among on-reserve Aboriginals, there is no intergenerational improvement at this education level. Among both on- and off-reserve

Figure 8.10 Education Profiles of Aboriginals On and Off Reserve and Non-Aboriginals, 2001.

A. Ages 15 and older

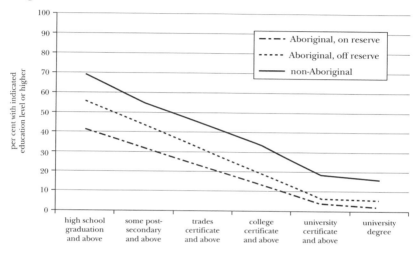

Source: Author's calculations from Canada, 2003c.

B. Ages 15 to 24

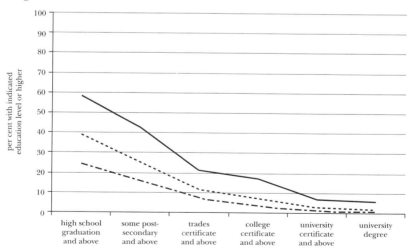

Source: Author's calculations from Canada, 2003c.

C. Ages 25 to 44

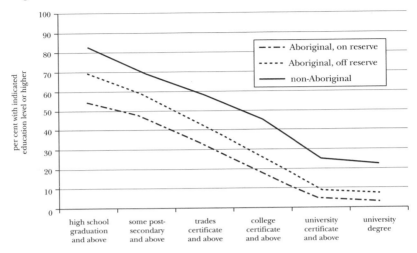

Source: Author's calculations from Canada, 2003c.

D. Ages 45 to 64

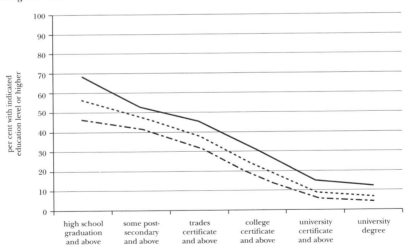

Source: Author's calculations from Canada, 2003c.

Figure 8.11 Changes in Education Profiles of Aboriginals On and Off Reserve and Non-Aboriginals, 25–44 Age Cohort less 45–64 Age Cohort, 2001.

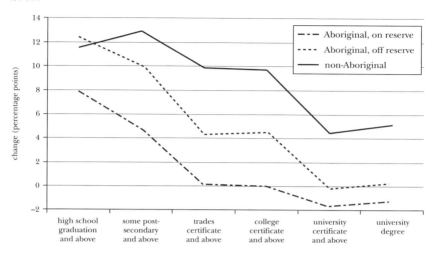

Source: Author's calculations from Canada, 2003c.

Aboriginals, the proportions with university degrees are essentially unchanged across age cohorts. Except at the high school graduation level, improvements among younger non-Aboriginals clearly dominate any analogous improvements for Aboriginals. In conclusion, there appears to be no intergenerational convergence of Aboriginal to non-Aboriginal education profiles at levels above high school graduation.

Indeed, as Figure 8.10, panel B, shows disconcertingly, 15-to-24-year-old Aboriginals are proportionately further behind the education attainments of the generation ahead of them than are 15-to-24-year-old non-Aboriginals.[9] At a minimum, here is evidence that should prompt a sense of urgency among those responsible for Aboriginal education. Low Aboriginal education outcomes are condemning the next generation to poverty.

What to Do about Aboriginal Education

Switching from description to policy, the obvious question to pose is, how can education levels be improved? Band control of on-reserve schools may have contributed to improved results since the 1969 White Paper, but it is not a panacea. Education outcomes are lower among on-reserve Aboriginals than among those off reserve and, as we have seen, young 15-to-24-year-old on-reserve Aboriginals are not making acceptable educational progress.

In 2000, Canada's Auditor General documented the glacial pace at which high school completion rates for on-reserve Aboriginals and non-Aboriginals were converging (Canada, 2000b). The report admonished the federal Department of Indian Affairs on "the need to articulate its role in education, to develop and use appropriate performance measures and to improve operational performance" (Canada, 2000b, pp. 4–5). In the 2004 report, the Auditor General returned to the issue, in a tone of frustration at the department's lack of urgency and dissatisfaction with its "hands-off" interpretation of its role (Canada, 2004c, s. 5.22). Noting that, according to 2001 census data, convergence rates had slowed, the report castigated the department's reluctance to evaluate on-reserve school outcomes.

> At the operational level, we found there is still ambiguity and inconsistency in the role of regional offices in fulfilling the Department's mandate and achieving its education objectives. The Department expects that the education delivered in schools located on reserves is comparable with what provinces offer off reserves and that students are able to transfer from band-operated to provincial schools without academic penalty. However, a number of school evaluations we reviewed clearly indicated that some students do not perform at their current grade level, suggesting that they cannot transfer to the same grade in the provincial education system. Yet, we saw no evidence that the regions consider this information in assessing whether First Nations meet the terms and conditions of their funding agreement and whether corrective action is required. Most regions continue to interpret their major role as that of providing a funding service. (Canada, 2004c, s. 5.37.)

With qualifications, the Auditor General's concerns also apply to the provinces. Aboriginal students attending provincially run schools outnumber those going to band-run reserve schools by nearly four to one. Furthermore, the school systems are not watertight compartments: Aboriginal families are much more mobile than most Canadians, and above-average numbers of Aboriginal students change schools, both within provincial systems and between on- and off-reserve schools. In both systems, high Aboriginal family mobility has a damaging effect on student performance.[10] Despite honourable exceptions, too many local school boards and provincial education ministries remain fatalistic about Aboriginal education outcomes. They are not exerting themselves to find out what is happening to Aboriginal students within their jurisdiction. They are reluctant to publish detailed school-by-school results.

Canada's Senate has also weighed in with an analysis of weak Aboriginal educational achievement in a report on urban youth.

There are many complex reasons why youth stop attending school. Some of these reasons include: racism; lack of parental involvement and guidance; resentment and embarrassment caused by feeling less successful scholastically than other students; instability caused by high rates of residential mobility; feelings of isolation caused by being in environments that are not culturally sensitive; an inability to afford text books, sporting equipment, and excursion fees; an unstable home life; and poverty.

Consistently, witnesses emphasized that the lack of parental involvement, guidance and support was partly responsible for the fact that Aboriginal youth continue to fare so poorly academically ….

The damaging effects of residential schools on Aboriginal peoples, cultures, and languages are now widely recognized …. [T]here is a deep mistrust among some Aboriginal people of mainstream educational institutions. The importance of obtaining a good education becomes secondary to what may be perceived as a further assimilative assault on Aboriginal culture, language and traditions. (Canada, 2003d, s. 1.4.)

The primary focus of the Senate report was the problems of poor, inner-city neighbourhoods, where Aboriginals are disproportionately likely to live (Richards, 2001). Fortunately, many urban Aboriginals are succeeding, but the senators are right: closing the education gap, particularly in poor neighbourhoods, will not be easy. But if more Aboriginals are to escape poverty, it is a gap that must be closed.

There is no inherent contradiction in studying the importance of Louis Riel in Prairie history *and* mastering geometry. What community leaders, both Aboriginal and non-Aboriginal, need to do is encourage learning that embodies both Aboriginal culture *and* the core academic skills and knowledge that contemporary society requires. Translating this obligation into pragmatic policy, however, means measuring school performance—championing the good and reforming the weak.

Aboriginal Students in British Columbia Schools

There is one exception to the critique made earlier that provinces are reluctant to publish data on performance of Aboriginal students in provincial schools. Since the late 1990s, the British Columbia education ministry has published a wealth of relevant information. In the 2002–2003 school year, 49,000 students in the British Columbia school system—8.2% of the total student count—identified themselves as Aboriginals. Of the Aboriginal students who entered grade eight in 1996, 42.5% graduated from high school within six years, compared with 79.2% of non-Aboriginals (see Figure 8.12).[11] Although Aboriginal high school completion rates are low, there has been improvement in recent years. For example, the 1996 Aboriginal cohort had

Figure 8.12 Student Retention and Graduation Rates, British Columbia Provincial Schools, Cohort Entering Grade Eight in 1996.

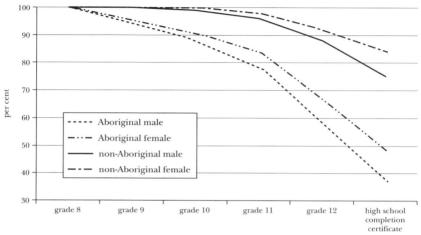

Source: British Columbia, 2003.

a completion rate that was 8.7 percentage points higher than that of the Aboriginal cohort that entered grade eight in 1991. Moreover, between 1991 and 1996, Aboriginal students slightly closed the gap between their high school completion rate and the non-Aboriginal rate, which increased by 6.4 percentage points (British Columbia, 2003, p. 26).

Quality of schooling matters as much as quantity. The importance of measuring school quality and of providing incentives to schools to perform better is a recurring theme in contemporary education policy analysis.[12] Over the past decade, and following an international trend, many provinces have set up province-wide tests intended to measure performance in core subjects at various stages of students' careers. Since 1999, British Columbia's education ministry has organized annual province-wide Foundation Skills Assessment (FSA) tests in reading, writing, and numeracy for nearly all students in grades four, seven, and 10.[13]

Students who take the FSA tests receive one of three results: "not meeting expectations," "meeting expectations," or "exceeding expectations." To preserve confidentiality, results are not reported for individual students, but they are available at the level of the individual school. In addition, each school's results are reported by a number of student characteristics, including whether the student identifies as being Aboriginal.[14] The most frequently used statistic from these tests is the "meet/exceed" score, which is the percentage of student tests in a school or larger unit that "meet" or "exceed" expectations. The score may refer to a particular grade, to a particular subject, to boys or girls, and so on.

If the quality of schools matters, as it undoubtedly does in explaining student performance, it is important to look at how particular schools are faring in terms of their Aboriginal students. Since the FSA program began in the 1999–2000 school year, approximately 400 British Columbia schools have annually reported results that include Aboriginal as well as non-Aboriginal students. A useful measure among these "mixed schools" is the meet/exceed score for Aboriginal and non-Aboriginal students, respectively, in a particular school. This statistic averages FSA results within a particular school over all relevant grades and all test components.

Figure 8.13 shows the distributions of both Aboriginal and non-Aboriginal school meet/exceed scores in 391 mixed schools for the four school years 1999–2000 to 2002–2003.[15] Consider the distributions of scores ranked from high to low. At the upper end, the gap between Aboriginal and non-Aboriginal results is fairly small. At the *ninth decile*—by definition, the point at which 10% of schools perform better and 90% perform worse—the gap is somewhat over eight percentage points. Moving down to schools performing less well, deciles diverge dramatically: the median school score for non-Aboriginal students is 16 percentage points higher than the median score for Aboriginal students, while in the *first decile*—the point at which 90% of schools perform better and 10% perform worse—the gap reaches 25 percentage points.

Some schools—including some in which Aboriginal scores are more than a fifth of the total—are doing well by their Aboriginal students. If one defines "doing well" to mean a school's Aboriginal meet/exceed score is above the non-Aboriginal median, 30 of the 391 schools qualify; unfortunately, the great majority do not.

Figure 8.14 shows the result of a similar exercise among the 391 schools in which school scores are calculated in terms of the percentage of FSA scores that exceed expectations. Once again, the score averages FSA results within a school over all relevant grades and test components. In 40 schools, the maximum score was actually slightly higher for Aboriginal students than for non-Aboriginal students. In general, however, results are not satisfactory. At all deciles, the school exceed scores for Aboriginal students are well below the analogous decile scores for non-Aboriginals. In nearly a quarter of the 391 schools there were no Aboriginal "exceeds expectations" scores,

Figure 8.13 "Meet/Exceed" Decile and Minimum-Maximum Scores for Aboriginal and Non-Aboriginal Students in Mixed British Columbia Schools, Academic Years 1999–2000 to 2002–2003.

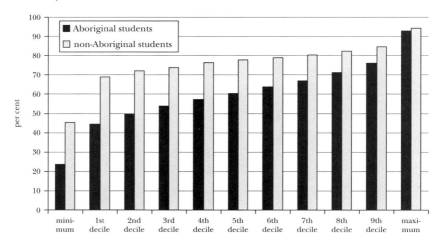

Note: The distributions include 391 schools. Each of these schools reported both Aboriginal and non-Aboriginal FSA scores for at least three of the four school years. The British Columbia Department of Education has recently revised procedures for designation of Aboriginal students. These revisions are not reflected in these calculations. See the text for definitions of mixed schools, school meet/exceed scores, and school exceed scores. The correlation between the school meet/exceed scores for Aboriginal and non-Aboriginal students is 0.51. The analogous correlation between school exceed scores is 0.34.

Source: Author's calculations from FSA data provided by the British Columbia Department of Education.

whereas only two schools recorded no "exceeds expectations" among their non-Aboriginal students.

Why do Aboriginal students fare so much worse in some schools than in others—or, to be optimistic, why do Aboriginal students fare so much better in some schools than in others? The statistics assembled in Table 8.3 afford a number of insights. The school groupings—from bottom tenth to top tenth—are constructed by ranking a sample of mixed schools by their Aboriginal FSA school meet/exceed scores for the 2000–2001 school year. The first column presents average Aboriginal FSA meet/exceed scores for schools within each group, while the second column does the same for non-Aboriginal scores. The third column gives the average Aboriginal share of total scores among schools within each group. The remaining five columns display relevant statistics for neighbourhood characteristics. As the table shows, average Aboriginal meet/exceed scores ranged from 31% in

Figure 8.14 "Exceed" Decile and Minimum-Maximum Scores for Aboriginal and Non-Aboriginal Students in Mixed British Columbia Schools, Academic Years 1999–2000 to 2002–2003.

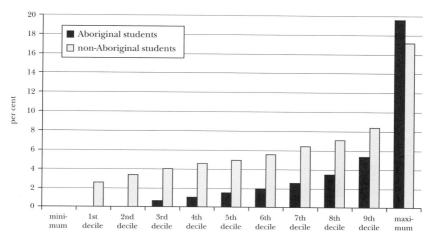

Source: Author's calculations from FSA data provided by the British Columbia Department of Education.

the bottom tenth of schools to 91% in the top tenth. Although the data do not allow for assessment of individual family characteristics on individual student outcomes, it is possible to consider the effect of the socio-economic characteristics of the school's *catchment area*—the census tract (or tracts) in which the school and its immediate neighbourhood are located and from which the school draws its students.

The first variable of interest is neighbourhood family income (Table 8.3, column four). Average neighbourhood family incomes are somewhat lower for schools with lower Aboriginal performance, suggesting that family income matters to some extent. Although families that value education can be found at all income levels, family income can influence children's education attainment through a number of routes. First, poor families often have more humble expectations for their children's careers and hence place less emphasis on their academic performance. Second, even if individual parents have high academic expectations, peer pressure can spread the low expectations of poor families through a school population. Third, wealthier parents are likely to monitor school teaching quality more aggressively than do parents of poor families. If parental monitoring matters, schools in wealthier neighbourhoods may recruit better teachers and, in general, perform better.

Table 8.3 Racial and Neighbourhood Characteristics, Sample of Mixed British Columbia Schools, Academic Year 2000–2001 (Averages by School Cohort, Ranked by Aboriginal FSA Meet/Exceed Scores)

	School Racial Characteristics		
	Aboriginal Meet/Exceed Score *(1)*	Non-Aboriginal Meet/Exceed Score *(2)*	Aboriginal Share of Total Student Scores *(3)*
School Cohorts[a]	*(per cent)*		
Bottom Tenth	30.5	63.1	17.8
Bottom Quarter	39.4	68.3	19.5
Second Quarter	56.4	74.4	11.2
Third Quarter	68.0	76.5	10.4
Top Quarter	82.9	82.8	9.3
Top Tenth	90.7	83.8	9.8

	School Neighbourhood Characteristics				
	Average Family Income[b] *(4)*	Poverty Rate[c] *(5)*	Lone-Parent Families[d] *(6)*	Family Head with Trade Certificate or Higher *(7)*	School in "Very Poor Neighbour-hood"[e] *(8)*
School Cohorts[a]	*(dollars)*	*(per cent)*	*(per cent)*	*(per cent)*	*(per cent)*
Bottom Tenth	45,097	22.0	19.1	47.6	13.3
Bottom Quarter	45,262	22.5	20.0	47.8	15.8
Second Quarter	49,517	17.9	16.7	51.2	8.1
Third Quarter	48,163	17.6	15.5	49.4	10.8
Top Quarter	50,124	14.4	14.7	50.6	0.0
Top Tenth	49,519	16.0	14.0	50.6	0.0

a Schools are ranked by average meet/exceed score of all Aboriginal students in the school; averages are calculated for schools in the relevant school cohort.

b *Average family income* in a school neighbourhood refers to the relevant weighted mean total income of census families. The income of a census family includes the total 1995 incomes of all family members ages 15 and older.

c The neighbourhood *poverty rate* is the percentage of families below the relevant Statistics Canada low-income cut-off (LICO).

d Total number of lone-parent families as a proportion of total number of census families.

e A *very poor neighbourhood* is defined as the school being in a census tract or subdivision in which the LICO poverty rate exceeds twice the national average of 16.3%.

Sources: Author's calculations from FSA data provided by the British Columbia Department of Education; data for school neighbourhood characteristics are from the 1996 census.

Neighbourhood poverty rates—by definition, the fraction of families in a neighbourhood with incomes below a defined threshold—are another potentially relevant variable (Table 8.3, column five). Since the income effects on education are particularly acute for low-income families, and since Aboriginal incomes are, on average, lower than non-Aboriginal incomes, a high overall neighbourhood poverty rate implies an even higher poverty rate among the neighbourhood's Aboriginal families.

Column six of Table 8.3 gives the average incidence of single-parenthood for each of the school groupings. Whether poor or not, parents without partners typically face more demands on their time than do parents with partners who share in the tasks of earning income and parenting. Single parents typically have less time to devote to helping children with their homework or participating in school affairs. Column seven offers some data on parental education levels, the significance of which is that the children of parents who have achieved a reasonable level of education may, for various reasons, be more likely to succeed at school. Such parents may be more effective in monitoring school performance, more able to help with homework, and so on.

In the final column of Table 8.3 is the probability that a school is located in a very poor neighbourhood. Many urban analysts emphasize the idea of a neighbourhood "tipping point." The concern is that in very poor neighbourhoods adverse socio-economic factors are likely to interact and to have a cumulative effect that is larger than simple addition would imply. Poverty, low education, single-parenthood, high concentrations of culturally marginalized groups, and a culture of welfare dependency may combine to "tip" a neighbourhood into ghetto-like status. One of the adverse outcomes of a poor neighbourhood is likely to be poor school results. Not only are parents less likely to monitor school outcomes of their children, it may be particularly difficult in such neighbourhoods to organize effective teams of teachers. A proxy for this tipping point effect is a neighbourhood poverty rate that exceeds some threshold—in this case, a 1995 neighbourhood poverty rate that was more than twice the national average of 16.3%. Nearly one in six of the bottom quarter of schools, in terms of Aboriginal school meet/exceed scores, is in such a neighbourhood, but no school in the top quarter is so situated.

Besides neighbourhood characteristics, it is also worth considering the ethnic composition of the 391 mixed British Columbia schools. There is evidence that schools with large minority racial cohorts have problems with academic performance—one reason is that good teachers are hard for weaker schools to retain. In the United States, for example, some of the weakest schools are in inner-city neighbour-hoods with high African American and Hispanic populations, and something analogous may be taking place in Canadian schools with proportionately large Aboriginal student cohorts. If this dynamic matters, Aboriginal student performance may be inversely related to their share of the student population. Consistent with such a story, the share of Aboriginal students in poorly performing schools is roughly twice that in schools that are performing well in terms of Aboriginal FSA scores (see Table 8.3, column three).

Finally, Aboriginal students appear to perform better in schools that achieve better non-Aboriginal test scores (see column two), perhaps due in part to peer pressure from non-Aboriginal students. In the end, although neighbourhood characteristics and in-school dynamics matter, there is much uncertainty as to the importance of the various factors that influence the academic performance of children.[16]

Policy Goals and Alternative Strategies

Improving Aboriginal education is not a simple exercise. It entails trade-offs among multiple goals that are rarely stated explicitly or in a way that encourages consideration of the trade-offs.

The Goals of Aboriginal Education Policy

In an earlier C.D. Howe Institute study, my colleague Aidan Vining and I attempted to summarize the literature evaluating education reforms, in the United States and Canada, intended to improve educational achievement among minority ethnic communities (Richards & Vining, 2004). We summarized by posing a number of implicit goals and policy alternatives.

ENHANCE ABORIGINAL ACADEMIC ACHIEVEMENT

The most important goal is to enhance student academic achievement. Three distinct aspects of achievement matter when considering any policy option: its potential effect on the performance of students with weak academic records, many of them in poor neighbourhoods; its effect on the performance of average students, mostly in nonpoor neighbourhoods; and its effect on the student dropout rate.

CONTAIN SCHOOL PROGRAM COSTS

A second goal is to contain school program costs. This is not to deny resources to Aboriginal schooling, but recent research (see, for example, Hanushek, 2002) suggests that the link between extra resources and improved education outcomes is weak—one cannot improve outcomes simply by spending more money.

MINIMIZE INTERRACIAL DIVISION

Attempts to focus on improving education outcomes for Aboriginals, rather than for all students, could exacerbate interracial jealousies. Any policies should thus seek to minimize tensions and promote reconciliation.

ENABLE PARENTAL CHOICE

The idea that all local children should attend the neighbourhood public school is intimately bound up with the rationale for public financing of education. It expresses important ideals: equal education opportunities for all children, independent of parents' incomes and social standing; the imparting to children of tolerance for social and ethnic differences; the imbibing by children of the values necessary for a sense of shared citizenship. For many, the goal of ensuring that local children attend the neighbourhood public school is second in importance only to educational achievement per se. There is, however, incontrovertible evidence that some neighbourhood schools, especially in poor areas, perform inadequately. What are we to do about them?

One possible policy response is to encourage parental choice. The idea of "parental choice" could be as modest as permitting parents to send their children anywhere within the school district, rather than having to attend the public school in their local catchment area. Parental choice might mean enabling multiple publicly funded school systems within the same community. More controversially, it might entail giving parents vouchers with which to buy education services from any public or private schools they choose.

An argument for choice is that parents are the best judges of their children's interests, and as such should have the right to choose which school their children attend. If parents chose good schools and shunned bad ones, it would benefit their own children and might encourage improvements in the overall quality of all schools.

Those who oppose choice raise concerns about equity. Prosperous, well-educated parents would make sure their children attended good schools, many of them private. Such parents likely would abandon their interest in neighbourhood public schools, leaving them to be monitored by less-educated, poorer parents who typically are less interested in education quality and less able to lobby school boards effectively over quality. The result, critics say, could be a downward spiral for public schools in poor neighbourhoods, and there is evidence to suggest that this fear is not groundless—see, for example, Ladd and Fiske (2001), and Weiher and Tedin (2002).

Given these problems, it is naive to analyze Aboriginal school reform without acknowledging the tension between the education ideals promoted by partisans of parental choice and those of believers in the neighbourhood school for all local children.

MINIMIZE THE INSTITUTIONAL COMPLEXITY OF REFORM

Institutional complexity raises at least two problems. First, the more complex the proposed education reorganization, the more likely it is that some unexpected event will intervene to confound expectations. Second, the more complex the proposed school reorganization, the more it entails disruption of established interest groups and the less likely it is to be fully implemented. Holding other things equal, even though they often are not, incremental reform is both more feasible and preferable.

Policy Alternatives for Aboriginal Education Reform

Throughout the twentieth century, black Americans migrated in large numbers from farms and villages to live and work in urban America, hoping to build better lives for themselves and their families. Mexicans cross the Rio Grande in search of the same goal. Migration is usually rational: in general, those who migrate improve their situation. But life in cities is far from perfect.

Among the problems ethnic minorities have faced in urban America is the quality of their children's education. For the past half-century, American education leaders have striven to close the education outcome gap between the children of new migrants and those of well-established urban Americans. There has been some success: many American school districts have improved outcomes, and the scores of black and white students on tests of core curriculum performance have converged somewhat. Cook and Evans (2000) conclude that "nearly 75% of the convergence is due to changes within schools, that is, to a narrowing in the gap in test scores between white and black students with the same level of parental education and who attend the same school" (p. 749). Cook and Evans note an important problem, however: black students increasingly are found in schools of lower quality. To the extent this is so, the explanation appears to be some combination of neighbourhood residential segregation by race and income, and abandonment of the public school system by many middle-class urban parents.

The Canadian analogue to the American experience of large-scale migration of ethnic minorities has been the migration of Aboriginals from rural communities, both on and off reserve, to cities. One-half of all Aboriginals now live in a city and, as noted above, the great majority of Aboriginal children attend off-reserve schools run by their province, not a band-run school on reserve. Like black and Mexican minorities in American cities, Canada's urban Aboriginals live disproportionately in poor neighbourhoods and their children attend schools whose academic outcomes are, in general, below those in more affluent neighbourhoods.

Vining and I defined the following four policy alternatives:

- *Create separate schools:* enable Aboriginals within a community to create autonomous school authorities and control public funds for some public schools in the community.
- *Enhance student mobility:* enable Aboriginals to attend good schools that already exist by eliminating limits to mobility posed by school catchment boundaries, and perhaps subsidize mobility as well.
- *Designate magnet schools:* designate one or more schools within a school district that will concentrate on Aboriginal cultural studies.
- *Enrich certain schools:* provide additional resources to improve the performance of schools with proportionately large Aboriginal student populations.

Table 8.4 summarizes our assessment of these four strategies. Here, in more detail, are our conclusions.

THE "SEPARATE SCHOOL" ALTERNATIVE

Given the concentration of Aboriginal students in relatively weak schools, some argue for an Aboriginal school system that engages Aboriginal families more intimately and makes more extensive use of Aboriginal culture in the school curriculum. Such schools would attempt to replicate in an urban environment what former Saskatchewan Premier Allan Blakeney has termed the "cultural comfort" of the reserve:

> *I see it as next to impossible for us to be able to create reserves which provide an appropriate economic base for all or most of the growing population of Aboriginal people. We know that some will wish to remain [on reserve] .... We know that some will move to the cities and integrate with the economic mainstream. We know that some will move back and forth—a transitional group .... [Aboriginals] leave the reserve because there is no economic opportunity for them and particularly for their children. It seems to me that they return to the reserve because on the reserve they experience a sense of place ... and also because on the reserve they have a level of cultural comfort. (as cited in Richards, 2001, pp. 24–25)*

Table 8.4 Policy Alternatives for Aboriginal Education Reform

Goals	Alternative 1: Separate Schools	Alternative 2: Student Mobility	Alternative 3: Magnet School	Alternative 4: School Enrichment
Enhancing Academic Achievement				
Effect on Students in Poor Neighbourhoods	Potential to increase Aboriginal parental involvement; probably positive effect	Modestly positive effect (based on evaluation of US school-choice experiments)	Positive cultural aspect might benefit low-achieving students from poor neighbourhoods	Small but not trivial; subject to Hawthorne effect; innovations must be evaluated
Effect on Students in Typical Neighbourhoods	Small or no effect	Negligible, provided migrating students are small share of receiving school	Uncertain result, much depends on relative quality of magnet, neighbourhood schools	As above
Effect on Dropout Rate	Potential to reduce	Small impact	Cultural aspect might help lower rate among low-achieving students	As above
Lowering School Program Costs	Highest incremental costs, requires administrative duplication	Medium incremental costs, much depends on premium for migrating students	Low incremental costs, requires staffing or more magnet schools	Low-to-medium incremental costs, depending on scope of enrichment programs
Minimizing Interracial Cleavage	Potential to improve interracial relations in medium term; potential for short-term conflicts over access to financial resources and perceived threat to racially integrated schools	May provoke non-Aboriginal opposition	As with separate school model	Little effect
Enabling Parental Choice	Significant increase in school choice for Aboriginal parents	As with separate school model	Provides school choice for students who gain access	No change from status quo
Minimizing Administrative Complexity of Reform	Entails major administrative adjustments	Few administrative problems; many precedents exist	More complexity than alternative 2, less than alternative 1	Minor administrative problems

There is evidence to suggest that "separate schools" controlled by cultural minorities do increase educational attainment among their children (see Evans & Schwab, 1995; Neal, 1997). Inspired by the precedent in many provinces of distinct public school systems based on the attributes of language and religion, Blakeney has informally broached the idea of an Aboriginal-based system in cities with large Aboriginal communities.

Administratively the most complex of the four alternatives, the establishment of separate schools would explicitly challenge the ideal of the universal neighbourhood school. Such Aboriginal-controlled schools are unlikely, however, to be a panacea for urban Aboriginals hoping to preserve their cultural distinctiveness. The analogous establishment of autonomous francophone school boards in communities outside Quebec has not guaranteed the preservation of French-language use in those areas. Nevertheless, the greater engagement of Aboriginal parents and the provision of "cultural comfort" in a separate school system would probably improve the academic performance of weak students and lower their dropout rates. A separate Aboriginal school system might also create a group of Aboriginal leaders with a stake in the success of urban, as opposed to reserve-based, Aboriginal communities. One potential drawback is the danger that separate schools develop a reputation for low standards—we already know that schools with large numbers of Aboriginal students do not, in general, enjoy high academic standards.

Any province that considers undertaking the separate school approach should impose clear guidelines in order to minimize potential problems. The conditions that seem most important are as follows:

- Both Aboriginal and non-Aboriginal parents should be free to choose to send their children to either an Aboriginal school or a conventional school.
- An Aboriginal school authority should be democratically elected by all parents, including non-Aboriginal parents, with children in the system.
- To maintain standards, all schools should be required to teach the provincially mandated core curriculum, and all students should sit province-wide exams in core subjects.
- School administrations must be shielded from political pressures that may arise to lower standards.

Similar conditions have been important for the successful coexistence of Catholic and nondenominational public school systems and for systems based on one or other of the two official languages. The fourth point raises the requirement that any urban Aboriginal school authority must address outcomes. Pressure to avoid outcome measurement would not be unique to this model of Aboriginal-run schools. But the need to resist such pressure and establish educational legitimacy would be greater for such schools, particularly in the short term.

ENHANCING STUDENT MOBILITY

Student mobility is of particular relevance for parents who want to avoid sending their children to poorly performing schools. A choice of schools is usually not feasible in rural areas, where schools are widely dispersed, but is an option for the increasing numbers of Aboriginals living in urban areas.

One of the best-known and most radical experiments in school choice has been under way in Milwaukee, Wisconsin, since 1990. Targeted at families whose incomes are less than 175% of the designated poverty line, the state-funded Milwaukee program offers vouchers that enable students to attend private schools—worth US$4,700 per student in the 1997–1998 school year. The number of vouchers is limited and students are selected randomly from eligible applicants. In a survey of this and similar experiments, Sawhill and Smith (2000) conclude that results are "modestly encouraging." They note, however, the mixed evidence that the Milwaukee experiment improves student achievement:

> One study, by Paul Peterson and his colleagues, found that by the third and fourth year of the program, [students in the program] had made sizable gains relative to their public school counterparts in both reading and math. Another study, by John Witte and his colleagues, found no differences between the two groups. And a third study, by Cecilia Rouse, found gains in math but not in reading. There are several reasons for these differences, including how each research team selected its control or comparison group and how they chose to adjust for any remaining differences between students who took advantage of the voucher and those who remained in the Milwaukee public schools. After carefully reviewing these three studies, we conclude that … it is simply not possible at the current time to render a clear verdict on the outcomes of the experiment. (Sawhill & Smith, 2000, pp. 274–275)[17]

The evidence suggests, at worst, that the experiment has made no difference.

There is, however, support for the claim that enabling modest levels of competition between schools and between school districts—reforms less radical than the Milwaukee voucher scheme—does improve school outcomes.[18] Cowley and Easton (2004) enthusiastically argue that "all Aboriginal parents should have the unfettered right to enroll their children in any school that they choose" (p. 3). Vining and I also defend the expansion of school choice, although with more qualifications. One modest parental choice model that could improve Aboriginal school outcomes is to let Aboriginal parents send their children to any school in the school district, rather than be restricted by school catchment boundaries—a reform rendered more feasible by recent legislation in British Columbia.

With the passing of the School Amendment Act in 2002,[19] British Columbia parents can now choose to send their children to any public school in the province—if they can find the space. Children within the school's catchment area have first priority, and how much space to make available to students beyond the catchment area is up to the school district, a discretion that weakens the effect of the reform for all students. Despite that weakness, the act seems to have had some impact within the Vancouver school district, where Steffenhagen (2003) finds informal evidence that parents are choosing schools that perform better on test scores.

Any strategy involving choice should include appropriate incentives for good schools to accept Aboriginal students, perhaps including paying them a "mobility bonus" for the number of migrating children they accept. School boards anxious to avoid explicit racial targeting could make such a bonus contingent on income, as is the case in the Milwaukee experiment.

The mobility alternative would primarily benefit Aboriginal parents who are conscious of the value of academically good schools and willing to incur the costs of sending their children to such a school even if it is not in the neighbourhood. This reform would be much less administratively complex than the separate school option and less controversial than school vouchers.

DESIGNATING MAGNET SCHOOLS

A *magnet* school—also called a "charter" school—is a tax-funded school within a public school system that enjoys a charter allowing it to specialize in a particular field of study. Any student in the school district can elect to attend the school, subject to its capacity.

An interesting Canadian example of a magnet school is Amiskwaciy Academy.[20] A secondary school in the Edmonton school district, it has a mandate to specialize in Aboriginal cultural studies. It follows the same core curriculum as other Alberta schools but supplemented with courses on Aboriginal history, literature, and culture.

All students who live in Edmonton, whether Aboriginal or not, are eligible to attend.

In terms of meeting the goals laid out earlier, magnet schools offer a compromise between the school enrichment and separate school alternatives. It allows for schools that explicitly encourage Aboriginal studies and concerns, without the administrative complexity that would accompany the establishing of a separate school authority.

ENRICHING CERTAIN SCHOOLS

A fourth strategy is for governments to provide additional resources to schools with large Aboriginal student contingents. The British Columbia government already includes the number of Aboriginal students in determining the funding formula for school boards, and the Vancouver board provides such schools in its district with extra library resources bearing on Aboriginal literature, arts, and history. School boards may also supplement the budgets of these schools to engage Aboriginal elders as counsellors and to hire highly motivated teachers. The strategy could be extended to include early childhood education programs attached to particular schools and targeted to attract Aboriginal children.

A weakness of such a strategy is that it relies exclusively on the supply side to improve school quality. The three previous alternatives, in contrast, invoke parental choice as, in effect, a demand-side check on quality in addition to the checks made by school authorities themselves. A separate Aboriginal school system would enable parents to choose between systems; enhanced mobility would add more choices for Aboriginal parents in urban school districts and could offer financial payments to recipient schools; and magnet schools also promise some degree of choice.

Another potential problem with enriching certain schools is the *Hawthorne effect*— the frequently observed phenomenon that short-term results improve immediately following an experimental intervention, regardless of the nature of the intervention. The immediate improvement may have more to do with the change in routines and increased attention paid by supervisors than with the efficacy of the reform itself, the determination of which would require a longer-term evaluation.

Conclusion

Any school board prepared to tackle Aboriginal education reform aggressively should probably have as its agenda a combination of the second, third, and fourth alternatives discussed above—namely:

- relaxation of neighbourhood school boundaries and payment of a financial bonus to schools to encourage them to accept Aboriginal students who migrate from beyond the relevant school catchment area;
- in large urban communities, creation of one or more magnet schools concentrating on Aboriginal cultural studies; and
- provision of generous enrichment programs for schools with large Aboriginal student populations.

It is probably more important to experiment actively than to seek the single optimum strategy. Edmonton, for example, is undertaking a natural experiment. While the city's nondenominational public school board is pursuing a magnet schools strategy, its Catholic school board has chosen the school enrichment approach. In a survey, the great majority of Aboriginal parents of children in the Catholic system expressed a preference for Aboriginal content within neighbourhood schools that otherwise remained integrated with non-Aboriginal students. In response, the Catholic board has embarked on an ambitious program to enrich Aboriginal content in schools with sizable Aboriginal student populations; the program includes hiring Aboriginal teachers and involving elders in schools (Sparklingeyes, 2005).

Beyond these specific recommendations is the matter of political priorities. Realizing the convergence of education outcomes will require a more consistent commitment to Aboriginal education success on the part of all concerned. This means a commitment by Aboriginal leaders and federal and provincial politicians on targets. Realizing targets requires, in turn, detailed benchmarking of the status quo (as British Columbia is doing via the FSA), a willingness to experiment (as, for example, is happening in Edmonton), and evaluation of outcomes (which, as the Auditor General notes with respect to on-reserve schools, Ottawa and band councils are not doing).

When the prime minister, premiers, and leaders of the major Aboriginal organizations met in Kelowna, British Columbia, in late 2005, they agreed to address social problems and not to debate disagreements among themselves over the respective powers to be exercised by Ottawa, the provinces, and band governments. With respect to education, they committed themselves to "the goal of closing the gap in K–12 educational attainment between Aboriginal learners and other Canadians by 2016" (Canada, 2005d, p. 4). It is highly unlikely they will realize this goal, but stating it is worthwhile—for at least two reasons.

First, this is an implicit acknowledgement by the prime minister and Aboriginal leaders that past education performance by both the Department of Indian Affairs and band councils has been woefully inadequate. It is also an acknowledgement by the premiers that their provincial education ministries must assume major responsibilities with respect to improving Aboriginal education, and that they can no longer sidestep the difficulties by reference to federal or band responsibility.

Second, it is in the nature of organizations to pursue goals that are explicitly stated. Having stated the target of eliminating the Aboriginal-non-Aboriginal gap in K–12 education levels, national leaders have almost certainly set in motion an invigorated dynamic to improve education outcomes. An initial result will probably be more adequate documentation of the current gap between Aboriginal and non-Aboriginal education levels. Those interested can cite this commitment in order to obtain evidence with respect to the size of the gap among Aboriginal children living on and off reserve, with respect to the size of the gap among children across provinces, across school districts within a province, and, finally, across individual schools within a school district.

As I have noted, it is highly unlikely that the K–12 education gap will be closed by 2016. A skeptic might ask whether it will ever be closed. One reason for skepticism—there are others—is to ask how serious the reserve-based Aboriginal leadership is about realizing social policy goals, such as closing the education gap, that ignore the agenda of treaty rights and blur the distinction between Aboriginals living on or off reserve.

REFERENCES

Allard, J. (2002). Big Bear's treaty. Excerpt from unpublished manuscript with foreword by Gordon Gibson. *Inroads, 11,* 108–169.

Antecol, H., & Bedard, K. (2002). The relative earnings of young Mexican, black, and white women. *Industrial & Labor Relations Review, 56*(1), 122–135. http://dx.doi.org/10.2307/3270652

Bishop, J. (1997). The effect of national standards and curriculum-based external exams on student achievement. *American Economic Review, 87*(2), 260–264.

Bishop, J. (2000). Privatizing education: Lessons from Canada, Europe, and Asia. In C. Steuerle, V. Ooms, G. Peterson, & R. Reischauer (Eds.), *Vouchers and the Provision of Public Services* (pp. 292–335). Washington, DC: Brookings Institution Press.

Bishop, J. (2001, Winter). A steeper, better road to graduation. *Education Next.* Retrieved from http://www.educationnext.org120014156.html

Boothe, P. (1998). *Finding a balance: Renewing Canadian fiscal federalism. Benefactors Lecture.* Toronto: C.D. Howe Institute.

Borland, M., & Howsen, R. (1992). Students' academic achievement and the degree of market concentration in education. *Economics of Education Review, 11*(1), 31–39. http://dx.doi.org/10.1016/0272-7757(92)90019-Y

Bradbury, K. (2002). Education and wages in the 1980s and 1990s: Are all groups moving up together? *New England Economic Review, First Quarter*, 19–46.

British Columbia. (2003). *How are we doing? Demographics and performance of Aboriginal students in BC public schools 2002–2003*. Victoria, BC: Ministry of Education. Retrieved from http://www.gov.bc.ca/abed

Cairns, A. (2000). *Citizens plus: Aboriginal peoples and the Canadian state*. Vancouver: UBC Press.

Cairns, A., & Flanagan, T. (2001). An exchange. *Inroads, 10*, 101–122.

Canada. (1966–1967). *A survey of the contemporary Indians of Canada*. 2 vols. (Also known as the Hawthorne Report.) Ottawa: Queen's Printer. Retrieved from http://www.ainc-inac.gc.ca/pr/pub/srvy/sci_e.html

Canada. (1969). *Statement of the government of Canada on Indian policy. Presented to Parliament by the Hon. Jean Chrétien, Minister of Indian Affairs and Northern Development*. Ottawa: Department of Indian Affairs.

Canada. (1980). *Indian conditions: A survey*. Ottawa: Department of Indian and Northern Affairs.

Canada. (1996). *People to people, nation to nation: Highlights from the report of the Royal Commission on Aboriginal Peoples*. Ottawa: Royal Commission on Aboriginal Peoples.

Canada. (1999). *A second diagnostic on the health of First Nations and Inuit people in Canada*. Ottawa: Health Canada. Retrieved from http://www.hc-sc.gc.ca

Canada. (2000a). *Diabetes among Aboriginal people in Canada: The evidence*. Ottawa: Health Canada. Retrieved from http://www.hc-sc.gc.ca

Canada. (2000b). Indian and Northern Affairs Canada: Elementary and secondary education. In *The Report of the Auditor General of Canada* (Chapter 4). Ottawa. Retrieved from http://www.oag-bvg.gc.ca

Canada. (2002a). *Building on values: The future of health care in Canada*. Ottawa: Commission on the Future of Health Care in Canada, also known as the Romanow Commission. Retrieved from http://www.hc-sc.gc.ca/english/care/romanow/indedx1.html.

Canada. (2002b). *Non-insured health benefits program: 2001–2002 annual report*. Ottawa: Health Canada. Retrieved from http://www.hc-sc.ca/fnhib-dgspni

Canada. (2003a). *A statistical profile on the health of First Nations in Canada*. Ottawa: Health Canada. Retrieved from http://www.hc-sc.gc.ca/fnihb

Canada. (2003b). *Aboriginal peoples of Canada: A demographic profile* (Catalogue no. 96F0030XIE2001007). Ottawa: Statistics Canada.

Canada. (2003c). *Aboriginal peoples survey*. Ottawa: Statistics Canada.

Canada. (2003d). *Urban Aboriginal youth: An action plan for change*. Final Report of the Senate Standing Committee on Aboriginal Peoples. Retrieved from http://www.parl.gc.ca/37/2/parl-bus/commbus/senate/com-e/abor-e/rep-e/repfinoct03-e.htm

Canada. (2004a). *2001 Aboriginal peoples survey community profiles*. Ottawa: Statistics Canada. Retrieved from http://www12.statcan.ca/english/profilOl/PlaceSearchForml.cfm.

Canada. (2004b). *Basic departmental data, 2003*. Ottawa: Department of Indian Affairs and Northern Development.

Canada. (2004c). Indian and Northern Affairs Canada: Education program and post-secondary student support. In *The Report of the Auditor General of Canada* (Chapter 5). Ottawa. Retrieved from http://www.oag-bvd.gc.ca

Canada. (2004d). *HIV/AIDS among Aboriginal peoples in Canada: A continuing concern.* Ottawa: Public Health Agency of Canada. Retrieved from http://www.phac-aspc.gc.ca/publicat/epiu-aepi/epi_update_may _04/9 _e.html

Canada. (2005a). *Aboriginal peoples living off-reserve in western Canada: Estimates from the labour force survey, April 2004–March 2005* (Catalogue no. 71-S87-XIE). Ottawa: Statistics Canada. Retrieved from http://www.statcan.ca/english/freepub/71-S87-XIE/71-S87-XIE200S001.pdf

Canada. (2005b, November 25). *Government of Canada invests in immediate action to improve lives of Aboriginal peoples in Canada.* Press release. Retrieved from http://www.pm.gc.ca/eng/news.asp?id=661

Canada. (2005c, June 3). Readmission to Saskatchewan correctional services among Aboriginal and non-Aboriginal adults. *The Daily.* Retrieved from http://www.statcan.ca/Daily/English/OS0603/dOS0603a.html

Canada. (2005d, November). *Strengthening relationships and closing the gap.* Paper released at First Ministers' and National Aboriginal Leaders' Meeting, Kelowna, BC. Retrieved from http://www.ainc-inac.gc.ca/nr/iss/fmm_e.html

Centers for Disease Control and Prevention (CDC) (1997, Oct 31). Trends in the prevalence and incidence of self-reported diabetes mellitus – United States, 1980-1994. *Morbidity and Mortality Weekly Report (MMWR), 46*(43), 1014–1018. Medline:9367135

Centers for Disease Control and Prevention (CDC) (2003, Aug 1). Diabetes prevalence among American Indians and Alaska Natives and the overall population–United States, 1994-2002. *Morbidity and Mortality Weekly Report (MMWR), 52*(30), 702–704. Medline:12894056

Chandler, M., & Lalonde, C. (1998). Cultural continuity as a hedge against suicide in Canada's First Nations. *Transcultural Psychiatry, 35*(2), 191–219. http://dx.doi.org/10.1177/136346159803500202

Cook, M., & Evans, W. (2000). Families or schools? Explaining the convergence in white and black academic performance. *Journal of Labor Economics, 18*(4), 729–754. http://dx.doi.org/10.1086/209975

Coon Come, M. (2003). Assembly of First Nations national chief expresses disappointment with Federal Court of Appeal ruling on Treaty 8 tax promise. Retrieved from http://www.afn.ca/Media/2003/june/june_11_03.htm

Cornell, S., & Kalt, J. (1998). Sovereignty and nation-building: The development challenge in Indian country today. *American Indian Culture and Research Journal, 22*(3), 187–214.

Cowley, P., & Easton, S. (2004). *Report card on Aboriginal education in British Columbia.* Vancouver: Fraser Institute.

Cutler, D., Glaeser, E., & Shapiro, J. (2003). Why have Americans become more obese? *Journal of Economic Perspectives, 17*(3), 93–118. http://dx.doi.org/10.1257/089533003769204371

Drolet, M. (2002). New evidence on gender pay differentials: Does measurement matter? *Canadian Public Policy, 28*(1), 1–16. http://dx.doi.org/10.2307/3552156

Drost, H., & Richards, J. (2003). *Income on- and off-reserve: How Aboriginals are faring. C.D. Howe Institute Commentary 175.* Toronto: C.D. Howe Institute.

Evans, W., & Schwab, R. (1995). Finish high school and starting college: Do Catholic schools make a difference? *Quarterly Journal of Economics, 110*(4), 941–974. http://dx.doi.org/10.2307/2946645

Flanagan, T. (2000). *First Nations? Second thoughts.* Montreal: McGill-Queen's University Press.

Florence, J.A., & Yeager, B.F. (1999, May 15). Treatment of type 2 diabetes mellitus. *American Family Physician, 59*(10), 2835–2844, 2849–2850. Medline:10348076

George, D. (1970). My very dear good friends … In Waubgeshig (Ed.), *The Only Good Indian, Essays by Canadian Indians* (pp. 184–188). Toronto: New Press.

Gibson, G. (1999). A principled analysis of the Nisga'a treaty. *Inroads, 8,* 165–178.

Greene, J., Peterson, P., & Du, J. (1996). *The effectiveness of school choice in Milwaukee: A secondary analysis of data from the program's evaluation.* Cambridge, MA: Harvard University Press.

Hanushek, E. (2002). *Publicly provided education.* NBER Working Paper 8799. Cambridge, MA: National Bureau of Economic Research.

Howe, E. (2002). Education and lifetime income for Aboriginal people in Saskatchewan. Unpublished working paper, Department of Economics, University of Saskatchewan.

Indian Chiefs of Alberta. (1970). *Citizens plus: A presentation by the Indian chiefs of Alberta to the Right Honourable P-E. Trudeau. The Red Paper, prepared under direction of Harold Cardinal.* Edmonton, AB: Indian Association of Alberta.

King, T. (2003). *The truth about stories: A Native narrative.* Toronto: House of Anansi.

Ladd, H., & Fiske, E. (2001). The uneven playing field of school choice: Evidence from New Zealand. *Journal of Policy Analysis and Management, 20*(1), 43–64. http://dx .doi.org/10.1002/1520-6688(200124)20:1<43::AID-PAM1003>3.0.CO;2-4

Léger & Léger. (2005, May 14). Quebec survey. Opinion poll commissioned by *Le Journal de Montréal* and *The Gazette.*

Matas, R., & Mickleburgh, R. (2002, April 18). Most in BC survey believe referendum harms treaty talks. *Globe and Mail* (Toronto), pp. A1, A8.

McRae, D., & Pearse, P. (2004). *Treaties and transition: Towards a sustainable fishery on Canada's pacific coast. Report prepared for the Federal-Provincial Post Treaty Fisheries Joint Task Group.* Ottawa: Department of Fisheries and Oceans.

Moffitt, R. (2003). The negative income tax and the evolution of US welfare policy. *Journal of Economic Perspectives, 17*(3), 119–140. http://dx.doi. org/10.1257/089533003769204380

Moscovitch, A., & Webster, A. (1995). Aboriginal social assistance expenditures. In S. Phillips (Ed.), *How Ottawa spends, 1995–1996: Mid-life crisis.* Ottawa: Carleton University Press.

Neal, D. (1997). The effects of Catholic secondary schooling on educational achievement. *Journal of Labor Economics, 15*(1), 98–123. http://dx.doi. org/10.1086/209848

Norris, D., Siggner, A., & Costa, R. (2003, October). *What the census and the Aboriginal peoples survey tell us about Aboriginal conditions in Canada.* Paper presented at the Aboriginal Strategies Conference, Edmonton.

Organisation for Economic Co-operation and Development (OECD). (1996). *Employment Outlook, 62.* Paris, France: Author.

Pendakur, K., & Pendakur, R. (2002). Colour my world: Have earnings gaps for Canadian-born ethnic minorities changed over time? *Canadian Public Policy, 28*(4), 489–512. http://dx.doi.org/10.2307/3552211

Ponting, J., & Gibbins, R. (1980). *Out of irrelevance.* Butterworth: Scarborough.

Richards, J. (2001). *Neighbors matter: Poor neighborhoods and urban Aboriginal policy. C.D. Howe Institute Commentary 156.* Toronto: C.D. Howe Institute.

Richards, J. (2002). Indian/non-Indian life expectancy: Why the gap? *Inroads, 12,* 48–59.

Richards, J. (2003). *A new agenda for strengthening Canada's Aboriginal populations: Individual treaty benefits, reduced transfers to bands and own-source taxation. Backgrounder 66.* Toronto: C.D. Howe Institute.

Richards, J. (2005). Labour markets and social policy: A qualified agenda for the future. In D. Laidler & W. Robson (Eds.), *Prospects for Canada: Progress and challenges twenty years after the Macdonald Commission* (pp. 83–97). Toronto: C.D. Howe Institute.

Richards, J., & Vining, A. (2004). *Aboriginal off-reserve education: Time for action. C.D. Howe Institute Commentary 198.* Toronto: C.D. Howe Institute.

Rouse, C. (1998). Schools and student achievement: More evidence from the Milwaukee parental choice program. *Economic Policy Review, 4*(1), 61–78.

Sawhill, I., & Smith, S. (2000). Vouchers for elementary and secondary education. In C. Steuerle, V. Ooms, G. Peterson, and R. Reischauer (Eds.), *Vouchers and the provision of public services* (pp. 251–290). Washington, DC: Brookings Institution Press.

Scott, D. (1991). The forsaken. In M. Ross (Ed.), *Poets of the Confederation.* Toronto: McClelland & Stewart. [Original work published 1905].

Siggner, A., & Costa, R. (2005). *Aboriginal conditions in census metropolitan areas, 1981–2001.* Ottawa: Statistics Canada. Retrieved from http://www.statcan.ca/english/research/89-613-MIE/89-613-MIE2005008.pdf

Sparklingeyes, P. (2005). Aboriginal learning services, Edmonton Catholic schools. Retrieved from http://www.sfu.ca/mpp/aboriginal/colloquium

Steele, S. (2002, November). The age of white guilt and the disappearance of the black individual. *Harper's Magazine,* pp. 33–42.

Steffenhagen, J. (2003, June 3). East pupils meet west schools. *Vancouver Sun,* pp. Bl, B7.

Tjepkema, M. (2002). *The health of the off-reserve Aboriginal population* (Catalogue no. 82-003). Ottawa: Statistics Canada.

Trudeau, P.-E. (1968). Separatist counter-revolutionaries. *Federalism and the French Canadians.* Toronto: Macmillan of Canada. (Reprinted and translated from the original in *Cite libre,* 1964)

Tuomilehto, J., Lindström, J., Eriksson, J.G., Valle, T.T., Hämäläinen, H., Ilanne-Parikka, P., … , Uusitupa, M., & Finnish Diabetes Prevention Study Group. (2001, May 3). Prevention of type 2 diabetes mellitus by changes in lifestyle among subjects with impaired glucose tolerance. *New England Journal of Medicine, 344*(18), 1343–1350. http://dx.doi.org/10.1056/NEJM200105033441801. Medline:11333990

United Nations (UN). (2004). *Human development indicators.* Retrieved from http://www.undp.org/hdr2003/indicator

Weiher, G., & Tedin, K. (2002). Does choice lead to racially distinctive schools? Charter schools and household preferences. *Journal of Policy Analysis and Management, 21*(1), 79–92. http://dx.doi.org/10.1002/pam.1041

Witte, J. (2000). *The market approach to education: An analysis of America's first voucher program.* Princeton, NJ: Princeton University Press.

World Health Organization (WHO) (2004). *Prevention of mental disorders: Effective interventions and policy options.* Summary report. Geneva: Author. Retrieved from http://www.who.int/mental_health/evidence/en

Young, T.K., Reading, J., Elias, B., & O'Neil, J.D. (2000, Sep 5). Type 2 diabetes mellitus in Canada's first nations: status of an epidemic in progress. *Canadian Medical Association Journal, 163*(5), 561–566. Retrieved from http://www.cmaj.ca Medline:11006768

Young, T.K., Szathmary, E.J., Evers, S., & Wheatley, B. (1990). Geographical distribution of diabetes among the native population of Canada: a national survey. *Social Science & Medicine, 31*(2), 129–139. http://dx.doi.org/10.1016/0277-9536(90)90054-V. Medline:2389148

Zanzig, B. (1997). Measuring the impact of competition in local government education markets on the cognitive achievement of students. *Economics of Education Review, 16*(4), 431–441. http://dx.doi.org/10.1016/S0272-7757(97)00003-4

NOTES

1 This chapter draws heavily on Richards and Vining (2004).

2 The *identity* definition of Aboriginals refers to those persons who reported in the census as identifying with at least one Aboriginal group (North American Indian,

Métis, or Inuit), even though they may not necessarily have Aboriginal ancestry. Thus, to some extent, "identity" is a matter of individual choice. The economic fortunes of an individual with one or two Aboriginal parents but who chooses not to identify as Aboriginal are as important as those of someone who embraces his or her cultural heritage. Among those living on reserve, the difference between the Aboriginal identity count and the Aboriginal origin count is negligible. Among those living off reserve, however, roughly three report themselves as Aboriginal in terms of origin for every two who report an Aboriginal identity— hence the usefulness of showing these two groups separately in Figure 8.1.

3 These data are derived from the 2001 *Aboriginal Peoples Survey* (Canada, 2003c), part of the 2001 census. For discussion of the meaning and limitations of the census income concept in the context of Aboriginal surveys, see Drost and Richards (2003).

4 For studies that consider education achievement and income distributions among ethnic groups, see Antecol and Bedard (2002); Bradbury (2002); Drolet (2002); and Pendakur and Pendakur (2002).

5 Using 1996 census data for Saskatchewan, Howe (2002) estimates that expected lifetime financial returns to Aboriginals who complete high school are much larger than expected incomes of Aboriginals who fail to do so.

6 This correlation between education and employment exists whether the measure of education is the percentage with high school graduation or higher, or the percentage with a trade certificate or higher. For Aboriginals on reserve, those with trade certificates tend to have higher employment rates than those with high school graduation. Many of the relatively few, usually band-council-financed, on-reserve jobs require some post-secondary education.

7 Over the two decades, the Aboriginal identity population more than doubled in these eleven cities. Siggner and Costa (2005) decompose this increase into natural increase (births less deaths), net migration, changes in under-reporting, and "ethnic migration." As social stigma against Aboriginals diminishes and Canadians accord Aboriginal culture more respect, increasing numbers of people choose to identify themselves as Aboriginal in census counts. This "migration" in ethnic identity explains roughly half the population increase since 1981. It likely also explains some of the improvement in education levels, as larger numbers of relatively educated young people identify as Aboriginal.

8 As with the 1981 to 2001 comparisons discussed earlier, some portion of the improvement by the younger cohort may be due to changing patterns of identity.

9 For example, non-Aboriginal 15-to-24-year-olds have achieved 70% of the high school and above level of the non-Aboriginal cohort ages 25 to 44 (70% = 58.3%/82.9%). On-reserve 15-to-24-year-old Aboriginals have realized only 45% of the comparable level among on-reserve 25-to-44-year-olds (45% = 24.2%/54.2%). Off reserve, the ratio is 57%. Similar results exist at higher education levels. Does this evidence mean young Aboriginals are slipping back relative to the education attainment of the generation ahead of them? Not necessarily, since the evidence from the 15-to-24-year-old cohort is incomplete. Obviously, we do not know the future, but it could turn out that Aboriginals complete their education on average at an older age than do non-Aboriginals, in which case the data for 15-to-24-year-olds represent proportionately less of the ultimate education attainment of Aboriginals than of non-Aboriginals.

10 See Richards (2001) for a review of evidence on Aboriginal student mobility.

11 Of course, some would have left the province and others will finish high school at a later date. However, as Cowley and Easton (2004, p. 13) point out, although such adjustments apply disproportionately to Aboriginal students, they are minor and do not affect the overall conclusion that dropout rates for Aboriginal students are unacceptably high.

12 Hanushek (2002) offers an excellent survey of empirical studies of the outcomes of policies to improve school performance. Bishop (1997, 2001) has written extensively on the value of jurisdiction-wide tests on core subjects as means to improve average school system performance by providing information to parents, students, and teachers on a basis that permits comparison across schools and among all children.

13 Subsequent to the years under review, British Columbia has organized province-wide exams in core subjects in grade 10 in lieu of FSA tests.

14 Readers interested in the Aboriginal education performance of individual British Columbia schools should look at Cowley and Easton (2004), who provide a great deal of useful information beyond the FSA results.

15 For the 391 mixed schools included in these distributions, school rankings differ for the Aboriginal and non-Aboriginal scores.

16 My colleague Aidan Vining and I undertook a preliminary regression analysis to assess the relative importance of variables (Richards & Vining, 2004, pp. 14, 25). Attempting to explain Aboriginal FSA scores using overall neighbourhood characteristics, it turns out, does not take us far. The regressions provide fairly strong evidence that FSA results decline, for both Aboriginal and non-Aboriginal students, as the Aboriginal share of the student population rises in any school. The most important single variable, in terms of its ability to explain the variation in Aboriginal outcomes across schools, is the school non-Aboriginal meet/exceed score, which supports the thesis that a rising tide lifts all boats. As a school improves, students tend to rise academically as an overall group, independent of race.

17 For access to the three studies of the Milwaukee school choice experiment mentioned in this quotation, see Greene, Peterson, and Du (1996); Rouse (1998); and Witte (2000).

18 See, for example, Borland and Howsen (1992); Zanzig (1997); Bishop (2000).

19 For a summary of the act's provisions, see http://www.bced.gov.bc.ca/legislation/legpS02.htm.

20 See the academy's website, http://amiskwaciy.epsb.net.

9

A New Approach to Understanding Aboriginal Educational Outcomes: The Role of Social Capital

Jerry White, Nicholas Spence, and Paul Maxim

This chapter is a revised version of a paper originally published in the Policy Research Initiative's *Social Capital Thematic Studies Book* in 2005. Reprinted from Jerry P. White et al. (Eds.) *Aborginal Policy Research: Moving Forward, Making a Difference, Volume III.* Toronto: Thompson Educational Publishing, 2006. pp. 69–86. Reproduced with permission.

Introduction

In recent years, social capital has received much attention and has been the subject of great debate in the social sciences and policy arenas. Whether social capital has the capacity and utility to produce meaningful change in achieving the goals of society is one focus of that debate.

This chapter examines the impacts of social capital on Aboriginal educational attainment in Canada, Australia, and New Zealand. The focus for Canada is First Nations, and in other countries it is a similar population. Our aim is to explore how social capital theory has been applied to Aboriginal contexts in each country, and we seek to determine if social capital plays or can play any role in improving educational attainment for Aboriginal populations. Does social capital figure in the formation of programs and policies? Should it be a consideration? What are the specific contexts in which social capital can have an effect on educational attainment? We approached these questions by creating as extensive an inventory of policies and programs as possible for each of the countries. Also, we supplemented our inventory with email, phone, and face-to-face interviews with experts, such as Robert Putnam in the United States, David Robinson in New Zealand, Canadian Aboriginal students, and government policy officers in all three countries. We thank everyone who took time to work with us.

We developed a synthesis, looking for patterns and distilling the role of social capital. Our research looked at conscious applications of the concept but also where we could discern its implicit part in educational attainment. In writing our results, we chose programs and policies that illustrated our synthesis.

Why Aboriginal Education?

The focus on educational attainment and human capital development is strategic. Much research has illustrated the gap in the standard of living between the greater Canadian society and Aboriginal people, and the foundations for understanding these outcomes (White, Maxim, & Beavon, 2004). Recurring themes are the lagging levels of educational attainment and the consequent poor labour market outcomes among Aboriginals compared to the non-Aboriginal Canadian population. The 2001 census data demonstrates these gaps clearly. Among the population 15 years of age and over, 48% of Aboriginals have less than a high school graduation certificate compared to 30.8% of the non-Aboriginal population. The percentage of Aboriginals with high school and some post-secondary education is 22.4% compared to 25% for the non-Aboriginal population. For trades or college, 23.7% of Aboriginals possess this credential compared to 25.9% of the non-Aboriginal population. At the high level of attainment—university—only 4.4% of Aboriginals have achieved this credential compared to 15.7% of the non-Aboriginal population (Statistics Canada, 2003). The picture is not, however, totally bleak. For example, Indian and Northern Affairs Canada (personal communication, November 11, 2004) data shows there have been some improvements in educational attainment over time, but the gaps are still important.

Our chapter is anchored by the desire to develop more insight into the solutions to these problems using the social-capital lens. The trends we have documented are not exclusive to Aboriginal Canadians. Indeed, Aboriginal populations across all three countries have less attainment than the general population, and this issue has not gone unnoticed by their governments. Although our preoccupation with this issue originates within the Canadian context, a logical step is to compare the work done in other countries and develop a general framework of social capital as it relates to Aboriginal educational outcomes. This is what we have done.

Defining Social Capital

Conceptually and theoretically, social capital has various faces and dispositions. Recently, there has been a move to arrive at a single conceptualization and definition of social capital—these efforts have met with much resistance. We do not resolve this issue but match our working understanding with the definition set out by some members of the government, including the Policy Research Initiative. We leave the theoretical debates regarding the "correct" definition of capital for another forum.

We adopt a structural approach to the concept, which emphasizes networks as the focal point of investigation. *Social capital* is defined as the networks of social relations within the milieu, characterized by specific attitudes that serve the purpose of *potentially* enabling individuals' access to a pool of resources and supports. Social capital is conceptualized in three different forms: bonding social capital (intragroup relations), social capital (horizontal intergroup relations), and linking social capital (vertical intergroup relations in a society stratified by class, status, and power relations) (Woolcock, 2001).

Outline

In the introduction, we dealt briefly with the focus of the study, our approach to the data, and the definition of core concepts. Part I presents our model for understanding how social capital operates in the Aboriginal context we studied. The four dimensions of social capital we identify were derived inductively from the study of policy, practice, and outcomes in our target countries. We integrate a small number of examples into this section to make the model grounded and easier to understand. In Part II, we explore some examples of policies and programs that illustrate our synthesis. Finally, we return to the four dimensions, integrate our examples into the model, and draw some further lessons for policymaking.

Part I: The Four-Element Model

We can draw the following general conclusions from our study of social capital and Aboriginal educational outcomes: first, social capital is not an extremely powerful explanator. It functions as an independent variable that explains some variance in population and individual outcomes. However, understanding what seems to impact on the effectiveness of social capital provides interesting insights into its potential strengths and weaknesses.

We found that there are four elements that interact to influence the policy-program effects of social capital. They are:

1. Levels of Social Capital

Social capital seems to have more influence at set threshold points. For example, in the case of Port Harrison (now Inukjuak, Quebec), the movement of the community to a new location led to the destruction of social capital as it broke generational ties. Parents and elders used to teach the young how to hunt and build ice houses. The relocation to a place where there were no hunting possibilities led to a breakup of the traditional system where young people travelled with the elder skilled hunters, learning many skills, such as language, traditions, etc., during the hunting season. Prior to the move, this community had high levels of educational attainment, because in the off-season the community studied at the school. After the relocation, this community spiralled downward as evidenced by many social indicators: suicide increased; school nonattendance became endemic; fertility rates declined; and rates of illness rose (White & Maxim, 2003). Thus, the state had destroyed, perhaps inadvertently, the social capital of the community.

As social capital approaches zero, there seems to be a relatively great effect on population outcomes. In communities that are decimated of social capital networks, educational attainment is very low. The rebuilding of social capital in these communities can have a positive effect; however, given the threshold effect, as we build social capital to even moderate levels, the effect may be negligible, or, depending on the existence of the following three other elements, we may see declines in positive outcomes as social capital grows very strong.

2. Norm Effects

Increasing levels of social capital are not necessarily related to increasing educational attainment. This can be understood by examining what we call *norm effects*. Simply put, where parents and family have low educational attainment and high levels of bonding social capital, the child's educational attainment is likely to be low. This is why we see a high correlation between mothers' and children's educational attainment (White & Maxim, 2002). The post-secondary students we interviewed for this study all came from communities where their family-clan networks had relatively high educational attainment. Ward's (1992) work examining the Cheyenne found that the level of educational attainment in the clan group is critical to the educational success of the children. In another American examination of policy, Ward (1998) notes that the more successful community of Busby, Montana, and its tribal school utilize the highest educational achievers where "adults with education are the role models and sources of support for students" (p. 102). This is a case where the norms available for the child are critical, and substituting higher-norm adults for the bonded network of the family has positive effects.

Where we have low educational norms embedded in a child's family, it is counterproductive to build bonding social capital. The higher the bonding social capital, the more the low norms are reinforced and the lower the educational attainment is likely to be. In Part II, we have several indications of this process. In Queensland, Australia, they had truancy problems and developed a program whereby buses went to the homes of every Aboriginal student to get them in the morning. They discovered that the parents who had little schooling would not wake the children to get on the bus—they preferred to have them sleep.

3. Cultural Openness Contexts (Building Relationships Based on Cultural Context)

Where bonding social capital networks are integrated into wider society (either bridged or linked), there is greater potential for increasing educational attainment. Even remote communities can experience more improvement if culturally open. Open cultures can exist in a few ways. For example, where language use includes dominant languages, people engage in the wider economy and traditions are not exclusionary. Openness is a relative concept; hence, if that which is "outside" can be made more like the target group's culture, it simulates a more open situation and allows bridging and linking. Highly closed dominant cultures and marginalized or nonintegrated ethnic groups can have high levels of social capital and very low levels of educational attainment. Integrated and open cultural contexts that have much lower social capital will have more potential for educational attainment.

This phenomenon can be understood in different ways. For example, if we look at the more successful endeavours in our target countries, we can understand the process as one where the dominant cultural group gathers a clear appreciation of the Aboriginal culture. This appreciation is translated into behaviours that are consistent with the norms within the Aboriginal culture, which facilitates the development of relations and allows linking and bridging to take place. We find this process most clearly manifested in New Zealand. Williams and Robinson (2002) have sought to identify Indigenous applications of social capital. Interestingly, they argued that "the nature of social capital in New Zealand can only be understood by taking into account elements of social capital important to the Maori," which led to their development of a Maori concept of social capital (Williams & Robinson, 2002, p. 12). Robinson and Williams (2001) argued that there were nine key factors or emphases in a Maori concept of social capital. Our review of their work indicates that the key differences involve the role of primary network. For example, in their estimation, social capital is not produced outside of family. The extended family in Maori thinking is the community. Imposition of networks outside the family or community are deemed to be less functional. Robinson and Williams (2001), outline their theory:

> A Maori concept of social capital emphasises the following elements: Extended family relationships are the basis for all other relationships. The whanau [family] is the nucleus of all things. Maori community values and norms come from traditional values that are rooted in the whanau … It is essential to have knowledge of, and to know one's place in … the hierarchy of whanau, hapu and iwi[1] … Relationships in Maori society develop around informal association rather than formal organisations … The connectedness that is derived from this association … The holistic, integrating nature of relationships and networks are of primary importance, while their use or functional activity is secondary … Family, tribal and community networks may take priority over functional contracts with specified agencies such as health, education or welfare …

> Membership in customary Maori associations is based on an exchange of obligations and acceptance by the group. Conditions for joining are verbal, implicit and obligation-driven—rather than rule-driven, specified and written down … The concept … includes obligations based on a common ancestry and the cultural dimension that obliges one to act in certain ways that give rise to the development of social capital. Key concepts of Maori society that relate to social capital include hapai (the requirement to apply the concept of uplifting/enhancement) and tautoko (providing support within the community). (pp. 55–60)

So New Zealand views of social capital imply that relationships must be built through informal associations as opposed to formal institutionalized structures, and the informal relations that lead to the connectedness and networks that are created have specific functions and expectations at the family kin group (whanau), subclan (hapu), and tribal (iwi) level. According to Williams and Robinson (2002), these relationships take precedence over formalized contractual relations in things such as education. The traditional culture has two social capital–related processes that New Zealand policy can utilize: hapai (bridge or connect) and tautoko (support or commitment) that we will see in the form of drawing the family into preschool.

From a practical point of view, the problem is how to utilize the strong-bonding social capital networks within the community at the family and clan level to enhance population outcomes. The simple approach to this would include bridging and linking them to wider social capital networks. Robinson (2004) notes that success depends on two factors: creating or drawing on a collective historical memory of relations held by the iwi (tribe) with another community that facilitates the bridging process (i.e., the memory and history of relations with the central government in this case); and the perception of, or lack of, shared understandings. These are assessed and developed through interaction. Interaction takes place in traditional forums such as the *hui*—a ceremonial gathering that allows people to get to know each other in a recognizable context. It seems from our assessment that this recognition can, therefore, manufacture a collective knowledge/memory of shared understandings that permits linkages.

New Zealand has developed a Maori concept of social capital where it is only produced in the extended family (whanau) and cannot be created for the Maori from the outside through linking or bridging networks. Thus, programs that involve the imposition of networks outside the family or community are deemed to lack functionality. Success rests on bridging networks based on relationships that must be built through engagement in informal associations at the whanau (family), hapu (clan), or iwi (tribe) level. Informal associations that work can eventually be translated to more formal institutionalized structures.

The Maori have specific practices where whanau, hapu, and iwi levels develop understandings of each other. These specialized meeting and exchange structures, such as the hui, are used to create higher-level linkages and bridges between social capital networks. You will see, in the program and policy examples below, how this has been used.

So, in New Zealand, we found that government policy and program development was preceded by an understanding of Maori culture. Implementing programs to help with educational attainment issues could only be done by creating the conditions for bridging and linking, which meant opening the cultural context by adopting the Maori ways.

There are many examples around the world where Aboriginal cultures have changed and become more open. Exogamy creates more openness, for example. In Australia and Canada, the residential schools were an attempt to force assimilation. We can see that these attempts to create linkages were very destructive.

4. Community Capacity

Strong-bonding social capital networks, with high-attainment members who are bridged to school networks and linked to resources, seem to have a positive effect on the transitions to high school and post-secondary institutions, graduate rates, and overall educational success. The context within which social capital works seems much more important than the "strength" or "level" of the bonded network. Networks cannot hold all the resources necessary to ensure educational attainment. They must operate in capital-rich environments; that is, they require other forms of capital in order to have a positive influence on educational attainment. This is why we observe that communities with low economic development (high unemployment) have low educational attainment. Those willing or able to integrate with wider capital formations (e.g., physical capital), or who have the capacity to develop such capital based on their infrastructures tend to have high educational attainment.

Our investigation of Australia demonstrated this dimension very clearly. Stone, Gray, and Hughes (2003) argue that using social capital generated by low-capacity communities can reinforce low capacity. They are looking at this in the context of job-searching, but it has implications for education. Interventions to network low-achievement parents with the schools may encourage a reproduction of the lower achievement according to the Australian approach.

Hunter (2000) notes that unemployment of adults is a key problem in creating and sustaining poor educational results for children. Community capacity is once again seen as playing a fundamental role in educational processes. Hunter's (2000) study of social capital concludes that reinforcing social capital in a community with low employment levels reinforces lower norms of achievement and leads to children uninterested in educational attainment.

A study by the Centre for Aboriginal Economic Policy Research (Hunter, 2000), however, does call for Australia to vet all policies (as per Putnam's call) to determine the effects on social capital and how to ensure that policies increase the involvement and connection of

Aboriginal society with wider Australian society. This "connectiveness" may actually increase integration and mitigate the effects of high levels of bonding capital, which works with low-education norms to reinforce separateness. There has been considerable research on Portes's four negative attributes of social capital and their application to the Australian Aboriginal context. Hunter (2004) notes that the "exclusion of outsiders" prevents access to services, especially in the area of education; "excessive claims on group members" plays out as "demand sharing" that may undermine educational involvement by youth; "restrictions on group members' freedom" can undermine autonomy where norms dictate noninvolvement; and "downward leveling of norms" creates a non-achievement context as we noted in the previous studies.

The Australians are developing a theoretical model that differs from the one used in New Zealand. They advocate the need to intervene to build community capacity, including at the level of network construction. They have also placed cultural specificity at the core of approaching the issue of social capital and educational attainment, but it appears somewhat differently (more interventionist) in practice, as we will see in the policies we review in Part II.

Conceptual Modelling of the Four Elements

If we examine some combinations of cases, the interrelationships and impacts of the four dimensions may become clearer:

> *Scenario One: Aboriginal children with moderate to high social capital, where educational attainment norms in their networks are moderate to high, who live in communities with cultural openness and low unemployment levels, will have high educational attainment.*

> *Scenario Two: Aboriginal students who have high levels of social capital with low educational attainment norms in their network and low economic development will have low educational attainment. This scenario is often compounded by being resilient to outside network bridging and linking—a result of being culturally closed.*

> *Scenario Three: Aboriginal children with zero or extremely low social capital will have no educational attainment norms to draw upon and will have low educational attainment. In this case alone, building social capital is a key prerequisite to increasing educational attainment.*

Part II: Selected Policy and Program Examples in New Zealand, Australia, and Canada

Part II explores some of the policies and programs aimed at confronting problems of educational attainment among Aboriginals in New

Zealand, Australia, and Canada. This is not designed to be an exhaustive review of the activities in each region; instead, it examines some key illustrations of the four-dimension model we presented earlier.

New Zealand

New Zealand has targeted educational attainment for the Maori as the key to reversing the negative population indicators all too common among Indigenous populations worldwide. The New Zealand Ministry of Education report small yet positive improvements based on two identified factors that have made the biggest difference in engaging students and raising their achievement: the quality of teaching and the relationship between whanau/home and school (New Zealand Ministry of Education, 2003). We will concentrate on the second issue, the relationship between family and school, because this is clearly connected to the use of social capital to increase educational outcomes, and provides the clearest indication of opening relationships based on cultural context.

Since 1988, the New Zealand government has moved to "hand over responsibility for governing educational institutions to the local community and make communities accountable … reforms have encouraged more innovative ways for communities and education institutions to work together" (Ministry of Maori Development, 1997, p. 10). The evaluation of the reforms, overall, cited that successful initiatives occurred when there was a developed community-school co-operation, and when the community families proposed, developed, or participated in and supported the programs (Ministry of Maori Development, 1997, p. 10).

One of the first policies developed and translated into programs was the stepwise creation of pathways for parents to be involved in supporting their children's learning. The Parent Support and Development Program (PSDP), Study Support Centres (SSC), and Parents as Mentors (PAM) initiatives were set up as partnerships between schools, whanau (family), and communities. If social capital is created in the kin group (whanau), and social capital in the form of networks of support are key to improving school achievement, then building network connections between schools and whanau would be the way to proceed. This is exactly what they have done. The building block of their improvement program is increasing Maori involvement, which cannot be done top-down but only bottom-up (recall our discussion in Part I).

The Parents as First Teachers (PAFT) program is one of the most illustrative. It focused on providing support and guidance to parents with children zero to three years of age. Maori children tend to come less prepared for elementary school, which leads to performance and discipline issues. This led to a widespread discussion between those running the program and the whanau and communities about establishing and running preschools in those communities to increase the preparedness of the children. From our modelling perspective, we have to ask: how did the Ministry get the whanau to be involved? The Ministry set up stalls at community events, attended hui (special meetings with dialogue), etc., and the Ministry networks became "known" to the Maori. Recall that relationships in Maori society develop around informal association rather than formal organizations, and so family, tribal, and community networks may take priority over functional contracts with specified agencies. Thus, building the personal informal links was a precursor to more formalized relations. After being known to Maori families, the New Zealand Ministry of Education explained the benefits of preschool and helped parents set up their own early childhood programs or helped children enroll in the founding ones. In 2003, three thousand Maori families were involved in the PAFT program (Farquhar, 2003; New Zealand Ministry of Education, 2003).

The case of New Zealand illustrates the need to build culturally sensitive pathways that open the bonding social capital networks up to linking and bridging resource-rich networks. Also demonstrated is the role of norms and the relative unimportance of levels of social capital in the basic bonding networks.

Australia

In this section, we want to highlight what is distinctive in the Australian approach and point out how their understanding contributes to our model. While the Australians have launched a myriad of programs to improve teacher cultural understanding, train new teachers, develop preschools, and integrate parents, they see building community capacity as integral to making education relevant to Indigenous peoples. Thus, jobs and access to markets are the foundation of success. They also see that the skills of the labour force have to increase in order to take advantage of any development. There is little evidence that the Australians are looking at any particular strategies that involve using or developing social capital in this process. Some exceptions are, however, notable. The Gumala Mirnuwarni (Coming Together to Learn) Program, in West Australia, was established in 1997. The House of Representatives Standing Committee (2004) reports that the impetus for this program was the community's desire to see their children more actively participate in school: "It has involved collaboration and partnership between children, parents, schools, State and Commonwealth education authorities, three resource partners and a philanthropic organization, in a program designed to improve educational outcomes for local Indigenous students" (p. 189). A representative of Rio Tinto outlined one element of the project, a personal commitment contract that reads: "'I, the child, agree to go along to school and I, the family member, agree to support my child going to school.' ... If the child does not participate in school, then they are not welcome at the afterschool program ... that has been set up for them. So there is an expectation that their participation in school will lead to enhanced benefits" (House of Representatives Standing Committee, 2004, p. 189).[2]

The Gumala Mirnuwarni has been successful because of the attempts to link family networks, students, and school networks together using reciprocity mechanisms. The government noted that they recognize the success of the project and have proceeded to use it as a foundation for other initiatives. They have developed the notion of compacts around the country in which diverse stakeholders forge beneficial working relations, for example, families with schools and industry (House of Representatives Standing Committee, 2004). This has the effect of increasing the apparent benefits of school. The use of networks in the community is less developed and less widespread than in New Zealand; however, an analysis of policy development does show the employment of networks. The Australians are cautious on social capital issues.

The Australian experience indicates the relationships between the goals of being educated and the motivation to be involved in the process of being educated. Where there is development in the community (higher capacity), there is a tangible reward or return for the work of going to school. Where there are no opportunities for work or societal involvement, the rewards are unclear and involvement in the educational process diminishes.

Canada

The last set of examples we will cover are from Canada. This section is broken into two parts, as we want to look at examples from national programs and policy, delivered under the auspices of Indian and Northern Affairs Canada (INAC), and some provincial examples.[3]

NATIONAL POLICIES IN CANADA

INAC operates two major sets of programs. First, The Elementary/ Secondary Education National Program aims to "provide eligible students living on reserve with elementary and secondary education comparable to that required in provincial schools ... where the reserve is located" (INAC, 2003a, p. 3). Funding is transferred to a variety of deliverers that can include the bands (communities) themelves, the provincial school boards if they are delivering the services, or federal schools maintained by the government. INAC outlines the expenditures acceptable for funding. Second, the Post-Secondary Education Program's objective is to "improve the employability of First Nations people and Inuit by providing eligible students ... access to education and skill development opportunities at the post-secondary level" (INAC, 2003b, p. 3). Moreover, this program aims to increase participation in post-secondary studies, post-secondary graduation rates, and employment rates (INAC, 2003b).

Canada launched a review in 2002 to identify and address the factors of a quality First Nations education (INAC, 2002). Several initiatives have been started in the past few years, but more time will have to elapse before we can evaluate these initiatives. However, we can see that many of these initiatives parallel those that have been successful in other countries.

PROVINCIAL INITIATIVES

There are many policies and programs across the country affecting Aboriginal people that are aimed at enhancing their educational and labour market outcomes. We look at only a few illustrative examples in British Columbia, where the work that has been done is quite extensive.

The Best Practices Project by the First Nation Schools Association and First Nations Education Steering Committee of British Columbia (1997) is a very successful initiative. For example, the First Nations Role Model Program in School District 52 (Prince Rupert) involves the use of very successful First Nations role models in the classroom. The goal is to promote awareness of First Nations cultures and issues for all students and teachers, while promoting self-esteem and pride in cultural heritage. There is a benefit to the school and students as the mentor links the students to the resources of the outside world, and they substitute for the low-educational norm context of the parental networks. Not only can the mentor's resources be potentially drawn upon but they establish a relationship that is grounded in a culturally familiar context. The provision of a higher-norm model substitutes for lower attainment levels in the child's bonding capital group (family) while fostering openness. The key is not building bonding social capital, which can reinforce low attainment (recall Scenario Two previously).

The Summer Science and Technology Camps Initiative, funded by INAC and coordinated by the First Nations Education Steering Committee, targets First Nations youth to engage them in science and technology issues and expose them to the numerous education and career opportunities available. The program includes local elders and other community members through the process of having First Nations communities and organizations develop the initiatives in accordance with their local priorities. Through partnerships with institutions outside of the community, such as BC Hydro, BC Gas, ministries of fisheries and forestry, Science World BC, and the University of British Columbia, the reason for education becomes clear. In a way, this initiative connects the students directly to the job market and makes education seem to have a purpose. In that respect, it plays the role that higher levels of community capacity and development would play. This is an illustration of what the Australians are arguing, concerning the need for resource-rich environments for social capital to operate. As well, links are forged between the communities (children) and resource-rich institutions. The immediate effects are increased interest in science subjects and the long-term establishment of relations between the community and the labour force.

Policy and Program Implications

As we developed Parts I and II above, we drew some tentative linkages between the policy and program initiatives and the four elements that we feel interact to enhance success generally and optimize social capital–based initiatives particularly. We can draw some more general conclusions in this section and push a little deeper into how we can approach the critical issue of Aboriginal educational attainment. Policy and program success seems highly sensitive to context.

In New Zealand, where the Maori are a large proportion of the population, we find well-developed programs to build educational attainment levels. They are also based most closely on a homegrown, culturally specific notion of social capital. As we noted, New Zealand has determined that social capital is only created in the communities at the family level. Given that the families and subclans all have high-bonding social capital levels, and that the higher tribal organizations are built on this social capital base, any bridging or linking that is going to take place must be rooted in the core family networks. They have a restricted, yet functional, view of using social capital, where the high levels of bonding social capital must be shaped and used in the wider institutions to promote the norms of external networks. We saw, for example, that the programs began at the preschool with the families running the preschool, which changed attitudes toward schooling. Parents (the whanau) became involved in preparing children for school, which was often done in the school setting, by passing school skills on to them. It is through this process that the school system becomes a part of the family. The school networks, including teachers, principals, etc., became "known" and began to "share a history" with the Maori while developing "knowledge of the customs and norms." This process allowed the whanau to be bridged and linked to the educational institutions that precipitated the flow of the bridged and linked resources. The policy aimed at creating a context of cultural openness in this case.

Openness can be created in two ways. First, one can transform aspects of the cultural norms of the target populations, although this is the most difficult and runs the risk of being seen as assimilationist. A second approach is to make sure the program is delivered in a way that is not challenging to the Aboriginal culture, using the ways of the people to the greatest possible degree. This has the effect of making the institution, such as a school, more like the people and less "outside." A closed cultural context is one that has two approaches that are culturally distant. Narrowing the gap through the introduction of Aboriginal language, community elder participation, and using the forums that are acceptable (e.g., the hui in New Zealand) helps create a more open context.

Specific policies and programs across our three countries all reinforce the importance of this condition being fulfilled. Many have aspects of their programs tailored, albeit often unconsciously, to reinforce openness. This process is clearly seen in initiatives such as "Teaching the Teachers," which teaches Aboriginal culture, as well as programs that integrate community cultural leaders and make use of family and elders.

The Australians have a greater focus on economic development as a necessary condition for improving educational attainment. They are generally more skeptical of the concept noting that high levels of bonding social capital combined with poor norms around schooling reinforce nonattainment. Australia seeks a more stepwise process to improving educational attainment, where the key is community development and improved community capacity. Having access to jobs enables citizens to understand the utility of education. Also, this strategy retains those with human capital in communities, which in turn provides better norm models. Recall, Queensland had a problem with school attendance and developed a program to have buses drive to each student's house every morning to take them to school. The result was poor because parents would not wake the kids if they were sleeping. Attendance, leading to graduation, leading to jobs, was the needed understanding. The successful programs have developed partnerships with the business community, creating job opportunities. These partnerships around the country link industry and community interests, giving meaning to educational attainment. They created the integration of the family bonding social capital networks with the resources that made education more important. In these cases, it was the building of community capacity that was key, and the other elements, while important, needed to be less prominent. Building social capital at the community level (bonding) was of little importance and may have been detrimental in the absence of economic development given the low educational norms.

Using our framework, and incorporating the Australian experience, we might argue, given our examination of initiatives, that in the unsuccessful programs, the parents were not easily involved because they had little understanding of the importance of schooling, given their low educational attainment. Given the low community capacity in terms of economic development, the purpose for supporting the schools and promoting higher educational attainment for the children was unclear to both the community and the students. The more successful programs were, indeed, linked to job paths.

In Canada, at the federal level, some of the recent initiatives that have been started in the past few years parallel initiatives that have been successful in other countries. These initiatives have not had sufficient time to develop and be evaluated at this stage. The provinces have developed programs that address specific local needs. The provincial programs that are most successful target the specific problem associated with our model. For example, in the Science and Technology Camps, the inclusion of local elders and other community members such as teachers led to the First Nations communities and organizations developing the initiatives in accordance with their cultures; consequently, family networks were bolstered by having adult participants who came back and encouraged support for education. In the case of the First Nations Role Model Program, the mentors substituted for the low educational norm context of the parental networks. Other initiatives examined but not reported showed similar patterns.

In conclusion, we would argue that understanding social capital is important in promoting educational attainment. However, it has a moderate influence and rarely acts alone. It influences outcomes for Aboriginal educational attainment in conjunction with other resources (human and economic/physical capital). It is contingent on the context, and this can be assessed by using the four elements we have discussed throughout our chapter. We have argued the following:

1. It is key to identify the specific context and interrelation of the four identified elements, and address programming toward the specificity of the situation. Just building social capital would rarely be the most effective strategy. Where communities, families, and clans face grave social problems and have low-bonding social capital, then it is appropriate to build that resource. It could, however, under certain conditions, be the wrong strategy.

2. Where there are very low educational norms in the child's networks, reinforcing social capital in those networks is the wrong approach. It will reinforce low norms and nonattainment strategies. Substituting higher-norm roles is one strategy for overcoming this problem; however, that involves bridging and linking to the child and their networks, which depends on the appropriateness of strategies and the degree of openness of communities to outsiders.

3. The ability to engage children depends on how open their communities are. Schools, ministries of education, federal departments, and teachers will have to depend on the target groups having accepted or incorporated aspects of the dominant culture and goals in order to connect with their programs and resources; or the dominant culture and its institutions can adopt, and adapt to, the Aboriginal minority culture and create an openness context to connect in that manner. Such adaptation must be context specific. However, even where connections can take place, there is no guarantee of any "buy-in" to goals of educational attainment.

4. Enthusiasm for education is linked to seeing a purpose for the effort. This point is key, particularly where past experience has been negative for the parents. For example, residential schooling in Canada and Australia created a legacy of mistrust and anger among Aboriginal peoples. The key to providing purpose is related to the development of community or related capacity.

Future Research

The development of a better understanding of the interrelationship between the four identified elements is the next step. This should involve two separate processes. First, the development of methods to measure the different elements will allow us to produce useful diagnostic tools. The second process is to develop a simple planning tool that gives its user a way to draw conclusions about the relative problems across the four dimensions: levels of social capital, norm effects, cultural openness, and community capacity. The planning tool could be a crude guide to assess existing programs, diagnose problems, and design improvements.

REFERENCES

Farquhar, S.E. (2003). *Parents as first teachers: A study of the New Zealand PAFT program.* Wellington, New Zealand: Early Childhood Development.

First Nations Schools Association & First Nations Education Steering Committee. (1997). *First Nations education: Best practices project* (Vol. 1). Vancouver: First Nations Schools Association and First Nations Education Steering Committee.

House of Representatives Standing Committee on Aboriginal and Torres Strait Islander Affairs. (2004). *Many ways forward: Report of the inquiry into capacity building and service delivery in Indigenous communities.* Canberra, Australia: The Parliament of the Commonwealth of Australia.

Hunter, B.H. (2000). *Social exclusion, social capital, and Indigenous Australians: Measuring the social costs of unemployment.* Technical Report Discussion Paper No. 204, Centre for Aboriginal Economic Policy Research, Australia National University.

Hunter, B.H. (2004). Taming the social capital Hydra? Indigenous poverty, social capital theory and measurement. Retrieved October 2, 2004, from http://www. anu.edu.au/caeprlPublications/topical!Hunter_social%20capital.pdC

Indian and Northern Affairs Canada (INAC). (2002). *Our children–keepers of the sacred knowledge: Final report of the Minister's National Working Group on Education.* Ottawa: Government of Canada.

Indian and Northern Affairs Canada (INAC). (2003a). *Appendix A: Elementary and secondary education–national program guidelines.* Ottawa: Government of Canada.

Indian and Northern Affairs Canada (INAC). (2003b). *Appendix B: Post-Secondary education–national program guidelines.* Ottawa: Government of Canada.

Ministry of Maori Development. (1997). *Making education work for Maori: Talking points for parents and whanau.* Wellington, New Zealand: Government of New Zealand.

New Zealand Ministry of Education. (2003). *Nga Haeata Maturauranga: Annual report on Maori education.* Wellington, New Zealand: Government of New Zealand.

Robinson, D. (2004, July 11–14). *Forming norms and implementing sanctions— deliberation and sustained dialogue in a social capital framework.* Notes prepared for panel presentation at ISTR Conference, Toronto.

Robinson, D., & Williams, T. (2001). Social capital and voluntary activity: Giving and sharing in Maori/non-Maori society. *Social Policy Journal of New Zealand, 17,* 51–71.

Statistics Canada. (2003). *Selected educational characteristics, Aboriginal identity, age groups, sex, and area of residence for population 15 years and over, 2001 census—20% sample data (Catalogue no. 97FOOIIXCBOI042).* Ottawa: Author.

Stone, W., Gray, M., & Hughes, J. (2003). *Social capital at work: How family, friends and civic ties relate to labour market outcomes.* Research Paper 31. Melbourne, Australia: Australian Institute of Family Studies.

Ward, C. (1992). *Social and cultural influences on the schooling of Northern Cheyenne youth.* Ph.D dissertation, University of Chicago.

Ward, C. (1998). Community resources and school performance: The Northern Cheyenne case. *Sociological Inquiry, 68*(1), 83–113. http://dx.doi.org/10.1111/j.1475-682X.1998.tb00455.x

Western Australia Department of Education. (n.d.). GUMALA MIRNUWARNI—coming together to learn. Retrieved September 20, 2004, from http://www.dest.gov.au/archive/iae/analysis/learningll/gumala.htm

White, J., & Maxim, P. (2003). Social capital, social cohesion, and population outcomes in Canada's First Nations communities. In J. White, P. Maxim, & D. Beavon (Eds.), *Aboriginal conditions: Research as a foundation for public policy* (pp. 7–34). Vancouver: University of British Columbia Press.

White, J., & Maxim, P. (2002, November 26–28). *Correlates of educational attainment in First Nations communities.* Paper presented at the Aboriginal Policy Research Conference, Ottawa.

White, J. Maxim, P. & Beavon, D. (Eds.). (2004). *Aboriginal policy research: Setting the agenda for change.* (Vol. I). *II.* Toronto: Thompson Educational Publishing.

Williams, T., & Robinson, D. (2002). Social capital based partnerships, a Maori perspective—a comparative approach. In D. Robinson (Ed.), *Building social capital* (pp. 14–30). Victoria, New Zealand: Institute of Policy Studies, Victoria University.

Woolcock, M. (2001). The place of social capital in understanding social and economic outcomes. In J.F. Helliwell (Ed.), *The contribution of human and social capital to sustained economic growth and well-being. International Symposium Report* (pp. 65–88). Human Resources Development Canada and OECD. Paris: OECD Publications.

NOTES

1 *Whanau* is family, *hapu* is subclan, and *iwi* is tribe.

2 "The programs involved Education Enrichment Centres where students can study after school, with supervision and support. Homework and individual tutoring was undertaken. The centres were set up with educational resources including computers with internet access … Students were assigned to a school-based mentor … who also worked on well-being. Extracurricular activities could be arranged to develop confidence and abilities including … visits to industry … and cultural awareness camps" (Western Australia Department of Education, n.d.).

3 In Canada, education falls under provincial jurisdiction in the Constitution. However, note that INAC funds basic elementary and secondary education for the 120,000 students who live on reserve (INAC, personal communication, 2004). The federal government also provides funding that supports roughly 26,000 First Nation and Inuit students in post-secondary education each year. About four thousand of these students graduate annually (INAC, personal communication, 2004).

10

Why We Need a First Nations Education Act

Michael Mendelson

This chapter was originally published by the Caledon Institute of Social Policy, Ottawa, October 2009. Reproduced with permission.

Introduction

In its path-breaking 1972 policy statement "Indian Control of Indian Education," the National Indian Brotherhood (forerunner of the Assembly of First Nations) demanded First Nations control of First Nations education (National Indian Brotherhood, 1972). This demand does not constitute a form of special status for First Nations. On the contrary, communal control over education is embedded in Canadian history.

Canada was made possible by section 93 of the Constitution Act of 1867, explicitly giving provinces sovereignty with respect to education (except on reserves), within the confines of constitutional provisions protecting confessional education rights. These constitutional provisions were a necessary accommodation to make the Canadian federation possible, resulting in parallel Catholic and secular school boards. Today we continue to accept the inconvenience and expense of multiple school boards in many of our cities, towns, and rural areas— e.g., there are four school boards in the city of Ottawa alone. There is nothing unusual, or in any way un-Canadian, about a community seeking to protect its capacity to use schools to enhance cultural continuity. First Nations are just as protective of their rights to determine the education of their children as are Canada's other peoples.

The first step in achieving Indian Control of Indian Education was for the federal government to cede its control over First Nations education, and this has largely been done. But the second and more crucial step is for First Nations to step into the vacuum and create the necessary organizational and financial infrastructure for a high-quality First Nations education system, and this has not been done. Despite many First Nations' attempts to establish needed educational infrastructure, only bits and pieces of an education system have so far been set up on various reserves across Canada. For the most part, the major elements of an education system for First Nations are missing.

This chapter describes those missing pieces and sets out a plan for how they may be put into place across Canada. It is a proposal for a new Act of Parliament that would allow First Nations who wished to do so to establish properly funded First Nations school boards with clear legal empowerment and the necessary regional educational agencies to support them.

Whole System Reform

The renowned educational scholar Michael Fullan argues that the revitalization of a school system requires what he calls "whole system reform" (2009). Fullan says that whole system reform must take place simultaneously at the school, district, and state level, with dedicated unrelenting leadership from the state, focused ultimately on what goes on in the classroom. As a practical example, he and Ben Levin describe the process of whole system reform in Ontario, which has resulted in improved educational outcomes across the province— except, of course, on reserves that are not under provincial jurisdiction (Levin, 2008; Fullan & Levin, 2009).

Whole system reform is exactly what is urgently required for First Nations education, yet education on Canada's First Nations reserves is characterized by the absence of First Nations' school systems and the isolation of individual First Nations schools. Whole system reform is impossible when there is no "system" to begin with. While there is a significant body of literature on how to improve schools (much of it controversial), this research almost always presupposes there is a mechanism in place to organize and implement whatever reform is being advocated. To initiate whole system reform of First Nations education, a First Nations education system must first be constructed.

There is no doubt that reform is desperately needed. There are approximately 113,000 students resident on reserves in elementary and secondary education. About 60% of these students attend 515 schools located on reserve, with the remainder attending mainly public high schools off reserve (Aboriginal Affairs). According to census data, the proportion of young people on reserve who have completed high school has not increased in the last 10 years, and the high school completion gap between youth on reserve and those in the general population is getting larger, not smaller (Richards & Scott, 2009; Mendelson, 2008). While some First Nations on-reserve schools are providing better education (Bell, 2004), many other on-reserve schools are doing worse. Piecemeal improvement of individual schools and even clusters of schools is failing to keep up with the continued deterioration of many other schools. On-reserve education is failing First Nations students, parents, and society as a whole.

A plethora of social ills is associated with low educational achievement (Riddell, 2005). For example, lack of educational attainment has an important negative effect on health and longevity (Wolfe & Haveman, 2001). Parental education is a significant determinant of child health and intellectual development (de Coulon, Meschi, & Vignoles, 2008). Lochner (2007) has reviewed empirical data and has concluded that "an increase in educational attainment significantly reduces subsequent violent and property crime yielding sizeable social benefits" (p. 1). Perreault (2009) shows that incarceration rates for Aboriginal people are much higher for those without high school graduation than for those who have graduated from high school. Lochner (2007) estimates that in the US, each additional male high school graduate saves the public $1,600 to $2,900 just as a result of the reduction in crime—not taking account of savings in any other area (p. 12). Such costs and potential savings are doubtless similar in Canada.

The list of costly and harmful social consequences of poor education could likely go on and on, but besides social costs, the destructive effect of the failure of First Nations education is also economic. The chances of getting and holding a good job are diminishingly small for those without a high school education (Richards and Scott, 2009). A young and dynamic First Nations population could be adding to the common wealth and well-being of Canada by fulfilling the demand for increasingly skilled workers and contributing to arts and culture, while also taking advantage of opportunities to start up exciting new businesses—and some of those businesses might be rooted in First Nations culture in ways we have not yet imagined. Instead, we likely will have continuing and escalating dependency, resulting in a heavy financial cost to society, especially on the Prairies where First Nations are an increasing proportion of the working-age population (see Table 10.1).

Given these costs, an investment that resulted in improved educational results for First Nations students on reserve would have a high rate of return and be well worth the expenditure. In their extensive study of the effects of improved Aboriginal educational outcomes on the economy and government budgets, Sharpe, Arsenault, Lapointe, & Cowan (2009) concluded that "Investing in Aboriginal education will not only benefit the Aboriginal population itself, but will also benefit Canadian government and, by extension, the entire Canadian population" (p. 70). The researchers found that gross domestic product (GDP) growth would be up to 0.03 percentage points higher and government's fiscal balances considerably improved if the Aboriginal population's educational attainment could be brought to the 2001 level of educational attainment of the general population.

But under the present circumstances, it is not clear how additional funding can be provided for First Nations education so as to maximize its effect on improving educational outcomes. As is discussed further below, more money is probably necessary but in itself will not automatically redress the deficiencies of the existing nonsystem of First Nations education. The public policy challenge is to spend

Table 10.1 Total Full-Time Equivalent (FTE) Students Normally Resident on First Nations Reserves Attending School On and Off Reserve

2000–2001 to 2007–2008 Fiscal Year					
Fiscal Year	**Total FTE Students Attending School**	**On-reserve Students**		**Off-reserve Students**	
2000–2001	112,701	69,131	61%	43,571	39%
2001–2002	112,546	68,578	61%	43,968	39%
2002–2003	113,216	68,373	60%	44,843	40%
2003–2004	113,138	68,737	61%	44,401	39%
2004–2005	114,720	69,589	61%	45,131	39%
2005–2006	115,299	68,434	59%	46,865	41%
2006–2007	113,121	67,478	60%	45,643	40%
2007–2008	112,996	68,576	61%	44,420	39%

Source: Office of the Parliamentary Budget Officer, 2009. Data provided by Indian and Northern Affairs, as identified in the nominal roll call. On-reserve includes approximately 1,500 FTE students in federal (non-band operated) schools and off-reserve includes approximately 2,055 FTE students in private schools.

effectively—to find ways to invest more money into First Nations education on reserve in such a way that the spending has a good chance of resulting in sustainable improvements in educational outcomes. A viable public policy strategy requires financing and educational reforms to be addressed simultaneously.

What Sorts of Reforms Are These?

As has been discussed extensively elsewhere (see Mendelson, 2008, for a review of reports), First Nations schools on reserve are unlike any other public schools in Canada in that they usually operate as independent, individual, or very small groups of schools with relatively few students. Since the 1930s, all off-reserve public schools in Canada have been brought under the supervision of school boards, most of which have substantial educational and administrative resources. In British Columbia, for example, 830 school districts in 1932 were reduced to 89 by 1947 and 57 today (Fleming and Hutton, 1997). In a later reform movement (some would say following the Soviet Sputnik and the consequent fear of falling behind Russia), provincial ministries of education were modernized to provide significant resources and supports to school boards.

The old village school, sometimes operating under the administration of the town mayor, is long gone everywhere—except on First Nations reserves. In a speech to the House of Commons upon introduction of the First Nations Jurisdiction over Education in British Columbia Act, former Minister of Indian and Northern Affairs Jim Prentice (2006) put it succinctly: "First Nation children, frankly, have been the only children in Canada who have lacked an education system."

Why is this important? School boards and provincial ministries play a vital educational role and are much more than added layers of bureaucracy. Each has functions that are crucial to the quality of education and especially to sustainable quality education over the long term. It is these institutions that make geographically dispersed schools into an education system. It is only through these organizations that a process of whole system reform can be led.

Viable school boards and ministries are essential, but they do not automatically result in improved educational outcomes. There would be no great surprise in uncovering a poorly functioning school board or a provincial education ministry that does not do its job. Rather, school boards and ministries are a necessary but not sufficient condition to organize the process of improving on-reserve schools. This is like the relationship of a factory and a manager: it is possible to have a manager who does a terrible job, yet without a manager, the factory will be chaotic and all but certainly go under. School boards and ministries are the required organizational infrastructure upon which may be built a better system of schools, but the "heavy lifting" of changing what actually goes on in the classroom must still be taken on. However, without boards and ministries there will be no one to ensure that the heavy lifting occurs—to improve on-reserve schools systematically.

In the next sections, we look at the functions of school boards and ministries in more detail, and discuss how these functions can be performed within a First Nations education system.

The Need for School Boards

School boards perform two types of function in the school system: they are the executive managers of schools *and* service providers for schools. As executive managers, school boards supervise their schools' performance and, if the school board is doing its job properly, intervene when schools are not succeeding. School boards oversee the human resources within their school system, negotiating contracts and the terms of employment for teachers and providing for stable employment with opportunities for professional training and advancement. School boards develop the leadership that is critical to successful schools by nurturing a cadre of principals, usually out of the ranks of teachers, with experience and knowledge. School boards administer the finances of the school system within their jurisdiction and the allocations to individual schools, including responsibility in some provinces for raising a portion of their own revenue.

In addition to management functions, school boards provide a range of centralized services. The school board service function is especially valuable where economies of scale require a shared specialty among many schools, such as speech therapy. But beyond the obvious examples of specialized educational services, there are many mundane and concrete services performed by school boards. To pick one example of a centralized service that does not involve the direct provision of educational services, most school boards have a building department including skilled and experienced professionals, such as architects and engineers, who are responsible for developing and maintaining the physical plant. For example, Winnipeg School Board, with 77 schools and 33,000 students, has approximately 20 people working directly for the board in its building department (Winnipeg School Board, n.d.). Of course, simply having lots of engineers on staff does not guarantee that a board will do a good job of capital planning and maintenance, but inadequate staffing will likely guarantee it will do a poor job.

On a comparative basis, and ignoring the relatively more challenging infrastructure demands of many on-reserve schools, there should be about 130 to 150 centralized, specialized staff serving on-reserve educational infrastructure needs across all of Canada. Based on a rough interpretation of staffing charts, it appears there is only

---

The Ontario government lists school boards' responsibilities as:

- determining the number, size, and location of schools;
- building, equipping, and furnishing schools;
- providing education programs that meet the needs of the school community, including needs for special education;
- prudent management of the funds allocated by the province to support all board activities, including education programs for elementary and secondary school students, and the building and maintaining of schools;
- preparing an annual budget;
- supervising the operation of schools and their teaching programs;
- developing policy for safe arrival programs for elementary schools;
- establishing a school council at each school;
- hiring teachers and other staff;
- helping teachers improve their teaching practices;
- teacher performance;
- approving schools' textbook and learning materials choices, based on the list of approved materials provided by the Ministry of Education;
- enforcing the student attendance provisions of the Education Act;
- ensuring schools abide by the Education Act and its regulations.

---

a handful of engineers and other professionals working for INAC on general infrastructure (not necessarily specializing in education) in national headquarters and in the regions, perhaps fewer than a half-dozen. Most on-reserve schools have no specialized building support at all. An Asset Condition Report is required every three years on all reserves, but the technical inspection is performed by outside contractors. The absence of in-house, education-specialized technical physical plant capacities places severe obstacles in the path of good capital maintenance and development.

Most First Nations' schools on reserve do not have the support of a fully empowered school board (some exceptions are discussed below). However, many First Nations have attempted to redress this deficiency, at least in part, by forming multischool service organizations with some pooled resources. Indian and Northern Affairs has often encouraged and helped finance multischool organizations. Many on-reserve schools are part of a multischool service organization, at least as best as can be determined from a casual survey.

Examples of First Nations Multischool Organizational Initiatives in 2006

First Nations Education Steering Committee

Treaty Seven First Nations Education Consortium

Treaty Six education initiative

Treaty Eight education initiative

Federation of Saskatchewan Indian Nations

Northwest Nations Education Council

Prince Albert Grand Council

Northern Nishanawbe Education Council

Fort Frances—Treaty 3

Union of Ontario Indians

Indigenous Education Coalition

Association of Iroquois and Allied Indians

Cree School Board

L'Institut Culturel Educatif Montagnais

New Brunswick Education Initiative

Mi'kmaq Kina'matnewey (McCue, 2006)

Most of the First Nations multischool service organizations are relatively small, with few resources and a limited range of services. Some are called a "school board" or a "school authority," but when these organizations involve several bands, only rarely do they have the range of responsibilities that are vested in off-reserve school boards. Nevertheless, it is at least theoretically possible for on-reserve schools to obtain some of the centralized service benefits of a school board through multischool service organizations—without an actual school board operating like an off-reserve school board. By contrast, the school board's executive management function will always be missing without a true school board that is fully responsible for the schools under its administration. Yet it is the executive management function that is especially critical for the challenges now facing on-reserve schools—management of human resources, finances, development of a cadre of principals, identification and correction of underperforming schools, and so on.

First Nations School Boards

First Nations schools need First Nations school boards.[1] First Nations school boards might be named something else, but whatever they are called, the functions they need to perform are the same. They must be fully vested with authority to manage the schools on reserves in their catchment area, as well as provide shared services to these schools. In short, and to be as explicit as possible, if First Nations are to have a school *system*, and not just a collection of schools, full control and ownership of schools must be vested in First Nations school boards and not in individual bands. Specialized agencies that are concerned solely with education—First Nations school boards— should become fully responsible for education on reserves, taking over from band government and from small education authorities set up, and sometimes appointed by, band governments.

In addition, First Nations school boards should have a responsibility that is not generally required of non–First Nations boards. As noted, many students normally resident on reserve will have to attend high school off reserve—and sometimes lower grades as well. In some instances, students living off reserve, particularly in isolated areas, attend on-reserve schools. First Nations school boards should negotiate and administer agreements with off-reserve school boards, providing for expectations and accountability on behalf of their students attending schools off reserve, and the reverse in the relatively rarer instances where off-reserve residents attend schools on reserve. These arrangements should include the payment and receipt of tuition fees so that funds on behalf of students would be paid by the First Nations school board responsible for a geographic area. At present, funding on behalf of on-reserve students attending off-reserve schools is paid either directly by INAC to the off-reserve school, or to the band council, which then pays the off-reserve school. A board-to-board relationship is more appropriate than a band-governance-organization-to-board relationship, and more likely to focus on educational requirements.

First Nations school boards' districts need to be large enough to be able to provide centralized services efficiently to their schools. There can be little doubt that First Nations need school boards, but how large their districts should be is one of the most difficult questions facing any attempt to establish a First Nations education system.

The Royal Commission on Aboriginal Peoples considered the restructuring of First Nations education and recommended the recognition of what they called "Aboriginal Nations" as the basis for the First Nations equivalent of school boards. According to the Royal Commission (1996):

> An Aboriginal Nation should be defined as a sizable body of Aboriginal people that possesses a shared sense of national identity and constitutes the predominant population of a certain territory or collection of territories. Thus, the Mi'kmaq, the Innu, the Anishnabe, the Blood, the Haida, the Innuvaluit, the western Métis nation and other peoples whose bonds have stayed at least partly intact, despite government interference, are nations. There are about 1,000 reserve and settlement communities in Canada, but there are 60 to 80 Aboriginal nations. (5.10)

Although the commission's approach would represent a dramatic consolidation, even with the Royal Commission's definition of Aboriginal nation, many of the school districts would be small, averaging only six or seven schools with few students. Is this large enough?

Unfortunately, there is no clear guidance from the existing research as to the optimal size of a school district. The question of optimal school district size has always been a difficult pedagogical and political issue in Canada, and not just for First Nations. School district consolidation has vexed all politicians, particularly on the Prairies and especially in Saskatchewan due to a sparsely distributed rural population and a history of many small school districts that were not as forcefully amalgamated as in other provinces in the 1930s and 1940s.

A 1993 task force report commissioned by the Saskatchewan School Trustees Association recommended that the minimum student enrolment for each district be 2,500 to five thousand, though "Exceptions to these enrolment guidelines might occur in areas where the population is sparse or dense" (as cited in Manitoba School Divisions/Boundaries Review Commission, 1994, p. 59). Apparently the 1993 task force did not end the discussion, as a further review of optimal school board size was undertaken on behalf of the Saskatchewan School Trustees Association in 1997 by Gord Erhardt, who observed that

> The literature on school jurisdiction size and school jurisdiction consolidation is inconclusive and does not present a clear picture for policy-makers. There is no substantial evidence that school jurisdiction size alone is a major factor in determining the costs or the quality of a school system. Furthermore, there is no solid foundation upon which to base a belief that school division consolidation will improve education or cost effectiveness. The research shows little evidence suggesting a causal link between the variables.

Much of the research, Erhardt points out, is from the United States and may not be applicable to Canada. In his own report, Erhardt simulates the amalgamation of several smaller school districts (mainly with fewer than two thousand students each) in Saskatchewan. He concludes that savings of about 4% could be achieved. However, about half of this amount would come from hypothesized school closings. Similar savings through closing smaller schools on reserves might not only be politically impossible, the geography itself might make this infeasible. Nor does Erhardt draw any conclusions about the effects on educational results.

In 1994, the Manitoba School Divisions/Boundaries Review Commission explicitly asked the question, "Is there an optimal size for a school division?" (p. 55). The commission heard several well-researched submissions on both sides of the "bigger is better" controversy, as well as commissioning its own independent review of the issue. It concluded the literature did not provide a clear answer to the question of optimal size but did arrive at a conclusion as to minimum size, which was the same as the initial recommendation of the Saskatchewan Trustees Association:

> It is very difficult to rationalize a board and full administration for less than 2,500 students. In fact, that minimum should range closer to the 5,000 figure were it not for distance, density and transportation limitation factors in rural areas. (Manitoba Schools, 1994, p. 61)

American economic research in 2002 concluded that "sizeable potential cost savings in instructional and administrative costs may exist by moving from a very small district (500 or fewer pupils) to a district with approximately 2,000 to 4,000 pupils" (Andrews, Duncombe, & Yinger, 2002, p. 1).

Overall, the research does not suggest an optimal size, but it does point toward a minimum size, likely in the order of 2,500 students. A more comprehensive review of the existing literature on optimal school board size should be undertaken—whether or not the recommendations in this chapter are followed—since multiband educational alliances are being formed all the time, and this research could help inform that process. However, if we assume this lower threshold as a rough guideline, there would be about 30 First Nations school districts across Canada, which implies about half of the number suggested by the Royal Commission.

To achieve a larger threshold size, First Nations school boards could consist of two or more Aboriginal nations. Alternatively, flexible arrangements could be negotiated according to local conditions, in which some services would be centralized among multiple First Nations boards, while the boards' executive management functions would remain unconsolidated. There is an existing example of shared resources among First Nations schools today—the First Nations SchoolNet, which has successfully connected all First Nations schools to the Internet. SchoolNet is sponsored by Indian and Northern Affairs and run regionally by six nonprofit First Nations SchoolNet Regional Management Organizations, listed in the text box below. Service-sharing agreements are also in place for many off-reserve school boards—e.g., the four City of Ottawa school boards share a single transportation agency.

However, it is not the *size* of First Nations school boards, based on the Royal Commission's concept of an Aboriginal nation, that would constitute the biggest difference between a true First Nations school board and existing multischool First Nations organizations. The most important divergence from what exists today would be the *management* of the schools by the First Nations school board. This is in contrast to the current First Nations multischool organization in which, in most cases, bands continue to manage the schools either directly or indirectly through educational authorities.

First Nations school boards as proposed here would be governed by First Nations trustees, preferably elected by the members of participating bands, so they would be entirely within First Nations' control. Of course, this approach would present some of the same governance challenges as does the current system, due to the colonial history of First Nations and the consequent deficit in expertise that confronts many bands. It is hoped that definitively separating school and general band governance, including two entirely separate budgets, would encourage over time a growth in knowledge and the selection of trustees deeply interested in matters of education. In addition, regional organizations, Indian and Northern Affairs, and the Assembly of First Nations could look at various measures to improve governance capacity as part of the reform process. For example, a one- or two-week training course to accelerate the development of education governance capacity could be established for newly elected First Nations trustees of school boards from across Canada, set up as part of the reformed system outlined here.

The concept of a First Nations school board is not only consistent with "Indian control of Indian education," as set out in the foundational statement by the National Indian Brotherhood that began the process of decolonizing First Nations education (National Indian Brotherhood, 1972): the development of First Nations school boards is the next step in asserting real First Nations control over their own education. Having wrested the management of schools away from non–First Nations governments, the establishment of First Nations school boards involves First Nations setting up effective management organizations for their own schools. Nevertheless, the proposal for individual bands to grant full authority to a special purpose First Nations organization made up of a number of bands should be acknowledged as challenging the current status quo in First Nations governance.

Independent Schools

None of this is to deny that, from time to time, a self-standing school (private or charter or whatever name is attached to it) may be established that thrives and provides excellent education. A dynamic and dedicated leader, with a clear philosophy of education, can build an exceptional school—although if such a school is to take on all comers, as must a public school, and not just expel students who do not fit, it, too, needs the backup of specialized resources that can only be provided economically to larger groupings of schools.

It may be possible to establish private or charter schools on a few reserves, with potential for positive results given the right combination of people and circumstances. If successful, these could provide good ideas and inspiration for other schools, and if unsuccessful, they could provide equally important lessons for other schools. But in the meantime, the other approximately five hundred–plus schools on reserves would continue to worsen unless there is a practical plan to reverse this trend.

The private or charter schools alternative does not provide a realistic alternative for whole system reform of First Nations education on reserve precisely because it is not systemic. There is no prospect of five hundred–plus wonderful principals springing up spontaneously and being offered the leadership of on-reserve schools, backed up by groups of empowered and engaged parents, with financial arrangements in place with the band and Indian and Northern Affairs. As Levin (2008) puts it:

> The issue of scale [meaning improving not just one school but "scaling" up to improve hundreds of schools] also raises the need to organize change in a way that is manageable for ordinary people. So many accounts of change seem to depend on heroic efforts by seemingly superhuman people. Yet entire education systems cannot depend for their success on having large numbers of extraordinary people—who, by definition, are always in short supply. (p. 4)

If there are to be competent leaders for on-reserve schools, there must be a concerted plan to create these leaders and get them in place with the support they need to do an excellent job, despite their being ordinary human beings with families who like to get home in time for dinner most nights and go on holidays. Human resource development, supervision, and monitoring performance are the mandate of school boards. There is no guarantee that a school board will perform its functions well, but without a school board, there is a guarantee that the functions will rarely be performed at all.

Similar considerations need to be brought to proposals for a "voucher" type of system or other mechanism to allow the money to follow the student rather than the student to follow the money. This approach would see First Nations students able to take the dollars of a "tuition agreement" on their own to any school they wanted to attend and which would accept them. In practice, almost all First Nations students normally living on reserve do not have the choice of several different schools: geography imposes strict limitations. Even for those few urban and semi-urban reserves where such a choice could be meaningful, this option would be helpful only for those students whose parents were engaged, confident, and knowledgeable enough to take advantage of this opportunity. Others would be left behind, and there is nothing to suggest that the pressure of losing a handful of relatively good students would turn nonperforming schools into good schools. It seems more likely that bad schools would get worse.

Ministries of Education

Provincial ministries of education fulfill the vital role of executive leadership for the overall off-reserve education system in each province. In fact, it is the ministries, together with the school boards, that stitch it all together to make it a *system*. Provincial ministries work mainly with school boards and only indirectly with individual schools, principals, teachers, and students. School boards for off-reserve schools are accountable to provincial ministries of education as well as their electorate.

Like school boards, ministries have both a management function and a service function. As a manager, the ministry of education is the executive leader of the whole education system, establishing the broadest goals, total budgets for K–12 (and in some provinces, pre-K), and other aspects of executive leadership. Ministry service functions include setting standards for educational attainment, establishing certification, codes of conduct, and the establishment and continuous development of the provincial curriculum. Much of what the ministries do is mandatory for schools, usually also including some mandatory requirements for private and independent schools in the province (although provinces differ substantially from one another).

The provincial ministry of education is also responsible for the laws that govern education in each province, and will maintain and submit proposed revisions to their minister and cabinet, who may bring revisions to these statutes to legislatures as required from time to time. Off-reserve schools operate within a framework of law.

Provincial education ministries' service functions are often expensive and may demand highly specialized knowledge, if they are to be done well. Consequently, these functions are most efficiently performed within a large system that provides substantial economies of scale. Some First Nations multischool on-reserve organizations have attempted to take on some of the functions of provincial ministries, especially with respect to curriculum. Although many have reportedly done a good job, this is not an efficient use of resources over the long run, as curriculum design and implementation need to be done on a large scale to minimize expense and concentrate expertise. Nor is the job ever completed. Curriculum requires constant revision and updating and is never completed.

Current agreements between Ottawa and First Nations require schools on reserve to educate to levels comparable to those found in similar off-reserve schools. For example, the Comprehensive Funding Arrangement with First Nations states that "education standards (e.g., certified teachers) shall allow students to transfer to an equivalent grade in another school within the school system of the province/territory" (Aboriginal Affairs, 2009/2010). In practice, these policies are at best implemented unevenly, and some observers would contend they are implemented hardly at all. While transfers from a grade on reserve to the same grade off reserve do frequently occur, the anecdotal evidence is that most on-reserve students find themselves far behind (Mendelson, 2008). Evidence from British Columbia cited in Richards and Scott (2009) shows that 57% of First Nations students are one or more years behind in reading and 66% of students are one or more years behind in mathematics.

To the extent that on-reserve schools do attempt to meet the goal of "educating to levels comparable to those to be found in similar off-reserve schools," the expectation is that they will do so by adopting the standards and instruments of the provincial system, including most prominently the provincial curriculum. Teachers on reserves must also be certified by the provincial body responsible for teacher certification. Some provinces have additional requirements of any secondary school, be it public, private, or on-reserve, if that school is to be permitted to offer a high school diploma recognized in the province.

The provincial ministries of education perform a necessary role to create and maintain a high-quality education system, and these roles—be it standards-setting or curriculum design—are also needed to support First Nations schools. So why cannot First Nations schools just fall under the responsibility of their respective provincial ministries of education? While superficially appealing, upon deeper consideration this option is, at the very least, impractical and would tie First Nations educational reform in knots for another generation or more, stalling needed change in a morass of political, financial, and legal battles. To understand why this option is unworkable, it is necessary to review the historical and legal context of First Nations education.

Any attempt to force First Nations education under the control of provinces would be fiercely resisted by most First Nations. Nor is resistance to a "provincial takeover" merely paranoia on the part of First Nations. It was within living memory that schools were consciously used as a tool of "internal colonisation" (as this policy is called in Australia)—deliberately designed to erase all aspects of Indigenous culture and language from students. Thankfully, this effort did not work. Today we see the re-emergence of rich Indigenous cultural heritages from which all Canadians benefit, but history reminds us that it is not mere fantasy propelling First Nations to be vigilant about guarding their right to control their own schools. Nor is this all safely buried in the past. While all provincial governments are today to varying degrees sensitive and responsive to First Nations cultures, this could change in the blink of an eye just through a single provincial election.

Nor would such a transfer of responsibility be acceptable to most provincial governments. On a practical level, putting aside issues of principle, most provinces would not accept a jurisdictional transfer without ironclad guarantees from the federal government regarding financing. This is especially true of the Prairie provinces with the largest numbers of First Nations peoples on reserves, relative to the size of these provinces. The financial negotiations would drag on, likely for decades, before a province would accept such a transfer—unless the federal government was willing to pay a huge premium to "bribe" a province into accepting. The financial negotiations would be difficult not only because of the challenge of setting the amount to be transferred in the first few years, but also because some formula would have to be established for resolving how the amounts would be fixed far into the future.

From a legal perspective, many First Nations would certainly challenge any attempt to apply provincial education statutes on reserves without First Nations consent. It is generally accepted that First Nations education on reserve is not subject to provincial education laws (for an interesting review of the law from an Aboriginal perspective, see Henderson, 1995). It seems likely that First Nations would win such a challenge, especially given the recognition of Aboriginal rights in the Constitution (section 35).

A strategy of forcing all First Nations on-reserve education under provincial jurisdiction is one of those public policy chimeras that haunt policy development, presenting a seemingly attractive alternative that cannot actually be implemented but serves to obstruct the evolution of more complex but realistic strategies. It is a recipe for stagnation or, worse, continued decline.

Yet the practical reality is that students who graduate from schools on reserve will want and deserve certification that does meet provincial standards and will also want the freedom to enter into further education just as would any other graduating student in the provinces. Moreover, even with effective First Nations regional organizations (discussed below), the number of students on reserve will be relatively small given the scale that is required to take on all the responsibilities of a provincial ministry. Further, from a public expenditure perspective, it makes little sense to duplicate what already exists at the provincial level. The opposite strategy—of trying to set up a completely parallel and independent First Nations education system that has little relationship and no reliance upon the provinces—is equally a chimera.

What is therefore needed is neither a holus-bolus handover of on-reserve education to the provinces, nor the development of a separate education apparatus. Rather, a partnership is required in which a First Nations regional education authority has many of the managerial responsibilities of a provincial education ministry to oversee First Nations school boards but relies substantially on a voluntary partnership with the provincial education ministry for many services under the terms of a written agreement.

Notwithstanding the above discussion, there may be instances in which First Nations voluntarily wish to become part of a public school board, operating under provincial authority. There are at least two examples of this in Canada today.

The Cree School Board was set up as part of the James Bay Quebec Hydro development in 1978. The Cree School Board now includes nine schools with about 3,600 students. The Cree School Board is one model of voluntary integration into the provincial education system, with the Cree School Board operating as a special board under Quebec's Education Act. The board is governed by commissioners from each of the Cree communities in the James Bay development agreement. Financing is 75% from Indian and Northern Affairs and 25% from Quebec, originally roughly meant to reflect the ratio of "status" and "non-status" students attending Cree School Board schools. The budget is negotiated between Ottawa and Quebec, supposedly reflecting funding levels for comparable Quebec schools, plus an additional mandate for activities such as development of a Cree language curriculum. The Cree School Board has consistently maintained—at least up to a few years ago—that funding did not, in fact, reflect their special mandate or needs. Moreover, the board itself had been excluded from the Budget setting intergovernmental discussions, at least in the early years (Diamond, 1987).

The educational outcomes of the Cree School Board are discussed further below, but it is a model in which a First Nations school board opts voluntarily to operate as a provincial school board, with funding shared between the province and Ottawa. Assuming that satisfactory legislative and financing arrangements could be negotiated, other First Nations school boards might wish voluntarily to become part of a provincial system and opt for recognition under a provincial system. So long as there is no compulsion involved, there is no reason to stand in the way of such an arrangement.

Another unique arrangement in Canada is in northern Manitoba where eight First Nations have opted to have their schools become part of the public school board covering northern Manitoba, called the Frontier School Division. The Frontier School Division on-reserve schools are financed by a tuition agreement whereby Indian and Northern Affairs pays the division tuition for each student resident on reserve in the reserve schools. Frontier is unusual in generally having a majority of Aboriginal trustees on its governing board at any given time. Frontier also has a "bottom-up" method of electing its trustees. Each school elects a community board for the school. Each community then elects two of its community board trustees to sit on an area board, of which there are five in the Frontier School Division. Trustees are then elected from each of the five area boards. This structure has led to good representation and a highly experienced and skilled board of trustees.

The Frontier arrangement makes a great deal of sense in a sparsely populated area such as northern Manitoba, with a large First Nations population and many people identifying themselves as Aboriginal who are not living on reserve (but this does not encompass the majority of First Nations students, as about 75% of First Nations students live in urban and rural areas, not in remote areas, according to the *Indian and Northern Affairs Band Classification Manual* cited in Richards and Scott, 2009). As a consequence, Frontier has always had substantial focus on First Nations language and culture as part of its curriculum. It might be possible to consider a similar arrangement in other areas sharing these features, such as northern Saskatchewan or perhaps northwest Ontario. However, the Frontier arrangement has evolved (and was not planned) over many decades with a good deal of trust and deep relationships built up over time. Frontier is careful to go through a long process of community engagement and consensus, reportedly taking about two years before agreeing to bring a new reserve school into the division. Even with willing First Nations and public school boards, it may not be easy to replicate the Frontier experience elsewhere in Canada.

The Frontier and the Quebec Cree experiences show that many different forms of partnership are possible, and some First Nations may wish to relate directly to a province either at a school board or at an individual school level. But if First Nations are not to be compelled to enter into these kinds of arrangements with their respective provinces—and such compulsion is unworkable as well as undesirable—First Nations regional education authorities, working in partnership with provincial education ministries, are needed to provide both services and management for a First Nations education system.

First Nations Regional Education Authorities

Several First Nations regional education authorities could be established across Canada to partner with provincial ministries and provide the equivalent of provincial education ministry functions to First Nations school boards. The First Nations regional education authorities would, in some instances, develop and deliver services themselves, and, in other instances, would contract with the provincial ministry to do so. First Nations school boards would relate to the First Nations regional education authorities analogously to the relationship between off-reserve school boards and provincial ministries of education.

The arrangements between the First Nations regional authority and the provincial ministry of education would be negotiated on a region-by-region basis, allowing flexibility to reflect regional differences. For example, as part of the negotiations surrounding the First Nations Jurisdiction over Education in British Columbia Act, 2006, a British Columbia First Nations Education Authority was to have been established. The proposed British Columbia First Nations Education Authority shares many of the characteristics of both school boards and regional authorities as proposed here but also differs in several respects. The British Columbia initiative is discussed further below. However, the terms of reference for the proposed British Columbia First Nations Education Authority provide a good example of the specific kinds of regional interests that a First Nations education authority might pursue.

In the case of British Columbia, the aspects of the education system to be developed by the First Nations Education Authority were:

- teacher certification (except for language and culture teachers);
- school certification;

- standards for curriculum and examinations for courses necessary to meet graduation requirements (First Nations Education Steering Committee, 2006).

A First Nations regional authority in Ontario might want to take a different approach and continue using the provincial processes now being used in on-reserve schools for teacher and school certification, while developing other areas.

As the First Nations regional education authorities matured, federal financing for education on reserve could be transferred to the regional authorities, rather than the regional office of Indian and Northern Affairs, and the First Nations regional education authority would fund the First Nations school boards (as is discussed further under financing below). Most of the current Indian and Northern Affairs regional staff positions allocated to education-related matters would be transferred over time to the regional authorities.

Current regional funding for Indian and Northern Affairs education internal administration is about $10 million annually. Although the total cost of First Nations regional education authorities would be more than this, the existing regional administrative allocation does provide a major source for financing the new authorities.

In many ways, the proposal for First Nations regional education authorities should be seen as a transfer of Indian and Northern Affairs regional education responsibilities to First Nations control. It is crucial that any such transfer be done carefully and in stages, as other attempts to "dismantle" Indian and Northern Affairs functions at the regional level have floundered on inadequate planning and preparation.

There are several different possible models for governance of the First Nations regional education authority. The Frontier School Division model would see trustees elected from each of the school boards with the regional authority, perhaps supplemented by a certain number of directly elected trustees. As with First Nations school boards, the development of governance capacity should be built into the reform process and not become a mere afterthought, including, for example, special training and perhaps coaching for authority trustees.

There has been no research to provide guidance as to the needed number of First Nations regional education authorities. Provinces vary in size from tiny Prince Edward Island to Ontario, so they hardly constitute a model of efficiency. The Royal Commission on Aboriginal Peoples spoke of this function being undertaken by multi–First Nation organizations but was not specific on how this would be accomplished. This question would require further investigation, but

First Nations and governments would need to appreciate the real relationship between the size of authorities and their independence. The larger the First Nations education authorities, the more they will be able to do on their own. The smaller the authorities, the more they will have to rely upon the provinces. On this basis, and subject to investigation and research, it would seem that something like six First Nations regional education authorities across the country would be appropriate.

Financing

Finance Minister Paul Martin's 1995–1996 Budget brought strict constraints into place in an effort to bring the federal deficit under control. In most departments, the budget was frozen or reduced for a number of years. Transfers to provinces were severely reduced, essentially eliminating one major multibillion dollar transfer program—the Canada Assistance Plan. In what was at the time seen as a concession to the extraordinary needs of Aboriginal peoples, the 1995–1996 Budget announced that Indian and Northern Affairs would be one of a small number of departments in which spending would be allowed to grow by 3% each year to 1997–1998 (excluding land claims and northern programs). In the following year's Budget—1996–1997— Indian and Northern Affairs was restrained by another percentage point to 2% (Department of Finance, 1996, p. 111).

Given the substantial cuts and freezes in 1996 and the prevailing fiscal climate, the 2% limit was not at the time widely seen as overly onerous. To some extent, allowing any increase at all still recognized the special circumstances of First Nations. But it is now 13 years later. In the meantime, many of the provinces have invested substantial amounts in education. Even if Indian and Northern Affairs and its regional offices have diverted substantial amounts from other areas into education (the 2% applies to a wider range of programs than education and reallocations are permitted within the departmental budget), and even with the addition of substantial amounts in specially targeted programs (discussed further below), it seems doubtful that funding for on-reserve education could have kept up on average with provincial off-reserve education financing over the last decade.

The need to update the funding of on-reserve education has long been recognized by First Nations and, in this author's view, by Indian and Northern Affairs officials as well. But the problem has been finding a way to do so that will satisfy all the diverse requirements of both First Nations and the federal government.

In 2004, Ottawa and the Assembly of First Nations established a Band Operated Schools Federal Funding Formula Working Group to review the funding formula and recommend changes. The first task of the working group was to try to understand the current real status of funding. To do so, it initiated a number of detailed analyses of funding in provincial schools compared to similar schools on reserves (e.g., see Matthews, 2001). Only a few of these studies have been completed and made public and none seem especially conclusive—the morass of details in this kind of accounting sometimes becomes too large to allow any kind of clear assessment. In any case, the working group appears to have evaporated.

It would be possible to spend a good deal of time and effort attempting to establish whether on-reserve schools have been funded the same as comparable schools off reserve, but is this the question that really needs to be answered? Even if it were found that many First Nations on-reserve schools had been funded less than comparative schools off reserve, what then? What if, as seems possible, some First Nations schools in a few regions are funded more than their comparators off reserve while most are funded less? Enquiring as to the past funding of schools is essentially backward-looking. Spending a lot of time, money, and energy on one-off studies about the level of funding over the past dozen or so years does not do much for the next dozen years. Even a large boost in funding in one year would last only so long, and then First Nations would be back in the same situation all over again. The demise of the Band Operated Schools Federal Funding Formula Working Group suggests that this path to reform may be another dead end.

Instead of looking backward, what is needed is a forward-looking strategy that would address funding as part of systemic reform of First Nations on-reserve schools in the future. The *method* of financing First Nations schools has to change so that the amounts provided as a result of a renewed process are adequate now and into the future.

A new method of funding would require turning the current financing system upside down as it applies to the "reformed" First Nations school system. Payments to recognized First Nations school boards ("recognition" is discussed below) would become what is known as statutory spending. *Statutory spending* refers to expenditures that are authorized by a specific law that "sets out both the purpose of the expenditures and the terms and conditions under which they may be made" (Treasury Board Secretariat, 2009/2010). Statutory expenditures are not approved annually but instead are paid as required under the terms of their governing statute.

Many payments in all governments are statutory. For example, in provinces, social assistance payments are statutory. Hundreds of payments in the federal government of Canada are statutory. A small sample of federal statutory payments is included in the accompanying text box below to show this is not a radical or unusual proposition.

Making education financing for on-reserve schools statutory allows that financing to be an obligation of the federal government of Canada, consistent with the terms of the statute. This permits a financing process to be established with an external determination of the amounts to be paid annually. A statutory payment does not mean that the government has no control over the amount paid out. An override mechanism can be written into the statute allowing Cabinet to limit the total paid out or otherwise to determine the amount if it is necessary to do so in unusual circumstances. For example, the Employment Insurance Act empowers the Canada Employment Insurance Commission to set premiums for employment insurance, but section 66.3 of the act provides that "on the joint recommendation of the Minister and the Minister of Finance, the Governor in Council may, on or before November 30 in a year, substitute a premium rate for the following year that is different from the one set by the Commission" (Employment Insurance Act, 1996, s 66.3).

Looked at purely from the perspective of financial risks involved in making these payments statutory, and ignoring for the moment what the payments would achieve, the potential cost increases are relatively small for the federal government of Canada. For example, if funding increased by, say $2,000 per student per year in on-reserve schools, the total additional costs would be less than $140 million and that maximum amount would be reached only when all First Nations schools came under the responsibility of a recognized First Nations school board. The process of restructuring would take several years, so the annual financial "risk" would likely be relatively small, say in the order of $20 million to $40 million. Adding a ballpark guess at all other costs, mainly for regional education authorities, the total cost at maturity of these aspects of reform would likely be in the order of $50 million. The annual incremental costs would be much less.

Total additional costs at maturity approaching $200 million is a huge amount of money for any individual, but it is a modest amount in comparison to other "incentive funds" that have been set up by the federal government—e.g., the Wait Times Reduction Transfer

Sample of Existing Federal Statutory Spending

- all contributions to employee benefit plans
- grant payments for the AgriStability Program
- payments in connection with the Agricultural Marketing Programs Act
- grant payments for the AgriInvest Program
- grant payments for the Agricultural Disaster Relief Program/AgriRecovery
- Canadian Cattlemen's Association Legacy Fund
- grants to agencies established under the Farm Products Agencies Act
- Payments to provinces under the Softwood Lumber Products Export Charge Act
- Children's Special Allowance payments
- loans to immigrants and refugees to facilitate the arrival of newcomers
- interest and other costs
- Canada Health Transfer
- fiscal equalization
- Canada Social Transfer
- territorial financing
- payments to International Development Association
- Wait Times Reduction Transfer
- Incentive for Provinces to Eliminate Taxes on Capital
- Old Age Security payments
- Guaranteed Income Supplement payments
- Universal Child Care Benefit
- Canada Education Savings Grant payments to Registered Education Savings Plan (RESP)

to the provinces of $250 million annually that was also made into a statutory payment. It is a fraction of the amount that provinces, such as Ontario, have invested in improving their education systems. This is small change to address what is likely the biggest social challenge facing Canada—if indeed taking this relatively small financial risk could establish one of the essential elements of a strategy to bring First Nations and government together in a process of building a First Nations education system. Furthermore, as previously discussed, any successful investment in First Nations education will result in substantial future savings to government.

Against this financial risk, we have the risk of failure to reform First Nations education. Without the federal government being willing to make a firm financial commitment of this kind, it is unlikely to be able to obtain the co-operation of First Nations in a reform project. There must be a quid pro quo to make First Nations education reform work, and a statutory undertaking of adequate financing is the kind of dramatic "quid" that would be needed to obtain First Nations' "quo."

Rather than the new financing process being one of Ottawa telling the regions how much they have, and the regions then telling the schools how much they in turn will get, the budgeting process would begin with the First Nations regional education authority (or the Indian and Northern Affairs region and recognized First Nations school board until a regional authority is established) working with the province to apply the results of the province's education funding formula (which is extremely complex in most provinces) to First Nations school boards under its jurisdiction. The estimated requirement would then be forwarded to Ottawa.

The statute would require that this amount be paid, subject to a simple and expeditious review mechanism built into the statute. The review mechanism would be open to any of the interested parties— schools, school boards, provinces, First Nations, and the federal government itself. The review would provide for an impartial, expert, third-party review of the amounts to be paid. As noted, the amounts could be overridden by Cabinet should it feel necessary to do so due to fiscal circumstances, but this is not likely to happen. If the economy turns sour, provinces will probably be in at least as bad fiscal circumstances as the federal government. It is the provinces' funding to their schools that would determine the amount of payments to the First Nations school boards, so it is unlikely that circumstances would arise in which provinces are making a payment larger than can be afforded by the federal government. And, at the end of the day, if Cabinet did use the "special override" route to reduce payments, it would at least have the virtue of making the amount of shortfall measurable public information, so it could presumably be made up at a later time.

The core concept here is one of reciprocal accountability. In the new reformed system, First Nations school boards and First Nations regional education authorities would be accountable to First Nations peoples and to government for spending to implement quality education. But in return, Ottawa would be accountable to First Nations peoples to provide them with the means to deliver quality education. This deal is discussed further below.

Attempts at Reform

As noted throughout this chapter, there have been numerous attempts over the last few decades to reform and improve schools on reserves. Most of these efforts have originated from First Nations themselves, often with assistance and support from Indian and Northern Affairs.

The organization of the northern Quebec Cree School Board has been discussed above, but not its educational outcomes. There has been little evaluation available to the public of the successes and failures of the Cree School Board, which is both surprising and disappointing given its unique status in Canada. What reports there have been of student outcomes seem to indicate that the Cree School

---

The Cree School Board's Development in Its Own Words

The early years of the Cree School Board were difficult. The Board inherited three school systems, which it had to integrate into one, and was expected to develop a uniquely native education system without proper funding and support. In 15 years, the Board has come a long way. The Board now controls a substantial budget and provides services to more than 3,600 students at the primary, secondary and post-secondary levels. It has implemented a distinctively Cree curriculum in geography, history and economics, and established in service training for Cree teachers. Efforts are under way to develop a land based Cree hunting and trapping vocational option. With these accomplishments, the Board is an outstanding example of Native determination and it sets a precedent for other First Nations to take control of responsibilities directed by others. (Cree School Board, n.d.)

Board has not necessarily done much better than other on-reserve schools in northern and remote locations in Canada in respect of graduating students from high school (Visser & Fovet, 2007).

If the educational outcomes of the Cree School Board schools are indeed as dismal as the few reports suggest, this should serve as a cautionary tale regarding our expectations of the effectiveness of school reform—both for those looking for the provincial system to "save" the on-reserve schools and those (as in this chapter) looking for First Nations self-government to improve the schools. In many northern communities, children may make a calculation that there is not much sense in continuing in school—and this may not be irrational. The knowledge they learn in school may appear to have little practical application to their future lives, especially if they do not see post-secondary education as a possibility, while in the meantime they are forced to sit in classrooms and not acquire the needed knowledge of the land that they must have to survive with dignity in their own communities. And the students may also face a barrage of social barriers. If doing well in school is disparaged by the youth culture in a small community and not supported tangibly by parents, it is a lot to expect any young person to overcome these obstacles. In addition, where English (or French) is not the first language, difficult barriers are going to be encountered in taking on the provincial curriculum even if it is supposedly taught in a First Nations language, let alone transferring to a non–First Nations high school or post-secondary institution.

All of these barriers and more reportedly exist to some degree in many reserve communities, especially those that are isolated. It would be foolish to think that better schools in and of themselves will overcome all challenges in a few years. There is no panacea and no silver bullet. Nevertheless, better schools are an essential ingredient in a community effort to better itself. If even a few students get a chance they would otherwise not have had, they may begin to create a nucleus of success upon which further success can grow. But we should also be wary of becoming mesmerized by the most extreme and difficult situations. Most First Nations students living on reserves are not in isolated and remote areas but in rural or urban areas. For these First Nations students, there are visible and tangible benefits from education and these obstacles do not loom so large.

On a more down-to-earth note, the Cree School Board had a lot of difficulty in its first decade getting the recognition and resources it needed to develop a program adapted to its students' needs, and encountered many other organizational challenges. Perhaps a more conscious and deliberate plan to assist and resource the board adequately to deal with these kinds of issues could have been more successful. Finally, it appears that the Cree School Board has attempted to take on some of the tasks that would ordinarily be performed at a regional level, such as curriculum development and Cree language textbooks. This imposes a large extra burden on the board, which has limited resources to begin with.

We should be better equipped to learn from some of the exceptional arrangements that do exist in Canada. To this end, it would be useful to have a public and culturally sensitive independent review of the Cree School Board experience of the last 30 years.

Ten years ago, the Mi'kmaw Kina'matnewey (MK) was organized in Nova Scotia. MK was set up under the terms of the federal Mi'kmaq Education Act. The Mi'kmaq Education Act is essentially an administrative statute, recognizing the MK as an organization outside of the Indian Act. The Mi'kmaq Education Act contains little or no content relevant to the substance of education. It appears that the act was passed without a great deal of planning. Like the Cree School Board, MK reportedly had substantial problems in its initial years. It seems to be doing much better today, with 10 schools under its administration.

MK receives all of the funding for its schools and distributes these to its community-based schools. In 2005, MK signed an agreement on funding with the government of Canada, which provided for its base funding plus increases to reflect changed enrolment and prices (by the Final Domestic Demand Implicit Price Index, which is similar to the more familiar Consumer Price Index). However, MK believes it is still underfunded compared to Nova Scotia schools and has requested a funding increase at least sufficient to allow it to pay teachers' salaries at a comparable level to those paid off reserve.

MK has several projects under way to improve the quality of education in its schools, including school success planning. In many respects, MK seems to be evolving into a true First Nations school board. For example, MK recently took the large step of equalizing the per capita funding of all of the schools within the organization.

MK is an optimistic story. Of course, none of the reserves in MK are remote and some of them (prominently Membertou) are well known for their success. Unfortunately, once again, there does not seem to be a publicly available independent review of the MK experience. Such a review would be useful for the lessons from the MK experience for other First Nations and for First Nations education policy generally.

On the other side of the continent, a coalition of British Columbia First Nations has been working, together with the British Columbia Regional Indian and Northern Affairs office and the province, for many years on measures to improve education on British Columbia reserves through the First Nations Education Steering Committee. The steering committee has been a leader in relentlessly pursuing quality education and First Nations cultural relevance for British Columbia First Nations. Over time, an impressive organization providing many valuable services to British Columbia First Nations schools has grown up under the auspices of the steering committee.

The coalition of British Columbia First Nations involved in the steering committee undertook to enhance the committee's role and to obtain formal recognition of First Nations' jurisdiction in education, initiating negotiations with the federal and provincial governments to this end. After negotiating a detailed understanding of the role of community education authorities and a new First Nations Education Authority in British Columbia but not the details of the financing, the federal government passed the First Nations Jurisdiction over Education in British Columbia Act in 2006. Like MK, a special purpose act was required because the Indian Act does not provide for recognition of First Nations' authority over education—or even for the recognition of First Nations education authorities of any kind.

The new First Nations Jurisdiction Act gives legal standing to a First Nations Education Authority in British Columbia, which will be a kind of successor to the steering committee and will become responsible for support of the K–12 education program in Participating First Nations (PFNs), including teacher certification, curriculum design, and other important functions. The provincial government of British Columbia also passed parallel legislation—the First Nations Education Act—providing for complementary changes in provincial laws.

Unlike MK, the British Columbia First Nations Education Authority would not act as a kind of nascent school board; rather, it would have very specific delegated responsibilities from the PFNs. In fact, the British Columbia agreement with PFNs is careful to stress that the jurisdiction for education remains in the individual bands and not in the new First Nations Education Authority. Unlike MK, the school budgets will not flow through the new British Columbia authority. If anything, it appears that the First Nations Education Authority is to be more like a provincial ministry, resembling the proposed First Nations regional education authorities discussed here—except only with delegated powers, no responsibility for school budgets, and, of course, smaller geographic reach. Aside from this and a few other differences, it does appear that the British Columbia initiative could be accommodated as an interim form of regional authority as envisaged here. This would also clarify that the British Columbia authority is, in fact, a tertiary-level, and not a secondary-level, education service provider.

Despite the British Columbia act having been passed a year and a half ago with great fanfare, as of the publication of this chapter in September 2009, the British Columbia First Nations Education Authority has not yet formally begun its work because negotiations on financing have not been successfully completed. Doubtless a financial agreement will emerge at some point and the new authority will officially come into being. Since financial problems bedevilled both MK and the Cree School Board for many years as they tried to establish their organizations—and still are problems for both organizations—it may well be a prudent strategy for the British Columbia First Nations to take their time until they arrive at a financial arrangement they believe will allow them to have a viable organization, given their mandate. Indian and Northern Affairs will doubtless also want to ensure that the British Columbia First Nations Education Authority is as successful as possible and perhaps can avoid some of the growing pains experienced by the Cree School Board and MK.

The Cree School Board, MK, and the British Columbia First Nations Jurisdiction Act are three examples of First Nations–initiated reforms covering three different decades. There are many other examples, both successful and not so successful.

Indian and Northern Affairs has also initiated targeted programs attempting to improve First Nations schools. Most recently, in 2008, Indian and Northern Affairs introduced a new strategy in an effort to assist and encourage First Nations wanting to take steps to reform their education programs. The new strategy is called the Reforming First Nations Education Initiative. So far, two programs have been implemented under the Reforming First Nations Education Initiative—the First Nation Student Success Program and the Education Partnerships Program. Both these programs are application-driven in that interested First Nations education organizations must submit an application with a proposal that fits within the criteria established by the programs.

The First Nation Student Success Program is a multiyear program only for schools on reserves. The program consists of three components, all of which must be part of any application—a school success plan, student learning assessments, and performance measurement of schools. The goal is to help schools establish an ongoing planning process focusing on literacy, numeracy, and student retention. The

Role of the British Columbia First Nations Education Authority

- certify teachers in PFNs schools using standards comparable to British Columbia provincial certification standards
- certify schools operated by PFNs
- establish education standards for PFNs schools that reflect the importance of First Nations culture and language
- ensure that curriculum, exams, and other programs delivered by PFNs schools will enable students to transfer to provincial schools and enter the British Columbia post-secondary education system

components are meant to work together to assist schools in implementing reforms and to measure the results to know whether the plans are succeeding. There have been more than 40 applications for grants under the First Nations Student Success Program in 2009–2010, almost entirely from tribal councils and other multischool organizations, including both the British Columbia First Nations Education Steering Committee and MK.

The Education Partnerships Program is also in the implementation stage. This program provides funding for First Nations multischool organizations to develop a partnership with the province, including negotiating or renegotiating agreements regarding provisions for on-reserve students who must attend off-reserve schools, curriculum adaptation to First Nations culture, and other measures. Some First Nations are reportedly suspicious that the program is an attempt to begin forcing First Nations schools to fall under provincial jurisdiction. But a careful reading of the program reveals that it is instead encouraging a business-like partnership wherein each partner—province and First Nations—can gain from using the resources of the other.

As the implementation has barely begun for either program, we are a long way from knowing how successful these initiatives will be. The strength of these programs is that they provide carefully targeted funding for specific and needed reforms. Unlike the three initiatives discussed above (Cree School Board, MK, and First Nations Jurisdiction Act), these programs are also open to all First Nations on an equitable basis. In addition, there is nothing coercive in these targeted programs. First Nations can either apply or not, at their discretion.

The weakness of this strategy is that it attempts to build needed reforms within a structure that is systemically failing. Many First Nations schools will doubtless use the funds effectively to, for example, set up a school success plan. But if the school cannot sustain a good teaching staff and is underfunded and working with an inappropriate curriculum, any progress made will likely not be sustainable. The targeted initiatives are positive in and of themselves but not sufficient. They do not fill in the big pieces that are missing from the First Nations school nonsystem. Given the continued systemic failure, while one school may move ahead with targeted initiatives, two others may be falling still further behind.

How can we encourage a process of systemic change?

A First Nations Education Act

The above discussion has described some of the "holes" in First Nations education that need to be filled in order to construct a modern education system. It has also described briefly a few of the attempts that have been made at reform. In our view, these attempts—both by First Nations and by Indian and Northern Affairs—are in the right direction and demonstrate the commitment of all parties to the need for vast improvements in First Nations education. But they are like chipping away at a glacier with an ice pick—during an ice age. No system involving tens of thousands of people can be changed overnight, but the current processes are too little and too slow. We are losing another generation or perhaps two.

The idea of a First Nations Education Act (FNEA) has been proposed elsewhere by this author and the approach has been endorsed by others as well (Mendelson, 2008; Richards, 2008; "Two ways forward," 2009). The FNEA would allow First Nations that wish to form a school board to do so, set up First Nations regional education authorities, provide for reasonable funding of the new structures and the schools within them, and other measures. The proposed FNEA is meant to provide a base that will allow First Nations to undertake the systemic reform of their education and build a First Nations education system. Equally important, the proposed FNEA is also meant to provide Indian and Northern Affairs with the tools it needs to support First Nations in the process of systemic reform. The FNEA is a legal and policy framework to build the necessary organizational infrastructure for whole system reform—and, over time, quality education in First Nations classrooms.

But the FNEA is best understood as a *strategy* for accelerating re-form of First Nations education. Most of what is contemplated by a FNEA could be achieved, in theory, through other government instruments such as individual statutes for each First Nations multiservice organization that requires a legal existence beyond incorporation; treasury board authorities for financial arrangements; negotiation of a new funding formula; and so on. The FNEA would do all of this, and more, except in an open, legally binding form with the consent of Parliament. Perhaps the most significant difference between the FNEA and the current piecemeal approach is its presentation of a comprehensive vision for a system of First Nations education.

The FNEA is an act of *trust*. It would say to First Nations that their educational rights and responsibilities are set out by Parliament and transcend the discretionary decisions of the government of the day. It would represent an enforceable commitment by the federal government of Canada that could be the foundation for a new trusting relationship in working toward the goal everyone is seeking—an education system that gives First Nations' children the best possible opportunity in life.

Following are some of the ways in which a FNEA would build a foundation for change.

Creating a National Plan for a First Nations Education System

The FNEA would enshrine the plan for the new First Nations education system in law, to be endorsed (or otherwise) by Parliament. The process of writing, discussion, and debate of the FNEA would demand further clarification of the plan and, if the process were successful, create a national guiding vision for restructuring over the next few decades. It would answer the question: What should a First Nations education system look like?

Grounding First Nations Education in Law

The FNEA would provide for the creation, purpose, and roles of all of the main organizations required in the new system, just as does any other statute setting up a system of governance and administration for a public service. It would establish the administrative requirements such as financing, reporting, and accountability. The FNEA would set out the legal duties and responsibilities of the federal government, First Nations regional education authorities and First Nations school boards, the First Nations Education Financing Review Commission, and any other organizations needed for the new reformed First Nations education system.

The FNEA would empower and require First Nations regional education authorities to establish and maintain a First Nations regional educational regulation that would have the status of a regulation under the FNEA, and so be fully recognized in Canadian law within the jurisdiction of each regional authority. The FNEA would set out the major topics to be covered in each First Nations regional educational regulation, likely reflecting the main topics in most provincial education acts, as well as topics unique to First Nations culture and language.

The FNEA would make it clear that the First Nations regional education authorities and school boards operate under the auspices of the federal law and not provincial law, removing the jurisdictional concerns of some First Nations. The FNEA should also affirm existing treaty rights regarding education.

Recognizing the Jurisdiction of First Nations over Their Education

As we have seen in the case of MK and the British Columbia First Nations Jurisdiction Act, each time a First Nations multischool organization needs to be recognized by federal authorities, a separate piece of federal legislation is required. There is inconvenience, cost, and delay in this for a government, but this is not the critical problem. The critical problem is that there is no legislation that recognizes First Nations' right to control their own education and to set up the organizations that allow them to do so effectively. The Indian Act does not recognize First Nations as entities with whom the federal government of Canada may contract to run their own schools. Today's relation with First Nations education is all based on obscure uses of the federal Treasury Board authority.

As noted above, the FNEA would be important from a practical perspective, providing a clear legal basis for the new structures—so that we preserve the principle of "rule of law"—but it would also be an Act of Parliament, recognizing for the first time the right of all First Nations to assert their jurisdiction over their education.

Removal from the Indian Act

The Indian Act's provisions regarding education are completely obsolete, colonialist, and an embarrassment to Canada. First Nations schools recognized under the FNEA would be removed from sections 114–122 on education under the Indian Act.

Enshrining the Principle of Reciprocal Accountability

The FNEA would set out the criteria for recognition under the act of First Nations multischool organizations, and it would also set out the responsibilities of the government of Canada. Provincial education statutes all establish the duties of the province. Parliament should also spell out in law the duties of the federal government with respect to that portion of the education system for which it is responsible, namely on First Nations reserves. The FNEA would make it clear how First Nations educational bodies that are recognized in the legislation are responsible to both their own peoples and to the government of Canada for First Nations education. The FNEA would also make it clear how the federal government is responsible to its own electors and to First Nations. Reciprocal responsibility is the principle upon which a trusting relationship may be built.

Facilitating Restructuring by Setting out Clear Criteria

When a group of First Nations want to initiate a reform, they must each time start afresh. The responsible government officials whom they contact must obtain a new mandate to negotiate. The whole process can take years or even decades and end up going nowhere. No one knows what the expectations should be from the start. Regional Indian and Northern Affairs officials can be put in a difficult position, not knowing what they can agree to, and caught between Indian and Northern Affairs headquarters and the First Nations in the region.

The FNEA would set out clearly the criteria for recognition of First Nations school boards and set the parameters for negotiation from the beginning. This would also provide government officials with their parameters. An orderly and reasonably efficient process could be established that would see a number of First Nations school boards set up within a few years.

Encouraging and Recognizing Real School Boards for First Nations

The FNEA would encourage the establishment of First Nations school boards, fully empowered as are off-reserve school boards, especially if the result would be an enforceable federal commitment to financing. The FNEA would set out the criteria for recognition, which should then follow simply and more or less automatically through regulatory listing under the act when a new First Nations school board meets the criteria. The FNEA would also establish parameters for election of the board members, financial accountability, and, in general, the other requirements of school boards analogous to those in provincial education acts setting up their school boards. As First Nations regional education authorities are established, they would assume the responsibility for the supervision of First Nations school boards.

Providing Stable and Fair Funding for First Nations Schools

As discussed above, the FNEA would include a statutory requirement for financing of First Nations school boards to a level of comparable boards in the province. The FNEA would also set out the process by which budgets would be decided and would obligate the federal government to pay that amount, unless it decided to use an "emergency" override. The FNEA would provide a mechanism for speedy, inexpensive, and fair resolution of financial disputes, and appeals could be made by First Nations or the federal government. This would put to bed the ongoing discussion of funding levels that is dominating much of the current debate.

Conclusion

This chapter describes the structural and financial fault lines in the current nonsystem of First Nations education on reserve. It proposes establishing a legislative framework through an Act of Parliament that would encourage systemic reform of First Nations schooling, essentially by setting up the kind of educational structures we have enjoyed off reserve. Of course, this is only a proposal. The final form of any mechanism would have to be negotiated with responsible First Nations organizations, and should also call on the views of experts in educational systems. But it is hoped that the proposal for a First Nations Education Act, and the reasons for it as set out here, will help stimulate governments and First Nations to consider bold proposals to begin a process of radical reform of First Nations education and establish the foundations for whole system reform.

REFERENCES

Aboriginal Affairs and Northern Development Canada (2009/2010). Comprehensive funding arrangement: National model for use with First Nations and Tribal Councils for 2009/2010. Section 6.1.2. Retrieved from http://www.ainc-inac.gc.ca

Aboriginal Affairs and Northern Development Canada. Retrieved from http://www.ainc-inac.gc.ca.

Andrews, M., Duncombe, W., & Yinger, J. (2002). Revisiting economies of size in American education: Are we any closer to a consensus? *Economics of Education Review, 21*(3), 245–262. http://dx.doi.org/10.1016/S0272-7757(01)00006-1

Assembly of First Nations. (2006). *Fiscal fairness for First Nations.* Ottawa: Author. Retrieved from http://www.afn.ca/misclRFBS.pdf

Bell, D. (2004). *Sharing our success: Ten case studies in Aboriginal schooling.* Kelowna, BC: Society for the Advancement of Excellence in Education (SAEE). Retrieved from http://www.saee.ca

Cree School Board. (n.d.). Retrieved from http://www.cscree.qc.ca/GIHistory.htm.

de Coulon, A., Meschi, E., & Vignoles, A. (2008). *Parents' basic skills and children cognitive outcomes.* London, UK: Centre for the Economics of Education, London School of Economics.

Department of Finance. (1996). *Budget plan: Including supplementary information and notices of ways and means motions.* Ottawa: Government of Canada.

Diamond, B. (1987). The Cree experience. In J. Barman, Y. Herbert, & D. McCaskill (Eds.), *The Indian experience in Canada: The challenge* (Vol. 2) (pp. 86–106). Vancouver: University of British Columbia Press.

Employment Insurance Act, SC 1996, c 23.

Erhardt, G. (1997). *Doing more with less: A simulated amalgamation of school boards.* Saskatchewan School Trustees Association Research Centre Report #97–04. Retrieved from http://www.saskschoolboards.caloldlResearchAndDevelopmentl ResearchReportslGovernancei

First Nations Education Steering Committee (2006). Draft British Columbia First Nations Education Authority Terms of Reference 2006. Retrieved from http://www.fnesc.ca/

Fleming, T., & Hutton, B. (1997). School boards, district consolidation, and educational governance in British Columbia, 1872–1995. *Canadian Journal of Educational Administration and Policy, 10.* Retrieved from http://www.umanitoba.ca/publications/cjeap/articles/jleming10.htm

Fullan, M. (2009). Large-Scale reform comes of age. *Journal of Educational Change, 10*(2), 101–113. Retrieved from http://www.edweek.org. http://dx.doi.org/10.1007/s10833-009-9108-z

Fullan, M., & Levin, B. (2009, June). The fundamentals of whole-system reform: A case study from Canada. *Education Week.* Retrieved from http://www.edweek.org/ew/articles/2009/06/17/35fullan.h28.html

Henderson, J.Y. (1995). Treaties and Indian education. In M. Battiste & J. Barman (Eds.), *First Nations education in Canada: The circle unfolds* (pp. 5–46). Vancouver: University of British Columbia Press.

Levin, B. (2008). *How to change 5000 schools: A practical and positive approach for leading change at every level.* Cambridge, MA: Harvard Education Press.

Lochner, L. (2007). Education and crime. In B. McGraw, P. Peterson, & E. Baker (Eds.), *International Encyclopaedia of Education* (3rd ed.). Amsterdam: Elsevier. Retrieved from http://economics.uwo.ca

Manitoba School Divisions/Boundaries Review Commission. (1994). *Report of the commission.* Winnipeg: Government of Manitoba.

Martinez, M., & Harvey, J. (2004). *From whole school to whole system reform. Consortium for Policy Research in Education sponsored by the National Clearinghouse for Comprehensive School Reform and the Annenberg Institute for School Reform.* Washington, DC: National Clearinghouse for Comprehensive School Reform.

Matthews, N. (2001). *First Nations education financing.* Paper prepared for the First Nations Education Steering Committee, British Columbia. Retrieved from http://www.fnesc.bc.ca

McCue, H. (2006). *First Nations 2nd and 3rd level education services.* A discussion paper for the Joint Working Group Indian and Northern Affairs—Assembly of First Nations. Retrieved from http://www.turtleisland.orgl.education

Mendelson, M. (2008, July). *Improving education on reserves: A First Nations education authority act.* Ottawa: Caledon Institute of Social Policy. Retrieved from http://www.caledoninst.org

National Indian Brotherhood. (1972). *Indian control of Indian education.* Ottawa: Assembly of First Nations.

Office of the Parliamentary Budget Officer (2009). *The funding requirement for First Nations schools in Canada.* Ottawa: Library of Parliament. Retrieved from http://www.parl.gc.calpbo-dpb

Perreault, S. (2009). *The incarceration of Aboriginal People in adult correctional services.* Statistics Canada Catalogue No. 85-002-X. Vol. 29 No. 3. Published by authority of the Minister responsible for Statistics Canada. Ottawa: Minister of Industry. Retrieved from http://www.statcan.gc.calpubI85-002-xI2009003Iarticlel10903-eng.pdf

Prentice, J. (2006). Jim Prentice on First Nations Jurisdiction over Education in British Columbia Act. Retrieved from http://openparliament.ca/debates/2006/12/5/jim-prentice-1/only/.

Public Works and Government Services. (1996). *Report of the Royal Commission on Aboriginal Peoples.* Ottawa: Author.

Richards, J. (2008). Closing the Aboriginal/non-Aboriginal education gaps. C.D. Howe Institute Backgrounder. Retrieved from *http://www.cdhowe.org*

Richards, J., & Scott, M. (2009). *Aboriginal education: Strengthening the foundations.* Ottawa: Canadian Policy Research Network.

Riddell, W.C. (2005). The social benefits of education: New evidence on an old question. In F. Iacobucci & C. Tuohy (Eds.), *Taking public universities seriously* (pp. 138–163). Toronto: University of Toronto Press.

Riddell, W.C. (2006). *Skill formation and economic outcomes.* Presentation to the Population, Work and Family Policy Research Collaboration Symposium, Gatineau, Quebec.

Royal Commission on Aboriginal Peoples. (1996). Report. Ottawa: Minister of Public Works and Government Services.

Sharpe, A., Arsenault, J.-F., Lapointe, S., & Cowan, F. (2009). *The effect of increasing Aboriginal educational attainment on the labour force, output and the fiscal balance.* Research Report 2009–3. Ottawa: Centre for the Study of Living Standards.

Statistics Canada (2005). *Projections of the Aboriginal populations, Canada, provinces and territories: 2001 to 2017.* Ottawa: Minister of Industry, Government of Canada. Retrieved from http://www.statcan.gc.ca

Treasury Board Secretariat. The Government Expense Plan and the Main Estimates, 2009–2010. Retrieved from http://www.tbs-sct.gc.ca/est-pre/20092010/me-bd/docs/index-eng.pdf

Two ways forward. (2009, August 26). *Globe and Mail,* A10.

Visser, J., & Fovet, F. (2007). *The Cree School Board experiment in northern Quebec: An eco-systemic review on curriculum and performance.* Burnaby, BC: Imaginative Education Research Group, Simon Fraser University. Retrieved from http://www.ierg.net

Winnipeg School Board. (n.d.). Retrieved from http://www.sd1.org/.

Wolfe, B., & Haveman, R. (2001). Accounting for the social and non-market benefits of education. In J.F. Helliwell (Ed.), *The contribution of human and social capital to sustained economic growth and well-being: International symposium report.* Ottawa: OECD and HRDC.

NOTE

1 The situation in the territories is unique and the proposals made here would have to be adapted to their requirements. These proposals for structural reform do not apply at all to Nunavut.

11

Free to Learn: Giving Aboriginal Youth Control over Their Post-Secondary Education

Calvin Helin and Dave Snow

This chapter was originally published in *True North*. (2010) Ottawa:
Macdonald-Laurier Institute for Public Policy. pp. 7–24, 26.
Reproduced with permission.

The gap in living standards between Aboriginals and non-Aboriginals in Canada is shocking. On nearly every social and economic indicator of well-being, Aboriginal people trail other Canadians. Life expectancy, for example, is often similar to that in developing nations (Flanagan, 2008, pp. 226–227). Although Aboriginals are making some progress, they continue to fall behind other Canadians, who are progressing even faster. The gap that separates Canada's most vulnerable group from the rest of its population is growing (Richards, 2006, pp. 34–41). Moreover, the plight of Aboriginals is not confined to certain regions; the gaps are consistent across Canada.

There are countless variables that determine Aboriginal well-being. Arguably, the most important is education. From secondary to post-secondary education, many studies demonstrate that increased education is highly correlated with material well-being

(Mendelson, 2006a; Sharpe, Arsenault, Lapointe, & Cowan, 2009). As with other social and economic indicators, Aboriginals in general fall far behind other Canadians in terms of their level of formal education. Aboriginals are not getting the education they need to thrive in Canada, and they are not getting an opportunity to determine their own future.

What is true of Aboriginals in general is especially true of "Indians." Constitutionally, "Aboriginal peoples" includes Indians, Inuit, and Métis. The category "Indians" includes both "status" Indians, who are registered under the Indian Act, and "non-status" Indians, who are not (Statistics Canada, 2008a). Registered status Indians are in turn divided between those who live on reserves and those who do not. Virtually all of the gaps between Aboriginals and non-Aboriginals are even more pronounced for Indians, especially those who live on reserves. Although this study discusses the situation of Aboriginals generally, it focuses particularly on the egregious plight of registered status Indians. The term "First Nations" is often used to designate registered Indians, but for clarity and ease of exposition, we will use the constitutional terminology.

Despite much goodwill, in the past, Canadians have too often tolerated ineffective programs intended to close the gap between Aboriginals and non-Aboriginals even as the gap persists and worsens. Now, however, looming demographic change associated with a greying population and low levels of fertility will soon create a labour shortage unlike anything Canada has ever experienced. Starting next year, the Canadian population will grow faster than the labour force. Not long after, the number of net new workers entering the labour force will drop to zero (Crowley, 2009, p. 32). In the face of this demographic crisis, Canadians' future prosperity depends on their being able to get the greatest value possible from every potential member of the workforce, in addition to the moral imperative of improving the lot of Aboriginal Canadians. Unlike the rest of the population, however, Aboriginals are young, on average, and the Aboriginal birthrate is high. As Canada's labour force ages and shrinks, Aboriginals represent a young population capable of entering the workforce and helping to fill the gap created by retiring boomers. But will we succeed in equipping them with the education they need to do so successfully?

Integrating Aboriginals into the workforce will by no means be an easy task. Although a labour shortage may be a worker's best friend, the modern knowledge economy requires highly skilled and educated workers. It is thus imperative that we ensure as many young

Aboriginals as possible enter the workforce with the highest possible levels of education. Post-secondary funding is an excellent way to encourage Indian youth, particularly those with low incomes, to harness their potential and take control of their educational future.

Canada's record in Aboriginal education, particularly through the residential schools and Indian day schools, offers Aboriginals every reason to be wary and skeptical about federal education policy. This chapter offers an approach that at once will improve access to funding for young Aboriginals while keeping control over education in the hands of Aboriginals themselves.

The federal government has constitutional responsibility for the education of Indians, particularly those living on reserve. In recognition of this responsibility, Indian and Northern Affairs Canada (INAC) spends $314 million annually through the Post-Secondary Student Support Program (PSSSP) in support of post-secondary education for registered Indian and Inuit students.[1] Yet the program's funding structure for Indians is counterproductive and stifling. *Indian bands*—the bodies entitled to exercise legal power for individual First Nation communities—receive "block" funding that they are then supposed to distribute to students. In practice, accountability mechanisms are non-existent. According to the evidence we have been able to gather, this has led to misuse of surplus funds, rationing, long waits for funding, regional variations in access to funding, and allegations of nepotism and favouritism. Because they have no relationship with on-reserve chiefs and councils, Indians living off reserve rarely receive PSSSP funding. Indian youth are too often not receiving the money they so desperately need. The program needs to change, and it needs to change soon.

For the funding to have its desired effect, there must be transparency and accountability. Most importantly, the authority for determining how the funding is used must move downward, from individual bands to individual students. This study proposes phasing out the PSSSP and replacing it with Aboriginal Post-Secondary Savings Accounts (APSSAs) for all registered Indians. The creation of these accounts would allow for more efficient and transparent use of taxpayer dollars, and it would empower Indian youth to make decisions about their own educational future.

This chapter unfolds in four sections. The next section examines the social and economic gaps between Aboriginals (particularly Indians) and the rest of Canadians. It then discusses the urgent need for integrating Aboriginal youth into the Canadian workforce, and demonstrates that education is the most important factor in lifting

Aboriginals out of poverty. The subsequent section examines the federal Post-Secondary Student Support Program, and outlines the numerous problems that have hindered its potential. Following that, this chapter examines proposals for reform to the PSSSP and shows that none of them effectively get to the root of the problem. The final section recommends a movement to Aboriginal Post-Secondary Savings Accounts.

Education: Closing the Gap between Aboriginals and the Rest of Canada

After decades of policy aimed at improving the social and economic conditions of Aboriginal Canadians (a group that includes Indians, Inuit, and Métis), Canada's most vulnerable group remains far behind the rest of the country on nearly every quality of life measure available, especially education, the particular concern of this chapter. Not all Aboriginals are eligible for federal assistance toward their post-secondary education, however. While there may be a case for assistance to other classes of Aboriginals, the Macdonald-Laurier Institute, as a public policy institute concerned with federal government policy, has asked that this chapter focus on reforming current federal programs for the current beneficiaries, who are registered Indians falling under Ottawa's jurisdiction. According to Statistics Canada, of the more than 1.17 million Aboriginal people in Canada in 2006, 698,025 (nearly 60%) identified as North American "Indian." Over 80% of Indians are registered "status" Indians.

Indians lag behind other Canadians on virtually every social indicator. As regards housing, Indians were five times more likely than non-Aboriginals to live in crowded homes: more than one-quarter of on-reserve Indians live in crowded housing (Flanagan, 2008, p. 225; Statistics Canada, 2008a, p. 8). As for life expectancy, Indians live on average 5.1 fewer years than other Canadians—a life expectancy comparable to China and the Dominican Republic. Registered Indians, particularly those living on reserve, have higher incidence rates than other Canadians for suicide, alcoholism, diabetes, smoking, tuberculosis, and obesity. More than 36% of on-reserve Indians receive welfare, compared with 5.5% of the general Canadian population (Flanagan, 2008, pp. 226–227; Richards, 2006, pp. 34–35, 41). Indians are more likely to be unemployed than the rest of Canadians, and have much lower incomes (Mendelson, 2006a, p. 35).

The substantially lower quality of life of Indians—indeed, of Aboriginals more generally—is especially evident with respect to education. In 2006, fully 38% of Indians aged 25–64 had less than a high school education, compared to 15% for non-Aboriginals in the same age bracket. Likewise, only 8% of all Aboriginals in the same age group had a university degree, compared to 23% for non-Aboriginals. This gap actually widened between 2001 and 2006 (Statistics Canada, 2008b, pp. 19–24). Sadly, only 3% of all registered Indians have a university degree, compared to 18% of the entire Canadian population (Usher, 2009, p. 5).

It should be noted that Aboriginal educational attainment is increasing, albeit slightly. Between 2001 and 2006, for example, the rate of Aboriginals with a university degree moved from 6 to 8% (Statistics Canada, 2008b, p. 19). This rate of increase, which is by no means negligible, held for Indians in general (by 1.1%) and on-reserve Indians in particular (by 0.7%). As one recent study noted, "even though the absolute educational gap between Aboriginal and non-Aboriginal populations is increasing, the strong rate of growth in the proportion of Aboriginals holding a university degree remains encouraging for the future" (Sharpe et al., 2009, p. 17).

Yet Canadians should hardly take comfort from these figures. Across the board, the educational data all tell the same story: Aboriginal attainment is increasing very slowly, at a much slower rate than non-Aboriginal Canadians. The gap between Aboriginals and non-Aboriginals is growing. Indians fare even worse than Aboriginals more generally. And finally, the on-reserve Indian population has poorer social indicators than Indians living off reserve. In 2006, for example, more than 50% of Indians living on reserve had not completed high school, compared to 30% of off-reserve Indians. Likewise, 9% of Indians living off reserve had a university degree, compared with only 4% living on reserve (Statistics Canada, 2008b, p. 22). To no one's surprise, this poor educational attainment leads to substantial dependency. As Aboriginal author and entrepreneur (and co-author of this study) Calvin Helin (2008) notes, "While only 29 percent of the Aboriginal population live on reserves, they receive 88 percent of the federal government program spending. The 50 percent that live in cities receive only 3.5 percent of this amount" (p. 55).

Why Canada Needs Indian Youth

Canadians clearly find the social and economic conditions experienced by Indians, particularly on reserves, deplorable. Yet Canadians have been complacent about our most vulnerable citizens, being "content to put Aboriginal challenges out-of-mind and into the backwater bureaucracy" (Helin, 2008, p. 44). Our national prosperity has unfortunately afforded us the luxury of overlooking the plight of all

Aboriginals, and with it their shockingly high unemployment, welfare rates, and poor living conditions.

In the coming years, such complacency will no longer be an option. Canada is about to experience an unprecedented labour shortage. The demographic shift associated with the looming retirement of baby boomers, combined with a shrinking labour force due to decades of declining fertility, presents a substantial change in the very structure of our population base. As Brian Lee Crowley (2009) explains,

> Starting in 2011, population will grow faster in Canada than the labour force, and that trend will continue for forty years … By 2016, a few short years away, the number of net new workers entering the workforce will be zero and will be slightly negative for a decade after that. We are teetering on the edge of a demographic cliff, and we have one foot out in the air. (p. 32)

All projections of Canada's future population, no matter how rosy, recognize this essential fact: the workforce is shrinking and the labour market is going to look very different in a few short years. Between 1956 and 2006, Canada's labour force grew by a whopping 200%; by contrast, in the next 50 years, it will grow by a mere 11% (Crowley, 2009, p. 24). At the same time, an aging workforce and the burgeoning number of retirees will create even greater dependency and will make labour force growth even more important. In 2030, the ratio of Canadian workers to retirees is expected to be a mere two to one, down from the current 3.25 to one (Crowley, 2009, pp. 255–256). One recent Statistics Canada report predicts that Canada's senior population (65 and older) could be more than double the number of children under the age of 15 by the same year (Chow, 2005). Canada needs workers, and it needs them urgently.

Thankfully, with crisis comes opportunity. Along with encouraging older workers to keep working, Canada can mitigate the labour shortage by employing workers from populations with traditionally lower labour force participation rates: young men, rural populations, recent immigrants, Canadians trapped in welfare dependency, and, of course, Aboriginals (Crowley, 2009, p. 260). The coming era "will be an age of inclusiveness such as the social engineers of the employment equity movement could never have imagined" (Crowley, 2009, p. 261), not because governments will force people to employ nontraditional workers, but because it will be an economic necessity to do so.

Some may feel that we can overcome the labour shortage simply by increasing immigration. However, immigration alone cannot stop

Canada's population from aging. The average age of immigrants, who often bring their aging parents to Canada, is not substantially different from the average age of Canadians as a whole, and the economic success of recent immigrants has fallen significantly behind that of Canadian-born workers. Even if Canada were to increase its immigrant intake fourfold—an average of one million immigrants per year for the next 50 years—by 2056, Canada's median age would still rise from 38.8 to 44.1 years, and the proportion of seniors from 13.2% to 22.3% (Statistics Canada, 2006). A dramatic increase in immigration levels would "mitigate only very partially the economic consequences of a broad social phenomenon like aging" (Crowley, 2009, pp. 218–219). Moreover, as competition for immigrants intensifies in the rest of the world, Canada's relative attractiveness as an immigrant destination will continue to decline. We can no longer blithely assume that we can "attract as many immigrants as we wish at whatever levels of education and skills we need" (Crowley, 2009, pp. 222–223).

By contrast, Aboriginal demographics present a clear opportunity in this regard, as Aboriginals (particularly Indians) and non-Aboriginals are essentially moving in opposite demographic directions: Canada's population is growing slowly and greying, while the Aboriginal population is growing rapidly and is much younger. One-third of the Aboriginal population is 14 and under, compared with a mere 19% for non-Aboriginals. In 2006, the median age of the Aboriginal population was 27. For the non-Aboriginal population, it was 40. Aboriginals account for 3.3% of the total Canadian population but 5.6% of Canadian children. The population increase for status and non-status Indians in the decade between 1996 and 2006 was 26%, three and a half times the 8% increase for non-Aboriginals (Helin, 2008, pp. 44, 48; Statistics Canada, 2008a, pp. 8, 14).

Whatever way one looks at it, the data say the same thing: as the Canadian labour force remains stable or stagnant while the economy is growing, the potential labour pool of Aboriginals is growing rapidly. The labour force implications are already here. The working age (15–64) Aboriginal population increased by 25% between 2001 and 2006 compared to 6% for other Canadians, and this trend is expected to continue; between 2001 and 2026, more than 600,000 Aboriginal youth will enter the labour market, an expected growth of 37% (INAC, 2006; Hull, 2008). This "Aboriginal demographic tidal wave" could not come at a more opportune time. This extraordinarily high rate of Aboriginal unemployment "is occurring precisely at the time when Canada needs the workers most" (Helin, 2008, pp. 44, 56).

Implications of Indian Labour Force Participation

Integrating Aboriginal youth into the Canadian workforce will by no means be an easy task. The economic and social ills plaguing Aboriginals, particularly those living on reserve, have been documented above. Merely coming of working age does not guarantee a job, even in a labour shortage. The employment rate for Aboriginals aged 25–64 is 63%, up from 58% in 2001, but much lower than 76% for non-Aboriginal Canadians. Of greater concern, in 2006, the unemployment rate for Aboriginals aged 25–64 was a whopping three times the Canadian average, exceeding the Canadian rate in every single region (INAC, 2006).

Thus, getting Aboriginal entrants into the Canadian labour market is not just a moral imperative in order to improve the well-being of Aboriginals: it is absolutely essential to easing Canada's coming labour shortage. Michael Mendelson (2006a) is not overstating the fact when he argues that "Canada's future prosperity depends on how successful we are in achieving equitable results in our labour market for Aboriginal Canadians" (p. 56).

A recent analysis by the Centre for the Study of Living Standards, which detailed the fiscal implications of improving Aboriginal living standards, lends credible evidence for this conclusion. The authors found the cost of Aboriginals' above-average use of government services was $6.2 billion in 2006, and will rise to $8.4 billion per year by 2026 if unchecked. On the other hand, if by 2026 Aboriginal Canadians were able to increase their educational attainment to the 2006 level of non-Aboriginals, gross domestic product (GDP) would grow by an additional $179 billion between 2001 and 2026. Government tax revenues alone would be $3.5 billion higher in 2026 (Sharpe et al., 2009, pp. v–vii).

The implications for the Canadian labour force would be enormous. Assuming that Aboriginal economic and social conditions remain the same as today, Aboriginals are expected to account for 12.7% of labour force growth and 11.3% of employment growth between 2006 and 2026; by contrast, if employment and participation rates reached 2006 non-Aboriginal levels by 2026, Aboriginals would account for 19.9% of the labour force growth and 22.1% of employment growth in the same period (Sharpe et al., 2009, p. vi). The authors recognize that such potential is unlikely to be fully realized, as many older Aboriginals are unlikely to go back to school. Nonetheless, they conclude that increasing Aboriginal well-being is not just in the interests of Aboriginals themselves—it is in the interests of all Canadians:

Not only would it contribute to the personal well-being of Aboriginals, it would address Canada's two most pressing economic challenges: a looming labour short-age caused by an ageing population and low birthrate; and a lackluster growth in productivity which has eroded Canadian industry's ability to compete. (Centre for the Study of Living Standards, 2009)

The best way to cope with this challenge will be to focus on increasing the educational attainment of Aboriginals. The next section examines this more closely, focusing principally on Indians.

Education Is the Means

Education is not simply another social indicator; in many senses, it is the most important cause of social mobility and progress. Study after study identifies education as the most important way to improve the life of Aboriginals. After completing post-secondary education, for example, Indians fare as well as the general population on most social indicators, though they fare slightly worse in terms of employment (Mendelson, 2006a, p. 35). As education level rises, so does median income (Richards & Vining, 2004, pp. 2–4). Although Aboriginals have much lower incomes than non-Aboriginals, Aboriginals with a high school diploma or higher obtained "significantly better labour market outcomes, both in absolute terms and relative to non-Aboriginal Canadians than those who did not" (Sharpe et al., 2009, p. vi).

Whether in the form of a secondary school diploma, a trade certificate, a college diploma, or a university degree, education matters (Usher, 2009, p. 6). As such, Canada will benefit from a sustained effort to ensure that Aboriginal youth are completing secondary school and moving on to post-secondary education. The authors of a recent study on the economic implications of Aboriginal success contend that "increasing the number of Aboriginal Canadians who complete high school is a low-hanging fruit with far-reaching and considerable economic and social benefits for Canadians" (Sharpe et al., 2009, 70).

For Indians, "there is no question that education really is the only path out of poverty" (Helin, 2008, p. 205). Secondary education is clearly a priority, and many studies have looked at ways to reform primary and secondary education for Indian students living on and off reserve (Richards, Hove, & Ofalabi, 2008; Mendelson, 2006b). However, making the transition from secondary to post-secondary education as seamless as possible also remains a crucial issue. Given the fact that Indian students, particularly those living on reserve, come from lower-income families than the rest of Canadians, funding is an obvious issue. Many young non-Aboriginals can graduate debt-free because they have the support of their families, who can often bear an important part of the cost. Young Aboriginals, on the other hand, often come from a background of poverty and cannot count on the same level of family support.

The educational and financial factors are mutually reinforcing. Insufficient funding (or the perception of insufficient funding) is one of the primary reasons Aboriginals do not complete post-secondary studies; nearly one-quarter of Aboriginals cited finances as a reason for not completing their post-secondary studies in 2001 (Statistics Canada, 2003, p. 19). Moreover, inadequate financial support and a desire to avoid debt are major factors that prevent Indian youth from beginning post-secondary education in the first place (Malatest & Associates & Stonechild, 2008).

Offering Indian students the means to harness their own educational potential and determine their future can close the gap between Indian and non-Indian Canadians. As the above section demonstrates, education is the most powerful force lifting Indian youth out of poverty and dependency and into prosperity. Given the uniformity of poor social, economic, and educational outcomes for Indian students across the country, this is an issue that warrants national attention. The national significance is magnified by the fact that education for registered status Indians falls under Ottawa's jurisdiction, a unique state of affairs. The next section examines the federal government's current policy for improving the post-secondary education success rate of all Indian youth.

Good Intentions, Bad Policy: The Post-Secondary Student Support Program

Although education is constitutionally an area of provincial jurisdiction, the federal government has authority over "Indians, and Lands reserved for the Indians" under section 1.24 of the Constitution Act, 1867. The federal Indian Act provides primary and secondary on-reserve education for all status Indian students. For post-secondary education, the jurisdictional question is less clear. The federal government considers Indian post-secondary education a matter of social policy, and thus an area of provincial jurisdiction. By contrast, Indian bands and First Nations organizations claim education at all levels is a treaty right recognized in the Canadian Constitution. When surveyed, Indian youth consistently espouse the same view (Canada, 2007, p. 3; Malatest & Associates & Stonechild, 2008, p. 23).

The federal government funds post-secondary education for Indians but views such funding as discretionary rather than constitutionally required. As Paul Leblanc, a former Senior Assistant Deputy

Minister, explained to the Standing Committee on Aboriginal Affairs and Northern Development, "Our interpretation is that there is nothing in the Act that requires a contribution at the post-secondary level, and that there is nothing in the Act that limits the possibility of contributing at the post-secondary level" (Canada, 2007, p. 3).

Federal funding for Aboriginal post-secondary education exists in the form of the Post-Secondary Education (PSE) Program of Indian and Northern Affairs Canada, which dates from 1977 and is designed to provide eligible Indian and Inuit students with access to post-secondary education. It contains three components:

- PSSSP: Provides money to Registered Indian and Inuit students[2] enrolled in post-secondary programs. These programs include community college and CEGEP *(Collège d'enseignement général et professionnel)* diploma/certificate programs, undergraduate programs, and advanced/professional degree programs.
- University and College Entrance Preparation: Provides money for Registered Indian and Inuit students enrolled in university and college entrance preparation programs.
- Indian Studies Support Program: Provides Indian organizations and post-secondary institutions with money for creating and administering university- and college-level courses specifically for registered Indian and Inuit students.

The Post-Secondary Student Support Program is by far the largest component of the PSE Program, at a current (2008–2009) annual cost of $314 million, increasing by a maximum of 2% annually. The money is intended to cover tuition, books, supplies, travel, and living allowances for students and their dependents, as well as tutoring, guidance, and counselling services. Inuit students and registered Indians living on and off reserve and residing in Canada are eligible for funding. In 2008–2009, the program funded approximately 22 thousand students, down from a high of 27 thousand in 1997–1998. The goal of the program, consistent with the goal of INAC's PSE Program in general, is to get more Indian students into post-secondary education, and eventually into the workforce.

Although INAC regional offices administer the program, almost 100% of the funding is delivered by Indian bands,[3] their administering organizations, or educational institutions. For the Inuit component of the program, the money goes from the federal government to the territorial governments, which then fund individual Inuit students (Canada, 2007, p. 13). For the Indian component, the money flows directly from INAC to individual bands via either a

Comprehensive Funding Agreement, which consists of funding on a program basis, or an Alternative Funding Agreement, which consists of multiyear "block" funding. In either case, the money is distributed from INAC to the Indian bands, which then distribute it to individual students. The federal government determines the objectives and provides the money, but the bands ultimately determine which students are funded.

In 2009, an INAC audit (INAC Audit and Assurance Services Branch) unearthed countless problems with the administration and effectiveness of the program. These problems include surplus funds, wait-listed students, regional variation, favouritism and nepotism, and a lack of performance measurement. Each problem underscores fundamental issues with the program's transparency and accountability structure. They are examined below.

Surplus Funds and Abuse of Expenses

To the extent that minimum program requirements are met (and these requirements, as seen below, are hardly arduous), individual bands are allowed to retain "unexpected balances" at the end of the year. In a classic case of a perverse incentive, if there is money left over, it does not go to the students for whom the money was intended. It stays with the bands, to be spent at the discretion of chiefs and councils. Revealingly, the audit found "such annual program surpluses are not uncommon," as individual bands "are not required to report on specific program spending" (INAC Audit and Assurance Services Branch, 2009, p. 6). Although some bands claim they "reallocate" funds for other community priorities, INAC keeps no records on such reallocations (Canada, 2007, p. 21).

When the bands do report information, there is evidence of mismanagement and abuse. The financial statements submitted to INAC routinely report the use of program funds for "non-eligible" expenses including, but not limited to, "administration costs, capital expenditures, child care costs, staff salaries and benefits, staff training/meetings, staff or council travel expenses, office expenses and utility costs" (INAC Audit and Assurance Services Branch, 2009, p. 18). Because the bands are allowed to retain surplus funds, they have the authority to spend such funds on "non-eligible" program expenses. Thus, the lack of transparency and accountability built into the program effectively turns any "non-eligible" expense into an "eligible" expense.

In itself, this program flaw speaks volumes. Surplus funds from a national program intended to cover Indian students' post-secondary education should be spent on the students, not on band council travel expenses or staff child care arrangements. The audit found that these uses of surplus funds "could be denying other eligible students from intended program support" (INAC Audit and Assurance Services Branch, 2009, p. 17). There is no evidence that anything has been done to rectify this shameful practice.

Wait-Listed Students and Rationing

In spite of surplus funds, the audit found evidence that some eligible students are unable to obtain funding, which results in students being "wait-listed" for funding. There is no data on precisely how many students are wait-listed (INAC Audit and Assurance Services Branch, 2009, p. 8; Malatest & Associates & Stonechild, 2008). The program's distribution structure has thus created a second perverse outcome: while on the one hand certain bands are able to retain surplus funds originally intended for students, on the other hand, students from other bands are unable to receive the funding to which they are entitled. For such variance to occur in a national program aimed at all Indian students is downright scandalous.

These problems, severe as they are today, will only be exacerbated in the future: the cost of post-secondary education is rising faster than the maximum rate of growth of the PSSSP. As the young Indian population continues to grow, more students will inevitably be forced to wait to have the chance to pursue their studies in the years to come. The lack of accountability and absence of clear guidelines for dealing with insufficient funds only exacerbates this problem, creating huge disparities between and even within reserves.

A recent examination of the program found that in addition to problems with oversight and accountability, stagnating resources per eligible recipient has led to rationing. Even where the program is administered properly, a 2% annual growth in expenditures cannot keep pace with the rapid growth of Indian youth, even if tuition costs were to grow at roughly the same rate rather than the 4.3% of the last decade (INAC Audit and Assurance Services Branch, 2009, p. 7). Absent spending increases, funding will inevitably be rationed in one of two ways under the current structure: by reducing the amount of funding per student, or reducing the number of students assisted (Usher, 2009, p. 12). As it stands, there is no policy guideline for how the necessary rationing should occur. Prospective students are left at the whim of the band council, who can allocate the funding however they see fit. The growth of the young Indian population combined with the rise in tuition costs mean this problem will only get worse in the absence of serious reform.

Regional Variation

Indian and Northern Affairs Canada is a federal government department with a mandate to serve the needs of Aboriginals across the country. Likewise, the PSSSP is a national program, designed to assist all registered Indian and Inuit students in Canada. Yet this ostensibly national program does not have a national funding formula. Rather, different regional INAC offices use different formulae to distribute the funds to individual bands (Usher, 2009, p. 10).

These formulae vary widely. Some regions base their funding on 18–34 age cohorts in the region, others on 18–34 age cohorts within individual bands, and others still on prior year funding. The result is considerable regional variance without any clear rationale. In 2008, the Ontario region disbursed $1,609 per individual in the 18–34 age cohort, whereas the Atlantic region disbursed only $941 per individual for the same cohort (INAC Audit and Assurance Services Branch, 2009, p. 12). This is in spite of the fact that Atlantic Canada has some of the highest tuition fees in the country: Nova Scotia has the highest average undergraduate tuition fees of any province, while New Brunswick has the third highest (Statistics Canada, 2009). The audit offered no explanation for this disparity, nor any evidence that anything was being done to rectify it.

Favouritism and Nepotism

Fundamentally, the major problems with the program are transparency and accountability, both of which are sorely lacking. As might be expected in a program with virtually no oversight, this lack of accountability has created conditions in which favouritism and nepotism often determine funding.

In 2008, the Canadian Millennium Scholarship Foundation commissioned R.A. Malatest & Associates and Dr. Blair Stonechild to look into the factors affecting the use of student financial assistance by Indian youth. The goal was to understand Indian youth awareness of post-secondary financial assistance programs and examine how that awareness differs from non-Indian youth. The researchers gathered information through 40 focus groups with secondary school students, youth in post-secondary education, and youth not in post-secondary education. The groups included Indian and non-Indian youth. The researchers also held interviews with 41 key stakeholders representing a wide range of people employed in occupations related to Aboriginal post-secondary education (Malatest & Associates & Stonechild, 2008, pp. 2–7). The authors concluded:

Many First Nation students expressed frustration with the "lack of transparency" with respect to how such funds are allocated. Some youth felt that receipt of band funding often depended on relationships with band leadership, proximity to the band (those living on reserve were seen as having a higher probability of being funded than those living off reserve) or other factors. (Malatest & Associates & Stonechild, 2008, p. viii)

Even more telling, some students stated that the past performance of their family members affected their ability to receive funding. Others were allegedly passed over because of their age, the fact that they had children, or the type of study (e.g., graduate studies) they were pursuing. Some students felt the application process was arduous and stressful, and they sometimes did not receive notification of funding until mere weeks before beginning their studies (Malatest & Associates & Stonechild, 2008, pp. 30–32). Others could not fulfill course requirements because the courses were filled by the time students received notification. Another study notes that the creation of "tiers" has become commonplace, with more "promising" students given top priority for funding (Usher, 2009, p. 12). While there is nothing wrong with meritocratic funding in principle, there is no evidence that such "tiers" have been created based on objective criteria. Such overt discrimination and cumbersome bureaucratic obstacles were certainly not an intended part of a program designed to enhance access to post-secondary education for all Indian youth.

No Performance Measurement

None of the above problems can effectively be rectified as long as the program is immune to any objective and accurate assessment of its performance. The bands are only required to submit an enrolment report that identifies the number of students receiving funding through the program, and a graduation report of the number of students who completed their studies in the previous year. While some bands report specific receipts and disbursements, this is not mandatory.

Because of these reporting procedures, INAC has no data on the average or median funding disbursed to students, the number of years of support provided to individual students, drop-out rates, wait-listed students, or the percentage of students graduating (INAC Audit and Assurance Services Branch, 2009, pp. 9–10). Moreover, the 2009 INAC audit found that "[n]o analysis has been conducted to determine the minimum amount of recipient funding required to achieve program objectives" (p. 7). INAC provides money to individual bands with no assurance that the money will be delivered to the people for whom it is intended, nor any assurance that the funding is adequate (or, alternatively, excessive). In short, INAC has no real way of measuring program success.

A major problem with the current program design is the capability of smaller bands to effectively distribute funding. Many reserves are small, with fewer than one thousand residents. Individuals who oversee PSSSP funding often lack the academic knowledge and understanding of post-secondary institutional operation, yet they are expected to administer highly complicated programs for the disbursement of funds. In this situation, administrative inefficiency and overload are to be expected (Usher, 2009, p. 11). Another study found that Indian high school students commonly used informal channels, such as family and friends, rather than formal channels (teachers and counsellors) to obtain information about post-secondary funding Malatest & Associates & Stonechild, 2008, p. vi).

In sum, it is remarkable that a national program designed to give money to registered Indian students across the country:

- allows individual bands to retain surplus funds to use at their discretion;
- is subject to regional variations to such an extent that the variation between Ontario and Atlantic Canada is nearly two to one per eligible student.

With virtually no transparency and accountability mechanisms in place, it is little wonder that the system has led to nepotism, favouritism, and wait-listed students. The current system devolves authority to INAC regional offices and to band councils and administrators but gives no authority where it truly belongs: Indian youth. The next section examines several proposals for reform and offers one solution that can overcome all the obstacles listed above.

Reforming the Post-Secondary Student Support Program

Clearly, the problems related to the PSSSP—accountability, transparency, capability, and regional variation—are not easily overcome. The program requires more than a minor tweak in order to achieve its goal of getting more Indian students into post-secondary education. A recent review of the program by the Educational Policy Institute (EPI) suggested five possible options for change in PSSSP program delivery (Usher, 2009). The five options were:

- status quo with improvements in accountability;
- administration by a regional First Nations' education organization;

- administration by a pan-Canadian First Nations foundation;
- direct administration by Indian and Northern Affairs Canada;
- direct administration by Human Resources and Skills Development Canada (HRSDC).

The EPI study did not make a recommendation as to which of the five alternatives were superior. Instead, it merely laid out the advantages and disadvantages of each option, using the criteria of efficiency, accountability, capability for innovation, and "Indian control of Indian education." The study also assumed, for simplicity's sake, that the policy would still involve the distribution of grants and that the funding level would remain the same. The remainder of this section briefly discusses these five options, before offering a sixth.

Status Quo with Accountability Improvements

Of the five solutions offered, the status quo "with accountability improvements" is perhaps the least satisfying. All the problems with efficiency would remain, and students would still be at the whim of the chief and council for funding. Moreover, it is not clear what precisely is meant by "accountability improvements." Even if one suspends disbelief and assumes that all funding would be subject to full accounting and that all surplus funds would be given to the students, the status quo cannot effectively address concerns with rationing, waitlisted students, and regional variation. Nor does such a change touch on the very difficult issue of administrative capability—namely, that reserves with fewer than one thousand people are expected to deliver a complex program with efficiency and transparency.

It is unlikely that minor accountability adjustments could effectively rid the program of the discrimination, nepotism, and favouritism that currently exists. Because of the myriad problems with the program noted above, it is clear that the status quo is unacceptable. Minor tweaking will do little to address the systemic flaws with this program.

Administration by a Regional First Nations' Education Organization

Administration by a regional First Nations' education organization could potentially address the concerns over the institutional capacity of small reserves. However, several problems would arise. First, as the EPI study itself noted, where these "second and third-level" organizations do exist, they vary widely in terms of size, scope, and administrative capacity. Not all bands participate in these organizations and not every region has one. Moreover, the problems of regional variation and institutional capacity would not effectively be fixed and could even be exacerbated. The administrative costs of creating these organizations where none currently exist would divert the money from helping young Indian students get their education. Finally, there is no guarantee that such an organization would eliminate the problems related to transparency and accountability. Without a clear accountability structure from INAC to the student, rationing, nepotism, and favouritism could occur within a regional education organization just as easily as within individual bands.

Administration by a Pan-Canadian First Nations Foundation

Under this option, one of two things could occur: a nongovernmental organization would be created to disburse money to students, with a board composed mainly of Indians; or, an existing organization such as the National Aboriginal Achievement Foundation could be charged with distributing the money.

It is difficult to see why either option is necessary. Again, such organizations could theoretically avoid the problems of institutional capacity that plague smaller reserves. But the above concerns related to accountability, rationing, and transparency would remain. How would the accountability within a pan-Canadian organization differ from the current accountability structure? How would the creation of an organization help the students who are unaware of the existence of the funds as it is? Creating a new organization would be cumbersome, time-consuming, and divert important funds from students. By the same token, there is no guarantee that an existing organization created for a purpose other than distributing funds to students would be effective or efficient at distributing these funds (Usher, 2009, p. 23). Although this option and the second option do retain some "Indian control of Indian education," there is little evidence that the systems would give any more control to Indian youth.

Direct Administration by Indian and Northern Affairs Canada/Direct Administration by Human Resources and Skills Development Canada

Both of the final two options, which would take control of the funding away from chiefs and band councils and put it in the hands of the federal government, would resolve many of the issues related to accountability, efficiency, regional variation, and administrative capability. Nepotism and favouritism would likely be reduced, if not eliminated. Distribution of funds would likely be similar to the Inuit component of the PSSSP, whereby funds are disbursed through territorial governments. Yet several problems would persist. As the EPI study itself notes, the government would need to create a rationing mechanism, whether based on need, merit, or some other criteria (Usher, 2009, p. 26). Although the Inuit component of the program may lack the problems of nepotism, regional variation, and abuse of expenses, there is no evidence that it has effectively dealt with problems of wait-listed students and rationing of funds. Making prospective students aware of the available funding would be another problem.

Given the scandalous problems that currently exist, either option would be preferable to the status quo. As long as the PSSSP funding continues to be based, in principle, on universality rather than need (e.g., under the current system, a student's family income does not determine whether he or she receives funding), there is no inherent reason why HRSDC rather than INAC should operate the program. INAC has the list of registered Indians and would be far more capable than HRSDC of ensuring the money reaches the students.

It is also worth noting that the EPI study acknowledges that these two options "would command little or no support among First Nations" (Usher, 2009, p. 29), as these options effectively abandon the principle of "Indian control of Indian education." The federal government, not the chief and council, would have to determine which students received funding and how rationing would occur. In this sense, bands, or at least the political leaders within the bands, would be opposed to such a policy. At the end of the following section of this chapter, we discuss this principle in greater detail.

Thus, if the above five options were the only options available, direct administration by INAC would be the most preferable to the status quo. However, picking the "least worst" policy option is hardly a strategy for success. There is another option the federal government can take that would erase nearly all of the problems with the PSSSP outlined in this chapter. Moreover, it would maintain "Indian control of Indian education," albeit in a way that is very different from what several First Nations organizations have proposed. The next section puts forward a policy proposal that would give control directly to individual Indian students.

The Aboriginal Post-Secondary Savings Account: Empowering Indian Students

As the Post-Secondary Student Support Program currently exists, the federal government distributes approximately $314 million per year to bands, who then distribute the money to students. There is virtually no accountability and students are being wait-listed. There is no effective formula for rationing. Accusations of waste, mismanagement, and nepotism abound. Indian students are often unaware that the funding is even available. A program designed to increase Indian participation in post-secondary education is not working nearly as well as it should.

Other proposals have been offered, but they fail to address the fundamental problem with the program: Indian students are powerless to determine whether they receive funding. Authority currently rests with band councils; under other proposals, it would rest with Aboriginal organizations or with the federal government. The following proposal puts authority exactly where it belongs: with Indian youth, who will be empowered to get the education they want and so badly need to choose for themselves. Moreover, it creates an incentive structure for Indian students to complete secondary education and move on to post-secondary education.

This study proposes that the PSSSP gradually be phased out and replaced with an Aboriginal Post-Secondary Savings Account (APSSA), created at birth for all registered Indians, regardless of whether they live on or off reserve. This savings account would contain $4,000 at the birth of the child and earn interest over their youth. After the completion of each grade, from six to 12, the account would be credited with an additional $3,000. This would create an incentive for Indian youth to complete secondary school by providing a tangible financial reward.

Creating such an incentive is of considerable importance. Currently, Indian high school completion rates are four times lower than non-Aboriginal rates. Over half of on-reserve Indians aged 25–34 have not completed secondary school, compared to 10% for non-Aboriginals in the same age bracket (Richards, 2009, pp. 7–8; Sharpe et al., 2009, p. 14). Completing secondary school leads to higher income and higher employment; Indians who have only completed secondary school are nearly twice as likely to be employed and nearly half as likely to be unemployed than Indians who have not (Sharpe et al., 2009, p. 22).

Thus, the savings account would first create an incentive to complete secondary school and then assist Indian students with post-secondary education. This financial incentive would total $25,000 upon graduation from secondary school, before adding in the substantial interest that would have accrued. This money would be placed in an account at a registered financial institution in the name of each registered Indian student. Once the student enrolls in a bona fide post-secondary educational institution, the money in the individual's APSSA would then be available to him or her through a payment system discussed below. Recognized institutions could potentially include members of the Association of Universities and Colleges of Canada, the Association of Canadian Community Colleges, Polytechnics Canada, the National Association of Career Colleges, or the Canadian Education and Training Accreditation Commission. Membership in organizations such as these could ensure a national minimum standard for acceptable programs. Moreover, if students wish to apply to use the funds for educational institutions that do not fall within this list of "recognized institutions," there would be an approval process to ensure the program is acceptable. For up to 10 years after graduation, the funding would be available to Indian youth (at this point, young adults), after which point it would lapse and be redistributed to other students' accounts and/or be used to deal with transition costs (discussed below).

As with many existing Canadian scholarships and bursaries, there would be strict controls to ensure that money intended to cover institutional costs such as tuition would be paid directly from the account to the post-secondary institution. Tuition and mandatory post-secondary fees would transfer directly from the student's account to the educational institution at the beginning of each academic semester. Money for living expenses would be disbursed to the student on a monthly or per-semester basis, provided the student remains registered with the post-secondary institution. Acceptable monthly living expenses could be set at a specific monthly amount, which would likely vary depending on the location. There could also be controls to ensure that the account balance does not fall below the amount of tuition that remains for the completion of the program. With these mechanisms in place, students would have access to the funds only while enrolled in the post-secondary institution with good academic standing, thus providing a strong incentive to complete their studies.

Currently, there are approximately 105,000 registered Indian students who will be completing grades 6–12 in 2011.[4] At $3,000 per student, this proposal would cost $315 million, which is nearly identical to the amount of funds currently disbursed under the PSSSP. However, creating the APSSA would involve administrative costs associated with setting up the accounts, and there would have to be overlap between the creation of the savings accounts and phasing out the PSSSP. This chapter proposes that during a six-year transition period from the PSSSP to the APSSA, Indian students enrolling in post-secondary education would get the same $25,000 that younger Indian students will receive for completing secondary school.

Under this proposal, costs would rise, temporarily but substantially, during the transition period. Creating the $4,000 accounts for every registered Indian at birth will also necessitate an overall increase in program spending. However, the reward would be an efficient, transparent, and accountable system that allows Indian students to have the funding necessary to pursue a post-secondary education. Moreover, the "lapsed" funds from the accounts of Indians who choose not to pursue post-secondary education could be used to defray some of the transition costs. In any event, it is prudent to deal with these transition costs as soon as possible, while the young Aboriginal population has not yet reached post-secondary age. Funding individual education is one of the best investments Canada can make, particularly when it is funding its most vulnerable population.

The funding numbers proposed in this study are not set in stone. Rather, they demonstrate that substantial funding can be made available to each and every registered Indian student, if only the current spending were invested properly. The $4,000 initial fund and $3,000 per year are flexible numbers that can certainly be raised depending on resources available to government and the number of registered Indian youth. The key point of the proposal is not the exact dollar amount; rather, it is to change the structure of the way the federal government funds post-secondary education for Indian students. The creation of an Aboriginal Post-Secondary Savings Account would create incentives for Indian youth to complete secondary school and empower them to take control of their educational future.

Moreover, there is no reason that post-secondary funding would need to stop with the government. The policy could easily be tweaked so that nonprofit and private donors could "top up" the students' savings accounts. This has already happened with Aboriginal education at the primary level: the Royal Bank of Canada has contributed nearly $200,000 dollars to the Grandview/Uuquinak'uuh Elementary School in East Vancouver, BC, a school with a remarkable success story (Helin, 2008, pp. 212–215). If the federal government could guarantee that a system funding post-secondary education for young Indians was transparent and accessible, there is every reason to think that nonprofit and private organizations might contribute.

Addressing the Unique Plight of Aboriginals

Phasing out the PSSSP and replacing it with a savings account would accomplish several goals. First, it would provide an incentive for Indian students to complete grades 6–12. Knowing that the successful completion of a grade means $3,000 to be put toward future costs is a powerful incentive for both Indian students and parents. Like property ownership, which is also critical to moving people out of economic dependency (de Soto, 2000), this incentive would effectively give Indian youth ownership of their educational funding. Indian youth would also benefit from being informed at an early age that there are educational opportunities after secondary school.

Second, it would eliminate many of the bureaucratic and administrative costs with the current system that lead to inefficiency and confusion. The money would go directly, and automatically, from INAC to the student upon completion of a grade. All students would be aware the funding existed. No students would be forced to wait. Rationing and regional disparities in funding would become a thing of the past. Nepotism and waste would disappear. Surplus funds and "non-eligible" staff expenses would no longer be issues. Relationships with band figures could not determine funding. On-reserve students and off-reserve students would be funded equally. Most importantly, control of the funds would rest with Indian youth themselves. The decision of whether to pursue post-secondary education would be entirely in the students' hands.

Some commentators will doubtless view the creation of the APSSA, like the PSSSP, as a way of privileging Indian students during a period in which non-Aboriginal Canadians often have difficulty paying for post-secondary education. However, as the earlier sections demonstrate, Aboriginals in general, and Indians in particular, do not have the same opportunities as other Canadians. Non-Aboriginals, who have higher income and employment than Aboriginals, are far more capable of contributing to Registered Education Savings Plans and other educational savings accounts. The Aboriginal Post-Secondary Savings Account is a targeted poverty reduction strategy for Indians, who cannot hope to have access to education savings programs that many non-Aboriginals do. It also provides an opportunity to confront Canada's looming shortage of young workers. The plight of Aboriginals is unique, and no other community in Canada is more deserving of the opportunity that the APSSA would provide.

A Final Word on "Indian Control of Indian Education"

Of course, the political implications of such a change have to be considered. For example, the EPI study described above was criticized for even mentioning approaches that deviate from the principle of "Indian control of Indian education," even though it did not even advocate a change away from the status quo. In response to the EPI report, the First Nations Education Steering Committee and the First

Nations Summit issued a joint press release that gave that report a "failing grade." The reason? "Any plan that removes authorities from First Nations is unacceptable" (First Nations Summit and First Nations Education Steering Committee, 2009).

Indians have a justifiable desire to have control over education funding. As a principle, the call for "Indian control of Indian education" grew initially out of Aboriginal experience of federal control of Indian day schools, which delivered poor educational results and offered Indians virtually no control over their educational future. Even more tragically, many Aboriginals experienced shameful treatment and abuse at schools that were not controlled by Aboriginals. Any policy change with respect to Aboriginal education that is interpreted as a loss of Aboriginal control over education is likely to bring back dark and horrible memories of residential schools, which forcibly removed Aboriginal students from their homes to promote assimilation:

> Aboriginal children were often subjected to unspeakable humiliation, and physical and sexual abuse. Children were beaten for speaking the Aboriginal languages and practising their traditions. A deliberate effort was made to make Aboriginal people feel ashamed of their Aboriginalness. (Helin, 2008, p. 97)

These painful and shattering events justify an attitude of Aboriginal distrust toward federal involvement in Aboriginal education. However, this paper's proposal ensures that Indian students would be subject neither to the whims of paternalistic government institutions nor to unaccountable chiefs. The creation of APSSAs would indeed shift authority from the band councils, which have been proven incapable of fairly and effectively disbursing the money to the target populations. But control would remain with First Nations, as Indian youth would gain control over their own educational future. If grassroots economic empowerment does not constitute "Indian control of Indian education," then what does? What institutional arrangement could possibly be more empowering than allowing all Indian students the opportunity to spend money on their education as they see fit?

It is true that the problems of nepotism, rationing, and corruption with the PSSSP do not exist in every single band: certain bands have effectively disbursed the funds to students in need. Nonetheless, the evidence suggests that many bands, particularly those that are smaller and less developed, have not effectively and fairly administered the funding to students. The goal of Aboriginal post-secondary funding should be to move the entire Aboriginal population forward by ensuring that every Aboriginal student gets access to their funding in the same open and fair way.

Another potential criticism stems from the fact that Indians view post-secondary funding as a treaty right, and the PSSSP is based at least in part on this principle. However, treaty rights are meaningless if they fail to protect and promote the interests of individual Indians. Our proposal does not seek to deprive Indians of these established rights; rather, it seeks to ensure that money intended to procure post-secondary education for Indians accomplishes its objective. The Aboriginal Post-Secondary Savings Account recognizes treaty rights by establishing a mechanism by which individual Indians are given responsibility and accountability for their own education. There is also no better guarantee of future treaty rights than a well-educated population.

The proposal put forward in this chapter demonstrates that there is a way to maintain "Indian control of Indian education" while increasing efficiency, transparency, and accountability. It would create an incentive for Indian youth to finish secondary school and begin post-secondary education, and encourage individual confidence, independence, and responsibility. It would solve nearly every problem associated with the current PSSSP, and could begin to fund all Indian youth immediately. Most importantly, it would offer Indian youth an opportunity to get the education they want and need to change the future of First Nations people in Canada for the better.

Conclusion

The importance of closing the gap between Aboriginal and non-Aboriginal Canadians cannot be overstated. Improving the well-being of Aboriginals, particularly registered Indians living on reserve, is a moral imperative for Canadians. With demographic change threatening a labour shortage across the country, it is also a social and economic imperative. Canada faces a demographic crisis that will require young, educated workers to enter the labour force. The young and booming Aboriginal population has the potential to enter the workforce precisely at the time they are most needed.

The single best way to improve the quality of life for Aboriginals is through formal education. Such education must start with the completion of primary and secondary school, but in the modern knowledge economy, it cannot stop there. Access to post-secondary education, whether through the completion of a trade, a certificate/diploma, or university, will enable Aboriginals to lift themselves out of poverty and determine their own future. As one of the authors of this paper, Calvin Helin (2008), frames the situation:

At the end of the day, given the demographic tsunami, the looming economic costs, and the savage toll that the welfare trap is taking on the poorest group in Canada, a real investment in education is key not only to moving Aboriginal people forward but to moving Canada forward. (p. 216)

Canada's experience with Aboriginal education is not a pretty one. The abuses suffered by Aboriginals at the paternalistic residential and Indian day schools are etched in Aboriginal memory, and they justify a distrust of federal educational policy. In this vein, the best way to empower Canada's most vulnerable citizens is to give them the tools to pursue an education and provide a better life for themselves. The federal government, through its PSSSP, offers significant funding for Indian students to enter post-secondary education. Yet the program, in which Indian bands receive block funding and are expected to provide it to Indian youth, is not achieving its goal. There is widespread evidence of misused funds, regional disparities, rationing, and wait-listed students. The program lacks accountability, transparency, and any means by which to measure performance. Indian students are not receiving the money that is meant for them. That is unacceptable.

If Canada wants to harness the potential of Indian students, this program needs to change, and it needs to change soon. Fundamentally, this requires ensuring that authority for post-secondary education rests with Indian youth, not band councils. Phasing out the Post-Secondary Student Support Program and replacing it with an Aboriginal Post-Secondary Savings Account would achieve this. It would maintain "Indian control of Indian education," providing Indian students with the incentive and the means to complete their secondary education and move on to post-secondary studies.

The money is theoretically being made available to Indian students. With the Aboriginal Post-Secondary Savings Account, we can make sure they actually get it.

REFERENCES

Canada. (2007). *No higher priority: Aboriginal post-secondary education in Canada.* Report of the Standing Committee on Aboriginal Affairs and Northern Development. Ottawa: Government of Canada.

Centre for the Study of Living Standards. (2009, May 20). Aboriginal education key to bolstering productivity, labour force. Press Release. Retrieved December 29, 2009, from http://www.csls.ca/reports/csls2009-3-pressrelease.pdf

Chow, K. (2005, December 16). Seniors could outnumber children by 2–1 in 25 years. *Vancouver Sun*, A3.

Crowley, B.L. (2009). *Fearful symmetry: The fall and rise of Canada's founding values.* Toronto: Key Porter.

de Soto, H. (2000). *The mystery of capital: Why capitalism triumphs in the West and fails everywhere else.* New York: Basic Books.

First Nations Summit and First Nations Education Steering Committee. (2009, December 3). *Federal government's First Nations post-secondary report earns a failing grade*. Joint Press Release. Retrieved December 29, 2009, from http://www.fnesc.ca/Attachments/Post-Secondary/Press%20Releases/FNS%20FNESC%20Joint%20Statement%20FINAL.pdf

Flanagan, T. (2008). *First Nations? Second Thoughts* (2nd ed.). Montreal: McGill-Queen's University Press.

Helin, C. (2008). *Dances with dependency: Out of poverty through self-reliance*. Woodland Hills, CA: Ravencrest Publishing.

Hull, J. (2008). Aboriginal youth in the Canadian labour market. *Horizons, 10*(1), 40–44.

Indian and Northern Affairs Canada (INAC). (2006). *Fact sheet: 2006 census Aboriginal demographics*. Retrieved December 29, 2009, from http://www.ainc-inac.gc.ca/ai/mr/is/cad-eng.asp

Indian and Northern Affairs Canada (INAC) Audit and Assurance Services Branch. (2009). *Audit of the post-secondary education program*. Ottawa: Indian and Northern Affairs Canada. Retrieved December 29, 2009, from http://www.ainc-inac.gc.ca/ai/arp/aev/pubs/au/psep/psep-eng.pdf

Malatest, R.A., & Associates, & Stonechild, B. (2008). *Factors affecting the use of financial assistance by First Nations youth*. Montreal: Canadian Millennium Scholarship Foundation.

Mendelson, M. (2006a). *Aboriginal peoples and postsecondary education in Canada*. Ottawa: Caledon Institute of Social Policy.

Mendelson, M. (2006b). *Improving primary and secondary education on reserves in Canada*. Ottawa: Caledon Institute of Social Policy.

Richards, J. (2006). *Creating choices: Rethinking Aboriginal policy*. Toronto: CD Howe Institute.

Richards, J. (2009). *Dropouts: The Achilles' heel of Canada's high-school system*. Toronto: CD Howe Institute.

Richards, J., Hove, J., & Ofalabi, K. (2008). *Understanding the Aboriginal/non-Aboriginal gap in student performance: Lessons from British Columbia*. Toronto: CD Howe Institute.

Richards, J., & Vining, A. (2004). *Aboriginal off-reserve education: Time for action*. Toronto: CD Howe Institute.

Sharpe, A., Arsenault, J.-F., Lapointe, S., & Cowan, F. (2009). *The effect of increasing Aboriginal educational attainment on the labour force, output and the fiscal balance*. Ottawa: Centre for the Study of Living Standards.

Statistics Canada. (2003). *Aboriginal peoples survey 2001 initial findings: Well-being of the non-reserve Aboriginal population* (Catalogue no. 89-589-XIE). Ottawa: Government of Canada.

Statistics Canada. (2006, October 26). Canada's population by age and sex. *The Daily*. Ottawa: Government of Canada. Retrieved from http://www. statcan. gc.ca/daily-quotidien/061026/dq061026b-eng.htm.

Statistics Canada. (2008a). *Aboriginal peoples in Canada in 2006: Inuit, Metis and First Nations, 2006 census* (Catalogue no. 97-558-XIE). Ottawa: Government of Canada.

Statistics Canada. (2008b). *Educational portrait of Canada, 2006 census* (Catalogue no. 97-560-X). Ottawa: Government of Canada.

Statistics Canada. (2009). *Average undergraduate tuition fees for full time Canadian students, by discipline, by province*. Ottawa: Government of Canada. Retrieved January 5, 2010, from http://www40.statcan.ca/ 101/cst01/educ50a-eng.htm.

Usher, A. (2009). *The post-secondary student support program: An examination of alternative delivery mechanisms*. Toronto: Educational Policy Institute.

NOTES

1 This report focuses solely on the Indian component of the program.

2 For brevity, this chapter focuses solely on the Indian delivery of the program. For the Inuit component of the program, the territorial governments disburse funds to individual Inuit students. Thus, many of the problems related to accountability and transparency within the Indian component of the program do not exist within the Inuit component.

3 The funding is given from INAC to the First Nations community, for which the official legal term is "Indian band." The legal decision-making body for most bands consists of a chief and a band council. To avoid confusion, this study uses "Indian bands" or "bands" to refer to the body entitled to exercise the band's legal power.

4 Information gathered through correspondence with Indian and Northern Affairs Canada in 2010.

12

Retention of Aboriginal Students in Post-Secondary Education

Judy Hardes

This chapter was originally published in *The Alberta Counsellor* (Summer 2006), 29(1), pp. 28–33. Reproduced with permission.

Statistics Canada (1998) defines *Aboriginal* as "those people who are North American Indian (First Nations), Metis, or Inuit." Current demographics on Aboriginal culture in Canada suggest that the number of Aboriginal post-secondary education students could largely increase in the future. This could have many positive effects if the retention rates are high, but there are socio-economic, educational, and cultural needs unique to the retention of Aboriginal students in mainstream colleges and universities. *Retention* is defined by the number of students remaining in their chosen program until graduation. This chapter focuses on the retention of Aboriginal students in post-secondary education, specifically where the Aboriginal student population is a minority group. It outlines some issues and then discusses some strategies that have been developed to retain Aboriginal students in post-secondary education.

Socio-Economic, Educational, and Cultural Retention Issues

Socio-Economic Issues

The Aboriginal culture in Canada has been affected by a long history of substance abuse, disease, violence, low employment rates, poverty, high mortality, and depression. In the past few decades, an increasing number of Aboriginal people have been migrating from reserves to urban settings. Aboriginal people enrolling in post-secondary education bring with them a host of social issues that may interfere with their academic success. Many students are among the first in their families to leave their home communities in pursuit of higher education. These first-generation attendees do not have role models or mentors to help personally or academically with the transition to post-secondary education.

The Saskatchewan Women's Secretariat (1999) identifies several facts about Aboriginal women that affect enrolment in post-secondary education. More women than men live in urban areas and are enrolled in post-secondary education. More single-parent families are headed by women and living in poverty than single-parent families headed by men. Aboriginal women have more children than white women, increasing the need for child care, family supports, and educational facilities.

Based on traditional Native cultural values, Aboriginal people are not future-focused; hence, they are less willing to go into debt to finance their education. Budgeting is difficult because they tend to share rather than save for the future. Many students rely on funding from sponsors, such as bands, Métis Nations, and bursaries when educational costs are rising and resources are dwindling. The costs of food, housing, daycare, health care, and transportation add to the financial strain. Many Aboriginal students must move away from their communities to attend college. Transportation to and from the reserve can be expensive, and funding agencies usually do not fund regular trips. If the success of Aboriginal students revolves around parental encouragement and support (McInerney, 1990), then when regular contact with family is in jeopardy so is the retention of the student.

Educational Issues

Education has been "the traditional enemy of Indian people" (Rodriguez, 1997, p. 40). Historically, Aboriginal students are half as likely to finish high school or complete a post-secondary diploma and one-fifth as likely to complete a university degree as the general population (Statistics Canada, 1998). Residential schooling, assimilation, and integration have all been blamed for the many educational difficulties facing the Aboriginal race.

Schools that Aboriginal students attend vary widely, as do curricula and academic standards, which affect entrance to post-secondary education. Some students entering post-secondary education lack study skills, program requirements, and academic preparedness, especially in mathematics and English. For many students, English is a second language. Few colleges provide instruction in Native languages or integrate Aboriginal culture into their curricula. Learning styles and teaching styles are different. Often students do not have a clear sense of purpose, which is important for success in the future-oriented environment of colleges. The lack of a clear career goal affects motivation and, ultimately, academic achievement.

Traditional Aboriginal teachings involved the promotion of peace and harmony arrived at through the "suppression of conflict practiced through the ethics of non-interference, non-competitiveness and emotional restraint" (Gorman, 1999, p. 114). These values do not mesh with the mainstream emphasis on competitiveness, especially for marks in post-secondary education.

Cultural Issues

The transition from living on a reserve to living in a college environment creates a culture shock for Aboriginal students. The adjustment to urban living includes changes in lifestyle, spirituality, and even simple things, such as eating different foods. Adjusting to the multicultural nature of Canadian society can lead to a conflict in values and beliefs. Students have to adjust not only to a non-Native culture but also to various Aboriginal backgrounds, including Status Indian, Métis, Inuit, and other Aboriginal students from various bands, all with their own cultural identities.

To "Dance in Two Worlds" (Betz, 1991) refers to Native people trying to maintain an allegiance to their traditional Native culture while actively participating in the mainstream society to get an education. Leaving their home communities in pursuit of higher education sometimes leads to ostracism by friends, family, and community. Students fear that once they become educated, they will "return home only to be treated like outsiders" (Steinhauer, 1998, p. 115). Racism and discrimination, whether actual or perceived, can be detrimental to the success of Aboriginal students in a predominately white environment.

The mainstream educational system is one of competition, saving, individualism, futurism, and verbosity, all of which conflict with the traditional Native values of co-operation, sharing, group identity, emphasis on present and past, and listening rather than talking (Friesen, 1991, p. 186). Native culture does not see education as a necessity that must be completed within a specific amount of time, but rather as Gorman (1999) points out, "the talents, skills, and interests of the Native child are nurtured to fulfillment and are part of a life-long learning process." Many Aboriginal students leave and return to college several times; this is referred to as "stepping out" (Rodriguez, 1997, p. 38). Although this may be quite acceptable for Aboriginal people, it is a source of frustration for staff and faculty in mainstream post-secondary institutions.

Socio-Economic, Educational, and Cultural Retention Strategies

Socio-Economic Strategies

The social issues that Aboriginal people bring with them to college have a major affect on their retention. Based on enrolment numbers, many social issues affecting retention revolve around serving the needs of Aboriginal women. Housing, child care, and transportation are three key areas that women need assistance with. Providing family housing and daycare on campus can help to alleviate these pressures, as does providing transportation for children to attend school. To balance home and school, women need support in the form of parent support groups, parenting classes, and time management.

Traditionally, the Aboriginal woman's role was to care for her home, husband, and children. As Aboriginal women assert themselves, men feel threatened in their roles, which can create relationship problems. Individual and group counselling, peer-support groups, and family housing associations can provide support for students to deal with many social issues.

Post-secondary students who move from their home communities to attend college leave behind a support network that they have relied on throughout their lives. Colleges can fill that gap with "family like support systems that one can find on campus, or through native organizations in urban areas" (Steinhauer, 1998, p. 115). Aboriginal student associations, Aboriginal liaison offices, and Native friendship centres are examples of these support services. Post-secondary institutions must provide continual understanding and support for students when these social issues put them at risk of dropping out.

Financial aid offices on campus can provide a liaison between students and funding agencies. Information on financial aid programs specific for Aboriginal students, including scholarships, bursaries, and loans, should be available prior to admission and throughout the college year. In case of emergencies, small loans, grocery coupons, or taxi vouchers can be available either through the Aboriginal liaison office, student services, or the Aboriginal students' council. Workshops on budgeting and economical shopping, as well as establishing collective kitchen programs, can help prevent financial difficulties. To alleviate the transportation issue, some institutions have developed "ride boards," where students with vehicles post when they are driving to a certain location, and students needing a ride can post their requests. Students then share the transportation costs. Aboriginal student housing programs provide affordable accommodations that are culturally responsive. An Aboriginal work placement office can assist Native students in finding practicum placements during the school term and employment after college.

Educational Strategies

Nora and Cabrera (1996), Wells (1997), and the New Mexico Commission on Higher Education (1996) all agree that a lack of academic preparedness profoundly affects retention of Aboriginal students in post-secondary education. Organized tutoring and remedial courses can help students with writing and mathematical skills. Being on time for classes and meetings, handing assignments in on time, and keeping appointments are basic expectations of the white population, but these are often barriers to success for a culture that is not time-conscious. Workshops on time-management skills, study skills, and organizational skills can help prepare students for academic success. Spreading a two-year program over three years can allow students the extra time to cope with academic pressures.

Mentoring programs can help facilitate transition into a college environment. Typically, such programs match first-year students with second-year students who act as role models, are familiar with the support services available, and can share experiences with new students so that they do not have to struggle through the system on their own. Summer bridge programs and career preparation programs can help students gain the necessary prerequisites for college entrance. These programs could be offered prior to admission and throughout the academic year.

Having students identify their learning style and develop strategies focusing on their strengths would help to retain students. Ongoing recognition of academic achievements is important to retaining Aboriginal students who traditionally are not future-focused or committed to long-term goals. Recognizing short-term accomplishments could be done monthly in the form of Round Dances. Historically, Aboriginal people learned best by doing; hence, many students today benefit from hands-on learning. Programs with practicums, co-operative education, and work experience programs are examples of educational programs that lend themselves to kinesthetic learning styles.

Students who have specific career aspirations are more motivated to succeed; thus, linking academic programming to a realistic and achievable career goal is useful. Academic advising and career counselling go hand in hand to provide meaningful educational choices. Especially for Aboriginal students, emphasizing the practicality of the program and making explicit the relation of the courses to the career goal are important to retention. Academic advising and career counselling programs must be cognizant of the cultural needs of Aboriginal students in selecting an appropriate career goal if they are to facilitate retention.

Cultural Strategies

Betz (1991) explains that "retention and graduation will continue to fall far below those of majority students until everyone involved becomes aware of, and sensitive to, cultural and racial differences and acts to eliminate the external as well as the internal barriers to education." Hiring a liaison worker of Aboriginal descent is important in establishing a post-secondary institution that will respond to the unique needs of Aboriginal students. The Aboriginal liaison worker will usually establish an Aboriginal liaison office to complement the existing student services that are available for all students. The worker will assist students with recruitment, admission, advising, financial aid, counselling, job placement, college adjustment, and referrals. Developing and co-ordinating new initiatives in response to the needs of Aboriginal students is an important part of this role. The Aboriginal liaison worker will liaise between the college, Native communities, and the urban community where the college is located. Having access to a specific contact person through the Aboriginal liaison office simplifies communication. Above all, the Aboriginal liaison worker is a role model for Aboriginal students. A section on the application package for students to identify themselves as Aboriginal students and benefit from services provided by the Aboriginal liaison office shows prospective students that the institution recognizes, and is sensitive to, the unique needs of Aboriginal students.

Prior to registration day, the transition to college is made easier by conducting student orientation programs, such as campus tours, open houses, information evenings, and meet-the-faculty sessions.

The hope is that prospective students will be more familiar with the physical setting and the support services available at the college prior to attending. A summer bridge program not only assists students with the essential academic skills but also helps them to create "their own community within a White structure" and an "inter-tribal system among themselves" (Rodriguez, 1997, p. 39).

An Aboriginal students' council can provide support and advocacy for students by addressing issues and concerns, promoting understanding and awareness, and ensuring them a comfortable transition to college life. Examples of the functions and services that an Aboriginal students' council can provide include organizing peer support through sharing circles, co-ordinating cultural events such as Round Dances and traditional graduation ceremonies, distributing a newsletter, producing a student handbook, and providing access to elders on campus. Establishing a meeting place, such as an Aboriginal students' centre, provides a hub for cultural activity, and as Rodriguez (1997) suggests, "Schools which provide cultural centers do best at retention (p. 39). To foster communication among all students, a representative of the Aboriginal student population should be included in the general students' association.

Awareness, understanding, and acceptance of the differences between cultures and how this affects the success of Aboriginal students are important to their retention. Betz (1991) writes that faculty members directly and profoundly affect the motivation and desire of Indian students to remain in school. Instructors must seek to "understand the minority students' communication skills, modalities, and behaviors (body language, facial expressions, eye contact, silence, touch and public space); teachers must understand and decrease their stereotypes about, and fears of, minority students" (Ford, 1998). Training administrators, faculty, staff, and students about Aboriginal culture and its history is important and perhaps best provided by elders from Aboriginal communities. "Hearing elders compare and contrast the educational and political structures of the dominant society with native approaches to life produces more genuine and substantial cross-cultural understanding" (Marker, 1998).

Perhaps Lenning, Beal, and Sauer (1980) sum it up best when they say: "a genuine concern about student retention and a commitment to develop and implement retention strategies must be visible at all levels of the institution." The role of board members, administrators, faculty, and support staff, as well as their presence on campus, has a bearing on the retention of Aboriginal students. The establishment of Native advisory boards, the appointment of Aboriginal people to board positions, and the active recruitment of Aboriginal staff and faculty shows a commitment to the Aboriginal student and fosters awareness and communication between Aboriginal and non-Aboriginal people.

Conclusion

The debate is ongoing as to whether minority groups should have special programs within the post-secondary system. Giroux (1997) examines the defensive posture taken up by many white college students, who view the emergence of multiculturalism as an attack on whiteness and concludes that some white students resent the benefits that Indian people receive as a result of treaties with the federal government. Rodriguez (1997) notes that the University of New Mexico established three minority student service centres for Hispanics, African Americans, and Native Americans. Rodriguez claims that not only were the centres seen as racist but the "existence of these patronizing services unavoidably and intolerably stamp these race/ethnic identities as academically inferior" (p. 30). His belief is that the existence of the centres is counterproductive and promotes tribalism and groupthink, not individuality (p. 30). In contrast, Richardson (1989) states that retention strategies are rungs on the ladder to success that must be in place for minority students to succeed. These rungs or retention strategies are necessary and must therefore be provided by the institutions that seek to retain and graduate minority students.

According to Wells (1997), the vast majority of institutions recognize the unique needs of Aboriginal students and offer special programs to address those needs. Even the New Mexico Commission on Higher Education (1996) provided numerous examples of colleges that recognize, support, and serve the educational and cultural needs of the Native Indian student populations through special programs.

Post-secondary institutions in Alberta are at various stages of development and implementation in regards to programs and services for the Aboriginal population. Some institutions have fully established services for recruitment and retention. Others are currently developing initiatives to implement in the near future. Evidence shows that colleges and universities in Alberta recognize the unique needs of a growing population of Aboriginal students and are striving to meet those needs.

REFERENCES

Betz, D. (1991). International initiatives and education of Indigenous peoples: Teaching and learning to "dance in two worlds" (ERIC Document Reproduction Service No. ED339561). Oklahoma City, OK: Sovereignty Symposium IV, the Circles of Sovereignty, The Next Generation: Educating the American Indian Child.

Ford, D.V. (1998). The underrepresentation of minority students in gifted education. *Journal of Special Education, 32*(1), 4–14. http://dx.doi.org/10.1177/002246699803200102

Friesen, J.W. (1991). *The cultural maze.* Calgary, AB: Detselig.

Giroux, H. (1997). Rewriting the discourse of racial identity: Towards a pedagogy and politics of whiteness. *Harvard Educational Review, 67,* 285–320.

Gorman, W. (1999). Canadian Native students and inequitable learning. *Canadian Social Studies, 33,* 114–116.

Lenning, O.T., Beal, P.E., & Sauer, K. (1980). *Retention and attrition: Evidence for action and research.* Boulder, CO: National Center for Higher Education Management Systems.

Marker, M. (1998). Going Native in the academy: Choosing the exotic over the critical. *Anthropology & Education Quarterly, 29*(4), 473–480. http://dx.doi.org/10.1525/aeq.1998.29.4.473

McInerney, D.M. (1990). *Sex differences in motivation of Aboriginal students in school settings.* Paper presented at the AARE Annual Conference, University of Sydney, Australia.

New Mexico Commission on Higher Education. (1996). *Native American student recruitment and retention at college and universities in New Mexico.* Albuquerque, NM: Author.

Nora, A., & Cabrera, A.F. (1996). The role of perceptions of prejudice and discrimination on the adjustment of minority students to college. *Journal of Higher Education, 67*(2), 119–148. http://dx.doi.org/10.2307/2943977

Richardson, R. (1989, January 11). If minority students are to succeed in higher education, every rung of the educational ladder must be in place. *The Chronicle of Higher Education.* Retrieved from http://chronicle.com

Rodriguez, R. (1997). Learning to live a warrior's life. *Black Issues in Higher Education, 14,* 38–40.

Saskatchewan Women's Secretariat. (1999). *Profile of Aboriginal women in Saskatchewan.* Regina, SK: Government of Saskatchewan Women's Secretariat.

Statistics Canada. (1998, January 13). 1996 census: Aboriginal data. *The Daily.* Retrieved from http://www.statcan.ca/Daily/English/980113/d980113.htm.

Steinhauer, N. (1998). Higher education and Native students. *Canadian Social Studies, 32,* 115.

Wells, R.N., Jr. (1997, May 23). The Native American experience in higher education: turning around the cycle of failure II. *The Chronicle of Higher Education.* Retrieved from http://chronicle.com

13

Aboriginalism and the Problems of Indigenous Archaeology

Robert McGhee[1]

Reproduced by permission of the Society for American Archaeology from *American Antiquity* 73(4), 2008.

The past two decades have seen a significant amount of academic energy invested in professing the urgent need for developing an Indigenous archaeology in North America, and indeed throughout the world. Books, essays, and academic conferences have discussed, defined, and designed a multiplicity of paths toward this goal (cf. articles and references cited in Conkey, 2005; Dongoske, Aldenderfer, & Dochner, 2000; McNiven & Russell, 2005; Nicholas & Andrews, 1997a; Peck, Siegfried, & Oetelaar, 2003; Smith, 2004; Watkins, 2000, 2005). Very little effort has been expended, however, in examining the intellectual viability or the social and cultural desirability of this project.

This chapter developed from an endeavour to explore the extent to which the disciplines of anthropology and archaeology are implicated in constructing a concept that might be conveniently named "Aboriginalism." The word has some currency in Australia, but with variable meanings referring either to support for Aboriginal rights, or to beliefs related to the relationship of contemporary Aboriginals to "authentic" Aboriginality (Attwood, 1992). The term will be used here in a broader sense, based on the model of Said's (1978) "Orientalism" and referring to the concept that Indigenous societies and cultures possess qualities that are fundamentally different from those of non-Aboriginal peoples. This notion has wide currency in European and North American academic and public thought, although it bears little resemblance to any reality outside the world of scholars and the politicians who appropriate academic theories. The idea of "Indigenous archaeology" is very much an artifact of this process, and archaeologists' acceptance or promotion of a distinct form of their discipline that is appropriate to the study of Aboriginal history implicates the discipline in the production and maintenance of the dubious discourse on Aboriginalism. It also links archaeologists to the potentially negative impact this discourse may have on the contemporary and future well-being of Indigenous communities in North America and elsewhere.

In dealing with a subject that is fraught with misunderstandings and emotional associations, a writer is well advised to begin by summarizing his personal viewpoint. My perspective differs little from that espoused by Wylie (2005), who describes it as "modest realism" and "moderate pragmatic objectivism" (p. 63). As a secular humanist, my training and experience supports a rationalist scientific approach to the investigation of the world and it's past. I view archaeology as a set of techniques developed for the recovery of information related to human history, and as a project that is equally applicable to the history of all human communities. I also see the discipline of archaeology as a means of maintaining candour, integrity, and an approach to objectivity in the work of its members through established methods of peer judgement in accord with a set of transnational standards. Although agreeing that the construction of historical narratives is necessarily influenced by the cultural assumptions and personal situation of the narrator, I argue that a reasonably objective view of the past is attainable by historians who are conscious of bias arising from their individual ideologies and life situations, as well as of alternative views held by others both within and beyond the academy. I recognize archaeology as one among several means of talking about the past. Religious discourse, family and community history that may be either oral or written, and fictional narrative are other important means of dealing with and using the past. The past is a universe that is open to all, and if archaeologists choose not to base their interpretations on the evidence of oral tradition, religious faith, or the imaginative use of other forms of information, they should have no part in denying others the right to do so. I argue that such alternate methods must, however, be of only peripheral interest to archaeology lest their un-critical acceptance compromise the attributes of the discipline that make it a particularly effective means of talking about the past.

Over several decades, I have enjoyed the acquaintance of many In-digenous individuals—mainly Canadian First Peoples and Inuit—in a variety of circumstances ranging from dogsled trips and commercial fishing crews to archaeological projects, museum consultation com-mittees, and land claims negotiation tables. The ideas presented in the following chapter have largely sprung from the contrast between these individuals and the stereotypical view of the Aboriginal that is common in both the academy and among the publics of Western nations.

The growing interest and involvement of Indigenous peoples in the archaeology of postcolonial states is a development that is undoubt-edly beneficial to the continued growth of historical knowledge. The expansion of Indigenous sovereignty over lands containing archaeo-logical remains has often enhanced the protection, preservation, and archaeological use of these remains. The specific interests brought to the field by Aboriginal scholars have encouraged a welcome shift in emphasis toward an appreciation of historical, rather than system-atic, explanation and of the role of the individual in history. The fol-lowing discussion should not be interpreted as questioning the many beneficial archaeological projects that encourage the participation and collaboration of Indigenous people, or that promote the use of archaeological findings and interpretations in Indigenous programs of education and cultural revival. Difficulties arise, however, when archaeologists accede to claims of Aboriginal exceptionalism and in-corporate such assumptions into archaeological practice. These are the proponents of the "Indigenous archaeology" that is perceived as problematic in the title of this chapter.

Randall McGuire's often-cited paper "Archaeology and the First Americans" provides a good point of entry into our exploration of Aboriginalism and Indigenous archaeology, with its question, "Why are scholars (archaeologists, historians and anthropologists) the stew-ards of Indian pasts?" (McGuire, 1992, p. 817). The obvious answer is that historians and archaeologists are the stewards of the past for most nations and ethnic communities. McGuire, however, assumes the American situation to be both anomalous and negative, and ar-gues unconvincingly that it arises from the perception of Natives as a vanishing race and from government policies deriving from that assumption. The more appropriate question would seem to be "Why are so few Native Americans engaged in archaeology?" An important part of the answer to this query lies in the lack of educational and economic opportunity available to many Aboriginal communities. However, another very significant factor is the widespread assumption that techniques developed in a rationalist scientific tradition are not appropriate to the investigation of the Aboriginal past.

The assumption of exceptionalism also allows Aboriginal individuals and groups to assume rights over their history that are not assumed by, or available to, non-Aboriginals. These privileges go beyond those that are normally accorded to the governments of sovereign territories and include proprietary rights over archaeological and other heritage materials, jurisdiction over how these materials are investigated, and claims to authority over the dissemination of information recovered by archaeological and historical research. Rather than question the assumptions from which such privileges are derived, archaeologists have proposed a variety of accommodations. Some are benign, involving constructive efforts to communicate, engage, and work in collaboration with local Indigenous communities. However, the proponents of a more directed form of "Indigenous archaeology" seek to appease Indigenous opposition by incorporating non-Western values and perspectives as sources and methods of investigation, or by explicitly aligning their efforts with the historical interests of specific communities or groups. This chapter argues that such efforts are not only theoretically unsound but are detrimental to both archaeology and to Indigenous communities.

What Is the Problem with Archaeology?

This chapter assumes that the central purpose of archaeology, whether as an academic discipline or as a resource management practice, is the increase of knowledge regarding human history. Interestingly, this crucial concern seems of little relevance to those who are most vigorous in promoting the development of Indigenous archaeology. Rather than discussing potential contributions to knowledge of the past, the interest of these proponents is focused on mitigating the presumed negative effects of archaeological practice on the living descendants of the communities that are studied by archaeologists.

During the past several decades, the representatives of Indigenous cultural and political organizations have made archaeologists very aware of the prevalently negative perceptions of their discipline: archaeology's narratives regarding Native history compete with, and often deny, traditional Indigenous views on the subject; archaeology removes ancient Native artifacts and human bones from their natural resting place and converts them into commodities that are owned by non-Native institutions; archaeology uses Indigenous history as a resource that archaeologists and museums exploit to build their reputations in non-Native society. Deloria's (1995) monograph *Red Earth, White Lies* provides a definitive catalogue of such complaints, in which archaeology takes the brunt of a more general attack on the problematic aspects of Western science.

The view that archaeological interpretations of the past denigrate Native cultural heritage and belief is widely held in the world of Indigenous political and cultural leadership. However, the most explicit and serious charges come from archaeologists themselves, some of whom accuse the discipline of inadvertently, implicitly, or in collusion with state governments, depriving Indigenous peoples of both their past and their rightful existence in the present world. Watkins (2003, p. 137) charges that the rationalist perspective of science segregates humans from nature, and thus views Indigenous history as merely a segment of global human heritage; Native American philosophy, however, "serves to integrate humans with the natural world through a philosophical understanding of the interrelationship of human and nature" (Watkins, 2003, p. 137). This relationship presumably operates on a local level, linking people with the land that they occupy, so that the concept of the American past as part of a global human heritage that is amenable to scientific investigation "removes American Indians from the stage. It also removes American Indians from the present by denying them their past as the foundation on which their current cultures are based" (Watkins, 2003, 137).

Taking a somewhat different approach, Zimmerman (2006) argues that conflict arises from fundamentally opposed conceptions of the past. To archaeologists, the past is a distant entity that is evidenced by artifacts and other remains, whereas "Indians know the past because it is spiritually and ritually a part of daily existence and is relevant only as it exists in the present" (Zimmerman, 2006, p. 171). The outcome of archaeological practice and perspective is seen to be identical to that postulated by Watkins: "When archaeologists say that the Native American past is gone, extinct, or lost unless archaeology can find it, they send a strong message that Native Americans themselves are extinct" (Zimmerman, 2006, p. 171). This diagnosis resembles that proposed by Martin (1987a), who argues that Native Americans fascinate historians "with their astounding ability to annul time, their remarkable capacity to repudiate systematically time and history" (p. 16). By constraining the study of Indigenous peoples to the perspective of rationalist linear history, invalidating their cyclical world of myth, "we surely strangle these people" (Martin, 1987a, 16).

Smith (2004) goes beyond the commonplace linking of archaeology to colonialism and scientific imperialism in proposing that "archaeological discourse and knowledge may become mobilized as a technology of government to govern particular social problems and issues" (p. 17). With a specific focus on practices in the United States and Australia, she concludes that archaeology is used as a means "to define, understand and regulate truculent populations and the social problems and issues that they present for the state" (Smith, 2004, p. 17).

Whether seen as an instrument of a coercive state or simply as a tool for sustaining academic life and reputation, these scholars assert that archaeology serves to deprive Indigenous peoples of their right to define their own place in the modern world, and that it is an effective weapon of assimilation to mainstream cultures. This analysis is well summarized by Custer (2005), who enthusiastically embraces the view that "Archaeologists have created a thought world which serves to support their own power and privilege, harms the interests of American Indian people, and aids the ongoing cultural genocide focused on Native Americans" (p. 3).

The arguments and conclusions listed in the previous paragraphs are based on a number of assumptions regarding Indigenous peoples, suppositions that are highly dubious but which are rarely and very quietly questioned in the current academic world. Clifton (1990, p. 13) noted almost two decades ago that standards of etiquette in the academic environment include norms and taboos of deferential behaviour in any dealings with Indigenous people. "The taboo on scholars writing anything that is likely to annoy native peoples is one expression of this explicitly partisan, condescending ethos" (Clifton, 1990, p. 13), an ethos that extends to scholarly organizations, law, the mass media, and government. This characterization of scholarly etiquette continues to be valid. Sheridan (2005), referring to relations between Native and non-Native scholars, characterizes current American ethnohistory as a field in which "No one is exactly sure what the ground rules are, yet no one seems willing to have them spelled out because of confrontations that might ensue" (p. 63). In ethnology, Suzman (2003) notes that "Despite the fact that the indigenous rights doctrine is out of step with much contemporary anthropological thinking, few anthropologists have criticized it. Of the few who have, most have been careful to add the caveat that their critique is intended for theoretical consumption only" (p. 399). Dyck (2006) analyzes the development of similar limitations on the work of Canadian ethnographers during the late twentieth century, noting that *in the late stages of an age of identity politics, considerable care has been invested in grooming anthropologists not so much as intellectuals but rather as practically oriented professionals who wish to proclaim their sympathies and solidarity with Indigenous peoples and to place their services at the disposal of Aboriginal leaders. (p. 87)*

He remarks that the self-deprecation and self-censorship adopted by anthropologists working with Canadian Aboriginals "contrasts vividly with the determinedly independent and critical stances exhibited by ethnographers who strive to chart the politics of nationalism, civil war, violence, and human rights abuses around the world" (Dyck, 2006, p. 87). This analysis can quite validly be extended to the training and work of archaeologists who support the notion of an Indigenous archaeology.

As a result of the assumed harm caused by archaeology to Indigenous people and societies, support for the concept of Indigenous archaeology is almost universally set in a framework of "ethics" of archaeological practice. The fact that this framing has remained unexamined and unquestioned must be attributed to the etiquette described in the previous paragraph. This silence has given rise to a sense that archaeologists who champion forms of Indigenous archaeology are somehow "more ethical" than those who might question the concept. I suggest that we might best lay aside this inference of comparative integrity before examining the arguments presented in the remainder of this chapter.

An equally questionable assumption that is made by proponents of Indigenous archaeology relates to these individuals' essentialist views on the nature of Aboriginal peoples and societies, and of the unique qualities and abilities that set Indigenous peoples apart from European and Euro-American populations (excellent examples of such views have been previously cited from Martin, 1987a; Watkins, 2003; and Zimmerman, 2006). Aboriginals are assumed to have a special relationship with, and understanding of, the natural world. Their perception of time as cyclical or continuously present is more complex and less limiting than the linear concept of time on which Western historical scholarship is based. Some follow Deloria (1995) in characterizing Indigenous peoples as having access to a superior understanding of the past than that offered by the Western historical tradition and Western scientific methods. This ability is presumed to result from an enduring relationship with local landscapes, and from a unique capacity of Aboriginal historical and cultural traditions to preserve a deeper, and in some sense a more truthful, narrative of the past than that available to non-Aboriginal societies (Trask, 1987, p. 178).

These characteristics of an essentialized Aboriginal culture can be rationalized only through an assumption that contemporary Aboriginals are the inheritors of long and essentially unchanging cultural traditions that are tied to specific regions and environments. Identification with local lands, a profound understanding and commitment to stewardship of local environments, and the creation and transmission of deep historical and cultural knowledge are generally understood as arising from countless generations of persistent occupation in a specific region. The projection of current ethnic definitions and identities into the past, as well as the assumption that local societies have been historically stable and enduring over great periods of time, may be psychologically rewarding to contemporary communities. It has also proved legally useful in negotiations regarding land use and ownership.

However, history and archaeology attest that assumptions regarding the endurance of unchanging local cultural identities are unlikely to reflect what actually happened in the past. On the contrary, the accumulated evidence of history demonstrates that all of our ancestors have at some point lost their homelands, taken over the homelands of others, and mixed with other societies and changed beyond recognition over time (Lowenthal, 2005, p. 407). Claims of Aboriginal uniqueness, like those of national or any other ethnic distinctiveness that are based on belief in the persistence of ancient and unchanged societies, are clearly untenable from the viewpoint of Western historical and scientific scholarship.

The fact that archaeologists choose to participate in the essentializing of the Aboriginal, despite the fact that their knowledge and their rationalist view of the past denies the historical prerequisites for such a view, is difficult to comprehend. It is clearly associated with the fact that Indigenous interests and demands regarding archaeological practice are enmeshed in the entire complex situation of negotiation and accommodation between Aboriginal and settler populations in the Americas, Africa, Australia, New Zealand, and elsewhere. More specifically, Smith (2004) notes that Aboriginal historical assertions are "part of wider negotiations with governments and their policy makers about the political and cultural legitimacy of Indigenous claims to specific rights, not least of which are rights to land" (p. 16). In the analogous case of social/cultural anthropology, Plaice (2003) suggests that "In its guise as the discipline interested in cultural diversity, it [anthropology] could be construed as the academic wing of the indigenous rights movement, whose role is to advocate the rights of vulnerable cultural minorities" (p. 397). She notes that individual anthropologists, as members of liberal Western society, condone the "seemingly racist policies" of ascribing exceptional qualities and rights to Aboriginal peoples simply because they find it distasteful to watch the disintegration of traditional societies (Plaice, 2003, p. 397). There is little doubt that archaeologists in settler societies are susceptible to the same temptations.

Sheridan (2005) suggests that the only intellectually honest way for a historian to approach such situations is by taking a stance of "strategic essentialism" (p. 76), through conjecturing an essential difference between Aboriginals and non-Aboriginals in order to help shift the centre of power away from the hands of the colonizer. Sheridan's intellectual honesty would seem to be more fairly characterized as political commitment. It is also worth noting that the social theorist G.C. Spivak (1988), who initially defined the concept of strategic essentialism as an effective tactic in colonial struggles, has long since renounced its use. Duncanson (2005) quotes Spivak as remarking in a 1990 interview that "Essentialism is like dynamite, or a powerful drug: judiciously applied, it can be effective in dismantling unwanted structures or alleviating suffering; uncritically employed, however, it is destructive and addictive" (p. 28).

In a broader context, the intellectual stance of archaeology with regard to the Indigenous is a sidebar to discussions regarding human rights, cultural pluralism, and modes of accommodation in multicultural societies (Ignatieff, 2001; Kymlicka, 1995; Niezen, 2003; Taylor, 1994). These debates necessarily revolve around questions of cultural relativism in contest with assumptions regarding the universality of rights, moral values, and the will to political self-determination. Do universal human rights trump local traditional or religious practice? Is there a place for collective rights as opposed to the rights of the individual? What are the limits of self-determination in pluralist societies? Questions such as these hang in the background of any confrontation between the universality of scientific practice and the particular values and beliefs of local societies. Unfortunately, these debates have produced little guidance to the negotiation of specific situations such as those arising in the archaeology of ancestral Indigenous peoples.

Savages, Primitives, Natives, Aboriginals, Indigenes: A Short History of Aboriginalism

Niezen (2003) notes with astonished approval the momentum that the concept of "Indigenous people" has recently acquired on the world stage of political and social ideas:

The interesting thing about the relative newness of this concept is that it refers to a primordial identity, to people with primary attachments to land and culture, "traditional" people with lasting connections to ways of life that have survived "since time immemorial." That this innovation should be so widely accepted is a startling achievement. (p. 3)

Other anthropologists view the same phenomenon less optimistically, interpreting it as the resurgence in both anthropological and political discourse of the concept of "primitive people" under a new disguise (Béteille, 1998; Clifton, 1990; Kuper, 2003). The official recognition by national governments, as well as by the United Nations and other international organizations, of Indigenous peoples as societies with common attributes, common problems, and common rights appears to have rescued this long-discredited concept from the anthropological rubbish heap. As noted above, anthropologists and archaeologists have been susceptible to abetting this resurrection by agreeing to ascribe to Indigenous communities a common set of intellectual and moral characteristics that set them apart from non-Aboriginal societies.

This development is perhaps not surprising, despite a century of social theorizing on cultural diversity that has valourized the equality of human capabilities and drawn clear distinctions between the genetic and cultural attributes of societies. Biolsi (1997) suggests that "Anthropology as a discipline has not been able to escape [the] conceptualization of the primitive, which is deeply embedded in the way Western civilization in general and American civilization in particular, constitutes itself. In fact, the Western, modernist concept of the primitive is what makes anthropology intellectually possible" (p. 136). Whether or not we agree that this is true with regard to the discipline of ethnology, it is certainly not for the archaeological study of ancestral Indigenous peoples. If archaeologists are tempted to perceive the subjects of their study (and their contemporary descendants) as primitives, they do so not from intellectual necessity but from consciously or unconsciously drawing on stereotypes that have a long and compelling allure within the Western cultural tradition.

The seductiveness of these abstractions may be illustrated by the great historical depth that they possess and the use to which they have been put. Following Diamond (1974) and others, Biolsi (1997) summarizes the view that Western society requires a fictional "primitive" to define its "civilized" self: "The primitive is a concept generated out of the social and cultural dynamics of state-level societies and modernity .... The self-identity or subjectivity of people in state societies ...

requires a concept of the primitive both to bound and to give content to the concept of the civilized" (p. 135). The argument derives from the same dialectical thinking that spawned Said's (1978) contention that "the Orient" was invented as a necessary contrast through which Western scholars could celebrate the social efficiency, technical pre-eminence, and the moral and intellectual superiority of their own societies. Although this may be true in the case of Orientalism, an examination of the historical use that Western society has made of the fictional primitive suggests a very different inverse mode of comparison. Among social theorists and other academics, primitive societies are more often ascribed splendid qualities that are lacking in those of the civilized world. This perception may also explicate the mechanism by which the concept of the "Noble Savage" became a basis for the self-definition of many contemporary Indigenous peoples.

Scholars in the Western intellectual tradition have long compared their own societies with that of a mythological Golden Age, or with the societies of barbarian or savage peoples that retained the characteristics of that age. Like the social theorists of the past few centuries, those of Imperial Rome experienced ever-widening knowledge of strange lands and stranger populations. Roman poets and philosophers reacted to these new peoples in an interesting fashion: they consistently admired the hospitality, courage, morality, and love of freedom that appeared to characterize barbarian societies, and that mitigated their indolence and ignorance. Some barbarians were described in terms reminiscent of the ancient inhabitants of the Golden Age, and this period of simplicity and ease seems to have continued in some manner to exist among the peoples who lived beyond the bounds of civilization.

The description of barbarian societies also served as a means of commenting on the immorality and corruption that poets and scholars saw in their own world. Tacitus's (1914) *Germania*, an ethnography of the peoples who lived beyond the Rhine frontier, blended repugnance of their sloth and disorder with respect for their honour, hospitality, bravery, sexual morality, and democratic mode of governing. Historians such as Publius Cornelius Tacitus (1914, pp. 29–32) and Cassius Dio (1925, pp. 3–5) wrote fictional speeches for barbarian military leaders in which they praised the barbarians' bravery, endurance, and ability to live with and from nature, in contrast to the weakness and cowardice of Romans who depended on their military technology to secure victory. These exercises in fictional rhetoric were meant for Roman ears, and their format was clearly designed to allow critical views of Roman society to be expressed by scholars who obviously preferred that such views not be openly expressed as their own.

The concept of the noble barbarian seems to have disappeared with the decline of Roman civilization, perhaps because of an increase in first-hand experience of tribal peoples and the transformation of Europe into semi-autonomous social units that no longer had a barbarian "*Other*" with which to compare themselves. However, the penchant for romanticizing barbarian character, for relating this character to an idealized Golden Age when humans were closer to the land, and for using the barbarians as a foil to demonstrate the failings of contemporary European society reappeared in the descriptions of peoples that were encountered by the explorers of the European Renaissance. It is quite apparent that these similarities are more than coincidental, as fifteenth-century voyages of discovery coincided with the efforts of scholars and translators to recover the long-forgotten texts of the classical past. The historical and geographical knowledge of the classical world was a primary source of information for the explorers of the Renaissance and for those who recorded and interpreted their accounts of discovery. Porter (1979) notes that antiquity supplied "ready made 'myths' which literate explorers could use as an allusive framework for the accounts of their exploits" (p. 45). Classical allusions occur throughout the reports of fifteenth- and sixteenth-century discoveries and most prominently in discussions of the Native peoples encountered.

Ellingson (2001, pp. 22–26) credits the Parisian lawyer Marc Lescarbot with inventing both the discipline of anthropology and the concept of the Noble Savage. After spending the year 1606–1607 at the fur-trading post of Port Royal on the Bay of Fundy in eastern Canada, Lescarbot argued that the local Mi'kmaq shared with European nobility the patterns of moral and social life that had been preserved from an ancient Golden Age. The lawyer saw these patterns as deriving from the practice of hunting, an activity that in France was reserved to the nobility, and that was associated with the charity and generosity of an ancient world (Lescarbot, 1609/1925, p. 267). Lescarbot's analysis of New World society was widely translated and played an important role in the development of social theory during the following century.

In contradiction of standard histories of anthropology, Ellingson (2001) is correct in asserting that neither Jean-Jacques Rousseau nor any other social philosopher of the Enlightenment thought of the

Noble Savage as anything more than an ancient theoretical possibility, a hypothetical creature who served as a useful rhetorical foundation for theories on the development of human society. Despite Locke's (1690/1980) famous dictum that "Thus in the beginning all the world was America" (p. 49), he used the descriptions of Aboriginal peoples in the same way as he did those of biblical and classical times, as examples of those that have progressed to various points along the theoretical pathway from nature to the development of civil society. A century later, Hume's (1777/1975) *Enquiry Concerning Human Understanding* clearly states the view that noble savagery did not exist and that human nature was consistent throughout the world and throughout history (p. 65).

Lewis (1998) derives the discipline of anthropology, and especially the Boasian school of Americanist anthropology, from this intellectual tradition. He laments what he takes to be the recent abandonment of its basic principles in favour of an "us and them" perspective in which comprehension of other cultures is illusory. However, this postmodernist perspective also has a long intellectual tradition in anthropology. Whereas Boas's (1911) *The Mind of Primitive Man* argued that all human minds operate on identical principles and differ only through cultural input, Lévy Bruhl's contemporaneous *Les fonctionnes mentales dans les sociétés inférieures* (published in English as *How Natives Think* [1966]) characterized primitive thought as prelogical, mystical, and impervious to "rational" learning through experience.

The rationalist tradition in anthropology, arguing the psychic and intellectual unity of mankind, has always been challenged by a Romantic tradition that has perpetuated a view of the primitive as a special class of human who is probably not quite ready to join contemporary world culture and society. This perspective survived the Enlightenment discussions of social philosophy, gained strength in the literature and oral traditions of nineteenth-century colonial administration and Christian missionary activities, and gained academic credibility with the development of anthropology as a scholarly discipline.

The Culpability of Anthropology

A reading of the history of anthropology supports Ellingson's (2001) contention that "the Noble Savage was indeed associated with both the conceptual and the institutional foundations of anthropology" (p. 4). Following Stocking's (1987, pp. 243–256) close analysis of the discipline's origins, he detects the concept arising in scholarly disputes carried out against the background of the US Civil War that was being fought over African slavery. On the one side were the anatomists who argued the biological inferiority of Africans and other Indigenous peoples, on the other were the archaeologists and ethnologists who believed in the equal capacity of all humans. By the late 1860s, the latter faction had triumphed and their views, which in England had developed from those of the Quaker-led Aborigines Protection Society, became the defining discourse of the new discipline of anthropology. "Equal but very different" could have been their watchword, as the developing field defended the position of its philanthropic intellectual ancestors against the racialist views of colonial soldiers and administrators. Of the later nineteenth century, Stocking (1987) notes that "If few in this period questioned the white Europeans' evolutionary mission, many anthropologists continued in kindly scholarly fashion to play the roles of defender of savage ways of life and explicator of savage modes of thought—roles clearly premised on a sense of moral obligation" (p. 273).

Of the same period, Kuper (1988) argues that the development of a concept of "primitive society" was sustained by the dynamics of scholarly behaviour: "Primitive society then became the preserve of a new discipline, which soon developed a sophisticated set of techniques for kinship studies. When this happened, the survival of the idea of primitive society was ensured" (pp. 9, 14). The concept, together with related notions concerning primitive mentality, primitive religion, and primitive art, became the central orthodoxy of anthropology. From this base, it permeated the political and historical consciousness of Western intellectual society, where it has persisted to the present day.

Extending Kuper's analysis, we could note that although anthropology announced itself as "the study of Man," this assertion was eroded during the early twentieth century by a florescence of academic disciplines that also studied humanity, including economics, psychology, Oriental studies, and sociology. Anthropology retreated to a smaller but more defensible academic niche: the study of ancient humans and of the small societies that lived beyond the mainstream of world events. Social and cultural anthropology became the study of the Indigenous, the "peoples without history" whose ways of life were thought to have changed little since ancient times. The interests of anthropology, as an academic discipline, would seem to have lain in emphasizing the unique characteristics of Aboriginal cultures, those traits that set them apart from the peasant and urban societies that at the time were studied by other academic disciplines.

This allowed great scope for developing the "equal but very different" concept, especially as it could be applied not only to social and economic life but to the worldview, languages, and belief systems of Aboriginals. Although Indigenous people generally lived with less technology, and at a less complex socio-economic level than the colonial peoples who had displaced them, the doctrine of "equal but very different" suggested their potential for possessing and developing less tangible qualities, and such qualities began to emerge from anthropological descriptions. The unique character of these subjects, developed especially during the period of "culture and personality" studies in the first half of the twentieth century, provided clearly defined boundary markers for the discipline of anthropology, markers that could be used to repel the poaching of economists, sociologists, or Orientalists.

By the mid-twentieth century, the unique thought patterns of Aboriginals had become an academic reality. Anthropological linguists (Hoijer, 1950/1964; Lee, 1938; Sapir, 1931; Whorf, 1937/1956) convinced many scholars that thought processes were necessarily conditioned by the construction of individual languages. The great diversity of Aboriginal languages became a measure of the diversity that could be expected in thought patterns and of how different these could be from those of Europeans. The evidence suggesting wide diversity in thought patterns and worldviews, however, did not prevent anthropologists from continuing their long tradition of sustaining the stereotype of the "primitive" mind. Although *La Pensée Sauvage* is not as prescriptive as the English title *The Savage Mind* would suggest, as late as the 1960s, Claude Lévi-Strauss (1966) could still essentialize the primitive mind:

> The characteristic feature of the savage mind is its timelessness; its object is to grasp the world as both a synchronic and a diachronic totality …. The savage mind deepens its knowledge with the help of imagines mundi. It builds mental structures which facilitate an understanding of the world in as much as they resemble it. In this sense savage thought can be defined as analogical thought. (p. 262)

In this early phase of the postmodernist movement, the Aboriginal had become a class of humans whose minds worked in ways that were different from those of civilized Westerners and that might be incomprehensible to Western science. In more recent years, this idea has been most thoroughly expounded by Sahlins (1995) in his celebrated debate with Gananath Obeyesekere on whether Western rational analysis can comprehend why Native Hawaiians chose to kill Captain James Cook.

Kuper (1988) contends that the concept of primitive society was developed and maintained by the structural needs of the academic discipline of anthropology. This argument can be extended through consideration of Keesing's (1989) important, yet very little recognized, article titled "Exotic Readings of Cultural Texts." Keesing argues that the reward structure of anthropology (like those of geographical exploration and travel writing) has encouraged the announcement of new and increasingly exotic phenomena and interpretations. He cites the example of a colleague, invited to prepare a paper in honour of Claude Lévi-Strauss, who eagerly set to work analyzing the concept of "direction" as it was perceived by the Indigenous people whom he had studied. Eventually, he realized that their concept and practice of direction-naming and orientation was identical to his own, so he did not bother to complete and publish the paper. This sort of contribution would return little reward to its author, and would rarely, if ever, get published or even written. I suspect that the process of selective reporting has been very significant in the development of a paradigm defining Aboriginals as peoples who possess, among other unique or unusual attributes, an extraordinary and holistic understanding of their environments; who recognize time as a synchronous or cyclical, rather than a linear, phenomenon; who have enhanced qualities of spiritual realization; and whose oral traditions provide all of the information required to preserve an ancient and unchanging view of the world and how it should be inhabited.

The preceding pages have argued that Aboriginalism, the paradigm of "The Aboriginal" as an individual and a society that is essentially different from the non-Indigenous, is a delusion that has been fostered by the practice of anthropology. But, of course, Aboriginals have had their own say in the matter. Lescarbot's characterization of the Mi'kmaq, described above, may have been based less on observation than on discussions with French-speaking Native acquaintances. His leading informant on Mi'kmaq life, Membertou, was also the local leader who explained Mi'kmaq society to the Jesuit Fr. Pierre Biard five years later. Biard reported that

> They consider themselves ... braver than we are, boasting that they have killed Basques and Malouins .... They consider themselves better than the French; "For," they say, "you are always fighting and quarreling among yourselves; we live peaceably. You are envious and are all the time slandering each other; you are thieves and deceivers; you are covetous, and are neither generous nor kind; as for us, if we have a morsel of bread we share it with our neighbor." (Thwaites, 1896–1901, p. 173)

This rhetoric had no effect on the Jesuit's negative views of the Mi'kmaq, but the lawyer-ethnologist Lescarbot may have been less critical. Mi'kmaq self-regard as braver, more honest, and more generous than the French may have been a primary source of Lescarbot's depiction of the native Acadians as inheritors of the same moral qualities that characterized the royalty and nobility of Europe. Lescarbot, whose decision to come to Acadia was occasioned by a recent injustice and his consequent disenchantment with Parisian society, may have been more disposed to accept Mi'kmaq opinion of their own culture. A shared view of social comparisons may have been developed during a long winter of discussions between Membertou and the lawyer. Such a mutually reinforcing process would have served different purposes for the disillusioned French philosopher of society, and for the Mik'maq engaged in defining their relationship with the new settlers, but it would have supported the establishment of a shared belief in the unique differences that existed between European and Aboriginal societies.

An important mechanism in the self-identification of Indigenous peoples with the fictional primitive of European scholarship has been the development of recursive feedback between the writings of European scholars and the Aboriginal subjects of their texts. The process began very early in the encounter between European and American peoples. Thomas More's 1515 fiction *Utopia* described the discovery of an island in the West Indies that was home to a perfected human society characterized by common ownership, religious tolerance, and a political system based on consensual decision rather than imposed authority. *Utopia* is Plato's *Republic* crossed with the idealized New World societies described from the voyages of Columbus and Vespucci. It is clear that More did not invent the Utopian community as a plan for an ideal civilization but as a foil designed to highlight the problems and faults of contemporary English society. Yet, barely 20 years after its publication, Bishop Vasco de Quiroga began to found communities in Michoacan based on the customs of the Utopians. The creation of an ideal society seemed appropriate, as the bishop explained that "with much cause and reason is this called the New World, not because it is newly found, but because in its people, and in almost everything, it is like as was the first Golden Age" (Porter, 1979, p. 47). It seems likely that these ideas were promulgated to the bishop's subjects, the actors in his experiment to recreate the Golden Age.

A remarkable and much more recent example of feedback between European scholarship and Aboriginal belief can be found in the use of the "Adario dialogues" written by the Baron de Lahonton, a soldier who spent several years in Canada during the late seventeenth century. The most interesting section of Lahonton's (1703) published account of his ventures is a series of long and obviously imaginary conversations with a Huron chief named Adario, a character who is usually thought to have been based on a noted warrior and diplomat named Kondiaronk who had died after failing to sabotage the Great Peace of Montreal.

Adario is presented as a philosopher of the Golden Age, and his role is to describe the superiority of Huron culture in order to point out the absurdity of Christian beliefs, the immorality of priests, the dishonesty of French legal and commercial practices, and the corrupt nature of French society. The argument is presented clearly and affably, and Lahonton is obviously using his imaginary debater in the same way as Roman historians used barbarians, or as Thomas More used Utopia, to speak truth to power without endangering his own prospects. However, the Adario dialogues have become a favourite of Aboriginal historians and cultural leaders, perhaps best exemplified by Georges Sioui's (1992) *For an Amerindian Autohistory*. Here, a leading Aboriginal historian presents Adario as an actual Huron philosopher recording, through his friend Lahonton, the truth about the Aboriginal way of life in ancient North America. This paragon not only demonstrates the clear superiority of Native American culture and society but "Adario had already foreseen the need for a world government and may be said to have helped lay the intellectual foundations for the great social revolutions of our own time" (Sioui, 1992, p. 81). A carefully nuanced but flattering introduction to the book was written by a leading archaeologist, the late Bruce Trigger (1992), and epitomizes the intellectual dilemma faced by archaeologists in attempting to accommodate the historical perspectives of Indigenous peoples.

Although a careful reading of Trigger's testimonial absolves the scholar of supporting Sioui's interpretations, on the surface his statement appears to validate the concept of Aboriginalism. Other archaeologists (Watkins, 2003; Zimmerman, 2006) are less careful in expressing essentialized stereotypes of Aboriginal people. Such voices of scholarly authority serve to support the myths of Aboriginalism in the public mind, and Indigenous people in particular must be susceptible to such a gratifying view of their inherent qualities. Simard (1990, p. 360) compares the situation to that of traditional Québécois who were prone to accept the dominant *Anglais* view of themselves. "Generation after generation [Aboriginals] have integrated into their own practical and intellectual life the dominant culture's Owner's Manual for being Indian" (Simard, 1990, p. 358). The chapters of the manual written by scientists who describe Aboriginals as possessing uniquely admirable qualities of thought and exceptional abilities to understand the world would be especially tempting to integrate into the self-perception of Indigenous people.

The transformation of scholarly writing into traditional knowledge has been well documented by Symonds (1999, p. 119), who notes that in the Scottish Highlands oral histories telling of the traumatic eighteenth- and nineteenth-century clearances of agricultural populations have been replaced by traditions based on the accounts of popular historians. The work of writers such as John Prebble (1963) are now incorporated into traditional knowledge and "have become the new oral history" (Symonds, 1999, p. 119). Nicholas and Andrews (1997b) note the problem of "readback" (p. 277) when interpreting historical information provided by Aboriginal consultants; this caution should perhaps be expanded to include information on the self-perception of the consultants and their culture. The readback process must have occurred repeatedly among literate Indigenous communities whose culture and history have been described by anthropologists and archaeologists, sometimes in clearly essentialist terms. The assimilation of the Aboriginal stereotype is unquestionably abetted by the acceptance of the obverse Whiteman stereotype—materialistic, uncharitable, dishonest, cowardly, environmentally ruthless—as formulated by Lescarbot, Lahonton's Adario, and countless other critics of Western society from Tacitus to contemporary anthropologists (Marcus & Fischer, 1986, p. 111).

Aboriginalism and Indigenous Archaeology

Do Indigenous people and societies possess inherent qualities and abilities, with special reference to historical matters, that distinguish them from non-Aboriginals? Despite the prevalence of assumptions based on the traditional construction of the primitive, neither anthropology, archaeology, or any other field of study provides persuasive evidence in support of the view that Indigenous people possess a distinctive view of time and of history, a unique understanding of the natural world, or oral traditions that allow recovery of knowledge related to the distant past. Recent approaches to the subject rely on the presentation of rhetoric rather than of empirical evidence. Donald Fixico's (2003) *The American Indian Mind in a Linear World* enumerates significant differences between Indigenous and European ways of understanding the world, the most basic of which is the assumed fact that Indian thought proceeds from the understanding that circles and cycles are central to the universe, relating all times and all things. Thus, "the linear mind looks for cause and effect, and the Indian mind seeks to comprehend relationships" (Fixico, 2003, p. 8) among phenomena as disparate as events, dreams, and ceremonies.

In a work subtitled *Towards a Critical Indigenous Philosophy*, Dale Turner (2006) repeatedly states the duty of Indigenous intellectuals to protect and defend the legitimacy of Indigenous ways of knowing the world. He is particularly interested in the power of Indigenous philosophy as the basis for political discussions and negotiations of rights, sovereignty, and nationhood. Turner stresses the idea that if they are to be politically effective, Aboriginal worldviews must be made comprehensible to dominant Euro-American societies. However, Turner (2006) is uncertain whether "indigenous philosophies are articulable in English" (p. 116) (and presumably in other non-Indigenous languages), and makes no attempt to articulate the ways of knowing that are basic to his argument. Rather than providing empirical evidence of Indigenous difference, both Fixico and Turner argue that empirical evidence, in the sense familiar to the rationalist scientific tradition, is irrelevant to an understanding of Indigenous thought.

Layton (1994) discusses the problem of setting up an intellectual dichotomy between Western and non-Western modes of thought, noting that "such dichotomies obscure equally interesting differences between the diverse cultures in the 'other' category," and that in the particular case of historical perspectives, "such simplistic thinking tends to attribute opposed functions to oral art forms and written literature" (p. 4). The series of essays collected by Layton from scholars on all continents presents a diversity of non-Western, Indigenous, and rural approaches to history, yet provides no evidence of a simple nonlinear view of time past. Statements by individuals that they and their community view time as cyclical, or think of the past as eternally present, cannot be judged as other than anecdotal. Similar anecdotal evidence can be cited from the experience of the present author, who has found that Indigenous individuals have no obvious problem internalizing the concept of linear time that is a necessary component of living in the contemporary world. The same class of evidence suggests that Westerners share with other humans a sense of cyclical time in the recognition that every seasonal and communal celebration, be it Halloween, Christmas, Passover, Eid, Diwali, or Green Corn Festival, is the same celebration come round again, carrying its own freight of emotional recognition. Indeed, the notion of cyclical time as a unique attribute of non-Western peoples may be traceable to the questionable assertions made by the student of religions Mircea Eliade (1954) in *The Myth of the Eternal Return*.

On the related subject of the historical accuracy of oral traditions, those of Aboriginals seem to be at most marginally different from those of any other society. Nabokov's (2002) wide-ranging and sympathetic analysis of American Indian modes of history "endorses efforts to transcend old characterizations of Indians as victims or stereotypes and their traditions as monolithic and intractable. The many Indian pasts ... are as much stories of philosophical, ideological, and symbolic creativity and synthesis, inevitably processed through definitions of self, community, and destiny, as they are beads of discrete incidents hung on narrative strings" (p. 237). Instead of supporting claims of superior and more accurate knowledge of historical events, Nabokov stresses the importance of the individual storyteller, the context of narration, and the importance of multivocality as a foundation of Native historical approaches. He compares this complex perspective with the simple essentialism displayed by Martin (1987b), much to the detriment of the latter. In discussing the San Pedro Ethnohistory Project, one of the most sophisticated and rewarding examples of collaboration between archaeologists and Indigenous historians, Ferguson and Colwell-Chanthaphonh (2006) state, "We do not advocate that archaeologists simply accept traditional histories in their entirety as literal truth .... Nonetheless, we think archaeologists should seek to identify the social and cultural processes implicated in tribal narratives about the past" (p. 247).

Turning to other presumed qualities of the Indigenous, Krech (1999, 2005) and Mann (2005) have assembled sufficient evidence to discredit the Romantic idea of Native Americans as natural conservationists whose ancestors did nothing to alter or harm the natural environment. No evidence has been presented to support a belief that Indigenous people possess a greater knowledge of their land or a more intense feeling for their land than do non-Aboriginal individuals, especially those who spend a great deal of time outdoors in one particular patch of country. The frequent assertion that Aboriginal lives are permeated by a sense of spirituality that is not available to non-Aboriginals has been criticized even by Deloria (1997), who laments that "a self-righteous piety has swept Indian country, and it threatens to pollute the remaining pockets of traditionalism and produce a mawkish unreal sentimentalism that commissions everyone to be 'spiritual' whether they understand it or not" (p. 213).

In summary, scholarly literature provides considerable evidence hostile to the tenets of Aboriginalism. In support of the concept that Aboriginal peoples have unique attributes that distinguish them from all other societies, one finds only assertions that are unsubstantiated by evidence or interpretation. The idea of Indigenous societies that are morally and spiritually superior to those of European ancestry has an intellectual allure, perhaps parallel to that of benevolent extraterrestrial visitors. Such uncorroborated beliefs, however, do not form a useful base for the construction of a special form of Indigenous archaeology that is appropriate to the unique needs of Aboriginal peoples. In fact, most archaeologists' assertions of these needs, and their proposals for accommodating them, are distinctly condescending to those whom they intend to honour or placate.

The supposed problems that current archaeological practice causes for Indigenous communities were discussed earlier in this paper. The discipline is accused of disrespecting the religious and historical beliefs of Indigenous people, of disregarding the desire of Indigenous communities to define their own pasts and therefore their unique places in the contemporary world, of denying sophisticated Aboriginal concepts of cyclical or eternally present time and imposing on Indigenous history the simple Western notion of linear time, and of being an agent of coercive governments in abetting acts of cultural genocide.

Proposed solutions to these problems involve the development of forms of Indigenous archaeology that depart radically from the practice of archaeology as an academic and heritage-management discipline. Few of these proposals have the clarity of Deloria's (1995) direct statement that "Much of Western science must go" (p. 15) before Aboriginal people can obtain a clearer understanding of their past. Some (Custer, 2005) argue that archaeology can be practiced with a clear conscience only if it is carried out at the request of, and under the direction and control of, an Indigenous community. Others simply assume that "indigenous rights should always trump scientific inquiry," as Gillespie (2004, p. 174) notes of the papers collected by Zimmerman, Vitelli, and Hollowell-Zimmer (2003). With particular reference to Australia, McNiven and Russell (2005) see the claims of archaeologists to academic freedom as no more than "part of the colonial fantasy of naturalized superiority and hegemonic control" (p. 239). Nicholas (2005, p. v) recommends that archaeology be willing to accept restrictions placed by Indigenous communities on the dissemination of data, and to accept publication moratoriums that may allow the subject community time to explore ways of benefiting from the data before others do.

Beyond the sharing of authority over the use of archaeological resources and the information derived from them, proponents of Indigenous archaeology generally require what Ridington (1999) calls "sharing theoretical authority" (p. 20) by moving beyond the canons/cannons of formal academic discourse. Such projects strip archaeology of the scientific attributes that make it a particularly powerful narrator of the past, and accord it, at most, equal weight relative to Indigenous oral tradition and religious discourse. Zimmerman (2006) predicts that "Accountability to Native Americans will create a very different discipline, one that will not be scientific, according to our current standards" (p. 173). He proposes that the loss of scientific credibility may be compensated by access to a greater range of Indigenous Knowledge, especially in the realm of the sacred, a suggestion rooted in the stereotyped view of Indigenous peoples as holders of sacred knowledge.

The problem of accommodating scientific demands to the requirements of local communities has been addressed more honestly and profitably by anthropologists. Noting the difficulties of reconciling empirical positivism with the faith-based assertions that underlie the belief systems of most communities, Brown (2006) states that

> *Collisions between faith and fact are inevitable … and there will be difficult moments when cultural anthropologists must decide whether we are* griots *and* griottes *[praise-singing bards] for our ethnographic partners or active participants in a transcultural community of scholars who answer to truth standards that many of our ethnographic collaborators find incomprehensible or offensive. Presumably we are both. (p. 992)*

Playing a game that has two distinct and often opposed sets of rules is neither easy nor often useful to either the player or to disparate audiences. Kuper (2003) notes that

> *If anthropology becomes … "the intellectual wing of the indigenous rights movement," if we report only what is convenient and refrain from analysing intellectual confusions, then our ethnographies will be worthless except as propaganda. Even as propaganda they will have a rapidly diminishing value, since the integrity of ethnographic studies will be increasingly questioned by the informed public. (p. 400)*

The doubts of an informed public regarding the veracity of anthropological reporting were expressed by Chief Justice Allan McEachern of the British Columbia Supreme Court in the important Canadian land claims case of *Delgamuukw v. British Columbia*. The judge excluded the testimony of anthropologist Richard Daly, which was considered suspect because he adhered to the American Anthropological Association's code of ethics that states, "in research, an anthropologist's paramount responsibility is to those he studies" (Culhane, 1992, p. 72).

Trigger (1997) offers a similar warning that "If archaeologists knowingly treat the beliefs of Indians differently than those of Euro-Canadians, there is a danger that the discipline will descend into mythography, political opportunism, and bad science" (p. x). He also warns that "For archaeologists to take sides in political issues of this sort [in this case, denial of the Asiatic origin of Native Americans] risks interference in Native life that may be scarcely less patronizing than the interference of Indian agents and missionaries was in the past" (Trigger, 1997, p. x). We cannot foresee the consequences of archaeological support for statements and perspectives that are consistent with Aboriginal belief but not with scientific evidence, any more than Indian agents and missionaries could accurately forecast the outcome of their activities. In any case, as Kuper (2003) reminds us, "Even if we could accurately weigh up the medium- and long-term political costs and benefits of saying this or that, our business should be to deliver accurate accounts of social processes" (p. 400).

Predicting the benefits of Indigenous archaeology is a theoretical exercise, because the thorough revision of the discipline envisaged by its advocates has yet to be implemented, and the advantages of accommodating a scientific discipline to the desires of a specific nonscientific community are not at all clear. Proctor (2003) perceptively notes that "Historians are familiar with the obstructive impact of ill-willed ideologies on science; less familiar are examples of political goodwill's stifling science" (p. 223). Indigenous archaeology, as proposed by its supporters, would appear to provide an exceptionally apt example of such a negative outcome. If the harmful effects of such a practice were restricted to its influence on the disciplines of archaeology and history, our concerns might be limited. However, it can be argued that the impact of subverting scientific archaeology to the wishes or the control of local communities extends beyond the boundaries of the academy.

As one example of such an impact, we might examine the relationship between archaeology and the Native land claims process in North America and elsewhere. Smith (2004) and others charge that archaeology often serves, or is seen to serve, as a pawn of coercive government. There is no doubt that archaeology is useful to national governments engaged in dealing with Aboriginal populations, but perhaps not in the way suggested by the proponents of Indigenous archaeology. Anyone who has participated as an archaeologist in Canadian land claims negotiations soon realizes that government negotiators generally encourage, or do little to mitigate, the development of an emotional atmosphere surrounding the subject of archaeological remains. Such an atmosphere increases the value of control over the treatment and disposition of these remains, which then becomes a significant token that can be traded away in return for concessions on economic resources or other items of greater interest to government. Trigger (1997) has also noted that politicians favour "ceding control over cultural matters to Native people as a less expensive and dangerous way to compensate them for centuries of injustice than giving them extensive political and economic powers" (p. viii). If archaeologists are concerned at the thought of becoming government pawns, they should realize that—in Canada at least, and I suspect elsewhere—this process is most easily accomplished by acceding to the belief that Aboriginal peoples have unique needs to possess and control their archaeological past, thus artificially inflating the value of this resource when measured against the provision of economic and political powers to Indigenous communities.

A more important outcome of the legitimization of Indigenous archaeology lies in its reinforcement of stereotypes of Indigenous uniqueness. Wax (1997) has identified the problems caused by the ease with which Native American leaders find political leverage in presenting themselves to the world "as passive and abused 'noble savages,' torn from the mythic wilderness of the ages of European exploration" (p. 53). Sahlins (1995) notes that academic efforts to defend Aboriginal ways of life by "endowing them with the highest cultural values of western societies" have the paradoxical result of "delivering them intellectually to the imperialism that has been afflicting them economically and politically" (p. 119). In preserving and maintaining this essentialist self-image, they encourage perpetuation of their public stereotype as primitives, as a special class of human who will always be marginal to the dominant culture and society.

The demands for Indigenous archaeology do not arise in response to an intellectual problem but, rather, from the emotions and political reactions of scholars to Aboriginal communities that are socially and economically marginal, and that conceive of this situation as the result of historical mistreatment at the hands of Western society. Nicholas and Andrews (1997a) feel that "As archaeologists and anthropologists from a dominant society, we have an obligation to contribute to the well-being of First Peoples" (p. 12). Such a reaction is indeed admirable, if very patronizing. Any community must find means to alleviate the misery of its most marginal members, and archaeology's association with the heritage of such peoples is a profoundly political engagement.

However, archaeologists must recognize that by using the authority of their discipline as a means of advancing causes based on assumptions of the unique needs and capabilities of Indigenous peoples, they risk following the trail blazed by ancestral anthropologists who first established Aboriginals as a special category of humans. This academic concept was to prove extremely useful in the theory and practice of colonial administration, generally to the detriment of the peoples administered. In conspiring to believe in the paradigm of Aboriginality, and in reinforcing it by providing historical justification, archaeologists are complicit in maintaining the intellectual conditions under which poor and marginalized Indigenous societies can continue to exist into the future. Rather than abetting such tragedies, we might emulate Kuper (1988) in hoping that "although certain things have been done badly in the past, we may still aspire to do them better in future …. If we liberate ourselves, we may be able to free others. Anthropologists developed the theory of primitive society, but we may make amends if we render it obsolete at last, in all its protean forms" (p. 243). Archaeologists can make an important contribution to this goal by exposing the myths of stable enduring societies on which the idea of the primitive or the Aboriginal is founded.

Changing Archaeology

As many readers will conclude, there is little in this chapter that has not been said before. In fact, the use of extensive quotations has been meant to fortify that impression. This poses the question, why, despite such broad agreement among analysts of archaeology and anthropology, do many practitioners of the disciplines continue to pursue, or at least accept, the legitimacy of Aboriginalist goals?

The broad majority of archaeologists who are opposed to Aboriginalist views, and to archaeological practice based on these perspectives, appears to be constrained by the same code of silence regarding disagreements on Aboriginal issues that was reported by Clifton (1990) and more recently by Sheridan (2005). The prevalent and inappropriate framing of discussions on Indigenous archaeology as an issue of ethics arises from this situation, and in turn has contributed to its reinforcement. Removal of the debate from the context of ethics, and resituating it as a matter of intellectual and political concern, would do a great deal to advance clarification and ultimately a resolution of the issues involved.

Another factor in the silencing of critics arises from the fact that archaeologists are enmeshed in an academic culture that is still committed to the tenets of a declining postmodernist movement. Tenure, advancement, and the adjudication of research grants often involves the judgement of academic colleagues whose perspectives include the encouragement of equivocality in historical interpretation, and the importance of political perspective as a major factor influencing the reliability and trustworthiness of scholarly research. As noted by Clifton almost two decades ago, universities, granting agencies, academic societies, museums, and other institutions still have an almost irrational fear of offending Indigenous groups, and of the potential problems that might result.

Many archaeologists are also concerned regarding access to the Indigenous archaeological resource, which in most jurisdictions is now dependent on consultation with, or the permission of, local Indigenous communities. Continued access to archaeological materials is the subtext of many publications proposing the development of Indigenous archaeology. Ferris (2003), after documenting recent changes in legal attitudes that can be expected to provide increasing rights of North American Native groups over archaeological materials, suggests that archaeologists adapt to this situation by shifting from "a parasitic to a symbiotic" (p. 172–173) relationship with Aboriginal partners. McNiven and Russell (2005) propose that archaeologists accept a "host/guest" relationship with Indigenous communities, which "have every right to control archaeological research in whatever way they wish" (p. 236). Neither these nor other proponents question the intellectual grounds on which Indigenous peoples require unique interests in, and rights over, heritage materials. This may be a convenient stance at the present moment, but there are no assurances that such a position will be of long-term benefit to anyone. On the contrary, refraining from questioning the intellectual basis of current political assumptions can be expected to reinforce the political and legal constraints under which archaeology currently works. The consequent neglect of historical research on the history of Indigenous peoples will be interpreted, correctly, as the result of the racist attitudes of Western scholars toward the interests of Indigenous populations.

Dyck (2006) notes that North American ethnographers who do not insist on their rights to a free and independent anthropological voice will be increasingly constrained by "habits of self-censorship and situational silence" (p. 92). This analysis applies equally to North American archaeology. It is surely absurd that many members of a mature academic discipline refrain from publicly stating their commitment to one of the most basic intellectual tenets of their field, that all humans are ancestrally related and have similar ranges of capabilities. Or that these same scholars publicly endorse, or at least do not oppose, a belief that they know to be patently false—that Indigenous people form a class of humans with unique qualities and abilities that are not shared by non-Aboriginals. The situation seriously impairs a field of study that could potentially make a significant contribution to the understanding of Indigenous cultures and their place in the contemporary world. It can be resolved only by full and candid discussion, yet such a debate seems unlikely to take place under present circumstances.

Lacking the opportunity for open discussion of these matters, Sheridan's (2005) concept of an intellectual division of labour in historical studies may be relevant to archaeologists: "The challenge of Native American studies ... is to present indigenous perspectives in rigorous and reflexive ways. The role of non-Indian scholars is to learn from these perspectives without surrendering the insights and rigor of their disciplines" (p. 77). In this view, Indigenous archaeology should be considered a branch of Aboriginal studies, rather than as a component of the academic discipline of archaeology.

Beyond this definitional solution, change in the archaeological discipline can be effected primarily through the actions of individuals, actions that reflect a belief in the universal nature of human history and the value of historical knowledge. These actions include getting to know Indigenous people as individual acquaintances, rather than as contemporary avatars of an ancient ideal; dealing with the past as a place inhabited by real people and real communities, rather than by the abstract entities postulated by both processual paradigms and Aboriginalist belief; and working co-operatively with Indigenous people toward this goal, engaging them in archaeological research and learning from their genuine knowledge of their societies and the historical processes that have formed them (McGhee, 2004).

Archaeologists who are convinced that their discipline is engaged in a project that is capable of contributing to a better understanding of the present world must be willing to support this conviction with determination. On the one hand, they cannot be intimidated by those who claim ethnically based special rights of access to archaeological materials, or special historical knowledge and abilities that are not available to those who practice science in the Western tradition. On the other hand, they must stand against those in the academic world who claim extreme forms of cultural relativism, equivocality among diverse approaches to knowledge, and the impossibility of relatively objective historical research. Something as important as the human past deserves both courage and thoughtful scholarship on the part of those who claim to make it their study.

REFERENCES

Attwood, B. (1992). Introduction. In B. Attwood & J. Arnold (Eds.), *Power, knowledge and Aborigines* (pp. i–xvi). Melbourne, Australia: La Trobe University.

Béteille, A. (1998). The idea of Indigenous people. *Current Anthropology, 39*(2), 187–192. http://dx.doi.org/10.1086/204717

Biolsi, T. (1997). The anthropological construction of "Indians": Haviland Scudder Mekeel and the search for primitives in Lacota County. In T. Biolsi & L.J. Zimmerman (Eds.), *Indians and anthropologists* (pp. 133–159). Tucson: University of Arizona Press.

Boas, F. (1911). *The mind of primitive man.* New York: Macmillan.

Brown, M.E. (2006). Comment on Strang (2006). *Current Anthropology, 47*(6), 992.

Bruhl, L. (1966). *How Natives think.* New York: Washington Square Press.

Clifton, J.A. (1990). Introduction: memoir, exegesis. In J.A. Clifton (Ed.), *The invented Indian: cultural fictions and government policies* (pp. 1–28). New Brunswick, NJ: Transaction.

Conkey, M.W. (2005). Dwelling at the margins, action at the intersection? Feminist and Indigenous archaeologies, 2005. *Archaeologies, 1*(1), 9–59. http://dx.doi.org/10.1007/s11759-005-0003-9

Culhane, D. (1992). Adding insult to injury: Her Majesty's loyal anthropologist. *BC Studies, 95,* 66–92.

Custer, J.F. (2005). Ethics and the hyperreality of the archaeological thought world. *North American Archaeologist, 26*(1), 3–27. http://dx.doi.org/10.2190/E0Y2-L9N8-43W0-RLT2

Deloria, V., Jr. (1995). *Red Earth, White Lies.* New York: Scribner.

Deloria, V., Jr. (1997). Anthros, Indians and planetary reality. In T. Biolsi & L.J. Zimmerman (Eds.), *Indians and anthropologists* (pp. 209–221). Tucson: University of Arizona Press.

Diamond, S. (1974). *In search of the primitive: A critique of civilization.* New Brunswick, NJ: Dutton.

Dio, Cassius. (1925). *Roman history VIII, Cassius Dio books 61–70.* Loeb Classical Library. Cambridge, MA: Harvard University Press.

Dongoske, K.E., Aldenderfer, M., & Dochner, K. (Eds.). (2000). *Working together: Native Americans and archaeologists.* Washington, DC: Society for American Archaeology.

Duncanson, I. (2005). Refugee meanings. In A. Wagner, T. Summerfield, & F.S. Benavides Vanegas (Eds.), *Contemporary issues of the semiotics of law* (pp. 19–34). Oxford: Hart.

Dyck, N. (2006). Canadian anthropology and the ethnography of "Indian administration." In J. Harrison & R. Darnell (Eds.), *Historicizing Canadian anthropology* (pp. 78–92). Vancouver: University of British Columbia Press.

Eliade, M. (1954). *The myth of the eternal return.* Princeton, NJ: Princeton University Press.

Ellingson, T. (2001). *The myth of the noble savage.* Berkeley: University of California Press. http://dx.doi.org/10.1525/california/9780520222687.001.0001

Ferguson, T.J., & Colwell-Chanthaphonh, C. (2006). *History is in the land: multivocal tribal traditions in Arizona's San Pedro Valley.* Tucson: University of Arizona Press.

Ferris, N. (2003). Between colonial and Indigenous archaeologies: legal and extra-legal ownership of the archaeological past in North America. *Canadian Journal of Archaeology, 27,* 154–190.

Fixico, D.L. (2003). *The American Indian mind in a linear world: American Indian studies and traditional knowledge.* New York: Routledge.

Gillespie, J.D. (2004). Review of Zimmerman, Larry J., Karen D. Vitelli and Julie Hollowell-Zimmer (2003). *Canadian Journal of Archaeology, 28,* 172–175.

Hoijer, H. (1964). Cultural implications of some Navaho linguistic categories. In D. Hymes (Ed.), *Language in culture and society* (pp. 142–148). New York: Harper and Row. (Original work published 1950)

Hume, D. (1975). *Enquiry concerning human understanding.* Oxford: Clarendon Press. (Original work published 1777)

Ignatieff, M. (2001). *Human rights as politics and ideology.* Princeton, NJ: Princeton University Press.

Keesing, R.M. (1989). Exotic readings of cultural texts. *Current Anthropology, 30*(4), 459–469. http://dx.doi.org/10.1086/203765

Krech, S., III. (1999). *The ecological Indian. Myth and history.* New York: Norton.

Krech, S., III, (2005). Reflections on conservation, sustainability, and environmentalism in Indigenous North America. *American Anthropologist, 107*(1), 78–86. http://dx.doi.org/10.1525/aa.2005.107.1.078

Kuper, A. (1988). *The invention of primitive society.* London, UK: Routledge.

Kuper, A. (2003). The return of the Native. *Current Anthropology, 44*(3), 389–402. http://dx.doi.org/10.1086/368120

Kymlicka, W. (1995). *Multicultural citizenship: A liberal theory of minority rights.* Oxford: Oxford University Press.

Lahonton, L.-A. Baron de. (1703). *New voyages to North America.* London, UK: Benwicke, Goodwin, Wotton, Tooke and Manship.

Layton, R. (1994). Introduction. In R. Layton (Ed.), *Who needs the past: Indigenous values and archaeology* (pp. 1–20). London, UK: Routledge.

Lee, D. (1938). Conceptual implications of an Indian language. *Philosophy of Science, 5*(1), 89–102. http://dx.doi.org/10.1086/286489

Lescarbot, M. (1925). *Nova Francia, a description of Canada, 1606.* London, UK: Routledge. (Original work published 1609)

Lévi-Strauss, C. (1966). *The savage mind.* London, UK: Weidenfeld and Nicolson.

Lewis, S.H. (1998). The misrepresentation of anthropology and its consequences. *American Anthropologist, 100*(3), 716–731. http://dx.doi.org/10.1525/aa.1998.100.3.716

Locke, J. (1980). *Second treatise of government.* Indianapolis, IN: Hackett. (Original work published 1690)

Lowenthal, D. (2005). Why sanctions seldom work: Reflections on cultural property internationalism. *International Journal of Cultural Property, 12*(3), 393–423. http://dx.doi.org/10.1017/S0940739105050216

Mann, C.C. (2005). *1491: New revelations of the Americas before Columbus.* New York: Knopf.

Marcus, G., & Fischer, M.M.J. (1986). *Anthropology as cultural critique: An experimental moment in the human science.* Chicago: University of Chicago Press.

Martin, C. (1987a). An introduction aboard the *Fidele.* In C. Martin (Ed.), *The American Indian and the problem of history* (pp. 3–26). New York: Oxford University Press.

Martin, C. (Ed.). (1987b). *The American Indian and the problem of history.* New York: Oxford University Press.

McGhee, R. (2004). Between racism and romanticism, scientism and spiritualism: The dilemmas of new world archaeology. In B. Kooyman & J. Kelley (Eds.), *Archaeology on the edge, new perspectives from the northern plains, occasional paper 4* (pp. 13–22). Calgary, AB: Canadian Archaeological Association.

McGuire, R.H. (1992). Archaeology and the first Americans. *American Anthropologist, 94*(4), 816–836. http://dx.doi.org/10.1525/aa.1992.94.4.02a00030

McNiven, I.J., & Russell, L. (2005). *Appropriated pasts: Indigenous peoples and the colonial culture of archaeology.* New York: AltaMira.

Nabokov, P. (2002). *A forest of time: American Indian ways of history.* Cambridge, UK: Cambridge University Press.

Nicholas, G.P. (2005). On mtDNA and archaeological ethics. *Canadian Journal of Archaeology, 29*(1), iii–vi.

Nicholas, G.P., & Andrews, T.D. (1997a). Indigenous archaeology in the post-modern world. In G.P. Nicholas & T.D. Andrews (Eds.), *At a crossroads: Archaeology and First Peoples in Canada* (pp. 1–18). Burnaby, BC: Archaeology Press.

Nicholas, G.P., & Andrews, T.D. (1997b). On the edge. In G.P. Nicholas & T.D. Andrews (Eds.), *At a crossroads: archaeology and First Peoples in Canada* (pp. 276–279). Burnaby, BC: Archaeology Press.

Niezen, R. (2003). *The origins of Indigenism: Human rights and the politics of identity.* Berkeley: University of California Press. http://dx.doi.org/10.1525/california/9780520235540.001.0001

Peck, T., Siegfried, E., & Oetelaar, G. (Eds.). (2003). *Indigenous peoples and archaeology.* Calgary, AB: University of Calgary Archaeological Association.

Plaice, E. (2003). Comment on Kuper (2003). *Current Anthropology, 44*(3), 396–397.

Porter, H.C. (1979). *The inconstant savage, England and the North American Indian 1500–1660.* London: Duckworth.

Prebble, J. (1963). *The Highland Clearances.* London: Seeker and Warburg.

Proctor, R.N. (2003). Three roots of human recency. *Current Anthropology, 44*(2), 213–239. http://dx.doi.org/10.1086/346029

Ridington, R. (1999). Theorizing coyote's cannon: sharing stories with Thomas King. In L. Philips Valentine & R. Darnell (Eds.), *Theorizing the Americanist tradition* (pp. 19–37). Toronto: University of Toronto Press.

Sahlins, M. (1995). *How "Natives" think, about Captain Cook, for example.* Chicago: University of Chicago Press. http://dx.doi.org/10.7208/chicago/9780226733715.001.0001

Said, E.W. (1975). *Orientalism.* New York: Random House.

Sapir, E. (1931). Conceptual categories in primitive languages. *Science, 74,* 578.

Sheridan, T.E. (2005). Strategic essentialism and the future of ethnohistory in North America. *Revista de Antropologia, 34,* 63–78.

Simard, J.-J. (1990). White ghosts, red shadows: The reduction of North American Natives. In J.A. Clifton (Ed.), *The invented Indian: cultural fictions and government policies* (pp. 333–369). New Brunswick, NJ: Transaction.

Sioui, G. (1992). *For an Amerindian autohistory.* Montreal: McGill-Queen's University Press.

Smith, L. (2004). *Archaeological theory and the politics of cultural heritage.* London: Routledge. http://dx.doi.org/10.4324/9780203307991

Spivak, G.C. (1988). Subaltern studies: Deconstructing historiography. In G.C. Spivak (Ed.), *Other worlds: Essays in cultural politics* (pp. 197–221). New York: Routledge.

Stocking, G.W., Jr. (1987). *Victorian anthropology.* London, UK: Collier Macmillan.

Suzman, J. (2003). Comment on Kuper (2003). *Current Anthropology, 44*(3), 399–400.

Symonds, J. (1999). Songs remembered in exile? Integrating unsung archives of highland life. In A. Gazin-Schwartz & C.J. Holtorf (Eds.), *Archaeology and folklore* (pp. 105–125). London, UK: Routledge.

Tacitus, Cornelius. (1914). *Tacitus I: Agricola, germania, dialogus. Loeb Classical Library.* Cambridge, MA: Harvard University Press.

Taylor, C. (1994). *Multiculturalism.* Princeton, NJ: Princeton University Press.

Thwaites, R.G. (Ed.), (1896–1901). *The Jesuit relations and allied documents* (Vol. I). Cleveland, OH: Burrows Brothers.

Trask, H.-K. (1987). From a Native daughter. In C. Martin (Ed.), *The American Indian and the problem of history* (pp. 171–179). New York: Oxford University Press.

Trigger, B. (1992). Foreword. In G. Sioui (Ed.), *For an Amerindian autohistory* (pp. ix–xv). Montreal: McGill-Queen's University Press.

Trigger, B. (1997). Foreword. In G.P. Nicholas & T.D. Andrews (Eds.), *At a crossroads: archaeology and First Peoples in Canada* (pp. vii–xiii). Burnaby, BC: Archaeology Press.

Turner, D. (2006). *This is not a peace pipe: Towards a critical Indigenous philosophy.* Toronto: University of Toronto Press.

Watkins, J. (2000). *Indigenous archaeology.* Walnut Creek, CA: AltaMira.

Watkins, J. (2003). Archaeological ethics and American Indians. In L.J. Zimmerman, K.D. Vitelli, & J. Hollowell-Zimmer (Eds.), *Ethical issues in archaeology* (pp. 129–141). Walnut Creek, CA: AltaMira.

Watkins, J. (2005). Through wary eyes: Indigenous perspectives on archaeology. *Annual Review of Anthropology, 34*(1), 429–449. http://dx.doi.org/10.1146/annurev.anthro.34.081804.120540

Wax, M.L. (1997). Educating an anthro: The influence of Vine Deloria, Jr. In T. Biolsi & L.J. Zimmerman (Eds.), *Indians and anthropologists* (pp. 50–60). Tucson: University of Arizona Press.

Whorf, B.L. (1956). Linguistic consideration of thinking in primitive communities. In J.B. Carroll (Ed.), *Language, thought and reality, selected writings of Benjamin Lee Whorf* (pp. 65–86). New York: Wiley. (Original work published 1937)

Wylie, A. (2005). The promise and perils of an ethic of stewardship. In L. Meskell & P. Pels (Eds.), *Embedding ethics* (pp. 47–68). Oxford: Berg.

Zimmerman, L.J., Vitelli, K.D., & Hollowell-Zimmer, J. (Eds.). (2003). *Ethical issues in archaeology*. Walnut Creek, CA: AltaMira.

Zimmerman, L.J. (2006). Sharing control of the past. In K.D. Vitelli & C. Colwell-Chanthaphonh (Eds.), *Archaeological ethics* (2nd ed., pp. 170–175). Walnut Creek, CA: AltaMira.

NOTE

1 I wish to thank the many colleagues and associates whose discussions contributed to the ideas presented in this chapter. Over the past 15 years, these have included fellow members of the Assembly of First Nations/Canadian Museums Association Task Force on Museums, members of the Consultation Committee on the First Peoples Hall at the Canadian Museum of Civilization, and my curatorial colleagues at the latter institution. We have often found ourselves in disagreement over the matters discussed here but have hopefully come to appreciate each others' sincerity and intentions. I am also grateful to the four anonymous reviewers who provided useful critiques of an earlier draft.

14

Running the Gauntlet: Challenging the Taboo Obstructing Aboriginal Education Policy Development

Albert Howard with Frances Widdowson

Since 2002, the Department of Indian and Northern Affairs and the University of Western Ontario have cohosted a number of Aboriginal policy research conferences. The purpose of these conferences has been to provide a neutral forum promoting evidence-based policy where "ideas and beliefs can be openly discussed and debated" (Beavon, White, & Maxim, 2004, pp. 9–10). As a result of the papers presented at these conferences, a number of volumes documenting the current research being undertaken on Aboriginal policy have been compiled.

Of special importance in these discussions is the research undertaken on Aboriginal education policy. It is noted that Aboriginal education is "a central preoccupation of both Aboriginal and non-Aboriginal policy makers," since improving Aboriginal educational achievement will "enrich not only individuals and First Nation communities, but will also provide more systemic benefits for the entire country" (Beavon et al., 2004, pp. 9–10). Increasing educational levels will enable Aboriginal people to contribute their skills and expertise to Canadian society as a whole.

The evidence-based character of the research pertaining to Aboriginal education policy, however, is absent in one of the articles included in the selection of papers compiled to represent the 2006 Aboriginal Policy Research Conference. This paper, written by Anthony N. Ezeife and entitled "Culture-sensitive Mathematics: The Walpole Island Experience," speculates about the poor educational achievement of Aboriginal students. According to Ezeife (2006), substandard Aboriginal educational achievement "is a surprising development considering the historical fact that Aboriginal people of old were keen students of nature, astronomy, science, and math" (p. 54).

This argument is not based on a rigorous analysis of the evidence available. Although three sources are cited as supporting this viewpoint, few specifics are provided.[1] There is little to indicate how this could be the case when Aboriginal people had no written language, number system, or instruments to aid the study of these disciplines.[2] These technologies did exist before 1500, in the Old World, in various cultures—Greek, Chinese, Indian, and Persian—and influenced the development of European educational systems in North America after contact. Therefore, to claim that Aboriginal proficiency in astronomy, science, and math is a "historical fact" evades the evidence-based distinction that will help us to understand and address Aboriginal educational deficiencies today.

As will be shown below, Ezeife's 2006 article is very similar to the vast amount of literature concerning Aboriginal education policy, where it is argued, often in the absence of evidence, that a revitalization of Native cultural traditions will enable Aboriginal peoples to more fully participate in Canadian life and achieve economic self-sufficiency. This assumption, in fact, has been largely sustained by a number of vested interests that have made taboo all discussion of the developmental differences between Aboriginal traditions and modern educational processes (see Widdowson & Howard, 2008). It is imperative that this taboo be overcome because evidence-based policy development, an essential step in addressing Aboriginal deprivation, requires that all ideas be openly presented, discussed, and debated with material available for public evaluation. To facilitate more effective policy formulation, this chapter will show that some cultural traditions, artificially imposed in Aboriginal education, including Native pedagogy, Indigenous languages, and "traditional knowledge," are associated with small and relatively unproductive kinship-based groupings and incompatible with participation in much larger, complex, and productive modern nation-states. This has resulted in the impetus to create completely separate educational systems with culturally relative standards, such as the development of Native studies programs, so as to hide the educational deficit that is being perpetuated by this policy direction.

Policy Development and the Current Aboriginal Educational Deficit

In discussions about Aboriginal education, it is generally recognized that "Aboriginal students experience profound disadvantage relative to the general population" (School Community Safety Advisory Panel, 2008, p. 528). Richards and Vining (2004) note, for example, that, according to the 2001 census, it was documented that 48% of Aboriginal people had not completed high school, in contrast to only 31% for the non-Aboriginal population. More disturbing is the fact that there does not appear to be a convergence of Aboriginal and non-Aboriginal educational achievement, and a substantial gap between the two continues (Richards & Vining, 2004, pp. 5–7). Michael Mendelson (2006) has noted that "an astonishing 43 percent of Aboriginal people aged 20 through 24 reported in 2001 having less than high school education" and that this cohort "would have been in high school in the 1990s, not in some distant past of discredited old policies and old programs" (p. 16).

It is important to note that dropout rates are only part of the problem. Because of political pressure to increase the number of Aboriginal graduates, questions have to be asked about whether Aboriginal students are simply being "passed through" the system, regardless of their educational levels.[3] Aboriginal leaders often resist standardized testing on the grounds that Canadian requirements are inappropriate for Aboriginal students.[4] There also have been suggestions by some policy researchers that the measurement of Aboriginal learning outcomes should be changed to reflect the priorities of Native communities. It is maintained that analyzing Aboriginal educational outcomes should not just "focus on ... standardized assessments" but "holistic learning," which includes "physical, spiritual, mental and emotional dimensions" (Canadian Council on Learning, 2007, p. 2). One study of Aboriginal curriculum development even suggests that grading systems might not be appropriate in Aboriginal courses since "this can conflict with community systems that ... do not recognize failure" (Evans, McDonald, and Nyce, 1999, p. 197).

The difficulties that Aboriginal peoples are facing in the educational system have resulted in many attempts to analyze the problem. One of the most common explanations is that the current educational system is culturally alienating for Aboriginal students, and therefore Aboriginal teachers and curriculum that reflects Aboriginal culture are needed (Demmert, Grissmer and Towner, 2006). It is maintained that it is important for Aboriginal students to "know who they are" (School Community Safety Advisory Panel, 2008, p. 528). Incorporating Aboriginal traditions into the school system, it is claimed, will help to instill pride within the Native population, facilitating their educational success. This has resulted in the teaching of Aboriginal languages and Native cultural traditions (James, 2001, p. 7).[5]

Schools that are most active in teaching Aboriginal traditions, however, are often those that rank lowest in graduation rates and testing results.[6] British Columbia reserve schools, for example, where traditional teachings are more prominent, have lower educational levels and graduation rates than is the case for students who attend provincial schools (Richards, Hove, & Afolabi, 2008). In fact, a recent study shows that Aboriginal students do best when they attend schools with a significant mix of Aboriginal and non-Aboriginal attendance. Segregating Aboriginal students so they can retain their traditions results in a "negative peer effect" due to reduced expectations.

These results raise questions as to whether the current attempts to let Aboriginal people know "who they are" (whatever that means), as well as to develop culturally sensitive programming, are effective in improving educational outcomes. One of the reasons why these approaches may be dubious, though not discussed in the literature, is that there is a large developmental difference between modern educational processes and Aboriginal traditions. This is to be expected, considering that Aboriginal cultures had no writing before contact— a circumstance that has inhibited literacy development. As will be shown below, Native pedagogy, Aboriginal languages, and Indigenous Knowledge are all aspects of a preliterate culture. The lack of a culture of literacy makes it doubtful that these will help Aboriginal peoples to master the skills, values, and attitudes they need for success in a highly structured educational system.

Native Pedagogy: Enculturation, Not Education

One of the key areas deemed necessary for cultural sensitivity in the educational system is the teaching methods used for Aboriginal students. It is maintained that mainstream educational institutions need to recognize that Aboriginal peoples traditionally have developed their own pedagogy for teaching their children (Harp, 1998, pp. 67–69). Because Aboriginal people lived according to an "oral tradition," knowledge was not disseminated with the written word but through storytelling, ceremony, and allowing children to "learn by example" (what also has been referred to as "looking, listening, and learning—'the three Ls'" (Miller, 1996, pp. 16–17). We are also told that teaching was task oriented. Abstract principles were not featured; education was concerned with helping a person to understand their place in the community and giving them the skills for subsistence living and to be a member of the group (Swan, 1998, pp. 49–58).

These different "educational methods," the argument goes, make Canadian institutions alienating for the Aboriginal student, causing them to drop out and perform poorly in comparison with non-Aboriginals (Cajete, 1994, pp. 196–197). The solution to this problem, according to this reasoning, is to incorporate the above forms of "Aboriginal pedagogy" into the curriculum. Aboriginal students are encouraged to "apply" abstract concepts instead of completing assignments involving "number-based mathematics" (Leavitt, 1995, p. 130). The curriculum should not be organized according to abstract categories but in the "context of the children's daily lives" (Leavitt, 1995, p. 132; MacIvor, 1995, p. 77). We are told that in Indigenous pedagogy, "overt intellectualization is kept to a minimum in favor of direct experience and learning by doing" (Cajete, 1994, p. 225). Experience on the land is perceived as being more important than being in the classroom, as direct instruction is regarded as a "disservice to the learner" since the animals are the "greatest teachers" (Nadasdy, 2003, pp. 97–101). It is even considered offensive in traditional Aboriginal cultures for a person to tell someone else what to do (Brant, 1990).[7]

In addition to practical, as opposed to abstract, forms of instruction, an aspect of Native pedagogy often referred to is the use of the Medicine Wheel. The Medicine Wheel is a "centred and quartered circle" and is used as "a teaching device" by many Aboriginal educators (RCAP, 1, 646–647). According to RCAP (1996), this device "represents the circle that encompasses all life and all that is known or knowable, linked together in a whole with no beginning and no end. Human beings have their existence in this circle of life, along with other beings and the unseen forces that give breath and vitality to the inhabitants of the natural world" (Vol. 1, pp. 646–647). In RCAP's (1996) view, Medicine Wheels are important because they "help people examine experience by breaking down complex situations into constituent parts, while reminding them not to forget the whole" (pp. 646–647).

As well as transforming teaching methods, "different" forms of communication are advocated for Aboriginal students. It should not be expected that students will be able to structure information in terms of arguments and evidence. Instead, they should listen to stories where a "multifaceted conversation" and "narration ... presenting accounts of many experiences" result in a "conceptualization of ever-increasing completeness, without a stated conclusion" (Leavitt, 1995, p. 128). In fact, this is due to the lack of writing in Aboriginal traditions, as well as the fact that Native groups are socialized into high-context, as opposed to low-context, cultures. *Low-context* cultures are those, like European societies, where precise forms of communication are relayed through the spoken word. *High-context* cultures, on the other hand, are common to Native communities. In these cultures, communication is not explicit and "a great deal is left unsaid and situational factors deliver the greater part of an intended meaning" (Taylor, 1995, p. 233).[8]

Aboriginal communication also differs in that it avoids criticizing the viewpoints of others. Thus, teaching critical thinking skills to Aboriginal students becomes problematic since it "may be viewed as challenging the traditional etiquette of respectful listening" (MacIvor, 1995, p. 80). It is argued, for example, that the "sacredness" and "fundamental truth" of myths should be honoured (Leavitt, 1993, p. 3),[9] even though this would obviously interfere with scientific skepticism. The resistance to critical thought is especially strong if the viewpoint in question comes from an elder. Questioning the knowledge claims of elders is often perceived as an attack on their integrity and this is "the most disrespectful thing that you can do" (White, 2005, p. 18).[10]

But how will making educational systems more "culturally sensitive" toward the Native population by incorporating Aboriginal pedagogy help the Native population participate in modern society? If Aboriginal peoples are not able to master "number-based mathematics," are resistant to developing their critical faculties, or must rely on "nonexplicit" forms of communication, how will they ever be able to become the "engineers, managers, business people, natural resource specialists, and all the other experts" that are claimed to be needed in Native communities (Hampton, 1995, pp. 6–7)? It is often argued that integrating Native pedagogy will facilitate this process by providing a bridge between Aboriginal learning processes and those that are used today. However, this fails to consider that Native pedagogy, since it emerged in the context of preliterate cultures, is not really a method of teaching in the classical sense. Modern education imparts information formally so as to develop abstraction, and all the examples referred to above indicate an avoidance of these procedures. They are actually an aspect of the more general process of enculturation, where children learn through empathy, identification, and imitation (Mead, 1965; see also Miller, 1996). Therefore, there are no teaching methods found in Aboriginal traditions that can facilitate the dissemination of abstract ideas and the organization of complex information.

While it appears that the Medicine Wheel is an exception, by offering a more systematic pedagogical technique, this turns out to be a mirage. The "constituent parts" that emerge from the "breaking down [of] complex situations" are arbitrarily constructed, the only basis for which is a spiritual belief about the significance of the number four.[11] Platitudes about "holistic" teaching methods are provided (Canadian Council on Learning, 2007, p. 6), but there is no indication of how using this approach will enable Native students to master the complex information that is needed to become proficient in subjects like mathematics, medicine, or astronomy. It is even difficult to determine exactly what this term means, and it often ends up just becoming a synonym for the word "spiritual" (RCAP, 1996, Vol. 3, p. 357; see also Smith, 2001, p. 80). This is because holism's value is not to enhance understanding but to help its proponents avoid scrutiny. As John Ruscio (2002), a psychologist at Elizabethtown College in Pennsylvania, points out, holism is actually "a scientists' curse and a charlatan's dream" (pp. 49–50). According to Ruscio (2002), holism is "an empty retreat from reality, a method by which pseudoscientists muddy rational thought, avoid clear and concise communication, and follow their own idiosyncratic beliefs to justify doing whatever they please in the name of all that sounds nice and feels good" (pp. 49–50).

The fact is that teaching by example, high-context forms of communication, the uncritical acceptance of the views of elders, and "holistic" thought are associated with an early historical period, where small kinship groups were organized around subsistence activities. Today, the world is a much more complicated place. Nation-states require elaborate and universalized educational systems to transmit the vast knowledge of a technologically advanced, global economy and society. Reading, writing, and mathematics require abstract thought and more formal methods of instruction—pedagogy that is developed in the context of a culture of literacy. This cultural influence is undeveloped in many Aboriginal communities, where the presence of reading materials at home is not part of Native life experience.[12] It is also being exacerbated by the promotion of Indigenous languages in the educational system that are preliterate and do not have the vocabulary or complexity to facilitate educational achievement today.

Indigenous Languages: Preserving Orality or Promoting Illiteracy?

In addition to Aboriginal "teaching styles," it is argued that a revitalization of Aboriginal languages is necessary to improve Aboriginal educational outcomes. According to those who advocate language revitalization, Indigenous languages "constitute precious verbal media for conveying and institutionalizing ideas, concepts, and emotions that relate to the experience of Canada in its ecological totality" (Morris, McLeod, & Danesi, 1993, p. i).

These arguments, once again, fail to recognize that Aboriginal cultures had not developed writing before contact—one of the most significant aspects in the evolution of language. Carl Sagan (1977) describes the relationship between writing and the development of human cognition by placing it in the context of three different kinds of information: genetic preprogramming, commonly referred to as instinct; extragenetic information, which is learned; and, finally, extrasomatic knowledge, which is unique to humans and stored outside the body—primarily in writing (pp. 4, 26). This development came about due to the need for more reliable communication than could be expected from a messenger's memory or relying on the oral transmission through a series of individuals (Childe, 1936, pp. 144–145). Records could be kept and referred to at a date in the future without depending on the word of possibly partial or subjective reporters. The ability to store information externally also increased access to knowledge and ideas across both space and time. As Maryanne Wolf (2007) puts it, "while reading, we can leave our own consciousness, and pass over into the consciousness of another person, another age, another culture" (p. 7).

Wolf (2007) also has pointed out that "educated members of an oral culture had to depend entirely on personal memorization and meta-cognitive strategies to preserve their collective knowledge," and this limited "what could be said, remembered, and created" (p. 65). Therefore, "as humans learned to use written language more and more precisely to convey their thoughts, their capacity for abstract thought and novel ideas accelerated" (Wolf, 2007, p. 66). This increasing development of abstract thought made possible the emergence of academic enterprises such as history, logic, science, and philosophy—disciplines requiring that observations and arguments be recorded so they could be referred to at a later date, and analyzed (Ong, 1988, pp. 15, 52, 57, 174). As Walter Ong (1988) explains, writing is necessary for "explicative understanding" since cultures lacking literacy "cannot organize elaborate concatenations of causes in the analytic kind of linear sequences which can only be set up with the help of texts" (p. 55). The preliterate character of Aboriginal languages, in fact, explains why they "do not necessarily organize reasoning according to a linear sequence of cause-and-effect, or axioms-theorems-corollaries, as do speakers of European languages" (Ong,

1988, pp. 130–131). Without writing, the verification and refutation of ideas becomes impossible, because there is no mechanism to determine what was originally said.

The less developed capacity of Aboriginal languages for abstraction is also shown by their small vocabularies. All written languages have far more words than those that are preliterate, which must store their entire vocabulary in the memory of the living generation. A 1925 Inuktitut-English dictionary, for example, documents only 2,600 Inuktitut words, and many of these would be concepts brought by literate Europeans (these words were being *written* in a dictionary, after all) (Peck, 1925). The vocabularies are sparse because of the oral nature of the language. The inability to write down concepts means few abstractions are possible (Jenness, 1977, pp. 24–25).[13] This lower level of abstraction in Aboriginal languages has been attributed to the less developed character of Aboriginal economies before contact, which resulted in an absence of the surplus value and division of labour that makes the existence of an intelligentsia possible (Jenness, 1977, p. 25).

The lower capacity for abstraction in Aboriginal languages also makes them less specific than those that have evolved with the development of writing. The lack of specificity impedes the exact translation of scientific principles into Aboriginal languages. Although it is possible to translate Aboriginal stories and legends into modern languages such as English, French, or German, one can imagine the difficulties of trying, in an Aboriginal language, to write about the engineering requirements for building skyscrapers, organic chemistry experiments, Renaissance paintings, or Hegel's *Philosophy of Right*. In these cases, no concepts would be present in Aboriginal culture to make any kind of meaningful translation possible. This is because Aboriginal culture has not gone through the developmental stages in art, science, or philosophy that have occurred in literate societies.[14]

Although there have been attempts to modernize Aboriginal languages by "Aboriginalizing" various concepts, this has really meant that new words are grafted on to what is still basically a preliterate form of communication. Problems arise because the values, attitudes, concepts, and knowledge needed to become fully literate do not exist in the history of Native cultures. So even though a new word might be created in an Aboriginal language, there are no related concepts that exist in the culture to give it meaning. This leads to much less specific ideas being applied to new concepts. Domestic animals, for example, are described in Inuktitut as *nujuattaittut*, or "animals that do not run away," (Meekitjuk Hanson, n.d.), thereby including injured animals, a turtle hiding in its shell, or a snake that has become too cold to move. Legal phrases such as "reasonable doubt" and "pleading guilty or not guilty" also have been impossible to translate into Indigenous languages. The former has been translated as "exactly what happened without the aid of magic" (Ashbury, 1997), and the latter as "did you do it or not?" (Betty Harnum, personal communication, August 1994). Furthermore, Native languages tend to use the same term for a range of different meanings. The verb "to lie" is used to describe being misinformed or wrong, which poses problems for modern justice systems.[15]

These difficulties with Aboriginal languages are disguised by discussions about the number of words that exist to describe particular elements of the environment or the irrelevant assertion that Aboriginal languages are "verb-oriented" versus "noun-oriented." With respect to the latter, it is not shown how this is the case, or how this difference will enable Aboriginal students to master modern educational requirements.[16] Arguments about the number of words that exist for natural phenomena such as snow or eels, on the other hand, are offered to show that Aboriginal languages are "complex" and therefore capable of meeting the requirements of advanced educational processes. But such assertions fail to make a distinction between the complexity that comes with being highly organized and that which is associated with irregularity. The fact that something is difficult to understand does not mean that it is "complex" in the first sense. As languages progressed, rules were developed so that they could be learned more easily. In other words, languages became more organized as they evolved. This is why the verb "to be" is irregular in almost all European languages. It is the oldest and therefore the most primitive (i.e., the closest to its ancestral roots). And regardless of the number of words used to describe eels or snow, discussions about this aspect of Aboriginal languages misses the most important point: this sort of "complexity" is relatively unimportant in the modern context. Much more important are the various abstractions that are used to understand developments in engineering, chemistry, logic, history, art, social relations, and philosophy, as well as the specificity in meanings that are required for clear communication with large numbers of people. It is these skills that must be acquired if Aboriginal peoples are going to participate in, and contribute to, the wider society.

"Traditional Knowledge": Protoscientific Observations and Spiritualism?

In addition to changes in Aboriginal pedagogy and the revitalization of Indigenous languages, it is maintained that Aboriginal academic achievement can be improved by incorporating Indigenous "traditional knowledge" into all aspects of the educational system. This claim was extensively elaborated upon in the 1996 *Report of the Royal Commission on Aboriginal Peoples*—a source that is used as evidence in many current discussions about Aboriginal education policy.[17] The report maintains that recognizing traditional knowledge is important for affirming Native identity and maintaining cultural diversity, and therefore it is necessary that traditional knowledge be recognized in educational processes. It also asserts that such recognition does not amount to an act of condescension, since traditional knowledge can help everyone, regardless of their culture, to better understand the world. This argument presumes that "ethnocentrism" led Europeans to be prejudiced against traditional knowledge and to imprudently disregard it as a primitive relic. RCAP (1996) maintains that this assumption is now being rethought (Vol. 3, p. 215; Vol. 4, p. 139), even arguing that "'Native science' can offer valuable insights and teachings in areas such as astronomy, medicine, pharmacology, biology, mathematics, and environmental studies, to name but a few" (Vol. 4, p. 128).[18]

But what is not clear from RCAP's analysis is what these "valuable insights" consist of, and how incorporating these "teachings" will improve educational outcomes. RCAP (1996) notes, for example, that traditional knowledge assumes that "spirituality" is a major component of "knowledge." It points out that

> the fundamental feature of Aboriginal world view was, and continues to be, that all of life is a manifestation of spiritual reality. We come from spirit; we live and move surrounded by spirit; and when we leave this life we return to a spirit world. All perceptions are conditioned by spiritual forces, and all actions have repercussions in a spiritual reality. Actions initiated in a spiritual realm affect physical reality; conversely, human actions set off consequences in a spiritual realm. These consequences in turn become manifest in the physical realm. All these interactions must be taken into account as surely as considerations of what to eat or how to keep warm in winter. (Vol. 1, p. 628)

What is downplayed, however, is the fact that these beliefs are inconsistent with the scientific assumptions that influence modern educational systems. Some of these "spiritual forces" to which RCAP (1996) refers, for example, concern "vision quests" where Aboriginal people claim to have communicated with animals (Vol. 1, p. 642).

Prayers, prophecies, and Aboriginal peoples' "special relationship to the Creator" are also constantly referred to as being important aspects of the Aboriginal "world view" that others should appreciate (RCAP, 1996, Vol. 1, pp. 617–618, 620, 632–633). RCAP (1996) even recognizes the unscientific character of these aspects when it acknowledges that "the validity or truth value of the spiritual aspects of traditional knowledge cannot be assessed scientifically" (p. 640). It even attempts to justify this circumstance by arguing that rational thought and logic might be "highly efficient for some tasks," but "by narrowing the field of perception to gain focus, searching for cause/effect sequences in a time-limited frame, and dismissing the influence of non-material forces, the logical mind may screen out much of the knowledge considered essential by many Aboriginal people for living well" (RCAP, 1996, Vol. 1, pp. 640–641).

Aside from the inclusion of beliefs in supernatural forces in the educational system—a development that actually contradicts scientific methods—it is not clear how RCAP perceives that "Native science" has extended our grasp of "astronomy, medicine, pharmacology, biology, mathematics, and environmental studies." Contributions to mathematics, astronomy, and physics supposedly relate to the assumption that "[the Aboriginal conception of] the nature of the cosmos is consistent with many of the fundamental principles set forth in modern science, particularly quantum physics and its offshoot, chaos theory" (RCAP, 1996, Vol. 4, pp. 127–128).[19] This view is supported by the claims of Leroy Little Bear, who maintains that Aboriginal languages are very "action- or verb-oriented" and, as a result, Aboriginal peoples have "'always thought in terms of energy, energy fields and constant motion'" (as cited in RCAP, 1996, Vol. 1, p. 621; Vol. 4, p. 123). The only concrete example of a "contribution" provided by RCAP is the Akwesasne Science and Mathematics Pilot Project. In this project, there are "units on the Haudenosaunee teachings of the four winds" and the "concept of oneness with the universe" (RCAP, 1996, Vol. 3, pp. 458–459). "Aboriginal cosmos mythology" is also taught so as to demonstrate the "intricate thought" of Haudenosaunee ancestors (RCAP, 1996, Vol. 3, pp. 458–459).

But even if one were to accept that cultures without writing and lacking the possession of a rudimentary counting system were able to develop the advanced understanding of mathematics, physics, and astronomy that emerged in the twentieth century only after hundreds of years of scientific experimentation,[20] these excerpts do not show us what traditional knowledge has *added* to our understanding of these scientific fields. All the quotations from Little Bear do is make the dubious claim, on the basis of the unsubstantiated and vague arguments of one Native studies professor who has no background in physics,[21] that Aboriginal conceptions are *similar* to current scientific theories.[22] The case of the Akwesasne Science and Mathematics project is also not very helpful since it is not clear what the "teachings of the four winds" consist of, or how Haudenosaunee "cosmos mythology" improves our understanding of astronomy.[23]

Similarly questionable claims are made with respect to the "valuable insights" that traditional knowledge has provided to the field of biology. Although it is noted that "there is increasing interest in integrating traditional knowledge with the knowledge of biologists, botanists, climatologists and others in deliberations about environmental regulation" and "growing legitimacy for these ideas," it is also pointed out that "just what is involved in integrating the two forms of knowledge is still a matter of some uncertainty, although various attempts have been made" (RCAP, 1996, Vol. 4, pp. 456–457). There is no explanation of what these "attempts" consisted of, however, except that "the views and knowledge" of certain Aboriginal groups have been "considered." All we are provided with is the vague assertion that "the credibility of native hunters as accurate interpreters of nature has become more widely accepted" (Milton Freeman as cited in RCAP, 1996, Vol. 4, p. 457).

The one specific reference concerns Aboriginal classification systems of plants and animals. According to RCAP (1996), the insights from these systems supposedly pertain to the fact that Aboriginal people "need to gain knowledge of the land by direct experience," enabling "individuals to see relationships connecting phenomena rather than discrete objects" (p. 640). As a result, RCAP (1996) maintains that "the skills to observe and the expertise to describe reality in ecological terms constitute part of the knowledge that elders possess to an exceptional degree," but they have "begun to find a place in the classification systems of western science only recently" (Vol. 1, p. 640).

The evidence RCAP (1996) provides as support for this is a 1990 study prepared by Douglas Nakashima for the Canadian Environmental Assessment Research Council that discusses the "Inuit system of classifying animals according to their relationships within the ecosystem as a whole" (Vol. 4, pp. 139–140). The study maintains that "although ecological classification is a relatively recent development in the Western scientific tradition, it has long been a fundamental organizing principle for the traditional Inuit taxonomy" (RCAP, 1996, Vol. 4, pp. 139–140). It also argues that this system "reveals a strong ecological logic and reflects a dichotomy of land and sea which is a central theme in traditional Inuit mythology and world-view," resulting in the categorization of plants and animals as to whether they "rise to the surface," "walk," or are large birds, small birds, "large motile fish," or bottom-dwelling organisms (RCAP, 1996, Vol. 4, pp. 139–140).

Dividing organisms in this way, the report argues, is beneficial because it "directly reflects the Inuit world view," and this "will advance our understanding of arctic ecosystems and improve our ability to protect them" (RCAP, 1996, Vol. 4, pp. 139–140). But it is not shown how this is the case. The only evidence offered for improving the protection of ecosystems is the concern of elders that current economic processes are destroying the earth—a sentiment that could exist regardless of the classification system used. It is also not apparent how such a system would "advance our understanding of arctic ecosystems." What is to be gained, from a biologist's standpoint, by classifying animals according to whether or not they "rise to the surface" or "walk"? "Walking" is a characteristic of a large number of animals, and if scientists classified them according to this attribute, we would have a nebulous category of thousands of organisms with diverse characteristics. Even more problematic is the last category— "bottom-dwelling marine organisms, that includes fish, clams, sea urchins and seaweeds [sic]" (RCAP, 1996, Vol. 4, pp. 139–140). How would biology's "understanding of arctic ecosystems" be advanced by using this kind of system? These categorizations, in fact, obviously would be useful only in the context of Inuit subsistence.[24] Animals rising to the surface are perceived differently from "those that walk" because of the hunting methods required.[25]

A similar lack of substantiation occurs with respect to many of the arguments that RCAP makes about another kind of traditional knowledge that it believes will improve education today—Aboriginal "insights" into the field of medicine. This area, in fact, is the most extensively discussed in RCAP's report, where there are numerous references to the importance of "traditional medicine" or "traditional healing."[26] RCAP maintains that one of the major mechanisms to combat ill health in Aboriginal communities, and to some extent in the wider society,[27] is through the use of traditional medicine and traditional healers.[28] This was not only because Aboriginal peoples themselves believe that traditional medicine is effective in alleviating their health problems; RCAP (1996) also assumes that the "concepts and understandings" in traditional healing "are affirmed by the leading edge of scientific research on the determinants of health" (Vol. 3,

p. 215). It notes that "for Aboriginal people, the conviction that they have a contribution to make [to enhanced health] is deeply held and a source of strength," and it will elucidate "the solid ground on which this belief stands" (RCAP, 1996, Vol. 3, p. 202).

The report, however, provides little evidence to sustain this argument. Most of its support for the importance of Aboriginal health and healing consists of quotations from Aboriginal people themselves;[29] even descriptions of what traditional healing entails are hard to find. In its chapter on "Health and Healing," for example, there are only five cases of "traditional healing" put forward—spiritual ceremonies, using the principles of the aforementioned Medicine Wheel; diabetes prevention programs; midwifery; and traditional herbs.

These five cases, however, would in no way be considered to be on the "leading edge of scientific research." The unscientific spiritual ceremonies and Medicine Wheel were discussed earlier in this chapter. Diabetes prevention concerns communicating in a manner consistent with Aboriginal cultures,[30] and midwifery simply involves making childbirth more family-oriented and less of a medical procedure.[31] The final case—the use of the medicines of "traditional healers" or Native "pharmacology"—on the surface appears to offer some promise for making a contribution to scientific medical education, as it concerns the historical use of various herbs by Aboriginal peoples to cure ailments.[32] But RCAP offers no evidence that this "herbal lore" is on the "leading edge of scientific research."[33] The "methodology" was generations of trial and error that enabled Aboriginal peoples to discover certain remedies that have had beneficial health effects. RCAP (1996) also notes a number of unscientific practices involving the use of plants in spiritual ceremonies,[34] including burning sweetgrass and smoking tobacco.

Despite RCAP's enthusiastic promotion of the benefits of "traditional healing," therefore, there is really not much support for its claims that this "knowledge" will facilitate Aboriginal participation in the field of medicine or improve educational processes. This view, in fact, is expressed in one of the studies prepared for RCAP that asserts that "there is little scientific evidence for or against the efficacy of current treatment programs based on traditional Aboriginal healing practices" (Kirmayer et al., 1997).

Consequently, in all the areas where RCAP refers to "traditional knowledge" as making important contributions to education, there is little evidence that it has enhanced scientific research and educational processes. This is why, as RCAP (1996) itself acknowledges, "scientific scepticism" is one of the "barriers to the integration of traditional knowledge" into modern research and educational systems. It maintains that "scientists are sceptical about the credibility or reliability of aboriginal information gathered through interviews, preferring 'hard' data such as biophysical data. Some may dismiss Aboriginal knowledge as subjective, anecdotal and unscientific" (RCAP, 1996, Vol. 4, p. 457). RCAP (1996) also notes that "the gatekeepers of western intellectual traditions have repeatedly dismissed traditional knowledge as inconsequential and unfounded" (Vol. 3, p. 526). Rather than delving into these criticisms, however, RCAP just dismisses them as prejudicial attitudes. It maintains that these "gatekeepers" have "failed to recognize" that "[western] knowledge building is also defined by culture and that Aboriginal intellectual traditions operate from a different but equally valid way of construing the world" (RCAP, 1996, Vol. 3, 526).

What RCAP's analysis of traditional knowledge actually does is deny the developmental gap that exists between traditional views of the world and modern understanding. This denial that knowledge develops with technological advancements such as literacy and numeracy is common in current examinations of Aboriginal educational policy. This obscures the nature of the educational problems that many Aboriginal peoples are currently experiencing. Because hunting and gathering/horticultural societies lack a culture of literacy, incorporating Aboriginal traditions will not facilitate the values, skills, and attitudes that Aboriginal people will need to obtain a scientific understanding of the world and participate fully in modern societies. It is generally recognized that it is inappropriate to uncritically teach what our ancestors believed five hundred years ago, but this is not the case with respect to the Native population. The result is to keep Aboriginal people isolated from the scientific developments that have occurred in the rest of the world.

Native Studies: Hiding the Educational Deficit

The denial that there is a developmental gap between Aboriginal traditions and modern educational requirements has created a problem for post-secondary educational programs. Students who have not acquired the knowledge needed in the school system now do not have the prerequisites necessary for successfully completing university programs. Because there is political pressure to increase the number of university-educated Aboriginal people, the result is the development of a number of initiatives to hide the educational deficits of Native students. The most significant is the development of an entirely separate academic field known as Native studies.

The lack of rigour in Native studies is hidden by arguments that Aboriginal cultures have worldviews that must be perpetuated or reclaimed, and that questioning them amounts to "colonialism" (Riding In, 2008, p. 65), therefore theories and methodologies should be developed that place "Indian spirituality, worldviews, cultural values, origin stories, oral histories, and beliefs at the center of analysis" (Riding In, 2008, p. 65). These different theories and methodologies have been excluded from universities historically because of alleged racist attitudes and practices that are intent on keeping Aboriginal people subordinate. The development of Native studies programs is promoted because they are perceived as enabling the interests and values of Native communities to achieve the representation they have been denied historically (Riding In & Pexa, 2005, p. 5).

This representation is important, it is argued, because it enables the actual circumstances of Aboriginal people to be more accurately represented in universities. Stress is placed on the fact that Aboriginal people are not like other ethnic minorities. They are the original inhabitants of the Americas and have a treaty relationship (in the case of the United States and Canada) with governments. Their aim is not for increased representation within the wider society but in preserving their traditions and maintaining Native sovereignty (Riding In & Pexa, 2005, p. 11). Because Aboriginal histories and goals are unique, advocates assert, Native studies is necessary to give full recognition to the specificity of Native circumstances.

As well as helping to underline the uniqueness of Aboriginal circumstances, Native studies is claimed to support the interests and values of the Native population by promoting the political agenda of Aboriginal organizations. As Elizabeth Cook-Lynn (2005) points out, "the thrust of Indian studies was to form an educational strategy in the defense of tribal nations, the defense of land and native rights" (p. 182). This largely involves promoting scholarship that affirms Aboriginal tribes' historical sovereignty and the preservation of Aboriginal traditions in the future (Cook-Lynn, 2005, p. 186). It also encourages presumptive research to enhance the self-esteem of Aboriginal peoples. As Devon Mihesuah (2003) points out, Aboriginal students "want to hear that they have rich histories and cultures and that the mean stereotypes they see and hear everyday are fabrications designed to make the colonizers feel better" (p. 463). This, according to Mihesuah (2003), will "help students respect themselves so that they in turn can assist their communities" (p. 465).

But why does the fact that Native circumstances are "different" mean that completely unique theories and methodologies must be developed to understand them? And why is it assumed that an Aboriginal person has a particular worldview in the first place? There are different cultures throughout the world, and yet it is not suggested that all Chinese or African people have immutable philosophies that must be maintained by completely separate disciplines such as Chinese archaeology or African political science. To understand what makes Aboriginal circumstances different from other cultures, in fact, requires a common frame of reference. If not, how can it be generally accepted that Aboriginal circumstances are unique? For this argument to be sustained, there has to be a common understanding of other cultures and how their circumstances, values, and interests differ from those of Aboriginal people. This common understanding is made possible by methods that value objectivity and avoid rationalization.

In addition to the problem of demanding unique approaches for developing a common understanding of human differences, it is not clear why the theories and methodologies that are used in other disciplines are seen as being contrary to Aboriginal values and interests. Although there may be stereotypes that exist in disciplines outside of Native studies, does not the solution to this problem lie in changing these inaccurate characterizations? And why is the self-esteem of Aboriginal people today seen as being influenced by the description of their ancestors? Should the Holocaust in Nazi Germany or the Spanish Inquisition be eliminated from the curriculum because of the possibility that this might damage the self-esteem of Spanish or German youth?

The disciplines in modern universities exist to increase human understanding, and questions must be raised about the extent to which Native studies programs are able to contribute to this endeavour. The development of theories and methodologies that are special to Native studies, in fact, has dramatic implications for the educational process. Many of the people who enrol in Native studies are Aboriginal, and they will be encouraged to embrace a number of ideas that cannot be supported with evidence acceptable to other academic disciplines. The real concern of Native studies is, in fact, advocacy, not approaching the study of Aboriginal circumstances in a multidisciplinary context. While this will perhaps support the political aspirations of Aboriginal organizations, it will not provide the Native population with the knowledge they need to become truly self-actualizing in the world today. It will lead the Aboriginal graduates of these programs to remain forever isolated in "Native only" areas, limiting their contribution to, and participation in, the wider society.

One of the best examples of such a circumstance concerns Native studies' response to the question of Aboriginal origins in the Americas. Because Aboriginal peoples' historical occupancy of land has implications for legal claims about land title, some Native political organizations have been opposed to the idea that Aboriginal people migrated out of Africa just like all other human beings (Friesen & Friesen, 2005, p. 43). And as a result of Native studies' relationship to political advocacy, pressure has been placed on the discipline to reject this idea. Devon Mihesuah (2003), for example, notes that she refers to Aboriginal people as either "Indigenous" or "Native" in her courses because she believes that both terms "imply that the people of this hemisphere were created here and did not migrate from the Old World" (p. 467). Cook-Lynn (2005) also opposes the teaching of the Bering Strait theory, responding to it thusly: "We know that the scientists of the world are unhappy with our views of the universe and their continued arguments are still out there. We in Indian studies will not give in to their failed imaginations" (p. 179). Michael Yellow Bird (Yellow Bird, Lujan, & Trujillo, 2005) even admits to feeling a little uneasy about a faculty member who had his class boycotted by Native studies students after presenting research that supported the Bering Strait theory. According to Yellow Bird (Yellow Bird, Lujan, & Trujillo, 2005), "on the one hand, I think [the boycott is] a very courageous and important thing to do. On the other hand, I think they lose the benefit of challenging that methodology and that individual. Whenever we shut down that kind of discourse, I think we shut down an opportunity to learn" (p. 193). Jace Weaver (2007) raises similar concerns when he notes that

> we [in Native studies] sometimes seem pushed into taking what is perceived to be the most "Native-affirmative" position on any issue, and to state such positions as absolute fact, any evidence to the contrary notwithstanding. From the Bering Strait and Native creation myths to Iroquois influence on the U.S. Constitution, we take tantalizing skeins and insist that they are bolts of whole cloth, when more nuanced readings would be more in conformity with the data while being no less affirmative of Natives and their agency. (p. 238)

Native studies' denial of Old World origins, in fact, has serious implications for the teaching of archaeology, the geosciences, and evolutionary biology. The academy generally rejects the teaching of Creationism as science, and the Genesis myth is not taught in Old World archaeology. Therefore, why should there not be the same response to the demands to integrate some Aboriginal peoples' unscientific beliefs into post-secondary education? As Steve Lekson, an archaeologist at the University of Colorado Museum, points out, "some people who are not sympathetic to fundamentalist Christian beliefs are extraordinarily sympathetic to Native American beliefs … I'm not sure I see the difference" (as cited in Johnson, 1996). Clement Meighan, an anthropologist at the University of California at Los Angeles, has noted that New World archaeology is now being threatened by the anti-intellectual sentiment that "Indians have a revealed wisdom that is not to be challenged, not to be questioned or investigated" (as cited in Johnson, 1996). This has resulted in attempts to "repatriate" prehistoric skeletons so as to prevent them from being analyzed by archaeologists. As Meighan insightfully points out, this trend actually has the most negative implications for the Native population because "it's their history that's being destroyed" (as cited in Johnson, 1996).

The idea that separate theories and methodologies should be developed in Native studies, therefore, supports the continuing isolation of Native people in the education system and their marginalization in Canadian society more generally. Instead of helping Aboriginal people to feel more comfortable in participating in universities, Native studies segregates Aboriginal people from the mainstream by not demanding the evidence and rigour expected in other academic disciplines. These lower standards obscure the educational problems that currently exist in the Native population, preventing evidence-based solutions from being adopted.

Overcoming Taboos and Addressing the Developmental Gap

Instead of hiding the educational deficits in Aboriginal education with "culturally sensitive" initiatives, there needs to be an honest recognition of the developmental differences between modern education and preliterate traditional enculturation. Once this is acknowledged, evidence-based Aboriginal educational policy development can begin. Because of the advocacy-driven character of Aboriginal education policy initiatives, and the resulting construction of taboos that constrain the recognition of developmental differences, addressing the educational deficits facing many Aboriginal people has not been effective.

There have been a number of evidence-based attempts to develop a culture of literacy in countries with deprived and marginalized groups, but the most effective, by far, has occurred in Cuba. Although there were no hunting and gathering tribes on the island, a large peasant population lived in isolation from the modern world and was mired by poor health, unsanitary living conditions, and low educational levels. With the success of the Cuban revolution in 1959, however, the government made a concerted effort to provide universal education and health care to its population. By analyzing the experiences of countries like Cuba, policymakers can better understand what is required to improve Aboriginal educational levels.

In the 1950s, under the oppressive Battista regime, half of Cuban children did not attend school, only 17% went to high school, and a quarter of the population was illiterate. In a United Nations address in 1960, Fidel Castro set the goal of eliminating illiteracy in one year. To accomplish this, he sent huge numbers of volunteers to the countryside to teach the entire population (including adults) to read and write. By 1961, over 270,000 volunteers were working as literacy instructors, and by December 1961, illiteracy had dropped to a remarkable 3.9% of the population. And once this basic level of literacy was achieved, the Castro government set on raising the level of the population's education to the sixth grade. Once 1.3 million Cubans had achieved this in 1980, the "battle for the ninth grade" began. Because of the socialist goal of raising the educational levels for the entire population, and concerted state action designed to carry it out, it has been noted that "the revolutionary reform of Cuban education from 1959 to 1987 must rank as one of the more extraordinary efforts in the history of education" (Padula & Smith, 1988, p. 135). Today, despite being a poor country, Cuba has one of the most advanced educational systems in the world.

Dramatic improvements were also made in the area of health care. To achieve this, the most backward rural areas of the country were targeted; instead of ignoring the countryside, doctors were sent to all corners of the territory. It was recognized in the early 1960s that people in these areas lived in squalor and suffered from illnesses such as tuberculosis, which were linked to poor sanitary conditions and inadequate nutrition (much like the circumstances in Aboriginal communities). Besides a "lack of economic resources, doctors and medicines," the Cuban government also noted that these conditions were aggravated "by the ignorance and superstition of the population who go to spiritualists and healers, thinking to find some remedy for their ills" (Padula & Smith, 1988, pp. 47–48). This statement was not made to insult peasant culture. Rather, it recognized it as a problem that needed to be overcome in order to improve the health and education of the entire population (Wald, 1978, p. 89).

Encouraged by the Cuban example, Venezuela, under the late President Hugo Chavez, established publicly funded education with an emphasis on universal literacy. The Venezuelan education policy adopted scientifically oriented programs, preschool access for children under the age of five, and a differentiation after grade nine to choose humanities or sciences for their continued education. It is important to note that the teacher profile is that they be "critical thinkers who can stimulate others and generate questions" (Brant Castellano, 2004). With an Indigenous population proportionally similar to Canada's, Venezuela's literacy rate is over 95% (Pearson, 2010). These modern approaches to educational policy provide examples of proven effectiveness far beyond the cultural-indoctrination character of the Canadian system.

It is these kinds of labour-intensive, scientifically based services that are needed to improve the educational levels in Aboriginal communities. Instead of promoting the incorporation of unsystematic teaching methods, preliterate languages, and superstitions into the educational system, it needs to be recognized that this misguided effort to raise Aboriginal self-esteem entrenches the ignorance experienced by all of our ancestors before they developed literacy and an understanding of the material nature of the universe. The work that needs to be undertaken in Aboriginal education policy is to determine the steps needed to bridge the gap between traditional cultural features and the modern world with the least trauma to the Native population.

The Cuban and Venezuelan examples above indicate that much can be accomplished when clear policy objectives are undertaken, but effective policy first requires an acknowledgement of this developmental gap. The government's role in Aboriginal education must move beyond that of a funding service and take responsibility for policy. Writing, controlled experimentation, logic, and mathematics are necessitated by the increasing productivity, size, and complexity of modern societies. To not recognize these fundamental features of human intellectual development is to deny it to the Aboriginal population, preventing many Natives from ever becoming participants in the modern world. This, of course, acts to keep things just as they are, reinforcing Aboriginal dependence on the various consultants and lawyers who make their living by keeping the Native population segregated and isolated from wider human developments (see Widdowson & Howard, 2008).

REFERENCES

Ashbury, D. (1997, November 24). Legal languages a world apart. *News/North*.

Beavon, D., White, J., & Maxim, P. (Eds.). (2004). Introduction. In *Aboriginal policy research: Setting the agenda for change* (Vol. I). Toronto: Thomson Educational Publishing.

Begoray, D.L. (2001, November 17). Reading tests flawed. *Victoria Colonist*, p. A11.

Brant, C.C. (1990, August). Native ethics and rules of behavior. *Canadian Journal of Psychiatry*, 35(6), 534–539.

Brant Castellano, M., Davis, L., & Lahache, L. (2000). Conclusion: Fulfilling the promise. In M. Brant Castellano, L. Davis, & L. Lahache (Eds.), *Aboriginal education: Fulfilling the promise* (pp. 251–255). Vancouver: University of British Columbia Press.

Butterworth, B., Reeve, R., Reynolds, F., & Lloyd, D. (2008a, July 15). Language without numbers. *Science Daily*. Retrieved February 2009, from http://www.sciencedaily.com/releases/2008/07/080714111940.htm

Butterworth, B., Reeve, R., Reynolds, F., & Lloyd, D. (2008b, Sep 2). Numerical thought with and without words: Evidence from Indigenous Australian children. *Proceedings of the National Academy of Sciences of the United States of America*, 105(35), 13179–13184. Retrieved from http://www.pnas.org/content/105/35/13179.full. pdf+html. http://dx.doi.org/10.1073/pnas.0806045105 Medline:18757729

Cajete, G.A. (1994). *Look to the mountain: An ecology of Indigenous education*. Skyland, NC: Kivaki Press.

Canadian Council on Learning. (2007). *Redefining how success is measured in First Nations, Inuit and Métis Learning*. Ottawa: Author.

Castellano, M.E. (2004, September 19). Revolutionary university. Znet. Retrieved March 2013, from http://www.zcommunications.org/revolutionary-university-by-maria-ejilda-castellano

Childe, V.G. (1936). *Man makes himself*. London: WATTS and Co.

Cohen, B. (1997). Health services development in an Aboriginal community. *For Seven Generations* [CD-ROM]. Ottawa: Libraxus.

Cook-Lynn, E. (2005, Spring). Keynote address: Indian studies—how it looks back at us after twenty years. *Wicazo Sa Review*, 20(1), 179–187. http://dx.doi.org/10.1353/wic.2005.0006

Dehaene, S., Izard, V., Spelke, E., & Pica, P. (2008, May 30). Log or linear? Distinct intuitions of the number scale in Western and Amazonian indigene cultures. *Science*, 320(5880), 1217–1220. http://dx.doi.org/10.1126/science.1156540 Medline:18511690

Deloria, V., Jr. (2001). American Indian metaphysics. In V. Deloria & D.R. Wildcat (Eds.), *Power and place: Indian education in America* (pp. 1–6). Golden, CO: Fulcrum Resources.

Demmert, W.G., Grissmer, D., & Towner, J. (2006). A review and analysis of the research on Native American students. *Journal of American Indian Education*, 45(3), 5–23.

Evans, M., McDonald, J., & Nyce, D. (1999). Acting across boundaries in Aboriginal curriculum development. *Canadian Journal of Native Education*, 23(2), 190–205.

Ezeife, A.N. (2006). Culture-sensitive mathematics: The Walpole Island experience. In J.P. White, S. Wingert, D. Beavon, & P. Maxim (Eds.), *Aboriginal policy research: Moving forward, making a difference* (Vol. III, pp. 53–66). Toronto: Thomson Educational Publishing.

Fletcher, C. (1997). The Innuulisivik maternity care centre. *For Seven Generations* [CD-ROM]. Ottawa: Libraxus.

Friesen, J.W., & Friesen, V.L. (2005). *First Nations in the twenty-first century: Contemporary educational frontiers*. Calgary, AB: Detselig Enterprises.

Hampton, E. (1995). Towards a redefinition of Indian education. In M. Battiste & J. Barman (Eds.), *First Nations education in Canada: The circle unfolds* (pp. 5–46). Vancouver: University of British Columbia Press.

Harp, J. (1998). Traditional parenting. In L.A. Stiffarm (Ed.), *As we see it: Aboriginal pedagogy* (pp. 67–69). Saskatoon: University of Saskatchewan Press.

Hatfield, M.M., Edwards, N.T., & Bitter, G.G. (1994). *Mathematic methods for elementary and middle school teachers.* New York: Wiley and Sons.

James, K. (2001). Fires need fuel. In K. James (Ed.), *Science and Native American communities* (pp. 1–8). Lincoln: University of Nebraska Press.

Jenness, D. (1977). *Indians of Canada.* Toronto: University of Toronto Press.

Johnson, G. (1996, October 22). Indian tribes' creationists thwart archaeologists. *New York Times.*

Kaufert, J.M. (1997). Health status, service use and program models among the Aboriginal population of Canadian cities. *For Seven Generations* [CD-ROM]. Ottawa: Libraxus.

Kewayosh, A. (Ed.). (1993). *Sociocultural approaches in diabetes care for Native peoples.* Ottawa: Assembly of First Nations.

King, H.C. (1955). *The history of the telescope.* London: Charles Griffin and Company.

Kinnon, D. (1997). Health is the whole person. *For Seven Generations* [CD-ROM]. Ottawa: Libraxus.

Kirmayer, L., Gill, K., Fletcher, C., Ternar, Y., Boothroyd, L., Quesney, C., … & Hayton, B. (1997). Emerging trends in research on mental health among Canadian Aboriginal peoples. A Report Prepared for the Royal Commission on Aboriginal Peoples. Montreal: Culture and Mental Health Research Unit, Jewish General Hospital and the Department of Psychiatry, McGill University.

Leavitt, R. (1993). Language and cultural content in Native education. In S. Morris, K. McLeod, & M. Danesi (Eds.), *Aboriginal languages and education: The Canadian experience.* Oakville, ON: Mosaic Press.

Leavitt, R. (1995). Language and cultural content in Native education. In M. Battiste & J. Barman (Eds.), *First Nations education in Canada: The circle unfolds* (pp. 124–138). Vancouver: University of British Columbia Press.

Macaulay, A.C. (1988, Jul). Diabetic education program in the Mohawk community of Kahnawake, Quebec. *Canadian Family Physician Médecin de famille canadien, 34,* 1591–1593. Medline:21253033

Macaulay, A.C., Montour, L.T., & Adelson, N. (1988, Aug 1). Prevalence of diabetic and atherosclerotic complications among Mohawk Indians of Kahnawake, Quebec. *Canadian Medical Association Journal, 139*(3), 221–224. Medline:3395936

MacIvor, M. (1995). Redefining science education for Aboriginal students. In M. Battiste & J. Barman (Eds.), *First Nations education in Canada: The circle unfolds* (pp. 73–98). Vancouver: University of British Columbia Press.

McNeney, M. (2002, Autumn). Making minds strong. *UVic Torch Alumni Magazine.*

Mead, M. (1965). *Continuities in cultural evolution.* New Haven: Yale University Press.

Medicine, B. (2001). *Learning to be an anthropologist and remaining "Native."* Urbana: University of Illinois Press.

Meekitjuk Hanson, A., with Otokiak, J. (n.d.). Language. Retrieved March 2002, from http://www.nunavut.com

Mendelson, M. (2006, July). *Aboriginal peoples and postsecondary education in Canada.* Ottawa: Caledon Institute of Social Policy.

Mihesuah, D.A. (2003, Winter/Spring). Basic empowering strategies for the classroom. *American Indian Quarterly, 27*(1 & 2), 459–478. http://dx.doi.org/10.1353/aiq.2004.0068

Miller, J.R. (1996). *Shingwauk's vision: A history of Native residential schools.* Toronto: University of Toronto Press.

Minogue, S. (2006, April 17). Iqaluit students lacking basic skills. *The Globe and Mail,* p. A9.

Montour, L.T. (1993, May 5). Royal Commission on Aboriginal Peoples transcripts, Kahnawake. *For Seven Generations* [CD-ROM]. Ottawa: Libraxus.

Morris, S., McLeod, K., & Danesi, M. (Eds.). (1993). *Aboriginal languages and education: The Canadian experience*. Oakville, ON: Mosaic Press.

Nadasdy, P. (2003). *Hunters and bureaucrats*. Vancouver: University of British Columbia Press.

Nakashima, D.J. (1990). *Application of Native knowledge in EIA: Inuit, elders and Hudson Bay Oil*. Montreal: Canadian Environmental Assessment Research Council.

National Indian Brotherhood. (1972). *Indian control over Indian education*. Ottawa: Author.

Ong, W.J. (1988). *Orality and literacy*. New York: Methuen.

Padula, A., & Smith, L.M. (1988). The revolutionary transformation of Cuban education, 1959–1987. In E.B. Gumbert (Ed.), *Making the future: Politics and educational reform in the United States, England, the Soviet Union, China, and Cuba* (pp. 117–139). Atlanta: Center for Cross-cultural Education, Georgia State University.

Pearson, T. (2010, January 27). UNESCO: Education in Venezuela has greatly improved. Retrieved March 2013, from http://venezuelanalysis.com/news/5107

Peck, E. (1925). *Eskimo-English dictionary*. Hamilton, ON: Anglican Church of Canada.

Price, J. (1979). *Indians of Canada: Cultural dynamics*. Englewood Cliffs, NJ: Prentice-Hall.

Richards, J., Hove, J., & Afolabi, K. (2008). *Understanding the Aboriginal/non-Aboriginal gap in student performance*. Toronto: C.D. Howe Institute.

Richards, J., & Vining, A. (2004, April). Aboriginal off-reserve education: A time for action. C.D. Howe Institute Commentary 198.

Riding In, J., & James Riding In. (2008, Fall). Presidential address: American Indian studies: our challenges. *Wicazo Sa Review, 23*(2), 65–75. http://dx.doi.org/10.1353/wic.0.0006

Riding In, J., & Pexa, C. (2005, Autumn). Editors' commentary. *Wicazo Sa Review, 20*(2), 5–13. http://dx.doi.org/10.1353/wic.2005.0022

Ross, P.E. (2004, Apr). Draining the language out of color. *Scientific American, 290*(4), 46–47. http://dx.doi.org/10.1038/scientificamerican0404-46 Medline:15045753

Royal Commission on Aboriginal Peoples (RCAP). (1996). *Report of the Royal Commission on Aboriginal Peoples [final report]*. (Volumes 1, 3, & 4). Ottawa: Supply and Services.

Ruscio, J. (2002, March/April). The emptiness of holism. *Skeptical Inquirer, 26*(2), 46–50.

Sagan, C. (1977). *The dragons of Eden: Speculations on the evolution of human intelligence*. New York: Ballantyne Books.

Saskatchewan Federated Indian College. (1997). Aboriginal post-secondary education Indigenous student perceptions. *For Seven Generations* [CD-ROM]. Ottawa: Libraxus.

School Community Safety Advisory Panel. (2008). *The road to health: A final report on school safety*. Toronto: Author.

Slide rule sense: Amazonian Indigenous culture demonstrates universal mapping of number onto space. (2008, May 30). *ScienceDaily*. Retrieved February 2009, from http://www.sciencedaily.com/releases/2008/05/080529141344.htm

Smith, M. (2001). Relevant curricula and school knowledge: New horizons. In K.P. Binda (Ed.), *Aboriginal education in Canada: A study in decolonization* (pp. 77–89). Mississauga: Canadian Educators' Press.

Smith, M.R. (1994). Scientific knowledge and cultural knowledge in the classroom. In K.P. Binda (Ed.), *Critical issues in First Nations education* (pp. 38–54). Brandon, MB: BUNTEP, Faculty of Education, Brandon University.

Sokal, A., & Bricmont, J. (1998). *Fashionable nonsense: Postmodern intellectuals' abuse of science.* New York: Picador USA.

Swan, I. (1998). Modelling: An Aboriginal approach. In L.A. Stiffarm (Ed.), *As we see it: Aboriginal pedagogy* (pp. 49–58). Saskatoon: University of Saskatchewan Press.

Taylor, J. (1995). Non-Native teachers teaching in Native communities. In M. Battiste & J. Barman (Eds.), *First Nations education in Canada: The circle unfolds* (pp. 101–112). Vancouver: University of British Columbia Press.

Tsioniaon LaFrance, B. (1993, July). *Culturally negotiated education in First Nation communities, empowering ourselves for future generations.* Paper presented at the National Round Table on Education, Royal Commission on Aboriginal Peoples, Ottawa.

Wald, K. (1978). *Children of Che: Childcare and education in Cuba.* Palo Alto, CA: Ramparts Press.

Weaver, J. (2007, Spring). More light than heat. *American Indian Quarterly, 31*(2), 233–255. http://dx.doi.org/10.1353/aiq.2007.0026

White, G. (2005, May 13–20). *Culture clash: Traditional knowledge and EuroCanadian governance processes in northern claims boards.* Paper presented at the First Nations, First Thoughts Conference, Centre of Canadian Studies, University of Edinburgh.

Widdowson, F., & Howard, A. (2008). *Disrobing the Aboriginal industry: The deception behind Indigenous cultural preservation.* Montreal: McGill-Queen's University Press.

Windschuttle, K. (1997). *The killing of history: How literary critics and social theorists are murdering our past.* New York: The Free Press.

Wolf, M. (2007). *Proust and the squid.* New York: HarperCollins.

Yellow Bird, M., Lujan, C., & Trujillo, O.V. (2005, Spring). Second panel: Reclaiming American Indian studies. *Wicazo Sa Review, 20*(1), 189–197. http://dx.doi.org/10.1353/wic.2005.0016

NOTES

1 Ezeife cites Cajete (1994), M.M. Hatfield et al. (1994), and M.R. Smith (1994). No page numbers are provided, and a cursory examination of Cajete's book (which has no index) does not show how this is the case. Cajete's book is mostly about Aboriginal spirituality, not science. It maintains, in fact, that "in traditional American Indian life, the foremost context for understanding is the *Spiritual,* the orienting foundation of Indigenous Knowledge and process. It is the spiritual that forms not only the foundation for religious expression, but also the ecological psychology underpinning the other foundations" (Cajete, 1994, p. 39, emphasis in original). Ezeife (2006) does point out that Smith refers to the case of the Skidi Pawnee who were supposedly "enthusiastic astronomers" and "actually so accomplished that they went as far as identifying and describing the planet Venus," as well as tracking celestial bodies so that they "conceptualized the summer solstice" and "predict[ed] reoccurring solar phenomena" (p. 46). The important question, however, is how this knowledge compares to those with writing and more technologically advanced astronomical instruments. Is Ezeife suggesting that this understanding of astronomy equals that found in more technologically developed societies?

2 Diamond Jenness (1977), for example, notes that the Inuit counting system consists only of differentiating between "one," "two," and "many" (p. 22), and Price (1979) explains that amounts in Inuktitut are clumped together in a way that makes simple arithmetic impossible (pp. 31–32). This is also claimed to be the case for Aboriginal groups in Australia and South America (see Butterworth, Reeve, Reynolds, & Lloyd, 2008a, 2008b). Astronomical instruments in the Old World include the antikythera mechanism, armillary sphere, astrolabe, dioptra,

equatorial ring, gnomon, mural quadrant, and triquetrum. For a discussion of some of these developments, see King (1955).

3 A survey taken of Iqaluit teachers in 2006, for example, notes that 13% of Iqaluit children do not have the skills they need when they enter kindergarten, and substandard skill levels increase to 22% in grade one, 28% in grade two, 30% in grades four and five, and 53% in grade eight (Minogue, 2006, p. A9).

4 See, for example, National Indian Brotherhood (1972, p. 10), Brant Castellano, Davis, and Lahache (2000, p. 251), and Royal Commission on Aboriginal Peoples (RCAP) (1996, Vol. 3, p. 462). Deborah L. Begoray, an associate professor and graduate adviser in the Faculty of Education at the University of Victoria also maintains that reading tests are flawed and should not be applied because they will reveal that Aboriginal students are lagging behind non-Aboriginals. Instead, she recommends "construct[ing] a picture of literacy abilities in B.C. which has depth and breadth" by "learn[ing] from our aboriginal community about the strengths of their children (for example, oral storytelling and reading the land) which are not revealed on any large-scale reading test" (Begoray, 2001, p. A11).

5 The Toronto First Nations School, for example, has instituted an "Honour Feather Society" to deal with low educational levels and suspensions. This initiative is described as follows: "at the end of each term, the school assembles to hear the announcement of the names of students who have been granted a feather. The feathers are small, metal pins that can be attached to a coat or hat. Students who earn three feathers are entitled to have their name engraved upon a small metal plate that is attached to a 'clan staff of honour'. An Honour Feather is attached to the staff, so that students can see that they have honoured their clan. Students earn feathers through good performance in the areas of academics, attendance, behaviour, promotion of traditional values, or the promotion of traditional language and culture" (School Community Safety Advisory Panel, 2008, p. 528).

6 It is noted that, in the case of the Toronto First Nations School, "students at the school rank last in the Board on Education Quality and Accountability Office ("EQAO") testing results" (School Community Safety Advisory Panel, 2008, p. 528).

7 Brant, a Mohawk psychologist, refers to this as the "ethic of non-interference" that is common in Aboriginal culture (p. 534).

8 RCAP (1996) links this circumstance to a historical absence of literacy in Aboriginal cultures. It maintains that literacy results in a "one dimensional … approach to knowing" because "persons schooled in a literate culture are accustomed to having all the context they need to understand a communication embedded in the text before them" (Vol. 1, pp. 622–623). This is different from the experience of preliterate cultures that are "taught to use all their senses" (RCAP, 1996, Vol. 1, pp. 622–623). These persons "may well smile at the illusion that words alone, stripped of complementary sound and colour and texture, can convey meaning adequately" (RCAP, 1996, Vol. 1, pp. 622–623).

9 This concern with promoting "respectful listening" has even led the University of Victoria to change teaching methods and curricula to "accommodate aboriginal traditions and values" (McNeney, 2002, p. 4).

10 A curriculum guide for the Sacred Circle Project in Edmonton puts it this way: "Elders emphasized listening and not asking WHY … A learner must sit quietly and patiently while the elder passe[s] on his wisdom. Listening is considered to be very important. Questions were not encouraged. Asking questions was considered rude. Clarification of a certain point or comments was considered okay" (as cited in Medicine, 2001, p. 79).

11 RCAP (1996), for example, notes that the "cycle of life" is broken down into child, youth, adult, and elder, yet no rationale, except for the importance of "four directions" is given for categorizing human beings in this way. The same is true for other Medicine Wheels that break down health into four categories—spiritual, mental, physical, and emotional—and the "cultural worlds" of

Aboriginal people (Aboriginal, between worlds, assimilated, bi-cultural). Even more perplexing is Figure 15.2 in RCAP's *Final Report* (1996)—"Anishnabe Teachings" (pp. 654–655). These "teachings" connect four virtues (sharing, honesty, strength, and kindness) with "animals," "tree," "rock," and "sweetgrass." This association is based on an elder's belief that "[the Creator] gave them sweetgrass, the tree, the animal and the rock. The sweetgrass represents kindness; the tree represents honesty; the animal, sharing; and the rock is strength" (Elder George Courchene, as cited in RCAP, 1996, Vol. 1, pp. 654–655). For further discussion of the Medicine Wheel, see RCAP (1996, Vol. 1, p. 647; 1996, Vol. 3, pp. 446–447, 476).

12 The problems of "lack of supervision" and neglect were also identified by government authorities in the late 1960s and early 1970s. See RCAP (1996, Vol. 1, p. 349, notes 99–102).

13 It has been discovered, for example, that preliterate languages, in general, tend to have only two to four words for different colours (Ross, 2004). Preliterate cultures, because of a lack of numeracy, also only have the capacity to develop "logarithmic mapping," unlike numerate cultures that can develop linear mapping ("Slide rule sense: Amazonian Indigenous culture demonstrates universal mapping of number onto space," 2008). See also Dehaene, Izard, Spelke, and Pica (2008).

14 The problem of Aboriginal language translations was shown in the book that I wrote with Frances Widdowson. In this book, two paragraphs on Aboriginal traditional knowledge had been translated by a government report into French, Dogrib, and Inuktitut. When these paragraphs were back-translated into English, large discrepancies between the English and the Aboriginal languages were noted. While the back-translation from French into English was almost identical, much of the meaning in the English text was lost in the back-translations from Dogrib and Inuktitut. For an elaboration of this back-translation experiment, see Widdowson and Howard (2008, pp. 205–208).

15 This circumstance became apparent in the Northwest Territories during the hearings for the proposed BHP diamond mine in 1996. At these hearings, numerous elders would speak in their Indigenous language, and a native speaker would translate this phrase as "no one can call me a liar when I say this." This statement would be used even when the elder obviously meant that they had an accurate recollection of the detail in question.

16 This comment was made by James Frideres during a presentation at Mount Royal College on December 1, 2008, in Calgary, Alberta, but he provided no evidence to support this contention. The assertion is questionable as all languages begin with nouns ("Mama" is often the first word uttered by children), and so it does not make sense to distinguish between "noun-oriented" and "verb-oriented" languages.

17 See, for example, Canadian Council on Learning (2007, pp. 5–7).

18 RCAP (1996) also notes that "traditional knowledge consists of a world view, organizing principles of life, laws of behaviour, and a knowledge of the sciences, from archaeology to zoology, framed and presented in a unique way through the power of the spoken word" (Vol. 4, p. 117).

19 It is also debatable that chaos theory is an offshoot of quantum physics.

20 This appears to be the view of a research study prepared for RCAP that maintains that Aboriginal students "had researched the teachings of physics, chemistry and biology, and they knew that ancient Indigenous scholars had studied these areas too. They had a sense of carrying on these traditions, and they respected professors who were able to teach these subjects in unique ways. 'They [the professors] demonstrate that the way Indians think is a legitimate way in its own right. It is just as legitimate as the so-called 'scientific' way'" (Saskatchewan Federated Indian College, 1997). This study then goes on to state that "students need to see Aboriginal faculty teaching physics, chemistry, mathematics, philosophy, engineering, medicine, psychology and metaphysics—all subjects

that were highly developed by Aboriginal peoples before contact with Europeans, and all subjects that are now considered difficult by mainstream society" (Saskatchewan Federated Indian College, 1997).

21 The physicists Alan Sokal and Jean Bricmont (1998) have examined similar claims within the humanities and social sciences more generally. They provide a detailed analysis of how the works of a number of prominent intellectuals such as Jacques Lacan, Julia Kristeva, Luce Irigaray, Bruno Latour, Jean Baudrillard, Gilles Deleuze, Félix Guattari, and Paul Virilio all "have repeatedly abused scientific concepts and terminology: either using scientific ideas totally out of context, without giving the slightest justification ... or throwing around scientific jargon in front of their non-scientist readers without any regard for its relevance or even its meaning" (pp. x–xi). More specifically, Sokal and Bricmont (1998) document how the sociologist Bruno Latour provides a "semiotic analysis of the theory of relativity," which "illustrates perfectly the problems encountered by a sociologist who aims to analyze the content of a scientific theory he does not understand very well" (p. 124).

22 It is often stated that Aboriginal peoples had knowledge of quantum physics or the theory of relativity, but no evidence is provided to show how this is the case. See, for example, Cajete (1994, p. 196) and Deloria Jr. (2001, p. 5).

23 This example is drawn from a research study prepared for RCAP by Brenda Tsioniaon LaFrance (1993). No information is provided in this report either to shed light on how this program enhances our knowledge of the world.

24 Another Aboriginal "classification system" with respect to plants contains "plant stories" where there are "long descriptions explaining when a plant may be used, the part of the plant used, the time of the year the plant is used, and so on" (Smith, 2001, p. 84).

25 Keith Windschuttle (1997) makes a similar point when he discusses Marshall Sahlins's use of the taxonomy of the Chewa people of Malawi, who do not classify domestic ducks in the same category as birds or even wild ducks, as evidence of "the existence of an entirely different system of rationality" from Western cultures (p. 280). Windschuttle (1997) notes that the classification system of the Chewa people is more of an indication that

> human beings who share the same rationality are quite capable of adopting a variety of methods for classifying the same things and a variety of ways of looking at things depending on how they intend to use them. Different uses generate different classifications. There is nothing surprising about a Malawi tribe that puts domestic ducks and wild ducks into different categories ... The big difference between our culture and theirs is that we *also* have a method of classification derived from the science of biology. In this case we classify creatures not from our own interest but from the relations we find in nature. In fact, biology is the most obvious example of a science that adopts classifications that derive objectively from nature, despite the claims of postmodernists that such a thing is impossible. Our scientific taxonomies of species are in no way human-inspired or arbitrary but, rather, correspond precisely to the patterns of reproduction we find in nature. If animals or plants do not reproduce with each other they do not constitute a species. This is a taxonomy that exists in nature and did so eons before the emergence of Western science; indeed, it would still have existed even if human beings had never evolved to discover it. (p. 283)

26 It also identifies "traditional healers" as a "wide range of people whose skills, wisdom and understanding can play a part in restoring personal well-being and social balance, from specialists in the use of healing herbs, to traditional midwives, to elders whose life experience makes them effective as counsellors, to ceremonialists who treat physical, social, emotional and mental disorders by spiritual means" (RCAP, 1996, Vol. 3, p. 361, note 1).

27 As RCAP (1996) puts it: "traditional medicine and healing practices are a source of ideas that may ultimately benefit not just Aboriginal peoples, but all peoples" (Vol. 3, p. 353). It also argues that the combination of Aboriginal and "bio-medical" knowledge offers "real hope for enhanced health among Aboriginal people and, indeed, enhanced health for the human race" (RCAP, 1996, Vol. 3, p. 202).

28 RCAP (1996) maintains that "in the face of continuing threats to well-being, effective action is possible—and already under way—by drawing on community strengths, traditional knowledge and creative use of professional services" (Vol. 3, p. 110; see also Vol. 3, pp. 290–293, 348–361 for RCAP's promotion of traditional healing).

29 RCAP (1996), for example, refers readers to three research studies to support its claim that "support for traditional Aboriginal healing and medicine was expressed ... from many sources" (RCAP, Vol. 3, p. 325). These include Cohen (1997), Fletcher (1997), Kinnon (1997), and Kaufert (1997).

30 One concerns an Ojibwa program, where the only detail provided of its "success" is the use of "the Ojibwa story of Nanabush and the Pale Stranger as a metaphor to explain the effects and management of diabetes" (RCAP, 1996, Vol. 3, p. 351). See also Kaufert (1997). Three other prevention programs mentioned include the Diabetic Outreach Program in the High Prairie region of northern Alberta, the "Walking in Balance Program" of the Anishnabe Spiritual Centre on Manitoulin Island, and an initiative at the Kateri Memorial Hospital Centre at Kahnawake, Quebec (RCAP, 1996, Vol. 3, p. 148). RCAP (1996, Vol. 3, p. 328), however, does not specify how these programs are effective but refers readers to the following sources: Kewayosh (1993); Montour (1997); Macaulay, Hanusaik, and Delisle (1988); Macaulay et al. (1988). Despite of the lack of evidence provided, they are used as support for RCAP's (1996) claim that "control over the design of diabetes prevention ... led to culture-based materials that increased their effectiveness" (Vol. 3, p. 207).

31 Although RCAP (1996) maintains that midwifery programs were instituted to recognize "indigenous birthing knowledge" (Vol. 3, pp. 134–135) and have subsequently led to "excellent health outcomes" (Vol. 3, p. 228), it provides no evidence that this is because Native midwives understand pregnancy and childbirth as much or more than "bio-medical" practitioners or non-Aboriginal midwives. Instead, it is due to the fact that, in the "bio-medical" system, "a woman must leave her family behind and live in a hostel for a two-week waiting period, then enter a hospital for delivery. She may find that no one speaks her language or understands her background. She may give birth attended by strangers. What was traditionally a joyous, even sacred event can be frightening and alienating. Her family and community are denied the life-affirming experience of sharing in the miracle of new life. The father, siblings, grandparents and other relatives are excluded from the birth and from the all-important first days or weeks of the infant's life when the bonds of love and responsibility are forged" (RCAP, 1996, Vol. 3, pp. 134–135).

32 RCAP (1996), for example, provided an assertion of Chrestien LeClercq, quoted by the historian Olive Dickason, that "Amerindians are all by nature physicians, apothecaries and doctors, by virtue of the knowledge and experience they have of certain herbs, which they use successfully to cure ills that seem to us incurable" (Vol. 3, p. 112). This was followed by the comment from Dickason herself that "the process by which the Amerindians acquired their herbal lore is not clearly understood, but there is no doubt about the results" since "more than 500 drugs used in the medical pharmacopoeia today were originally used by Amerindians" (RCAP, 1996, Vol. 3, p. 112).

33 The problematic character of this research area—often referred to as "ethnobotany"—is discussed extensively in Widdowson and Howard (2008, pp. 183–189).

34 Besides the use of plants, RCAP (1996) also mentions the spiritual ceremonies of sweat lodges, prayers, and fasting, which it maintains are important aspects of "traditional healing." (RCAP, 1996, Vol. 3, p. 224).

15

The Unintended Outcomes of Institutionalizing Ethnicity: Lessons from Maori Education in New Zealand[1]

Elizabeth Rata

Introduction

Education systems in liberal democratic countries with ethnically diverse populations face a common problem: how to increase participation and achievement by marginalized groups yet maintain the role of schools as integrating institutions for the national polity. In the 1980s, New Zealand education became committed to a bicultural project that was grounded in ideals of "difference in unity" between Maori and settler-descendants (*pakeha*). No institution was more influenced by biculturalism than education. The separate *kaupapa* Maori system from early childhood to tertiary education was developed in the 1980s and 1990s and a cultural approach was adopted for the vast majority of Maori students within mainstream education.

My purpose in this chapter is to compare the intentions of the early biculturalists with the present situation and to ask: What is the current state of the separate Maori education system created by the biculturalists? Has separate Maori education revived the Maori language? What about the achievement of Maori children? What is the situation of Maori children in mainstream education? And finally: What are the consequences of institutionalizing ethnicity in education for New Zealand's liberal democratic society? Although the intentions of the early biculturalists were to increase participation and achievement by Maori while maintaining the role of schools as integrating institutions for the national polity, I argue that biculturalism has led instead to the inclusion of ethnicity as a political category in state institutions. Undoubtedly, ethnic and cultural affiliation can be accommodated within liberal societies. This has been the case with religious differences through the separation of church and state and the use of secularism as the means to ensure the tolerance of difference in the public sphere. However, the elevation of ethnic identity to a political status removes the boundary between ethnic identification and political status. By doing so, that politicization of ethnicity corrodes the concepts of universalism and equal citizenship upon which liberal democracies are based.

The Politics of Culture

New Zealand, like other liberal democracies in the 1970s, rejected liberal ideas of integrating diverse populations into the social contract of the modern nation-state, turning to culturalism instead as a more socially just way to ensure the social contract. *Culturalism* is a premodern concept of social organization. It includes multiculturalism, biculturalism (the New Zealand version), and monoculturalism.[2] It is the idea that a social group's historical identity, which has a contemporary manifestation in various combinations of physical appearance, language, religion, cultural beliefs and practices, and so on, is the primary source of social belonging—one to be acknowledged politically. However, despite the rights discourse used to promote bi- and multiculturalism, and the racist discourse used to promote monoculturalism, all three forms are racial ideologies. This is the case because the criteria for belonging to the social group is set down in the genetic link to the historical group. In New Zealand, Maori leaders are quite clear about this genetic criteria (Mahuika, 1998). For example, "If you are born a Maori, then you have to accept the consequences of that biological fact, and the culture that comes with it" (Mead, 1997). As stated by Winiata, "A person who is 1/1024 requires only nine or ten generations ancestry to be identified with a full Maori. By contrast, a person who does not have one dot of Maori ancestry is unable to do this" (as cited in Tremewan, 2006, p. 110).

This causes one of several conundrums for liberals who support biculturalism. Efforts to gloss the race concept mean that there are two opposing official definitions of Maori identity. According to Statistics New Zealand (2005), *ethnicity* is the ethnic group or groups that people identify with or feel they belong to. "Ethnicity is a measure of cultural affiliation, *as opposed to race*, ancestry, nationality or citizenship. Ethnicity is self perceived and people can belong to more than one ethnic group" (Statistics New Zealand, 2005, emphasis added). Yet in an Orwellian separation of a word from its meaning and then attaching the word to the completely opposite meaning, the actual official practice contradicts the rhetoric and uses the genetic descent criteria. For example, a person must be a descendant of a Maori to be on the Maori electoral roll and education scholarships require evidence of Maori descent. This is not "ethnic identity of one's choosing."

The second conundrum facing biculturalists is the changing face of the project. Originally an attempt by the liberal Left section of the new middle class to redistribute New Zealand's considerable wealth to the marginalized—a group in which Maori dominated—biculturalism was propelled by a rights-based, redistributive agenda featuring a social justice rhetoric. For the first decade, what I refer to as *inclusive biculturalism* (Rata, 2008) was designed to bring Maori in from the margins of society, to give the liberal Left an ethnic identity as *pakeha* (a Maori term meaning white British settlers), and to revive the Maori language and other cultural practices. However, by the late 1980s, biculturalism had taken an exclusive form. It referred increasingly to a relationship between the corporate tribes and the government. The former emerged as major players when the Treaty of Waitangi settlements, originally intended to compensate for historical injustices such as illegal land confiscations and to benefit all Maori, were awarded to those tribes that could prove their existence in 1840—the year of the signing of the treaty (Round, 2000, p. 668). From 1987, the corporate tribes have developed considerable economic and political ambitions (Rata, 2011a) that have more in common with neoliberalism than with the rights-based social democratic agenda of redistribution. Tribal wealth is based on the privatization or proposed privatization of considerable public resources, including land, fisheries, forests, minerals, geothermal resources, the foreshore and seabed, freshwater, and capital infrastructure (Ministerial Taskforce on Maori Economic Development, 2010, p. ii). Tribal political ambitions now extend beyond the idea of a "partnership" with the government—an interpretation of the treaty that dates only to 1987—to proposals for a constitutional arrangement (Durie, 2009).

Those Maori for whom biculturalism initially received its support have not benefitted. Chapple's (2000) warning that the treaty settlements "risk being captured by the considerable number of Maori who already have jobs, skills, high incomes and good prospects" (p. 115) added to an earlier warning by Poata-Smith (1996, p. 110) and also to my own (Rata, 1996). According to Poata-Smith (1996), the emphasis on culture in the struggle for equality "resulted in a dramatic expansion of opportunities for middle-class professional Maori in the state apparatus, education system, health and the media," but has been "an unmitigated disaster for the vast majority of working-class Maori whanau [extended families]" (p. 110). The unelected Maori Statutory Board on the Auckland City Council illustrates the types of positions and remuneration[3] available to the middle-class professional Maori who occupy the structural positions made available by biculturalism. Indeed, the board's task of auditing the council's adherence to the Treaty of Waitangi exemplifies such treaty-informed work. In addition, there is a small and highly influential corporate tribal elite whose wealth is the direct result of the treaty settlements.[4] A third group of Maori are those in whose name biculturalism was first developed. These are Maori with no tribal affiliation who are "some of those most disadvantaged in society" (Gill, Pride, Gilbert, & Norman, 2010, p. 19). As a consequence of treaty settlements, inequality between the elite, the new professional class, and the poor has actually increased. Callister (2007) notes that "Maori living standards in 2004 showed increased within-group inequality" (p. 24) as the number of Maori in severe poverty increased, from 7% in 2000, to 17% in 2004 (Jensen, Krishnan, Hodgson, Sathiyandra, & Templeton, 2006).

The initial social justice redistributive agenda that first justified biculturalism and ensured support for its goals has not been realized, with the result that increasing numbers of New Zealanders are troubled by the adherence to the Treaty of Waitangi that is well institutionalized in New Zealand's public organizations and policies as a result of its inclusion in legislation. A 1999 survey of attitudes to the treaty and the Waitangi Tribunal found that the treaty "is a major point of division within the country" (Perry & Webster, 1999, p. 74). Only 5% of those surveyed "think that the Treaty should be strengthened and given the full force of law." (Perry & Webster, 1999, p. 74). "About 34 percent want the Treaty abolished" (Perry & Webster, 1999, p. 74). Ten years later, and despite considerable promotion (see, for example, the Treaty Roadshow that toured the country for four months in 2006), the Human Rights Commission's (HRC's) annual progress report on treaty issues for 2009 (HRC, 2009) found *declining* numbers who agree that the treaty is the country's founding document (a central idea of the latter period of biculturalism). A third conundrum facing New Zealand as a consequence of its adherence to exclusive biculturalism is the unintended consequences for education.

Maori Education[5]

Approximately 14% of the school age population are identified as Maori. Of these, about 84% are educated in the mainstream system while about 16% of Maori students are in *Maori-medium education.* This is where the Maori language makes up 12% or more of the instruction. Nearly 4% are in the separate *kaupapa* Maori education system where 80–100% of the instruction is in the Maori language. This Indigenous education system includes institutions for early childhood, primary, secondary, and tertiary sectors, and the production of Maori Indigenous Knowledge. Kaupapa Maori is committed to educating children and young people into tribal society and into Maori knowledge through the medium of the Maori language. For example, a recent Ministry of Education document states that "As Maori, tribal identity is paramount in development a strong sense of self" (Takao, Grennell, McKegg, & Wehipeihana, 2010, p. 15). "Iwi-specific [tribal] curriculum enables the child to know their [*sic*] place in the world" (Takao et al., 2010, p. 15).

Considerable claims are made for the success of the kaupapa Maori Indigenous system. According to three leading Maori educationalists, kaupapa Maori is successful in its goals of raising Maori achievement and reviving the Maori language. Smith states, "Maori have experienced a 25-year revolution and are on the threshold of a new wave of development and change" (as cited in Gerritsen, 2009, p. 11). "The significance of the transformation of thinking created by the development of Te Kohanga Reo [Maori early childhood language centres] was that, in the absence of organised resistance, there was enough critique to provide a counter hegemonic possibility" (Smith, 2006, pp. 250–251). Durie claims that "Maori participation in early childhood education and tertiary education or in health programmes would not have reached the heights it has if cultural frameworks such as kohanga reo had not been employed. The experience of the past 25 years is where a Maori cultural framework has been used; it has led to some quite major transformations" (as cited in Laugesen, 2009, p. 26). These claims are also found in Ministry of Education reports. Separate Maori institutions have "made a major contribution to the education system as a whole by giving learners a new means through which to achieve education success" (Education Information and Group Analysis/Group Maori, 2009, p. 2). "Recent NCEA [National Certificate of Educational Attainment] results confirm strongly the academic success of kura [Maori language and culture schools] graduates" (Takao et al., 2010, p. 18).

International agencies draw on such claims, using them in some cases to justify similar programs in other countries. For example, according to the United Nations Education, Scientific and Cultural Organization (UNESCO) report, *Education for All* (2010), "New Zealand's *kohanga reo* movement has demonstrated what a powerful force indigenous language revitalisation can be, not only for education but also for social cohesion" (p. 206). "The movement began in 1981 and thirteen years later there were 800 kohanga reo catering for 14,000 children" (UNESCO, 2010, p. 206). The Canadian Nunavut Project, in recommending that "a strong program of bilingual education must be adopted" for the Inuit of the Nunavut territory, proposes a model based on New Zealand Maori language tests (Berger, 2006, p. iv). The leading role played by New Zealand in developing Indigenous Knowledge and research methodologies is acknowledged by Weis, Fine, and Dimitriadis (2009) who, in referring to the "intellectual and political ascendancy gained by critical Indigenous scholarship which privileges local knowledge and cross-site Indigenous knowledges" (p. 438), specifically mention kaupapa Maori theorists G.H. Smith (2000) and L.T. Smith (1999, 2005).

However, the reality of kaupapa Maori education is at odds with the claims. There has been a huge decline in the numbers of children attending both the kohanga and the kura. The kohanga were established in 1982 and rapidly increased to 767 in 1996. However, by 2005 the number had dropped to 501, a decline that continues with 464 kohanga in 2009 (Education Counts, 2009a). Similarly, the number of students attending kura kaupapa Maori (primary Maori schools based on tribal principles where instruction is 80–100% in the Maori language) is also in decline. In the kura, the number of Maori learners dropped from 1,092 in year eight to 545 in year nine (Education Counts, 2009b). In addition, there is also a decline in student numbers in Maori-medium education (not kura kaupapa Maori), where 52–80% of the instruction is in the Maori language from 610 students in year eight to 257 in year nine (Education Counts, 2010).

The kaupapa Maori approach is also promoted as a successful means of addressing long-term Maori educational underachievement for students in higher education. According to Linda Smith (2006), "The achievements in Maori education have been determined if not remarkable. Maori participation rates in tertiary education are high and Maori educational institutions have proven to be sustainable and resilient in the face of inequalities in the system" (p. 251). *Wananga* (Maori government-funded tertiary institutions based on an Indigenous Maori approach) are promoted as the way to attract young

Maori males, who have failed at school, back into education by offering culturally appropriate basic education. There is a widespread perception that this approach is successful. According to media commentator, Garth George (2009), "There is a quiet revolution occurring in education throughout the nation and it is taking place in Maori-led institutions, the largest of which is Te Whare Wananga o Aotearoa" (p. A11). However, Paul Callister's (2009) research into the choice of tertiary institution, if any, "that have been successful at bringing young Maori men into basic level education" found that while "wananga as a group have overall achieved real success in attracting Maori students, both numerically and as a percentage of their overall rolls, they are attracting relatively few young Maori men in level 1–3 courses" (p. 13). Contrary to his expectation, Callister (2009) found that the nonethnic "polytechnic sector have been the most successful in enrolling young Maori men" (p. 13).

The long-term and ongoing underachievement of Maori, especially males (Clark, 2007), is a serious problem for New Zealand education. If ethnic or racial categories are used to differentiate student achievement, Maori students are at the bottom of the scale. According to Salmond (2009), "66 percent of Asian and 44 percent of European students leave school with University Entrance and/or Level 3 NCEA (National Certificate of Educational Achievement), only 20 percent of Pacific and 18 percent of Maori students gain these qualifications" (p. 5). However, the Ministry of Education continues to support the cultural immersion approach in Maori-medium schools. The results for year 11 students in immersion education are used to justify this support. "Year 11 candidates at Maori-medium schools were more likely to meet both the NCEA literacy and numeracy requirements than the other Maori candidates" (Education Information and Group Analysis/Group Maori, 2009, p. 2). The UNESCO report, *Education for All* (2010), also uses the year 11 figures: "Year 11 Maori students in immersion schools have recorded *significantly better* achievement rates than their Maori peers in English-medium schools" (p. 206, emphasis added).

Yet the comparison of Maori achievement in these schools with those in the mainstream system is not straightforward, with the UNESCO claim that rates are "significantly" higher not standing up to scrutiny. The only indepth comparative analysis of year 11 Maori student achievement is a study of the 2003–2004 results by Murray (2005), updated in 2007. This does support Ministry findings that there was "a higher rate of attainment for year 11 Maori-medium students" doing NCEA levels one and two compared with Maori in mainstream schools (Ministry of Education, 2005, p. 12). "Candidates in these settings were more likely to gain NCEA level two compared with their Maori peers in English-medium (mainstream) schools" (Ministry of Education, 2005, p. 13) and "candidates at immersion and bilingual schools (in 2003 and 2004) were more likely to gain a National Certificate of Educational Achievement (NCEA) than Maori candidates in English medium schools" (Murray, 2005, p. 2).

However, it is a matter of which statistics are used. Despite this comparison, other statistics show a problem. Murray (2005) also found that the "proportion of immersion school candidates to meet both the literacy and numeracy requirements was similar to the proportion of Maori in mainstream schools who met both requirements. In addition, mainstream Maori candidates were more likely to meet the numeracy than the literacy requirement" (p. 9). Of serious concern is the "low achievement of (immersion and bilingual) students in the science learning area" (Murray, 2005, p. 2). "Around half (51%) of the Year 11 immersion school candidates who gained an NCEA (at any level) achieved no credits in science subjects. In comparison, 88% of Maori candidates in mainstream schools who gained an NCEA gained some credits in science subjects" (Murray, 2005, p. 5). In addition, Murray (2005) points out that comparisons between Maori achievement in Maori-medium with mainstream schools need to be read with considerable caution. Given the small numbers of students in Maori-medium education, it is not yet possible to say that Maori-medium education offers greater success to Maori students. Indeed, the 2007 comparison is between only 509 year-11 students in Maori-medium and a much larger number (11,079) Maori at other schools (Education Information and Group Analysis/Group Maori, 2009, p. 26).

Murray is not alone in urging caution with respect to the statistics. Wang and Harkess (2007) note that from 2004 to 2006, years 11–13 candidates at Maori-medium schools were more likely to gain a typical level or higher NCEA qualification than their Maori peers at English-medium schools. But they, too, warn that the statistics must be treated with caution given that there are vastly more students in mainstream schools than in Maori-medium schools. I have included Wang and Harkness's figures because they show the extent of the difference in numbers, a difference that gives considerable weight to the need for caution in using the figures. Indeed, the difference is so great that the figures do not tell us anything useful. In Maori-medium education the figures are: year 11, 460–540 students; year

12, 280–340 students; year 13, 150–250 students. Maori students in English-medium schools are considerably larger: year 11, 11,394 students; year 12, 7,118 students; year 13, 4,115 students (Wang & Harkess, 2007, pp. 1–2). For these reasons, Earle (2008) has also urged caution in interpreting the statistics. In Earle's (2008) case, a comparison of Maori achievement at university found that "students from kura kaupapa Maori were somewhat less likely than other Maori students to pass all their courses" (p. 13).

Explaining Maori Education

There are two directly opposing explanations for the persistent low achievement of Maori students and subsequently for the solutions that are prescribed. One argues that educational achievement is directly related to the resources available to, and the family cultural practices of, people at the lower end of the working class or in the intergenerational unemployed. The second—the Indigenous Maori orthodoxy—argues that the cause of low Maori educational achievement is the result of unequal power relations established in the colonial period and remaining into the present day. In this section, I discuss the class-based explanation before turning to the culturalist understanding that informs New Zealand education.

It is important to note that not all Maori students are underachieving. There is "wide variation in the achievement levels within the Maori pupil population with the largest difference between Maori pupils who were high achievers and those who were low achievers related to the availability of educational resources in the home" (Programme for International Student Assessment [PISA], 2000, p. 21). It is likely that the increasing wealth gap *within* the Maori population (Callister, 2007) will affect education outcomes given that the differences in formal attainment between students from schools in different socio-economic locations suggests a strong link between social-economic class and educational achievement.

For example, 25% of Maori who left school in 2005 had little or no formal attainment, two and a half times higher than for pakeha (i.e., British descent) students (Ka Hikitia, 2006). The majority of those Maori students are in low-decile schools. (In New Zealand, decile categories are used to rank schools' socio-economic location, with low decile indicating low socio-economic location and high decile referring to schools in wealthy areas.) Twenty-one per cent of students from decile 1–3 schools left school in 2004 with no formal attainment compared to 6% from schools in the decile 8–10 band (Data Management and Analysis Division [DMAD], 2006, p. 82). Given the high proportion of Maori students in decile 1–3 schools (78,952 in decile 1–3 compared with 20,643 in the decile 8–10 range [DMAD, 2006, p. 60]), it can be assumed that socio-economic class location is strongly implicated in Maori educational achievement (as it is with all other groups).

A number of sociologists of education in New Zealand do support the socio-economic class explanation for the educational underachievement of a group of Maori. Research by Marie, Fergusson, and Boden (2008, p. 183) found that educational underachievement among Maori can be largely explained by disparities in socio-economic status during childhood. This supports earlier research by Roy Nash (2001) and Simon Chapple (2000). According to Chapple (2000),

> it is sole Maori with low literacy, poor education, and living in geographical concentrations that have socio-economic problems, not the Maori ethnic group as a whole. There are probably also sub-cultural associations with benefit dependence, sole parenthood, early natality, drug and alcohol abuse, physical violence, and illegal cash-cropping. In other words the policy issue may need to be viewed primarily at a sub-cultural and socio-economic level rather than the coarse ethno-cultural level of Maori/non-Maori binaries. (p. 115)

Wylie (2001) also noted that "While we found some differences in mathematics and literacy scores for children who came from different ethnic groups, most of these differences were reduced or were no longer significant once we took family income and maternal qualification into account. In other words, it is the resources available to children which matter to their progress, not their culture or ethnicity" (p. 31).

Roy Nash's family resource approach has spearheaded the class explanation over several decades (Nash, 1993, 2001, 2005, 2006a, 2006b). According to Nash (2001), the "bulk of the Maori population is located in the working-class, indeed, into the lower skilled fraction, and as a consequence of that has adopted, through processes of acculturation into specific class cultures, practices with a distinctive character" (p. 35). It is the link between the class-located resources available to families and the type of cultural practices associated with class location that has fuelled the often-heated debate among sociologists of education in New Zealand.

While cultural theorists support the view that resources matter, any suggestion that "practices with a distinctive character," especially cultural practices associated with an ethnic group, are implicated is attacked as "deficit theorizing." Chapple's (2000) description of subcultural factors was condemned in this way. Since the 1970s, Marxist sociologists of education, and their social constructivist "descendants" in the 1980s and 1990s, have joined with culturalists in rejecting what is called the "blame the victim" approach of deficit theorizing (Rata, 2010, 2012). Worse still was research that found fault with Maori culture itself. This was the research of the pre-New Sociology of Education era. For example, Bray (1971) had concluded from his research into delayed gratification that many "Maori boys among both higher- and lower-ability groups, tend to view their main goals as relatively immediate" (p. 75). His findings supported earlier research by Beaglehole and Beaglehole (1946), Ritchie (1963), and Metge (1967) that, as Metge (1967) notes, there is a "concentration of interest on the present rather than the future" and "a happy-go-lucky attitude to time and money" as "distinctly Maori" (pp. 59–60).

With the turn of the sociology of education to first Marxist New Sociology of Education in the 1970s, and then to the relativism promoted by postmodernism, social constructivism, and culturalism in the 1980s and beyond (Rata, 2010), explanations that found cultural reasons for poor achievement were soundly rejected. Deficit theorizing was now considered part of the problem. Since that time, the reasons for low educational achievement are explained using either a class or cultural determinism approach, with strict avoidance of any causes that could be laid at the feet of family practices, especially if those families are Maori. Accordingly, what determines poor educational performance can be found in the school's adherence to the white middle-class capital of the colonizing class, not in the family circumstances of the students.

Nash's attempts to introduce a more sophisticated explanation that recognized both the effects of class location, such as poverty, and the types of class practices associated with particular subgroups, particularly those in the intergenerationally unemployed section of the working class, continue to be rejected as deficit theory by culturalist theorists. In the current sociology of education climate in New Zealand, located as it is within the bicultural orthodoxy, any explanation that focuses on family practices as the problem is not just unacceptable to the discipline, but if those practices are related to Maori, they are considered to be anti-Maori racism.

The culturalist explanation for Maori underachievement is so far opposed to Nash's family resource explanation that it is difficult to believe that the same social phenomenon is being described. According to cultural theorists, Maori continue to live in colonial-imposed, structural inequality, expressed through culturally oppressive pedagogical relations between teachers and Maori students. For example, "what precludes significant advancement being made in addressing Maori achievement in mainstream education institutions, including teacher education institutions and classrooms, is that current educational policies were developed and continue to be developed within a framework of colonialism and as a result continue, consciously or unconsciously, to serve the interests of colonialism" (Bishop, 2000, p. 3).

Bishop, Berryman, Tiakiwai, & Richardson (2003) are quite clear about the reason for Maori educational failure: "The quality of the in-class face-to-face relationships and interactions between the teachers and Maori students is the most important influence on Maori students' educational achievement" (p. 190). Teachers who maintain low expectations of Maori students, or who fail to recognize their cultural identity, continue the colonial oppression. Roy Nash totally rejected this explanation. Using a quantitative study[6] that "Maori students have broadly favourable perceptions of their teachers whereas a Ministry of Education funded interview-based research study (*Te Kotahitanga*) has produced an exactly contrary finding," Nash (2006b) questioned the motives of the "Ministry of Education that presents such information to school principals as important and reliable knowledge" (p. 26).

Despite these strong objections, the official solution is the culturalist one—to recognize cultural identity by providing separate Maori institutions—the Indigenous Maori system of kohanga reo; Maori-medium primary schools, especially kura kaupapa Maori; and whare wananga. According to the Ministry of Education, these separate Maori institutions have "made a major contribution to the education system as a whole by giving learners a new means through which to achieve education success" (Education Information and Group Analysis/Group Maori, 2009, p. 2). For those Maori who do not attend a kaupapa Maori–type institution, in other words, the approximately 85% of Maori students who are in mainstream education, the solution is to change teachers' pedagogy. This is the reason for the Ministry's considerable and long-term support for the very well-funded Te Kotahitangi project being rolled out in New Zealand's secondary schools (Bishop et al., 2003).

Culturalism is an orthodoxy not confined to education. The hegemonic nature of these ideas throughout the country is most clearly shown in the favourable reception to a speech by the Maori Party's co-leader, Tariana Turia, to the 2000 New Zealand Psychological Society Conference. Turia (2000) evoked a "holocaust suffered by indigenous people including Maori as a result of colonial contact and behaviour," one that "inevitably wounds the soul," requiring "generations of oppression since colonial contact" "to be articulated, acknowledged and understood." The outcome is "post-colonial trauma" "passed down from the period of the Land Wars to current generations" (Turia, 2000, n.p.).

The solution to postcolonial trauma is to strengthen the essentialized Maori identity through cultural affirmation (Durie & Kingi, 1997). It is considered that identification with the ancestral group will enable the descendants to first acknowledge, then reject, oppressive experiences, and to benefit from the revival of precolonial, pre-oppressive cultural integrity. Yet research into *marae*-based courses found that this approach "does not support all categories of Maori people who are struggling with their ethnic identity" (Van Meijl, 2006, p. 930). Rather, it creates an unexpected crisis of identity for those Maori who are unable to identify in terms of cultural ideology, as they believe they can never meet the orthodox criteria for recognition as "genuine Maori" (Van Meijl, 2006, p. 930). Van Meijl (2006) suggests that "the presentation of Maori cultural identity is fundamentally different from the self-representation of alienated young urban Maori people" (p. 931), leaving the self of some Maori bewildered with their personal yet deviating notions of Maoriness.

Despite nearly four decades of the culturalist orthodoxy in education, the fact remains that a proportion of Maori children and young people continue to fail at school and spend their lives living with the consequences of this failure. The kaupapa Maori system has yet to prove it deserves its accolades. Indeed, it is likely that the kura are contributing to student failure as a consequence of the lack of English language teaching in the schools (Rata & Tamati, 2013).

All schools are legally required to teach English (Education Review Office [ERO], 2007a), yet this appears not to be happening in almost all of the kura. Of the 25 kura kaupapa Maori ERO reports written between 2005 and 2009, only three kura provided information on the teaching of English. Comments in the reports were minimal and did not provide information about the type of transition pedagogy nor the level of achievement reached by students in either conversational or academic English. According to one report, "there are high expectations that students, staff and whanau [extended family] will be multilingual in te reo Maori [the Maori language], Spanish and English" (ERO, 2007a, p. 10). The second stated, "[s]tudents in years 5 to 8 are learning the skills of reading and writing in English as a separate subject" (ERO, 2006a, p. 12), while the third report provided only slightly more information, saying that "[t]he whanau and staff fully support students to achieve full competency in the English language. Formal English language programmes are provided to students from year six" (ERO, 2006b, p. 14). This was followed by a brief description of assessment methods.

Despite the absence of any meaningful information about what English is provided in the kura, if any, the Ministry of Education document, *Te Piko o te Mahuri, The Key Attributes of Successful Kura Kaupapa Maori* states that "Successful kura continue to develop strategies for the teaching of English as a second language so that their children may become fully competent in both Maori and English. The willingness to continually develop English language programs has eventuated in clear policy and effective practice in this area" (Takao et al., 2010, p. 14).

The Maori Language

The commitment by biculturalists to the kaupapa Maori approach is further strengthened by the claim that Maori-medium education will revive the Maori language. However, as with the claim for improving educational achievement, the evidence is contradictory, even confusing, and suggests a less optimistic picture. For example, the Ministry of Education *Annual Report on Maori Education 2007/08* records the "research from Te Puni Kokiri (the Ministry of Maori Development) as showing 'significant gains across all language skills and most age groups. Overall, results show more people are actively using their Maori language skills at home and in the community. Overall, between 2001 and 2006, speaking proficiency rose 4.2%, reading proficiency rose 9.6% and writing proficiency rose 5.2%'"(Education Information and Group Analysis/Group Maori, 2009, p. 20).

But, in the next paragraph, with reference to the 2006 census and the Survey on the Health of the Maori Language, the Ministry report presents opposing evidence—strangely described as "highlights." Apart from a very small increase in "the total number of Maori who can hold a conversation about everyday things in Maori language, an increase of 1128 people from the 2001 census," the remaining statistics show a static or declining trend in Maori language use (Education Information and Group Analysis/Group Maori, 2009, p. 20). "One-quarter of Maori aged 15 to 64 years can hold a conversation in Maori language (unchanged from 26.4% in 2001)." "Just under half (47.7% of Maori aged 65 years and over) can hold a conversation in Maori language (compared to 53.1% in 2001)." The statistic that is worth noting, however, is that which shows a decline in Maori language use by younger people: "More than one in six Maori

(35,148 people) (16.7%) aged under 15 years can hold a conversation in Maori language (compared to 19.7% in 2001)" (Education Information and Group Analysis/Group Maori, 2009, p. 20). Given these statistics, it is difficult to understand the statement in the Ministry report that "the survey shows *significant* increases in the number of Maori adults who speak, read, write and understand Maori language" (Education Information and Group Analysis/Group Maori, 2009, p. 21, emphasis added).

The picture of Maori language decline is supported by Winifred Bauer's (2008) research. Bauer (2008) describes "a fairly bleak" picture of Maori language use in the home in 2001, with children who attend Maori-medium education "not particularly likely to respond in Maori: only 9% of respondents in 2001 said that under twelves spoke Maori half or more of the time" (p. 41). According to Bauer (2008), this "suggests that for the most part, children are developing passive skills, and if they have active skills, they are not taking them out of the educational domain into the home" (p. 41). Skeptical of a reported increase in 2006, she argues that "the overall picture is one of decline rather than increase in the younger age groups" (Bauer, 2008, p. 43). The children's stronger language is English despite total immersion education in the Maori language for the small percentage of Maori children in Maori-medium education. It is important to remember, too, that of the small numbers of learners in Maori-medium education, the majority are in schools where the use of Maori as the language of instruction is less than 50% and may indeed be at the lower end—closer to 12%.

Ethnic Identity and Ethnic Boundary-Making

Maintaining the culturalist approach to Maori education receives considerable support from the claim that the approach is working. Given this claim and the belief that because the numbers of Maori children are increasing exponentially, it is important to not only maintain the approach but to strengthen it. It is commonly accepted, indeed it is now a truism (e.g., Brooker et al., 2010) that "future demographic realities" (Ministerial Taskforce on Maori Economic Development, 2010, p. ii) point to a "browning" of New Zealand. According to the report, "in Census 1951 we were 6.9% of the population. In Census 2006 that had grown to 14.6%. Statistics New Zealand's future projections predict that in 2026 we will be 17% of the population. It is entirely probable there will be more Maori and Pasifika children in our schools than Pakeha [white] well before the middle of this century" (Ministerial Taskforce on Maori Economic Development, 2010, p. ii).

The social reality is far more complex. While the raw statistics state that the numbers of young Maori are increasing at a rapid rate, this may or may not be the case. As Bromell (2008) notes, "Maori are neither a homogeneous group nor a closed population—all Maori also have European or other ancestry, and around half the Maori population identifies as both Maori and European" (p. 41). This is the result of the widespread intermarriage that has occurred for about two hundred years, so that today "all Maori have some degree of non-Maori ancestry" (Butterworth and Mako, 1989, p. 1).

There is a range of possible identifications available to the population that identifies as Maori. Callister (2003) notes that "of all those who recorded Maori as one of their ethnic groups in the 2001 census, only 56% recorded *only* Maori" (p. 15). Indeed, it is quite possible that many New Zealanders identified with several ethnic groups including Maori prior to 2006, but the prioritization principle used by the Department of Statistics until that year meant that those who included Maori as one of their ethnic identities were automatically assigned to the Maori category. This would increase the numbers of Maori but the actual situation is less straightforward.

In reality, the situation is as Chapple (2000) describes: "Some people of Maori descent have a strong ethnic Maori identity; others have little or none. For some, their Maori identity is central to their lives; for others, different aspects of their social and personal identities … seem to take precedence" (p. 104). A study by Kukutai and Callister (2009) that asked young people who were Maori and European which main group they would identify with found that for those who were happy to pick a main group, over half picked European. Callister (2008) has also found that a Maori person with a "white" physical appearance is more likely to identify as both Maori and non-Maori, a group tending to be "socially and economically much better off than all other Maori" (p. 21).

For children in the education system, the allocation of Maori identity to those with Maori ancestry or to those who look Maori or to those who identify as Maori is a moving feast. The vagaries of allocation are captured in an education newsletter reporting on Ministry of Education views: "it is sometimes a difficult task for schools to identify which of their students are Maori" (*Team Solutions Newsletter*, 2009, p. 2). Many New Zealand families have Maori and non-Maori members (including growing numbers of people from non-European countries) and as Chapple (2000) found, "the majority of Maori ethnic children growing up today have a non-Maori parent" (p. 105).

Conclusion

This chapter has analyzed the claims made for separate Maori Indigenous education in New Zealand and argued that the claims cannot be substantiated. The question that needs to be asked is why, given the evidence and logic supporting the family resource explanation, has the culturalist one maintained its place as the orthodoxy in New Zealand education? It is an orthodoxy that pervades all areas of New Zealand public life. An example of the far reach of culturalism is Christopher Tremewan's (2006) critical analysis of New Zealand's Anglican Church's almost inexplicable division into three racial groups. There are other areas that suffer the same fate—in health, social welfare, and justice.

Any understanding of the reach of culturalism in New Zealand needs to consider the role of biculturalism as a secular religion for some and a means for economic and political advancement for others. Indeed, one role feeds into the other. The quasi-religious commitment serves to justify the extent of interest group advancement for the small group of tribalists who have benefitted from the cultural turn taken by the liberal Left since the 1970s. Biculturalism began as a progressive project based on liberal ideals of universal human rights. State institutions such as education were to be used to promote both the recognition of Maori culture and greater social cohesion. However, the inclusion of ethnic or racial categories within state institutions is outside the logic of liberal universalism. Once an ethnic category is included in state institutions, that category adheres to itself rights and status justified by the ethnicity itself. Therein lies the fundamental contradiction between liberal democracy and culturalism—a social group created in the past and organized according to the principle of status claims political recognition according to the universalist social contract. In the New Zealand case, Maori education provides a sobering insight into the unintended outcomes of a progressive liberal project aligned to the reactionary nature of ethnic politics.

REFERENCES

Bauer, W. (2008). Is the health of the Maori language improving? *Te Reo, 51*, 33–77.

Beaglehole, E., & Beaglehole, P. (1946). *Some modern Maoris*. Wellington: New Zealand Council for Educational Research.

Berger, T.R. (2006, March 1). *The Nunavut project, conciliator's final report, Nunavut land claims agreement, implementation contract negotiations for the second planning period 2003–2013*. Vancouver: Craig E. Jones, Counsel to the Conciliator, Bull, Housser & Tupper.

Bishop, R. (2000). Nau te Rourou, Naku te Rourou Maori education: Setting an agenda. *Waikato Journal of Education, 6*, 3–17.

Bishop, R., Berryman, M., Tiakiwai, S., & Richardson, C. (2003). *Te Kotahitanga: The experiences of year 9 and 10 Maori students in mainstream classrooms*. Wellington, NZ: Ministry of Education. Retrieved from http://www.minedu.govt.nz

Bray, D.H. (1971). Maori adolescent temporal values: Distance of goals perceived as important and of delayed gratification, as compared with Pakehas. *New Zealand Journal of Educational Studies, 6*(1), 62–71.

Bromell, D. (2008). *Ethnicity, identity and public policy.* Wellington, NZ: Institute of Public Policy.

Brooker, B., Ellis, G., Parkhill, F., & Brailsford, I. (2010). Maori achievement in literacy and numeracy in Canterbury schools. *New Zealand Journal of Educational Studies, 45*(1), 49–66.

Butterworth, G., & Mako, C. (1989). *Te Hurihanga o te Ao Maori: Te Ahua o te Iwi Maori Kua Whakatatautia.* Wellington, NZ: Department of Ministry Affairs.

Callister, P. (2007). *Special measures to reduce ethnic disadvantage in New Zealand.* Wellington, NZ: Institute of Policy Studies, School of Government, Victoria University of Wellington.

Callister, P. (2008). Skin colour: Does it matter in New Zealand? *Policy Quarterly, 4,* 18–25.

Callister, P. (2009, July). *Which tertiary institutions are educating young low skill Māori men? A research note.* Wellington, NZ: Institute of Policy Studies Working Paper.

Callister, P. (2003, July 3–4). The allocation of ethnicity to children in New Zealand: Some descriptive data from the 2001 census. Paper presented at the Population Association of New Zealand Conference, Christchurch.

Chapple, S. (2000). Maori socio-economic disparity. *Political Science (Wellington, N.Z.), 52*(2), 101–115. http://dx.doi.org/10.1177/003231870005200201

Data Management and Analysis Division (DMAD). (2006). *Education Statistics of New Zealand for 2005.* Wellington, NZ: Ministry of Education.

Durie, M. (2009, July 14). Pae Mana: Waitangi and the evolving state. Presented at the Paerangi Lectures, Maori Horizons 2020 and Beyond. Massey University Te Mata O Te Tau Lecture Series.

Durie, M., & Kingi, K. (1997). *A framework for measuring Maori mental health outcomes. A report prepared for the Ministry of Health. Research report TPH 97/5.* Palmerston North, NZ: Massey University, Department of Maori Studies.

Earle, D. (2008). *Hei Titiro Ano I Te Whainga: Maori achievement in bachelors degrees revisited.* Wellington, NZ: Ministry of Education.

Education Counts. (2006). *Maori medium education as at 1 July 2006. School roll report.* Retrieved October 6, 2009, from http://www.educationcounts.govt.nz/statistics/maori_education/schooling/6040maori.

Education Counts. (2009a). *Annual ECE summary report.* Retrieved January 11, 2010, from http://www.educationcounts.govt.nz/statistics/Māori_education

Education Counts. (2009b). *Maori medium education as at 1 July 2009. School roll summary report.* Retrieved October 6, 2009, from http://www.educationcounts. govt.nz/statistics/maori_education/schooling/6040/maori

Education Counts (2010). *Number of enrolments in Maori-Medium learning by highest level of learning and year of schooling at 1 July 2009.* Retrieved January 13, 2010, from http://educationcounts.govt.nz/statistics/maori_education/schooling/6040/5747

Education Information and Group Analysis/Group Maori [Ministry of Education]. (2009). *Nga Haeata: The annual report on Maori education 2007/08.* Chapter 4: Maori language education. Retrieved January 13, 2010, from http://www.educationcounts.govt.nz/publications/series/5831/3

Education Review Office (ERO). (2006a). *Te Aho Matua review report: Te Kura Kaupapa Māori o Te Hiringa.* Retrieved December 16, 2009, from http://www.ero.govt.nz/ero/reppub.nsf/0/A554EE7855153060CC2571EE0004EF54/$File/3100.htm?Open

Education Review Office (ERO). (2006b). *Te Aho Matua review report: Te Kura Kaupapa Māori o Tupoho.* Retrieved December 16, 2009, from http://www.ero.govt.nz/ero/reppub.nsf/0/8184B74FC28880F5CC25723E000CDDA4/$File/2377.htm?Open

Education Review Office (ERO). (2007a). *Evaluation indicators for education reviews in Te Aho Matua Kura Kaupapa Māori.* Wellington, NZ: Author.

Education Review Office (ERO). (2007b). *Te Aho Matua review report: Te Kura Kaupapa Māori o Te Koutu*. Retrieved December 16, 2009, from http://www.ero. govt.nz/ero/reppub.nsf/0/F0BE4C6CB1BC403DCC257324001534A6/$File/1153.htm?Open

George, G. (2009, July 2). The Maori education revolution is here. *New Zealand Herald*, p. A11.

Gerritsen, J. (2009, August). Wananga at the crossroads. *New Zealand Education Review, 28*, 10–11.

Gill, D., Pride, S., Gilbert, H., & Norman, R. (2010). *The future state, working paper 10/08*. Wellington, NZ: Institute of Policy Studies, Victoria University of Wellington.

HRC (Human Rights Commission). (2010). *Treaty of Waitangi in review*. Retrieved March 2010, from http://www.hrc.co.nz

Jensen, J., Krishnan, V., Hodgson, R., Sathiyandra, S.G., & Templeton, R. (2006). *New Zealand living standards 2004: An overview*. Wellington, NZ: Centre for Social Research and Evaluation, Ministry of Social Development.

Ka Hikitia. (2006). *Ka Hikitia managing for success: The draft education strategy 2008–2012*. Wellington, NZ: Ministry of Education.

Kukutai, T., & Callister, P. (2009). A "main" ethnic group? Ethnic self-prioritisation among New Zealand youth. *Social Policy Journal, 36*, 16–31.

Laugesen, R. (2009, October 10). It's about Whanau. *NZ Listener*, pp. 24–26.

Lourie, M., & Rata, E. (2012). A critique of the role of culture in Maori education. *British Journal of Sociology of Education*, 1–18. http://dx.doi.org/10.1080/0142569 2.2012.736184

Mahuika, A. (1998). Whakapapa is the heart. In K.S. Coates & P.G. McHugh (Eds.), *Living relationships—Kokiri Ngatahi: The treaty of Waitangi in the new millennium* (pp. 214–221). Wellington, NZ: Victoria University Press.

Marie, D., Fergusson, D., & Boden, J. (2008). Educational achievement in Maori: The roles of cultural identity and social disadvantage. *Australian Journal of Education, 52*(2), 183–196. http://dx.doi.org/10.1177/000494410805200206

Mead, S. (1997). *Landmarks, bridges and visions. Aspects of Maori culture*. Wellington, NZ: Victoria University Press.

Metge, J. (1967). *The Maoris of New Zealand*. London: Routledge and Kegan Paul.

Ministerial Taskforce on Maori Economic Development. (2010, May). *Iwi infrastructure and investment*. Retrieved from http://www.iwichairs.maori.nz

Ministry of Education New Zealand. (2005). *Ngā haeata mātauranga: Annual report on Māori education*. Wellington, NZ: Author. Retrieved November 5, 2007, from http://www.educationcounts.govt.nz/publications/series/5851/nga_haeata_matauranga_-_annual_report_on_Māori_education_2004

Ministry of Education New Zealand. (2009). *Ka Hikitia managing for success Māori education strategy 2008–2012*. Retrieved May 11, 2010, from www.minedu.govt.nz

Murray, S. (2005). *Achievement at Maori immersion and bilingual schools 2004*. Wellington, NZ: Ministry of Education.

Murray, S. (2007). *Achievement at Maori immersion and bilingual schools 2004 update for 2005 results*. Wellington, NZ: Ministry of Education.

Nash, R. (1993). *Succeeding generations: Family resources and access to education in New Zealand*. Auckland, NZ: Oxford University Press.

Nash, R. (2001). Models of Maori educational attainment: Beyond the "class" and "ethnicity" debate. *Waikato Journal of Education, 7*, 23–36.

Nash, R. (2005). Cognitive *habitus* and collective intelligence: Concepts for the explanation of inequality of educational opportunity. *Journal of Education Policy, 20*(1), 3–21. http://dx.doi.org/10.1080/0268093042000322801

Nash, R. (2006a). Challenging ethnic explanations for educational failure. In E. Rata & R. Openshaw (Eds.), *Public policy and ethnicity: The politics of ethnic boundary making* (pp. 156–169). Houndmills, UK: Palgrave Macmillan.

Nash, R. (2006b). Fancy that: Discrepant research evidence on what Maori children think about their teachers. *Delta, 58*(1), 15–27.

Orsman, B. (2011, February 9). Council's Maori board to cost $3.4m after budget blowout. *New Zealand Herald*, p. A1.

Perry, O., & Webster, A. (1999). *New Zealand politics at the turn of the millennium.* Auckland, NZ: Alpha Publications.

Poata-Smith, E. (1996). He Pokeke Uenuku i Tu Ai: The evolution of contemporary Maori protest. In P. Spoonley, C. Macpherson, & D. Pearson (Eds.), *Nga Patai: Racism and ethnic relations in Aotearoa/New Zealand* (pp. 97–116). Auckland, NZ: Dunmore Press.

Programme for International Student Assessment (PISA). (2000). *Focus on Maori achievement in reading literacy.* Retrieved from http://www.educationcounts.govt.nz data/assets/pdf file/0007/6973/pisa-00-maori.pdf

Rata, E. (1996). Goodness and power: The sociology of liberal guilt. *New Zealand Sociology, 11*(2), 231–274.

Rata, E. (2008). Educating for citizenship in a bicultural society. In A. St. George, S. Brown, & J. O'Neill (Eds.), *Facing the big questions in teaching: Purpose, power and learning* (pp. 51–62). Melbourne, AU: Cengage Learning.

Rata, E. (2010). A sociology "of" or a sociology "for" education? The New Zealand experience of the dilemma. *International Studies in Sociology of Education, 20*(2), 109–128. http://dx.doi.org/10.1080/09620214.2010.503060

Rata, E. (2011a). Encircling the commons: Neotribal capitalism in New Zealand since 2000. *Anthropological Theory, 11*(3), 327–353. http://dx.doi.org/10.1177/1463499611416724

Rata, E. (2011b). Theoretical claims and empirical evidence in Maori education discourse. *Educational Philosophy and Theory, 44*(10). http://dx.doi.org/10.1111/j.1469-5812.2011.00755.x

Rata, E. (2012). *The politics of knowledge in education.* London, UK: Routledge.

Rata, E., & Tamati, T. (2013). Indigenous politics and language provision in New Zealand's Maori schools. *Journal of Language, Identity, and Education, 12*(5), 262–276.

Ritchie, J.E. (1963). *The making of a Maori.* Wellington, NZ: A.H. and A.W. Reed.

Round, D. (2000). Judicial activity and the treaty: The pendulum returns. *Otago Law Review, 19*(4), 653–671.

Salmond, A. (2009, July 24). Open entry for Maori. *The University of Auckland News*, p. 5.

Smith, G.H. (2000). Protecting and respecting Indigenous Knowledge. In M. Battiste (Ed.), *Reclaiming Indigenous voices and vision* (pp. 209–224). Vancouver: University of British Columbia Press.

Smith, L.T. (1999). *Decolonizing methodologies: Research and Indigenous people.* Dunedin, NZ: University of Otago Press.

Smith, L.T. (2005). On tricky grounds. In N. Denzin & Y. Lincoln (Eds.), *Handbook of qualitative research* (pp. 85–107). Beverly Hills, CA: Sage Publications.

Smith, L.T. (2006). Fourteen lessons of resistance to exclusion: Learning from the Maori experience in New Zealand over the last two decades of neo-liberal reform. In M. Mulholland (Ed.), *State of the Maori nation: Twenty-first-century issues in Aotearoa* (pp. 247–259). Birkenhead, Auckland, NZ: Reed Publishing Ltd.

Statistics New Zealand (2005). *Statistical standard for ethnicity 2005.* Wellington, NZ: Author. Retrieved February 2009 from http://www.stats.govt.nz

Tahana, Y. (2010, March 19). Tainui leader fuming over double-dip insinuation. *New Zealand Herald*, p. A4.

Takao, N., Grennell, D., McKegg, K., & Wehipeihana, N. (2010). *Te Piko o te Mahuri: The key attributes of successful Kura Kaupapa Maori*. Wellington, NZ: Ministry of Education.

Team Solutions Newsletter. (2009, April). Issue 2. Auckland, NZ: University of Auckland Faculty of Education. Retrieved from http://www.education.auckland.ac.nz/webdav/site/education/shared/about/centres/school-support/docs/tsnewsletter-t2-2009-final.pdf

Tremewan, C. (2006). Re-politicising race: The Anglican Church in New Zealand. In E. Rata & R. Openshaw (Eds.), *Public policy and ethnicity: The politics of ethnic boundary making* (pp. 95–112). Houndmills, UK: Palgrave Macmillan.

Turia, T. (2000). *Speech to New Zealand psychological society conference 2000, Waikato University, Hamilton*. Retrieved January 28, 2000, from http://www.converge.org.nz/pma/tspeech.htm

United Nations Education, Scientific and Cultural Organization (UNESCO). (2010). *Education for all global monitoring report: Reaching the marginalized*. Retrieved February 23, 2010, from http://www.unesco.org/un/education

van Meijl, T. (2006). Multiple identifications and the dialogical self: Urban Maori youngsters and the cultural renaissance. *Journal of the Royal Anthropological Institute, 12*(4), 917–933. http://dx.doi.org/10.1111/j.1467-9655.2006.00370.x

Wang, H., & Harkess, C. (2007). *Senior secondary students' achievement at Māori-medium schools 2004–2006 fact sheet*. Wellington, NZ: Demographic and Statistical Analysis Unit, Ministry of Education.

Weis, L., Fine, M., & Dimitriadis, G. (2009). Toward a critical theory of method in shifting times. In M. Apple, W. Au, & L.A. Gandin (Eds.), *The Routledge international handbook of critical education* (pp. 437–448). New York: Routledge.

Winiata, W. (1988). *Response to Te Roopu mo te Whakatika I te Pouhere o te Hahi Mihinare. ANG139/1/6(1)*. Auckland, NZ: Kinder Library Archives.

Wylie, C. (2001). *Ten years old and competent—the fourth stage of the competent children project: A summary of the main findings*. Wellington, NZ: NZCER.

NOTES

1 This chapter is based on a presentation given to the Department of Education at Cambridge University on May 4, 2011.

2 A discussion of the three types of culturalism, including their similarities and differences, is available in Rata (2012, Chapter 8).

3 The cost of the unelected Maori Statutory Board to the Auckland City Council illustrates the positions and remuneration for professional Maori in local government:

Pay and expenses for nine board members $494,500

Pay and expenses for non-board members sitting on council committees $50,500

Staff costs $946,500

Legal, communication, professional advice, tikanga $470,000

Engaging and reporting to the Maori community $280,000

Audit of council performance relative to Treaty of Waitangi $175,000

Research on wellbeing of Maori $650,000

Council support services $369,000

Total $3,435,500

(Orsman, 2011, p. A1)

4 The third brokerage stage was the actions of these representatives in pursuing the interests of the two "partners." For example, brokering the transfer of

ownership of the Auckland volcanic cones and "untangling the claims in Tamaki Makaurau" (Auckland) (a process conducted away from public involvement) earned "Sir Douglas Graham $177,264 in government fees" (Tahana, 2010, p. A4). Treaty claims facilitator, Tukoroirangi Morgan "was paid $141,000 in director's fees as well as a $100,000 success fee for completing Tainui's Waikato River settlement. The Government also contracted Mr Morgan as a Crown facilitator to help move the iwi through the settlement process. Between November 2008 and March 1, 2010, the Office of Treaty Settlements (OTS) paid Mr Morgan $171,093.61" (Tahana, 2010, p. A4).

5   Extracts in this section are taken from Rata (2011b).

6   Nash (2006b) used data from PISA research and the Progress at School study.

16

Native Studies and Canadian Political Science: The Implications of "Decolonizing the Discipline"

Frances Widdowson

● ● ● ● ● ● ● ● ● ● ● ● ● ● ● ● ● ●

The desire for the truth is in itself a legitimate motive, and it is a motive that should not be sacrificed to gratify social, professional, or spiritual desires. Those who violate their own intellectual integrity, for the sake of values they hold more dear, corrupt the very values for which they make the sacrifice. To sacrifice intellectual integrity for spiritual yearnings or political hopes is sentimental and weak-minded, and to sacrifice it for professional ambition is cynical and ignoble. (Carroll, 1995, p. 32)

For a number of years, Canadian political scientists have expressed concern about Native dependency and deprivation. This concern is not limited to political scientists with a particular ideology; it is expressed across a wide political spectrum, and includes neo-Marxist arguments as well as various liberal viewpoints (see Bedford & Irving, 2000; Tully, 1995; Cairns, 2000). Even political conservatives, who oppose state intervention in the economy to redistribute wealth, are uneasy that a *particular* ethnic group continues to suffer from disproportionate levels of poverty, unemployment, and social, educational, and health problems (Flanagan, 2000).

With a few exceptions,[1] this concern has resulted in the conclusion that "decolonization" is the solution to Native dependency and deprivation. *Decolonization*, as it is currently defined with respect to Aboriginal–non-Aboriginal relations, is closely linked to what Alan Cairns has referred to as "parallelism" (Cairns, 2000, pp. 70–73, 117, 132). Also called the "Two Row Wampum" approach, parallelism is the view that Aboriginal cultures and the wider Canadian society should exist separately from one another, continuously reproducing distinctive economies, political systems, and worldviews.[2] Such a conception is opposed to the idea that cultural osmosis will eventually lead to Aboriginal and non-Aboriginal peoples becoming part of a larger, integrated, and species-oriented whole because it is believed that "individuals are born into [distinct] cultures, and they secure their personal identity through the group into which they are born. This is their birthright, and it demands the recognition and respect of all Canadians and the protection of the state" (Royal Commission on Aboriginal Peoples [RCAP], 1996, pp. xxiii–xxiv). The most racially segregationist account of this vision can be found in H. Millar's "Record of the Two Row Wampum Belt," provided approvingly as the opening quotation in an article by the Canadian anthropologist Marc G. Stevenson (2006):

> The Whiteman said, "… I confirm what you have said …. Now it is understood that we shall never interfere with one another's beliefs or laws for generations to come." The Onkwehonweh replied: "I have a canoe and you have a vessel with sails and this is what we shall do: I will put in my canoe my belief and laws; in your vessel you will put your belief and laws; all of my people in my canoe; your people in your vessel. We shall put these boats in the water and they shall always be parallel. As long as there is Mother Earth, this will be everlasting. The Whiteman said, "What will happen if any of your people may someday want to have one foot in each of the boats we have placed parallel?" The Onkwehonweh replied "If this so happens that my people wish to have their feet in each of the two boats, there will be a high wind and the boats will separate and the person that has his feet in each of the boats shall fall between the boats; and there is not a living soul who will be able to bring him back to the right way given by the Creator, but only one: The Creator Himself." (p. 167)

These assumptions about Aboriginal–non-Aboriginal relations have resulted in challenges to the discipline of political science itself. This is because parallelism promotes the recognition of Indigenous worldviews as an aspect of decolonization, resulting in some political scientists arguing that attempts to reach a universal understanding in the discipline have made it complicit in the oppression of Aboriginal peoples (see, for example, Ladner, 2000a; Alfred, 2004). Pressure has increased to incorporate "Indigenous theories and methodologies"— often drawn from the field of Native studies—so as to "decolonize the discipline" of political science.

But how do Aboriginal approaches to understanding politics and government differ from those that are non-Aboriginal, and how will incorporating the former into political science aid the decolonization process and address Native deprivation? In order to answer these questions, it is necessary to understand what Aboriginal theories and methodologies are and how they are perceived to be linked to decolonization. As will be shown below, however, the linkage between the use of Native studies' approaches and Aboriginal liberation is not self-evident; in fact, promoting Indigenous theories and methodologies can act to obscure the causes of Aboriginal dependency and entrench Native marginalization.

What Are "Indigenous Theories and Methodologies"?

In 2007, the political scientist Kiera Ladner presented the paper "Decolonizing the Discipline: Indigenous Peoples and Political Science" at the University of Alberta. In the abstract of this paper, Ladner argues that political science espouses a "western-eurocentric understanding of the world," limiting the acquisition of knowledge about Indigenous politics in this country. Incorporating Indigenous theories and methods into political science, according to Ladner (2007), would contribute to the "decolonization and destabilization of the discipline," thereby supposedly facilitating Native empowerment and liberation.

Arguments such as Ladner's have transformed the discipline of political science, and there is an increasing tendency for positions in Aboriginal politics to be jointly offered with Native studies. The University of Toronto, for example, advertised such a position in 2007. As it was to be located in both departments, the job description stated that "interest in applying Aboriginal methodologies to the study of politics" would be an "asset" (POLCAN, 2007).

While the use of Aboriginal theories and methodologies is promoted, their specific character often remains elusive.[3] When I asked the chair of the University of Toronto's political science department "what 'Aboriginal methodologies to the study of politics' are, and how these methodologies differ from non-Aboriginal methodologies used in political science," he was unable to shed light on the matter. He merely stated that *with respect to the job description, as reflected in our advertisement, we have found it best to let the ad stand on its own, without further interpretation, and invite everyone interested in the position to apply on that basis, framing their application as they see fit. (David Cameron, personal communication, October 2007)*

This response, of course, poses difficulties for applicants. If it is not known what methods are considered to be "Aboriginal" by the hiring committee, how can an application be constructed to increase the likelihood of a candidate's success? Surely the declaration that the use of these methodologies would be an "asset" indicates that there is some understanding of what they are and how they can contribute to political science.

One of the disturbing possibilities is that the University of Toronto's reluctance to describe these methodologies could be an attempt to avoid transparency in the hiring process; the vagueness of the job description enables the hiring committee to avoid accountability for promoting a methodology that could, if scrutinized publicly, be found wanting. The University of Toronto does not assume that other ethnically based "worldviews" are necessary for the study of, say, Chinese politics, and so why has it privileged "Aboriginal methodologies" in the discipline?

Despite the reluctance to identify the specific nature of Indigenous theories and methodologies, it is possible to investigate their distinctiveness through a review of the literature. This literature relates to the incorporation of Indigenous worldviews in a wide variety of academic disciplines, including political science. RCAP, for example, discusses Aboriginal theories and methodologies with respect to understanding history, which is applicable to all the social sciences. It maintains that there are actually two "conceptions of history"—one espoused by Aboriginal peoples and another by non-Native Canadians.[4] The main difference between the two, according to RCAP, is that while non-Aboriginal peoples see history as being "linear" in character, to Native cultures it is "cyclical."[5] More specifically, RCAP argues that these "conceptions of history" can be distinguished from each other in terms of four criteria: secularity, objectivity, conceptions of evolution/progress, and the sources that are used (RCAP, 1996, p. 33). It points out that the Aboriginal tradition, in conceptualizing history, "crosses the boundaries between physical and spiritual reality" and "is less focused on establishing objective truth and assumes that the teller of the story is so much a part of the event being described that it would be arrogant to presume to classify or categorize the event exactly for all time" (RCAP, 1996, p. 33).

One of the main distinctive characteristics of Aboriginal methodologies, therefore, is that they do not strive for objectivity,[6] enabling any belief about the past to be considered an Aboriginal "conception of history." This holds, even if it is contradicted by written records or archaeological findings. Furthermore, there is generally no attempt to reconcile contradictions *between* oral accounts (see Widdowson, 2006, pp. 75–134).

Eschewing objectivity is related to two other characteristics of Aboriginal methods referred to in the literature—the oral character of Aboriginal historical traditions and assumptions about the existence of a "spiritual reality." Both contribute to subjectivity because there is no way for spiritual beliefs and "legends, stories and accounts handed down through the generations in oral form" (RCAP, 1996, p. 33) to be verified as accurate by the wider academic community. When it is asserted, for example, that "the Creator placed each nation on its own land and gave the people the responsibility of caring for the land— and one another—until the end of time" (RCAP, 1996, p. 24; see, also, Ladner, 2000b, pp. 44–45), there is no way of determining that this is the case because the contention is a matter of faith, not evidence. The same can be said of claims that prayers, dreams, prophecies, and spiritual ceremonies are pathways to "knowledge" (see RCAP, 1996, pp. 617–618; 620; 632–633). As no "spiritual world" has been shown to exist, it does not make sense to claim that there are methods and theories that can access this realm and increase human understanding.

The use of oral accounts as evidence in Aboriginal methodologies also contributes to their subjective character (Ladner, 2000a, pp. 39–49). Although Ladner (2000a) "perceive[s] oral tradition to be a source of information which is superior to the written tradition" (p. 41), this assertion is completely without evidential support and fails to consider the added difficulties in using oral accounts. Unlike interpretations of the past using written records, "oral histories" cannot be "pinned down," making it possible for them to change dramatically over the years. As the anthropologist Alexander von Gernet (1996) points out,

> *a written document, while often biased in its original formulation, at least becomes permanent, as it is archived and "subtracted from time." The original biases may be compounded by the interpretations of the historian who makes use of the document, but at least the content remains unaltered and may be interpreted by other parties. (p. 11)*

In the case of "oral histories," on the other hand, von Gernet (1996) explains that

> a primary or "original" version (if such existed to begin with) is lost to modern scrutiny since it is replaced by later versions. What is left may be multiple layers of interpretations which have accumulated over time and a content that may only vaguely resemble an "original" oration. (p. 11)

This is especially relevant when one considers that oral traditions have been passed down through a number of generations; the longer the passage of time between an event and a recollection, the more likely the memory will be distorted by other events.[7] Such a problem exists even when mnemonic aids like petroglyphs or wampum belts are used.[8]

Oral accounts also present the additional possibility that they could have been completely changed from the original version after the fact (either consciously or unconsciously) to put forward a particular view of history.[9] This makes their incorporation different from the historian's use of written documents, since, as Keith Windschuttle (1996) points out, very little of the written record that is available for historical interpretation "has been deliberately preserved for posterity" (p. 221). According to Windschuttle (1996), "the biggest single source of evidence comprises the working records of the institutions of the past, records that were created, not for the benefit of future historians, but for contemporary consumption and are thus not tainted by any prescient selectivity. Most of these documents retain an objectivity of their own" (p. 221).

Bruce Trigger makes a similar point with respect to archaeological data. According to Trigger (1989),

> the past ... had, and in that sense retains, a reality of its own that is independent of the reconstructions and explanations that archaeologists may give of it. Moreover, because the archaeological record, as a product of the past, has been shaped by forces that are independent of our own beliefs, the evidence that it provides at least potentially can act as a constraint upon archaeologists' imaginations. (p. 381)

Although Trigger (1989) recognizes that the "propensity of value judgments to colour our interpretations" must be taken into consideration in analyzing archaeological data, he notes that

> the deliberate construction and testing of two or more mutually exclusive interpretations of data can ... increase the capacity for the constraints that are inherent in the evidence to counteract the role played by subjective elements in interpreting archaeological data. (p. 400)

This capacity of both archaeological data and written documents to constrain "Western-Eurocentric" interpretations is very different from oral testimonies, which are obtained specifically for the purpose of constructing history.

The "Western-Eurocentric" Promotion of "Indigenous Thought"

The subjective character of Indigenous theories and methodologies, and how these are reinforced by spiritual beliefs and oral accounts, means they cannot be considered "theories" or "methodologies" at all. There is no attempt to develop any kind of systematic approach for evaluating the evidence that is deployed to reach an understanding of the natural world. A spiritual belief, for example, is not a "theory," since there is no evidence that can be evaluated to determine its validity. And although it is often claimed that Aboriginal peoples have their own standards for evaluating oral histories, elaboration of these methods actually reveals a lack of systematic assessment (see Widdowson, 2006, pp. 87–91).

It is also difficult to determine why these worldviews are designated as "Indigenous." Does this mean that all Aboriginal people believe in the supernatural and that "the Creator" made their ancestors the custodians of "Mother Earth"? This is obviously not the case since a number of Aboriginal people do not accept these spiritual beliefs. Furthermore, many people with Native ancestry wish to become doctors, wildlife biologists, and physicists, and these careers require the use of methods that strive for objectivity.

Indigenous theories and methodologies also are not contrary to all "Western-Eurocentric" thought. One particular worldview of Western European origin, which has come to be referred to as post-modernism, enthusiastically embraces subjective Indigenous theories and methodologies. Defined by Alan Sokal and Jean Bricmont (1998) as "an intellectual current characterized by the more-or-less explicit rejection of the rationalist tradition of the Enlightenment, by theoretical discourses disconnected from any empirical test, and by a cognitive and cultural relativism that regards science as nothing more than a 'narration', a 'myth' or a social construction among many others," (p. 1), this particular conceptualization of the world has profoundly influenced many academic disciplines, especially anthropology, history, and sociology. It has also led to the development of a number of interdisciplinary programs—ethnic studies, women's studies, disability studies, queer studies, and, most importantly, Native studies.[10]

The support for integrating approaches from Native studies into political science is due to the belief that Aboriginal peoples' "subjective understandings of their conditions" must be accepted for them to be the "agents of their own liberation" (Simmons, 2006, p. 15). These subjective understandings, it is argued, will give Aboriginal peoples power by enabling them to become stronger and better able to resist colonization (Wilson, 2004). According to this view, colonization occurred because Indigenous worldviews were devalued, enabling Europeans to demobilize the Native population and establish sovereignty over them (Simpson, 2004, p. 377). As Angela Wilson (2004) asserts, "if Indigenous cultural traditions had been deemed to be on equal ground with the colonizer's traditions, colonialist practices would have been impossible to rationally sustain" (p. 360). This sentiment is found in the postcolonial writings of Frantz Fanon (1963), Albert Memmi (1991), and Paulo Freire (1998), who maintain that colonization requires the colonized to believe in their cultural inferiority.[11] Consequently, restoring the cultural pride of oppressed groups, including respect for Indigenous theories and methodologies, is essential for overcoming colonization.

In the case of Aboriginal peoples, preserving culture is seen as necessary for decolonization because traditional cultures are perceived to be an essential aspect of Indigenous existence (see Alfred, 2009, pp. 4–6, 9). This is related to the belief of a number of Aboriginal peoples that culture, knowledge, and spirituality are tied to their ancestry and are, therefore, unchangeable. Indigenous Knowledge is believed to be the "original directions given specifically to our ancestors" and that colonization is resisted "by carrying that knowledge into the present" (Wilson, 2004, p. 361).[12] It is argued that the "relationship with Creation and its beings was meant to be maintained and enhanced and the knowledge that would ensure this was passed on for generations over thousands of years" (McGregor, 2004, p. 389).[13] These assumptions, in fact, explain why some Aboriginal people are opposed to the "spread of white-minded thinking" within the Native population (Hart-Ross & Simmons, 2006, p. 26).

Aboriginal Subjectivity, Political Science, and Decolonization

The connection between Aboriginal subjectivity and decolonization, therefore, concerns the postmodern assumption that the liberation of oppressed groups can be facilitated by the preservation of differences, including their distinctive conceptualizations of reality. This argument is sustained by postmodernism's claim that all attempts to strive for common understanding are power ploys aimed at maintaining subaltern marginality. Bruce Robbins (1996), an editor of the prominent postmodern journal *Social Text*, for example, maintains that it is in the interest of oppressed people to insist that truth is socially constructed (i.e., not universal) because "truth can be another source of oppression" (p. 58). To illustrate this, Robbins (1996) notes that "it was not so long ago that scientists gave their full authority to explanations of why women and African Americans ... were inherently inferior" (p. 58).

But how can the claim that oppressed groups are "inherently inferior" be true? By linking the words "truth" and "source of oppression," Robbins appears to be claiming that there is convincing evidence showing that this is the case. Robbins's irrational claim, however, is made possible by the fact that he is misusing the word "truth." As Alan Sokal (1996) correctly points out (in response to Robbins),

> *claiming something doesn't make it true, and the fact that people ... sometimes make false claims doesn't mean that we should reject or revise the concept of truth. Quite the contrary: it means that we should examine with the utmost care the evidence underlying people's truth claims, and we should reject assertions that in our best rational judgment are false.*

Similar problems of logic exist in the study of Aboriginal politics in the discipline of political science. A number of political scientists argue that the Native population has been historically characterized as inferior, but this is the result of an incorrect analysis of many theories in the discipline (Ladner, 2000a, p. 3, note 3; Tully, 1999, pp. 416–417) and the erroneous assumption that attempting to scientifically evaluate a group's level of development is a value judgement intended to either denigrate or admire the culture being examined.[14] Consequently, these political scientists are politically opposed to theories that accept notions of historical progress and cultural evolution, such as neoclassical economics, Weberian sociology, and Marxist political economy.

What these evolutionary theories are actually arguing, however, is that humanity *as a whole* progresses with the increasing productivity of economic systems (see Widdowson, 2006, pp. 135–188). Increasing productivity, according to evolutionary perspectives, enables larger and more complex societies to come into existence, resulting in a number of political and intellectual developments. It is on the basis of the linkage between economic systems, institutional complexity, and advancements in human knowledge that these frameworks have been able to conclude that the cultures associated with hunting and gathering economies are less developed than those that have emerged in the context of industrialization.

But what has led to the inference, made by some political scientists, that societies with less productive economies are *inferior*? This, in fact, is an incorrect interpretation of the developmental theories currently used in the discipline. It is based on the assumption that these theories must be arguing that there is some biological (i.e., racial) reason for developmental differences, when they could be relying on environmental explanations. Marxist political economy's conception of hunting and gathering cultures, for example, is largely based on the writings of the anthropologist Lewis Henry Morgan, who linked human development to "enlarging the basis of subsistence" (as cited in Widdowson, 2006, p. 161). Morgan maintained that human beings around the world were essentially the same, and that cultural evolution involved advancements in controlling nature with thought processes that were universal; it was just the fortuitous distribution of various plants and animals, making technological advancements such as iron, the wheel, and alphabetic writing possible, which resulted in different rates of development (Morgan, 1974, pp. 3–21).[15]

Opposition to developmental theories also results from what Jared Diamond (1999) has referred to as "confus[ing] an explanation of causes with a justification or acceptance of results" (p. 17). As Diamond (1999) explains, "what use one makes of a historical explanation is a question separate from the explanation itself" (p. 17). In other words, recognizing the unevenness in development that led to European conquest does not mean condoning the terrible harm wreaked upon the Aboriginal population. Acknowledging that the developmental gap between hunting and gathering societies and industrial capitalism contributed to Aboriginal deprivation, on the other hand, can aid decolonization by addressing the roots of Aboriginal dependency.

The assumption that all evolutionary theories were invented for the *purpose* of expropriating Aboriginal lands, undermining Native political systems, and destroying Indigenous cultures (RCAP, 1996, pp. 260, 600–601, 695), however, has resulted in a reluctance to apply them to Aboriginal–non-Aboriginal relations in political science. There is a tendency to deny that there is a developmental gap, and assertions about the sophistication and complexity of Aboriginal political traditions abound within the discipline. With one exception (Dickerson & Flanagan, 2006, p. 8),[16] even introductory textbooks in political science do not discuss developmental differences between kinship-based systems and governance in modern nation-states.[17]

"Indigenous political thought" rejects developmental theories on the basis that they harbour the "false assumption" that Aboriginal political systems are relatively simple in comparison to those that developed in Europe (RCAP, 1996, p. 188). But there is no way for subjective worldviews to determine what is "false" or "true." Claims by Ladner (2005), for example, that the Mi'kmaq had a precontact "constitutional order" similar to the one developed by the British (pp. 936–937), that "Indigenous nationalisms are nationalisms with histories that pre-date colonization" (Ladner, 2000b, p. 36), or that "Indigenous ideas and practices contributed to how rights, liberty, happiness, equality, democracy, and federalism were understood by American founding fathers and institutionalized in the unique federal and constitutional system they created" (Ladner, 2000a, p. 8) are all truth claims, but none are supported with convincing evidence. They either rely on redefining "governance" and "nationalism" in a way that is not generally applicable in the discipline of political science, or they use oral accounts that could have been refashioned for political reasons.[18]

Political scientists like Ladner, however, are able to prevent their own truth claims from being scrutinized by arguing that their views are rooted in "Indigenist thought," and therefore any challenging of their veracity is an indication of "Eurocentrism." The tactic of name-calling is used to prevent exposure of the irrationality of Indigenous theories and methodologies. The result is that many of the arguments linking Indigenous perspectives to decolonization have not been critically analyzed. This has enabled ideas that actually maintain Aboriginal dependency and marginalization to be put forward under the banner of "decolonization."

Justifying Aboriginal Dependency and Deprivation

In political science, Indigenous theories and methodologies are largely supported because doing so is seen as aiding the decolonization of Aboriginal peoples. Academics who would not support, for example, holding prayers at political science meetings, accept this imposition when it is claimed to be associated with Aboriginal decolonization.[19] Canada's Native population has been terribly oppressed historically, and it is argued that recognizing and respecting Native culture is a harmless way to right past wrongs.

But, as Alan Sokal (1996) points out, in response to a British archaeologist, Roger Anyon, who maintained that Zuni spiritual beliefs were "just as valid" as archaeological theories based on evidence, "Dr. Anyon has quite simply allowed his political and cultural sympathies to cloud his reasoning." Sokal (1996) goes on to note that this is without justification because

> *we can perfectly well remember the victims of a horrible genocide, and support their descendants' valid political goals, without endorsing uncritically (or hypocritically) their societies' traditional creation myths. Moreover, the relativists' stance is extremely condescending; it treats a complex society as a monolith, obscures the conflicts within it, and takes its most obscurantist factions as spokespeople for the whole.*

While rational thinkers should not prevent the superstitious from going about their rituals, intellectual integrity is compromised when one pretends agreement or becomes a participant. This, however, is often what occurs in interactions with Aboriginal people, when those who know better stand for prayers and participate in smudge ceremonies and sweat lodges out of a misguided display of solidarity. Political scientists who act in such a sentimental and weak-minded fashion, including those who promote the incorporation of irrational Indigenous theories and methodologies, are, as Joseph Carroll (1995) notes in the introductory quote, "corrupt[ing] the very values for which they make the sacrifice."

In addition to the hypocrisy and condescension that is involved in the promotion of subjective worldviews in political science, questions should be raised as to why "valid political goals" require such obfuscation in the first place. If the parallelist political vision for Aboriginal peoples will help the Native population achieve self-sufficiency and self-determination, why is it necessary to support this project with special pleading and sophistry?

Such obfuscation is necessary because parallelist political goals *are themselves* invalid. Instead of facilitating liberation from oppression, Indigenous theories and methodologies isolate Aboriginal people, both as political scientists and subjects of study, from everyone else in society. Political scientists of European descent can collaborate with, and criticize, the views of other academics regardless of their culture or ancestry, and so why is this not possible in the case of Aboriginal political scientists? Without honest interaction, in fact, Aboriginal peoples will never be exposed to the challenging ideas needed for intellectual progress. They also will be limited to undertaking research within the field of Native studies, since subjective theories and methodologies by definition cannot have universal applicability.

As well as preventing Aboriginal people from participating in Canadian society, the promotion of Indigenous theories and methodologies has an even more disturbing consequence. This is that their subjectivity enables the actual causes of Aboriginal dependency and deprivation to be obscured. "Indigenous thought," in fact, is deployed to undermine developmental frameworks that can help political scientists understand the Aboriginal question. Declarations that notions of historical progress and cultural evolution are "Western-Eurocentric" has meant that their application to Aboriginal–non-Aboriginal relations in political science is largely off limits.

The reluctance to apply notions of development to the Aboriginal question in political science has prevented the unviable and destructive character of the current policy direction from being recognized. Land claims and self-government initiatives are dependent on the racist assumption that Aboriginal peoples are inherently different from "Western-Eurocentric" cultures, making integration into the wider society impossible. At the same time, however, it is argued that Aboriginal people should achieve parity with the non-Aboriginal population in terms of income, employment, health, education, and housing. How this can be achieved, when small and unproductive Native communities remain separate from the wider society, is never addressed.

Arguments that Aboriginal cultures are both "different" and "developed," in fact, are used to support the professional ambitions of non-Aboriginal lawyers and consultants who negotiate and implement parallelist policies (Widdowson & Howard, 2008). They provide a rationale for the expensive, separate structures being created in hundreds of Aboriginal communities. But because the developmental gap between Aboriginal and "Western-Eurocentric" cultures is denied, Aboriginal problems continue, providing the necessity for more government funds. And since Indigenous methods and theories cannot be verified, and have no capacity to evaluate the consequences of land claims and self-government initiatives, there will be no way that this policy direction can be critically analyzed and changed. It is time for progressive political scientists in Canada to resist this cynical and ignoble agenda.

REFERENCES

Alfred, T. (2004). Warrior scholarship: Seeing the university as a ground of contention. In D. Abbott Mihesuah & A. Cavender Wilson (Eds.), *Indigenizing the academy: Transforming scholarship and empowering communities* (pp. 88–99). Lincoln: University of Nebraska Press.

Alfred, T. (2009). *Peace, power, righteousness: An Indigenous manifesto* (2nd ed.). Toronto: Oxford University Press.

Anuik, J., Battiste, M., & George, P. (2010). Learning from promising programs and applications nourishing the learning spirit. *Canadian Journal of Native Education, 33*(1), 63–82.

Bawer, B. (2012). *The victims' revolution: The rise of identity studies and the closing of the liberal mind.* New York: Broadside Books.

Bedford, D., & Irving, D. (2000). *The tragedy of progress: Marxism, modernity and the Aboriginal question.* Halifax, NS: Fernwood Publishing.

Borrows, J. (2006, January). *Indigenous legal traditions.* Report prepared for the Law Commission of Canada.

Brosius, P.J. (2000). Endangered forest, endangered people: Environmentalist representations of Indigenous Knowledge. In R. Ellen, P. Parkes, and A. Bicker (Eds.), *Indigenous environmental knowledge and its transformations: Critical anthropological perspectives* (pp. 293–317). Amsterdam: Harwood Academic.

Cairns, A. (2000). *Citizens plus: Aboriginal peoples and the Canadian state.* Vancouver: University of British Columbia Press.

Carroll, J. (1995). *Evolution and literary theory.* Columbia: University of Missouri Press.

Coulthard, G. (2006, September–October). Indigenous peoples and the politics of recognition. *New Socialist, 58,* 9–12.

Cruikshank, J. (1994). Oral tradition and oral history: Reviewing some issues. *Canadian Historical Review, 75*(3), 403–418.

Cruz Begay, R. (2004). Changes in childbirth knowledge. *American Indian Quarterly, 28*(3&4), 550–565. http://dx.doi.org/10.1353/aiq.2004.0092

Diamond, J. (1999). *Guns, germs and steel.* New York: W.W. Norton and Co.

Dickerson, M.O., & Flanagan, T. (2006). *An introduction to government and politics: A conceptual approach* (7th ed.). Toronto: Thomson Nelson.

Ermine, W. (1995). Aboriginal epistemology. In M. Battiste & J. Barman (Eds.), *First Nations education in Canada* (pp. 101–112). Vancouver: University of British Columbia Press.

Fanon, F. (1963). *The wretched of the earth.* New York: Grove Weidenfeld.

Flanagan, T. (2000). *First Nations? Second thoughts.* Montreal: McGill-Queen's University Press.

Freire, P. (1998). *Pedagogy of the oppressed.* New York: Continuum.

Hart-Ross, W., & Simmons, D. (2006, November–December). Wasáse FAQs. *New Socialist, 59.*

Ladner, K.L. (2000a). *When buffalo speaks: Creating an alternative understanding of Blackfoot governance.* (Unpublished doctoral dissertation). Carleton University.

Ladner, K.L. (2000b, Summer). Women and Blackfoot nationalism. *Journal of Canadian Studies. Revue d'Etudes Canadiennes, 35*(2), 35–60.

Ladner, K.L. (2005, December). Up the creek: Fishing for a new constitutional order. *Canadian Journal of Political Science, 38*(4), 923–953. http://dx.doi.org/10.1017/S0008423905040539

Ladner, K.L. (2007, March 22). Decolonizing the discipline: Indigenous Peoples and political science. Paper presented at the University of Alberta for the Subaltern Voices Speaker Series.

McGregor, D. (2004). Coming full circle: Indigenous Knowledge, environment, and our future. *American Indian Quarterly, 28*(3&4), 385–410. http://dx.doi.org/10.1353/aiq.2004.0101

McNaughton, C., & Rock, D. (2003). *Opportunities in Aboriginal research: Results of SSHRC's dialogue on research and Aboriginal peoples.* Social Science and Humanities Research Council of Canada. Retrieved May 2008 from http://www.sshrc.ca/web/apply/background/aboriginal_backgrounder_e.pdf

Memmi, A. (1991). *The colonizer and the colonized.* Boston, MA: Beacon Press.

Morgan, L.H. (1974). *Ancient society, or, researchers in the lines of human progress from savagery, through barbarism to civilization.* Gloucester, MA: P. Smith.

Murphy, M. (2000, Fall). Review of the book *Citizens Plus: Aboriginal Peoples and the Canadian State* by Alan Cairns. *Canadian Journal of Sociology, 25*(4), 517–520. http://dx.doi.org/10.2307/3341612

POLCAN. (2007, October 5). Tenure-stream position in the area of Aboriginal politics in Canada. Retrieved May 2008, from http://listes.ulaval.ca/cgi-bin/wa?A2=ind0710&L=polcan&P=R9394&I=3

Robbins, B. (1996, September/October). Anatomy of a hoax. *Tikkun, 11*(5), 58–59.

Royal Commission on Aboriginal Peoples (RCAP). (1996). *Report of the Royal Commission on Aboriginal Peoples. Volume One.* Ottawa: Supply and Services.

Sefa Dei, G.J. (2000). Rethinking the role of Indigenous Knowledges in the academy. *International Journal of Inclusive Education, 4*(2), 111–132. http://dx.doi.org/10.1080/136031100284849

Shahjahan, R.A. (2005, Spring). Mapping the field of anti-colonial discourse to understand issues of Indigenous Knowledges: Decolonizing praxis. *McGill Journal of Education, 40*(2), 213–240.

Simmons, D. (2006, September–October). Socialism from below and Indigenous peoples. *New Socialist, 58,* 13–15.

Simpson, L.R. (2004). Anticolonial strategies for the recovery and maintenance of Indigenous Knowledge. *American Indian Quarterly, 28*(3&4), 373–384. http://dx.doi.org/10.1353/aiq.2004.0107

Sokal, A. (1996). A plea for reason, evidence and logic. Retrieved April 2013 from http://www.physics.nyu.edu/sokal/nyu_forum.html

Sokal, A., & Bricmont, J. (1998). *Fashionable nonsense: Postmodern intellectuals' abuse of science.* New York: Picador USA.

Stevenson, M.G. (2006, Summer). The possibility of difference: Rethinking co-management. *Human Organization, 65*(2), 167–180.

Trigger, B.G. (1984). Indian and white history: Two worlds or one? In M.K. Foster, J. Campisi, & M. Mithun (Eds.), *Extending the rafters: Interdisciplinary approaches to Iroquoian studies* (pp. 17–33). Albany: State University of New York Press.

Trigger, B.G. (1989). *The history of archaeological thought.* Cambridge, UK: Cambridge University Press.

Tully, J. (1995). *Constitutionalism in an age of diversity.* Cambridge, UK: Cambridge University Press. http://dx.doi.org/10.1017/CBO9781139170888

Tully, J. (1999). Aboriginal peoples: Negotiating reconciliation. In J. Bickerton & A.-G. Gagnon (Eds.), *Canadian Politics* (3rd ed., pp. 413–441). Peterborough, ON: Broadview Press.

von Gernet, A. (1996, April). *Oral narratives and Aboriginal pasts: An interdisciplinary review of the literature on oral traditions and oral histories.* Ottawa: Department of Indian and Northern Affairs.

Wallace, A.F.C. (1984). Overview: The career of William N. Fenton and the development of Iroquoian studies. In M.K. Foster, J. Campisi, & M. Mithun (Eds.), *Extending the rafters: Interdisciplinary approaches to Iroquoian studies* (pp. 1–12). Albany: State University of New York Press.

Whittow, M. (1996). *The making of orthodox Byzantium, 600–1025.* Los Angeles: University of California Press.

Widdowson, F. (2006). *The political economy of Aboriginal dependency: A critique of the Royal Commission on Aboriginal Peoples.* (Unpublished doctoral dissertation). York University.

Widdowson, F., & Howard, A. (2008). *Disrobing the Aboriginal industry: The deception behind Indigenous cultural preservation.* Montreal: McGill-Queen's University Press.

Widdowson, F., Voth, E., & Anderson, M. (2012, June 13–15). *Studying Indigenous politics in Canada: Assessing political science's understanding of traditional Aboriginal governance.* Paper presented at the Annual Conference of the Canadian Political Science Association, Edmonton, Alberta.

Wilson, W.A. (2004). Introduction: Indigenous Knowledge recovery is Indigenous empowerment. *American Indian Quarterly*, 28(3&4), 359–372. http://dx.doi.org/10.1353/aiq.2004.0111

Windschuttle, K. (1996). *The killing of history: How literary critics and social theorists are murdering our past.* San Francisco: Encounter Books.

NOTES

1 The two main exceptions in political science are the arguments of Alan Cairns and Tom Flanagan. Cairns argues for "citizens plus" (i.e., differentiated citizenship), whereby Aboriginal peoples receive additional rights while being encouraged to participate within the wider Canadian society. Meanwhile, Tom Flanagan maintains that Aboriginal peoples should be perceived as individuals with the same rights and duties as other Canadian citizens (Cairns, 2000; Flanagan, 2000).

2 In a review of Cairns's book, *Citizens Plus*, Michael Murphy (2000) notes that parallelism's "primary metaphor of a nation-to-nation relationship governed by treaties conjures up the image of a mini-international system of separate communities whose paths never converge" (p. 517).

3 The Social Sciences and Humanities Research Council (SSHRC), for example, maintains that it "has the unique opportunity to support the development of research that uses and further develops an Aboriginal paradigm, emphasizing the theme of decolonizing research," which includes "the use of Aboriginal methodologies, as appropriate to local traditions and the subject matter being addressed" (McNaughton & Rock, 2003, p. 15). However, it does not attempt to define what these "methodologies" are, and merely provides the following in a footnote: "See Smith, *Decolonizing Methodologies*, pp. 42–57, for a discussion of some of the differences between Aboriginal and Western systems of thought in relation to concepts of time, space, the individual and society, and race and gender" (McNaughton & Rock, 2003, p. 18, note 32).

4 RCAP's analysis of these two different "conceptions of history" is drawn from three sources: Cruikshank (1994); Wallace (1984); and Trigger (1984).

5 The linear view envisions "time as an arrow moving from the past into the unknown future," where the present relationship between Aboriginal and non-Aboriginal Canadians "grows out of the past ... and can be improved upon." The cyclical view of Aboriginal peoples, on the other hand, perceives "time as a circle that returns on itself and repeats fundamental aspects of experience" (RCAP, 1996, pp. 35–36).

6 Ladner, in fact, refers to Willie Ermine's definition of "Aboriginal epistemology," arguing that it is the "search for subjective inner knowledge" (Ermine as cited in Ladner, 2000a, p. 29). Ermine also argues that "only through subjectivity can we continue to gain authentic insights into truth" (Ermine, 1995, p. 110).

7 The archaeologist Mark Whittow has noted that locals visiting a twelfth-century archaeological site in Jordan had "vivid and contradictory accounts of their father or grandfather living in the house the team was excavating," even though the site had not been occupied for hundreds of years. He goes on to point out that "anthropologists have demonstrated how fluid and adaptable oral history can be" and that "the oral history of a tribe was primarily concerned to explain the present" and "would adapt and shape its view of the past, creating stories with supporting details to explain and justify present circumstances." According to Whittow, even during continuous settlement of an area, accurate memory lasts no more than two generations and "in times of ... social upheaval change is quicker and more profound." See Whittow (1996, p. 83).

8 Alexander von Gernet, for example, recounts a particular case where the hereditary Mi'kmaq Chief Stephen Augustine read a wampum belt pertaining

to "Mi'kmaq law," where it was later determined that the belt had been made by a Quebec group and had nothing to do with the Mi'kmaq. Ideas generated after the fact had enabled Augustine to become the "self-proclaimed interpreter of wampum belts," thereby inventing a "document" asserting the existence of "Mi'kmaq law" (as cited in Borrows, 2006, p. 26).

9 This circumstance was documented by Peter Brosius (2000), when he showed that advocacy oriented anthropologists like Wade Davis often create an "ethnographic hall of mirrors" in their discussions with Aboriginal peoples. Brosius conducted interviews with the Penan—an Aboriginal group in Borneo—ten years before Wade Davis and his associates arrived on the scene, but uncovered no Indigenous pharmacological knowledge at that time. After Davis and other anthropologists and environmentalists talked to the Penan, however, Brosius discovered that the Penan began to assert that they did have this knowledge. Brosius claims that these anthropologists brought preconceived notions about the medicinal properties of plants to the Penan, who then would repeat what they had heard to others as authentic "indigenous knowledge" (p. 307)

10 For a discussion of the relationship between these programs and postmodernism, see Bawer (2012, pp. 8–10).

11 For an application of these ideas to the recognition of Indigenous Knowledge, see Glen Coulthard (2006), George J. Sefa Dei (2000), and Riyad Ahmed Shahjahan (2005).

12 This notion is muted somewhat by Anuik, Battiste, and George (2010). They maintain that "embodied spirits" connected to Aboriginal ancestors provide "inspiration, guidance, and nourishment to fulfill the purpose of the life journey," but this is tempered by the person's free will (Anuik, Battiste, & George, 2010, p. 67).

13 See also R. Cruz Begay (2004).

14 RCAP (1996), for example, dismisses evolutionary theories as inherently "racist," "ethnocentric," "intolerant," "contemptuous," "self-serving," "unflattering," and "demeaning" (pp. 260, 600–601, 695).

15 Morgan's view is essentially the one adopted by Jared Diamond. In addition to linking cultural development to the global distribution of plants and animals, Diamond also points to the fact that the Old World was aligned on an east-west axis (unlike the Americas, which stretched from north to south), which allowed for a greater diffusion of domesticated plants (because of similar growing seasons across the continent). He also notes that domesticating animals enabled Old World cultures to develop immunity to diseases that did not occur in the New World (Diamond, 1999, 195–214).

16 Interestingly, this discussion of developmental differences is greatly reduced in the latest edition.

17 I have discussed this circumstance extensively elsewhere. See Widdowson, Voth, and Anderson (2012).

18 The claim that the Mi'kmaq had a precontact "constitutional order that comprises and defines distinct political, economic, educational, property and legal systems," for example, was based upon a political declaration of the Union of Nova Scotia Indians (Ladner, 2005, pp. 936–937).

19 An editor from UBC Press, upon reading my letter posted on POLCAN, a listserve for political scientists, protesting the imposition of prayers at the Canadian Political Science Association's plenary session, "Decolonization Impulses on Turtle Island," held on June 14, 2004, stated that "it is a well composed letter that certainly made me face my own hypocrisy. While reading the first paragraph, I began to puff with outrage [that] a member of the Christian right was bringing Bush-ite prayer breakfast rituals to the CPSA" (UBC Press, personal communication, June 2004).

Part III: Exchanges

In Parts I and II, parallelist and integrationist approaches were represented separately. The purpose of Part III is to allow these two perspectives to speak to each other.

The idea for these exchanges was inspired by three forums that were held at Mount Royal University from 2009 to 2011. In an attempt to encourage discussion and debate, a variety of perspectives were solicited. This format was most effective in 2011, when opposing viewpoints were expressed on three specific questions, including the role of spirituality in Aboriginal education. The assumption of this format was that open and honest debate is essential for the development of knowledge, as well as for effective policy development. The forum, like the Intelligence Squared (n.d.) debates put on by the British Broadcasting Corporation (BBC), was "dedicated to creating knowledge through contest." This was in contrast to the position, often expressed in discussions about Aboriginal policy, that there should be an attempt to accept diverse viewpoints without consideration of whether or not they contradict one another.[1] Even works that claim to encourage critical thought and dialogue tend to exclude perspectives that promote notions of historical progress, cultural evolution, and human universality. For example, a recent book edited by Sandra Tomsons and Lorraine Mayer (2013), with the ironic title *Philosophy and Aboriginal rights: Critical dialogues,* claims to "[bring] Western and Indigenous world views together into a deeply meaningful discussion," to feature "frank, open dialogues," and to "[expose] students to a diversity of perspectives." An examination of the book, however, shows that almost all its contributors espouse the assumptions of parallelist approaches, albeit to varying degrees. A number of integrationist perspectives are excluded and are dismissed by the editors as being "Eurocentric" (Tomsons & Mayer, 2013, pp. 178, 260–262) and as justifying colonialism and inequality (pp. 259, 282), as well as having "epistemological misconceptions" and being untrue (pp. 1, 400). Tomsons (2013) even suggests that Widdowson's views should be "regarded as hate speech" (p. 400).

Part III is based on the same premise that prompted the Mount Royal University forums. To clarify the assumptions held by parallelists and integrationists with respect to Aboriginal education, two exchanges with opposing viewpoints have been compiled. The first concerns the interaction of liberal integrationism and parallelism. The liberal integrationist article, written by John R. Minnis, uses the idea of the rentier state, typically applied in the study of Arab countries in the Gulf region, to pose questions about the low educational levels that exist in Aboriginal communities. Minnis is unconvinced of the idea that colonialism is the root cause of educational problems on reserves; instead, he investigates whether government transfers, by creating what he calls a "rentier mentality," have contributed to poor Aboriginal educational outcomes.

Frank Deer responds to Minnis's position. Deer argues that rentier theory is an inappropriate framework with which to examine Aboriginal educational outcomes because the circumstances of the Arab states of the Middle East differ widely from those facing Aboriginal communities. Also, Deer questions Minnis's claim that colonialism is not a convincing explanation for the low educational levels on Aboriginal reserves. Deer is particularly skeptical of Minnis's assertion that private ownership is a remedy for Aboriginal peoples' socio-economic problems.

The second exchange is between parallelism and an integrationist position influenced by political economy assumptions. The exchange examines the value of incorporating Indigenous Knowledge (IK) into post-secondary education. David Newhouse begins the discussion with an article asserting that the incorporation of IK is necessary to cultivate what Haudenosaunee philosophers refer to as a "good mind." A good mind, according to Newhouse, results when reason is "tempered by passion." This circumstance, brought about by the inclusion of IK, improves the post-secondary educational experience for both Aboriginal and non-Aboriginal people.

Newhouse's arguments are critiqued by Frances Widdowson. Widdowson rejects the idea that Aboriginal and non-Aboriginal people have different kinds of knowledge. She maintains that Newhouse's arguments about the existence of an ethnically based way of knowing can be sustained only by including various elements that are contrary to knowledge. In contrast to the Haudenosaunee notion of a good mind, furthered by Newhouse, Widdowson explores Bertrand Russell's conception of the "good life." Widdowson maintains that Russell's vision is more compelling than Newhouse's because it distinguishes knowledge from mythology and spiritual beliefs.

Because parallelism is the dominant approach examining Aboriginal education policy, David Newhouse was offered the last word. Newhouse's response is interesting in that he challenges the premise that presenting oppositional viewpoints enhances our capacity to pursue the truth. Instead, Newhouse proposes a dialogue that assumes that there are "paths to truths"—a framework that he argues is less harsh and competitive than the oppositional exchanges we originally envisioned. In his dialogue, Newhouse accepts that empiricism and logic offer one valid path to pursuing the truth, but also argues that there are other kinds of knowledge with different methods of justification. Furthermore, Newhouse asserts there is evidence that rationality is linked to emotion and this must be considered in the pursuit of truths.

In addition to enabling the different approaches to speak directly to one another—a rare occurrence in discussions about Aboriginal education—these exchanges have raised other questions about the nature of knowledge, critical thinking, and the purpose of education. Is there one truth to be pursued or many truths? Can approaches originally developed to study non-Aboriginal societies be used to shed light on Aboriginal education? Why should reason be tempered? Are all passions unreasonable? Should critical thinking itself be thought about critically? What role should emotion, notions of "spirit," and deference to traditional authority play in education? How does the educational system respond to various perspectives when they appear to be based on contradictory assumptions? These questions hopefully will lead to further efforts at "hunting assumptions"—that is, "trying to uncover assumptions and then trying to assess their accuracy and validity, their fit with life" (Brookfield, 2012, p. 7).

REFERENCES

Brookfield, S.D. (2012). *Teaching for critical thinking: Tools and techniques to help students question their assumptions.* San Francisco: John Wiley & Sons.

Intelligence Squared. (n.d.). Retrieved April 2013 from http://www.intelligence squared.com/

Tomsons, S. & Mayer, L. (Eds.). (2013). *Philosophy and Aboriginal rights: Critical dialogues.* Don Mills, ON: Oxford University Press.

NOTES

1 In 2010, for example, Frances Widdowson invited a number of people with diverse perspectives on Aboriginal research ethics to participate in a roundtable at the Canadian Political Science Association. Particularly revealing was a response that was received from Dr. Jeff Reading, the inaugural director of the Centre for Aboriginal Health Research at the University of Victoria. Dr. Reading's reply to Widdowson's cordial invitation was as follows: "I cannot fathom why you have chosen to publically present 'conflicting viewpoints' rather than seeking consensus through mutual understand [*sic*] on this very sensitive and complex issue." He went on to say that he did not think this was "a respectful or even helpful means to address longstanding issues" (Jeff Reading, personal communication, November 25, 2010).

17

First Nations Education and Rentier Economics: Parallels with the Gulf States

John R. Minnis

This chapter was originally published in the *Canadian Journal of Education* (2006), 29(4), pp. 975–997. Reproduced with permission.

In this chapter, I compare select educational trends and patterns of First Nations[1] education with that of Arab populations of the oil-rich Gulf region. Drawing on pertinent literature, I focus on the links between the rentier nature of First Nations reserve economies, political decision making, and educational outcomes and the Gulf region. Of concern is the persistently high level of educational underachievement common to First Nations populations and how this might be linked to the dependence on external rents.

First Nations control the management and distribution of fiscal transfers that emanate from the Canadian government. As a result, political actors on reserves, much like government bureaucrats in the Gulf, manage and distribute the funds for education and other social services. Fiscal transfers and oil rents, despite emanating from different sources, constitute unearned income unrelated to domestic production. In the Gulf, extensive oil rents result in high per capita incomes, affluent lifestyles, and rapid modernization but also reinforce weak state institutions, authoritarian rule, and weak educational systems (Noreng, 1997).

Referred to as *rentier* or distributive states, Saudi Arabia, United Arab Emirates, Bahrain, Qatar, and Oman have created extensive cradle-to-grave welfare systems consisting of free education, subsidized housing, free medical care, and guaranteed public employment. Beblawi and Luciani (1987) were among the first economists to describe the negative effects of welfare capitalism on the social fabric of oil-rich Gulf nations. They noted the disdain for work and lack of interest in formal learning. They introduced the term *rentier mentality* to refer to the disjunction in the popular mind between work and education and between income and reward. Further research by Amuzegar (1999), El Ghonemy (1998), and Mazawi (1999) reinforced the prevalence of the rentier mentality as a causal factor in the poor educational performance of Arab students. By no means, however, are the Gulf nations unique in this regard (Ross, 2001). With few exceptions, resource-driven economies, whether they are mineral-based or oil-based, tend to be governed by autocratic elites, have weak civil societies, demonstrate high rates of illiteracy, and are prone to interethnic strife (Amuzegar, 1999). The balance of this chapter explores the possibility that First Nations' persistently low educational performance may be similarly linked to the rentier nature of reserve economics.

Background

Statistics indicate that despite quantitative improvements over the years, the record of educational achievement for First Nations people, as well as Métis and Inuit, continues to be much lower than that of other Canadians. According to Wotherspoon (2006, p. 673), about one-third (35%) of all Aboriginal people compared to 17% for non-Aboriginals aged 25–44 had not completed high school. About half (49%) of young Aboriginals aged 15–24 compared to 36% of non-Aboriginals in the same age group were not attending school. Data from other sources suggest that the dropout rate for Aboriginals before completion of grade nine is about 20% and 40% before completion of grade 12, compared to 3% and 16%, respectively, for the non-Aboriginal population (Macionis & Gerber, 2005).

A 2000 report from Indian and Northern Affairs Canada (INAC) (2000, p. 14) estimated that it will take roughly 23 years for the proportion of Aboriginal high school graduates to reach comparable national levels. The situation has apparently worsened over the last four years. A 2004 Auditor General's report states that it will now take

28 years for Aboriginals to achieve parity with non-Aboriginals (cited in Wotherspoon, 2006, p. 673).

At the post-secondary level, the number of Aboriginals attending university increased from about 900 in 1986 to 27,000 in 1996 (Hull, 2000). However, Aboriginal degree completion rates remain low. As a group, Aboriginals are far less likely to hold a post-secondary qualification of any kind—35% compared to 52% for the Canadian population—and most of these are community college credentials. The situation is most dire at the university level. According to Hampton (2000), most Aboriginal students drop out before the second year of university study. Schissel and Wotherspoon (2003) state that only 2.5% of on-reserve Aboriginals hold an undergraduate degree or certificate compared to 15% for non-Aboriginals.

The data indicate that large numbers of Aboriginal people are not acquiring basic academic skills. This situation is quite worrying given that the Aboriginal population is not only much younger than the Canadian population but is growing at a much faster rate. The median age of the Aboriginal population in 2001 was 25 years compared to 38 years for the non-Aboriginal population. The Aboriginal birth rate is presently 1.5 times that of the Canadian population. A third of the Aboriginal population is under the age of 14 compared to 19% of the non-Aboriginal population. Holmes (2006, p. 4) estimates that in the next decade, more than 315,000 Aboriginal children will be born who will eventually go through the K–12 system and potentially into post-secondary education.

The cost of Aboriginal education is bound to increase because of the population growth rate alone. On reserves, First Nations governments will control and distribute these funds. According to INAC (2000), the cost of elementary and secondary education, minus capital and maintenance costs, amounted to $1 billion in 2000. The annual cost of post-secondary education is rising and amounted to $287 million in 2000. In 2003, the most recent figures available, some 25,000 students at the post-secondary level were funded through INAC totalling about $300 million (Malatest & Associates, 2004). About 69,000 students are presently enrolled in First Nation–managed schools on reserves; an additional 46,000 are enrolled in provincial schools. Not surprisingly, expenditures for elementary and secondary education are among INAC's largest departmental allocations to a single program representing over 21% of budgetary funding.

On the surface, educational underachievement does not appear to be caused by underfunding; however, it must be acknowledged that although the number of funded post-secondary students has grown dramatically from 3,700 in 1977, funding has not kept pace with demand, particularly during the 1990s (Holmes, 2006, p. 13). The result is that some students are relatively well funded while many others are dependent upon loans, part-time work, and parental support.

The Problem

Fiscal transfers amount to unearned income for, and not profit from, ownership of natural resources or industrial production. First Nations assert that their economic and social problems can be solved primarily through increases in federal expenditures. At the same time, they also demand less government oversight and argue for more authority over the way federal funds are allocated (Assembly of First Nations, 2004).

The tendency to constantly rely on government funding is at odds with recent scholarship indicating that successful First Nations, whether as a result of gaming, resource extraction, or manufacturing, can indeed make important contributions to local, regional, and national economies (Taylor & Kalt, 2005). With reference to American Indians, Anderson (1995) argued that economic productivity is significantly higher on reserves where a relatively large portion of the land is privately owned as compared to land held in trust or land that is tribally owned. Furthermore, tribal governments in the United States that are constitutionally constrained support more economic growth than tribal governments that can arbitrarily change the rules of the game and redistribute wealth.

This story is not unlike that characteristic of First Nations reserve economics where individuals are forced to adapt to the incentives and constraints that exist. What are lacking on reserves are secure private property rights that create incentives to produce and expand wealth. Centralized political power in the hands of a few creates incentives for political leaders to pursue other peoples' wealth (de Soto, 2000). The result is rent-seeking.

It would be misleading, however, to assume that First Nations possess the necessary institutional infrastructure and human resource capacity to completely act on their own behalf (Anderson, 1998). Most reserves are protected from seizure and therefore cannot be used for collateral. Surety bonding and the acquisition of capital investment are therefore constrained. As long as external agencies carry primary responsibility for economic growth, development decisions will inevitably reflect the goals of those agencies, not necessarily the goals of First Nations individuals (Chiste, 1999). Such factors create a development milieu similar to that found in the Gulf but very different from that found on nonreserve lands.

On-reserve economic development, as a result, tends to be reduced to an endless search for temporary jobs funded by First Nations, most of which are within the First Nations bureaucracy. This jobs-and-income approach is managed by political actors who are not above handing out contracts and jobs to family and kin (Allard, 2002). Thus, rent-seeking solidifies the hierarchical relationship between the "haves" and "have-nots" as suggested in the work of Maxim, White, and Beavon (2003). The tendency is for political power to be held in perpetuity by elite groups supported by a steady flow of unearned income by way of fiscal transfers.

The crux of the problem is that on reserves, political power is not only highly centralized but also fused with financial decision making. Few mechanisms within the reserve political system allow grassroots involvement or wholesale resistance to political decisions. Real power and authority under the Indian Act are vested in political offices, and whoever gets into office enjoys a wide range of discretionary powers not unlike that enjoyed by political leaders in the Gulf. The poverty and suffering on reserves, and the lack of economic development, are only partly caused by lack of opportunity or funding; such outcomes are the product of an antiquated system of political and economic decision making (Carstens, 2000). First Nations governments, much like their Gulf counterparts, have but one major responsibility, that is, to leverage as much money as possible out of the federal government to support on-reserve bureaucratic mechanisms designed to distribute the rents in politically appropriate ways.

Old Theories: New Realities

Internal Colonialism

Internal colonialism is a Marxist-inspired theory that explains educational underachievement as an outcome of the deliberate subjugation of First Nations by the Canadian state. The colonization of First Nations, therefore, is an ongoing social and political process (Frideres & Gadacz, 2001). Advocates of this approach claim that the structure and content of Canadian schooling subjects First Nations to mainstream values and in the process, subordinates and destabilizes efforts to establish Aboriginal institutions and knowledge systems (Bird, Land, & MacAdam, 2002).

Further, colonization is assumed to have deepened rather than abated over the years, and mainstream education, a major agent of colonization, is responsible not only for poor academic performance but also for creating an unequal socio-economic relationship between First Nations and mainstream society, resulting in distrust and enmity. Attempts to reform mainstream schools and curriculum are thus nothing more than a covert strategy aimed at marginalizing First Nations values. Advocates claim that the only way to prevent further colonization is to reject Eurocentric knowledge and pedagogical practices completely. A central objective is the preservation of Indigenous languages and cultures (Battiste, 2001; Calliou, 1999).

The assumption that academic underachievement is caused by colonization is flawed from many perspectives. First, by defining reserves, of which there are over two thousand, as internal colonies, assumes that First Nations are politically powerless actors. Recent court decisions and employment equity practices have politically and economically empowered First Nations to an extent unimaginable 10 to 20 years ago (Burtch, 2003).

Second, demographic data indicate that First Nations are both a rural and an urban people with about 40 to 50% now living off reserve on either a permanent or semipermanent basis (Kerr, Guimond, & Norris, 2003). Migration data show that both reserve and off-reserve populations are increasing. Far from stationary, Canada's First Nations people are highly mobile. In fact, 70% of all Aboriginals (Indian, Métis, and Inuit) now live in towns or urban centres. And yet only $7 million is spent annually servicing off-reserve populations compared to $320 million for on-reserve populations. This means that approximately 80% of First Nations funding is going to 15% of the total population. This not only signals an urgent need for the development of policy frameworks for urban Aboriginals but also provides enormous potential for rent-seeking (Belanger, 2005).

Third, from a political perspective, First Nations reserves contain very few counterbalancing political structures. Major social and economic problems tend to be attacked through the singular field of politics, dominated by a small cabal of elected political leaders (Carstens, 2000). Those in political power also exercise control over band finances and dominate decision making pertaining to the distribution of fiscal transfers (Flanagan, 2000). To label First Nations as colonies is therefore misleading and ignores the autonomous decision-making power (and rent-seeking opportunities) that First Nations politicians possess.

Neither can internal colonialism explain why off-reserve students perform better than on-reserve students in the trades and at the secondary and post-secondary level (Schissel & Wotherspoon, 2003,

p. 109). Also, many on-reserve schools are now staffed with Aboriginal teachers and personnel who are brought up in the same culture as their students. Does this imply that First Nations teachers are colonizing First Nations students?

Influenced by demographic shifts to urban centres, present trends, particularly at the post-secondary level, indicate that First Nations are indeed moving toward, not away from, greater involvement in mainstream educational institutions (Hull, 2000). The shift in policy from federal to local control (ongoing since the early 1970s) has meant that the internal colonization process has fragmented and can no longer be claimed to be a significant factor in First Nations educational underachievement.

Cultural Discontinuity

An equally dubious explanation for low Aboriginal academic achievement is the cultural discontinuity thesis. This perspective asserts that culturally based differences in the communications and learning styles of First Nations students' home life, and the Anglo-bureaucratic ethos of Western schools, leads to conflicts, alienation, and ultimately school dropout (Kanu, 2005).

This approach understandably focuses on the process rather than the structure of education and concludes that making classrooms culturally appropriate will result not only in improved academic success but will ultimately strengthen First Nations culture. To achieve this end, a concerted effort has been made to make schools and teachers culturally sensitive. Universities and colleges have made great efforts to help First Nations students adjust to city living and the culture of the university (Holmes, 2006). More First Nations administrators and teachers are employed in reserve schools. Professional and cultural counselling and support services are available at most post-secondary institutions (Taylor, Crago, & McAlpine, 2001). Community-based teacher education degree programs have sprung up over the country in an attempt to reduce the cultural divide.

Despite these widespread efforts, few empirical studies conclusively confirm that culturally appropriate pedagogical or structural reforms have substantially reduced the level of academic underachievement on or off reserve (Binda, 2001). Interestingly, studies by Ledlow (1992) and Brady (1996) suggest that social class variables, specifically the quality of home and family life, and the role of literacy in early socialization, may have a greater positive effect on Aboriginal achievement than culturally appropriate interventions in the classroom. Moreover, Radwanski's (1987) and Mackay and Myles's (1989) research in Ontario indicate that First Nations culture in the typical Canadian classroom does not explain the high dropout rate. Unfortunately, Canadian scholars remain wedded to the cultural discontinuity thesis despite evidence suggesting that other theories may be equally plausible.

The stress on difference recognition embedded in the cultural discontinuity thesis was understandably a natural pendulum reaction to the historical stress on assimilation so pervasive throughout most of First Nations postcontact history. However, demographic and social forces, exemplified by the high intermarriage rates between First Nations and mainstream populations, are gradually undermining the notion of cultural difference. In their 1992 report, Clatworthy and Smith (1992) estimate an overall out-marriage rate of 34% for status persons and 62% for off-reserve status people. This pattern reflects a high level of cultural exchange and weakens assertions by cultural discontinuity theorists that ineffable cultural differences occur between First Nations and mainstream Canadian values. Cultural discontinuity also assumes that First Nations and mainstream cultures develop in relative isolation from one another, and that mainstream culture is essentially superior. Given these assumptions, educational success is assumed to be contingent on assimilating into the dominant culture.

Research by Guimond (2003) suggests that persons of Aboriginal origin who report more than one ethnic origin outnumber those who report a single origin. This represents the cumulative effect of multiple generations of ethnic mobility. Interestingly, Guimond found that more than a third of persons of Aboriginal origin do not identify with any Aboriginal group. He refers to this as *ethnic drift*—the tendency for Aboriginals to switch identities. Individuals drift in and out of Aboriginal populations, bringing with them their own set of demographic and socio-economic characteristics—mostly urban, lower fertility, and higher educational attainment.

In addition, the shift from rural to urban areas, which is ongoing and dynamic, offers numerous opportunities for cultural exchange and the development of multiple identities. To quote Cairns (2000), "Aboriginal societies, like all other societies, are penetrated societies. Their members live in many worlds at once, and relate to more than one community" (p. 101).

Rents and Rent-Seeking

Definition

The theory of rent dates to the classical eighteenth- and nineteenth-century economists Adam Smith and David Ricardo. Both defined rent as a distinct source of income. According to Smith (1776/1974), "rent enters into the composition of the prices of commodities in a different way than wages and profit. High and low wages are the causes of high or low prices; high or low rent is the effect of it" (p. 249). Ricardo (1817/1960) observed that rent was a reward for, and not profit from, ownership of natural resources. In making this distinction, Ricardo stated, "the laws which regulate the progress of profits and seldom operate in the same direction" (p. 270). To avoid misunderstanding, *rent* used in this context has nothing to do with rent, in the sense of rent for land or property. *Rent* strictly refers to financial income that is not matched by corresponding labour or investment. Rent-seeking behaviour aims at avoiding competitive or market pressures to bring about distortions in one's own interest in the political sphere.

More broadly, *rent-seeking* is the process by which government officials prescribe and reinforce rules that give *themselves* discretionary control over the allocation of valued resources. Rent extraction occurs when government officials exercise this discretion for personal gain. Theoretically, rent-seeking and corruption are often linked causally, although most economists believe that rent-seeking, more often than not, is a cause of corruption and not the other way around. Analysts who study the Gulf speak of rent-seeking regimes where the defining characteristic of governance, the end to which all political activity seems to be channelled, is the creation and control of rent-seeking opportunities (Gause, 1994).

In the Gulf, the national government is typically the principal recipient and dispenser of rents. Its responsibility is to manage the flow of rents and distribute them by means of outright grants, entitlements, contracts, licenses, or state employment. The political economy is, therefore, arranged as a hierarchy of rentiers, with the state at the top of the pyramid, acting as the ultimate support of all other rentiers (Karl, 1997).

Social, Political, and Economic Outcomes in the Gulf

Despite enormous rents derived from oil and gas exports, rentier states have been unable to diversify economically and as a result, display a remarkably uniform developmental path (Gause, 1994; Shafer, 1994). Analysts point to the following reasons. The steady flow of wealth prohibits the need for taxation on personal incomes. Oil revenues are owned by the government. Thus, the extraction of oil and gas is basically an isolated, capital-intensive enterprise dominated by expatriate workers. The relationship between the citizen and the state is therefore fundamentally different from that found in nonresource-based societies. By exercising dominance over the economy, governments vest a wide variety of private interests in its stability, privileging its allies and punishing its opponents.

In return for public acquiescence, governments are obliged to provide a wide array of services to citizens in the form of free education, health care, housing, and consumer subsidies. Peace and stability among these otherwise fragile states is maintained by the consistent use of various strategies, i.e., strong security services, political co-optation, divide-and-rule measures, allowing token democratic participation, and providing free public services (Byman & Green, 1999).

The dominance of external rents over time creates an extroverted economy. In his study of rentier states, Gunn (1993) found no nexus between production and income distribution because revenues accrue directly to the government from rents emanating from outside the country. This supports Beblawi and Luciani's (1987) notion of a *rentier mentality* that implies a break in the work-reward causation—where reward is not related to risk-taking or the perceived need to work hard or compete. Other analysts have observed that rent-seeking tends to produce an inverted pyramid of social classes (Noreng, 1997). In the Gulf, a large, nonproductive, consumer-driven, middle class dominates the social structure in the absence of a producer class. High levels of affluence create insatiable demands for foreign goods and products. Thus, from a development perspective, the modern Gulf state demands those skills that can be attained only by accessing Western-style training and education.

Parallels with Reserve Economies

First Nations land and resource ownership is highly constrained by the effects of more than 200 years of British and Canadian colonial policy. Chief and council (band) control the sale, lease, and use of reserve land, even though it is deemed as collective property. As a result, individual band members possess little in the way of collateral that allows them the freedom to buy property on or off the reserve. Without collateral, it has proven difficult for band members to obtain sufficient start-up capital to establish businesses (Flanagan & Alcantara, 2002). The lack of an integrated system of private property prohibits large-scale economic development and further reinforces the fusion of political and economic decision making. As pointed out by the Royal Commission on Aboriginal Peoples (1996), the consequence is that a disproportionate amount of federal funding is directed toward welfare and remedial programs (social and family breakdown) relative to economic development.

Through no fault of their own, First Nations as individuals have never enjoyed a workable system of property rights. This is not to suggest that reserve residents have no individual property rights whatsoever. In reality, the situation is much more complex. First Nations do indeed control much reserve land as collective property, but on some reserves individuals enjoy the benefits of customary rights and certificates of possession under the Indian Act (Flanagan & Alcantara, 2002). However, the numerous treaties, the many amendments to the Indian Act, and the necessity to rely on the courts rather than the political process to resolve land claims and other disputes have conspired to confine residents of reserves to a system of collective rights that constrains economic growth and diversification (Franks, 2000).

In the Gulf, analysts note that rent-seeking exacerbates political factionalism and systematizes patterns of patronage and cronyism. As a result, employment in the public sector is often created not to meet identified economic needs, but to provide jobs for friends and relatives (Devlin & Jewison, 1995). Mainly because reserves have not been the object of systematic economic study, it is not known to what extent patronage and cronyism are institutionalized. The political factionalism reported in the popular media over the years does indeed point to extensive interfamily jealousies and political factionalism (e.g., Cheney, 1998; Rabson, 2001; Redekop, 2001). Such cases must be judged on their own merits; however, it must also be acknowledged that political leaders on reserves, much like their Gulf counterparts, do possess broad discretionary control over spending.

How might discretionary control over resources lead to rent-seeking? Because the political elite on any reserve tends to control most aspects of reserve life, from the allocation of housing to who gets jobs and welfare, they are virtually unimpeded in using band funds to reward those who provide political support. Similar conditions exist on many reserves where select occupations, such as elected office, are subject to salary grids that are insensitive to market conditions (Allard, 2002). Although not all First Nations leaders can be assumed to be predatory, what are the checks and balances to prevent them from being so?

In addition, if leaders develop predatory as opposed to development aims, where are the collective actors within the reserve society to impose some domestic conditionality on how those in power exercise that power fairly and with a sense of accountability? The idea that the mere existence of rent-seeking opportunities will be used for predatory purposes is consistent with the experience in the Gulf.

Predation tends to occur as a consequence of the failure to adopt rules, clearly defined procedures, regulations, and appeal processes. If such conditions are in place, the probability of prolonged rent-seeking is reduced (Ross, 2001).

Increasing social stratification on reserves has led some analysts to comment on the increasing polarization between the haves and the have-nots. These groups are differentiated by educational attainment that creates a dual labour market where individuals are either limited in the band bureaucracy to low-skill, low-paying jobs, or high-skill, high-paying positions (White, Maxim, & Beavon, 2003). In the absence of taxation, and with traditional customs of sharing and redistribution no longer being practised on many reserves, there are few legal or normative mechanisms for redistributing wealth from the elite to the people (Allard, 2002).

Commenting on the prospects for the success of First Nations businesses, Flanagan (2000) concludes, "as long as reserves are small, impoverished and supported by external funding they will be prey to factionalism, nepotism and waste" (p. 107). Flanagan's view is supported by Cairns's (2000) observation that more than 80% of federal government transfers pay for costs associated exclusively with band administration.

Perhaps the most important lesson for First Nations to be drawn from the Gulf experience is that rent-seeking begets more rent-seeking and does not enhance economic development. There is also a covariance of weak states with oil rents. That is, reliance on external rents tends to transform social and political structures so that formidable barriers to change are erected. Similar outcomes are evident within reserve economies. There is an overabundance of service sector employment, an absence of private sector enterprises or initiatives, low direct investment from outside firms, and reliance on the jobs-and-income approach.

Discussion

Political leaders in both First Nations communities and the Gulf are failing to systematically address the notion that the causes of educational underachievement may in part emanate from the rentier nature of their dependence on external rents. In regard to First Nations, although it is true that political actors control educational policy and financing, they receive this money as part of a larger package from the government, not through taxation of their members. The lack of taxation removes an important variable from the political equation: no legitimate basis exists for citizens to demand accountability from elected officials as there is in mainstream society. Moreover, without clear rules of accountability and transparent budgetary practices, First Nations citizens may not be as informed as they should be as to how their money is spent on education or any other social service.

To prevent rent-seeking from taking hold, reserve politics must be separated from the process of managing band money. Successful First Nations in the United States have achieved this by creating a development corporation with an independent board (Taylor & Kalt, 2005). Long-term economic planning is left to the band while the board's responsibility is to conduct and manage business operations. Unless a clear separation of powers occurs, the risk of rent-seeking rises sharply and ultimately, as experienced in the Gulf, stifles entrepreneurship and political participation. The lesson for First Nations is that the adjudication of disputes over resources should be separated from politics. If dispute mechanisms internal to a band are controlled politically, they are obviously subject to manipulation and this may enhance corruption and further discourage risk-taking and joint economic ventures with outside agencies and firms.

The lack of citizen involvement in First Nations politics creates a vacuum in terms of addressing educational problems and issues. An analogy can be drawn to mainstream society to illustrate this: if the Canadian high school dropout rate were as high as that of First Nations, it would result in an angry public reaction followed by hurried political efforts to find solutions. Clearly, Canada could not afford the resultant loss of taxes, diminished economic production, and increased costs in social assistance. How long would mainstream parents tolerate high attrition and dropout rates such that their children were denied the necessary skills and credentials to compete in a global economy? Paradoxically, the financial costs of First Nations underachievement will be borne by the Canadian taxpayer while the social and psychological costs will continue to be borne by First Nations themselves.

Citizens of the Gulf region and the First Nations lay great stress on obtaining post-secondary qualifications. In Canada, this may be due in part to the increase in entrepreneurial activity on reserves but is more likely linked to the availability of jobs in the social services that require professional certification, such as teaching and social work. The close correspondence between public sector jobs and higher education is a characteristic of rentier economies as noted by Altbach (1998). Once on the rentier path, First Nations will be constantly under pressure to create more jobs. Because well-paid employment requires post–high school training, keen competition occurs for band sponsorship and educational funding. Given their control over funding and job creation, political leaders are free to offer financial support in return for political support. In the long term, no group or individual seeking funding for education can easily avoid rent-seeking. Evidence from the Gulf suggests that once established, rent-seeking regimes tend to become autonomous and intensify.

Despite quantitative improvements in educational participation, it is inevitable that the social returns to post-secondary education will remain low for reserve residents as long as noncompletion rates are high. The result is that individuals, not First Nations, will benefit the most from educational funding. Because superior employment opportunities are found off reserve, urban centres (and urban reserves) will continue to pull post-secondary graduates away from remote and under-resourced reserves. Human capital is held by individuals, not collectivities, and resides in the community only as long as the individual stays there and capitalizes on the educational skills and knowledge he or she has acquired. This demands the financial and other physical capital resources of the community to be both present and in motion for the community to develop economically. This is not the case for the majority of reserves.

If educational underachievement is indeed a serious problem, many First Nations are not responding in a constructive manner. For instance, some have refused to participate in provincial testing that compares their educational achievement interprovincially and internationally. In Alberta, for example, First Nations were requested but refused to release information on test results, arguing that such disclosure would be harmful to their relations with government (cited in Cowley & Easton, 2004). At the national level, similar concern over the lack of First Nations accountability and transparency is reflected in the 2000 Auditor General's report (INAC) that documented numerous reporting and accountability problems pertaining to the management of on-reserve education. Sadly, the Auditor General (INAC, 2000) concluded, "The Department of Indian and Northern Affairs does not know how much money is spent by First Nations on education" (p. 17).

Conclusion

With this chapter, I have attempted to reveal how the rentier nature of reserve economics affects political decision making, which in turn may be linked to First Nations educational outcomes. The following questions are put forth to stimulate further investigation:

- In reserve economies, where other dominant forms of wealth creation are absent, fiscal transfers provide the bulk of regular income. Because education is fully subsidized, to what extent are educational systems used by authorities as a means to distribute rents? For example, are funding opportunities and available jobs in education part and parcel of the reserve patronage system as they are in the Gulf region?

- Both the Gulf countries and First Nations reserves have been transformed into consumer societies by virtue of their rentier status. If rent-seeking is a condition for educational funding, how motivated will First Nations students be to achieve educational success? Will they be inclined to adopt an indifferent attitude toward education as is the case in the Gulf?

- Dependence on unearned income allows those in power to dispense favours and rents to the people for the dual purpose of providing benefits and, in the process, buying off dissidents and managing the flow of rents. In the Gulf, such a rent-seeking environment has created a situation in which citizens are constantly jockeying for the favour of the hand that feeds them. What are the personal experiences of First Nations students in this respect?

- In rentier states, the nexus between work and academic achievement is made problematic in so far as education and training, indeed risk-taking of any sort, is not strongly linked to future economic rewards, particularly when those rewards are perceived to be external to the individual. In regard to First Nations students, is dropping out a rational response relative to the expected rewards and probable outcomes?

Hopefully, within the context of renewed emphasis on First Nations economic development, the pitfalls associated with overdependence on external rents will be recognized and avoided. Perhaps a sensible place to start is for First Nations citizens to realize that development policies and outcomes have to represent their wishes and to ensure that their political masters are accountable to them.

REFERENCES

Allard, J. (2002). Big Bear's treaty: The road to freedom. *Inroads, 11*, 108–169.

Altbach, P.G. (1998). *Comparative higher education: Knowledge, the university and development.* Greenwich, CT: Ablex.

Amuzegar, J. (1999). *Managing the oil wealth: OPEC's windfalls and pitfalls.* London, UK: I.B. Taurus.

Anderson, R. (1998). *Economic development among the Aboriginal peoples of Canada: The hope for the future.* Concord, ON: Captus Press.

Anderson, T.L. (1995). *Sovereign nations or reservations? An economic history of American Indians.* New York: Basic Books.

Assembly of First Nations. (2004). *Federal government funding to First Nations: The facts, the myths and the way forward.* Ottawa: Author.

Battiste, M. (2001). Decolonizing the university: Indigenous contexts for academic freedom. In L.M. Findlay & P.M. Bidwell (Eds.), *Pursuing academic freedom: "Free and fearless"?* (pp. 190–203). Saskatoon, SK: Purich.

Beblawi, H., & Luciani, G. (Eds.). (1987). *The rentier state.* London, UK: Croom Helm.

Belanger, Y.D. (2005, May). *The politics of accommodation in Winnipeg: The dynamics involved in developing a policy of Aboriginal inclusion.* Paper presented at the Canadian Studies Centre, University of Edinburgh, Scotland.

Binda, K.P. (2001). Aboriginal education in comparative and global perspectives: What has research and practice done for Aboriginal education in Canada? *Canadian and International Education. Education Canadienne et Internationale, 30*(1), 1–16.

Bird, J., Land, L., & MacAdam, M. (Eds.). (2002). *Nation to nation: Aboriginal sovereignty and the future of Canada.* Toronto: Irwin.

Brady, P. (1996). Native dropouts and non-Native dropouts in Canada: Two solitudes or a solitude shared? *Journal of American Indian Education, 35*(2), 1–6. Retrieved from http://jaie.asu.edu/v35/V35S2nat.htm

Burtch, B. (2003). *The sociology of law: Critical approaches to social control* (2nd ed.). Scarborough, ON: Thompson-Nelson.

Byman, D.L., & Green, J.D. (1999). The enigma of political stability in the Persian Gulf monarchies. *Middle East Review of International Affairs, 3*(19), 1–20.

Cairns, A.C. (2000). *Citizens plus: Aboriginal peoples and the Canadian state.* Vancouver: University of British Columbia Press.

Calliou, S. (1999). Sunrise: Activism and self-determination in First Nations education. In J.H. Hylton (Ed.), *Aboriginal self-government in Canada* (2nd ed., pp. 157–186). Saskatoon, SK: Purich.

Carstens, P. (2000). An essay on suicide and disease in Canadian Indian reserves: Bringing Durkheim back in. *Canadian Journal of Native Studies, 20*(2), 309–345.

Cheney, P. (1998, October 28). How money has cursed Alberta's Samson Cree. *Globe and Mail,* p. A4.

Chiste, K.B. (Ed.). (1999). *Aboriginal small business and entrepreneurship in Canada.* Concord, ON: Captus Press.

Clatworthy, S., & Smith, A.H. (1992). *Population implications of the 1985 amendments to the Indian Act.* Ottawa: Assembly of First Nations.

Cowley, P., & Easton, S. (2004). Report card on Aboriginal education in British Columbia (2004 edition). Studies in Educational Policy. Vancouver: The Fraser Institute.

de Soto, H. (2000). *The mystery of capital: Why capitalism triumphs in the West and fails everywhere else.* New York: Basic Books.

Devlin, B., & Jewison, N. (1995). *The development of public education and training in the state of Qatar.* Working paper no. 8. The Centre for Labour Market Studies, Leicester University, UK.

El-Ghonemy, M.R. (1998). *Affluence and poverty in the Middle East.* London, UK: Routledge. http://dx.doi.org/10.4324/9780203301586

Flanagan, T. (2000). *First Nations? Second thoughts.* Montreal: McGill-Queen's University Press.

Flanagan, T., & Alcantara, C. (2002). Individual property rights on Canadian Indian reserves. Public Policy Sources 60. Vancouver: The Fraser Institute. Retrieved from http://www.fraserinstitute.org/research-news/display.aspx?id=13114

Franks, C.E.S. (2000). Rights and self-government for Canada's Aboriginal peoples. In C. Cook & J.D. Landau (Eds.), *Aboriginal rights and self-government: The Canadian and Mexican experience in North America* (pp. 101–134). Montreal: McGill-Queen's University Press.

Frideres, J.S., & Gadacz, R.R. (Eds.). (2001). *Aboriginal peoples in Canada: Contemporary conflicts* (6th ed.). Toronto: Prentice Hall.

Gause, F.G., III. (1994). *Oil monarchies: Domestic and security challenges in the Arab Gulf States.* New York: Council on Foreign Relations Press.

Guimond, E. (2003). Changing ethnicity: The concept of ethnic drifters. In J.P. White, P.S. Maxim, & D. Beavon (Eds.), *Aboriginal conditions: Research as a foundation for social policy* (pp. 91–107). Vancouver: University of British Columbia Press.

Gunn, G.C. (1993). Rentier capitalism in Negara Brunei Darussalam. In K. Hewison, R. Robinson, & G. Rodan (Eds.), *Southeast Asia in the 1990s: Authoritarianism, democracy and capitalism* (pp. 122–138). Singapore: Allen & Unwin.

Hampton, E. (2000). First Nations controlled universities in Canada. In M. Brant Castellano, L. Davis, & L. Lahache (Eds.), *Aboriginal education: Fulfilling the promise* (pp. 208–221). Vancouver: University of British Columbia Press.

Holmes, D. (2006, June). *Redressing the balance: Canadian university programs in support of Aboriginal students.* Report prepared for the Association of Universities and Colleges of Canada, Ottawa.

Hull, J. (2000). *Aboriginal post-secondary education and outcomes in Canada, 1996.* Ottawa: Research and Analysis Directorate, Indian and Northern Affairs Canada.

Indian and Northern Affairs Canada (INAC) (2000, April). *Report of the Auditor General of Canada.* Ottawa: Office of the Auditor General.

Kanu, Y. (2005). Teachers' perceptions of the integration of Aboriginal culture into the high school curriculum. *Alberta Journal of Educational Research, 36*(4), 346–362.

Karl, T.L. (1997). *The paradox of plenty: Oil booms and petro-states.* Berkeley: University of California Press.

Kerr, D., Guimond, E., & Norris, M.J. (2003). Perils and pitfalls of Aboriginal demography: Lessons learned from the RCAP projections. In J.P. White, P.S. Maxim, & D. Beavon (Eds.), *Aboriginal conditions: Research as a foundation for public policy* (pp. 39–90). Vancouver: University of British Columbia Press.

Ledlow, S. (1992). Is cultural discontinuity an adequate explanation for dropping out? *Journal of American Indian Education, 31*(3), 14–26. Retrieved from http://jaie.asu.edu/v31/V31S3cul.htm

Macionis, J.L., & Gerber, L.M. (Eds.). (2005). *Sociology* (5th Canadian ed.). Toronto: Pearson Education Canada.

Mackay, R., & Myles, L. (1989). *Native dropouts in Ontario schools.* Toronto: Queen's Printer Press.

Malatest, R.A. & Associates (2004). *Aboriginal peoples and post-secondary education: What educators have learned.* Montreal: Canada Millennium Scholarship Foundation.

Maxim, P.S., White, J.P., & Beavon, D. (2003). Dispersion and polarization of income among Aboriginal and non-Aboriginal Canadians. In J.P. White, P.S. Maxim, & D. Beavon (Eds.), *Aboriginal conditions: Research as a foundation for public policy* (pp. 222–247). Vancouver: University of British Columbia Press.

Mazawi, A.E. (1999). The contested terrain of education in the Arab states: An appraisal of major research trends. *Comparative Education Review, 43*(3), 332–352. http://dx.doi.org/10.1086/447566

Noreng, O. (1997). *Oil and Islam: Social and economic issues.* New York: John Wiley.

Rabson, M. (2001, September 8). Reserve's welfare fight leaves residents angry. *Winnipeg Free Press,* p. A8.

Radwanski, G. (1987). *Ontario study of the relevance of education and the issue of dropouts in Ontario schools.* Toronto: Ontario Ministry of Education.

Redekop, B. (2001, December 29). Deputy depleted $6-m special fund: Caribbean cruise grievance rejected. *Winnipeg Free Press,* pp. A1, A4.

Ricardo, D. (1960). *On the principles of political economy and taxation.* London, UK: J.M. Dent & Sons. (Original work published 1817)

Ross, M. (2001). Does oil hinder democracy? *World Politics, 53*(03), 325–361. http://dx.doi.org/10.1353/wp.2001.0011

Royal Commission on Aboriginal Peoples. (1996). *Report.* Ottawa: Ministry of Supplies and Services.

Schissel, B., & Wotherspoon, T. (2003). *The legacy of school for Aboriginal people: Education, oppression, and emancipation.* Don Mills, ON: Oxford University Press.

Shafer, M.D. (1994). *Winners and losers: How sectors shape the development prospect of states.* Ithaca, NY: Cornell University Press.

Smith, A. (1974). *The wealth of nations.* New York: Penguin Books. (Original work published 1776)

Taylor, D.M., Crago, M.B., & McAlpine, L. (2001). Toward full empowerment in Native education: Unanticipated challenges. *Canadian Journal of Native Studies, 20*(2), 45–46.

Taylor, J.B., & Kalt, J.P. (2005). *American Indians on reservations: A databook of socioeconomic changes between the 1990 and 2000 Censuses.* Retrieved December 19, 2006, from http://www.Ksg.harvard.edu/paied/pubs/documents/American IndiansReservatinsAdatabookofsocioeconoimcchanges.pdf

White, J.P., Maxim, P.S., & Beavon, D. (Eds.). (2003). *Aboriginal conditions: Research as a foundation for public policy.* Vancouver: University of British Columbia Press.

Wotherspoon, T. (2006). Teachers' work in Canadian Aboriginal communities. *Comparative Education Review, 50*(4), 672–694. http://dx.doi.org/10.1086/507060

NOTE

1 I use the term *First Nation* to denote an Indian tribal group that shares a common cultural heritage. Members of First Nations may reside on or off reserve. There are over two thousand reserves in Canada and most are governed by a First Nations band, normally consisting of a chief and council. The number of First Nations will presumably vary over time depending on population growth, migration patterns, success of land claims, and changes in federal government policy. First Nations people who are registered under the Indian Act fall under the legislative and administrative authority of the federal government. As a result, they are entitled to educational, social, and economic benefits.

18

First Nations Education and Minnis's Rentier Mentality

Frank Deer

This chapter was originally published in the *Canadian Journal of Native Education* (2009), 32(2), pp. 94–104. Reproduced with permission.

Introduction

The Eurocentric preoccupation with inferring the existence of social phenomena based on pre-acquired knowledge gained from other sources has had profound effects on Canada's Aboriginal population (Battiste & Henderson, 2000; Henderson, 2000a). Many social scientists who work in the Eurocentric tradition have used anthropological procedures to apply what they know from one society to try to understand what they do not know in another (Henderson, 2000a, 2000c). This process of filling the gaps in an effort to understand a social phenomenon may offer a superficially rational understanding of the phenomenon in question but does little to recognize the unique manifestations of localized knowledge and experience that are prevalent in First Nations communities (Little Bear, 2000). What may be observed and learned in one part of the world may not be appropriately applied to another; the diversity of thought, value, experience, and sensibility that is prevalent in the modern world does not always suit such metanarratives (Duran & Duran, 2000).

Many First Nations in Canada are in crisis (Deer, 2008). The problems that have been plaguing First Nations communities have been illustrated and compared with the lifestyles of non-First Nations peoples in Canada, much to the detriment of contemporary understandings of the phenomenon (Battiste & Henderson, 2000). The publicizing of these problems has focused public attention on the problems themselves and the ethnic origin of those who are experiencing them: discourse on the causes of institutional marginalization is frequently overlooked in Canada's popular consciousness (Indian and Northern Affairs Canada, 1996). In attempting to identify the causes of such problems, some scholars have attempted to use social phenomena prevalent in other societies to explain the crises that plague First Nations peoples in Canada.

Western society is replete with examples of minority groups that have struggled with socio-economic and political issues that their respective governments have attempted to remedy through social programming and the enactment of policy that espouses inclusivity (Dauvergne, 2005). Canada's First Peoples, however, represent a diverse group who have a noteworthy relationship with their colonizers: one that is governed in part by treaties (Lerat & Ungar, 2005). These treaties, accords that are derogatory in their language and subjugating in their implications, represent agreements that promise restitution for the vast areas of land that were surrendered so that all Canadians could live in what is contemporarily regarded as one of the best countries in which to live (United Nations Development Programme, 2007). Although the treaties established by Canada's First Peoples and their colonizers do provide for such restitution, they also represent the Canadian government's means of control through maintaining a status quo that supports oppression and provides marginal opportunity for social advancement (Tully, 2000). Canada's treaty arrangements with the First Peoples, whether perceived in a positive or negative light, are an inextricable part of Canada's First Peoples' identity. In spite of the establishment of treaties, Canada's First Peoples have struggled with the effects of colonialism and social dominance (Stidsen, 2006).

In some quarters, the reasons for the predicament in which many First Peoples struggle have been characterized otherwise. One sentiment that has prevailed in popular consciousness is similar to that put forth by Minnis (2006), who asserted that educational shortcomings among First Nations students could be attributed to fiscal transfers from the Canadian government to First Nations. The fiscal transfers that Minnis appears to focus on are those initiated by the Department of Indian Affairs and Northern Development to support existing treaty agreements (Indian and Northern Affairs Canada, 2007). Minnis's principal assertion is that such fiscal transfers represent unearned income and support a *rentier mentality*: the failure to develop an appreciation of the work-reward relationship (Yates, 1996). This work propagates a sentiment of Canada's First Peoples that is supported by a number of inaccuracies and problematic theoretical applications to the phenomenon in question. Furthermore, Minnis's work has failed to recognize the importance of the unique treaty agreements made between the First Peoples and their colonizers. To the extent that these histories, experiences, and accords are specific to a particular social context, Minnis's application of Arab states in the Gulf Region as a parallel is not appropriate. The negative sentiments echoed by Minnis's work are exacerbated by the fact that the work in question appears in one of Canada's most recognized scholarly journals for education. This chapter challenges the proposition that a rentier mentality among the First Nations of Canada has affected the educational performance of First Nations students. For the purposes of this chapter, the terms *Aboriginal* and *First Peoples* are used interchangeably to refer to those status Indians living in First Nations communities in Canada. In writing this chapter, I affirm that educational underachievements, as well as social, political, and economic problems, are urgent matters for First Nations in Canada.

First Nations and the Rentier Mentality

A rentier mentality is one that is developed when a community or nation acquires financial gain from external sources in return for the land that that community or nation owns or occupies (Yates, 1996). Contemporary scholars, when discussing such communities or nations, frequently cite oil-rich Arab states of the Middle East as cogent examples of such states (Beblawi, 1990). Countries such as Saudi Arabia and the United Arab Emirates lack economic diversification, and monies acquired through the oil trade are distributed to citizens and public-sector institutions (Gylfason, 2005). Thus, a rentier mentality allegedly emerges when civil workers and citizens become dependent on rents and fail to develop an appreciation of the work-reward relationship. Yates (1996) described this mentality.

> *The rentier mentality is a psychological condition with profound consequences for productivity: contracts are given as an expression of gratitude rather than as a reflection of economic rationale; civil servants see their principal duty as being*

available in their offices during working hours; businessmen abandon industry and enter into real-estate speculation or other special situations associated with a booming oil sector; the best and brightest abandon business and seek out lucrative government employment; manual labor and other work considered demeaning by the rentier is farmed out to foreign workers … in extreme cases income is derived simply from citizenship. (p. 22)

In asserting the prevalence of such mentality in First Nations in Canada, Minnis (2006) suggested that the receipt of fiscal transfers has affected educational achievement on reserves. In attempting to draw comparisons between First Nations in Canada and oil-rich Arab states in the Middle East, Minnis stated,

I focus on the links between the rentier nature of First Nations reserve economies, political decision-making, and education outcomes and the Gulf region. Of concern is the persistently high level of educational underachievement common to First Nations populations and how this might be linked to the dependence on external rents …. fiscal transfers … constitute unearned income unrelated to domestic production. (p. 976)

The suggestion that educational underachievement in First Nations is the consequence of fiscal transfers from the federal government in the form of rents is bold. Unfortunately, Minnis's work contains little information related to educational psychology and does not cite any empirical studies that infer that First Nations students have been underachieving as a result of their community having received rents from external agencies.

Contemporary and historical accounts of First Nations life in Canada may recognize and affirm the existence of a number of problems related specifically with First Nations in Canada, and particularly with the education of First Nations peoples. Educational achievement is problematic for First Peoples in Canada, as is the case with other aspects of First Nation life. These problematic aspects can include "suicide, conflict with the criminal justice system, child welfare apprehensions and intrusions, violence against women and children, [and] sexual abuse" (Monture-Angus, 1999, p. 11), as well as First Peoples being "more closely scrutinized, less likely to be promoted, more likely to be blamed for difficulties, and less likely to be recognized for successes" (Mills & McCreary, 2006, p. 41). Such social problems may have detrimental effects on educational achievement in such communities (Schissel & Wotherspoon, 2003). The problems associated with educational achievement may be exacerbated by the projected increase of First Nations populations, as well as anticipated funding issues for education (Stewart, 2006).

Educational problems on First Nations, and the broader social problems that often accompany them, may be better characterized as a result of colonialism and postcolonial oppression (Battiste & Henderson, 2000). To suggest that such problems are a result of a rentier mentality is grossly to simplify the phenomenon in question and focuses attention on social problems that were initiated and propagated by external agents. The rentier mentality theory put forth by Minnis (2006) is not presented such that it reflects the colonial roots that led to the establishment of the fiscal transfers that he discusses. *Treaties* may be characterized as agreements of restitution for those lands that were acquired by non-Aboriginals. *Rent*, as described by Minnis, is not an issue in this context; the fiscal transfers from the Canadian government may be better described as monetary transfers that account for Canada's treaty obligations.

Alleged parallels between fiscal transfers to First Nations and the rents that are acquired in oil-rich Arab states in the Middle East do not reflect the state of affairs in Canada for a number of reasons. First, the lifestyles of Arabs in the Middle East are in no way prevalent in Canada's First Nations; for most First Nations peoples on reserve, the standard of living is quite low (Gylfason, 2005; Lerat & Ungar, 2005). Collective outrage on the part of the First Peoples in Canada suggests that this state of marginalization is not desired, unlike those who enjoy the benefits of rents in the Middle East. Second, the government transfers to First Nations should not be regarded as unearned income. Money transferred to First Nations to satisfy treaty obligations are a result of transactions that took place many years ago through the struggles of negotiation that were burdened by the forefathers of Canada's First Peoples; the acquisition of money in return for something as precious as the lands of Turtle Island can hardly be regarded as unearned income. Just because the money in question is not closely related to domestic production does not mean it is unearned. Third, on the topic of rents, Minnis (2006) wrote, "Fiscal transfers amount to unearned income for, and not profit from, ownership of natural resources or industrial production" (p. 979). This may be the case; however, one may find it difficult to accept that those providing the income view such natural resources as the property of First Nations. Formal ownership of the natural resources from which the government acquires money to transfer appears to lie with those other than the First Nations, making the application of rentier economics to this phenomenon problematic.

Perhaps the most suspect aspect of Minnis's (2006) discourse is the suggestion that the socio-economic problems associated with First

Nations in Canada can be remedied by allowing private ownership of existing land and resources in First Nations territories. As Minnis states, "economic productivity is significantly higher on reserves where a relatively large portion of land is privately owned as compared to land held in trust or land that is tribally owned" (p. 979). Making reserve land private, certainly in the mainstream sense, is risky business if one considers the possibility that individual owners of land can treat such property in any way they see fit, possibly leading to large-scale resource extraction or even outright sale of the property to others. The possible results of private ownership of First Nations land may remind one of the assimilation policies put forth by the White Paper of 1969, when government authorities attempted to encourage Canada's Aboriginal population to become a more active part of mainstream society. Although private land ownership may lead to temporary prosperity, the existence of such lands in Canada's mainstream economy may ultimately lead to their permanent disappearance from the First Nations' sphere of control and will serve to nullify existing treaty relationships. For these reasons, First Nations lands must be protected (Turner, 2006). Private land ownership by individuals is a Eurocentric reality that Minnis appears to accept as imperative for the First Nations peoples of Canada.

In presenting his argument about the rentier mentality, Minnis (2006) suggests that colonization and cultural discontinuity are not sufficient reasons for contemporary educational underachievement in First Nations in Canada. Minnis's sentiments about colonization and cultural discontinuity, arguably flawed by problematic applications of inappropriate concepts, are addressed separately in the following two sections.

Colonization

In regard to educational underachievement, Minnis (2006) writes, "The assumption that academic underachievement is caused by colonization is flawed from many perspectives" (p. 981). Minnis attempts to substantiate this claim by suggesting that (1) political actors on First Nations have sufficient political and economic power to address the situation, and (2) First Nations people living off reserve have increased in number to the point that government transfers to First Nations should be the subject of policy development. These reasons for discounting the colonization argument as an explanation for educational underachievement in First Nations suffer from how Minnis employs the term *colonization*, which is defined as the act or instance of colonizing (Merriam-Webster Online, 2008). If one accepts that colonization refers to a series of events that led to Confederation and the signing of treaties (after which, European settlements could hardly be referred to as colonies), then one may also accept that *post-colonialism* is a better term to describe the phenomenon in question: this distinction is not made in Minnis's article and may cause confusion for readers.

The suggestion that political actors in First Nations possess sufficient political and economic power to address the crises in question is remarkably misguided. In the last four decades, developments in the area of First Nations governance have been encouraging but are still considerably insufficient (Bird, 2002). Traditional forms of First Nations community leadership still need to be made commensurate with mainstream democracy (Otis, 2006). Minnis's suggestion that First Nations people living off reserve have increased in number to the point that government transfers to First Nations should be the subject of policy development does not adequately support an argument for re-examining how money is transferred to First Nations. As Minnis (2006) writes, "70 per cent of all Aboriginals now live in towns or urban centres. And yet only $7 million is spent annually servicing off-reserve populations compared to $320 million for on-reserve populations" (p. 981). Regardless of how much money is used to service off-reserve Aboriginals, Canada's treaty obligations were established in reference to First Nations reserves; the monies used to address those obligations should not be the subject of policy development that adversely affects existing treaty obligations.

Minnis's (2006) failure to regard postcolonial phenomena as genuine reasons for Aboriginal underachievement is exacerbated by one of his more problematic statements:

> *Neither can internal colonialism explain why off-reserve students perform better than on-reserve students in the trades and at the secondary and post-secondary level …. many on-reserve schools are now staffed with Aboriginal teachers and personnel who are brought up in the same culture as their students. Does this imply that First Nations teachers are colonizing First Nations students? (p. 982)*

A reasonable answer to Minnis's query is *yes*; neocolonialism (Ashcroft, Griffiths, & Tiffin, 2000) is prevalent in such situations, because although the teachers in question may come from the same community as the students they teach, the pedagogical practices, curricular materials, and broad educational imperatives employed in First Nations schools can have an adverse effect on Aboriginal students (Battiste & Semaganis, 2002).

Cultural Discontinuity

Cultural discontinuity is a reason for educational underachievement among Aboriginals that Minnis (2006) regards as "dubious" (p. 982). Minnis's strongest evidence for this reason being inadequate appears to be that changes have been made in First Nations schools that have made them culturally appropriate. As he writes,

> A concerted effort has been made to make schools and teachers culturally sensitive. Universities and colleges have made great efforts to help First Nations students adjust to city living and the culture of the university. More First Nations Administrators and teachers are employed in reserve schools. Professional and cultural counselling and support services are available at most post-secondary institutions. Community-based teacher education degree programs have sprung up over the country in an attempt to reduce the cultural divide. (p. 983)

As encouraging as these developments have been over the last few decades, First Nations schools have not yet realized a form of education that is congruent with traditional ideals of learning and is respective of spiritual, environmental, and cultural aspects of First Nations communities; such an education would need to be localized and unique to the specific community in which it is employed (Abel, Dittburner, & Graham, 2000). To assert that sufficient changes have been made in the area of First Nations education in respect to cultural appropriateness is misguided. Cultural discontinuity is perhaps the most plausible reason for these difficulties, and such discontinuities may merit further research. The plausibility may be better appreciated by considering the following: bearing in mind that language is an important element of ethnic culture (Fettes & Norton, 2000), if the specific cultural discontinuity in First Nations classrooms were language (English instruction of students who converse only in a traditional language), would one really doubt the cultural discontinuity argument for educational underachievement in First Nations? Other aspects of culture such as history, oral traditions, spirituality, and connections to traditional lands may be every bit as essential to First Nations heritage as language.

Discussion: First Nations' Struggles in Postcolonial Canada

First Nations people have a treaty right to education (Friesen & Friesen, 2002). Treaty obligations are currently usually honoured through the transfer of money from government departments to First Nations (Frideres & Gadacz, 2008); these monies fund education in

First Nations. This financial relationship between government and First Nations in Canada may be characterized as a treaty relationship, but it would be remiss to overlook the notion that such relationships have their roots in the colonial activities of European settlers during their conquest of present-day Canada (Dickason, 2006). Although the colonial activities of European arrival, settlement, and eventual Confederation took place centuries ago, the effects of those activities are still present today and have had an extremely detrimental effect on the First Peoples of Canada (Lerat & Ungar, 2005). Rather than maintaining their ways of life on the traditional lands of their ancestors, Canada's First Peoples have been forced into small enclaves with little in the way of resources to live as they wish (Ray, 2005). These effects, the results of colonial activities of the past, can be referred to as postcolonialism.

Postcolonialism, the theory that "centralizes the issues emerging from colonial relations" (Cashmore, 1996, p. 285), has been manifest in the aftermath of European incursion onto Turtle Island and the marginalizing and oppressive social systems and institutions that continue to subjugate those who have been colonized. If one considers the notion that colonial activity in Canada came to an end with the establishment of treaties, the Indian Act, and Confederation, establishments that are still in force today, then the effect of those developments may merit discourse in the realm of Indigenous studies and other similar forums. The postcolonial mentality, one that perpetuates the appalling social status quo of Canada's First Peoples (Ashcroft et al., 2000), can be inferred by the state in which people exist in First Nations communities compared with how they existed when the postcolonial era began. With few exceptions, opportunities for personal and social development are still rare, economic opportunity is still dependent on government assistance, educational performance by First Nations students is still wanting, and non-Aboriginal perspectives on these problems continue to be characterized by a blame-the-victim mentality.

Education for First Nations people has suffered from the effects of postcolonialism (Alfred, 1999). Many have suggested, much as Minnis has, that underachievement in education is the result of a mentality of indolence, inferring that a sedentary lifestyle has developed among First Nations peoples in Canada that is associated with economic dependence on government transfers. To reiterate a point made above, the transfers discussed by Minnis are presented in a way that fails to communicate the reasons why such transfers exist in the first place. European conquest of present-day Canada involved the initiation on the part of European colonizers of a process of political, economic, and social domination of the First Peoples that reached a significant stage after two crucial events: Confederation (the formalization of the colonizers' ownership of Canada) and the signing of the treaties (events that took place over many years and solidified the colonizers' domination over First Nations of Canada). After this stage, government officials assumed the freedom to subjugate the First Peoples of Canada with little resistance (Adams, 2000; Henderson, 2000b). Fiscal transfers may be viewed as compensation for surrendered lands (Mainville, 2001), but such transfers may be viewed as tools of control as well (Cox, 2002). First Nations that have been forced to exist on small, remote, and resource-poor lands where genuine opportunities for social and economic development are rare must make use of these transfers to maintain community programming and ensure the health of their people as best they can (Indian and Northern Affairs Canada, 1996). Focusing on the mentality that emerges from this process of postcolonialism, as Minnis does, is to convey a minute portion of a larger story.

At present, educational underachievement in First Nations is being addressed through processes of decolonization related to curricular content and pedagogical practices. Armstrong, Corenblum, and Gfellner (2008) employed the use of traditional forms of art in First Nations schools in order to help students affirm and practice traditional cultural mores and improve academic achievement. Greenwood and de Leeuw (2007) espoused a form of education that incorporates connections to the traditional lands and teachings that are relevant to the students in question. Saunders and Hill (2007) called for the inclusion of traditional pedagogies and culturally sensitive curriculum as a remedy for educational underachievement on reserves. These examples speak to a movement in the field of First Nations education that emphasizes adaptation of contemporary educational processes to render them congruent with the cultural uniqueness of the students and communities in question. The unique manifestations of Indigenous Knowledge, heritage, and consciousness that are prevalent in a particular community should be reflected in how educational programming is developed and delivered to Aboriginal children; the inclusion of such components of culture can have important benefits to academic achievement (Armstrong et al., 2008; Friesen & Friesen, 2002), as well as language retention (Ionk, 2008). Transforming the Eurocentric school curricula and pedagogical practices employed in most schools in postcolonial Canada into culturally appropriate programming for First Nations students may be a more appropriate means of addressing educational underachievement than focusing on inappropriate economic theories.

REFERENCES

Abel, F., Dittburner, C., & Graham, K.A. (2000). Towards a shared understanding in the policy discussion about Aboriginal education. In M.B. Castellan, L. Davis, & L. Lahache (Eds.), *Aboriginal education: Fulfilling the promise* (pp. 3–28). Vancouver: University of British Columbia Press.

Adams, H. (2000). Challenging Eurocentric history. In R.F. Laliberte, P. Settee, J.B. Waldram, R. Innes, B. Macdougall, L. McBain, & F.L. Barron (Eds.), *Expressions in Canadian Native studies* (pp. 40–53). Saskatoon, SK: University Extension Press.

Alfred, T. (1999). *Peace, power, righteousness: An Indigenous manifesto.* Don Mills, ON: Oxford University Press.

Armstrong, H.D., Corenblum, B.S., & Gfellner, B.M. (2008). An initial report to a community university research alliance: Community-based Aboriginal curriculum initiatives. *First Nations Perspectives, 1,* 1–18.

Ashcroft, B., Griffiths, G., & Tiffin, H. (2000). *Post-colonial studies: The key concepts.* London, UK: Routledge.

Battiste, M., & Henderson, J.Y. (2000). *Protecting Indigenous Knowledge and heritage: A global challenge.* Saskatoon, SK: Purich.

Battiste, M., & Semaganis, H. (2002). First thoughts on First Nations citizenship: Issues in education. In Y.M. Hebert (Ed.), *Citizenship in transformation in Canada* (pp. 93–111). Toronto: University of Toronto Press.

Beblawi, H. (1990). The rentier state in the Arab world. In G. Luciani (Ed.), *The Arab state* (pp. 85–98). London, UK: Routledge.

Bird, J. (2002). Introduction. In J. Bird, L. Land, & M. Macadam (Eds.), *Nation to nation: Aboriginal sovereignty and the future of Canada* (pp. xiii–xvii). Toronto: Irwin.

Cashmore, E. (1996). *Dictionary of race and ethnic relations* (4th ed.). London, UK: Routledge.

Cox, B.A. (2002). Introduction. In B.A. Cox (Ed.), *Native people, Native lands: Canadian Indians, Inuit and Metis* (pp. xi–xv). Montreal: McGill-Queen's University Press.

Dauvergne, C. (2005). *Humanitarianism, identity, and nation: Migration laws in Canada and Australia.* Vancouver: University of British Columbia Press.

Deer, F. (2008). *The significance of citizenship development for Canadian Aboriginal students.* Paper presented at the 4th international conference on Indigenous education Asia/Pacific, Vancouver.

Dickason, O.P. (2006). *A concise history of Canada's First Nations.* New York: Oxford University Press.

Duran, B., & Duran, E. (2000). Applied postcolonial clinical and research strategies. In M. Battiste (Ed.), *Reclaiming Indigenous voice and vision* (pp. 86–100). Vancouver: University of British Columbia Press.

Fettes, M., & Norton, R. (2000). Voices of winter: Aboriginal languages and public policy in Canada. In M.B. Castellan, L. Davis, & L. Lahache (Eds.), *Aboriginal education: Fulfilling the promise* (pp. 29–54). Vancouver: University of British Columbia Press.

Frideres, J.S., & Gadacz, R.R. (2008). *Aboriginal peoples in Canada* (8th ed.). Toronto: Pearson Education Canada.

Friesen, J.W., & Friesen, V.L. (2002). *Aboriginal education in Canada: A plea for integration.* Calgary, AB: Detselig.

Greenwood, M., & de Leeuw, S. (2007). Teachings from the land: Indigenous people, our health, our land, and our children. *Canadian Journal of Native Education, 30*(1), 48–53.

Gylfason, T. (2005, September). *Institutions, human capital, and diversification of rentier economies.* Paper presented at the meeting Transforming Authoritarian Rentier Economies, Bonn.

Henderson, J.Y. (2000a). Ayukpachi: Empowering Aboriginal thought. In M. Battiste (Ed.), *Reclaiming Indigenous voice and vision* (pp. 248–278). Vancouver: University of British Columbia Press.

Henderson, J.Y. (2000b). Postcolonial ledger drawing: Legal reform. In M. Battiste (Ed.), *Reclaiming Indigenous voice and vision* (pp. 161–171). Vancouver: University of British Columbia Press.

Henderson, J.Y. (2000c). Postcolonial ghost dancing: Diagnosing European colonialism. In M. Battiste (Ed.), *Reclaiming Indigenous voice and vision* (pp. 58–76). Vancouver: University of British Columbia Press.

Indian and Northern Affairs Canada. (1996). *Royal Commission on Aboriginal peoples.* Ottawa: Author.

Indian and Northern Affairs Canada. (2007). *Canadian polar commission and Indian specific claims commission: Performance report for the period ending March 31, 2007.* Ottawa: Author.

Ionk, L.B. (2008). How do young children learn language: Perspectives of Aboriginal and non-Aboriginal mothers. *First Nations Perspectives, 1,* 74–97.

Lerat, H., & Ungar, L. (2005). *Treaty promises, Indian reality: Life on a reserve.* Saskatoon, SK: Purich.

Little Bear, L. (2000). Jagged world views colliding. In M. Battiste (Ed.), *Reclaiming Indigenous voice and vision* (pp. 77–85). Vancouver: University of British Columbia Press.

Mainville, R. (2001). *An overview of Aboriginal and treaty rights and compensation for their breach.* Saskatoon, SK: Purich.

Merriam-Webster Online. (2008). Colonization. Retrieved May 1, 2008, from: http://www.merriam-webster.com/dictionary/colonization

Mills, S., & McCreary, T. (2006). Culture and power in the workplace: Aboriginal women's perspectives on practices to increase Aboriginal inclusion in forest processing mills. *Journal of Aboriginal Economic Development, 5*(1), 40–50.

Minnis, J.R. (2006). First Nations education and rentier economics: Parallels with the Gulf States. *Canadian Journal of Education, 29*(4), 975–997. http://dx.doi.org/10.2307/20054207

Monture-Angus, P. (1999). *Journeying forward: Dreaming First Nations' independence.* Halifax, NS: Fernwood.

Otis, G. (2006). Elections, traditional Aboriginal governance and the charter. In G. Christie (Ed.), *Aboriginality and governance: A multidisciplinary perspective* (pp. 217–237). Penticton, BC: Theytus Books.

Ray, A.J. (2005). *I have lived here since the world began: An illustrated history of Canada's Native people* (rev. ed.). Toronto: Key Porter Books.

Saunders, S.E.R., & Hill, S.M. (2007). Native education and in-classroom coalition-building: Factors and models in delivering an equitous authentic education. *Canadian Journal of Education, 30*(4), 1015–1045. http://dx.doi.org/10.2307/20466677

Schissel, B., & Wotherspoon, T. (2003). *The legacy of school for Aboriginal people: Education, oppression, and emancipation.* Don Mills, ON: Oxford University Press.

Smith, L.T. (1999). *Decolonizing methodologies: Research and Indigenous peoples.* London: Zed Books.

Stewart, S.C. (2006). First Nations education: Financial accountability and educational attainment. *Canadian Journal of Education, 29*(4), 998–1018. http://dx.doi.org/10.2307/20054208

Stidsen, S. (2006). *The Indigenous world 2006.* Copenhagen: International Work Group for Indigenous Affaires.

Tully, J. (2000). A just relationship between Aboriginal and non-Aboriginal peoples in Canada. In C. Cook & J.D. Lindau (Eds.), *Aboriginal rights and self-government* (pp. 39–71). Montreal: McGill-Queens University Press.

Turner, D. (2006). *This is not a peace pipe: Towards a critical Indigenous philosophy.* Toronto: University of Toronto Press.

United Nations Development Programme. (2007). *Human development report 2007/2008.* New York: Author.

Yates, D.A. (1996). *The rentier state in Africa: Oil rent dependency and neocolonialism in the Republic of Gabon.* Trenton, NJ: Africa World Press.

19

Ganigonhi:oh: The Good Mind Meets the Academy

David Newhouse[1]

This chapter was originally published in the *Canadian Journal of Native Education* (2008), 31(1), pp. 184–197. Reproduced with permission.

Before all words are spoken, we send greetings to the universe and to all living things.

We give thanks for the rising of the sun and the light and life that it brings.

We give thanks for another day of life.

I start in this traditional fashion with words of thanksgiving: the words that come before all others. Historic Haudenosaunee protocol requires a formal acknowledgement of the other, a ceremony "at woods edge," as it is called. It signals to those whose village we are about to enter that we have arrived, asks for permission to enter, and gives time to refresh ourselves from the journey. It allows time to collect our thoughts, to pay our respects, to thank the universe and our protectors for their watchfulness, and allows our prospective hosts to ready themselves. The ceremony at woods edge is an important aspect of Haudenosaunee diplomacy. It begins with the Thanksgiving Address, which reminds us of the nature of the universe, its structure and functioning, the roles and responsibilities of all aspects of it, and creates an attitude of humility and gratitude.

I acknowledge the original inhabitants of this land and their descendants who have lived here for a few millennia and whose way of life has changed significantly over this time.

I also acknowledge the institution of the university in which we as professors and students work and study. Universities have their origins in a distant land close to nine hundred years ago. Like the original inhabitants of North America, they have survived the ages and have been transformed, often by forces that they have been unable to resist. The contemporary university has its roots in the European Enlightenment, an intense period of intellectual and philosophical debate that emphasized the primacy of reason as the way to knowledge and to the good life. Haudenosaunee philosophers of the good mind would agree that reason is indeed important. However, as I discuss below, they would add the importance of balancing reason with passion.

Starting in this traditional way helps us to consider how might we extend our traditional practices to our scholarly endeavours? Can we create norms of scholarship that are appropriate to our understandings of the work of the university? Ought our scholarly endeavours be consistent with our cultural practices? This chapter reflects my experience as a faculty member since 1993 and department chair of Indigenous studies at Trent University, bringing Indigenous Knowledge (IK) and Indigenous Knowledge-holders into the university. I was born and raised at Six Nations of the Grand River in the Longhouse religion in a family of ceremonialists. My family has been involved in thinking about tradition in a contemporary world for a century, starting with my great-grandfather Seth Newhouse, who challenged the prevailing view at the tum of the twentieth century about the need to begin to communicate what we now call Indigenous Knowledge in English, both written and oral. We are no strangers to controversy.

Trent brought Indigenous Knowledge into the university as cultural knowledge in the 1970s and Indigenous elders as holders of Indigenous Knowledge as professors of Native studies[2] at the same time. The project was seen as important for the university and Aboriginal communities. We have a 30-year history of working with Indigenous Knowledge in an academic setting. I start by placing the IK movement in the contemporary social political environment and then move on to our experiences at Trent. I hope this helps to demonstrate that addressing the issues surrounding IK are important to the future of Indigenous higher education and to Canada.

Indigenous Knowledge in the Contemporary Political and Social Environment

Indigenous people in Canada live in a time I call *after great pain*, although the effects of great pain are still evident. Indigenous peoples are in the process of creating political places of dignity and respect in the Canadian federation through the self-government movement, the treaty and land claims processes, and the healing movement. In many places, this work is undertaken in collaboration with non-Indigenous allies who wish to help Canada live up to its past promises and contemporary multicultural ideals. In universities, contemporary Indigenous scholars have developed a postcolonial[3] consciousness that imbues their work. Taiaike Alfred's (1999, 2005) writings on Haudenosaunee political theory, Marie Battiste's (2000) work on IK and education, John Borrows's (2002) work on Aboriginal law, and Willy Ermine's (2005) work on Indigenous philosophy and ethics are excellent examples of this consciousness. Their scholarship is imbued with an awareness of the history of the poor treatment by the Europeans who established this country, has a critical awareness of colonial effects, and proposes how to deal with these effects.

Indigenous peoples have been part of the university experience in North America since their establishment in the seventeenth century. We have been mascots, students, administrators, professors, and objects of research. There is, after one hundred years of research, much written about Indigenous peoples: some of it is even true and useful. It would be fair to say that Indigenous peoples did not go to universities to find themselves or to study themselves, or to learn about their culture or how their societies functioned. Indigenous peoples were enticed to enter universities as preparation for high-level participation in the labour market or to meet the goals established for them by groups outside Indigenous communities. The university served as another instrument of assimilation. The first Indigenous person, Caleb Cheeshahteaumauk, a Wampanoag, graduated from a North American university in 1665 (Monaghan, 2005). One of the oldest universities in the United States, Dartmouth College, was established in 1769 to train Indians to serve as ministers who would then spread Christianity and civilization among their people.

Despite the efforts directed to transforming them, Indigenous peoples shared their knowledge with those working inside the institution. The knowledge shared with early anthropologists helped to establish the discipline. The knowledge shared with professors like Abraham Maslow (in Hoffman, 1999) and Carl Jung (1963) added to the rafters[4] of the discipline of psychology. The work of William

Fenton, Arthur Parker, and other anthropologists and historians led to the development of the discipline of ethnohistory. Today, IK is shaping disciplines such as health studies and environmental studies. Political studies and law, among other disciplines, have similarly benefitted from their engagement with Indigenous peoples and their ideas. Indigenous peoples were often seen as a way of learning about the evolution of human beings, as a glimpse into a human past. It would be fair to characterize the relationship throughout most of its history as a one-way transfer of knowledge and benefit, that is, from Indigenous peoples to university. The history of Indigenous-university relations remains to be written, although there is a good start in *Science Encounters the Indian* (Bieder, 1995), which provides a foundation for examining the early relationship.

In 1972, the National Indian Brotherhood, now the Assembly of First Nations, released a position paper entitled *Indian Control of Indian Education*. This document argued that Indians ought to have control over their own education, both process and content. Indian control would enable Indian peoples to shape the education of their children in ways that would strengthen culture and provide a solid basis for societal participation as Indians. Over the last 30 years, Indigenous people in Canada have vigorously pursued this policy direction. It has stimulated discussion and change at all three levels of education: primary, secondary, and post-secondary. One of its results has been the development of a network of 52 Aboriginal-controlled post-secondary education institutions across the country. Some of these are independent diploma-granting institutions that are part of the provincial systems, such as the Nicola Valley Institute of Technology; others are private institutions similar to tribal colleges in the United States, such as the First Nations Technical Institute; and others are affiliated or partnered with universities or colleges, such as the First Nations University of Canada. In universities, departments or programs of Indigenous studies (or Native studies, First Nation studies, or Aboriginal studies), and other programs emerged, often as a way of attracting Indigenous students and making the institution relevant to Indigenous community needs.

The curriculum over the last few years has reflected an Indigenous desire for cultural transmission, identity development, and market skills. Much effort has been made to ensure that the system does not "get rid of the Indian" (Titley, 1986), as Duncan Campbell Scott would have wished, but to create a self-confident, modern Indigenous person fully capable of meeting the challenges of the contemporary world and living a good life as an Indigenous person.

Over the last three decades, Indigenous peoples have stood up and begun to speak for themselves, using the skills and knowledge gained from this curriculum. They speak back to a system that saw and generally continues to see them only in negative terms, that saw them as marginal and offering little to contemporary life and even less to the broad political, social, and cultural debates of the day. This speaking back in my view is an important aspect of the decolonization movement as we are experiencing it in Canada. Decolonization is a multifaceted process, but it starts with a single statement: I am a person, fully conscious, self-determining, and able to think and speak for myself. I am not you nor am I the image that you have created of me.

Through the process of decolonization, we as Indigenous peoples come to the table with something of value to offer to the world. This something has come to be called *Indigenous Knowledge*. IK is the knowledge that we have developed over generations: the theories of the universe and how it works; the nature of human beings and others; the nature of society and political order; the nature of the world and how to live in it; and human motivation among many other aspects of life. This knowledge has been transmitted from generation to generation, thought about, discussed, refined, discarded, reinforced, and subjected to continual analysis and testing. It has not been static. IK shows how to live in a world of continual change, for it is based on a foundational philosophical tenet: the world is constantly in process of transformation and movement. Hoping for stability and certainty in the material world leads to suffering. We live in a world where we as human beings are the last created and the most dependent on other forces for our survival. We are at once powerless and powerful: our bodies are powerless; our minds are powerful. These are Indigenous philosophical statements about the nature of human beings and the universe.

One of the central aspects of modern Indigenous societies is the desire to use IK as a key-informing basis of contemporary life. This is not to say that the knowledge of others is not useful or helpful. It is, however, to place IK at the centre, in a position of centrality or primacy. To ignore other knowledges would be inconsistent with traditional teachings about what it means to be an educated person. In fact, many Indigenous elders insist that we learn and engage with the knowledge of others. We can interpret the *Guswentah*, the two-row wampum that signified the relationship between Haudenosaunee and various European settlers in the early arrival period, in a way that supports their position. The Guswentah consists of two rows of purple beads separated by three rows of white beads. It looks like two purple parallel lines on a bed of white.

The separateness and parallel nature of the two rows has been used as an argument for the creation of a state of complete separateness from each other. We canoe alone, so to speak. The two rows denote a relationship and in my view a dialogue between nations and cultures; the three white rows signify the ethics of this dialogue: respect, honesty, and kindness. There is much to be said for noninterference in national political affairs, but not much in favour of other aspects of separateness. Not engaging with the knowledge of others, denying the knowledge of others, is inconsistent with a Guswentah philosophy of engagement. In fact, engagement is required in order to live well with those with whom one shares the world.

Learning, reason, and oratory have always been marks of an educated person in Haudenosaunee society. Similarly, so was a facility to speak languages other than one's own. Learning the other's knowledge was also considered important, as important as learning the knowledge of one's own society and culture. The highest compliment that one can make of an Iroquoian person is to say that they are *of good mind*.

The *good mind* is the consciousness ideal postulated by Haudenosaunee philosophical thought. What does it mean to be of good mind? A good mind is balanced of reason and passion, ever negotiating the dance that the two undertake. A good mind is ever thinking of how to foster peace between peoples, the world, and all its inhabitants. Important here is the idea of balance and the ideas of reason and passion. Haudenosaunee philosophers, not being influenced by Descartes, did not conceive of a separateness of mind and body; no statement *I think, therefore I am* animates Haudenosaunee philosophy. *Reason*—the ability to think logically, rationally, and to express oneself well in words and passion—that is, the feelings are related and mutually influential. Both are deemed necessary for the good life.

Passion, especially anger, is seen as destructive. The founding story of the Iroquoian confederacy conceives of a time when humans were ruled entirely by passion. There was war everywhere, brother fought brother, cousin fought cousin, blood was everywhere. Such was the effect of passion. Iroquoian philosophers say, "passion drives reason from the table." On the other hand, reason alone leads to sterility and is equally destructive. Reason robs one of passion, forcing one to look with coldness and distance at human beings and the world. Our minds are made up of reason and passion. Neither can be denied, nor should they be denied. We ought to act with reason tempered by passion.

The central ceremony of Iroquoian life is the condolence ceremony, invented by the Peacemaker and practiced by Hiawatha. Its purpose is to bring reason back to the table. With this feather, I wipe the obstructions from your eyes so that you may see again, from your ears so that you might hear again, from your throat so that you may speak again. Grief has driven reason from the table and impaired our ability to see, hear, and speak. It is a symbolic return to the good mind, a mind balanced of reason and passion.

Our preference is to build educational institutions that explore and transmit our ideas, ideas like that of the good mind. (I might go as far as to say that the foundational idea for an Indigenous university ought to be the good mind.) This project has proven to be somewhat difficult, mostly due to the single-mindedness of the adherents to the Enlightenment project. Enlightenment universities favour reason over passion. I am not arguing against reason, science, a desire for objectivity, or empiricism. I am arguing that reason is not enough. The idea of the good mind sustained us in the past and can continue to sustain us in the future.

In my view, one of the fundamental purposes of a university is to help us to understand the world and ourselves and to transmit our knowledge to a new generation of people. It ought also to help us explore what a good life is. And in the twenty-first century, it ought to foster highly creative, innovative human beings adept at creating or, if you will, uncovering new truths. A university ought to bring the best of human knowledges into dialogue so that we might better understand the universe.

Until recently, the knowledge of our ancestors as represented by Indigenous Knowledge was not considered worthy of inclusion in this dialogue. It was, however, considered worthy of study as folklore or local knowledge in the Geertzian sense (Geertz, 1985). Indigenous Knowledge as Indigenous Knowledge was not part of any university-level curriculum until the early part of the twenty-first century. It was present in the research reports of others, but not as taught by elders. The problem was that it was not produced as a result of the scientific method, did not result in peer-reviewed publications, and was, therefore, not part of the dialogue that academics have with each other, as my colleagues are fond of saying. The reasoning process behind it was not visible, and as a result, it did not meet the test of verifiability that was necessary for it to be accepted as real and true.

The construction of a category of knowledge called Indigenous Knowledge is a powerful act of decolonization. It makes visible in a real and tangible way the intellectual efforts of Indigenous peoples; in fact, it allows for Indigenous intellectuals and in the process creates something that can be explored by the academy. The construction of IK also attempts to place boundaries around colonization and provides the basis for a way forward. The desire to use IK in daily life creates an intellectual project that can be understood and explored by the university.

IK has some commonly accepted characteristics that have been agreed on by a growing group of Indigenous scholars such as Cajete and Little Bear (1999), Brant Castellano (2000), Battiste (2000), and Ermine (2005), among others. It comes about as a result of a long, intimate relationship with a particular environment, is based on careful, long-term observation and testing of hypotheses, is tested regularly through use and practice, is modified according to changing environmental conditions and reason, and is rooted in Indigenous understandings of the nature of the universe. In IK, reason and passion are intertwined. IK is transmitted through practice, ceremony, and instruction. IK rests on a spiritual foundation. By *spirit*, I mean a sense of the interconnectedness of things and a sense that we live in a sea of energy that animates everything. The universe is alive.

IK is multidisciplinary in nature. Its most common and best-known discipline is TEK, traditional environmental knowledge. The Inuit speak of Inuit Qaujimajatuqangit or Inuit traditional knowledge (ITK), and the government of Nunavut is working out how it might be incorporated into the daily workings of the government and its programs (Nunavut, 2003). Another example is Gayanashagowa: the Great Binding Law expresses the social and political philosophy of the Haudenosaunee and is at the centre of their self-government efforts (Dennis, 1993). The Wet'suwet'en described their approach to peacemaking based on their view of the nature of human beings and their interactions to the judge in the 1991 Delgamuukw case (Mills, 1994).

I hope that you have a sense that IK is a complex of ideas and practices based on Indigenous views of the universe. How do we bring IK into Enlightenment universities? Can we create IK scholars who research and teach in their intellectual spaces? Can we transmit IK through university courses? What is IK research? What constitutes an IK publication? How do we evaluate IK scholars? These are some of the questions we face when we bring IK into the university. I now turn to our efforts at Trent University.

Indigenous Knowledge at Trent

At Trent, since the 1970s, in Native studies, now Indigenous studies, we have been teaching about Indigenous cultures at the undergraduate level in a variety of ways: formal course-based teaching involving readings and discussions of elders' teachings, experiential placements, summer camps, annual elders' gatherings, and, more recently, weekly traditional teaching workshops. Our approach has been to provide a sufficient foundation so that students who wish to learn more can do so with the knowledge that they will not commit grave errors and can do so respectfully, that is, in accordance with Indigenous protocols.

This was not called Indigenous Knowledge teaching; we taught cultural knowledge. This changed in 1999 when we started a doctoral program in Indigenous studies. By this time, the discourse of IK was firmly established in intellectual discourse. We began an extended conversation about what it was, what aspects of it we could bring into the university, who could teach it, how they would teach it, and who could learn it. Our Ph.D. vision statement places IK at the centre of the program. This means in practice what we had to grapple with. Saying it was easier than doing it. We did have at the time two and a half decades of teaching cultural knowledge and working institutionally with elders as holders of traditional knowledge. What had we learned from this experience that might guide us as we developed the doctoral program?

Our first conclusion was that the teachers of IK should be elders. We have had elders as members of the faculty since 1975: Fred Wheatley, who taught Nishnaabewin and Anishnaabe culture, and Chief Jake Thomas, who taught Mohawk language and Iroquoian culture. Both were tenured faculty members appointed without the usual academic credentials but on the basis of their cultural knowledge and Indigenous credentials. Lately, we have had Shirley Williams and Edna Manitowabi: Shirley to teach Nishnaabewin and Edna to teach a course appropriately called Indigenous Knowledge. Shirley became the first professor in Canadian history to become a full professor on the basis of IK.

In order to do this, we have had to grapple with the idea of Indigenous scholarship and with the criteria that we would use to appoint Indigenous Knowledge-holders to tenured faculty positions. Our appointment and tenure criteria define scholarship broadly and allow for the use of elders, from the cultural group of the person under consideration, in the evaluation of Indigenous Knowledge scholarship.

The university-wide decision-making processes involving chairs' and deaconal committees and the board of governors approved our criteria. Our tenure review process rests on the widely accepted idea of peer review and extends the peers to a group not usually considered by the university as part of its internal process.

Second, we concluded that the historical structure of university courses based on reading, reflection, discussion, and writing did not suit well the teaching of IK. Teaching IK required a hands-on experiential approach, an apprenticeship of sorts consistent with Indigenous approaches to learning. The teaching had to engage both reason and passion. At the undergraduate level, we have created courses that provide this experience in a setting away from the university, in a natural environment, and that focus on the teachings of a particular group. We learned that a pan-Indigenous approach did not make sense and caused more confusion among students than it solved. Accordingly, we separated Anishnaabe IK from Haudenosaunee IK. At the graduate level, we also wished to provide an opportunity for extended study with elders. We put in place a Bimaadiziwin/ Atonhetseri:io option that would provide this. Students have an opportunity to spend a term working with an elder, learning in depth from him or her. This option occurs away from the campus under the leadership and direction of a director of studies, an elder himself. The inclusion of this option is important to our academic mission. Approximately half the students in the doctoral program have taken part in this option.

We also found that learning IK was different from learning about IK. The task of learning IK requires a mindful presence and a keen understanding of self, as well as an ability to reflect. Learning IK is in my view akin to studying the humanities. It requires not only knowledge of content but also knowledge of one's own values, perspectives, and attitudes, or at least a willingness to explore them. Learning IK is transformative. It changes a person in unexpected ways. It makes you keenly aware that you are living in an interconnected world, that the world is alive, that there is an animating energy/spirit, and that we are only a small part of the universe. Learning IK teaches humility, gratitude, and forgiveness, an awareness of the cycle of life and death, and how to begin to live in a powered universe. This is the knowledge that one gains from studying the humanities.

Third, we found that we could not ignore our own behaviour. Given the interwoven nature of knowledge and spirituality, how should we behave? How should our students behave? Deciding to study IK in the views of the elders with whom we were working required a high level of commitment, a sense of humility, and most important, an open and honest heart with a desire to use the knowledge for the betterment of humankind. Self-aggrandizement was not part of the package.

In terms of learning from elders, we had to learn how to question differently. In the university, everything is open to probing, to questioning, to examination through the use of reason. The knowledge-holders were also subject to examination, to challenge, and to continual questioning. What was unsettling was not that these things were occurring. After all, there is a long intellectual tradition in Indigenous societies. What was unsettling was that they occurred in a climate of disrespect or what many interpreted as disrespect. How does one question an elder? In the academy, we ask professors questions all the time, asking direct questions and expecting direct answers. A lack of understanding is often interpreted as a problem in explanation, a problem of telling rather than a problem of listening. Elders would respond to questions with stories, fully expecting the student to answer his or her own question. Students want answers. We have had both to teach how to respond to each other and to learn how to relate to one another in a new way.

Bringing IK-holders into the academy has also meant that we have had to think about expectations for a professor who is an IK-holder. The academy requires that as professors, we have a research program that results in a steady stream of published books, papers, and conference presentations, among other things. This research is often funded through a variety of grant programs. The university academic culture requires that we demonstrate that we are active and productive scholars. By active and productive, they mean that we produce a steady stream of output, that our research is funded, and that we transmit this knowledge through teaching and writing. Above all, our work is to result in "net new knowledge." It is important that this new knowledge be produced as a result of the research or inquiry efforts of the professor. When confronted with the question of newness about the output of Indigenous Knowledge scholars by my dean, who is a philosophy professor, I asked, what net new knowledge has European philosophy and philosophers contributed to humanity over the last few hundred years? Is not a significant part of philosophical scholarship grappling with the ideas of those who came before and interpreting them for a contemporary time? How is this different from what Indigenous Knowledge-holders do? The question has not been asked again.

The problem of expectations of IK faculty is illustrated by one of our elder faculty who was nominated for a research award. She had produced a lexicon of Nishnaabemowin (Ojibwa language) obtained by interviewing elder speakers. It was the first such text produced. The committee deliberated about whether her work was research; whether it was original, that is, was net new knowledge, or whether she had just written down something that was already in existence. I wondered aloud why an anthropologist could get a doctorate for doing the same thing and demonstrated that several scholars had received their degrees for producing Indigenous lexicon dictionaries. How can the same activity and output be research in one academic discipline and not in another?

We have had to convey what elders do in the language of the academy so that it can be understood in its terms rather than our own. We conceptualized and described the work of elder faculty as research. Attending and participating in medicine camps became fieldwork and plant research. Giving interviews to other academics for publication became published papers. Participation in ceremonies has become workshop participation; leading ceremonies has become keynote addresses. We began a conversation about oral texts, Indigenous research methods, Indigenous epistemologies, and cosmologies that was intended to help us and others understand better how to think of academics as knowledge-creators in addition to their role as knowledge-transmitters. The purpose of these conversations was to make some of the rules of knowledge creation visible and subject to review as they are in other disciplinary areas. An elder's CV would then look similar in some respects to those of other academics. The texts to which it refers would be written and oral like those of the rest of us in the academy.

Students also had expectations about what they would find when they arrived here. They came expecting to engage IK and IK-holders and to come to their own conclusions. They came expecting an intellectual dialogue similar to that with which they were familiar. Learning about IK was fairly straightforward and easy. Learning IK challenged their understanding of themselves. However, as they grappled with it, it began to appear in their written work: papers, thesis proposals, and dissertations. It also began to affect their individual behaviour in unexpected ways.

We were confronted with practical questions: what knowledge can we bring into this place? (All except ceremonial or sacred knowledge. How do we know what is sacred or ceremonial? Ask). Who can learn it? (All who desire and who come to learn it with an open heart and sincere desire to learn). How do we evaluate their learning? (In the standard way, through written papers and oral presentations. In the IK courses and the two apprenticeship options, students make presentations in the presence of elders who then question them on what they learned). What type of grades should we give: pass/fail or letter grades? What constitutes an A? This was the subject of much debate and is still not resolved to everyone's satisfaction. Those who argue for pass/fail speak of the difficulty of evaluating degrees of IK; those who argue for letter grades argue for the use of grades in scholarship and other awards evaluation processes.

We worked on our responses to questions like these through a process of dialogue and discussion, not only with ourselves as academics but with elders and community members. For us, the university is not an ivory tower, distant from everyday life and concerns, but an important part of everyday life. What we do within it affects others. We do not undertake our work only for our own egos, but with and for our communities. It makes sense, then, to have them involved. Our advisory councils—Elders' Council, the Aboriginal Education Council, and Indigenous Studies Ph.D. Council—provide guidance and advice. As in any community, there is diversity of opinion and here is no exception. We might describe our efforts as an effort to come to one mind, to use a Haudenosaunee metaphor again.

These are the issues that arise from our move to bring IK into the academy. I am reminded, however, that IK is already in the academy. It has been for many years. Many Ph.D.-holders have received their degrees studying, documenting, and teaching about it in a variety of fields. Yet few of the IK practitioners or knowledge-holders are present in the academy as fully fledged members of the academy like tenured professors.

A large and growing global dialogue in IK is taking place. In a Google search I found 2.0m sites. Google Scholar lists 275,000 articles. Scholars' Portal shows 4,300 articles published on IK since 1981. The global academic literature on IK has become voluminous and inexhaustible. The academic dialogue represented by this literature is divided into two parts: a large critical dialogue about IK situating it clearly in the postcolonial, anticolonial critique of the West, and a smaller content dialogue of IK. The first academic dialogue receives most of the attention; it is what gets us published and what provides us with legitimacy in the eyes of the academy. The second is the more challenging aspect of the dialogue as it involves learning with both reason and passion. It is also the most difficult part to teach.

With each change of administration, we learned that we had to educate a new group about IK: deans, vice-presidents academic, and presidents. It is not part of their education and experience as faculty members, and consequently they have many questions. We continually have to discuss and make visible the foundations of our discipline. Each administration states that they are in support of IK in the academy, yet a new generation seems reluctant to bring IK-holders into the academy, even given our 30-year history of success in doing so. The reluctance to bring IK-holders into the academy is akin to wanting to teach physics without hiring physicists.

The academy is a powerful institution. It is not immutable. Its rafters have been extended many times over the centuries. Bringing IK into it will not destroy it, nor will it shake its foundations. The primacy of reason is important to human survival, even to those who hold to the idea of the good mind. Bringing IK into it is a project of dialogue, discussion, and debate. It requires the creation of an atmosphere that supports a broad definition of inquiry, the inter-relatedness of reason and passion, the notion of truths rather than Truth, and above all, accepts that Indigenous people have something to offer beyond opportunities for research into social problems.

For many, the spiritual aspects of IK are problematic. They are seen as inappropriate for inclusion in an Enlightenment institution and as inimicable to the reasoned work of the academy. For us as Indigenous peoples, as for many others, the spiritual facilitates our work. It makes us think of relationships and connections, of impact and effect, and awakens our consciousness to new truths. The spiritual also reminds us of the ethics of our work, to approach it, as the Anishnaabe say, in a good way and as the Haudenosaunee say, with a good mind. The spiritual also reminds us of our responsibilities as academics to tell the truth, to be conscious of our method, to be aware of our emotions and their effects, and above all, to do no harm.

It is possible to do all these things without a spiritual foundation, as our Enlightenment colleagues will tell us. This is indeed true. Yet for us it would not be consistent with the idea of the good mind and would be asking us to forget who we are. It would not be in keeping with the dialogue postulated by the Guswentah. It would be asking us to continue the old assimilationist activities of the university.

I am reminded of Hiawatha and the Peacemaker's work to convince Atatarho of the message of peace. They came to him and told him the message. He was unable to hear, saying, "No, not yet." They continued their work, bringing others to the message. Each time they came back and were greeted with the response: "No. Not yet." Finally, they stood in huge numbers before Atatarho. He saw and was convinced. Hiawatha combed the snakes from his hair and his mind became the good mind. His body was straightened and he accepted the message. Our numbers are gathering.

These are the measure of my words. I hope that you found something of interest. I thank you for the opportunity to share them with you.

And now that the words have been spoken and our business is concluded, we cover the fire and return to our homes and families. May you find them in good health and joyful at your return. May you journey well.

REFERENCES

Alfred, T. (1999). *Peace, power, righteousness: An Indigenous manifesto.* Toronto: Oxford University Press.

Alfred, T. (2005). *Wasase: Indigenous pathways of action and freedom.* Peterborough, ON: Broadview Press.

Battiste, M. (2000). *Reclaiming Indigenous voice and vision.* Vancouver: University of British Columbia Press.

Bieder, R. (1995). *Science encounters the Indian, 1820–1880: The early years of American ethnology.* Norman, OK: University of Oklahoma Press.

Borrows, J. (2002). *Recovering Canada: The resurgence of Indigenous law.* Toronto: University of Toronto Press.

Brant-Castellano, M. (2000). Updating Aboriginal traditions of knowledge. In G. Sefa Dei, B. Hall, & D. Rosenberg (Eds.), *Indigenous Knowledges in global contexts: Multiple readings of our world* (pp. 21–36). Toronto: University of Toronto Press.

Cajete, G., & Little Bear, L. (1999). *Native science natural laws of interdependence.* Santa Fe, NM: Clear Light Books.

Dennis, M. (1993). *Creating a landscape of peace: Iroquois-European encounters in seventeenth-century America.* Ithaca, NY: Cornell University Press.

Ermine, W. (2005). *Ethical space: Transforming relations, A report for the Tri-Council on Ethics.* Ottawa: Tri-Council on Ethics.

Geertz, C. (1985). *Local knowledge.* Scranton, PA: Harper Collins.

Hoffman, E. (1999). *The right to be human: A biography of Abraham Maslow.* Toronto: McGraw-Hill.

Jung, C. (1963). *Memories, dreams, reflections.* New York: Pantheon Books.

Mills, A. (1994). *Eagle down is our law: Witsuwit'en law, feasts, and land claims.* Vancouver: University of British Columbia Press.

Monaghan, E.J. (2005). *Learning to read and write in colonial America.* Boston, MA: University of Massachusetts Press.

Nunavut. (2003). *Inuit Qaujimajatuqangit Katimajiit established.* Iqaluit, NU: Department of Culture, Language, elders and Youth, Government of Nunavut.

Titley, B.E. (1986). A *narrow vision: Duncan Campbell Scott and the administration of Indian Affairs in Canada.* Vancouver: University of British Columbia Press.

NOTES

1 This chapter is based on talks given at the University of Sudbury Ethics Project and Algoma University College in November 2007. I extend thanks to the faculty and students who provided commentary on the ideas and for helping me to clarify them.

2 The Department of Native Studies was established as the Indian-Eskimo Studies Program in 1969, became the Department of Native Studies in 1972, and the Department of Indigenous Studies in 2006. Its name change over the years reflects the changing nomenclature used to refer to the original inhabitants of Canada. In this chapter, I use the term "Indigenous" to reflect our recent

decision. It is intended to connote a commonality of global experiences of original peoples with nation-states.

3 I acknowledge that the term "postcolonial" is disputed and that some argue that the period of colonialism is not over, so there can be no "post" or *after*. I use it here as a marker in a change in consciousness, that is, an awareness of the forces of colonialism.

4 "Added to the rafters" is a term for the addition to a longhouse to accommodate another family. I believe that it is important that we use ideas and concepts from our own cultures inside the academy as part of our work as Indigenous scholars. This practice grounds our work in our own intellectual traditions and reinforces our desire to foreground Indigenous ideas.

20

The "Good Mind" and Critical Thinking: A Response to David Newhouse[1]

Frances Widdowson

In the article "Ganigonhi:oh: The Good Mind Meets the Academy," David Newhouse argues that it is important to incorporate "Indigenous Knowledge" into the academy. Newhouse claims that this is necessary so that reason can be "tempered by passion" (Newhouse, 2008, p. 189). While he acknowledges that reason is important, Newhouse maintains that its use must include an awareness of colonialism and its effects. "Humility and gratitude," as well as "respect, honesty and kindness," are also claimed to be aspects of Indigenous Knowledge, which is described by Newhouse (2008) as

> the knowledge that we [Indigenous peoples] have developed over generations: the theories of the universe and how it works; the nature of human beings and others; the nature of society and political order; the nature of the world and how to live in it; and human motivation among many other aspects of life. This knowledge has been transmitted from generation to generation, thought about, discussed, refined, discarded, reinforced, and subjected to continual analysis and testing. (p. 187)

Newhouse's arguments appear convincing on the surface. It is important that conceptions of the universe be "subjected to continual analysis and testing" in the development of knowledge—this is, in fact, the defining characteristic of scientific research. Emotional intensity also can motivate the search for the truth; a lack of social concern, on the other hand, could result, as Newhouse (2008) points out, in dehumanization—"look[ing] with coldness and distance at human beings and the world" (p. 189). This is one of the reasons why there is concern with ensuring that research is undertaken ethically. Ethics review boards are being formed in universities to determine the impact of research on those who are being studied.

However, Newhouse's article disguises a darker reality that can be uncovered through a closer analysis. This reality concerns his definition of knowledge, and its implications for human understanding. It is apparent that what Newhouse assumes to be "knowledge" is actually the concept's opposite. This confusion, shown in his notion of the "good mind," has serious consequences for incorporating Indigenous Knowledge into the academy.

The deficiency in Newhouse's definition of knowledge is shown when his conception of the good mind is contrasted to a much more convincing attempt to link knowledge with socially beneficial attitudes—the British philosopher Bertrand Russell's account of the "good life." As is shown below, Russell's conception contains all the "passion," "honesty," and "kindness" praised by Newhouse, but avoids the impediments to human understanding contained in the latter's advocacy for Indigenous Knowledge.

Bertrand Russell's "Good Life"

In 1925, Bertrand Russell first published his essay "What I Believe,"[2] which summed up his view of the "good life" as follows: "one inspired by love and guided by knowledge" (Russell, 1957, p. 56). This summation raises two questions: What does Russell mean by "love," and how is it connected to "knowledge"? From this essay, it is clear that Russell (1957) equates love with altruism—"the desire for another person's welfare" (p. 58)—as this increases co-operation and eliminates conflict.

"Knowledge" is not explicitly defined by Russell in this essay, but it appears that his notion of the concept would be similar to what the physicist Alan Sokal (1998) has proposed—"justified true belief" (p. 9). Sokal and Bricmont (1998) have noted that "both in philosophy and in everyday language, there is a distinction between *knowledge* ... and mere *belief*; that is why the word 'knowledge' has a positive connotation while 'belief' is neutral" (p. 195, emphasis in original). Thus, if we believe that the sun revolves around the earth, or that the earth is flat, these beliefs cannot constitute knowledge, for the simple reason that they are false. Similarly, if on the night of September 10,

2001, a person dreamt that the World Trade Center towers would collapse the next day, and then awoke believing it, that belief would still not constitute knowledge, for though it turned out to be true, it was so because of coincidence; there was no *good reason* to believe it was true—in other words, it was not a *justified* true belief relative to the evidence available at the time.

Knowledge, therefore, is acquired through critical thinking and is very different from faith or opinion. In order to determine if a belief is justified, one must use reason, evidence, and logic to investigate it. This does not mean that one needs to avoid asking political questions, however. As Sokal (1998) explains, "there is nothing wrong with research informed by a political commitment, as long as that commitment does not blind the researcher to inconvenient facts" (p. 5). A researcher, for example, could be motivated by the desire to develop a "critical awareness of colonial effects," as Newhouse (2008, p. 186) advocates, but such an investigation would need to show how historical accounts of Aboriginal–non-Aboriginal relations were flawed by rigorously examining all of the available evidence. Sokal (1998) goes on to point out that any critique needs "to stand or fall on its own merits," since "having good political intentions doesn't guarantee that one's analysis will constitute good science, good sociology or good history" (p. 5).

What, then, does Bertrand Russell's good life look like, and how does it differ from Newhouse's concept of the good mind? To illustrate Russell's concept, a quadrant has been constructed below to provide a visual representation of how the love and knowledge to which Russell refers, as well as their opposites, can occur in various combinations, resulting in four different "types" of life—good, arrogant, Panglossian, and evil (see Table 20.1).[3]

Table 20.1 Mapping the Good Life (adapted from Bertrand Russell's "What I Believe")

	Knowledge	Ignorance
Altruism	*The Good Life*	*The Panglossian Life*
	Benevolence and understanding	Being content to believe what one is told
	Example: socially available medicine	Example: holy men in the Middle Ages
Selfishness	*The Arrogant Life*	*The Evil Life*
	Cruelty, coldness, and egotism	Promoting irrationality for personal gain
	Example: the Brights movement	Example: televangelists

The upper left corner of the quadrant represents the good life, when both benevolence and understanding are combined. Ensuring that knowledge is influenced by altruism results in its use for socially positive goals. The example that Russell deploys to illustrate the good life is socially available medical knowledge (Russell, 1957, p. 57). Medicine is beneficial, not only when it is based upon the best scientific research available, but also when this knowledge is used to enhance the health of the whole society. As we can see with private health services, medical knowledge is withheld from large numbers of people. This is contrary to Russell's idea of the good life, as it results in profoundly unequal social outcomes where many are deprived of services that are necessary for their survival.

Knowledge, however, can also be combined with emotions that are the opposite of love, or what Russell characterizes as selfishness. This circumstance is shown in the bottom left-hand corner of the quadrant. According to Russell (1957), it results in cruelty, coldness, and a sense of superiority (p. 58). An example of this circumstance could be the Brights movement, cofounded by Paul Geisert and Mynga Futrell in 2003. A "Bright" is defined as "an individual whose worldview is naturalistic (free from supernatural and mystical elements)" (Brights, n.d.). Designating this as "bright" has been challenged by a number of people with a variety of ideological perspectives, because the word could be interpreted as meaning that the nonreligious are more intelligent (i.e., "brighter") than the religious (Mooney, 2003). Christopher Hitchens (2007), for example, referred to it as the "cringe-making proposal that atheists should conceitedly nominate themselves to be called 'brights'" (p. 5). To paraphrase Russell, such actions would constitute an "arrogant life," not a good life.

The top right-hand section of the quadrant shows what happens when ignorance (the opposite of knowledge) is combined with love. The example that Russell uses to illustrate this is from the Middle Ages, when priests assumed (erroneously) that prayer would cure the Black Death. As Russell (1957) points out, "holy men advised the population to assemble in churches and pray for deliverance; the result was that the infection spread with extraordinary rapidity among the crowded masses of supplicants" (p. 56). As this constituted "an example of love without knowledge" (Russell, 1957, p. 56), it can be characterized as a "Panglossian life,"[4] not a good life.

In the lower right section of the quadrant, ignorance and selfishness are combined. Such an example would be televangelists who exploit the gullibility of their followers in their own self-interest. The most abominable of these charlatans are those who encourage the poor to send money to the church so that God's favour will enable them to become rich, as well as the "faith healers" who offer false hopes to the afflicted, diverting them from seeking real medical treatment (Martz & Carroll, 1988). These actions could be characterized as an "evil life," perceived in purely secular terms.[5]

The "Good Life" versus the "Good Mind"

This deconstruction of Russell's conception of the good life raises questions about how it differs from Newhouse's idea of the good mind. Newhouse's vision is similar to the good life envisioned by Russell in that it stresses the importance of altruism in the acquisition and dissemination of knowledge. As was mentioned earlier, Newhouse discusses the importance of kindness (i.e., benevolence), as well as an awareness of colonialism and its effects (understanding).

Newhouse's conception, however, differs from Russell's in that he advocates a number of factors that are contrary to knowledge—spirituality, mythology, and "respect." Newhouse (2008) maintains that his notion of the good mind embraces knowledge, and to show this he focuses on Indigenous Knowledge's empirical aspects—that it has been "developed over generations" and "subjected to continual analysis and testing" (p. 187). But these characteristics disguise the fact that many of Indigenous Knowledge's claims are not analyzed or tested. It is maintained, for example, that "the world is alive," there is a "powered universe," and "that there is an animating energy/spirit" (Newhouse, 2008, p. 192). Newhouse (2008) even maintains that we should "give thanks" for the sun and the light that it brings (p. 184), implying that there is a conscious designer of the universe who responds to, as Ambrose Bierce has acerbically quipped, "a request that the laws of the universe be annulled on behalf of a single petitioner confessedly unworthy" (Bierce, 1993).

In addition to animistic beliefs, aspects of the Indigenous Knowledge discussed by Newhouse encompass mythology. This is shown by Newhouse's (2008) reference to the Guswentah[6] and the "condolence ceremony" that was "invented by the Peacemaker and practiced by Hiawatha" (p. 189). But there is no evidence that the Peacemaker existed, or that the Guswentah should be interpreted as Newhouse proposes. The Peacemaker appears in a legend that has been recounted by elders,[7] while the Guswentah is merely a belt consisting of "two rows of purple beads separated by three rows of white beads" (Newhouse, 2008, p. 188). In the case of the latter, Newhouse (2008) decides to give the belt the following politically desired meaning: "the two rows denote a relationship and in my view a dialogue between nations and cultures; the three white rows signify the ethics of this dialogue: respect, honesty and kindness" (p. 188). This is a general problem that exists with Indigenous Knowledge—the uncritical reliance on oral histories and unsupported opinion.[8]

The final aspect of Indigenous Knowledge that is inconsistent with Russell's idea of the good life is the demand that it must be given "respect." Although Newhouse (2008) maintains that "knowledge-holders" should be subject "to examination, to challenge and to continual questioning" (p. 192), the example that Newhouse provides contradicts this contention. Newhouse (2008) maintains that direct questions are perceived as being disrespectful because elders expect students to come to their own conclusions about the stories that are recounted (p. 193). This assertion inadvertently exposes, but does not clearly articulate, the reality that questioning the opinions of Aboriginal elders is considered rude in traditional cultures, as it is perceived as an attack on their intellectual integrity and social status (Widdowson & Howard, 2008, p. 196).

A similar problem is revealed concerning one's capacity to understand Indigenous Knowledge. Newhouse (2008) maintains that certain areas of Indigenous Knowledge—"ceremonial or sacred knowledge"—cannot be discussed or analyzed in the academy (presumably because this would result in "a climate of disrespect" [p. 192]). But what about the claim that knowledge-holders be subject to examination, challenge, and continued questioning? Newhouse (2008) also, in response to the question "who can learn [Indigenous Knowledge]?," replies: "All who desire and who come to learn with an open heart and sincere desire to learn" (p. 194). But again, the words "open heart" are an attempt to discourage critical thinking. This is why it is difficult to "evaluat[e] degrees of IK" (Newhouse, 2008, p. 194).

Because Newhouse's idea of the good mind contains many aspects that are contrary to knowledge, it is fundamentally different from Russell's conception of the good life. Although this difference is justified on the grounds that "the construction of a category of knowledge called Indigenous Knowledge is a powerful act of decolonization" (Newhouse, 2008, p. 190), just how the substitution of unsubstantiated beliefs for rational understanding is an act of decolonization is not evident.

The Good Mind and Decolonization

Newhouse's conception of the good mind, in fact, relies on a stereotyping of Aboriginal people as inherently "spiritual." This is ironic in that Newhouse (2008) claims to be opposed to stereotypes, admonishing those who make assumptions about his Aboriginality. Newhouse (2008) recognizes that "decolonization is a multifaceted process" that "starts with a single statement: I am a person, fully conscious, self-determining, and able to think and speak for myself. I am not you nor am I the image that you have created of me" (p. 187).

At the end of the article, however, Newhouse reverts to the same construction of stereotypes that he is criticizing. He maintains that "the spiritual facilitates [the] work" of all Indigenous peoples, even though it is possible, in Newhouse's opinion, for a non-Aboriginal person to engage in research and scholarship "without a spiritual foundation" (2008, p. 196). For Newhouse (2008), denying the spiritual "would not be consistent with the idea of the good mind and would be asking us to forget who [Indigenous peoples] are. It would not be in keeping with the dialogue postulated by the Guswentah" (p. 196). This would be similar to telling Italians that they must continue to remain Catholic, otherwise they would "forget who they were" and their research and scholarship would not be "in keeping with the dialogue postulated" by the bible.

Newhouse (2008) maintains that the idea of the good mind is important for decolonization because it "sustained us in the past and can continue to sustain us in the future" (p. 189). Even if this were true, and not some idealized version of the past, what sustained a culture historically is not necessarily what will be necessary today. A huge body of knowledge has emerged since the first colonizers arrived in the Americas, and it is important for Indigenous peoples, if they are to be intellectually self-determining, to develop the critical thinking skills needed to thrive in the world today. The myth of the Peacemaker is not history, and there is no evidence that there is an "animating ... spirit" in the universe. To pretend otherwise is condescension, and contrary to the good life so convincingly articulated by Bertrand Russell.

Newhouse (2008) argues that universities should "create a self-confident, modern Indigenous person fully capable of meeting the challenges of the contemporary world and living a good life as an Indigenous person" (p. 187). But why should "living a good life as an Indigenous person" differ from what is beneficial for non-Aboriginal people? It appears that Newhouse argues this because he thinks that Aboriginal people will always embrace the spirituality, mythology, and "respect" found in the worldviews of their ancestors. This confuses faith (ignorance) with knowledge—a mystification that disguises, and entrenches, the low educational levels within the Aboriginal population. Aboriginal people can become physicists and historians if they choose to pursue these occupations, but they will not be able to meet the challenges of these academic disciplines if they continue to embrace the concept of the good mind advocated by Newhouse.

REFERENCES

Bierce, A. (1993). Pray. In *The devil's dictionary*. Retrieved February 2012, from http://www.thedevilsdictionary.com/?P

Brights, The. (n.d.). The Brights' principles. Retrieved February 2011, from http://www.the-brights.net

Dewey, J., & Kallen, H.M. (1941). *The Bertrand Russell case*. New York: Viking.

Hitchens, C. (2007). *God is not great: How religion poisons everything*. New York: McClelland & Stewart.

Lemelin, R.H. (1996). *Social movements and the great law of peace in Akwesasne*. (Unpublished master's thesis). University of Ottawa.

Martz, L., & Carroll, G. (1988). *Ministry of greed: The inside story of the televangelists and their holy wars*. New York: Wiedenfeld and Nicolson.

Mooney, C. (2003). Brights: Not too "bright." (Doubt and about) Retrieved October 2012 from http://www.csicop.org/specialarticles/show/not_too_bright/

Newhouse, D. (2008). Ganigonhi:oh: The good mind meets the academy. *Canadian Journal of Native Education, 31*(1), 184–197.

Russell, B. (1957). What I believe. In *Why I Am Not a Christian*. New York: E.P. Dutton. (Original work published in 1925)

Simon, T. (2005/2006, December/January). Expunging evil. *Free Inquiry*, 26(1), Retrieved October 2012 from http://www.secularhumanism.org/index.php?page=simon_26_1&section=library

Sokal, A. (1998). What the social text affair does and does not prove. *Critical Quarterly, 40*(2), 3–18. http://dx.doi.org/10.1111/1467-8705.00151

Sokal, A., & Bricmont, J. (1998). *Fashionable nonsense: Postmodern intellectuals' abuse of science*. New York: Picador.

Widdowson, F. (2006). *The political economy of Aboriginal dependency: A critique of the Royal Commission on Aboriginal Peoples*. (Unpublished doctoral dissertation). York University, Toronto.

Widdowson, F., & Howard, A. (2008). *Disrobing the Aboriginal industry: The deception behind Indigenous preservation*. Montreal: McGill-Queen's University Press.

NOTES

1 This chapter follows from an exchange I had with David Newhouse at the New Directions in Aboriginal Policy Forum at Mount Royal University, Calgary, Alberta, May 5, 2010.

2 This essay was one of the pieces of evidence used in a court case that resulted in Russell being denied a professorial appointment at City College at the City University of New York on the grounds that he was morally unfit to teach philosophy (Dewey & Kallen, 1941). This case shows how much modern educational institutions have changed in terms of their capacity to allow a free exchange of ideas, and how demands for "respect" and "sensitivity" are a threat to intellectual progress.

3 I would like to thank Miriam Carey for suggesting the construction of this quadrant.

4 A word that combines both generosity and ignorance is difficult to find. The closest concept is *Panglossian*, which means misguided optimism. The word

"Panglossian" is derived from Voltaire's *Candide,* after the tutor Pangloss, who is a naive optimist. Definition from *Merriam-Webster online: dictionary and thesaurus.* Retrieved October 2012, from http://www.merriam-webster.com/dictionary/panglossian.

5 One of the problems of the term "evil," as it is currently defined, is that it has a religious basis, and therefore cannot currently be used in rational discourse. To give some meaningful content to the term "evil," one has to relate the word's meaning to social implications, and this is how the term is used here. Both ignorance and selfishness are socially negative, and therefore one can attempt to apply the term "evil" to human actions that have these characteristics. While there is merit to arguing that the term "evil" should be expunged from discussions of what is "good" (see, for example, Simon, 2005/2006), a more all-encompassing concept that can be used in opposition to "good" has not been put forward at this time.

6 The Guswentah is a "the two-row wampum that signified the relationship between Haudenosaunee and various European settlers in the early arrival period" (Newhouse, 2008, p. 188).

7 The story of the Peacemaker, in fact, refers to a number of mythological elements, including a stone canoe and a person named Tadadaho who had snakes in his hair. Another indication of the mythological nature of the tale of the Peacemaker is that "Haudenosaunee protocols and the Kaianerenkowa warn against using the true name of the founder of the Confederacy. For in times of great need, should the name of the Peacemaker be whispered by the Longhouse People, the Founder of The Confederacy will return to help his people" (Lemelin, 1996, p. 31). It is for this reason that Lemelin asserts the following: "therefore, the name of the Peacemaker will not be utilized in this paper; rather the terms 'Founder of The League' and 'Peacemaker' will be used it its place" (p. 31). Because of the problem of the inability to separate mythology from history, oral testimonies about the Peacemaker cannot be accepted verbatim; they must be analyzed alongside written accounts and then questions must be asked as to whether or not they are consistent with the body of knowledge that has been accumulated in social scientific disciplines.

8 I have critiqued "oral histories" extensively elsewhere and so will not do so here. For a discussion, see Widdowson, 2006, 78–94.

21

Paths to Truths

David Newhouse

Before other words are written, I want to bring greetings to all of creation, to acknowledge and honour the world that we live in and to acknowledge the life force that exists within all of creation.

Frances invited me to prepare a rebuttal to her critique of my chapter, "Ganigonhi:oh The Good Mind Meets the Academy." I replied that I would do so, not in the spirit of rebuttal (which seems to me to be a brutal way to find truths, evocative of the Hobbesian winner-take-all world that has come to characterize some parts of the contemporary academy) but in the spirit of dialogue. I do not set out to dispute the empiricism and rationality that is foundational to her critique of my chapter and her reading of my idea of the good mind. The ability to reason well, to present rational logically constructed arguments, and to engage in deliberative, reasoned, and data-driven inquiry are foundational to the idea of the good mind. I would also point out there is now ample scholarship that would demonstrate the veracity and usefulness of Indigenous Knowledge(s) (IK). My concern comes from her conception of "truth" that she contends is based upon critical analysis. *Truth* is defined as justified belief. The only possible justification in her view is knowledge derived from critical thinking. The basis of critical thinking is empiricism and logic. This is, in my view, a rather narrow view, unduly narrow in that from an Indigenous perspective it excludes other forms of knowledge and their justification methods. It also runs counter to contemporary scholarship in psychology and decision making that links rationality and emotion (Damasio, 1994).

One of the central aspects of modern Aboriginal society is its desire to use ideas from Indigenous intellectual traditions as one of the key informal aspects of the every day (Newhouse, 2000). Aboriginal scholars have taken up this desire, and new sites of scholarship that explore these ideas have begun to emerge within the academy (Waters, 2004; Warrior, 1994; Native Critics Collective, 2008). This scholarship has developed sufficiently over the last decade that we can begin to discern some of its features (Battiste & Henderson, 2000; Dei, Hall, & Rosenberg, 2000; Warrior, 1994).

The central notion of Indigenous scholarship is "complex understanding" (Newhouse, 2002, p. 5). *Complex understanding* occurs when we can see and examine a phenomenon from various perspectives, as well as the relationships among these perspectives. Complex understanding does not seek to replace one view with another but to find a way of ensuring that all views are given due consideration. It does not work in an either-or fashion. A phenomenon is not one thing or another but can be all things at once. Complex understanding allows for our understanding to change depending upon where we stand to see or upon the time that we look or who is doing the looking. Complex understanding is grounded in a view of a constantly changing reality that is capable of transformation at any time (Bastien, 2004; Peat, 2005).

Complex understanding is based on dialogue rather than dialectic. In this sense, it is deeply rooted in traditional Aboriginal notions of how one comes to understand. The notion can create a broader and deeper understanding of a phenomenon. It fosters a conversation among different disciplines, perspectives, knowledge systems, and methods of inquiry. It fosters understanding without necessarily inviting competition. Challenge is present through the attempt to understand and explain the sometimes differing, sometimes similar, views. Truths emerge from the dialogue.

Indigenous scholarship also brings to the table the notion of sensemaking. *Sensemaking* is the collective coming to understand and is rooted in identity. Making sense becomes a collective process. We see it in Aboriginal discourse: "Let us put our minds together"; "Let us come to one mind." These principles are similar to those introduced by Weick (1995). He and others describe sensemaking as "being thrown into an ongoing unknowable, unpredictable streaming of experience in search of answers to the question, 'What's the story?'" (as cited in Anconca, 2012).

Indigenous scholarship does not just engage the intellect. It engages the mind, spirit, and body, and it considers all in its exploration. The data that are available for coming to truth is much broader than just that available to the rational mind. Indigenous scholarship also brings with it a sense of agency, an ability to shape the world through one's thought, action, and feelings. Within the academy, Indigenous methodologies that reflect these ideas have emerged, starting with a seminal text by Linda Smith (1999), and are now considered part of standard research approaches involving Indigenous peoples (Sillitoe, Dixon, & Bar, 2005; Wilson, 2008; Kovach, 2010).

As Indigenous peoples, we start from these simple premises: that there is a universe; that its origins are unknown; that it is imbued with energy and life; and that it contains beings with consciousness and an ability to reason, feel, and wonder. As human beings, we have duties and responsibilities to each other and to all of creation. One of our responsibilities is to use our consciousness to live well within this world and to learn to live with and respect all aspects of our nature as human beings. We are also inquisitive creatures, wanting to know the nature of the universe we inhabit in order that we might use its forces for both good and evil. We start from the position that we are part of a web of relationships with all that surrounds us; that our actions affect others and we are, in turn, affected by the actions of others. We believe in an animating force that is manifest in our minds and bodies that some call "spirit." The entity we have come to call human is comprised of body, intellect, emotion, and spirit.

Starting from these premises, how do we know what is true? Fernandez-Armesto (1997), in *Truth: A History and Guide for the Perplexed*, argues that we as human beings throughout history have tried to end our confusion and get at what we consider to be truth in four different ways: through feeling (i.e., we feel the truth); through authoritarianism (i.e., the truth that we are told); through logical, abstract reasoning; and through thorough sense perception (i.e., evidence gained through experience or experimentation of the natural world). He argues against the use of one method to the exclusion of all others, suggesting that the truths of one may correct the untruths of another and through the process new truths may emerge. Truth, like love, is a multisplendoured thing.

This is not a dialogue about the truthfulness of science or the importance of reason or the structure and/or animation of the universe. This is a dialogue about knowing and truth and how we come to understand what is true. It is the "we" that is of concern to me. As Charles Peirce (1974), the reputed father of American pragmatism, writes:

"individualism and falsity are one and the same ... one man's experience is nothing if it stands alone" (p. 259). In coming to know truth, we have to come to the discussion with a doubt that we may be wrong or that others may be wrong. We always start from a position of doubt and proceed from there. The heart of critical rationality is doubt, a sense that one may be wrong rather than one may be right. Popper (1935/1992) places falsibility at the centre of the scientific method. Foucault (1972) also linked power, knowledge, and truth, arguing that truth was in the minds of the powerful. The search for truth becomes an exercise in the world of relationship, power, identity, and method. Critical thinking leading to justified belief, the central premise of Widdowson's argument, needs to be examined using the same lens we would use with any other argument. The basis of justification in Indigenous scholarship is broader. It does not, however, discard any notion of rationality and empiricism. Cajete (1999, 2004) describes the rationality of Indigenous science. Bielawski (1992) reports that "pure knowledge is never separated from moral or practical knowledge" (p. 7). She also refers to a study (Fineup-Riordan, 1990) on the Yup'ik view of the analogical relationship between humans and animals and describes how this assumption leads to a different set of empirical researches focusing on the explanation of how differentiation is created out of an original unity in contrast to that of Western science, which assumes humans and nonhumans are inherently different and seeks to understand the relationship between parts that are originally independent.

In Iroquoian psychology, the human mind is viewed as comprised of both reason and passion. Both are engaged in a dance; sometimes reason leads, sometimes passion leads. In a good mind, reason predominates but never excludes passion. The belief, confirmed by empirical and experiential evidence, is that strong passion drives reason from the table. At the same time, strong reason can push passion away. The core Iroquoian spiritual ceremony, the condolence, is designed to bring reason back to the table after a loss or traumatic event. The ceremony arose out of the need to find a way to heal the overwhelming and paralytic grief of Hiawatha, whose wife and daughters were killed. The ceremony "clears the eyes, so that you can see again; unplugs the ears so that you can hear again and clears the throat so that you can speak again."

The restoration of the good mind and the use of the good mind in the pursuit of knowledge and truth becomes an important foundation of Iroquoian scholarship and research. It does not prevent an Iroquoian individual from becoming a physicist. It may help them become a better physicist as they are able to conceptualize and perhaps see the unseen forces of the universe easier, as the use of all the senses may lead to intuitions and hunches that can then be explored empirically.

We can also use our good minds to discuss the boundaries of exploration and inquiry within the academy. The boundaries have been constantly shifting since the foundation of the University of Paris in the late twelfth century. Shattuck (1994) examines, from a popular historical perspective, the struggle with the boundaries between what we know, what we are meant to know, and what knowledge ought to be explored by our institutions of learning. At this historical moment, standing in an awareness of the colonial forces, including the academy, that have shaped Indigenous lives, the boundaries for what can be legitimately explored by the academy are drawn narrowly and maintained with a high level of vigilance. Said's *Orientalism* (1979) provides what is perhaps the best description of the way in which Indigenous knowledges and views have been treated by those within the academy—either systematically ignored and disregarded or treated as primitive and presented as curiosities, not worthy of serious consideration. For those who believe in an academy that can investigate or bring into itself anything, overcoming this legacy will be difficult. At a different time, after a different set of experiences, the boundaries may be drawn in different places and with different firmness. The modern academy is not a monolithic site where only one set of views dominates. It is a site of multiple contested views and where paths to truths are similarly contested.

I would be remiss if I did not address the questions of spirituality and faith raised by Frances in her critique. There is some confusion in the belief that spirituality impedes reason or inquiry and prevents humans from acquiring knowledge. While I acknowledge the centuries-long debate about the relationships of reason and faith, Indigenous spirituality is inherently practical and not dogmatic. Indigenous spirituality focuses on the ethical relationship between all aspects of the universe, not just human to human but human to nonhuman as well. It does not preclude inquiry into the nature of the physical or social universe; by conceptualizing the universe as sets of relationships, issues of ethics become central to Indigenous conceptions of inquiry. Spirituality, in my view, then becomes a vehicle for carrying out our ethical responsibilities to those humans and nonhumans we study. We are also reminded of our responsibilities to future generations as we embark on our paths to truths.

REFERENCES

Anconca, D. (2012). Sensemaking: Framing and acting in the unknown. In S. Snook, N. Nohria, & R. Kjurana (Eds.). *The handbook for teaching leadership knowing, doing, and being* (pp. 3–20). Thousand Oaks, CA: Sage Publications Inc.

Bastien, B. (2004). *Blackfoot ways of knowing: The worldview of the Siksikaitsitapi.* Calgary, AB: University of Calgary Press.

Battiste, M., & Henderson, J. (2000). *Protecting Indigenous Knowledge and heritage: A global challenge.* Saskatoon, SK: Purich Publishing.

Bielawski, E. (1992, Summer). Inuit Indigenous Knowledge and science in the Arctic. Northern perspectives. *Canadian Arctic Resources Committee, 20*(1), 5–8.

Cajete, G. (1999). *Native science: Natural laws of interdependence.* Santa Fe, NM: Clear Light Publishers.

Cajete, G. (2004). Philosophy of Native science. In A. Waters (Ed.), *American Indian thought* (pp. 45–57). Malden, MA: Blackwell Publishing.

Damasio, A. (1994). *Descartes' error: Emotion, reason and the human brain.* London, UK: Vintage.

Dei, G., Hall, B., & Rosenberg, D.G. (2000). *Indigenous Knowledges in global contexts.* Toronto: University of Toronto Press.

Fernandez-Armesto, F. (1997). *Truth: A history and guide for the perplexed.* New York: Thomas Dunne Books/St. Martin's Press.

Fineup-Riordan, A. (1990). A *problem of differentiations: Boundaries and passages in Eskimo ideology and action.* Paper presented at the Seventh Inuit Studies Conference, Fairbanks, Alaska.

Foucault, M. (1972). *The archaeology of knowledge.* New York: Pantheon Books.

Kovach, M. (2010). *Indigenous methodologies: Characteristics, conversations and contexts.* Toronto: University of Toronto Press.

Native Critics Collective. (2008). *Reasoning together.* Norman: University of Oklahoma Press.

Newhouse, D. (2000). From the tribal to the modern: The development of modern Aboriginal societies. In R.F. LaLibertie (Ed.), *Expressions in Canadian Native studies* (pp. 395–409). Saskatoon, SK: University Extension Press (University of Saskatchewan).

Newhouse, D. (2002). The promise of Indigenous scholarship. Keynote address given at the Aboriginal Policy Conference, Ottawa.

Peat, D. (2005). *Blackfoot physics.* York Beach, ME: Red Wheel/Weiser, LLC.

Peirce, C.S. (1974). *Collected papers of Charles Sanders Peirce. Volume Three.* Cambridge: Harvard University Press.

Perkin, H. (2007). History of universities. In J.F. Forest & P.G. Altbach (Eds.), *International handbook of higher education* (pp. 159–205). The Netherlands: Springer.

Popper, K. (1992). *The logic of scientific discovery.* London, UK: Routledge. (Original work published 1935)

Said, E. (1979). *Orientalism.* New York: Vintage.

Shattuck, R. (1994). *Forbidden knowledge: From Prometheus to pornography.* Orlando, FL: Harcourt, Brace and Company.

Sillitoe, P., Dixon, P., & Barr, J. (2005). *Indigenous Knowledge inquiries: A methodologies manual for development. Indigenous Knowledge and Development Series.* Dhaka: The University Press.

Smith, L. (1999). *Decolonizing methodologies: Research and Indigenous peoples.* London, UK: Zed Books.

Warrior, R. (1994). *Recovering American Indian intellectual traditions.* Minneapolis: University of Minnesota Press.

Waters, A. (Ed.). (2004). *American Indian thought.* Malden, MA: Blackwell Publishing.

Weick, K.E. (1995). *Sensemaking in organizations.* Thousand Oaks, CA: Sage.

Wilson, S. (2008). *Research is ceremony: Indigenous research methods.* Black Point, NS: Fernwood Publishing Company, Limited.

Contributors

Frank Deer is an assistant professor in the Faculty of Education at the University of Manitoba.

Anthony N. Ezeife is a professor in the Faculty of Education at the University of Windsor.

John B. Friesen is a lecturer in the Faculty of Education at Lakehead University.

Wayne Gorman is an instructor at Grant MacEwan University.

Linda Goulet is an associate professor of Indigenous education at First Nations University of Canada.

Judy Hardes is a career and education consultant in Alberta.

Calvin Helin is a lawyer, businessperson, and author in British Columbia.

Albert Howard is an independent researcher, writer, and consultant in Alberta.

Verna J. Kirkness has retired from her position as a professor at the University of British Columbia where she was a director of the First Nations House of Learning.

Paul Maxim is a professor of economics in the School of Business and Economics at Wilfrid Laurier University.

Robert McGhee is a curator of archaeology at the Canadian Museum of Civilization.

Yvonne McLeod is executive director of the Kwayaciiwin Education Resource Centre.

Michael Mendelson is senior scholar at the Caledon Institute of Social Policy.

John R. Minnis was a faculty member in the Department of Sociology at the University College of the North.

David Newhouse is the chair and associate professor of Indigenous studies at Trent University.

Mai Nguyen is a Ph.D. candidate and lecturer in the Department of Political Science at York University.

Elizabeth Rata is an associate professor in the School of Critical Studies in Education at the University of Auckland.

John Richards is a professor in the Public Policy Program at Simon Fraser University and holds the Roger Phillips Chair in Social Policy at the C.D. Howe Institute.

Verna St. Denis is an associate professor of educational foundations at the College of Education, University of Saskatchewan.

Dave Snow is a Ph.D. candidate in the Department of Political Science at the University of Calgary.

Nicholas Spence is an adjunct research professor in the Department of Sociology at the University of Western Ontario.

Blair Stonechild is a professor of Indigenous studies at the First Nations University of Canada.

Jerry P. White is associate dean of the Faculty of Social Science at the University of Western Ontario.

Frances Widdowson is an associate professor in the Department of Policy Studies at Mount Royal University.